WRITING, READING, AND RESEARCH

FOURTH EDITION

WRITING, READING, AND RESEARCH

Richard Veit

Christopher Gould

John Clifford

The University of North Carolina at Wilmington

Allyn and Bacon

Boston   London   Toronto   Sydney   Tokyo   Singapore

Vice President, Publisher: Eben Ludlow
Editorial Assistant: Liz Egan
Marketing Manager: Lisa Kimball
Production Administrator: Annette Joseph
Production Coordinator: Susan Freese
Editorial-Production Service: Russell Till
Text Design and Electronic Composition: Wendy LaChance/By Design
Composition Buyer: Linda Cox
Manufacturing Buyer: Megan Cochran
Cover Administrator: Linda Knowles

Library of Congress Cataloging-in-Publication Data

Veit, Richard
    Writing, reading, and research / Richard Veit, Christopher Gould,
John Clifford. — 4th ed.
      p.   cm.
    Includes bibliographical references and index.
    ISBN 0-205-26459-x (alk. paper)
    1. English language—Rhetoric.   2. Research—Methodology.
  3. Academic writing.   4. College readers.   I. Gould, Christopher.
  II. Clifford, John.   III. Title.
PE1408.V45 1996
808'.042—dc21   96-46885
                                        CIP

Printed in the United States of America

10 9 8 7 6 5 4 3 2 1   01 00 99 98 97

See text and figure credits on pages 520–21, which constitute a continuation of the copyright page.

Contents

PART II: RESEARCH PAPER REFERENCE HANDBOOK   435

To the Instructor

Writing, Reading, and Research, Fourth Edition, derives from the assumption that the three activities in the title are central to a college education. Every college student must be able to access information and ideas, analyze and synthesize them, and communicate the resultant knowledge to others.

What is more, writing, reading, and research are so closely and symbiotically related that they need to be studied together. We believe that the research paper should not be seen (as it often is) as just one among many isolated writing activities, noted chiefly for its intricacies of search protocols and citation formats. Research, in the broader sense we envision, includes activities both large and small. Every task involving sources is a research activity, whether it be reading a textbook, using a library, searching the Internet, asking questions, taking notes, or writing a summary and analysis in response to an essay-exam question. A text on research-based writing, as we see it, should reflect this inclusive definition of research, engaging students in its rewards and excitement and preparing them to do it well.

It follows that students need to develop the many skills involved in college research. Writing an essay based on library sources, for example, employs a wide range of skills that, in our experience, many first-year college students have not yet developed. Most basic of all is the need to read well. Students need to employ efficient strategies, to read with perception and understanding, to analyze and critique what they read, and to make productive use of the information and ideas that arise from their reading.

For these reasons, we believe that writing, reading, and research skills should be taught and practiced together. A composition course that prepares students for the actual tasks they will face in their college and professional careers can and should be a unified whole. That unity is the principle that informs this book.

Learning the skills of writing, reading, and research is a process that can be divided into successive stages. We have attempted to take a commonsense approach to this process by introducing concepts sequentially. Although each chapter has its own integrity, each also builds on the concepts developed in preceding chapters.

In general, the book's movement is from simpler to more complex tasks—from working with a single source to working with multiple sources, from basic reading strategies to analytical and critical reading, from paraphrase and summary to simple synthesis, and then to more advanced creative and synthetic writing skills.

We had many specific goals in writing this book:

- To broaden the traditional notion of undergraduate research
- To teach the process of college research in a practical sequence
- To blend the best features of a contemporary rhetoric text, an interdisciplinary reader, and a research guide
- To provide a book that instructors would find a serviceable teaching instrument and that students would find lively and readable, instructive as a text, and useful as a research handbook
- To illustrate writing activities with student examples and to show the processes the writers carried out to achieve their finished products
- To provide helpful and engaging exercises, frequent opportunities to write, and many occasions for discussion and critical interaction.

Changes in the Fourth Edition

In the first edition of this book, published in 1985, our chapter on the library gave scant attention to electronic research tools and sources, except to predict, "The time is fast approaching when all indexes and catalogs described in this chapter will be computerized, and you will be able to find materials on any subject from a computer terminal—without even visiting the library." That time has certainly arrived, bringing not just a profusion of online and CD-ROM indexes but also unanticipated marvels such as the Internet and the World Wide Web. This fourth edition of *Writing, Reading, and Research* takes ample note of those changes, and our "library" chapter, now renamed "Tools for Finding Sources," features the most extensive revision in the book's history. Chapter 9 now provides a thorough introduction to computer-related resources, including ways to find sources electronically and to access sources that are themselves electronic. Information on how to cite various electronic texts is provided in Chapters A and B of Part II, the reference handbook section. This information is made concrete for readers in the three sample student research papers provided in Chapters 8 and 14, which use a variety of electronic, as well as print, sources.

Citation information has also been updated for this edition to reflect changes introduced in the fourth edition of *MLA Handbook for Writers of Research Papers* (1995).

We have provided all new end-of-chapter readings, with a continued emphasis on cross-disciplinary and multicultural topics, freewritten responses, and collaborative inquiry.

Acknowledgments

We owe the greatest debt to our students, from whom we have learned most of what we know about teaching composition. In particular, we would like to thank the student writers who shared their notes and drafts with us and allowed us to use their papers and experiences in this book—Patrick Krause, Molly MacLaren, Julie Swain, and Helen Veit. (In case you are wondering, yes, Helen is the daughter of one of the authors.)

We would also thank the following reviewers, whose wise and thoughtful suggestions made an immeasurable contribution to this fourth edition: Patricia E. Connors, The University of Memphis, and Steven J. Rayshich, Westmoreland County Community College.

Finally, we acknowledge Eben Ludlow, Vice President at Allyn and Bacon, and our friends and colleagues at the University of North Carolina at Wilmington.

R. V.
C. G.
J. C.

WRITING, READING, AND RESEARCH

PART I

Writing, Reading, and Research

Introduction to Writing, Reading, and Research

1

WRITING, reading, and research are the three most important skills you can learn in college. It follows, then, that a course that teaches those skills—the course you are now taking—is as important and valuable as any in the curriculum.

You may well be skeptical. If you are planning a career in forestry, for example, or in biology, theology, or accounting, the courses in your major field are the ones that seem most important to you now. Yet every college course presupposes that you have certain skills. And the most essential skills of all—the ones most vital to your success in your courses and career—are writing, reading, and research. You have an enormous advantage if you are an articulate writer, an observant and insightful reader, and a resourceful researcher.

Writing, reading, and research are important not just in terms of higher grades and bigger paychecks; they are essential for your own education and development as well. Once you have mastered them, you are able to discover and teach yourself almost anything you care to learn. And teaching yourself, surprising as it may seem, is what college is about.

A college education must do more than pour information into your head. It must teach you how to learn on your own. The sum of knowledge in any field is too vast and the world is changing too rapidly for an education that merely imparts information. Instead, an education worthy of the name must provide access to whatever you need to know, both now and after you graduate. It must prepare you to learn what people have discovered in the past, to understand what you read today, to receive and adapt to tomorrow's ideas. It must train you to think, to find out other people's ideas and knowledge, to evaluate and use them, and to contribute new ideas and discoveries of your own. These are the skills we mean by writing, reading, and research. You can see why we say they are important.

The good news is that there is nothing mysterious, or even terribly difficult, about these skills. You are perfectly capable of acquiring them. For one thing, you have been reading and writing for years, and (whether you know it or not) you have been doing research tasks all your life, both in and out of school. For example, when you were deciding where to attend college, you probably researched the subject by examining college catalogs, consulting with your guidance counselor, talking with friends, or making campus visits. In fact, if you found and read a catalog and then wrote for an application, you used all three skills.

The aim of this book is to develop and expand those skills to meet the needs of your college career. Writing, reading, and research are interrelated activities, so it makes sense to study them together. Doing research often involves finding what other people have written, reading it, and then writing in response. Even as you write, you must read and reread what you have written, deciding whether further research and rewriting are needed. And finally, what you have written about your research becomes someone else's reading.

Because these skills can be learned only through experience, *Writing, Reading, and Research* will give you considerable practice in using them. In addition, since they can most easily be learned in a progression, with one accomplishment building on others already mastered, this book is arranged in a reasonable, practical sequence. The purpose of this first chapter is to provide a brief introduction to these three essential and interrelated activities.

WRITING

Unlike the skill of speaking, which we acquire early in childhood without formal instruction, we almost always learn to write in school, and it takes time and practice to become proficient at it. Writing is a complex process, involving many separate skills from the basics of handwriting and spelling to the subtler nuances of tone and organization. The fundamentals are mastered easily enough, but we can never truthfully claim to have perfected our writing skills. The most illustrious writers, after a lifetime of accomplishment, continue to learn from their experience and to develop their craft. A college course in composition or a book like this can assist your development as a writer, but repeated practice will always remain the best teacher.

The essence of writing is *choice;* as writers we are faced with constant decisions. Even when we know exactly what we want to say (which most writers will admit rarely happens), we still face an almost infinite range of options about how to say it. We must decide on an overall strategy, choose the appropriate level of formality for our audience, find the best opening and closing, and determine which facts, arguments, or supporting material to include and which to omit. Even the selection of individual words involves choosing from an array of available synonyms.

In one sense, choice is a burden in that it makes writing more difficult. Writing is undeniably hard work, and not just for beginners. If anything, experienced writers are aware of even *more* choices available to them. Every writer is familiar with writer's block in one form or another: staring at the page (or computer monitor) and agonizing over what to say next. There are also compensating periods when the right words seem to flow, but "the work that writes itself" is unfortunately a myth. Experienced writers accept the difficulty and persevere through periods when writing gets arduous, knowing that eventually they will work through them. They have also developed their own strategies for creating and clarifying ideas and overcoming obstacles.

Fortunately, choice provides us with opportunities as well as obstacles. It is what makes writing an art, not just a competency. As writers we are more than trained word mechanics turning out an assembly-line product. We are artists in the sense that we are able to use our imaginations, experiences, and talents to create, from the unlimited options available to us, works that are original and effective. Writing gives us the means to communicate whatever we wish in a way that is profound, or funny, or provocative, or highly persuasive. Despite, or perhaps because of, the hard work and hard choices involved in writing, the sense of achievement we derive from having created a work uniquely our own can be great and at times even exhilarating.

Writing Habits and Strategies

One characteristic of skilled writers is that they spend considerable time in the preliminary stages of writing—long before they produce a complete, polished draft. Everyone's writing practices differ, and one of your goals as a writer should be to discover the procedures that give you the best results. David Bartholomae, a professor of English at the University of Pittsburgh, is one professional writer who has developed a systematic routine for composing. In the following passage, Bartholomae describes part of that routine.*

> There are things that get in the way of my writing and things that I put in the path of my writing that are different now than they were when I was younger, but the essential resistance—both mine and writing's—remains.
>
> Writing gets in my way and makes my life difficult, difficult enough that I sometimes wonder why I went into this business in the first place. There is work that comes easier to me. Writing gets in my way, but when I write, I almost always put up barriers—barriers to show my sense of duty—to stand (like parentheses) in the way of writing. I feel, as a matter of principle, that writing should not go smoothly and that when it does, unless I'm writing a memo (but even there I try to plant buried jokes or unofficial countervoices), when it does go smoothly, it's not doing the work of a professional or showing proper respect for what Thoreau referred to as the "extra-vagrance" of things.
>
> I think of writing primarily as a matter of resistance. At the same time, however, I will quickly admit that I have developed habits and changed habits to make writing more efficient. I've learned to revise, I've learned to use a word processor, I've learned to develop a schedule and to find a place that can make regular writing possible. Writing still, often, makes me unhappy, makes me sick, makes me do things—like smoke, for instance—that disgust me. I have my habits and quirks and behaviors, like other writers, and I've learned that thinking about them has helped me to put them to use, and I've learned that talking about them can help me speak with greater authority to my students. . . .
>
> What are my habits and quirks? I revise a lot and, as a consequence, I push my students to do the same. I spend a lot of time letting a paper bounce around in my head before I start writing. I begin my papers always with *things,* never with ideas or theses. I begin, that is, with a folder full of examples, or two books on my desk that I want to work into an essay, or a paragraph that I cut from an earlier essay of my own, or some long quotations that puzzle me and that I want to talk about and figure out. . . . I like green pens, I never outline, I work with two yellow pads (one to write on; one for making plans, storing sentences, and taking notes). I've learned to do all these things and they are a part of who I am and what I do as I write, but they strike me as unimportant when weighed on the scales of the Western tradition.
>
> I'm not just being snide here. I feel a sense of historic moment when I write—not that I'm making history, but that I am intruding upon or taking my turn in a conversation others have begun before me. I feel a sense of the priority of others. Some of them, I think, are great writers, some of them are my colleagues and

*From "Against the Grain" by David Bartholomae in *Writers on Writing* (T. Waldrep, ed.). New York: Random House, 1985. Reproduced with permission of The McGraw Hill Companies.

contemporaries, some of them are my teachers, some of them are strangers or students. I feel a sense of historic moment when I write that I'll confess I never felt at marches and rallies and that I never feel at university committee meetings or other public occasions.

Notice how Bartholomae experiences the same self-doubts and insecurities that plague less-experienced writers. But through practice and reflection he has learned that such feelings are an unavoidable, even productive, stage in a predictable routine that almost always ends with an acceptable draft.

Many people mistakenly believe that proficient writers create polished essays in a single, effortless try. The truth is that even experts start out with vague, half-formed bits and pieces of an idea. Their thoughts are not focused or developed, certainly not expressed in language that they are ready to share with a reader. At this stage, your writing and that of the most accomplished authors are probably not too far apart.

The chief difference between experienced writers and most first-year college students is that the former, like David Bartholomae, have learned through trial and error to break down the complexity of writing by approaching it in manageable stages, so that what starts out confused and awkward ends up, several stages later, as a polished essay or a crafted report. If you strive for early perfection in your writing, you are doomed to failure and frustration. Polish and clarity evolve over time through patient drafting and redrafting. That is the secret of professional writers. Writing is not any easier for them. But they have confidence in the routines they have developed. They know that if they are patient and persistent, then good ideas, good sentences, and even good grammar will come. So they relax and settle down to the hardest part of writing—getting started.

In this book we assume that you already have had a course in college or even high school that introduced you to the stages of the writing process. Even so, we think it useful to outline and review a composing sequence used by many seasoned writers. Your writing habits are different from everyone else's and every time you write, the circumstances vary. So be prepared to make adjustments when necessary. But remember there are no shortcuts to good thinking and clear writing.

Several times in this book, we present papers by college students written in response to assignments in their composition classes. In the following pages you will read a paper by Julie Swain, a first-year college student, who responded to the following assignment. In addition, to illustrate the composing process that leads up to a finished paper, we have recorded the evolution of Julie's paper from her first reading of the assignment through the proofreading of her final draft.

ASSIGNMENT   Writing from Observation

Research involves seeking out what you want to know and making discoveries. Later in this course you will engage in *secondary research,* so called because it involves your finding out what *other* researchers have already discovered. Library research is an example of secondary research. This paper requires some *primary research,* in which you discover information about the world firsthand, through direct observation.

Here is the assignment in brief: *Focus your attention on a certain place or activity, learn what you can about it through careful, persistent observation, and write about your discoveries in an interesting, informative paper.*

The following suggestions and guidelines may be of help:

- Choose an organization, office, building, or outdoor locale where a particular activity takes place. Examples could include a homeless shelter, art gallery, university cafeteria, pet shop, singles bar, or police station.
- Select a place or activity that is new or almost new to you. If you choose a topic with which you are familiar, you will not be able to see it with fresh eyes, and might take for granted or miss what an observant outsider could see. For this assignment, it is important that you observe and write as a *reporter,* not as a participant.
- Observe carefully what goes on there, particularly what might not be obvious to the casual observer. Note how people behave, perhaps including how they react to each other, their style of behavior, and the unspoken rules of the place.
- Adopt one of two styles of gathering data: Be an unobtrusive "fly on the wall," listening and watching others who are generally unaware of your presence. Or be an inquiring reporter, talking to people and asking questions.
- Return as often as necessary until you know your subject well. Take copious notes during or immediately after each visit.
- Write about the institution/activity and about your personal experience there. Report on what *you* see, and feel free to use the word *I* in reporting on your observations. You can discuss what you intended to find, what you discovered, and how your ideas changed or were reinforced by the experience.
- Do not spend much time on the obvious surface facts about the place. Do not tell your readers things they already know. Get behind the obvious and tell your readers what is really going on.
- Describe particular events that occurred during your observation rather than generalizations about what happens on typical days. Use specific details.

Submit your prewriting, notes, and preliminary drafts along with your polished paper.

The nature and requirements of this assignment will become clearer, first as you read Julie's polished essay and then as you follow her progress through the stages that led to her final draft. Notice how the assignment calls for something beyond purely personal writing. By this, we mean that the instructor expected members of the class to draw upon sources other than just their own thoughts and past experiences; that is, they were expected to rely on direct observation and, possibly, an interview or informal survey. The procedure might involve visits to several locales or repeated observation of a single site.

Being a fair and open-minded observer does not require the writer to assume a completely detached, impersonal stance toward a topic. In fact, when you read Julie's essay, you will find she became personally involved with what she was writing about, her observation of an Alcoholics Anonymous meeting. The assignment calls for a type of writing that is not completely different from the personal essays Julie had written previously in high school and college, nor from the more formal research-based writing she would do later in her composition class. Although the assignment does not call for a traditional research paper—the kind that cites library sources and uses formal documentation—it does involve a certain type of research. (Later chapters of this book explain various methods of research in greater detail.)

Audience and Purpose

Whenever we engage in any type of discourse—that is, whenever we converse, write a letter, give a speech, compose an essay, or participate in any other kind of interaction involving language—we adapt our words and style of delivery to our intentions. Imagine, for example, an overheard dialogue between a male and a female college student who have just met at a party. The conversation might consist of little more than the customary phrases of introduction, followed by some routine questions about hometowns, majors, interests, and tastes in music. Nevertheless, an astute observer will recognize in this dialogue certain subtle attempts to manipulate a familiar ritual for complex purposes. Both speakers are trying to discover the degree of their attraction to the other, to make a deliberate impression, and to advance (or perhaps to slow or even to end) the progress of their relationship. Like these two speakers, all of us, since early childhood, have become experienced in adapting language behavior to different situations. So it is when we write.

Two factors that all writers must take into account are **purpose** and **audience**. That is, they consider their reasons for writing and the persons they expect to read what they have written. These considerations affect a wide range of decisions involving language, because there is no single all-purpose style or method of writing that suits every occasion. To illustrate this point, consider the following excerpt from the Declaration of Independence:

> We hold these truths to be self-evident, that all men are created equal. . . .

Contrast it with this excerpt from H. L. Mencken's comic paraphrase "The Declaration of Independence in American":

> All we got to say on this proposition is this: first, me and you is as good as anybody else, and maybe a damn sight better. . . .

Both passages are widely admired, but, because they were written for different purposes and addressed to different audiences, they exemplify vastly different styles. In the original version, Thomas Jefferson hoped to justify American independence to the world and persuade his fellow colonists of the rightness of armed rebellion. In contrast, Mencken wanted to amuse his readers while making a point about language; therefore, his writing is informal and humorous. Each style suits the writer's goals, but neither style would have been appropriate in the other situation, or for the assignment Julie Swain received from her instructor.

Julie's purpose and audience were defined by the assignment. She was expected to gather information and impressions that might benefit her or provide insight and to report her findings from a personal vantage point. In addition, she was to share any discoveries with an audience of classmates. She understood that her instructor wanted to simplify the task by having her address readers like herself. However, she could not entirely ignore the fact that her instructor—who would be reading and responding to her writing—was an important part of her audience as well.

With these considerations in mind, Julie began her research and writing, the stages of which are traced in the following pages. As you read these next pages, you can judge how effectively she took into account the demands of her purpose and audience. Here is the final draft of Julie's paper:

Swain 1

Julie Swain

English 102

Professor Pamela McLaughlin

The Meeting

"There's an AA meeting going on somewhere in this town almost all the time," said "Bob" when I called the phone number for Alcoholics Anonymous. I imagined that I was hearing the ravages of liquor and cigarettes in his gravelly voice. "There's a small meeting tonight near the college, but if you want to see a big meeting, come to St. James Church downtown at 8 o'clock."

What had I gotten myself in for, I wondered as I drove through the dark city streets, slick from a recent shower. I could have picked a more comfortable target for my observation than a meeting of Alcoholics Anonymous. I could even have visited a small, safe suburban AA meeting with businessmen and middle-class housewives who looked like my parents and their friends. Instead I was driving downtown after dark, about to face who knows what.

The city streets, busy during the day, were now nearly devoid of traffic, much less pedestrians, and the parking lot across from the church was empty. I locked my car and, with many misgivings, crossed the street. The church's stained-glass windows were dark. Where was the meeting, I wondered. Around the corner two men stood on the steps to the church hall. I forced myself to approach them and asked if the AA meeting was inside those doors.

It had been moved, the large man in the white T-shirt said. The church needed the hall for another function, so tonight's meeting was being held at the Rehab Center, far across town. I thanked him, returned to my car, and drove home. It was too late, I told myself. I would miss most of the meeting if I went. There would be another meeting Thursday night, in three days, and I would return for that one. I was secretly relieved.

As I look back, I wonder what I was fearing. Was I putting myself in the midst of unpleasant winos and hooligans newly released from detox? Would they view me as an intruder, a suburban teenager who clearly didn't belong there? Would they resent someone like me who could drink safely, even get high now and then, without becoming a problem drinker?

But it wasn't really any of those things. What I most feared was their thinking that I did belong there. How could I walk into a meeting of all those people without appearing to be an alcoholic? Hadn't I just seen the concerned look in the eyes of the big man, like I might need the meeting, like he was offering to help me if I wanted to say more? All my life I had made a habit of avoiding unpleasant situations like this. Despite what I told myself, it was no certainty that I would go back.

Swain 3

Three nights later, however, I again left my secure neighborhood and drove downtown. This time the streets were dry and the parking lot was filled to overflowing. At least two dozen people were milling on the steps to the church hall, many smoking, many holding paper cups of coffee, almost all talking in small groups. I walked through the crowd, up the steps, and into the hall. Although I avoided contact, I could see that many of these people looked just like what I was expecting. There were rough-looking characters in sleeveless shirts and ball caps, grizzled men with paunches and buzz cuts, women whose exotic jewelry and dramatic gestures practically shouted "urban arts community."

But these were a minority. I was surprised to see women who looked like my grandmother, prosperous sober-looking men in their thirties, a multiracial cross-section of the community. Most of all I was surprised to see so many young people, some of them barely old enough to be in high school. The biggest shock of all was to see people my own age, people I would expect to sit next to in a college classroom, people who looked very much like me.

Taking a seat on a folding chair in the last row of the hall, I realized I had been in this place before. The Gothic arches, the church banners hanging from the vaulted ceiling, the walls ringed with photographs of clergy who had served the church during the past century were all

Swain 4

familiar. Had I been eight or nine when my older sister
played in a piano recital here one long-ago Sunday
afternoon?

At eight o'clock, a woman in her twenties walked to
the front of the room and shook a bell to get our
attention. "My name is Kimmie," she said in a quiet voice,
"and I am an alcoholic." I wasn't prepared for the
thunderous response from the crowd, "Hi, Kimmie!" Nor was
I expecting the religious tone of the meeting. We rose and
recited a prayer:

> God grant me the serenity to accept the things I
> cannot change, the courage to change the things I
> can, and the wisdom to know the difference.

Kimmie then introduced Ben, who read the "twelve steps" of
AA, and Kurt, who read the "twelve traditions." One
tradition was a respect for the privacy of members, who go
only by their first names. (I resolved to go further by
changing all the first names in my paper.) I had planned to
take notes during the meeting, but taking out my pad and
pen now seemed as inappropriate as it would be in the midst
of a church congregation.

Kimmie asked for first-timers and visitors from other
towns to introduce themselves, and four people did so.
Each included the words "I am an alcoholic" or "I'm in
recovery," and each received the same enthusiastic welcome
from that crowd that had greeted Kimmie, Ben, and Kurt.

Swain 5

Should I introduce myself? But what could I say: "I'm Julie, and I'm writing a paper about you for my English class"? I remained silent.

The next person to talk was Ted, who said that both his sons had become alcoholics like himself. He was proud to introduce the main speaker of the evening, his son Art, who was 22 years old and had been sober for two years. Ted and Art hugged each other as the meeting showed their support with applause.

Art told us his life story, how his parents had divorced when he was small and his father had moved to a distant state. When he was ten, he and a buddy found four cans of beer lying in the sun by the highway. Since drinking was a badge of manhood in his family, he decided to get an early start. "Only an alcoholic would drink hot Stroh's," he said to appreciative laughter.

Art described the deterioration of his life to the point where he cared for nobody but himself, and he loathed himself. He lied to his mother and friends about whatever trouble he got into, and they were all too ready to believe him. He had a wonderful girlfriend, but he treated her badly, breaking promise after promise. Whenever their relationship was about to end, he would do just enough to rescue it while taking pleasure in his skill at manipulating people. Gradually, however, he lost his friends and everything he cared for. He thought he was a

Swain 6

flawed person with mental problems. It never occurred to
him to attribute his problems to the alcohol and drugs he
was taking.

When his younger brother became sober, Art felt
abandoned and alone. During a visit with his father,
however, he went to an AA meeting, and for the first time
he came to grips with his addiction. He tried to stop
drinking on his own but relapsed after a few weeks. He
returned to AA, and this time he listened to the message.
He realized he could not succeed without help from God and
other people. He has been sober now for two years.

When Art spoke about his refusal to face his problems,
I thought about myself. My problems were nothing compared
to what he had overcome, but I know that I too have always been
good at rationalizing and taking the easy way out.
Attending this meeting was the kind of hard thing I usually
avoid. Like Art, maybe I was led to an AA meeting for a
purpose--to learn the truth about myself and become a
better person.

Like me, most people at the meeting were captivated as
Art bared his soul to us. But during his talk others got
up to pour themselves a cup of coffee. Maybe they had
heard this story before. Maybe they just needed to
distract themselves from the same demons Art described.
When he had finished, even these people joined in giving Art an
ovation.

Swain 7

Art's brother Michael was there too, and he gave out different-colored chips to mark "birthdays," another AA ritual. One man who was completing his first full day of sobriety got a white chip. Others came forward to get chips of various colors to represent weeks, months, and even years away from drinking. Finally, we rose and, holding hands to form a circle, recited the Lord's Prayer. The meeting seemed unforgettable to me, powerful and real, yet it was over in less than an hour.

I walked quickly to my car. I wanted to write down my impressions while they were still fresh. I looked back from the parking lot and saw that many people had spilled out onto the sidewalk, but almost no one was leaving. People wanted to stay and talk with each other, to gain strength from the fellowship that was as important to them as the meeting itself.

As I drove away, I knew that this AA meeting had touched and affected me. I also knew that I was the outsider driving home to my protected environment. The alcoholics with whom I had spent a single hour were staying on to fight their fight together.

Julie's is only one of a wide variety of possible responses to the assignment on page 6. It is a polished piece of writing, but it did not get that way at once. The following pages trace the stages of her research and writing that culminated in the essay you have just read.

Prewriting

It is much easier to begin drafting a paper when you already have some ideas about what you might want to say. Therefore, it makes sense, before you begin drafting, to carry out some procedures that can help you generate and discover ideas and get them in writing. These procedures include **brainstorming, mapping, freewriting, collecting data,** and **outlining.** Julie Swain used all four techniques as a sequence to help her get started.

Brainstorming

Brainstorming is used by writers, business people, and scientists to help them unlock their thinking. It is a way of bringing to mind as many ideas about a topic as possible. Brainstorming not only provides raw material to work with; it also gets your creative juices flowing. You can brainstorm out loud or on paper. One way is to write down all the words or phrases about a topic that pop into your head, listing them down the page, one after the other as they occur to you. Don't judge them or worry about whether they're consistent with one another. Sometimes you have to go through three or four or even a dozen useless ideas before a good one comes along. The purpose of this technique is to let associations connect with each other in the mind, like rubbing sticks together to create a spark.

When Julie's instructor presented the writing assignment on page 6, she asked the class to brainstorm about possible topics for their paper. Here is an excerpt from the list that Julie produced:

Campus
—dorm suite
   moving in, fitting in with roommates, Kara and Jen
   establishing community, making "rules"
   how do people change once they leave home?
   effects of drinking, party ethic, lounge/TV
—male/female
   conversations in Caf, post office, coffee bar
   seating patterns (in this class self-segregation)
   sorority rituals, dating, bars, hair (Kutz Above)
—races
   could I observe black student gatherings?
   gospel choir? whites in union? ask opinions?
—breaking rules—what reactions when you wear the wrong clothes, say wrong
   thing, like wrong music?
   two females holding hands?
—discrimination: gay student union

Other Problems

—crime: police station, go on patrol with officer?
court, trial, jail??, detox??
parole officer

—drugs
cigarettes, smoking rituals outside smoke-free buildings
alcohol: bars, underage drinking
dorm drugs? campus antiabuse programs, counseling?
. . .

Julie was writing down ideas as they came into her head, without rejecting any-thing as inappropriate, unworkable, or silly. She wrote quickly, not worrying about punctuation or spelling. She was writing entirely for her own benefit, and some of the names and items on her list had meaning only for her. But you can see how her mind was working—and how brainstorming helped her thought process to gather momentum, with one idea triggering another. Her list shows her train of thought, moving from campus life to gender and race relations, then to problems outside campus, and finally to drugs and alcohol, the eventual focus of her paper.

Mapping or Clustering

When you map your thinking, you try to make ideas concrete, to get them in black and white so you can look at them and see the relationship of one thought to another. You try to make a pattern of words and phrases that radiate out from a central thought. In doing this, writers are often surprised how the process of link-ing helps them discover other ideas. Sometimes the visual pattern itself can suggest the idea for the essay's basic organization. As in brainstorming it is best to jot ideas down quickly, without trying to decide whether each one is good or bad.

From her brainstorming, Julie found herself focusing on various social prob-lems, which she further explored in the map printed in Figure 1.1. Each of the problems she listed led to a variety of issues, and in the process of filling out the map she came up with several interesting ideas for her assignment. Some of the paths her mind took proved to be dead ends ("white male attitudes" about reverse discrimination did not lead in her mind to an observation-paper topic), but others continued to be promising ideas. She considered visiting a nursing home, a Weight Watchers meeting, and a bingo parlor. One of the more adventurous topics was to drive with a friend who claimed that black drivers were routinely stopped by police far more often than white drivers. Another was to pretend to be gay so as to observe others' reactions. Also on her map was the topic of alcohol addiction, which for Julie proved to be the most promising of all.

Freewriting

After an unfocused invention activity such as brainstorming or mapping, the best way to arrive at more focused ideas is to freewrite. Begin writing about your topic at a steady, comfortable pace, jotting down whatever comes to mind, and continue, without stopping, for a planned amount of time, perhaps five or ten minutes. Don't try to screen ideas; simply let them flow. Don't worry about spelling or repetition

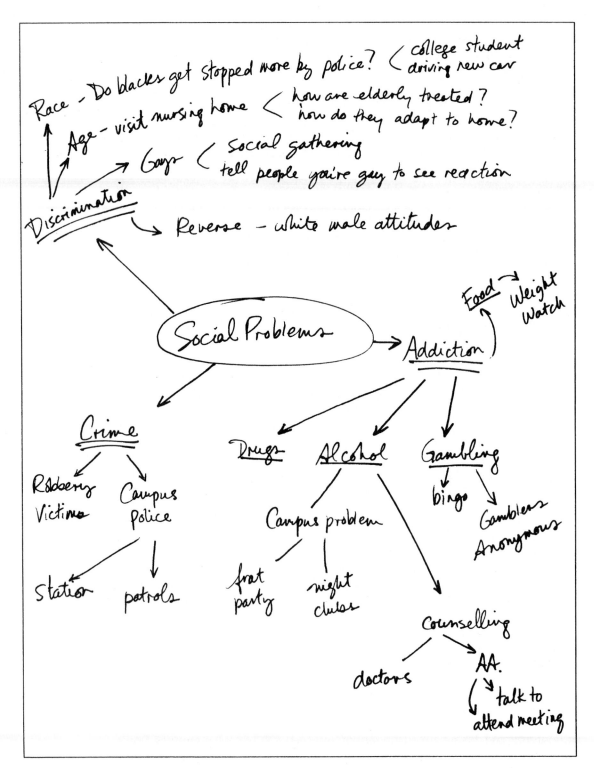

Figure 1.1 Julie Swain's map.

or punctuation or even making sense. You don't do freewriting for others to read; you do it for yourself so you can think through your topic and come up with ideas to use later. Julie's five-minute freewriting looked like this:

> Alcohol use and abuse could be my topic, including drinking on campus. In high school many students drank but most of my friends did not drink. Here it is far more common and expected. People who did not drink in high school get wasted even on weekdays. It is just normal, and no one pays attention to consequences, now or future. I could look at it from several points of view. I could observe dorm parties, Greek parties. Also (both/either) counseling, or talk to counselors (woman spoke at orientation). I doubt they would let me observe. I could attend AA meetings, see how alcoholics cope with addiction. We don't always see where we are going. There would be nice contrast doing both sides (frat kegger, AA). Both would be new learning experiences, plus I'm curious (about AA).

This is a typical piece of freewriting, rambling, conversational, and honest. This is as it should be. If it were tightly organized, well planned, and revised, it would not be true freewriting. Julie used it to further focus her thinking. As she started, she had several possibilities in mind. However, during the course of freewriting, she considered combining a description of alcohol abuse with a profile of treatment for addiction—a fraternity party and an AA meeting. Later, as she engaged in the observation, she decided that the AA meeting was in itself a fully adequate topic for her paper.

Collecting Data

At this point in her project, Julie made the telephone call that she described in her paper and, after an unsuccessful first attempt, visited a meeting of Alcoholics Anonymous. She did not know whether to find someone in authority and to introduce herself and explain her purpose. She decided to play it by ear. As she put it, "Actually, I was too embarrassed to say anything. That was probably a good idea, since nobody paid any special attention to me, and I think I saw a typical meeting." She brought a note pad and pen in her coat pocket, but it did not seem appropriate to take notes during the meeting. Instead, she waited until immediately afterward, when she wrote notes in her car, and she added to them after she arrived home. Here are some excerpts from her notes:

> Fifteen different 800 numbers for crisis lines, treatment lines, abuse lines. Called no. for "Alcoholics Anonymous Inter-Group Assn." "Bob," gravel voice: "There's a meeting going on here right now." Said I could attend, must respect privacy, no last names. Recommended St. Jas. Big meeting, group completing detox will be there.
>
> . . .
>
> *Place:* tan walls, aged appearance, same color as outside church stone, stained-glass window, dark wooden beams to form arches like Gothic church, church banners, churchlike feel, yet people friendly, informal
> —pictures of ministers from time church founded, late ones smiling, some recent women, now more informal
>
> . . .
>
> Bell rings, "My name is Kimmie, and I'm an alcoholic." Quiet voice. Wasn't expecting thunderous roar "HI, KIMMIE!" from audience. Serenity prayer. Men

read 12 steps, 12 traditions. Surrender because we're helpless, "higher power," accept no outside funds, no endorsements, respect for anonymity

People: assorted crowd
—12 rows, brown metal folding chairs, aisle, 80% filled, 60 or so people
—people milling, half wait till meeting start to sit, often in groups, many know each other, others single
—man to my left, nose once broken, woolly shirt, dirty jeans, loner, doesn't applaud, no smile, new person here?, his inside hidden
—woman row in front, closely cut black hair, large earrings, animated, mid 30s, pretty, no makeup, smiles often, exotic creature definitely city person, into the meeting
[Do these two represent stages (resistance/acceptance) or just personality differences?]
—old man on bench to right side, thin, worn face, baseball cap, never without cup of coffee, gets up two or three times, chewing something, looks around constantly, seeing everything and nothing?

. . .

Chips. White for first birthday. Other colors for week, month, three months, years. A black man for three months. 20-something woman for two years, lots of friendly applause, hugs. Shy about it but gives in since friends want to be happy for her. How did she do it? "A lot of prayer." Her friends chuckle.

These excerpts—a small part of Julie's notes—illustrate several different types of note-taking:

• *Listing of details.* Julie knew she would take notes as soon as possible after the meeting, and she forced herself to be observant and to pay particular attention to specific details. In the sections she labeled "Place" and "People," she jotted down details about her physical surroundings and the appearance of people.

• *Recording events.* In the section that begins "Bell rings," Julie described events she observed. Here she wrote sentences in a kind of shorthand that she expanded and elaborated in her paper.

• *Interviewing.* Julie did not directly interview participants, but she did quote and paraphrase words that were spoken during the meeting. She also took notes on the telephone call when she received permission to attend the meeting.

• *Analysis.* Throughout her notes, Julie presented her interpretation of what she observed. At one point she wrote, "new person here?, his inside hidden," and later, "Do these two represent stages (resistance/acceptance) or just personality differences?" Analytical details like these are often the most valuable part of note-taking, since they record what you have learned from the experience. They also help you discover a theme for your paper.

Outlining

Good notes furnish you with raw material for your paper, but at this stage the material is indeed raw. To use it in your paper, you have to *select* what parts of it you will use (good notes typically contain two or three times as much data as the writer will be able to include), and you must decide how you can *organize* it. These are not separate steps, however, and many decisions about selecting and organizing material are best made in the course of actually writing a draft. Most writers would find it futile at this point to attempt a detailed outline of their final draft, though many do find it useful to draw up a very brief and broad outline before they begin a draft—if only to test out a strategy for selecting and organizing their material. Such an outline should be a tentative and flexible plan, not a rigid blueprint. You should feel free as you write to alter your plan whenever you encounter new ideas or discover a better pattern of organization. Julie Swain drew up this brief outline before she began her first draft:

AA Meeting

Opening: history and goals of AA
Phone call
Meeting
    the hall
    introduction
        prayer and readings
        testimonial
        chips
        final prayer
    people
        appearance
        differences: different ages, races, incomes, stages of progress
           in the program
Impressions and conclusions

Julie's outline helped her get started on a first draft—a valuable impetus. But she was not a slave to this outline, and, as you have seen, she had departed considerably from it by the time she wrote the drafts reprinted on the following pages.

The First Draft

Having explored your topic in your mind and on paper through prewriting and having taken good notes, you have an important head start. You are now ready to begin a first draft. As you compose this draft, keep your prewriting plans in mind, but stay flexible. Since you are discovering ideas and since this is a first version, not the finished product, try not to worry yet about spelling or grammatical correctness. The time to put your paper into mechanically correct form is later, when you edit a revised draft. Pausing at this stage to check spelling or punctuation can be counterproductive if it interrupts composing. Unlike freewriting, a first draft should be composed in paragraphs, and ideas should be supported with examples, reasons, or illustrations.

After writing a first draft, Julie edited and polished it. She then produced the following revision and had a classmate read and respond to it—a process called *peer review*. As you read the draft, notice her classmate's brief marginal comments and his longer remarks at the end.

Swain 1

Julie Swain

Editing draft

This opening quotation captures my interest.   An Alcoholics Anonymous Meeting

"Hi. My name is Bill, and I'm an alcoholic." These

words were first spoken in 1938 when two men in Dayton,

Ohio met to talk about their drinking problem. Today that

Do you mean "a similar phrase"? Do they give their own names?

phrase is spoken thousands of times each day at Alcoholics

Anonymous centers throughout the world by men and women who

gather to conquer their addiction.

Once considered a character flaw that anyone with a

little gumption should be able to overcome on their own,

alcoholism is now regarded by the medical community as a

disease, one requiring outside help. Alcoholics Anonymous

exists to allow alcoholics to get that help from a higher

power and from their fellow man.

Visitors are welcome at meetings, said the man who

answered the phone under the AA listing, provided that they

respect the privacy of members. The "Anonymous" in

Alcoholics Anonymous is central to the program. Meetings,

he said, were held in many parts of town every day morning,

afternoon, and night. One would be held that night not far

from campus, but it would be relatively small. A larger

meeting with a greater variety of people, including some

who had just completed a detox program, would be held

downtown at St. James Episcopal Church.

Over twenty people were milling on the steps to the *I'm confused.*

church hall, many smoking, many holding paper cups of *Does this mean*

you went to the meeting at St. James?

Swain 2

coffee, almost all talking in small clusters. The group
was a cross section of humanity. It included rough looking
characters with tattooed arms extending from sleeveless
shirts, grizzled military vets, and exotic looking women. *I love these details.*
But also among the number were the same businessmen and
genteel housewives that could be found at a suburban
meeting. Most surprising of all was the number of young
people, some of them barely old enough to be in high
school, others looking like they could be my college
classmates.

at first I didn't understand why it was "medieval".

The atmosphere was casual, and many of the
participants looked out of place in this <u>medieval setting</u>.
The grey stone walls and the church banners hanging from
the high vaulted ceiling of the hall were reminiscent of a
Gothic cathedral. The walls were ringed with photographs
of clergy who had served the church during the past century
(the last few including women). This lofty locale seemed a
strange place for dealing with an earthy, modern-day
problem. *Now I see your point.*

Brown metal folding chairs filled the hall in a dozen
neat rows. Hanging from the front of the hall were two
banners, each with enumerated lists. One proclaimed <u>"The
Twelve Steps" and the other "The Twelve Traditions."</u>
Behind the chairs, two steaming urns of coffee set up on a
folding table were in constant use before, during, and
after the meeting.

Should I know what these are?

Swain 3

At eight o'clock, a woman in her twenties walked to
the front of the room and shook a bell to get our
attention. "My name is 'Kimmie,'" she said in a quiet
voice, "and I am an alcoholic." The crowd roared back its
welcome: "Hi, 'Kimmie'!" She led the audience in a
? standing prayer: *Do you mean a "typical" prayer - or did everyone stand up?*

God grant me the serenity to accept the things I
cannot change, the courage to change the things I
can, and the wisdom to know the difference.

"Kimmie" then introduced two members who read the "twelve
steps" and the "twelve traditions." Fellow alcoholics can
assist each other because they have been there themselves.
They never ridicule or judge but simply listen and
understand. Instead of thinking in terms of the ultimate
goal of never drinking again, the strategy at AA is to take
it "one day at a time." One tradition was a respect for
the privacy of members, who go only by their first names.
Another was that AA meetings should be self-contained.
They accept no outside funding, so financial support comes
exclusively from members.

"Kimmie" asked for first-timers and visitors from
other towns to introduce themselves, and four people did
so. Each included the words "I am an alcoholic" or "I'm in
recovery," and each received the same enthusiastic welcome from
that crowd that had greeted "Kimmie" and the other
speakers. *Is there a reason for putting names in quotation marks?*

Swain 4

The next person to talk was "Ted," who said that both his sons had become alcoholics like himself. He was proud to introduce his son "Art," who was 22 years old and had been sober for two years. "Ted" and "Art" hugged each other as the meeting showed their support with applause.

"Art" told us his life story, how his parents divorced when he was small and his father moved away. When he was ten he and a buddy found four cans of beer lying in the sun by the highway. Since drinking was a badge of manhood in his family, he decided to get an early start. He got a laugh from his listeners when he said, "Only an alcoholic would drink hot Stroh's."

"Art" described the deterioration of his life to the point where he cared for nobody but himself, and he loathed himself. He lied to his mother and friends about whatever trouble he got into, and they were all too ready to believe him. He had a wonderful girlfriend, but he treated her badly, breaking promise after promise. Whenever their relationship was about to end, he would do just enough to rescue it while taking pleasure in his skill at manipulating people. Gradually, however, he lost his friends and everything he cared for. It never occurred to him to attribute his problems to the alcohol and drugs he took. Instead he thought he was crazy.

This is powerful. I wonder what effect it had on you.

When his younger brother became sober, "Art" felt abandoned and alone. During a visit to his father, however, he went to an AA meeting, and for the first time

Swain 5

he came to grips with his alcohol problem. He tried to
stop drinking on his own, but he relapsed after a few
weeks. He returned to AA, and this time he listened to the
message. He realized he could not succeed without help
from God and other people. This time the message took
hold, and he has been sober now for two years.

Art spoke well, and his story was dramatic, but all
was not silent during his talk. A constant stream of
people made trips to refill their coffee cups. Perhaps it
is easier to take it "one day at a time" if you keep busy.
But when "Art" finished, everyone, including the most
distracted coffee drinkers, joined in giving him an
ovation.

"Art"'s brother "Michael" was there too, and he gave
out poker chips, another AA ritual. One man who was
completing his first full day of sobriety got a white chip.
Others came forward to get chips of various colors to
represent "birthdays" of weeks, months, and even years away
from drinking. Finally, we went to the outer edges of the
room to form a circle, grasping each other's hands while we
recited the Lord's Prayer. The meeting was over in less
than an hour.

But people didn't leave. Many stayed in the hall,   *again,
while others spilled out onto the sidewalk to light a   nice details.*
cigarette and drink still one more cup of coffee. Most of
all they talked with each other, gaining strength from the

Probably, but do you want to draw this conclusion for the readers?

fellowship that was as important to them as the meeting itself. Alcoholism is a terrible problem to face, but it (is clear) why Alcoholics Anonymous has been so successful in providing hope and effective results to so many since that first meeting in 1938.

This is a fascinating topic, Julie, and I admire you for writing about it. I've never been to an A.A. meeting, but I was always curious, and I have relatives who have drinking problems. You've given me information that I value. I also like the vivid descriptions you provide, and I think even more details would be worthwhile.

One question I have is about you. I don't quite know where you are coming from. What impact did the meeting have on you? I wonder what you felt about going to a downtown meeting at night. I would have been uncomfortable. Had you been to a meeting before?

I guess I'm looking for your reactions so I can draw a conclusion about the meeting.

Carson T.

Peer Review

As you can see by comparing Julie's editing draft with her final paper, she benefited from the careful review and helpful responses provided by Carson, her classmate. Most experienced writers are eager, even greedy, for this kind of feedback. By the time you have completed a draft that you are willing to submit for others to read, you have read it and reread it so often you can no longer view it objectively. A fellow student can help you to see your paper through his or her eyes and enable you to gain a fresh perception of it.

A peer reviewer's principal task, then, is to give the writer a sense of how another reader will respond to the draft. When you read and comment on another person's writing, you should not think of yourself as an instructor or grader of the paper. Instead, try to be yourself and simply respond as honestly and helpfully as you can. Notice several important features of Carson's response to Julie's draft:

- The longest comment is a final *holistic* response (a response reflecting on the entire draft and its impact on the reader rather than on isolated details). Carson was careful to provide two indispensable kinds of feedback in a few sentences: to tell the writer, truthfully but tactfully, what took place in his mind as he read the draft ("I was always curious. . . . You've given me information that I value.") and to make a very limited number of general suggestions for revision ("I guess I'm looking for your reactions. . . . ").

- The respondent has respected the writer's ownership of the draft: His comments are tentative rather than assertive. When he thinks a particular type of revision might be called for, he asks questions rather than issues directions ("do you want to draw this conclusion for the reader?").

- The respondent remarks on positive features of the text without being dishonest or patronizing. He is supportive ("I love these details") but lets the writer know where he had difficulties ("Should I know what these are?").

- The respondent gives scant attention to lapses in style and mechanics. Occasionally, a reviewer may point out an error that could easily escape the writer's attention, but that is far less important now than the other kinds of help a respondent can provide. (Proofreading for mechanical correctness will be an important concern later, and you may wish to enlist the assistance of an objective reader in carrying out that task also.) Notice, however, that Carson did call Julie's attention to problem phrases such as "standing prayer," and offered solutions ("Do you mean a 'typical' prayer—or did everyone stand up?").

- Comments tend to fall into several different categories: *responding personally* ("This opening captures my interest"), *praising strengths* ("This is powerful"), *pointing out unclear passages* ("I'm confused. Does this mean. . . ?"), *requesting amplification* ("I wonder what effect it had on you"), and *proposing revision* ("I think even more details would be worthwhile").

By far the most influential comments that Carson wrote were about Julie's distancing herself from the paper ("I wonder what you felt. . . . "). Many times in writing, a deliberately objective stance is called for. But Julie *had* experienced strong and conflicting emotions in researching the paper, and she decided the paper would be stronger and perhaps even more honest if she allowed the reader to see her reactions to her experiences. The final draft shows the results of her decision to place herself more directly into her narrative.

Rewriting

Careful, deliberate revision distinguishes the experienced writer from the novice. Experienced writers spend a large amount of time rereading, changing words, rearranging sentences and paragraphs, adding new material, and writing again. Some drafts require more revision than others.

A few things about revision hold true for almost any successful writer. First, you need feedback from an alert, objective respondent. You yourself can be that respondent, provided that you step back and view your work as a detached reader. After you have completed a draft, it is wise to let your paper sit (for a few days if possible, but at least overnight) so that you can see it from a fresh perspective. Some writers like to read their work aloud, either for themselves or for someone else. Some get ideas as they recopy or retype what they have written, since doing so forces them to read their work slowly and attentively. Frequently, however, the most valuable help can come from a trusted friend or classmate who reads your draft and offers suggestions. This is the kind of help that Julie Swain received from her classmate during a peer-review session.

Of course, not all writers are alike, and different writers prefer different strategies for revision. Some prefer all-at-once revisions. They write a draft all the way through, and then they compose a revised second draft, then a third, and so on. Others engage in ongoing revisions, altering one sentence or paragraph again and again before moving on to the next. Julie Swain probably falls somewhere in between. She composed her drafts on a word processor and made frequent changes as she went. But at least five times she printed out complete drafts and marked changes in pencil before entering them into the word processor. Here is how she revised one passage in her paper:

At least two dozen
~~Over twenty~~ people were milling on the steps to the church

hall, many smoking, many holding paper cups of coffee,

almost all talking in small, groups ~~clusters~~. ~~The group was a cross-~~

~~section of humanity.~~ There were ~~It included~~ rough-looking characters, ~~ball~~

~~with tattooed arms extending from~~ in sleeveless shirts, and ~~baseball caps~~

grizzled, ~~military vets~~, and ~~exotic-looking~~ women,

men with paunches
and ~~military~~ hair cuts
buzz cuts

~~with~~ whose exotic jewelry ~~earrings~~ and dramatic
gestures practically shouted
= urban arts community"

As you can see by comparing Julie's two drafts, reworking passages was only part of her revision strategy. She also deleted some passages altogether (for instance, the opening background information about the organization), moved her telephone conversation to the beginning of the paper, and added considerable information throughout about her personal experiences and reactions.

Writers often reassess their basic goals during revision. They consider the readers they are addressing, what they are trying to help them see or understand, and how they can provide more or better evidence to support their aims. Revision means *seeing again,* and often the best way to accomplish this is to look at your concluding paragraphs to see whether they reflect the same basic purpose as the earlier parts of your draft. Many writers discover their purpose in the act of writing a first draft, and it is not unusual for the ending of the draft to reflect the theme more than the beginning does.

Before completing her final draft, Julie drew up another brief outline—one that better reflected her paper's purpose:

The Meeting
1. Telephone call
2. First attempt to attend
   a. Talking with two men
   b. Secretly glad—my feelings
3. Return visit
   a. Outside steps
   b. Hall inside (description)
   c. People (descriptions)
   d. Meeting
      (1) Introductions, readings, prayer
      (2) Main speaker
      (3) Chips
      (4) Concluding prayer
4. Leaving
   a. People stay on
   b. Reactions and conclusions

Editing and Proofreading

As the final step, you will need to go over your revision to edit and proofread it. At this point you try to polish by eliminating any confusing words or ambiguous phrases. You also carefully check spelling and punctuation. After editing and proofreading, you are ready to type your paper and give it one final reading for typing errors. If you have composed your paper on a computer word processor, use the spell-check feature to find errors, but be sure to give the printed paper a careful visual proofreading as well.

Discovering Your Own Writing Rules

Learning to write is sometimes compared to learning tennis, woodworking, or some other skill. Basically, such comparisons are valid and reassuring; all college students *can* indeed develop their writing abilities to the point of proficiency. However, writing differs from certain other skills—long division, for instance—in that writing involves very few rigid rules, and those few are mastered at an early age. (For example: Begin every declarative sentence with a capital letter and end it with a period.) Well-meaning advice-givers sometimes try to reduce writing to a set of supposed rules such as "Never open a sentence with the word *and*" and "Never use the words *you* and *I* in an essay." However, experienced writers not only find such dictates unreliable (they routinely disregard those just mentioned, for example) but also have learned that writing is seldom systematic, orderly, and predictable. That is not to say that their approach is haphazard. Knowing that trial and error is rarely an efficient approach to the complexity of the task, experienced writers rely instead on a repertoire of procedures, which includes brainstorming, mapping, freewriting, and other techniques described in the earlier pages of this chapter.

Throughout this book you will be introduced to procedures for approaching each stage of the writing process. Keep in mind that these procedures do not always work in the same predictable fashion for every writer. They will not lead you to a single correct response to the writing tasks included in this book, nor to those assigned by your instructor. What they will do is encourage you to experiment with techniques that experienced writers use to get past the moments of writer's block that everyone encounters from time to time. The only way to find out which of these procedures will help you under which circumstances is to engage in as many of them as possible, merely going through the motions at first if necessary. Over time, however, you should learn to rely on a few standbys that can minimize the anxieties brought on by the interplay of complex skills involved in writing, particularly writing for academic purposes.

 READING

Reading is by no means a passive experience. It requires active participation. Without your involvement as a reader, the words on the printed page have no meaning. Only you can bring them to life. Your ability to interpret words, your knowledge of how sentences and paragraphs are put together, your past experiences with reading and with life, your current mood—all these work together to make your reading of an essay, a poem, or even a recipe different from anyone else's.

Interpreting Reading

No one can read exactly as you do. In some ways, reading is a very personal activity. When you read a book—even a book like this one—it is unlikely that anyone else will interpret it in exactly the same way that you do. In a class where most students have had similar experiences, responses will probably be similar, but they will not be identical. Since no one is an exact duplicate of anyone else, each person's reading experience will be unique.

The key to what you get out of reading is what you put into it. For example, if you bring an extensive background in music to the following passage, you will get much more from it than the average reader can:

> Although Schoenberg sometimes dreamed of serialism as a reassertion of German musical hegemony, he more commonly thought of it as a purely formalistic ordering device, and most American serialists share that view. So do the Soviets, with their crude denunciations of "formalism." But just as with psychoanalysis, dismissed by its opponents as a web of metaphors conditioned by time and place, serialism can be considered narrowly Viennese and, by now, dated. And not just dated and extraneous to an American sensibility, but out of fashion.
> —John Rockwell, *All-American Music*

Even if all the names and terms in this selection were explained, most readers would still find its meaning obscure. Actually the passage is neither difficult nor easy. The reader is the key here. To thousands of music experts, this passage is perfectly clear. But for those of us who do not bring the necessary meaning to it, very little emerges. Evidently, the passage is intended for a small, informed audience. If you were reporting on musical trends for a wider audience, you would not quote this passage. It demands too much of the average reader.

That is not to say that we cannot profitably read something that goes beyond what we already know and understand. Our purpose in reading is to do just that—to expand our knowledge and experiences. However, good writers are aware of their audience, and they modify their language accordingly. The author of the music passage was trying to reach only a musically sophisticated readership. Other authors, writing for a general audience, adjust their language for readers with varied backgrounds.

The following passage is written for a general audience. Although it may tell you something you did not know before, the point is crystal clear:

> On a cow-calf ranch, the first job of the summer begins after the spring branding when the calves are turned out. Freshly worked calves go through a period of stress which may last only a few days or up to a week. Stress is caused by several factors: loss of blood, the shock of dehorning and castration, soreness, and even a reaction to the vaccine. In small calves the stress is usually not severe. Their horns are small and the surgery that removes them is not radical, and the same holds true of their castration, so they don't lose much blood and don't suffer much shock. For several days they may lie around, their heads will be sore, and they may not drink much milk. But after that they bounce right back and are healed in a week's time. The healing process takes longer with larger calves, and they are the ones most vulnerable to stress. One day a nice, fat steer calf is walking slowly or lying off to himself, which you expect to see in a large calf that is stiff and sore. Then the next day you find him dead. You can never be sure exactly what it was that killed him, but you assume it had something to do with stress.
> —John R. Erickson, *The Modern Cowboy*

Even if you have had little experience with ranches and cattle, you can still get meaning from the passage. Erickson has introduced information that is new to most of us, but he has communicated it in familiar language and based it on concepts, such as stress, that most adults can readily understand.

So it seems that successful reading depends both on the reader's knowledge and skill and on the writer's sense of audience. Reading emerges from what both the writer and the reader have brought to the text. To do your part as reader, you must be alert, flexible, and open. If you are, reading can be as creative a process as writing—and as varied.

The expression "You find what you are looking for" makes good sense when applied to reading. When you read something just for information, you probably overlook such elements as style, tone, and metaphor. If a friend of yours accidentally swallowed a poison, you would immediately search the back of the bottle for the antidote. You would read rapidly, probably aloud: "Do not induce vomiting. Have the victim drink two quarts of fresh water." Needless to say, you would not comment to the victim about the style: "Hey, Louise, listen to these short, precise sentences!" Under the circumstances you just want information.

On the other hand, if you were asked to read and respond to the following poem, a *haiku* by the seventeenth-century Japanese poet Bashō, getting information would not be uppermost in your mind:

> *The ancient lagoon*
> *A frog jumps*
> *The splash of the water.*

These lines invite you to respond to images. You would not read them in hopes of advancing your knowledge of amphibian behavior or marine ecology. Someone experienced in interpreting poetry would respond differently than a novice, but each reader's response is personal and unique. One reader might be reminded of a childhood experience. For another reader, the images might create simply a sense of peace and beauty. Still another reader familiar with Zen Buddhism might have a more philosophical response. Such a reader might note the contrast between the poem's first line (an image of timeless stillness) and the second (a momentary action), and find in the last line, where the two contrasting images meet, an insight into an eternal truth. And someone totally unused to reading such an open-ended text might find it puzzling and useless.

Interpreting Reading   EXERCISE

As a test of what we have said, see how your responses to two very different passages compare with those of other readers. Reread the earlier paragraph about the cow-calf ranch and write a sentence or two stating what you think is its main idea.

Now read the following *haiku* by another Japanese poet, Buson, and write an equally brief interpretation of it.

> *On the bell of the temple*
> *rests a butterfly,*
> *asleep.*

Do not hesitate to write down your own response to the poem, even if you feel it is probably not correct. In fact, most experts would say that a single "correct" interpretation of such a poem simply does not exist. For this exercise, trust your personal response.

Now compare your responses with those of several classmates. Do they differ? Is there more agreement about the interpretation of the paragraph than of the poem? How do you account for such differences? Even with the ranch paragraph, is there room for differences in response?

Responding to Reading

Just as with writing, we read for different purposes and in different ways. There is no single right way to read. When we encounter the short, precise sentences of a set of directions, our purpose is practical, because we want to know how to do something quickly and efficiently. We do not want to be startled or challenged. But when we pick up a poem or a short story, we want more than information; we want to get pleasure out of the way words and images are used. We want to be surprised. And if our own values and experiences are not engaged when we read literature, we are disappointed. These very different ways to read are at opposite ends of a continuum.

Most of the reading you will do in this text lies somewhere between the objective prose of how-to directions and the subjective language of poetry. It will require your intelligent participation. When you conduct research, you cannot read a source without being critically alert, both to the information you read and to the author's attitude, purpose, and competence.

In addition to various exercises in writing, reading, and research, many chapters in this book conclude with a longer reading selection, followed by questions about your interpretations of the selection and about ideas that it raises. With most of the selections, you will be reading for multiple purposes. That will demand concentration and patience because, just as good writing involves revision, good reading often requires rereading.

When you respond to these readings, you will discover that you agree with your classmates about much of what you find there, but there will also be legitimate room for differences. As you read, you will form interpretations that other readers may not recognize. That is as it should be. We are all both alike and different—at the same time. Reading and writing demonstrate this fact.

The best way to respond to reading is to write about it. Writing stretches thinking by forcing us to connect one idea with another. And because it is visible, writing can help us see what we mean. It can also help us be clearer, more logical, more concrete. Freewriting is an especially useful form of writing about reading; when we freewrite, we respond openly, jotting down whatever we notice in our reading, whether it be a personal association, an observation on style, a restatement of what we think the author is getting at, or any other thought or feeling that comes to the tip of the pen.

EXERCISE   **Responding to Reading**

1. Here are four short reading selections. Read each passage carefully and then freewrite about it for five minutes. Remember, you create the rules for freewriting as you write (except for the basic rule that you should keep writing at your normal speed for a designated time).

    a. The following quotation is taken from *Newsweek*'s "Perspectives," a weekly column that features timely and controversial, sometimes outrageous, quotations that reflect current events and social trends:

    "Cappuccino. Nightcrawlers." *Sign at the convenience store Kum & Go in a resort town near West Lake Okoboji, Iowa*

b. The following column, titled "Dressed to Kill," comes from the *New York Times Magazine*. The author, Eric P. Nash, explains the historical origins of a particular type of traditional clothing worn by most American businessmen:

> Americans not only think of business as warfare, borrowing from Suntzu, Musashi and Attila the Hun, they also dress for it. Take your average foot soldier barreling out of Grand Central at rush hour: from his head to his toes, his uniform has been modeled by war. Consider the tie he wears. Four hundred years ago, it was called a cravat, after the 17th-century Croatian mercenaries who wore them on the battlefields of France. Chances are good our man's tie is a regimental stripe, whose colors originally connoted an officer's regiment, though now they could mean membership in anything from a country club to a bowling league. A typical man's shoe is called a blucher, from the Prussian General Gebhard Leberecht von Blücher, who battled Napoleon. Though defeated at Lübeck in 1806, Blücher survived to wear his namesakes to the battle of Waterloo.
>
> Modern outerwear and warfare is an even closer fit. Our commuter's trench coat has broad pockets, a removable lining and shoulder flaps, which made the coat highly practical for the British officers who wore them in Flanders during World War I. Those vestigial brass loops on the belt are actually grenade hooks. And that wristwatch our commuter anxiously consults is another military improvement (circa 1914) over the vest pocket watch then in popular use.
>
> Suppose our commuter is more casually attired in a blazer and khakis. The original blazer debuted on the British Naval ship, the H.M.S. Blazer, in the 1860's. Our commuter's button-down collar originated on the polo fields of Manipur, where British officers are said to have invented the game. And khakis, derived from the uniforms the Brits wore in India (in Hindi the word means "dust"), caught on with young vets returning to college after World War II.
>
> As Anne Hollander notes in "Sex and Suits," the origin of the tailored suit can be traced all the way back to the linen padding meant to be worn under a suit of armor. Men's coats are said to unbutton on the left, so that a right-handed man could reach his sword more easily, and later his six-shooter. Amazingly, the gesture endures today, each time a businessman reaches for his fountain pen, complete with scabbard and jeweled hilt. All of which brings to mind the words of Woody Guthrie in his ode to Pretty Boy Floyd: "Well, it's through this world I ramble/I've seen lots of funny men/ Some will rob you with a six gun/And some with a fountain pen."

c. This brief column from a recent issue of *Esquire* deals with the supposed sex appeal of shallow-minded men.

Shallow Waters Run Deep

> The stunning but unreflective man, playfully dismissed as a "himbo," knows a lot more than you think. Behind those big blank eyes and that deep tan is . . . well, there's not much. But it's something that women find hopelessly tempting: a healthy disdain for thinking too much.
>
> In a slender holiday from anything remotely resembling a meditation, Coerte V. W. Felske's *The Shallow Man* (Crown) makes a case for the unexamined life. Since he can't be bothered connecting the dots, he maps out the sexual politics of the jejune and Gitanes with an easy straight line. Reading the quick-witted prose, one begins to think less about things and more about Thing, the Shallow Man's tag for the women he dates: gorgeous, seemingly unattainable models.
>
> The Shallow Man is hardly stupid. He's more like Hamlet without the mental baggage, tumbling Ophelia by Act II. So what if behind all that cigarette smoke and charm lies a lean mentality? Oscar Wilde had his number: Only the shallow know themselves.

d. Eva Perón, wife of the former Argentine dictator, has become a popular legend since her premature death in 1952. The following newspaper article describes one of the more unusual manifestations of the preoccupation with Perón among the people of her country:

Eva Perón's Corpse Continues to Haunt Argentina
Calvin Sims

BUENOS AIRES, July 29—A new novel about Eva Duarte de Perón, which deals with the struggle over her remains after she died more than 40 years ago, has added to the fascination about her in a country with a long history of preoccupation with the dead.

Wife of the strongman Juan Domingo Perón, she was a champion of the poor until her death from cancer in 1952 at the age of 33. Her life was celebrated in the Broadway musical "Evita."

"No other corpse has meant so much to a nation than Eva Perón's to Argentina," said Tomás Eloy Martínez, whose novel, "Santa Evita," chronicles the unusual story of her embalmed body and how it was transported within Argentina and to Italy and then back to Argentina in a bizarre two-decade-long battle for possession between political forces.

Mr. Martínez, an Argentine who is chairman of Latin American studies at Rutgers University, received much of the information about the fight for Eva Perón's body from military informants who made contact with him several years ago after reading a novel he wrote about Mr. Perón.

The informants, who included officers in the Argentine intelligence service as well as an Argentine Ambassador to Spain, took part in the military's confiscation and eventual return of the body.

Explaining his reason for telling the story in a novel, which was published this month and was at the top of the best seller's list here this week, Mr. Martínez said what he learned about the fight for Eva Perón's body from the informants and from his own research was "so incredible, so unbelievable that it had to be written in the novel style."

"The novel is the most effective way of telling the truth especially about a person like Eva Perón, whose character has taken on mythical qualities in Argentina," said Mr. Martínez, who is one of Argentina's most prominent authors. While some names, places, and events have been altered, the novel is a reconstruction of the truth, he said.

So far, no one is disputing the basic facts in the book: Military leaders who overthrew Mr. Perón in 1955 confiscated Eva Perón's corpse because they were afraid that the opposition would use the body to rally the populace.

But wherever they hid the body, even in the most secure military buildings, there were problems keeping it from admirers, who would repeatedly place flowers and candles nearby, Mr. Martínez said. So the military eventually sent the body to a secret burial site in Italy, and after 16 years, her husband, exiled to Spain, recovered it and returned it to Buenos Aires.

"Her body was such a powerful symbol that everybody tried to control it," Mr. Martínez said. "I believe that this points to this country's tendency toward necrophilia."

Indeed, Argentina has a long history of preoccupation with the dead and of using the deceased for political purposes. In the 16th and 17th centuries, Spanish settlers often smeared the blood of their victims on their own wounds and paraded the bodies of the conquered around town.

In 1987, vandals broke into the tomb holding the body of Mr. Perón, who died here in 1974, and sawed off his hands. When the mutilation was discovered, labor unions and the Peronist party organized a protest that was attended by an estimated 50,000 people.

In 1989, before pardoning military officers for rebellion and political crimes, President Carlos Saúl Menem brought back the remains of Juan Manuel de Rosas, the most infamous of Argentina's 19th-century provincial warlords, from England as an example of the futility of continuing to nurture old hostilities.

But none of these cases comes close to matching Argentina's obsession with Eva Perón's body.

Mr. Martínez sees Eva Perón's body as symbolic for Argentina.

"It's the embalmed body of a beautiful woman who has not yet been resuscitated," Mr. Martínez said. "In the same way Argentina is a country of hope and promise that has never been fulfilled. This is the melancholy nature of Argentina."

From the start, Eva Perón's life after death was unorthodox. Her embalmer, Pedro Ara, wanted her embalmment to equal that of Lenin. Mr. Ara was so meticulous that he preserved the body with all its internal organs, which are normally removed, Mr. Martínez said.

Mr. Ara also made several wax and vinyl replicas of Eva Perón's body that were indistinguishable from the original, according to the book by Mr. Martínez. The military later used these body doubles, and others it commissioned, to deceive those who sought the real corpse.

After her death in 1952, the corpse was put on display at the headquarters of the General Confederation of Labor, where admirers came by the tens of thousands with candles and flowers and held vigils.

When Mr. Perón was toppled in 1955, military leaders determined that they had to keep Eva Perón's body from opposing political forces but they did not know how best to accomplish that.

"Evita was a symbol of the 'shirtless ones,' " Mr. Martínez said, referring to what she called the poor, who worshiped her. "And if the Peronists got hold of the body they would lead the masses, but the anti-Peronists were trying to destroy it and that would also mean trouble for the military."

After being moved to a number of military installations in Buenos Aires, the book says Eva Perón's body ended up in the house of an army major who stored it in his attic under old papers. But the body had to moved again after the major mysteriously shot his wife.

Finally, in April 1957, the military put the body on a ship bound for Italy where it was buried under a false name. Then in 1971, Gen. Alejandro A. Lanusse overthrew Gen. Juan Carlos Onganía, the Argentine military leader. In exchange for Juan Perón's blessing from exile, General Lanusse agreed to hold elections, restore Mr. Perón's citizenship, provide presidential back pay of $50,000 and give him the body of Eva.

The body was exhumed from a small cemetery near Rome and transported in a silver coffin to Juan Perón's villa in Madrid. Italian and Spanish police officers accompanied the hearse. Mr. Perón kept the body in an open casket on the dining room table of his villa, where he later built a shrine for it in the attic. His third wife, Isabel, combed the corpse's hair in a daily devotion, Mr. Martínez said.

In 1974, after Mr. Perón was elected President again, the Montoneros, the guerrilla organization that emerged from the leftist Peronist youth group, stole the coffin of Gen. Pedro Eugenic Aramburu, one of the military leaders who toppled Mr. Perón, and demanded Eva Perón's in exchange. They were unsuccessful and returned the general's coffin to its tomb.

In November 1974, after the death of Mr. Perón, Eva Perón's body was brought back to Argentina by Isabel, who succeeded him as President. It lay in state in the presidential residence until Mrs. Perón was overthrown in 1976, when the new military rulers had the body buried in the Duarte family tomb under three plates of steel in the Recoleta Cemetery in Buenos Aires.

So today, Eva Perón rests not among the "shirtless ones" she sought to care for but among the patrician families she despised and down the way from the tomb of General Aramburu, who had been instrumental in banishing her remains.

2. Exchange your freewritings with other members of the class. Are there differences in your responses? If so, how can they be explained? Why might different people respond in very different ways to these reading selections?

Reading Response Groups

Up to this point, we have presented reading as a process that engages individualism and independent thinking. Specifically, we have stressed the idea that readers actively *create* meaning rather than passively receive it from a "determinate" text—one that is supposed to elicit a single accurate interpretation that coincides with the author's intended meaning. Aiming to dispel the familiar notion that reading is simply a matter of retrieving information or ideas that writers have *put* in their texts, we have emphasized the *autonomy* of individual readers—their ability to assign personal interpretations to what they read.

Acknowledging that autonomy, we would grant a hypothetical reader the right to interpret the passage by John R. Erickson on page 32 as an animal-rights critique of ranching. To go a step further, let us suppose that some other reader viewed it as a metaphorical account of the process by which public education domesticates young American males. While most people would find that a misguided response, a carefully selected group of like-minded readers might accept it as a creative, possibly productive, interpretation—though probably one that the author would not have anticipated. Most reasonable people, however, would agree that there are limits. It is unlikely, for example, that any community of readers would acknowledge the possibility that Erickson is explaining the neutrality of Delaware during the Civil War. Such an interpretation is simply too eccentric to be supported persuasively.

The autonomy of individual readers, then, can be exaggerated. Like writing, reading is not a solitary act performed in total seclusion. Instead, both reading and writing are *social* acts, and readers often benefit from the responses of their peers just as Julie Swain did in writing her essay.

The following interaction among three experienced readers demonstrates the collaboration of a ***reading group,*** two or more individuals who share, often in writing, their personal responses to a text. Although reading groups come in various sizes, most are composed of three to six members. Your instructor may place you in a reading group and assign specific tasks, often called ***prompts,*** for you and your partners to address. (On the other hand, students enrolled in the same class can initiate groups of their own, and sometimes their collaboration can be spontaneous and unfocused.)

The following is a typical prompt designed to initiate discussion and collaborative response within a reading group. Take a moment now to read it, along with the essay to which it refers.

Freewriting

Read the article "A Short History of Love," which appeared in *Harper's*, a magazine of opinion that addresses current political and cultural issues. As you read, use your pencil to mark important or noteworthy ideas and any reactions or personal associations that come immediately to mind as you read. Keep this writing brief, using shorthand as much as possible, and try not to pause for more than a few seconds in perhaps three or four places at most. Then read the article again, this time looking more closely at the way Lawrence Stone presents the history of romantic love and draws conclusions from it. After you have completed both readings, freewrite for twenty minutes about the ideas in the article. In particular, consider whether or not you agree with the author's suggestion that there may be something dangerous and unhealthy in contemporary attitudes about love. Bring this freewriting to class next time, and be prepared to share it with other members of your reading group.

A Short History of Love

Lawrence Stone

Historians and anthropologists are in general agreement that romantic love—the usually brief but intensely felt and all-consuming attraction toward another person—is culturally conditioned. Love has a history. It is common only in certain societies at certain times, or even in certain social groups within those societies, usually the elite, which have the leisure to cultivate such feelings. Scholars are, however, less certain whether romantic love is merely a culturally induced psychological overlay on top of the biological drive for sex, or whether it has biochemical roots that operate quite independently from the libido. Would anyone in fact "fall in love" if they had not read about it or heard it talked about? Did poetry invent love, or love poetry?

Some things can be said with certainty about the phenomenon. The first is that cases of romantic love can be found in all times and places and have often been the subject of powerful poetic expression from the Song of Solomon to Shakespeare. On the other hand, as anthropologists have discovered, neither social approbation nor the actual experience of romantic love is common to all societies. Second, historical evidence for romantic love before the age of printing is largely confined to elite groups, which of course does not mean that it may not have occurred lower on the social scale. As a socially approved cultural artifact, romantic love began in Europe in the southern French aristocratic courts of the twelfth century, and was made fashionable by a group of poets, the troubadours. In this case the culture dictated that it should occur between an unmarried male and a married woman, and that it either should go sexually unconsummated or should be adulterous.

By the sixteenth and seventeenth centuries, our evidence becomes quite extensive, thanks to the spread of literacy and the printing press. We now have love poems, such as Shakespeare's sonnets, love letters, and autobiographies by women concerned primarily with their love lives. The courts of Europe were evidently hotbeds of passionate intrigues and liaisons, some romantic, some sexual. The printing press also began to spread pornography to a wider public, thus stimulating the libido, while the plays of Shakespeare indicate that romantic love was a concept familiar to society at large, which composed his audience.

Whether this romantic love was approved of, however, is another question. We simply do not know how Shakespearean audiences reacted to *Romeo and Juliet*.

Did they, like us (and as Shakespeare clearly intended), fully identify with the young lovers? Or, when they left the theater, did they continue to act like the Montague and Capulet parents, who were trying to stop these irresponsible adolescents from allowing an ephemeral and irrational passion to interfere with the serious business of politics and patronage?

What is certain is that every advice book, every medical treatise, every sermon and religious homily of the sixteenth and seventeen centuries firmly rejected both romantic passion and lust as suitable bases for marriage. In the sixteenth century, marriage was thought to be best arranged by parents, who could be relied upon to choose socially and economically suitable partners. People believed that the sexual bond would automatically create the necessary harmony between the two strangers in order to maintain the stability of the new family unit. This assumption is not, it seems, unreasonable, since recent investigations in Japan have shown that there is no difference in the rate of divorce between couples whose marriages were arranged by their parents and couples whose marriages were made by individual choice based on romantic love.

In the eighteenth century, orthodox opinion about marriage began to shift from subordinating the individual will to the interests of the group, and from economic or political considerations toward those of well-tried personal affection. The ideal marriage was one preceded by three to six months of intensive courting by a couple from families roughly equal in social status and economic wealth; that courtship, however, took place only with the prior consent of parents on both sides. But it was not until the Romantic movement and the rise of the novel, especially the pulp novel in the nineteenth century, that society accepted a new idea—that it is normal and indeed praiseworthy for young men and women to fall passionately in love, and that there must be something wrong with those who fail to have such an overwhelming experience sometime in late adolescence or early adulthood. Once this new idea was publicly accepted, the arrangement of marriage by parents came to be regarded as intolerable and immoral.

Today, the role of passionate attachments between adults is obscured by a new development: the saturation of the whole culture—through every medium of communication—with the belief that sexuality is the predominant and overriding human drive, a doctrine whose theoretical foundations were provided by Freud. In no past society known to me has sex been given so prominent a role in the culture at large, nor has sexual fulfillment been elevated to such preeminence in the list of human aspirations—in a vain attempt to relieve civilization of its discontents. We find it scarcely credible today that in most of Western Europe in the seventeenth century, in a society in which people usually married in their late twenties, a degree of chastity was practiced that kept the illegitimacy rate—without contraceptives—as low as 2 or 3 percent. Today, individualism is given such absolute priority in most Western societies that people are virtually free to act as they please, to sleep with whom they please, and to marry and divorce when and whom they please. The psychic (and, more recently, the physical) costs of such behavior are now becoming clear, however, and how long this situation will last is anybody's guess.

Here I should point out that the present-day family—I exclude the poor black family in America from this generalization—is not, as is generally supposed, disintegrating because of the very high divorce rate—up to 50 percent. It has to be remembered that the median duration of marriage today is almost exactly the same as it was 100 years ago. Divorce, in short, now acts as a functional substitute for death: both are means of terminating marriage at a premature stage. The psychological effects on the survivor may well be very different, although in most cases the catastrophic economic consequences for women remain the same. But the point to be emphasized is that broken marriages, stepchildren, and single-parent households were as common in the past as they are today.

The most difficult historical problem regarding romantic love concerns its role among the propertyless poor. Since they were propertyless, their loves and marriages were of little concern to their kin, and they were therefore more or less free to choose their own mates. By the eighteenth century, and probably before, court records make it clear that the poor often married for love, combined with a confused set of motives including lust and the economic necessity to have a strong and healthy assistant to run the farm or the shop. It was generally expected that they would behave "lovingly" toward each other, but this often did not happen. In many a peasant marriage, the husband seems to have valued his cow more than his wife. Passionate attachments among the poor certainly occurred, but how often they took priority over material interests we may never know for certain.

Finally, we know that in the eighteenth century—unlike the seventeenth—at least half of all brides in England and America were pregnant on their wedding day. But this fact tells us more about sexual customs than about passionate attachments: sex began at the moment of engagement, and marriage in church came later, often triggered by the pregnancy. We also know that if a poor servant girl was impregnated by her master, which often happened, the latter usually had no trouble finding a poor man who would marry her, in return for payment of ten pounds or so. Not much passion there.

Passionate attachments between young people can and do happen in any society as a byproduct of biological sexual attraction, but the social acceptability of the emotion has varied enormously over time and class and space, determined primarily by cultural norms and property arrangements. We are in a unique position today in that our culture is dominated by romantic notions of passionate love as the only socially admissible reason for marriage; sexual fulfillment is accepted as the dominant human drive and a natural right for both sexes; and contraception is normal and efficient. Behind all this lies a frenetic individualism, a restless search for a sexual and emotional ideal in human relationships, and a demand for instant ego gratification.

Most of this is new and unique to our culture. It is, therefore, quite impossible to assume that people in the past thought about and experienced passionate attachments the way we do. Historical others—even our own forefathers and mothers—were indeed other.

The freewritten responses of one reading group appear below. They have been edited a bit to remove crossed-out words and phrases, spelling errors, and other distractions that the writers did not have time to correct.

Janet's Freewriting

The author wants us to think more critically about romantic love, perhaps even to view it as unnecessary. Too many of us assume that living without romantic love is to be deprived. Stone wants us to examine and question that assumption. He addresses readers familiar with Shakespeare and Freud and comfortable with terms like *orthodox opinion* and *ego gratification*. He assumes an audience already a bit cynical about romance and passionate love. I think the reader most receptive to Stone's ideas has lost any idealism about such matters and is willing to believe that passion is not necessary, maybe unhealthy, in long-term relationships. The essay is for people more likely to sneer at Valentine's Day than to search for just the right greeting card.

Stone's point is that passion, romance, and sexual fulfillment are less crucial to happiness than our culture conditions us to believe. He argues that poets and playwrights created romantic love and that Freud added the notion that sex is an overriding drive. The presumed need for passionate attachments has been constructed by a culture in which the individual comes first and the needs of the group are relegated to a distant second. Stone warns that addiction to romance places us at peril, and he lists the increase of sexually transmitted diseases, divorce, depression, and even mental illness among the results.

Stone supports his ideas with evidence from history, with particular attention to the mass publication of novels, the Romantic Movement, and the influence of Freud. There's a gradual change in tone as the reading progresses. After the first few paragraphs, I expected a scholarly, informative piece with no earth-shaking point to it. But by the time I was finished, I realized that Stone was kind of up on a soapbox. As the essay develops, I get the picture of an embittered prude manipulating history to argue against something he either doesn't want or can't have.

Alex's Freewriting

Stone asks readers to consider a cultural norm in a fundamentally different and unconventional way. The trappings of romantic love so permeate our daily lives that we assume there's something wrong with an adolescent or young adult who doesn't experience the feeling. So Stone asks us to set aside this conditioning for a moment and to entertain the idea that a thing we all "know" to be natural and proper really isn't. Also he wants us to see that there's something at stake. I'm not sure he wants to alarm us and alter patterns of behavior, but he does want us to think about the consequences of our beliefs and to get a debate going. I think he makes two important points. First, love may be a form of learned behavior. Second, because of historical developments (democracy and individualism, invention of mass media, Freudian psychology), romantic love has run rampant and poses certain dangers.

I think Stone is addressing a well-educated, broad-minded audience—the sort of people who subscribe to *Psychology Today*. Ironically, that type of reader, like the people who perpetuated the concept of romantic love prior to the eighteenth century, are an elite. An essay like this is probably leisure reading for such persons. I think Stone envisions a reader who prides herself on being an independent, tough-minded skeptic—someone who isn't taken in by bunk just because it's popular or "nice." An iconoclast, I guess you could say. I'm not sure Stone is *addressing* this type of audience so much as he is *conjuring it up*.

I see a contradiction in the evidence. In paragraph one, Stone mentions the uncertainty of "scholars" (psychologists?) about whether love is "culturally induced" or "has biochemical roots." If it's biochemical, then aren't historians and anthropologists mistaken in the view that Stone attributes to them? Or are psychologists less certain about this than scholars in other fields? Has Stone expressed himself poorly, or am I reading his first paragraph carelessly? Stone introduces more specific support in paragraph five, when he refers to the divorce rate in Japan. It's interesting, though, that he relies on emotionally charged language in his next-to-last paragraph, with words like *frenetic*, *restless*, and *demand*. This seems out of keeping with the rest of the essay, which sounds more scholarly.

The essay is chronologically ordered, tracing the history of romantic love. But beneath that, I see a question–answer approach. Stone opens with a problem or dilemma, and the first paragraph ends with two questions. The next paragraph opens with "Some things can be said with certainty," and Stone lists those things. Paragraph four then opens with "another question," and that question leads to two others. Paragraph five goes back to certainty, beginning with "What is certain is that. . . . "

Agnes's Freewriting

Stone reminds an audience of psychoanalysts of the history of romantic love. He assesses where we stand today, with tremendous social pressures for people to seek and insist upon sexual fulfillment. For me, the essay doesn't make clear whether Stone sees romantic love and sexual love as the same thing. Stone fails, probably on purpose, to give a detailed explanation of how "love" took the place of arranged marriages and how, through the "saturation of the whole culture," sexual gratification was encouraged, even idealized. The chips seem to go down when he examines the influences of Freud. Is he trying to discredit the Freudian theory of human sexuality, now taken for granted in some circles? (When he speaks of "relieving society of its discontents," he alludes to Freud's justification of neurosis, *Civilization and Its Discontents*.) Stone seems to say that we pay a heavy price for license and excess. Is he trying to upset the Freudians? to urge therapists to stress social values rather than individual desires as they guide their patients out of a self-induced wilderness?

Stone is speaking to a group of professionals interested in new ways of thinking about mental illness and its treatment. The allusion to *Romeo and Juliet* isn't so important, since every high schooler has read the play. The Troubadors are less familiar, but anyone who's heard of Bing Crosby or Perry Como has heard the term. So I think Stone is flattering his audience without really demanding much of them. It seems scholarly, but is it really? His tone is earnest, though bias slips in near the end. There's not a great deal of hard evidence. Frankly, I think this essay could be adapted for the *Parade* section of the Sunday paper with only minimal editing. After all, we're all interested in what makes us tick, and all the emphasis on the demons of instant gratification, license, and unfettered individualism would hit home with people trying to figure out what's gone wrong with their relationships. Why not say something about the psychic toll taken by adulterous liaisons or arranged marriages?

Although "A Short History of Love" is not an obscure or difficult text, each of these readers responded to it a bit differently. One obvious contrast involves the way they interpret the aims of the author. Janet sees Lawrence Stone as "an embittered prude manipulating history to argue against something he either doesn't want or can't have." Alex is more inclined to take the article at face value, simply as one writer's attempt to provoke thought and debate. Agnes seems annoyed, reading the text as an effort to display knowledge and flatter the reader's self-image.

Other important differences emerge. Alex is very analytical, examining the structure of the article—right down to the author's choice of specific words. Agnes makes reference to things outside the text (from the title of a book by Freud to the names of popular singers of the 1940s and 1950s). Janet falls somewhere in between: She makes a few personal associations (such as her reference to greeting cards) but also focuses on Stone's ideas and the order in which he presents them. In addition, both Alex and Agnes arrive at their interpretations by asking questions, interrogating the text and even examining their own responses to it.

Although other differences can be highlighted, the important point has been made: The personality, preoccupation, and thinking style of each reader influence the way he or she reads "A Short History of Love." This does not mean that any one of the three readings is better than the other two. On the contrary, it suggests that the best reading would be one that is informed and enriched by a consideration of all three perspectives. Such a reading would exploit the benefits of Janet's speculations about the author, Alex's close analytical reading, and Agnes's skepticism. This formidable array of talent and personal response is something that no single member of the group (nor any one of their classmates) possessed individually.

The sharing of freewritten responses is not always an end in itself. Instructors may also ask groups to address a particular issue or problem introduced by a reading. For example, Janet, Alex, Agnes, and members of other reading groups were presented with the following assignment when they came to class with their freewritten responses to "A Short History of Love":

Group Work

Read your freewriting aloud to the other members of your group. As your partners are reading, take note of any comment or observation that you find noteworthy, but be particularly alert to the following:

1. Do the members of your group feel that romantic love is governed more by culture or by biology?
2. Do they recognize an unhealthy preoccupation with romance, sex, and individualism in modern society? Do they share Lawrence Stone's sense of alarm and urgency?
3. Did anyone in your group connect what Stone calls "frenetic individualism" and the desire for immediate self-gratification to other areas of life?

After everyone has read, try to reach some consensus in regard to the following questions:

1. Has Lawrence Stone identified a serious social problem that needs to be addressed?
2. What would be the most plausible solution to the tensions analyzed in this article?
3. Does extreme individualism and the desire for self-gratification cause problems in other areas of life?

Be prepared to share your group consensus with the entire class.

Approaching tasks such as these, reading groups strive for consensus—or at least mutual understanding—rather than a single best, most authoritative answer. After Janet, Alex, and Agnes had read their freewritten responses aloud, all three discussed ideas and observations that made an impact on them. For example, Alex remarked on Janet's belief that as Lawrence Stone gets further into his topic, he begins to sound more like a soapbox orator than a scholar. Alex connected that belief with something he had written about Stone's development—that "emotionally charged language" appears in the next-to-last paragraph of "A Short History of Love." Janet's observation thus helped Alex see the language in that paragraph in terms of a broader pattern. Janet, on the other hand, benefited from Alex's narrower focus on words in a specific segment of the text. Not only was her perception reinforced by what Alex noted, but she also had supporting evidence for what had been only a vague impression about tone.

As the group proceeded to discuss each other's responses, a number of similar transactions occurred. Agnes took issue with Janet's and Alex's notion that Stone hopes to alter public behavior. She reminded her partners that Stone delivered his paper at an academic conference and that his primary audience was psychoanalysts rather than a randomly selected group of single men and women. Acknowledging that they had lost sight of that fact, Janet and Alex modified their understanding of Stone's purpose. Later, Janet took note of her partners' doubts about Stone's authority in fields other than history and became more skeptical herself. All three group members continued their discussion for about fifteen minutes, after which their instructor asked them to share their conclusions with the entire class.

At the end of this and following chapters, you are invited to work in reading groups, engaging in similar processes of collaborative response. When you do so, try to adopt the constructive approach exemplified by these three readers.

 # RESEARCH

Many students expect research to be an excruciating ordeal, and the idea of THE RESEARCH PAPER looms in student mythology as the academic equivalent of a root canal session at the dentist's office.

Fortunately, the myth is wrong. Research needn't be drudgery or an ordeal, although it can be both to those who go about it without knowing what they are doing or why. *Research* is nothing more than finding out what you need to know. If you are good at it—if you have learned some elementary research skills—it can be useful and satisfying; it even can be a pleasure.

You are already skilled in certain kinds of research. Right now, for example, if you wanted to find your dentist's telephone number, you could easily do so, even though your phone book contains thousands of names. You have research skills that enable you to find out what movies are showing on television tonight and how much local bicycle stores are charging for Raleigh mountain bikes. Research in college involves additional skills, which you will find no less useful and which you are fully capable of mastering. One aim of this book and of the course you are now taking is to help you become a competent college researcher. These same skills will continue to prove useful after you graduate.

Research can take any number of forms, from looking up the meaning of a word to conducting an opinion poll. Depending on what you want to find out, you might need to ask the opinions of experts, undertake fieldwork or laboratory experiments, interview eyewitnesses, analyze photographs, or observe the behavior of people who don't know they're being watched. This more observational type of research is the kind that Julie Swain has used for her essay. Other research methods—ones we consider carefully in this book—involve written sources. You can discover general information in reference works such as encyclopedias and almanacs. More specific information and statements of ideas can be found in magazines, journals, pamphlets, and books. The college library collection and computer databases are two invaluable resources for college researchers.

When you like, you can use your research skills for your private benefit. For example, your knowledge of the library can allow you to research summer job opportunities for pharmacy majors or to find out which videorecorders are most reliable. One difference between such private research and the research you do as a college student is that the latter usually has a more public purpose. College research is often part of a larger project in which you share your findings with other scholars. Consequently, in order to communicate what you have learned as a result of your research, you will engage in *research writing.*

In short, any organized investigation can be called research, and any writing you do as a result—from poetry to scientific reports—can be called research writing. Research is important to your writing because you will not always know enough on your own. If you are writing about your own feelings, no research is needed; you are an expert already. But if the dating practices of a century ago are your subject, you will have to do research if you expect to produce anything worth reading. You owe it to your readers to produce writing that is informed and accurate. Research is essential to such writing.

Not all good writing, of course, is research writing. Your responses to the reading exercises on pages 34–38, for example, were probably based on reflection and personal opinion rather than on research. For the same reason, the following passage would not qualify as research writing:

> Marrying "early" before a career has caused a furor among my friends. . . .
> I've been accused of misrepresenting myself during college as someone trying to earn a MRS. degree rather than an education. When "feminist" friends hear that I am taking my husband's name, they act as if I'm forsaking "our" cause. One Saturday afternoon, a friend phoned and I admitted I was spending the day doing laundry—mine and his. Her voice resonated with such pity that I hung up.
> New York City, where we live, breeds much of this antagonism . . . [but] I've also experienced prejudice in my hometown in Colorado. At a local store's bridal registry, I walked in wearing a Columbia University sweatshirt and the consultant asked if I'd gone to school there. On hearing that I'd graduated 10 months earlier, she explained that she had a daughter my age. "But she is very involved in her career," she added, presuming that I, selecting a silverware pattern, was not.
> —Katherine Davis, "I'm Not Sick, I'm Just in Love"

This personal account is well written and honest, but it does not involve research in the way that we mean it. It is a reflection; it does not make use of outside sources. And it is not the result of systematic inquiry. On the other hand, if Katherine Davis had used quotations and facts gathered from formal interviews with friends, had researched published scholarship about attitudes regarding marriage and family, or had cited the writings of prominent feminist authors, then that would change her method from reflection to research. This is what we mean by research writing—using sources beyond your personal thoughts in your essay.

Distinguishing Features of Research Writing

Would you call Julie Swain's essay "The Meeting" research writing? Explain. Are any parts of this essay based on research? Does Julie's limited use of research make the essay less convincing? If she wished to strengthen the paper through additional research, what kinds of research would you suggest?

READING SELECTION

The following selection, "Precious Dangers," traces the invention and marketing of motorcycles during the past century; it then offers what may be a biased view of the culture of cycling since World War II. The passage is part of a longer profile published in the May 1995 issue of *Harper's*.

Precious Dangers

The Lessons of the Motorcycle

MELISSA HOLBROOK PIERSON

1   The first gas-powered motorcycle looked like an instrument of torture—an 1885 vehicle built by Gottlieb Daimler and Wilhelm Maybach of Würtemberg, Germany, wood-framed, rolling on iron-tired wooden wheels. After Daimler's son Paul took it on a six-mile ride from Cannstatt to Unterturkheim and back (successful unless you count as mishap the leather-covered saddle catching fire), Daimler abandoned the Einspur (one-track) to get on with his original interest, a four-wheel conveyance. The inventor of the motorcycle is to the rest of the world the father of the automobile.

2   In the new century motorcycles proliferated. At one time some 300 makes were going at one another on racetracks; by 1927 British manufacturers were putting out 598 different models, and Germany produced more than 151,000 bikes—nearly half the world output—in 1936. There was the Douglas Dragonfly, the Scott Flying Squirrel, the Matchless Silver Arrow, the BSA Rocket Gold Star, various Sunbeams ("The Gentleman's Motor Bicycle"), the Triumph Speed Twins, the Norton Commando, the Vincent Black Shadow, the Velocette Venom, the Ariel Red Hunter, the Royal Enfield Bullet ("made like a gun"). There was the Indian Scout, the Excelsior Deluxe, the Cleveland Century, the Henderson Ace, the Harley-Davidson Electra Glide, the Benelli Tornado, the Morini Settebello, the Gilera Saturno, the Moto Guzzi Falcone. They were cobbled together in backyard sheds or devised in factory studios, not only in Britain, America, Italy, and Japan but in Czechoslovakia, Germany, India, Spain, Scandinavia, Belgium, China. Many of this wild variety were named for things that fly, attack, show agility, or otherwise impress, and the names reek of advertising's peculiarly wishful derring-do. Then again, the hype had its reason. The motorcycle offered an artificially enhanced potency, a sort of stab at immortality: these man-made creations were constructed so that on them we could forget the sadness of not having been born this mighty. In other words, although we made them, they make us fly.

3   It was also significant that T. E. Lawrence met his end on one of his beloved Brough Superiors. (He named his bike Boanerges and loved to ride it flat out for pure speed, and sometimes to race a fighter plane flying overhead.) This is the man who was one of Colin Wilson's exemplary "outsiders" in his book of the same name, of whom he said, "His clear-sighted intellect could not conceive of moral freedom without physical freedom too; pain was an invaluable instrument in experiments to determine the extent of his moral freedom."

4   After World War II some alienated veterans came home to ride motorcycles in angry bunches, giving birth to the myth and the reality of gangs like the Hell's Angels. But after a short boom, even Indian Motocycle failed, leaving Harley the only U.S. maker. Incidents such as the 1947 biker riot in Hollister, California, in which 407 were arrested after police counterattacked with tear gas, spiced the era. The stinger that the biker riots left behind was in the movies, starting with *The Wild One* (1953), based on the Hollister episode, starring Marion Brando as a rebel without a cause and Mary Murphy as a good girl who naughtily reports of her first ride: "It's fast—it scared me—but it felt good." Although *Easy Rider* (1969) had a more sympathetic view of its chopper-riding heroes, the feeling was not shared by many people over thirty. The dozens of murder 'n' mayhem flicks that appeared in the Sixties and Seventies *(Hell's Angels on Wheels, Born Losers, Satan's Sadists)* left a mark that has been hard to remove, reducing "biker" to "bad guy."

5   The ethos of the Fifties—the conformity, cleanliness, safety, and impersonal modernity that helped wash away the residue of war—could not embrace motorcycling. But it made a brief return in the 1970s, as the result of the Mideast oil crisis, a back-to-nature movement, and one determined visionary, Soichiro Honda. His first test model, which arrived in the United States in 1958, was greeted with skepticism and disregard. But he soon proved the superiority of his motorcycles, and his pocketbook, on European race-tracks in the face of equal disdain. He also had a knack for giving people what they wanted before they knew they wanted it. By building small, unintimidating scooter-like "tiddlers," Honda easily hooked a new generation, who could then move up to faster models. Sales boomed, reaching 525,000 in 1982. Then, in Reagan's time, yearly bike sales free-fell to 178,000.

6   Biking has long welcomed the disenfranchised because no one else would have them, and because even outsiders must come inside sometimes. Wearing gang colors, iron crosses, and riding a Harley with straight pipes that amplify the blatting of a 45-degree V-twin engine to an all but unbearable pitch is as concise a way as any to tell the world you're pissed off and that you reserve the right to broadcast the news widely. The individuals who *look* like they might belong to gangs and who occasionally collect to proclaim their independence from family values (and at the same time show themselves to be the far right's great champions, with a rampant buy-American, anti-immigrant, misogynist conservatism) have merely adopted certain regalia and behavior (causing many to wonder just what it is about a Harley-Davidson that causes men to put on great weight in the midriff and grow unkempt beards). During the week they are your car's mechanic, a lift operator, a factory worker—the glorious, righteous proletariat. On the weekend they like to drink a bit to forget that they are the proletariat and to reassure themselves that everything is in its proper place ("Show your tits, baby!" they yell, or shell out twelve bucks for a T-shirt that reads "Hitler European Tour 1939–1945"). In the public imagination they are tattooed hellions, one step up from animals, acting out the antisocial rage of an entire nation.

7   But some of the alienation is real. Many of these men saw firsthand in Vietnam what an adventure the military can be. Unwilling to believe they had narrowly escaped the mortars and mines to which their friends succumbed only to return to less than the

American dream, they found themselves wishing for more—a just cause, some reason to keep going, a resuscitation of the dead, all those terrible dead. Every Memorial Day they roar into Washington, D.C., thousands and thousands of Hondas and Kawasakis and Harleys in low gear, decked and flapping with American flags and the black emblem of their only hope, the POW/MIA flag. To my mind this is not a gang; this is the dark wave from the bottom waters that has always buoyed America's more colorful toy boats on its surface.

I've encountered these men at rallies and races, and their sordid requests wear me down and rile me up. I think I should have the right to go where I want and do as I please as unmolested as these men demand to be. I have seen the women who acquiesce, seen them turn and raise their shirts to a grandstand of thousands at the races, or ride on the back of a bike through a resort town bare-breasted and waving. I've been told they are having fun. But I have looked into their eyes when their mouths were smiling. And I believe I know humiliation when I see it. **8**

Once, trying to be the reporter I was never meant to be, I may have put myself in danger by breaching Animal Hill at the annual race weekend in Laconia, New Hampshire. Although I was accompanied by male friends, they let me know that under no circumstances were they stopping in the midst of that sadists' heaven, the general aura of which was expressed by an inflatable love doll hung by the neck from a tree, every rubber orifice violated by whiskey bottles. Black smoke snaked to the sky from the embers of a burned Japanese motorcycle, a stolen truck, bits and pieces of furniture, and trees. Men stripped to the waist, some still bearing the mud they had fallen into the night before and stayed in till morning, lurched around, and beer was still appearing by the case on the backs of motorcycles slipping up the sodden trail. I heard that any woman who dared to spend the night up there would have to consider herself the property of all. **9**

I felt faintly sick at witnessing such desperation masquerading as fun. "Shit Happens" is the credo of men such as these, and they wear it on their chests and holler it to the sky. It is both what they believe has happened to them—nothing but shit—and an abdication of personal responsibility. **10**

Still, I acknowledge the fascination we have with excess, and how it appeals to our belief that humans are capable of anything. The outlaw biker is also a straightforward object of envy, in a peculiarly American style: animate the chrome and steel, turn back time a hundred years, and you have (what we imagine to be) the frontiersman on his tough little mustang, riding hell-bent for leather from danger or to it, a law unto himself in a lawless land. Bikes say: I am fast, faster than any pain you'd like to escape. Together, the motorcyclists I know are all busily painting in their own corner of the total work known as unhappiness; I'm working on it, too. . . . **11**

The legend of the motorcycle rider as rabble-rouser has remained into the Nineties, but in a transformed state. The miscreant's sidekick now helps sell a $12,000 beaded bustier on a magazine cover or becomes the theme of a New York tourist-trap burger joint (replete with rigged Harleys that vibrate and smoke for the patrons). The motorcycle, as a succinct image of power at once awesome and threatening, is ideal for advertising's purposes, particularly at a time when the will to buy has generally replaced the will to do. **12**

Once in this picture, however, limited to a role as semaphore or backdrop, the denatured bike suddenly ceases to be a bike at all. Its new fantasy world has been carefully arranged. It is a world in which external suaveness, animal appeal, hipness—at bottom, immortality—is frozen into permanent availability by the lens. To enter its safe precincts, the viewer need only amass all the props and re-create the scene. People who have no intention of ever riding a bike sport black leather jackets, the more zippers and buckles the better, and knockoff engineer boots à la Brando. In fact, actually riding a **13** bike would intrude on this dream, introduce incorrigible reality to a bargain struck precisely to banish reality's impermanence, uncertainty, failure. Nowhere is the reminder that the only purpose those togs originally had was to prevent severe skin abrasions or crushed foot bones in an accident. The real item for sale in the ads for motorcyclish goods is a sensation of pure magic: you get to feel like a rugged individualist while also becoming socially and sexually acceptable to a wide pool that shares the same standard of style. Reduced to a charm on the bracelet of fashion, motorcycles become safe for consumption while lending a sense of false danger to the riskless proceedings. Their appearance has no lasting effect except, like junk food, to provoke a hunger for more. Like holograms, they radiate their alluring substancelessness onto every surface. Near the end of the motorcycle's first century, actual motorcycles become fewer and fewer while the tidy simulations of them proliferate. Motorcycles are everywhere today, and the hand can pass right through them.

Freewriting

Freewriting can help you focus your thoughts and develop concrete ideas about your reading. Write a full page in your journal or notebook recording your reactions to "Precious Dangers" along with any thoughts inspired by what you read. Write at your normal pace about whatever comes to mind. Because this writing is not intended for others to read, you should concentrate on putting down your ideas without stopping to polish your language or to correct errors. Although you are free to write any of your thoughts related to the reading, you may, if you wish, respond to some of the following questions in your response: Are you surprised or offended by anything in Melissa Pierson's account of motorcycling? What is your reaction to the subculture (a group having socioeconomic traits distinctive enough to set it apart from others in the same society) Pierson describes? If reading the passage brought to mind any personal experiences with motorcycles or bikers, how were they similar to or different from those of the author?

Group Work

A reading group can be two or more students who share ideas about their reading. For the group work activities that follow the reading selections in this book, you can be a member of either a fixed group or one whose membership changes from reading to reading. For this reading, group members should do the following: First, take turns reading your freewritings aloud to the group. Then discuss your responses to Pierson's account of motorcycling and bikers. Compare your own experiences and observations with those of the author. Finally, try to decide whether you agree with the notion that modern advertising exploits the antisocial image that many Americans associate with bikers.

Review Questions

1. Why do few people think of Gottlieb Daimler as the inventor of the motorcycle?

2. Which Hollywood films and actors have contributed to popular perceptions of motorcycling? How?

3.   What caused the brief resurgence in cycling that occurred in the 1970s?

4.   What are some of the causes to which Pierson attributes the alienation of bikers?

Discussion Questions

1.   What are some possible benefits and dangers of channeling one's frustrations and hostilities into a hobby or enthusiasm?

2.   The passage can be divided into three sections: ¶s 1–3 (¶ is the paragraph symbol), which deal with the early history of motorcycles; ¶s 4–11, which trace the development of an antisocial image for bikers; and ¶s 12 and 13, which claim that today's mainstream advertising exploits that image. What facts and impressions regarding the motorcycle have remained consistent throughout its history? Do they help explain any of the changes that Pierson details?

3.   Is Pierson trying to make some point about American society or some segment of it larger than the community of motorcyclists? If so, why hasn't she stated it directly?

4.   Consult the passage by Robert Pirsig on pages 79–80 and decide how he might respond to Pierson's view of motorcycling.

Writing

1.   *Research*: In a dictionary, look up any of the following words of whose meaning you are uncertain:

Boanerges (¶3)   miscreant (¶12)
misogynist (¶6)   bustier (¶12)
proletariat (¶6)   semaphore (¶13)
acquiesce (¶8)

2.   Interview a person who sells or services motorcycles or a fellow student who has owned or driven one. Use the information that you gather to support or dispute some of the observations that Pierson makes.

ABOUT THE REST OF THIS BOOK

The chapters that follow in the first part of this book present an orderly program for developing your skills as a college reader, writer, and researcher. A number of chapters are concerned with reading, since an essential first step is to become a careful, perceptive reader. The early chapters are devoted to techniques and skills in reading for understanding. Later we introduce skills in reading critically and in writing analytically about a text. One area that receives special attention is reading argumentative writing and then writing to persuade others.

Our approach to research is systematic and consists of several steps. We first introduce important college skills that involve single sources, including paraphrase and summary. Those skills are then applied to working with multiple sources. The next step is to synthesize paraphrases and summaries of several readings.

We introduce you to various kinds of research, with particular attention to locating and using sources in the library. Our aim is to enable you to find almost any available information you are looking for. We show you how to compile information, select it, arrange and present it, and document it. In short, you will learn how to write research papers with skill and confidence.

The second part of this book, the Research Paper Reference Handbook, explains the formal conventions of research writing, including lists of works cited, parenthetical notes and footnotes, outlines, and typing requirements. In addition to the MLA style used in most composition classes, two alternative formats are also explained. For ease of use, conventions for lists of works cited and parenthetical notes are summarized in the Quick Reference Guides on the inside covers of the book.

We believe you will find this course rewarding and interesting. The activities you will engage in and the skills you will acquire are all eminently practical ones, and you will have ample opportunity to use them in the years to come. Being able to find the sources you are seeking, to read them perceptively, and to write clearly and articulately about what you have found can give you both a sense of power and a lasting satisfaction.

2 *Strategies for Reading*

ONE OF the most important skills for a college student to learn is reading. That statement may surprise you. Of course you can read quite well already, since you are reading this page. But we mean what we say. Good reading involves some very sophisticated skills, just as good writing does, and all of us can continue to improve our reading and writing abilities throughout our lives.

 ## INTERPRETATION

As you saw in Chapter 1, reading is much more than just recognizing the words on a printed page. It involves the ability to *interpret* what you read—recognizing the writer's intentions, perceiving what is implied but not stated, making connections between the ideas you read and other ideas you are aware of, and drawing conclusions. You already use sophisticated interpretive skills in your reading, as the following hypothetical example demonstrates.

Imagine that after having missed three meetings of your psychology class, you find in your mailbox the following communication from the Dean of Students' office:

> This is to inform you that this Office has been notified of your having reached the maximum number of absences permitted by the instructor of _Psychology 207_ . In accordance with University Academic Policy, further absence will cause a lowering of your course grade and may result in your failing the course. This Office will continue to monitor your academic progress. Do not hesitate to contact us if we can be of any help to you.

You might draw this interpretation: First, the fact that you received a formal notification from the office of a campus official, rather than a friendly verbal comment from your teacher, alerts you to the existence of a problem. The formality of the language ("This is to inform you") and the impersonal style ("this Office has been notified," rather than "your teacher has told me") give you the sense that a formidable bureaucracy has its eye on you. You conclude somewhat uncomfortably that the university takes its attendance policy seriously.

Besides the actual warning about lower grades, you also note the more vague, implied threat ("This Office will continue to monitor your academic progress"), which is only partially eased by the more benevolent final sentence. You decide from your reading that it would be wise not to miss additional classes if you can help it.

The knowledge that you had when you began reading the notice enabled you to interpret it as you did. Your previous experience of schools and school officials, of policies and grades, and of the way people use language all led you to the particular meaning you derived from the notice. Of course not every reader would respond precisely as you do to such a note, but the point is clear—your mind is actively at work whenever you read. Good readers think all the time—recognizing, understanding, comparing, and evaluating the information they encounter.

EXERCISE | **Interpretation**

Imagine the following situation:

It is two weeks before election day. Mr. and Mrs. Brown, both in their late thirties, are walking with their five-year-old daughter through a shopping mall. Suddenly a man, smiling broadly, grabs Mr. Brown's hand and shakes it. On the lapel of his suit jacket is a large button that reads "Bean for State Senate." He says:

> Hi, folks, I'm Phil Bean. I hope you're having a pleasant afternoon. What a beautiful child you have! *[To the girl:]* Hi, sweetheart. Aren't you pretty! *[To the woman:]* She looks just like her mother. But you're too young—you must be her older sister. *[To both adults:]* Say, I'm a candidate for the state senate, and I hope I can count on your support. I'm not one of those professional politicians, but I think we need some everyday folks like you and me in the state government for a change, don't you? You can compare my background with my opponent's, and you won't find any drunken driving arrests in *my* past. Of course, I don't want to say anything bad about my opponent, who seems to be a young, well-meaning kind of fella. I'm sure smart folks like you can see what's what and you'll vote for me, Phil Bean. Have a nice day.

In a flash, he is off, grabbing another shopper's hand and introducing himself.

1. Take a few minutes to write your interpretation of what you have read. Do you learn anything about Phil Bean, beyond the explicit content of the remarks he makes to the Browns? What kind of impression does he make on you? Is that the impression he is trying to make? Specifically, what qualities do you find in him? Why do you think he says the things he does? Give specific examples.

2. Now think about why you were able to read the passage as you did. What previous knowledge and experiences allowed you to interpret it in that way? Would a visitor from a country with a different political tradition, such as Albania or Zaire, be able to interpret Phil Bean's behavior and intentions as you did?

 CONTEXT

It is difficult—in fact, nearly impossible—to read a text if you begin with no idea of what it is about. Suppose someone were to lead you blindfolded through the stacks of your college library, asking you at some random point to reach out and take any book off the shelves. You flip open the book, point your finger somewhere on the open page, and, when your blindfold is removed, try to read from that point. In all probability, it would be quite some time before the words would begin to make sense to you—if indeed they ever did. With no initial idea of the book's topic, with no knowledge of why or when or by whom the book was written, with complete ignorance of what preceded the passage you turned to, you would find yourself groping for meaning.

The fact is that in order to read any passage, from a comic strip to a textbook chapter, you have to have some expectation of what it is likely to be about. Otherwise, even the simplest words will make no sense. We have all had an experience in conversation similar to this one: Two friends, Nancy and Jerry, are discussing the rain clouds that loom threateningly in the western sky. Nancy's mind then turns to an upcoming softball game that she has planned, and she says, "I hope they'll all be able to come." Jerry, who is still thinking about the clouds, stares at her with a puzzled look. He cannot understand Nancy because he did not have the right context for her words. She spoke on one subject while he was expecting another.

Like conversation, reading requires you to put words within a *context*—a situation that gave rise to those words. Context includes the background information and experiences that make utterances comprehensible. For example, if you are reading the directions on the box of a frozen dinner, your knowledge of that context enables you to anticipate what you are likely to encounter. You have no trouble, then, understanding what is meant when you are told to "Preheat the oven to 375°." It is just the sort of thing that the context would lead you to expect.

Several elements go into making up the context of any passage you read. Imagine, for example, that you are reading the final chapter of a detective novel. The context that enables you to read and understand it includes the following:

1. Your knowledge of what it is you are reading. (If you aren't aware that it is a detective novel, you will not make much sense of it.)

2. Outside knowledge (your familiarity with terms you encounter, such as *homicide* and *motive,* and your expectation from past experience with detective novels that it will end with a solution to the crime).

3. Your having read the preceding passages. (The last chapter of the novel would be baffling to a reader who had not read the chapters that led up to it.)

All these elements allow you to anticipate what you are likely to find as you read. Without such a context, reading becomes impossible.

Analyzing Context

EXERCISES

1. As a test of our claim that it is all but impossible to read a passage without a context that allows you to anticipate what you might find, try this experiment:

    Read, if you can, the following passage:

    . . . As the tellers passed along our lowest row on the left hand side the interest was insupportable—two hundred and ninety one—two hundred and ninety two—we were all standing up and stretching forward, telling with the tellers. At three hundred there was a short cry of joy, at three hundred and two another—suppressed however in a moment. For we did not yet know what the hostile force might be. We knew however that we could not be severely beaten. The doors were thrown open and in they came. Each of them as they entered brought some different report of their numbers. It must have been impossible, as you may conceive, in the lobby, crowded as they must have been, to form any exact estimate. . . .

a. Are there any words in the passage that you do not know? What is the passage describing? What guesses about its subject did you make as you read it?

b. Although its language is not especially difficult, it is likely that the passage did not make much sense to you, since you were deprived of the context that its readers would ordinarily have. If you had encountered the passage in its usual context, however, you would have known this information: The passage is an excerpt from a letter, written in 1831 by a well-known Englishman, Thomas Babington Macaulay. Macaulay was a Member of Parliament and, as earlier parts of the letter had made clear, he was present to vote in favor of the important Reform Bill. Macaulay and its other supporters had little hope that the bill would gain the more than three hundred votes it would need to be passed into law. Excitement grew as the clerks (tellers) began to count the two sides.

Given this context, try again to read the passage. Is it clearer now? If so, why?

2. Imagine you have been asked to read the following process description as a test of your powers of recall. Here are the directions: Read it once, put it aside, and then write down as many specific facts as you can remember.

The procedure is actually quite simple. First you arrange things into different groups. Of course, one pile may be sufficient depending on how much there is to do. It you have to go somewhere else due to lack of facilities, that is the next step; otherwise, you are pretty well set. It is important not to overdo things. That is, it is better to do a few things at once than too many. In the short run this may not seem important, but complications can easily arise. A mistake can be expensive as well. At first the whole procedure will seem complicated. Soon, however, it will become just another facet of life. It is difficult to see any end to the necessity for this task in the immediate future, but then one can never tell. After the procedure is completed, one arranges the materials into different groups again. Then they can be put into their appropriate places. Eventually they will be used once more, and the whole cycle will then have to be repeated. However, that is part of life.
—John D. Bransford and Marcia K. Johnson, "Cognitive Prerequisites for Understanding"

Although the vocabulary and sentence structure of this passage are simple, you probably faced difficulty recalling details. But suppose you had been provided the title, "Doing the Laundry." Is it likely you could have recalled more specific facts?

3. Now read the following narrative paragraph:

The Prisoner
Rocky slowly got up from the mat, planning his escape. He hesitated a moment and thought. Things were not going well. What bothered him the most was being held, especially since the charge against him had been weak. He considered his present

situation. The lock that held him was strong, but he thought he could break it. He knew, however, that his timing would have to be perfect. Rocky was aware that it was because of his early roughness that he had been penalized severely—much too severely from his point of view. The situation was becoming frustrating; the pressure had been grinding on him too long. He was being ridden unmercifully. Rocky was getting angry now. He knew that his success or failure would depend on what he did in the next few seconds.

—John D. Bransford, *Human Cognition: Learning, Understanding and Remembering*

Now reread the paragraph, substituting the title "The Wrestler." Does the title alter your reading experience? Consider the following questions: Why is it possible to play with the meaning of this paragraph by changing its title? What would happen if the paragraph had a well-written topic sentence? From a reader's perspective, what is the value of a title or a topic sentence?

STRATEGIES FOR UNDERSTANDING

As the preceding exercises demonstrate, familiarity with a context makes a passage easier to interpret. Since the context in which you place a text depends on your knowledge, as well as your experiences, values, opinions, and interests, two readers may not place a particular passage in precisely the same context and as a result will not interpret it in exactly the same way.

There are skills, however, that all good readers share. They are observant of context and seek clues to enrich it and to aid their understanding. In large part, these skills come from practice and experience. The more you read, the better reader you become. But it also helps if you are familiar with some of the principles and strategies of good reading. You can become a better reader very quickly with a little training.

Good readers routinely use several ***reading strategies.*** All of these strategies take additional time—and may therefore seem counterproductive at first—but they can save you a great deal of time in the long run, since they make your reading more alert and efficient.

Choosing the most appropriate and effective strategies is governed by your purposes in reading. Sometimes you read for entertainment; at other times, for information or ideas. Often you read for several reasons at once. Sometimes when you read, you accept the writer's authority and seek to understand and absorb what you read. At other times you read more critically, evaluating whether the writer's authority can be trusted and whether the ideas are worthy of acceptance. Chapter 7 presents strategies for critical reading. The focus of this chapter is on reading for understanding and information. Among the strategies that experienced readers find most important are these:

- Looking for clues in a text before you start to read it.
- Using the clues authors give you as you read.
- Reading with a pencil.
- Rereading if necessary.

Prereading Strategies

To read even the simplest passage, you have to be able to place it within a context and to anticipate what you are likely to find. The richer the context, the better you can anticipate and the easier your reading will be. It is to your advantage as a reader to discover in advance as much about your reading matter as you can. The strategy involved is simple: *Look over what you will read—quickly but alertly—before you begin to read it.*

Specifically, there are several clues to look for before you begin the actual reading, as the following situation demonstrates. Suppose you are reading an issue of *Newsweek* magazine and you come upon the "My Turn" article that appears on the facing page. What might you do before reading it (or even as you decide whether you want to read it)?

EXERCISE   **Finding Clues before Reading**

Before going any further, look now at the *Newsweek* article on the facing page and see what information you can gather about it *without actually reading its text*. What do you expect to be the topic of the article? What do you guess is the writer's point of view? What enabled you to make those assumptions?

Sources of Information

Good readers search for clues before they begin reading. Here are a few of the sources of information that will help you derive more meaning from your reading. While specific references are to the *Newsweek* article, being aware of and using these sources will improve all the reading you do.

Title

It may seem perfectly obvious to say that you should begin by reading the title, but a surprising number of students read assigned chapters and articles without paying any attention to their titles. In doing so, they miss an important source of information.

Titles of articles, chapter headings in books, and headlines of newspaper stories usually name the subjects they address, and they aid your reading by helping you anticipate what you are likely to find. We hope that the title of this chapter, "Strategies for Reading," led you to expect an explanation of how to get more from your reading. But not all titles are so plainly descriptive. Look at the *Newsweek* article and see what expectations you can derive from its title, "Knowing Isn't Everything." The title probably succeeded in its intended purpose of piquing your interest, while the subtitle indicates that the article deals with the value of genetic tests used to measure the likelihood that a person will contract a particular disease.

M Y   T U R N

Knowing Isn't Everything

Genetic testing is important but so are the people affected

BY SALLY SPAULDING

I AM ONE OF THOSE PEOPLE WHOSE LIFE HAS BEEN DRASTI-cally altered by the recent advances in genetic testing. In October 1989, shortly after predictive testing became available for Huntington's disease, my doctor told me there was a 92 percent chance I had inherited the gene for it from my father. In July 1994, after breakthroughs in testing, I learned that I have the gene, for sure.

Huntington's disease is a progressive, terminal neurological illness that causes mental and physical deterioration over a period of 10 to 20 years, usually beginning in a person's 30s or 40s. The gene is dominant and thus does not skip generations. Having the gene means I will get the disease. There is no treatment or cure, not even anything experimental. There's no way to stop its onset. I just turned 40.

One of the biggest arguments for genetic testing, even when there isn't any cure or treatment to offer the patient, is financial planning. If you know that you're probably going to be disabled and unable to work before reaching 50, you can plan for it. If you know you'll likely spend several years in a nursing home before you die, you can prepare. But there's a hitch: this sort of financial planning is almost impossible, except for the very wealthy.

I fit into a unique niche. Those of us now testing positive for Huntington's are the first to know for sure about future risks. Before testing, there was always hope. Somewhere down the road, there'll be hope again in the form of a cure—or a choice of treatments. However, even armed with knowledge that one has this gene, how can a person plan ahead financially for a devastating illness in this bleak anti-worker economy? Government and big business tell us that the economy continues to improve. But many in the middle and lower classes aren't any better off. What this means to those of us who've tested positive for Huntington's is that we slog along at jobs we don't love but can't leave. We are dependent on employer-provided health, disability and life insurance. We want to get in as many productive years as possible. We can't return to school to train for a new career because we don't have time. For us, there is no future.

Planning for the future with Huntington's is impossible, except for the very wealthy

We pray that there won't be a gap in our employment—without a paycheck and insurance. Many businesses are converting to long-term temporary employment (sometimes as long as two years) because it means not paying benefits or severance pay. Many of us who have the Huntington's gene don't have savings or investments. People at risk are offered gene tests, and few can resist the lure of knowing the future. But when the results are positive, those who are affected are on their own. There is no more research help. I knew I had to make financial plans for my family.

In September 1991, I was 36 and working as a legal assistant for a two-attorney law office—a successful father-and-son operation. I had a chance at a higher-paying job in the legal department of an insurance company. The man who ran my firm was in his 60s and had no plans to retire. But when I asked, I was told

that the firm would probably cease to exist without him if he became disabled or died. I needed to provide my family with health insurance for the first time. Up to that point, my husband, a Presbyterian minister, had provided us with medical benefits. He suffered from depression and changed jobs frequently. He was on the verge of another major breakdown. I knew it was now up to me to make sure we were covered.

The insurance company offered a higher salary, excellent benefits and stability. But one year and 9 months after being hired, I was laid off along with others in the department. Despite my extremely diligent efforts at finding work, I was unemployed for the next nine months. My benefits ($305 per week) ran out after six months. I was paying $500 a month to my former employer to continue health-insurance coverage for my family.

I finally found a job at another law firm. It lasted seven months before I was fired. I knew I'd done an excellent job. My employer's only complaint was that I couldn't keep up with the workload of the two young attorneys I was assigned to. The attorneys generated too much work for one person—50 percent of their assignments were due the same or next day. But the firm saw it as a personnel problem and let me go. I was shocked. I was also frightened that I was turning into my father, who couldn't hold onto a job after the age of 43 because of his illness. A long talk with my doctor convinced me that the disease wasn't setting in yet. I'd simply been the victim of a ruthless employer.

So I was out of work again for the second time in 18 months. I was ready to shoot every last perky staffer at the unemployment office who told me losing my job was a new beginning and anything was possible. I felt completely alone and out of place at the unemployment office's happy workshops.

This time my unemployment benefits would run out after three months. I didn't have the luxury to spend another nine months looking for a legal-assistant position making $33,000 a year, which was my salary at my last two jobs. I needed to act immediately. Because I can type 65 words a minute, I began looking for a secretarial or administrative-assistant position. I knew I would be lucky to make anything over $20,000. I didn't care. I needed that health insurance.

One week before my benefits ran out, I found a new job as a secretary with a national organization of neurologists. The medical benefits are excellent, but I'm earning only $19,200 a year, hardly enough to live on. My now ex-husband lost his job as a pastor and cannot be depended on for financial assistance. The only reason I'm afloat is that my mother is helping out. She went to work to support our family when my father could no longer hold a job. Now 70, she still works for the same company.

Going through predictive testing was supposed to help me gain control of my life, and I'm not sorry I had the test. I am thankful for the knowledge that I have the gene, even if I can't do anything medically about it. But I just wish today's economy would let me do something about it financially.

SPAULDING *lives in Minneapolis.*

Highlighted Quotations

Sometimes important passages will be excerpted and highlighted. These can give you clues to the central idea of the work. In the *Newsweek* article, for instance, a quotation from the text is reprinted in large type: "Planning for the future with Huntington's is impossible, except for the very wealthy." This clue allows most alert readers to predict that the article concerns the impact of genetic tests on financial planning. Along with the title, this quotation might also lead one to suspect that the author will dispute the notion that genetic testing is necessarily a good thing.

The Author

With many works, knowing some information about the author can enrich your reading. If you recognize the author's name, you may be able to make some useful predictions. If, for example, you were to encounter an article entitled "Teenagers and Sex," you would form very different expectations if its author were Billy Graham, the famous evangelist, than if it were Hugh Hefner, the publisher of *Playboy*. Professional titles, academic degrees, lists of other publications, or information about the author's occupation and accomplishments may give you clues about that person's point of view and expertise. Books frequently describe their authors on the flap of the dust jacket. Articles sometimes do so in a headnote before the article or in a footnote at the bottom of the first page or at the end of the article.

The *Newsweek* piece is accompanied by a photo of its author and followed by a one-sentence identification of her. Neither her name nor her face is familiar, and the description indicates only that she lives in Minneapolis, from which you may infer that the article concerns the personal experiences of someone who is neither a professional writer nor a celebrity. This, together with the subtitle and the highlighted quotation, suggests that the author herself has undergone genetic testing for a serious disease, a fact that will be confirmed in the first paragraph, where the author reveals that she has the gene for Huntington's disease.

Past Experience

Sometimes your prior reading can offer clues about what to expect. If you are a regular *Newsweek* reader, you recognize the "My Turn" column as a recurring feature of the magazine. Articles in this series are written by readers of the magazine, not staff writers, and usually relate personal experiences or express an opinion. This is further confirmation that the piece is a personal essay about how the diagnosis of a genetic disease can disrupt a person's ability to plan.

Section Headings

Scanning for headings and subheadings is especially valuable before reading a longer passage. One of the best and most important prereading strategies is to leaf quickly through a text for clues about the parts that make it up. Before beginning a book, examine its table of contents; before reading an article or chapter, page through it for headings and other clues. Having information in advance about a text's major ideas and organization can make your reading of it much more efficient. Although the *Newsweek* article has no subject headings, another reading that makes use of them is found on pages 69–72.

Date of Publication

Knowing when a piece was written can help you to evaluate it. When you are looking for information on advances in computer technology, for instance, it makes an enormous difference whether a source was written in 1976 or 1996. Knowing the date can also help put the author's viewpoints in perspective. You might consider whether attitudes toward genetic testing have changed since April 3, 1995, the date of the *Newsweek* issue in which the article appeared.

Length

Noting the length of an article or book chapter can give an indication of how thoroughly the author's point will be developed. It also helps to know where you stand within that development as you read.

Bold Type, Illustrations, and Captions

You can find additional clues to the contents of a book chapter by briefly examining it before you read. Key words that name central concepts are often printed in bold letters. (Look for examples in this chapter.) Other major ideas are often illustrated in drawings and photographs and explained in their captions. Open one of your textbooks that has illustrations and see what you can learn about the chapter from them.

With an article like the one we have examined, it takes only a few seconds of prereading to gather all this information. Prereading strategies amply repay the brief investment of time you make in them. Your mind is receptive as you begin to read, your reading is made easier, and you can read more alertly and profitably.

Textual Clues

Good writers help their readers in several ways. For example, they anticipate who their readers are likely to be, and they then write to be understood by them. They write clear sentences, using a vocabulary and style appropriate to their audience. They provide punctuation to signal when a pause in reading should occur or when one idea ends and another begins. Good readers, for their part, recognize and profit from the signals that writers give them.

Using Prereading Strategies   EXERCISES

1. Read the article "Knowing Isn't Everything" and determine the accuracy of the predictions you made using prereading strategies. Did these strategies enable you to read it more efficiently?

2. Using as many of the strategies in this section as you can, explain what predictions you can make about the rest of this chapter and about the reading that begins on page 69.

It is always easier for us to read a passage if we have a reasonably clear idea of what it is likely to be about. In a variety of ways, authors allow us to anticipate their ideas. Even inexperienced writers provide readers with a number of signposts to help them, as the following paragraph from a student's paper on teenage drinking demonstrates:

> Another cause of drinking among teenagers is peer pressure. They are told, "Go ahead, it can't hurt you. After all, everyone else does it." Before you know it, they are drinking along with the rest of the crowd. Soon they are even drinking before class, at lunch, and after school. They now have a serious drinking problem.

This paragraph is from a rough draft and would benefit from additional development and revision. Even so, it demonstrates the kind of signposts that writers provide for readers. Previous paragraphs in the paper had discussed other reasons for teenage drinking. The first two words here, *Another cause,* are **signal words,** also called **transition words,** telling us that a further reason is be introduced. The entire first sentence acts as a **topic sentence** for the paragraph, announcing the paragraph's general subject. After reading it, we anticipate that the rest of the paragraph will explain further how this pressure works. The writer does just that, detailing the process of how teenagers develop a drinking problem through peer pressure, and she uses transition words or phrases like *before you know it, soon,* and *now* to show us that a sequence of stages is being described.

Notice also how your mind works as you read the following passage, in which the sentences have been numbered:

> 1 Scarfe was always a tyrant in his household. 2 The servants lived in constant terror of his fierce diatribes, which he would deliver whenever he was displeased. 3 One of the most frequent causes of his displeasure was the food they served him. 4 His tea, for example, was either too hot or too cold. 5 The soup had either too much or too little seasoning. 6 Another pet peeve was the servants' manner of address. 7 God help the butler who forgot to add "sir" to every sentence he spoke to Scarfe, or the chauffeur whose tone was deemed not properly deferential. 8 On the other hand, when one of the more timid parlor maids would hesitate in speaking so as to be certain her words did not give offense, he would thunder at her, "Out with it, you stupid girl!"
> 9 Scarfe's wife and children were equally the victims of his tyranny. . . .

Notice how each sentence in the passage creates a context for sentences to come and so allows you to anticipate them. In the analysis that follows, we have made some assumptions about how you, or any typical reader, might have responded to the passage. Take some time to examine the analysis carefully and see if you agree with it.

In your first reading of the Scarfe passage, very likely your mind worked in this way:

First, since sentence 1 makes a general statement, you respond to it as a **topic sentence.** In other words, you guess that Scarfe's tyranny is the **main idea** of the paragraph. It comes as no surprise that sentence 2 tells you a more specific fact about his tyranny—Scarfe terrorized his servants. After sentence 2, you might expect either to learn which other members of his household Scarfe terrorized or else to get still more specific information about his treatment of the servants. The latter turns out to be the case.

The author provides a helpful *signal phrase* in sentence 3, "one of the most frequent causes of his displeasure," to show you where the paragraph is heading. The words *one of* inform you that food is one among several causes of Scarfe's anger and suggest that you may be told about others. The author makes the relationship between 2 and 3 clear by *repeating key words: his displeasure* in 3 refers back to *he was displeased* in 2, and *they* in 3 refers to *the servants* in 2.

Sentence 4 likewise uses a signal phrase, *for example,* to tell you that it will provide an example of Scarfe's displeasure. Although sentence 5 lacks a signal phrase, you can recognize that it is similar in purpose to 4 because it is similarly phrased, also containing the words *either too . . . or too. . . .* Sentence 6 begins with a signal word, *another;* the phrase *another pet peeve* refers back to sentence 3, which described the first pet peeve. Since 3 was followed by examples, you can expect the same of 6, and in fact both 7 and 8 also give specific instances of "servants' manner of address." Sentence 8 begins with a signal phrase, *on the other hand,* which signals a change in direction; that is, the sentence offers an example that is in some way opposite from the example in 7. It says that servants could be criticized for being too deferential, as well as for not being deferential enough.

By using *topic sentences,* repeating *key words,* and providing *signal phrases,* writers give readers clues to make reading easier. Without having to think about it, an experienced reader will respond to these clues, make predictions, and read with greater ease and effectiveness as a result. Chapter 4 pays special attention to topic sentences. The remaining sections of this chapter are concerned with other reading clues.

Responding to Textual Clues   EXERCISES

1. Only the first sentence (sentence 9) of the second paragraph is given in the passage about Scarfe. Make some predictions about the rest of that paragraph. Do you think sentence 9 is likely to be the paragraph's topic sentence? What would you expect the rest of the paragraph to be about? How is 9 related to the preceding paragraph? Does it contain any signal words or phrases linking it to the that paragraph?

2. Using your imagination to invent details, write the rest of the second paragraph, describing how Scarfe mistreated his wife and children. When you have finished, see what clues you provided to help your readers.

Transitions

Just as it is important for readers to recognize reading clues, it is also important for writers to provide them. *Signal words* make reading easier because they clarify the relationship between one sentence and another. It is for this reason that they are also called *transition words.* They help the reader see in which direction the ideas in a passage are moving. Relationships between sentences can be classified into several general categories. Four of the most important relationships, together with commonly used transition words for each, are listed below.

"And" Signals

And words signal movement in the same direction. They tell you that the new idea or fact will in some way be like the previous one. Here are the most common *and* signals:

and	similarly	furthermore	in fact	another
in addition	also	what's more	first	then
moreover	too	indeed	second	finally
likewise				

Example: Nixley's wisecracks got on his classmates' nerves. He *also* angered the teacher by snoring during the metaphysics lecture.

"But" Signals

But words signal a change in direction. They tell you that the new fact or idea will be different or opposite from the previous one.

but	however	on the other hand	still
yet	conversely	in contrast	instead
nevertheless	notwithstanding	the fact is	unfortunately
nonetheless			

Example: The doctor ordered Smedley to give up all spicy foods. *Nonetheless,* Smedley could still be found most nights by the TV set, munching happily on jalapeños and pickled sausages.

"For Example" Signals

For example words signal a movement from the general to the specific. They tell you that the new fact or idea will be a specific illustration of the previous general one.

for example	specifically	to illustrate
for instance	once	to begin with

Example: Pickleton is a splendid athlete. At a high school track meet, *for example,* she took firsts in both the low hurdles and the ten-kilometer race.

"Therefore" Signals

Therefore words signal a cause-and-effect relationship. They tell you that the new fact or idea will be the result of the previous one.

therefore	as a result	accordingly
consequently	hence	thus

Example: The Brunkin twins never remembered to set their alarm clocks. *As a result,* they were always late for their 8 o'clock statistics class.

Using Transitions	**EXERCISES**

1. The following passages are made difficult to read and sound choppy because signal words have been omitted. Supply signal words where you feel they would be useful to clarify relationships between sentences or to make the flow of the passage smoother.

   a. Colors are widely associated in people's minds with emotions. Red is traditionally associated with violence and anger. When people lose their tempers, they are said to "see red." Red has many positive associations. The poet Robert Burns wrote that his love was "like a red, red rose." Santa Claus is depicted wearing a red suit. Cheerfulness, as well as violence, is connected with red in our culture.

   b. We have taken it for granted that modern medicine is winning the war against contagious diseases. Fewer cases of malaria are reported each year. Smallpox has been eradicated. It comes as a shock to read that cases of venereal disease are rapidly increasing in number. New varieties have developed that are as yet incurable. No remedy for genital herpes is known to medical science. The traditional antibodies that once cured gonorrhea are proving ineffective against new, fast-spreading strains. Doctors are hopeful that in time venereal diseases, like other epidemics in the past, will be conquered once and for all.

   Practically every sentence in these two paragraphs has either an *and, but, for example,* or *therefore* relationship to the sentence that precedes it and so could take a signal word. So many signals, however, would probably clutter the paragraph. You have to decide where you will include them and where you will not. For each signal word you add, explain why you decided to use it.

2. Look at the article on pages 76–79, "The West at War." What transition words do you find in it?

3. Find a passage from one of your textbooks that uses a variety of signal words. Write a brief commentary on how the author uses them to alert readers to transitions between ideas.

4. Examine the paragraph you wrote for exercise 2 on page 63. What transitional words and phrases have you provided to help your readers? Supply additional signals if they are needed.

Reading with a Pencil

College students frequently face two problems when they read for academic purposes: maintaining interest and getting the most from their reading. Staying alert is sometimes no small challenge. Probably every student has had the disconcerting experience of losing that struggle and drifting into a trance, with the eyes continuing to plod across the page long after the mind has wandered elsewhere. When concentration is a struggle, your reading is slow, unpleasant, and—worst of all—

ineffective. Fortunately, there is a way of making your reading more efficient while maintaining your concentration: You can read better if you read with a pencil.

Two different activities are involved in reading with a pencil or a pen—*under-lining* and *note-taking.* If the book is your own, you may wish to carry out both procedures in the pages as you read them. In underlining, you mark the main ideas and the most significant information. In note-taking, you summarize the author's ideas in your own words or write your own ideas and responses.

Reading with a pencil has several advantages. One is simply that it keeps your mind alert and active. By combining writing with reading, you bring a larger area of your brain into the activity. Reading with a pencil also forces you to respond more actively to a text. When your mind is searching for the author's main ideas and connecting them to personal experience and other reading, you become directly involved with the text. You are forced to think, and you find that you better understand what you are reading.

Besides increasing alertness, reading with a pencil creates a useful record that later can give you easy access to the information you have read. For example, if you have marked a textbook chapter with underlining and notes in the margin, you can review that material quickly and effectively before an exam just by consulting what you have marked. You don't have to reread everything, since you have already marked what you consider most important. Moreover, by reading the highlighted passages, you stimulate your memory and recall most of what you read and thought the first time through.

Just as no two people will read a book in exactly the same way, no two readers will mark a book in the same way either. This is true partly because people bring into their reading different kinds of experience; consequently, they respond in different ways to the same words and ideas. But even the same reader will respond to a passage in different ways, depending on his or her purposes in reading.

Annotating and Underlining for Recall

Let's assume, for example, that a student in an introductory psychology class is studying the ways a society determines what kinds of behavior it considers normal versus unusual or deviant. She is assigned a selection from her textbook, from which the following passage has been excerpted.* The student knows that she will be tested on the chapter's content; therefore, her goal is literal comprehension of important facts. Here is how she might annotate the passage:

Abnormality and Society

Defining Abnormal Behavior

1   When we ask how a society defines a psychological abnormality, what we are asking is where that society draws the line between acceptable and unacceptable patterns of thought and behavior. There are several different measuring sticks for acceptability, but perhaps the most used is the society's norms.

---

*From *Abnormal Psychology: Current Perspectives,* Fifth Edition, by R. R. Bootzin and J. R. Acocella. New York: Random House, 1993. Reproduced with permission of The McGraw-Hill Companies.

Norm Violation. Every human group lives by a set of *norms*—rules telling us   2
what is "right" and "wrong" to do, and when and with whom. Such rules circumscribe every aspect of our existence, from our most far-reaching decisions down to
our most prosaic daily routines.

Let us consider, for example, the ordinary act of eating. Do we eat whatever   3
we want, wherever and whenever we want it? We do not. Eating is governed by
norms as to what is "good for us" to eat, how often we should eat, how much we
should eat, and where we should eat. Eating at a football game or at a rock concert is fine, but eating in church or at a symphony concert is not. Furthermore,
there are rules as to when and where certain things can be eaten. Drinking wine
with dinner is accepted practice; drinking wine with breakfast would be considered rather odd. Likewise, if a man lunches on stuffed squab in the bleachers at
the ball park, his sanity or at least his virility may well be questioned by the fans
seated around him; he is expected to eat a ball-park lunch—hot dogs and beer.
Conversely, if he serves hot dogs and beer at a candlelit dinner party, his guests,
expecting something closer to stuffed squab, will consider him either very daring
or very ignorant.

Some cultures even have strict taboos governing the question of whom one   4
can eat with. Certain tribes, for instance, prohibit eating in the presence of blood
relatives on the maternal side, since eating makes one vulnerable to being possessed by a devil, and such devils are more likely to appear when one is in the
presence of one's maternal relatives.

To outsiders, such norms may seem odd and unnecessarily complicated, but
adults who have been raised in the culture and who have assimilated its norms
through the process of socialization simply take them for granted. Far from
regarding them merely as folkways, they regard them as what is right and proper.
And consequently they will tend to label as abnormal anyone who commits serious violations of these norms.

norms are arbitrary yet most people assume they're "natural"

In a small, highly integrated society, there will be little disagreement over   6
norms. In a large, complex society, on the other hand, there may be considerable
friction between different groups over the question of what is right and proper. For
example, the Gay Liberation movement may be conceptualized as the effort of one
group to convince the society as a whole to adjust its norms so that homosexuality
will fall inside rather than outside the limits of acceptability. And it may be said in
general that American society is in the process of broadening its definition of nor-
mality, so that fewer and fewer kinds of behavior are being classed as abnormal.

In a sense, the use of norms as a standard for judging mental health might
seem inappropriate. Norms are not universal and eternal truths; on the contrary, as
we have seen, they change drastically across time and across cultures. Therefore,
they seem a weak basis for applying the label of abnormal to anyone. Furthermore,
whether or not adherence to norms is an appropriate criterion for mental health, it
might be called an oppressive criterion. Not only does it enthrone conformity as
the ideal pattern of behavior, it also stigmatizes the nonconformist. For norms
contain value judgments. People who violate them are not just doing something
unusual; they are doing something wrong. Yet despite these objections, norms
remain the dominant standard for defining abnormality. Though they may be
relative to time and place, they are nevertheless so deeply ingrained that they *seem*
absolute, and hence whatever violates them automatically appears abnormal.

Though oppressive and arbitrary, norms are the most common yardstick of conformity

Notice how the reader observed these guidelines to get more out of her reading:

GUIDELINES for Annotating and Understanding for Recall

- *Mark the most important ideas.* Let your underlining serve as an outline of the passage. Find the author's words that best express the main ideas and underline them. Usually that means underlining topic sentences and not underlining examples and other supporting material, unless they too are important.

  Notice that the reader did not underline anything in paragraphs 3 and 4, which consist entirely of examples that illustrate a point made in paragraph 2. She did underline part of that earlier paragraph: a sentence that states the main idea of the entire passage:

  > *Norm Violation.* Every human group lives by a set of *norms*—rules telling us what is "right" and "wrong" to do, and when and where and with whom. Such rules circumscribe every aspect of our existence, from our most far-reaching decisions down to our most prosaic daily routines.

- *Don't underline too much.* Underlining nearly every sentence that you read defeats your purpose; it makes your underlining nearly useless for review. Be selective and highlight only the most important ideas and information. The amount of material you underline will depend on what you are reading. Some passages that contain many important ideas will be underlined heavily. Others that contain examples or background material may not be underlined at all. Let your judgment and common sense be your guide.

- *Mark with rereading in mind.* Find and underline the words of the author that best express the main ideas. You don't need to underline entire sentences. In fact, since you are interested in brevity, underline only those phrases that are needed to make the main idea clear to you when you reread them. Sometimes parts of two different sentences can be underlined and connected to form a single statement. This passage shows an example of selective underlining with rereading in mind:

  > Norms are not universal and eternal truths; on the contrary, as we have seen, they change drastically across time and across cultures. Therefore, they seem a weak basis for applying the label of abnormal to anyone. Furthermore, whether or not adherence to norms is an appropriate criterion for mental health, it might be called an oppressive criterion. Not only does it enthrone conformity as the ideal pattern of behavior, it also stigmatizes the nonconformist.

  When she reviews her textbook the night before her exam, the reader can quickly recall the main idea simply by reading the underlined words: "Norms . . . change drastically across time and across cultures . . . [A]dherence to norms . . . also stigmatizes the nonconformist."

- *When the author's words are not convenient or clear, use your own.* If a passage is not phrased in words suitable for underlining, rephrase the main idea in your own marginal note. The reader of our sample passage wrote marginal notes to summarize ideas in paragraphs 5 and 7. Capsulizing important concepts in your own words is an aid to understanding what you read. When people talk about "writing to learn," one of the things they mean is that when students manage to translate difficult or unfamiliar ideas into their own language, their ability to understand and recall those ideas is enhanced.

• *Use special symbols to signal the most important passages.* Since some of the passages that you mark will be more important than others, let them stand out by drawing special symbols next to them in the margin. Stars, lines, exclamation and question marks, asterisks, and checks are only some of the marks you can use to make important passages stand out.

• *Mark only your own book.* Because no two readers think alike as they read, no one likes to read books that other people have marked. Writing in library books or books borrowed from friends is both a discourtesy and an act of vandalism. Use stick-on notes, or make photocopies of any borrowed materials that you want to mark. Of course, you are strongly encouraged to mark books that you own.

Reading with a Pencil   EXERCISE

Imagine that as part of a course in art, you are studying recent trends in portraiture. Read through the following article, and then reread it, this time underlining and annotating to recall specific facts and concepts. Mark especially the passages you might wish to review later for an exam on the material.

Portraiture Is Back, but, My, It's Changed
Celia McGee

When America's 19th-century art critics took it upon themselves to rank types of art, portraiture ended up at the bottom. Landscape painting had the depiction of the Romantic sublime and Manifest Destiny to recommend it. Still life coaxed nature into pretty arrangements loaded with symbolism. Genre promoted nationalism and pious sentimentality; history painting maintained its scholarly snob appeal.

But as if an association with vanity wasn't bad enough in portraiture, along came photography to challenge portraiture's role in recording the human visage. Despite a brief, brilliant comeback in the work of John Singer Sargent during the robber-baron decades and in Thomas Eakins's somber psychological realism, portraiture's reputation took further beatings from Cubism and other forms of modernist abstraction. Its low point coincided with the triumph of Abstract Expressionism and Minimalism in the 1950's and 60's. Next thing you knew, social types were commissioning their likenesses as Day-Glo silk-screens taken from Polaroids by a fellow in a blond wig.

Relegated to a place beyond the cultural pale, portraits have seemed social anachronisms, frumpy heirlooms, pictorial equivalents of gold watches, for retiring officialdom. A portrait at its best, wrote Charles Baudelaire, should be "a poem full of space and reverie." Where is the poetry in portraiture today? What has happened to the self reflected in the mirror of art?

A lot. The art world of the 90's is witnessing a resurgence of interest in portraiture— portraiture as diverse as it is full of contradictions. Portrait commissions are on the increase. Painters like Aaron Shikler, the dean of American portrait artists, are coming in from the cold. More and more, Mr. Shikler said, he is being invited to give lectures and teach master classes. "There's less of a stigma attached to painting portraits," he said. "There was a period when it was the lowest of the low, when you were laughed at."

Part of the revitalization of portraiture is owed to the revival of representation in art, both traditional and post-modern. "The visual arts are altogether different these days," said Alan Fern, director of the National Portrait Gallery in Washington. "There's more tolerance, more of an inclination to deal with figurative art than there was in the 70's. Portraiture has more of a place in what is happening."

That place is central because some of the most important trends in art today are responsible for portraiture's reinvigoration. The confrontation with identity, an emphasis on human physicality and its frailties, the politics of multiculturalism, and a continuing obsession with the mass media are everywhere.

"Portraiture isn't outdated and dead if you can reinvent it," said the New York artist Jonathan Santlofer, who makes what he calls constructed portraits, combining painting and sculptural elements. "I try to link my work with the very disparate history of portrait painting," he said, "to Greek and Egyptian reliefs, Flemish portraits, Cubism." He would like to portray a group of businessmen in the style of Rembrandt's "Nightwatch."

Portraiture's rehabilitation, however, is perhaps most noteworthy on the cutting edges of art. Taking many different forms, from installation art to abstraction, portraiture has produced fierce debates about formalism and realism, about irony in art, about politics, about tradition and breaking with conventions. Next month, the Hudson River Museum in Yonkers is opening "Making Faces: The America Portrait," an exhibition that will span 200 years. "There has been a move in contemporary art from broad investigations of culture to a search for individuality," Philip Verre, the museum's director, says. The intense examination of sex, ethnicity, sexuality and class has led naturally to portraiture and the ménage à trois it sets up among artist, subject and viewer.

Exhibitions
A Calendar Crowded with Faces

This fall, New York gallerygoers could visit shows featuring portraits by such historical figures as Elaine de Kooning or Pavel Tchelitchev, and by contemporary artists like Billy Sullivan, John Currin, Cindy Sherman, Janine Antoni, David Hammons and Hugh Steers, who paints drag queens, people with AIDS and his own patrician social circle. Philip Pearlstein will have an exhibition at the Robert Miller gallery next month. Even Julian Schnabel, until now uncharacteristically private about his portrait painting, is considering a show on the subject.

Last spring saw the most influential museum show of portraits in years, recent work by the English painter Lucian Freud at the Metropolitan Museum of Art, which is also planning a Chuck Close retrospective in 1996. The debut of the Andy Warhol Museum in Pittsburgh last summer refocused attention on Warhol's portraits.

The Museum of Modern Art is counting on a blockbuster with next year's "Picasso and Portraiture: Representation and Transformation." On the Jewish Museum's schedule is "Too Jewish," an exhibition that will introduce such variations in portraiture as Dennis Kardon's sculptured "Jewish Noses" series.

A number of historical shows—John Singleton Copley exhibitions next year in Boston and Washington and at the Metropolitan, for instance—will apply the social consciousness of contemporary art scholarship to portraiture's past. In July, the Parrish Art Museum in Southampton, L.I., will present the wide-ranging "Face Value: American Portraits," with 19th-century examples as well as contemporary ones.

Concepts
Finding Expression below the Neck

With so much traditional portraiture resurfacing, anti-establishment artists have felt provoked to deconstruct and redefine portraiture as a genre. "Portraiture is an incredibly complex topic," said Donna da Salvo, chief curator of the Parrish Art Museum and the organizer of "Face Value." "A lot of it doesn't even have faces in it anymore."

Many observers say that the past decade's preoccupation with the body—its fragility, its politics, its power to challenge taboos—has contributed to portrait-making's redefinition. "It's logical that the interest in portraiture would come out of all this concern with the body," said Marcia Tucker, the director of the New Museum of Contemporary Art in New York. "It's a question of the individual body in dialogue, or in confrontation, with the body politic. It's a way of being really honest and of signifying an interface between the self and the world. It's not a return to any kind of tradition."

Philip Pearlstein may not be the sort of artist Ms. Tucker had in mind. For decades, he has been considered a leading exponent of the body's formalist function in art, whether in his nude studies or his clothed portraits. But lately he has begun to express sentiments about his work that Ms. Tucker might find intriguing. "All my paintings are portraits," he said. "I don't go out of my way to capture personality—I'm not hot for soul-searching nervous breakdowns—but it's written all over the body." No matter how tiny. The artist Robert Greene paints fingertip-size likenesses of friends that he refers to as "thumb-print portraits."

Women's bodies, their appearance and their complicated roles in art and society, are a portraiture battlefield. The young artist Janine Antoni, know for her self-portrait busts carved out of chocolate and lard, went on to a project in which she spent a year studying with a prosthetic makeup artist to create a gender-bending, identity-confusing work about her parents. During three-hour sessions with wigs, putty and cosmetics, she literally switched her parents' identities, photographing the results. "I made my mom into my dad, and my dad into my mom," she explained. "They made me, so I turned around and remade them."

The physical details of Ms. Antoni's double portrait simultaneously hint at her parents' class, professional status and assimilated ethnicity. It is a sendup of the traditional society portrait, a personalized and affectionate version of the portrait as social critique, a commentary on portraiture as theatrical performance and on the trickiness of perception. Many artists involved with portraiture want to emphasize the fact that there is no such thing as fixed, single identity. "I participated in a project by the artist Kerri Scharlin," Ms. Antoni said, "who had a group of her friends each describe to a police sketch artist what she looked like. Each portrait was different."

The Subjects
Likenesses of Everyman

The questioning of mainstream portraiture's normally upper-crust subject matter has paved the way for the representation of others. The black artist David Hammons says his work is often a form of portraiture exploring the background and history of the so-called black underclass. He has taken stones unearthed by road work in Harlem, adorned them with hair from local barbershops and copied various hairdos from those he sees around his neighborhood. "They become portraits that make me feel close to the kids who wear these hair styles," he said.

Mr. Hammons's unslick, iconic likenesses are part of an effort to reclaim portraiture from advertising and the news media, to deflate the cult of celebrity and artifice. "The portrait has become a central part of advertising," said Donna da Salvo. "Look at the Gap ads, or American Express's 'Do You Know Me?' campaign. We are going to have selected advertisements and objects taken from material culture in 'Face Value' to analyze what advertising has done to the portrait tradition." Klaus Kertess, the curator of the Biennial, sees several of the artists he has selected "playing with the mass media's neutralized imagery" in their portraits.

Portraiture instead must establish an intimacy and trust between artist and sitter, points out Robert Storr, curator of painting and sculpture at the Museum of Modern Art. "It's a letting go of distances," he said. "And a portrait allows you to stare at somebody as much as you like and satisfy your curiosity."

Emotional rapport is usually the last thing associated with the billboard-size canvases of Polaroid head shots that Chuck Close first started to create in the late 60's in his desire to apply abstract patterning to the human face. Yet, said Mr. Close, "for the last few years I've been referring for the first time to my paintings as portraits rather than heads as I've been coming to grips with the tradition and conventions of portraiture.

"I paint people in order to get to know them," he said, "and my paintings always look more like the people than the Polaroids I paint them from."

If, in the last few years, he allowed himself to be more emotional and expressionist in his work, the development was accelerated after he was stricken by an aneurysm in 1992 that left him almost completely paralyzed. "When I was lying in the hospital," he said, "so many images of mine showed up to visit me. It became clear that the people I painted, my friends and family, were what mattered to me." Like many artists, Mr. Close paints mostly fellow artists. "It gives me a sense of community," he said.

Julian Schnabel, once of the broken-plate approach to art, agrees. "It's incredible to draw someone's face; it's like making a picture of their soul," he said. But Mr. Schnabel also likes to emphasize how much the emotional relationship between portraitist and sitter suggests the erotic. "It is an intense way of communicating with someone. My making a portrait is like a person tattooing their lover's name into their arm. There's something indelible about it."

Sometimes the contact between an artist and subject borders on clairvoyance. The painter Alex Katz, whose subjects derive their coolness from the artist's formalized depictions of urbane society, said: "I've always thought of emotion as one of the things I don't like. But five years ago, the novelist Anne Beattie wrote a book about my work in which she pointed out things about the relationships between the people in my paintings. She could tell from gestures, from appearances, what was buried way down in my work. She was 95 percent correct when it came to predicting which couples were going to break up."

Methods
Step No. 1: Go Inside the Skin

Many artists believe that no mechanical means of reproduction should come between artist and subject in their intense connectedness, a reason some feel that nonphotographic portraiture is getting back on an equal footing with photography. Although many traditional portraitists use photographs as aids to memory, Jamie Wyeth, who paints the famous and the unknown with the vernacular naturalism he learned from his father, Andrew, refuses to do even that. "I have to spend a lot of time with people when I paint them," he said.

He had just been approached by Oxford University to do a portrait of President Clinton, a former Rhodes scholar. "I'd love to accept, but accessibility may be a problem," Mr. Wyeth said, laughing. Retired Presidents are easier. The young realist painter Jacob Collins recently painted George Bush.

"It was strange bossing around a President," Mr. Collins said, "but I guess he's used to relying on experts. The only hard part was painting an official portrait without giving up my personal esthetic. I didn't become a painter to paint smiling people. All those faces by Rembrandt and Velázquez and Titian peering out from the ages look like they're thinking about something. Great portrait paintings avoid the false veneer of success."

Linda Nochlin, the Lila Acheson Wallace Professor of Modern Art at New York University's Institute of Fine Arts, thinks she knows why. "I believe a portrait is all about the artist," she said. Portraiture is self-portraiture. Professor Nochlin has been the subject of two well-known portraits, a picture with her husband, Richard Pommer, done by Philip Pearlstein in 1968, and one with her daughter, Daisy, by Alice Neel, an influential figure for many of today's younger artists. "Alice made everybody look anxious and full of anxiety about the times," she said.

But one artist's anxiety is another's grand illusion. A painting by Julian Schnabel is called "Portrait of God." "Just a title I gave it," he said.

Annotating to Stimulate Response

Now let's look at a passage from a different kind of text, an essay by historian and novelist Wallace Stegner. In this case, the reader is enrolled in a course in American history. His instructor has assigned a collection of short readings, all concerned with the development of public lands in the Far West. Students will be expected to participate in a class discussion of those readings, to be followed by an essay exam that will test their ability to make connections—to recognize points of agreement and disagreement—among the authors of the assigned readings. The reader's marking of the text indicates that he is reading for more than just factual information:

1

How many now?

Within the six Rocky Mountain states there lived in 1960 less than seven million people. They were densest in Colorado, at 16.9 to the square mile, and thinnest in Nevada at 2.6. Surprisingly, they were more urban than rural. Over half of Colorado's people were packed into the ten counties along the eastern face of the Rockies, the rest were scattered thinly across fifty-three counties. More than two thirds of Utah's population made a narrow dense band of settlement in the six counties at the foot of the Wasatch. The cause for this concentration is the cause that dictates so many aspects of Western life: water. As Professor Webb said, the West is an oasis civilization.

2

Fewer than 3 per sq. mi.!

3

Scarcity of water means population is concentrated in a few areas.

Room, then—great open spaces, as advertised. In reality as in fiction, an inescapable fact about the West is that people are scarce. For comparison, the population density of the District of Columbia in 1960 was nearly 13,000 to the square mile, that of Rhode Island was 812, that of New Jersey 806, that of Massachusetts 654. By the criterion of space, California at 100 to the square mile had already in 1960 ceased to be West, if it ever was, and Washington at 42.8 was close to disqualification; but Oregon, thanks to its woods and its desert eastern half, was still part of the family at 18.4, which is less than half the density of Vermont.

4

Paradox: Lots of land, yet not much of it liveable

5

Calif. isn't "west". Fla. isn't "South". Stegner sounds like one of those writers who defines what is and isn't Southern.

The natural resources of these open spaces are such as cause (heartburn) among corporations and individuals who wish the West were as open as it used to be, and were not watched over by so many federal bureaus. Now that the pineries of Wisconsin and Michigan are long gone, the Northwest holds our most valuable forests. Now that the (Mesabi) Range approaches exhaustion, Iron County, Utah, becomes a major source of iron ore; the steel industry based upon Utah ore and limestone, and Utah, Colorado, and Wyoming coal is a first step on the road that led to Pittsburgh and Gary. It has been estimated that the Upper Colorado River basin contains a sixth of the world's known coal reserves. The oil shales of Utah and Colorado, already in experimental reduction in Parachute Canyon, lie ready for the time when petroleum reserves decline. The Rocky Mountains contain most of our gold, silver, lead, zinc, copper, molybdenum, antimony, uranium, and these, depending on the market of the moment, may produce (frenzies) comparable with the gold rushes of last century. A few years ago, on a road across the Navajo Reservation near the Four Corners, I was stalled behind an oil exploration rig that had broken an axle fording Chinle Wash after a cloudburst. Behind me, in the hour I waited, stacked up fifteen or twenty cars and parts of three other exploration outfits. And who pulled the broken-down rig out and let us go on? A truck loaded with twenty tons of uranium ore. This on a road that only a little while earlier had been no more than ruts through the washes, ducks

6

Businessmen and developers suffer physically from their own greed.

7

where's this?

8

Natural resources of East and Midwest are depleted. Corporations now eye the West and its riches.

9

And now the steel industry is in decline. Does economic development set in motion an inevitable chain of events culminating in poverty?

10

Unusual word Erratic business cycles lead to "frenzies" and "panics"

11

Precious minerals but no water

12

Paradoxes: Sparsely populated but urban, great wealth but no water

on the ledges, and periodic wallows where stuck travelers had dug and brushed themselves out of the sand.

Enormous potentials for energy—coal, oil, shale, uranium, sun. But one source, water, has about exhausted its possibilities. The Rockies form the nation's divide, and on them are generated the three great western river systems, the Missouri, Columbia, and Colorado, as well as the Southwest's great river, the Rio Grande. Along those rivers and their tributaries most of the feasible power, reclamation, and flood-control damsites have been developed. Additional main-stem dams are not likely to recommend themselves to any close economic analysis, no matter how the dam-building bureaus promote them, and conservationist organizations in coming years can probably relax a little their vigilance to protect the scenery from the engineers.

—Wallace Stegner, *The Sound of Mountain Water*

In this case, the reader's annotations are a good deal more complex and diverse than those of the first reader, who was trying mainly to memorize facts and concepts. In fact, this reader's marginal notes fall into several different categories:

• *Summary.* Notes 3, 4, 8, and 11 differ little from the marginal notes attached to the passage from the psychology textbook. The reader is simply trying to recast Stegner's ideas into his own language.

• *Questions.* Questions help the reader identify the inevitable "gaps" in any selection—places that lead to confusion, places where the reader would like further details or explanation, places where the reader experiences doubt or reservation. In the first marginal note to the Stegner passage, for example, the reader wonders how much the population of the Rocky Mountain states has grown in the past twenty-five years. Is Stegner's assessment, published in 1969, still valid? Did Stegner fail to foresee population shifts? Have natural barriers to settlement kept the region relatively immune to change through growth and development, as Stegner seems to predict?

• *Reactions.* A reader may react either to the ideas brought out in a passage or to the author's way of expressing those ideas (tone of voice, vocabulary, bias). Note 2 illustrates the first kind of reaction. This type of response can be a simple statement of agreement, disagreement, outrage, or whatever. For example, note 2 says little more than "Imagine that!" On the other hand, reactions become more complex when a reader calls on personal experience or makes connections with facts outside the writer's text. In note 5, the reader seems to be saying:

> Isn't it funny that Stegner should say that California, the westernmost of the 48 states, isn't "really" Western? It reminds me of how most people say that Florida, the southernmost state, isn't "really" Southern. Stegner sounds like an old-time native talking to an audience of outsiders and newcomers who don't know from Western.

Here the reader is drawing some conclusions about the relationship between himself (the "listener") and Stegner (the "speaker"). More importantly, the reader is consciously resisting the role of a passive listener, one who might accept uncritically a rather subjective interpretation of what constitutes "the West."

Notes 6 and 10 comment on vocabulary. Specifically, they point to Stegner's tendency to view corporate greed in terms of illness ("heartburn") and emotional disturbance ("frenzy"). In contrast to the natural splendor and abundance of the West, attempts to exploit its wealth are presented in terms of sickness and imbalance. Again, the alert reader is conscious of the writer's attempt to manipulate his interpretation or understanding of the subject.

- *Definitions.* Every reader, regardless of educational level, is likely to encounter an unfamiliar word or name from time to time. The often-heard advice to stop and look it up is not always practical, unless the word or name in question represents a key idea that keeps reappearing. Instead, most readers learn to make satisfactory guesses on the basis of clues provided by context. (Of course, this process is not likely to work with a passage that has a high density of unfamiliar vocabulary.) Although these guesses can help a reader comprehend a passage, it still is a good idea to mark unfamiliar vocabulary with a circle or question mark, returning later with a dictionary, encyclopedia, or almanac. In the case of note 7, the reader, not knowing where the Mesabi Range is located, guessed from clues provided in the preceding sentence that it was somewhere in the upper Midwest. Using a dictionary, he later discovered that the Mesabi Range is in Minnesota.

- *Extrapolations.* To *extrapolate* means to take a given set of facts or interpretations and to project or predict other facts and interpretations that are not given or available. For instance, a business executive, examining sales records for the past ten years, might wish to extrapolate from those figures how much sales should increase or decline in the next six months. Readers extrapolate when they take a writer's ideas and extend them, expand on them, or apply them to other situations that the writer overlooked, did not know, or failed to predict. In note 9, for instance, the reader points out that since 1969, the steel industry of Pittsburgh and Gary has suffered the same kind of economic decline as the one brought on by the depletion of coal and iron ore deposits in the upper Midwest. This leads the reader to extrapolate an idea about business cycles—an idea that is not stated (or even necessarily implied) by Stegner.

- *Inventories.* Sometimes readers detect recurring ideas, images, or patterns of language in a passage. Or, perhaps during a second reading, they detect connections among their own annotations. For example, when the reader connects Stegner's use of the words *heartburn* and *frenzy* to describe corporate behavior, he is beginning to make an inventory in his mind. Note 12 is an attempt to put another type of inventory into writing: The reader sees that Stegner describes the West through a series of paradoxes or contradictions.

Not every annotation you can make when reading with a pencil falls neatly into one of the categories listed above. However, the important thing to do whenever you read with a pencil is to record some of the thoughts and responses that pass through your mind as you experience the text. As readers become more proficient at the process, they often engage in a kind of conversation or dialogue with what they read. In the process, they become independent of rules, formulas, and categories of response.

Annotating a Passage

Imagine that as part of the same course in history, you are assigned the following article, written twenty-five years after Stegner's essay. Read through the article, and then read it again, annotating to stimulate response. Annotate the text in a way that would help you contribute to a class discussion and, perhaps, prepare you to make connections between these two readings on the same general topic.

The West at War
Michael Elliott with Stryker McGuire

> *Culture Clash: With their gentrified new houses and chic art galleries, affluent newcomers are turning the traditional Mountain States into the nation's most fashionable—and most socially divided—region. Can the cowboys coexist with the Feds, the militias—and cappuccino bars?*

Each summer, in every culture with a cow, a man and a mountain, the same thing happens: the man drives the cow up the mountain to fresh pasture. Rod Lucas, 76, who ranches outside Jackson Hole, Wyo., has been doing it for decades—taking his cattle from the valley to alpine meadows high in the Gros Ventre range. No more. He tried, for the last time, a year ago, starting as soon as "it was light enough to tell a cow from a sagebrush." But before Lucas was half a mile down the road, there was a line of cars in both directions, and their drivers were screaming at him and his herd to get out of the way. "That was it," says Lucas. "The cow business as everybody knew it is gone. I need to get out of this tourist country."

Cows against cars: one of many skirmishes unfolding across the mountain west. Clashes that pit survivalists against the government are dramatic, political and—in the wake of the Oklahoma City bombing—well known. Other economic and cultural conflicts are less sensational but equally important in this, the nation's fastest-growing region. Ranchers lose grazing land to California software writers buying up real estate; small towns with shared values are swamped by chic new settlers. The West is at war with itself.

And so an old song continues. Despite the myths, the West has never been a peaceful idyll. Indians against settlers; sheep against cows; gringos against Mexicans; union men against the company—there has never been a single conception of what "the West" means.

Yet history doesn't make the current conflicts any less disturbing. For established Westerners, everything is fundamentally changing—and fast, as thousands of newcomers consume the available property. The West's traditional industries—mining, ranching and logging—are clear losers in the new order. That old economy, based on "extracting" wealth from rocks, grass and trees, is dying, pushed aside by market forces (it's a lot cheaper to raise cows on feedlots in Florida than on poor pasture in Wyoming), replaced by high-skilled workers in high-tech companies. There are only 3,000 miners left in all of Idaho—fewer than one lone company, Micron Technology Inc., employs in two counties near Boise. Currently, the region's most rapidly expanding employers are museums, amusement parks and fitness clubs. The steepest declines are in the traditional extractive jobs. So cowpats and coal mining are out; cappuccino and cilantro are in. On Yankie Street in the New Mexico mining town of Silver City, the A.I.R. Espresso Bar and Gallery says it all: "A.I.R." stands for "artist in residence."

The old West won't go quietly. Its stalwarts will fight, and fairly or not, one of their main targets is the federal government, blamed for regulating the old extractive industries to death. Throughout the West, federal rangers have been threatened; in some towns, militiamen openly swagger, guns in holsters. The Bureau of Land Management warns its Idaho employees never to leave their compounds without radio communication and to "avoid areas with a known potential for conflict."

Why can't traditional Westerners live and let live? Largely because of an unprecedented population increase over the last 10 years. At first glance, this shouldn't matter. Between the Mexican and Canadian borders, and between the Front Range of the Rockies to the east and the Cascades and Sierra Nevada to the west, live fewer than 20 million people. In Western Europe—about the same size—there are more than 300 million. Surely, there's room enough for everyone who wants to live there.

Perhaps not, for in the West, "space" isn't quite what it seems. Yes, there are vast empty reaches. But almost all of the mountain west is arid; much of it as steep as it is waterless; and in some states two thirds or more of the land is owned by the federal government. So the land actually available for private development is very limited. That has made the West an "oasis" civilization, with its people clustered mainly in towns and cities. Eagle County, Colo., whose population grew by more than 20 percent between 1990 and 1994, has more than 1 million acres. But only 14 percent of its land is privately owned, and geology dictates that most of that can't be built on.

Replicate that example a hundred times, and you've got a problem. Take St. George, Utah (population: 35,000, for now), where, one morning this spring, Jeff Knowles was busy running cable-TV hookups into new stucco houses in a development called The Legacy. About 40 such subdivisions are being built in St. George. "You drive by one day, and a hillside is wide, open pasture land," says Knowles. "Next time you go by, it's all cleared off, and they've got house pads laid out." That means plenty of work for cable-TV installers—but it also signals a profound change in the town. "Whatever was unique about St. George," says 20-year resident Bob Owens, "is being lost." Or, as it says on a bumper sticker in Silver City (where one planned development would double the size of the town): WELCOME TO SILVER CITY. NOW PLEASE GO HOME.

That orneriness is somewhat understandable. The West is being quickly transformed from someplace special into "rural sprawl," complete with strip malls and suburban tracts—albeit with a drop-dead beautiful backdrop. "We don't have any developments with guards and gates yet," says Will Petty, who runs a technical-translation business (classic "New West" industry, that) in Moab, Utah. "But they have them in Jackson Hole, and they're coming our way."

Throughout the West, longtime residents know whom to blame: "You must be a Californian" has become a mountain insult. The Census Bureau reckons that by 2020, an additional 4 million Californians will have fled, mostly to neighboring states, where they will join the likes of Roy Kee, who recently moved from southern California to St. George with his wife. "We left because of the crime," says Kee. "It got so it was nothing but Bloods, Crips, drug addicts and wetbacks," says his wife, Lisa. (One Utah mayor is said to have coined the phrase "Rodney King real estate" for the new boom-towns.) The newcomers push up housing and property prices—in southern Utah, they've quadrupled since 1990. Californians, locals note, build differently: "There's a lot more stucco and tiled roofs," says Bob Nicholson of the St. George planning department. "We never had that before." Never had 10,000-square-foot mansions whose plate-glass windows glint on a ridge line, either. Terry Anderson, a professor at Montana State, has an old shack outside town, and snorts about a new house there that has *Southern columns.* "A libertarian like me," says Anderson, "almost gets to believe in zoning."

Or in flattening tourists. In Moab, the world capital of mountain biking, one resident has a squashed-like-a-bug bike strapped to the front of his Jeep. Southern Utah has lived the quintessential boom-and-bust economic history of the West. After the Three Mile Island accident in 1979, nuclear power fell out of favor, uranium mining collapsed, and in the town of about 6,000 people, 2,000 jobs were lost. The unlikely savior of the local economy was the bike. Each weekend, there are *20,000* cyclists around Moab. Each year, 100,000 cyclists try the roller-coaster-like Slickrock Trail, parts of which have turned black from the rubber residue of the bikes' tires. And spring break turns Moab into Daytona West, with boozed-up tourists surfing big four-wheel-drive vehicles along the rocks up into the hills.

Yet the mountain west is a desperately fragile landscape. Aridity sees to that, and makes water the most precious commodity in the region. Most of the West's water has been devoted to farming, but urban development and tourism are putting a nearly unbearable strain on that scarce resource. Ask Pat Allen. Now 77, he has ranched 1,700 acres on the Payette River in Idaho all his life (his father bought the land). Allen uses a lake formed when the government built a dam back in the 1940s. But now he's been told to cut his grazing allotment on the lake's west bank by two thirds to reduce pollution. On the other side of the water, the Bureau of Reclamation just put up signs limiting the locals' four-wheel-drive access to the lake—too much erosion. And the nearby town of Cascade, whose new subdivisions are visible from Allen's land, has told him it's going to drill two wells on his land to meet clean-water regulations, whether he likes it or not. (He doesn't.) Meanwhile, new neighbors whose backyards used to be pasture complain when Allen's cattle graze too close to their lawns. "It's getting to where you don't sleep good at night," says Allen's wife, Marie. "It's just fight, fight, fight."

Water and grazing wars are proxies for a bigger issue—the collapse of community. "People in the West used to be poor together," says Ed Marston, publisher of the High Country News, based in the old coal-mining town of Paonia, Colo. "You didn't have enough people to have economic classes." In Paonia today, says Marston, "you can't buy socks . . . but you can buy real estate at four or five places." But paradoxically, in at least some Western towns, the force of the culture clash is bringing communities together. It's as if people have goaded each other to the edge of a canyon—and now, pondering their mutual fate, are stepping back.

In the Bitterroot Valley of western Montana, the thing that did it was the death threats to judges. Old-time residents had tolerated the incoming militia types (not all newcomers eat salad and like stucco). The right-wingers seemed to share the same inbred Western distrust of the federal government, liked their guns—regular guys, if a bit weird. Then came the black helicopters—or rather, then came warnings from the militias that government forces would soon descend from the choppers to take away their wives and children. Finally, early this year, Joe Holland, director of the North American Volunteer Militia, threatened to shoot a local judge in the head. For Gordon Read, minister of the First Christian Church in Hamilton, that was enough. He printed 1,000 WE SUPPORT OUR RAVALLI COUNTY OFFICIALS posters and organized an antimilitia rally. Fourth-generation Montanans joined with Californians; latter-day hippies held hands with church ladies; greens and businessmen found common cause.

Hamilton still isn't entirely at peace—at least not yet. Sally Edwards moved there from California with her husband last year, took over a small restaurant, dumped the menu's fatback and canned peaches and started serving huevos rancheros and rolled pancakes with fresh fruit. She's been treated pretty well, mostly, but the locals, Edwards says, don't like what they call "the changes" in town. Yet the extremes are giving way. Ravalli County Sheriff Jay Printz is no fashionable liberal; he's suing the federal government, arguing that the Brady gun-control bill violates states' rights. But he thinks the militias go too far. "They make me look like an idiot when they start talking about the goddammed Trilateral Commission and the Jews and the bankers and all that crap," says Printz. "We always get lumped into the same category, which really gravels me."

So, can the "new" Westerners—the Californians, the technical-translators, the mountain bikers—be generous enough to find room in *their* West for people who use "gravel" as a verb? For Sheriff Printz, and for Rod Lucas's cows? If espresso bars and fresh-fruit pancakes completely prevail, if mountain towns become a cross between Aspen and Orange County, probably not, and that would be a distinctive cultural loss. The future of the West is a test both of those who have always lived there, and of those affluent folk who would now like to. It asks both to tolerate ways of life that are superficially antithetical to each other. Now would be a good time for Westerners to offer each other a friendly hand—before the West's war with itself gets out of control.

Keeping a Reading Journal

There are times when writing marginal notes may not be the most effective strategy. Perhaps you have borrowed a book from the library or from a friend, or you may want to expand the range of your responses to a particular reading (that is, write at greater length than you would be able to do comfortably in the margins of a book). On those occasions, a reading journal is a good way to foster the same type of active engagement with a text that takes place when you write marginal notes.

Consider how one reader commented on the following passage, the opening of Robert Pirsig's book *Zen and the Art of Motorcycle Maintenance.* The reader was taking a course in contemporary literature and selected Pirsig's book from a list of non-assigned readings. Asked to compose a paper that explains and develops her personal interpretation of the book, she decided to use a reading journal as a stimulus for personal reflection. First read the passage from the book and then observe the way that the reader reflected on that passage in a reading journal:

> *What follows is based on actual occurrences. Although much has been changed for rhetorical purposes, it must be regarded in its essence as fact.*
>
> I can see by my watch, without taking my left hand from the left grip of the cycle, that it is eight-thirty in the morning. The wind, even at sixty miles an hour, is warm and humid. When it's this hot and muggy at eight-thirty, I'm wondering what it's going to be like in the afternoon.
>
> In the wind are pungent odors from the marshes by the road. We are in an area of the Central Plains filled with thousands of duck hunting sloughs, heading northwest from Minneapolis toward the Dakotas. This highway is an old concrete two-laner that hasn't had much traffic since a four-laner went in parallel to it several years ago. When we pass a marsh the air suddenly becomes cooler. Then, when we are past, it suddenly warms up again.
>
> I'm happy to be riding back into this country. It is a kind of nowhere, famous for nothing at all and has an appeal because of just that. Tensions disappear along old roads like this. We bump along the beat-up concrete between the cattails and stretches of meadow and then more cattails and marsh grass. Here and there is a stretch of open water and if you look closely you can see wild ducks at the edge of the cattails. And turtles.... There's a red-winged blackbird.
>
> I whack Chris's knee and point to it.
>
> "What!" he hollers.
>
> "Blackbird!"
>
> He says something I don't hear. "What?" I holler back.
>
> He grabs the back of my helmet and hollers up, "I've seen *lots* of those, Dad!"
>
> "Oh!" I holler back. Then I nod. At age eleven you don't get very impressed with red-winged blackbirds.

You have to get older for that. For me this is all mixed with memories that he doesn't have. Cold mornings long ago when the marsh grass had turned brown and cattails were waving in the northwest wind. The pungent smell then was from muck stirred up by hip boots while we were getting in position for the sun to come up and the duck season to open. Or winters when the sloughs were frozen over and dead and I could walk across the ice and snow between the dead cattails and see nothing but grey skies and dead things and cold. The blackbirds were gone then. But now in July they're back and everything is at its alivest and every foot of these sloughs is humming and cricking and buzzing and chirping, a whole community of millions of living things living out their lives in a kind of benign continuum.

You see things vacationing on a motorcycle in a way that is completely different from any other. In a car you're always in a compartment, and because you're used to it you don't realize that through that car window everything you see is just more TV. You're a passive observer and it is all moving by you boringly in a frame.

On a cycle the frame is gone. You're completely in contact with it all. You're *in* the scene, not just watching it anymore, and the sense of presence is overwhelming. That concrete whizzing by five inches below your foot is the real thing, the same stuff you walk on, it's right there, so blurred you can't focus on it, yet you can put your foot down and touch it anytime, and the whole thing, the whole experience, is never removed from immediate consciousness.

—Robert Pirsig, *Zen and the Art of Motorcycle Maintenance*

Here are the annotations the reader wrote in her journal:

1. Well, the title is certainly interesting, and the author's note is amusing. Most writers probably aren't so quick to tell you that something may not be factual.

2. Funny how this starts off seeming *not* to be the sort of thing I'd choose to read: I'm not an outdoorsy person, and I've been on a motorcycle exactly once— thought I'd never walk again after 34 miles of it! I'm still attracted to this. Maybe it's guilt feelings, sitting in the car openly admitting that the scenery is OK but sort of dull after a while, something for seeing through windows. Maybe I'm not, as Pirsig suggests, old enough to appreciate it. I don't like to sweat—have a compulsion about being clean, and I'm none too secure about the idea of being inches from pavement that could skin me clean if I made one wrong move.

3. I like what he says about smelling things, though. The smell of lawns being watered, wet pavement, honeysuckle, the ocean, even rotting logs. I even like some city smells, like diesel fumes. I used to find the smell of Greyhound buses very exciting—the lure of adventure. I guess the motorcycle thing is similar, though maybe both Pirsig and I have been unduly influenced by movies. I did sort of enjoy my one and only ride on a cycle, but I've never felt safe about repeating the experience.

4. Pirsig seems to be hinting at something about safety and risk. He's riding with his son—surely he's no hotdogging type, you just don't risk your children that way. So the risk is something else. My boyfriend once suggested how wonderful it would be to spend the rest of your life sailing around the world. I thought not, since I was afraid of drowning, sharks, sunburn (too many movies again?). He added, "However long it might be." There are various kinds of risk, not all of them physical. It's sobering to think how attached I am to safety. I've certainly taken some risks in my life, though seldom physical.

5. I wonder if Pirsig is talking about this a bit when he says you become part of the scene instead of just an observer?

This response to reading lies at the opposite extreme from the notes and under-linings written in the psychology textbook. It is a highly personal response and a greatly elaborated one. Of course, neither of these extremes (nor anything in between) is necessarily better than the other. Partly, it is a matter of individual pref-erence, but mostly it is a case of the reader's techniques being governed by her pur-poses for reading. The student responding to *Zen and the Art of Motorcycle Mainte-nance* is deliberately trying to record the personal impact of that book on her as a reader. She is doing so not because she is necessarily a more subjective, intuitive type of person than the first reader; rather, she is trying to meet the demands of an academic task that calls for a more personal type of response to reading.

The personal responses in this student's reading journal fall into several cate-gories:

- *Reactions to details outside the immediate text.* In her first annotation, the student has attended to the author's prefatory note and reflected in the book's title. In doing so, she makes use of previous experiences as a reader.

- *Personal associations and recollections.* To some, this reader's second anno-tation may seem digressive and unrelated to the passage from Pirsig's book. How-ever, one of the advantages of a personal journal—which is intended for the writer's own use, not the reading of others—is that a writer is free to explore ideas that are not always clearly connected. Sometimes surprising discoveries can occur.

- *Evaluations.* In her third annotation, the reader evaluates the effectiveness of Pirsig's writing before going on to another personal association.

- *Inferences.* In her fourth annotation, the reader begins to draw a conclusion about ideas brought forth in the passage. This type of response will be particularly useful later, when the reader tries to develop her thoughts in a more formal piece of writing intended for an audience of readers. Notice how the free play of seem-ingly irrelevant ideas in the earlier annotations appears to have primed the pump—to have led the reader spontaneously to draw an inference in the fourth annotation.

- *Speculations.* Making an inference often draws a reader into further reflec-tion. In her fifth annotation, the reader extends and amplifies her ideas from the previous annotation.

No list of categories will exhaust the range of responses that can appear in a reading journal. Independent of rules and formulas, experienced readers learn to become inventive and even playful in their journals. However, if you have not used a reading journal before, you may want to try out some of the following sugges-tions or prompts:

- Select a quotation from the reading:
  - –Explain it.
  - –Apply it to your life.
  - –Explain precisely why it is not clear.
  - –Supply a concrete illustration for it.
  - –Rewrite it so it communicates better.

–Examine its unstated assumptions.
–Examine its logic/evidence.
–Argue with it.
–Examine its implications and significance.
–Study its style.

- Make a list of the words you did not know and their meanings.

- Take a long or complex unit (section or chapter) and boil it down to its key ideas or segments.

- Try to pin down definitions of key terms.

- Pick out several impressive sentences or images.

- Point out contradictions from place to place.

- Study relationships among facts, opinions, generalizations, and value judgments.

- Examine the treatment of opposing views. Are they mentioned? tolerated? refuted? respected? insulted?

- Examine the writing's structure.

- Discuss the sort of readers for whom the work seems intended.

A useful variation of the reading journal is the ***double-entry notebook.*** Here, the reader draws a vertical line down the middle of each page and writes journal entries in the left-hand column. Later, she can record responses to her own notes on the opposite side of the page. Many readers find the double-entry notebook an effective way to engage in reflection and critical analysis by opening up a conversation or dialogue with themselves as well as with the text. Here is how some of the annotations written in response to the passage from *Zen and the Art of Motorcycle Maintenance* might have looked if they had been recorded in a double-entry notebook:

Respond to the text in the left-hand column as you read.	*Reflect on your responses later in the right-hand column.*
1. I like what he says about smelling things, though. The smell of lawns being watered, wet pavement, honeysuckle, the ocean, even rotting logs. I even like some city smells, like diesel fumes. I used to find the smell of Greyhound buses very exciting—the lure of adventure. I guess the motorcycle thing is similar, though maybe both Pirsig and I have been unduly influenced by	The "nature" thing is really a diversion. Not sure why I think so, but I don't think he is going to be raving on about nature.

movies. I did sort of enjoy my one and only ride on a cycle, but I've never felt safe about repeating the experience.

2. Pirsig seems to be hinting at something about safety and risk. He's riding with his son—surely he's no hotdogging type, you just don't risk your children that way. So risk is something else. My boyfriend once suggested how wonderful it would be to spend the rest of your life sailing around the world. I thought not, since I was afraid of drowning, sharks, sunburn (too many movies again?). He added, "However long it might be." There are various kinds of risk, not all of them physical. It's sobering to think how attached I am to safety. I've certainly taken some risks in my life, though seldom physical.

When he talks about being part of the scene, I also think of the idea that what's worth doing is worth doing well. The catch to that is, of course, that we can excuse any failure by saying, well, it wasn't worth doing.

3. I wonder if Pirsig is talking about this a bit when he says you become part of the scene instead of just an observer?

You hear people say that all the time—"it's stupid"—just because the outcome wasn't somehow satisfactory. There are a lot of people just going through the motions of things because they decide too quickly that the results *won't* be worth real involvement; so the bad outcome is predetermined.

In her double-entry notebook, this student has managed to sustain a dialogue between Pirsig's text and the personal associations that it arouses in her mind. Notice, for example, how the first annotation in the right-hand column carries the student from a purely personal reflection (found in the corresponding annotation in the left-hand column) back to an observation about Pirsig's text. The two following pairs of annotations, on the other hand, move in the opposite direction.

Successful college students learn to tailor their reading processes to meet varying purposes for reading. The different strategies presented in this chapter—annotating and underlining to recall specific facts and concepts, annotating to stimulate response, and keeping a reading journal—can help you regulate your reading processes, making them serve the needs at hand.

READING SELECTION

The following selection is an article from the *New York Times*. Imagine that you are taking an anthropology course titled "Human Behavior and Customs" and are asked to read the article. The discussion topic for your next class is what we humans can learn about ourselves from studying other primates. With that in mind, read the article and, as you do, make entries in a reading journal.

Meat Viewed as Staple of Chimp Diet and Mores

The finding may bear on the evolution of human behavior.

VERNE G. KOPYTOFF

1   If chimpanzees were human, their thirst for blood could be called barbaric. And if human morality applied to their practice of trading food for sex, many would spend the mating season in jail.

2   Researchers studying chimpanzee hunting habits are gaining new insight into the lives of man's closest animal relative. Once thought of as docile vegetarians, these able hunters forage for meat with a passion and motivation not chronicled until recently.

3   Dr. Craig B. Stanford, an anthropologist at the University of Southern California, has documented the chimpanzee's success in the pursuit of flesh. Given other similarities between chimps and man, he suggests that early humans could have chased game millions of years before current evidence suggests. Dr. Stanford described his research, the largest study to analyze the chimpanzee's predilection for meat, in the May-June issue of *American Scientist* magazine.

4   Dr. Stanford found that chimpanzees hunt with such gusto in Gombe National Park in Tanzania that each year they lay waste to one-fifth of their territory's population of the red colobus monkey, their preferred prey. These long-tailed victims, crowned with a thatch of red hair, are plucked with abandon from the trees where they forage near the border with Zaire.

5   The 45-member Kasakela chimpanzee community, living in the low-lying forest of Gombe, eats one ton of meat on average each year, said Dr. Stanford, a 38-year-old associate professor at U.S.C. During one hunting binge in 1992, they killed 71 red colobus monkeys in 68 days.

6   This level of predation is surprising to many primatologists, but seems less so when compared with the diet of humans, the only other primate known to eat meat regularly. According to Dr. Stanford, chimpanzees can consume up to a quarter-pound of meat a day when they hit their hunting stride, rivaling at times some contemporary tribes of hunter-gatherers.

7   "Every article ever written on human evolution up until now says, 'Isn't it fascinating that chimps eat meat, but it's trivial compared to what modern humans eat,'" Dr. Stanford said. "Well, the Pygmies of Zaire are among the lowest meat consumers on the human spectrum. And there is no question that chimpanzees are, in some months, very close to that amount or are already there."

8   Dr. William C. McGrew, an anthropologist at Miami University of Ohio who studies chimpanzee behavior, said: "You pick up any textbook and it would say that meat

eating by chimpanzees is insignificant. This is the first time meat has been shown to be important nutritionally."

Among the first scientists to debunk the myth of chimpanzees as banana-eating vegetarians was Dr. Jane Goodall, a British primatologist, who nearly 30 years ago announced to a startled scientific community that chimpanzees were part-time carnivores. Further research showed that these natives of equatorial Africa kill fellow chimps, use tools and mourn their dead—all behaviors once thought of as uniquely human.   9

As early as the 1960's, Dr. Geza Teleki, an American primatologist, said after observing male chimps swap meat for sex with females that nutrition was only one of several reasons chimpanzees ate flesh.   10

Dr. Stanford builds on this finding, saying that male chimpanzees often hunt as a way to finance their sexual barter when traveling with sexually receptive females. And the more such receptive females are present, the more likely a group of chimpanzees will hunt.   11

Time after time, Dr. Stanford documented how male chimpanzees dangle a dead red colobus monkey in front of a sexually swollen female, sharing only after first mating. He said that human sexual relationships could have been just as material-based.   12

"When chimps arrive at a tree holding meat on the hoof, the male chimps seem to have an awareness that, 'Well if I get meat I will maybe get more copulations because the females will come running over once I get a carcass,'" Dr. Stanford said.   13

Female chimpanzees are sexually promiscuous, with or without meat, copulating with more than a dozen males each day. But Dr. Stanford believes the attraction of flesh, consumption of which is shown by Dr. McGrew to be linked to the survival of offspring, could give lower-ranking males a better chance at matings; or that it could be "the difference between getting lots of sex and getting lots and lots of sex."   14

The ruthless manner in which chimpanzees hunt monkeys is best illustrated by a 1992 kill at Gombe, one of the largest ever recorded. Two chimpanzee parties traveling with 33 members, including two sexually receptive females, converged underneath trees in which up to 25 colobus monkeys were noisily feeding on fruit.   15

The colobus monkeys, weighing nearly 20 pounds, shrieked with alarm as the group of male chimpanzees (females hunt only on occasion at Gombe) made their way up to the canopy. In the frenzy of battle, some colobus monkeys were killed in the trees by the usual bite to the head. Others fell to the ground only to be flailed against the forest floor by chimpanzees weighing nearly 100 pounds.   16

By the time the "gruesome bloodbath" ended one hour later, Dr. Stanford said, seven monkeys were being eaten. The most prolific hunter at Gombe has killed 42 colobus monkeys in five years.   17

"Chimps absolutely love meat and get extremely excited about hunting," said Dr. Richard W. Wrangham, a Harvard anthropologist who said in a 1990 study that chimpanzees prey on at least 25 different species of mammals. "They will wait for an hour under a tree for just three drops of blood to fall off a leaf."   18

Most hunting is seasonal at Gombe, Dr. Stanford found. It takes place during the dry summer months, a time when females are generally sexually receptive and when the food supply of fruit, leaves and nuts is scarce. During the winter, however, when sex is not usually an issue and food is more plentiful, chimpanzees can go several weeks without a morsel of monkey, baboon, small antelope or baby bush pig.   19

But male chimpanzees sometimes hunt at Gombe when no sexually receptive females are nearby, primatologists report. This is when chimpanzee politics comes into play.   20

Dr. Toshisada Nichida, a Japanese zoologist, described in 1992 a primate patronage system that would be right at home in the back room of Capitol Hill. A male troupe   21 leader in the Mahale Mountains of Tanzania, doled out meat portions to allies, while denying the rewards to enemies. At Gombe, Dr. Stanford observed similar politicking at meal time.

22   "In the chimp society as in human society, being big doesn't get you everything," Dr. Stanford said. "It's being a politician. You have to know how to network. You have to use your political abilities to get what you want."

23   It is difficult to generalize about chimpanzee society. As an example, chimpanzees at Gombe capture mainly infant colobus monkeys using a pell-mell strategy, Dr. Stanford said. By contrast, Dr. Christophe Boesch, a Swiss primatologist, says male and female chimpanzees at Tai National Park in Ivory Coast prey mostly on adult colobus monkeys in coordinated attacks.

24   The difference in technique, Dr. Stanford says, could be accounted for by the local vegetation. The tall, densely packed trees of Tai provide more escape routes for the monkeys, and therefore requires more organized hunting.

25   "This demonstrates that chimps have behavioral plasticity," said Dr. C. Owen Lovejoy, an anatomist and anthropologist at Kent State University in Ohio. "It's very exciting news that chimpanzees are perfectly capable of enhancing their own fitness for success."

26   Dr. Stanford says chimpanzees are such efficient killers, successful nearly 90 percent of the time when 10 or more males are present, that he wonders whether early man was also quite skilled.

27   Archeological evidence indicates that humans hunted at least 2.5 million years ago, based on stone meat-cutting tools found at Olduvai Gorge in Tanzania. But Dr. Stanford said that from what he learned from watching chimpanzees, he believed that humans were avid hunters nearly three million years earlier than remains suggested.

28   "The amount of meat chimps eat suggests that early hominids, who would have presumably been more intelligent and better able to coordinate their actions and hunt together, were probably eating as much meat as chimps or more," he said.

29   Molecular biologists estimate that 98 percent of a chimpanzee's DNA matches that of humans. And since both humans and chimpanzees eat meat, Dr. Stanford said he thought it likely that so did their common ancestor who lived some six million years ago, when a branch in evolution created early man.

30   Scientists have been debating for some time when early man began hunting, believed by many to be a hallmark of human evolution linked to brain expansion. Some contend these human ancestors were mainly scavengers, too weak and slow on two legs to have hunted successfully, while others say Dr. Stanford's theory lacks evidence.

31   A team led by Dr. Timothy D. White, a paleontologist at the University of California at Berkeley, last year uncovered in Ethiopia a partial skeleton of the earliest hominid yet found, dating back 4.4 million years. Dr. White said that the hominid, known as Australopithecus ramidus, was probably capable of hunting, but that the remains provided no concrete evidence that it ever did so.

32   "Stanford's work is very provocative," Dr. White said. "And it's completely plausible; but it's totally unsupported by empirical evidence. That's why we're trying to find some kind of smoking gun, though I don't know what that would look like."

33   Dr. Stanford said it was unlikely that evidence to support his theory of early hominid hunting would ever be uncovered. To illustrate the point, he held the bone remains of five colobus monkeys (equal to about 60 pounds) in the palm of his hand—leftovers collected after a chimp feast.

34   "Chimps eat hair, skin, bones—there's nothing left," Dr. Stanford said. "Early hominids probably ate everything and you wouldn't find it in the fossil record."

Freewriting

Write for ten minutes about your thoughts as you read the article. What did you learn that you did not previously know? Is your knowledge of humans in any way expanded by what you learned about chimpanzees? If so, how? What are some of the similarities you observed between chimpanzees and humans? For example, ¶s 21 and 22 describe a "patronage system that would be right at home in the back rooms of Capitol Hill." Besides members of Congress, can you think of any other humans who have used food or other material goods in a similar fashion?

Group Work

As freewritings are read aloud by each group member in turn, jot down notes whenever you hear ideas you wish to comment on or question. Discuss what you have written, taking note of similarities and differences in your responses. (For example, do you respond similarly to the "patronage system" that is compared to chimp behavior in ¶s 21 and 22?) Can the group reach a consensus about some ways that humans and chimpanzees are alike or unalike? Does the group conclude that studying other primates can teach us anything about ourselves?

Review Questions

1. How has scientific knowledge about the diet of chimpanzees changed over the past thirty years?

2. Other than obtaining nutrition, what are some of the apparent reasons that chimpanzees hunt?

3. Why is it difficult to find empirical evidence to support the theory that humans began hunting very early in their evolutionary history?

Discussion Questions

1. If you eat meat, does reading this article affect your understanding of vegetarianism? If so, how? If not, why not?

2. Do you find yourself repulsed by any of the chimp behavior described in this article? Would you respond any differently if the behavior involved another species, say predatory birds or fish?

3. What similarities between chimpanzees and humans did you find most surprising? On the whole, did you find the article encouraging or discouraging? After reading it, are you more or less likely to agree with the following statement: "Humans are good by nature but have been corrupted by society"?

4. Do the sexual and political practices of chimpanzees provide any rationale for comparable practices among humans?

Writing

1. Craig Stanford, the anthropologist whose research is discussed in this article, observes: "In the chimp society as in human society, being big doesn't get you everything. It's being a politician. You have to know how to network. You have to use your political abilities to get what you want." Using the evidence cited in this article, along with any relevant personal experience or observation, present the most compelling case that Stanford's research uncovers some disturbing parallels between chimpanzees and humans. Then try to make the strongest case that the statement above is simply a realistic assessment of normal intelligent behavior. Finally, try to identify and examine any unstated assumptions about what is normal or ethical that can be found in each of your two arguments.

2. Choose an entry from your reading journal and develop it into a brief essay.

3   *Writing a Paraphrase*

W HEN you *paraphrase* a statement, a passage, or a longer text, you recast its ideas in different words. College students are called upon to paraphrase almost daily. When you take notes during a class lecture, for example, you probably jot down the instructor's ideas in your own words. Likewise, an essay examination often involves restating material from lectures, reading, and class discussion. In fact, your ability to explain concepts in your own language is a crucial academic skill, since it allows you to demonstrate understanding of significant facts, inferences, and opinions.

 ## PARAPHRASE AS A READING STRATEGY

Let's begin with the most informal, and probably the most common, type of paraphrase. Whenever they encounter an unfamiliar text, experienced readers immediately try to assign meaning to it. One way they do this is to paraphrase. Consider the following sentence from *Talking Power,* a book by Robin Lakoff, a prominent scholar in the field of language study:

> When it is important that language be forceful, we attempt to buttress it in some tangible ways.

A fluent reader might pause here, for less than a second, to interpret this sentence by mentally casting it in slightly different terms: "When words really matter, we try to back them up with something concrete." Sometimes, readers find it useful to write such interpretive paraphrases in the margins; other times, they simply read further to see whether their mental paraphrasing is correct. In the case of Lakoff's sentence, the accuracy of our paraphrase is confirmed by an illustration that follows in the same paragraph:

> Nowadays we often think of . . . oaths as mere words themselves, *pro forma* declarations. But they originated as dire threats. . . . The very words *testify, testimony* recall one ancient link between words and reality. They are derived from the Latin *testes,* its meaning the same as in current English. In swearing, the Roman male . . . placed his right hand upon his genitals; the implication was that, if he swore falsely, they would be rendered sterile.

Sometimes, a written paraphrase in the margins of a text proves useful later on. If, for example, you know that you must review material to prepare for an exam, a paraphrase of an important idea could be helpful. However, there are limits to how much you can write in the margins, as, indeed, there are limits to the amount of time you can profitably devote to paraphrasing, either in your head or on paper. And since a paraphrase, unlike a summary, restates every idea from its original source, a writer rarely paraphrases a passage longer than two or three contiguous sentences. Proficient readers, likewise, seldom recast sentence after sentence in their heads, even when they encounter difficult texts.

Take, for example, the following sentences, also from Lakoff's book:

> We are not mere passive recipients of manipulative communicative strategies. Orwell and other worriers ignore the truth, whether unpleasant or happy: we all manipulate language, and we do it all the time. Our every interaction is political, whether we intend it to be or not; everything we do in the course of a day communicates our relative power, our desire for a particular sort of connection, our identification of the other as one who needs something from us, or vice versa.

A common, but naive, bit of advice to someone who finds these sentences confusing would be to look up any unfamiliar words, thereby putting the passage into simpler language. Thus, a dutiful, though misguided, reader might spend five minutes with a dictionary in order to translate the first sentence as follows: "We are not inactive receivers of influencing talkative plans." The same industrious reader would learn that *Orwell* refers to George Orwell, a British novelist and essayist who lived from 1903 to 1950. All this effort provides little if any clarification. To make matters worse, the task becomes truly hopeless after the first sentence; since the vocabulary is now familiar to almost any literate adult, a dictionary provides no help at all.

Efficient readers, therefore, paraphrase sparingly. Often, they defer complete understanding for a few sentences, waiting to see if subsequent parts of the text provide help. Later in the paragraph from which we have just quoted, for example, Robin Lakoff says, "We are always involved in persuasion, in trying to get another person to see the world or some piece of it our way, and therefore to act as we would like them to act." Suddenly, the foregoing sentences become much clearer; Lakoff relieves most readers of the need to paraphrase preceding sentences.

This first type of paraphrase lies at one end of a spectrum on which we might place every act of reading and interpretation; more subjective types of response lie at the opposite end. When we want to explore our own responses and personal connections to a text, we read and write subjectively, less concerned with literal understanding of what the writer is trying to say. But when we want to try to get down exactly what a particular sentence or passage means, we paraphrase it. The figure below illustrates the spectrum of which we speak.

Responses to Reading

Objective	Subjective
Paraphrase (author's ideas)	Personal response (reader's ideas)

USING PARAPHRASE IN WRITING

Up to this point, we have treated paraphrase as a reading strategy—a way of understanding or coming to terms with concepts in academic texts. Whether performed mentally or recorded on paper, this private type of paraphrase is different from all others in one important way: It does not absolutely require an **acknowledgment phrase** (e.g., "according to Lakoff") or **formal documentation** (e.g., a parenthetical note keyed to a bibliographical entry). In other words, since this kind of paraphrase is not going to be read by anyone else, you are not obligated to identify its source explicitly. For example, were you to paraphrase the main points of this paragraph in a marginal note, you probably would not begin it with "Veit, Gould, and Clifford say that . . . " or end it with a note citing the authors' names and the page number.

Notice, however, that we qualify this advice: A private paraphrase—one that no one else is going to read—does *not absolutely require* acknowledgment and documentation. However, if you were to place such a paraphrase in a notebook or on an index card or on a photocopy that does not clearly identify the author, your failure to acknowledge and document the source could prevent any future use of the paraphrased ideas. If you ever wanted to use or even refer to those ideas in any kind of writing intended for other readers (including your instructor), you would have to relocate their original source and cite it appropriately. That would be necessary because every public use of paraphrase—every use involving one or more readers other than yourself—demands acknowledgment and proper documentation.*

One public use of paraphrase is to reword a difficult or highly technical passage for an audience unfamiliar with its concepts or terminology. Legal experts are often called upon to paraphrase complex or ambiguous texts such as contracts, court decisions, and legislation; in such cases, interpretation, as well as translation, is frequently involved. At other times, we may paraphrase an argument with which we disagree in order to demonstrate good faith and a willingness to listen. Finally, in research writing particularly, we paraphrase sources in order to cite important facts or information, to place a topic or issue in context, or to support an interpretation or opinion. The following sections of this chapter will consider these occasions for paraphrasing.

Before going on, however, we wish to emphasize one crucial point about paraphrasing for any purpose. Whenever you paraphrase, you must completely recast the phrasing of your source, using your own words and your own style. Simple word substitution does not constitute a legitimate paraphrase of another's language; neither does a mere rearrangement of word order. Suppose, for example, that you wanted to paraphrase the following sentence in an essay for your English class. The sentence is taken from the review of Walt Disney World by Manuela Hoelterhoff, writing for the *Wall Street Journal*.

> I did not have a great time, I ate food no self-respecting mouse would eat, stayed in a hotel that could have been designed by the Moscow corps of engineers and

The original passage

*The conventions of acknowledgment and documentation are discussed in subsequent chapters. In particular, the parenthetical note, a short annotation usually citing the source of paraphrased ideas or quoted words and the page(s) on which they can be found, is explained in Chapter 5. Although the scope of this chapter is confined to techniques of paraphrasing, the significance of proper documentation should not be overlooked or minimized.

suffered through entertainment by smiling, uniformed young people who looked like they had their hair arranged at a lobotomy clinic.

An acceptable paraphrase might look like this:

An acceptable paraphrase

Visitors to Disney World can expect unappetizing food, uncomfortable lodging, and mindless performances put on by cheery adolescents who all alike.

On the other hand, the following sentence would not be an appropriate paraphrase because it merely tinkers with Hoelterhoff's sentence:

An illegitimate paraphrase

You will not have fun; you will eat food unfit for human consumption, sleep in a hotel inferior to customary expectations, and endure performances by grinning teenagers who appear to have undergone brain surgery.

Whenever you write a paraphrase that others will read, as in a research paper, you are bound by certain rules of fair play. Specifically, you must completely recast material borrowed from your sources, using your own words and your own style. Failure to do so is *plagiarism,* an act of dishonesty. Unless you quote your source exactly (within quotation marks), readers will assume that the language they are reading is entirely your own. You must also give full credit for a source's contributions to your paper.

Upcoming chapters will provide more detail about the use of sources in research writing, including paraphrase and quotation, the citation of sources, and the avoidance of plagiarism.

Paraphrasing for a Different Audience

Writers are sometimes called on to paraphrase their own writing or the writing of others in order to make it clearer or more appropriate for a different audience.

For example, a passage written in an earlier century might need to be paraphrased for modern readers. A writer quoting Shakespeare, for instance, might feel the need to provide a paraphrase:

"That which we call a rose," wrote the Bard, "by any other name would smell as sweet." His point is that we should not judge things by their names, since names do not alter the essence of those things.

The second sentence is a paraphrase of the first. Notice that it is more than a simple restatement of the author's words in other language. It if were, it would say something like: "A rose would be just as fragrant no matter what we called it." Instead, this paraphrase goes further and states the meaning behind those words— the meaning that Shakespeare left unstated.

As a second example, a scientist might report in a technical journal about a significant discovery she has made in genetic engineering. She would write her article in the technical vocabulary and style appropriate for her fellow scientists. Non-scientists, however, would probably be unable to read the article; and a newspaper reporter describing that same discovery in a news story would need to paraphrase the scientist's words using less technical, everyday language.

Specialized and General Audiences

When you are writing for a specialized audience whose members share knowledge about a particular field, it is appropriate to use the special language, or *jargon,* of that field, even though that language is not comprehensible to outsiders. Browsing through the periodical section of your library will introduce you to a host of magazines and journals written for specialized audiences. Articles in *Field and Stream* assume knowledge of game animals and rifle scopes; *PC Computing* articles take it for granted that the reader knows the difference between RAM and ROM; and the scholarly journal *Linguistic Inquiry* expects its readers to comprehend terms such as *anaphoric dependencies* and *surface filters.* Each of us has special interests that enable us to understand some articles and books that might be baffling to others.

Often in your research you will need to translate from the specialized jargon of the publications in which you find your information into clear, general English for the nonspecialized readers you are addressing. Paraphrasing technical information so that it can be read easily by general readers is a skill that all college writers need to master.

Consider the following two passages about periodicity, the rhythmic behavior observed in many plant and animal species. The first passage, from *Physiological Zoology,* a scientific journal, is likely to present difficulties for most readers:

> Recent studies have provided reasons to postulate that the primary timer for long-cycle biological rhythms that are closely similar in period to the natural geophysical ones and that persist in so-called constant conditions is, in fact, one of organismic response to subtle geophysical fluctuations which pervade ordinary constant conditions in the laboratory (Brown, 1959, 1960). In such constant laboratory conditions a wide variety of organisms have been demonstrated to display, nearly equally conspicuously, metabolic periodicities of both solar-day and lunar-day frequencies, with their interference derivative, the 29.5-day synodic month, and in some instances even the year. These metabolic cycles exhibit day-by-day irregularities and distortions which have been established to be highly significantly correlated with aperiodic meteorological and other geophysical changes. These correlations provide strong evidence for the exogenous origin of these biological periodisms themselves, since cycles exist in these meteorological and geophysical factors.
> —Emma D. Terracini and Frank A. Brown, Jr., "Periodisms in Mouse 'Spontaneous' Activity Sychronized with Major Geophysical Events"

Passage for a specialized audience

If you were researching periodicity, you probably would derive enough information to get the gist of such specialized writing. But if you wanted to report that information to readers unlikely to share your background and interests, you would need to paraphrase what you discovered in plainer language. Consider how Frank Brown, coauthor of the passage cited above, recasts some of the same information in another article, published in the less technical *Science* magazine:

> Familiar to all are the rhythmic changes in innumerable processes of animals and plants in nature. . . . These periodisms of animals and plants, which adapt them so nicely to their geophysical environment with its rhythmic fluctuations in light, temperature, and ocean tides, appear at first glance to be exclusively simple responses of the organisms to these natural factors. However, it is now known

Passage for a less specialized but educated audience

that rhythms of all these natural frequencies may persist in living things even after the organisms have been sealed in under conditions constant with respect to every factor biologists have conceded to be of influence. The presence of such persistent rhythms clearly indicates that organisms possess some means of timing these periods which does not depend directly upon the obvious environmental physical rhythms. The means has come to be termed "living clocks."
—Frank A. Brown, Jr., "Living Clocks"

This rendering of facts is more accessible to the average educated adult. However, it still assumes the reader's interest in the particulars of scientific research—an assumption warranted by the author's awareness of who reads *Science* magazine. Notice how Frank Brown once again paraphrases these basic facts, this time adapting them to a still broader audience in an article published in the *Saturday Evening Post:*

Passage for a general audience

One of the greatest riddles of the universe is the uncanny ability of living things to carry out their normal activities with clocklike precision at a particular time of the day, month and year. . . . Though it might appear that such rhythms are merely the responses of organisms to rhythmic changes in light, temperature or the ocean tides, this is far from being the whole answer. For when living things . . . are removed from their natural habitat and placed under conditions where no variations occur in any of the forces to which they are generally conceded to be sensitive, they commonly continue to display the same rhythms they displayed in their natural environment.
—Frank A. Brown, Jr., "Life's Mysterious Clocks"

In each of these three cases, writing is adapted to the needs of a particular group of readers. The first passage is directed toward professional scientists. There, the authors are careful to avoid assigning "agency"—telling who performed certain actions. Readers are told, for example, that "*recent studies* have provided reasons" and that "organisms have *been demonstrated* to display"; the authors avoid saying "*scientists* have provided reasons" or "*we and our colleagues* have demonstrated." Although writing that does not assign agency is usually harder to understand, scientists prefer that type of writing because it is thought to be more objective. The third passage, directed toward the readers of *Saturday Evening Post,* uses simpler vocabulary, like *living things* instead of *organisms,* and explains concepts like *controlled conditions,* which are defined as "conditions where no variations occur in any of the forces to which [living things] are generally conceded to be sensitive."

You may be wondering whether a writer ever paraphrases in language more formal than that of the original source. Because the results often sound peculiar, writers may do this when they want to create a comical effect. In *Politics in the English Language* George Orwell, for example, translated a passage from the Old Testament into political jargon. The passage, taken from *Ecclesiastes,* reads:

I returned and saw under the sun, that the race is not to the swift, nor the battle to the strong, neither yet bread to the wise, nor yet riches to men of understanding, nor yet favor to men of skill; but time and chance happeneth to them all.

In order to ridicule what Orwell calls "modern English," he paraphrased the passage as follows:

Objective consideration of contemporary phenomena compels the conclusion that success or failure in competitive activities exhibits no tendency to be commensurate with innate capacity, but that a considerable element of the unpredictable must invariably be taken into account.

Orwell's aim is not to communicate the ideas and sentiments expressed in his source, but to show how a particular type of language makes those ideas and sentiments obscure and inelegant.

On the other hand, suppose you wished to paraphrase the following sentence from a magazine that targets an audience of gay readers:

Chubby, fat, and obese queers suffer outcast status.

The word *queers,* usually a term of abuse, is offensive to most readers. (Since the author himself is homosexual, we assume that he does not intend it as such.) Also, words like *chubby, fat,* and *obese* are loaded with connotation—implicit meaning, as opposed to objective "dictionary" definition. Therefore, if our aim is objective reporting of ideas, an appropriate paraphrase might be the following:

According to one observer, overweight homosexuals are shunned by other homosexuals.

Some might argue that we have unwisely recast the original sentence in euphemisms (polite equivalents for unpleasant or controversial words), because our paraphrase lacks the emotional impact of the original quotation. However, we believe that this is the best way to proceed under the circumstances.

Notice, too, the qualification, "According to one observer," which places distance between the source and the writer who paraphrased it. This seems appropriate in view of the fact that the statement is a controversial opinion, apparently based on personal experience or observation. Some textbooks draw a distinction between **informative paraphrases**—those that adopt the tone of a source, reporting facts and opinions as though they were the writer's own—and **descriptive paraphrases**—those that take a more detached stance, describing the source rather than presenting its views or information directly. Thus, an informative paraphrase of the foregoing sentence might begin as follows:

Some books differentiate between informative paraphrases and descriptive ones. . . .

An informative paraphrase

A descriptive paraphrase, on the other hand, would open like this:

Veit, Gould, and Clifford report that some books differentiate between informative paraphrases and descriptive ones. . . .

A descriptive paraphrase

Although the distinction between informative and descriptive paraphrase is valid, we do not emphasize it here, preferring to suggest at various points in this chapter how and when a writer might choose to adopt a more detached perspective toward a particular source. (This principle will be discussed also in Chapter 12.)

Paraphrasing for a Different Audience

EXERCISES

1. The following sentences come from another article about periodism, or "biological clocks," the topic addressed in earlier excerpts. This passage, also by Frank Brown, was written for the *Biological Bulletin.* Try to paraphrase the sentences for

a general audience, similar to the one Brown addresses in the article he wrote for the *Saturday Evening Post:*

> Much has been learned, particularly in recent years, as to the properties, including modifiability, of this endogenous rhythmicity. The fundamental problem, however, that of the timing mechanism of the rhythmic periods, has largely eluded any eminently reasonable hypotheses.

2. Recast the passage from Frank Brown's article in the *Saturday Evening Post,* adapting it to readers of *National Geographic World,* a magazine for children in elementary school.

3. Select a textbook from one of your advanced courses and copy out a passage that people who have not taken the course might be unable to understand. Paraphrase it so as to make it accessible to most readers.

4. The following regulations are taken from the Board of Governors' Code for a multicampus state university. This Code is a legally binding document that is likely to be cited in disputes that are taken to court. The passage below specifies circumstances under which a faculty member with tenure may be dismissed. Suppose a popular instructor on your campus (the Code refers to each campus as an "institution") were dismissed on grounds of "financial exigency." In order to assess the legality of the university's actions, you need to paraphrase the following section of the Code. Assume that your paraphrase will appear in an article for the student newspaper:

> The tenure policies and regulations of each institution shall provide that employment of faculty members with permanent tenure . . . may be terminated by the institution because of (1) demonstrable, bona fide institutional financial exigency or (2) major curtailment or elimination of a teaching, research or public-service program. "Financial exigency" is defined as a significant decline in the financial resources of the institution that is brought about by decline in institutional enrollment or by other action or events that compel a reduction in the institution's operations budget. The determination of whether a condition of financial exigency exists or whether there shall be a major curtailment or elimination of a teaching, research or public-service program shall be made by the Chancellor, after consulting with the academic administrative officers and faculty. . . , subject to the concurrence by the President and then approval by the Board of Governors. If the financial exigency or curtailment or elimination of a program is such that the institution's contractual obligation to a faculty member may not be met, the employment of the faculty member may be terminated in accordance with institutional procedures that afford the faculty member a fair hearing on that decision.

Formal and Informal Writing

When you paraphrased a section of a legal document in the preceding exercise, you wrote something that sounded different from the original. After all, the two versions were written for different purposes and for different audiences. Good writers have command of several styles and levels of formality, and they adapt their writing to specific occasions. Some documents, such as important official pronouncements, adopt a highly formal style. Informal notes to friends, on the other hand, are likely to use much more casual language. Between those extremes lies a whole range of stylistic levels. The examples that follow represent very different places along that range.

First is a passage from the Gospel of St. Luke as it appears in the King James version of the Bible, a translation undertaken by English scholars of the early seventeenth century, the age of Shakespeare:

> And it came to pass in those days, that there went out a decree from Caesar Augustus, that all the world should be taxed.
> (*And* this taxing was first made when Cyrenius was governor of Syria.)
> And all went to be taxed, every one into his own city.
> And Joseph also went up from Galilee, out of the city of Nazareth, into Judæa, unto the city of David, which is called Bethlehem; (because he was of the house and lineage of David:)
> To be taxed with Mary his espoused wife, being great with child.
> And so it was, that, while they were there, the days were accomplished that she should be delivered.
> And she brought forth her firstborn son, and wrapped him in swaddling clothes, and laid him in a manger; because there was no room for them in the inn.
> And there were in the same country shepherds abiding in the field, keeping watch over their flock by night.
> And, lo, the angel of the Lord came upon them, and the glory of the Lord shone round about them: and they were sore afraid.
> And the angel said unto them, Fear not: for, behold, I bring you good tidings of great joy, which shall be to all people.
> For unto you is born this day in the city of David a Saviour, which is Christ the Lord.
> And this *shall* be a sign unto you; Ye shall find the babe wrapped in swaddling clothes, lying in a manger.
> And suddenly there was with the angel a multitude of the heavenly host praising God, and saying,
> Glory to God in the highest, and on earth peace, good will toward men.
> And it came to pass, as the angels were gone away from them into heaven, the shepherds said one to another, Let us now go even unto Bethlehem, and see this thing which is come to pass, which the Lord hath made known unto us.
> And they came with haste, and found Mary, and Joseph, and the babe lying in a manger.
> And when they had seen *it*, they made known abroad the saying which was told them concerning this child.

The language of this passage is lofty and formal. Its vocabulary is elevated, even obscure in two or three instances; there are no contractions or colloquialisms (words or expressions more appropriate to informal conversation than to public speech or writing). Nevertheless, a good many, perhaps most, English-speaking Americans are so familiar with this account of the first Christmas that it presents no real difficulties for them. However, the following excerpt from *The Best Christmas Pageant Ever,* a play by Barbara Robinson, shows how the same biblical passage might confuse other native speakers of English. In this scene, the mother is directing a rehearsal for a Christmas pageant. The Herdmans—Ralph, Leroy, Claude, and Imogene—have never before attended a Christian worship service:

Mother: All right now *(finds the place and starts to read).* There went out a decree from Caesar Augustus, that all the world should be taxed... *(All the kids are visibly bored and itchy, except the HERDMANS, who listen with the puzzled but determined concentration of people trying to make sense of a foreign language.)*... and Joseph went up from Gailee with Mary his wife, being great with child....

Ralph: *(Not so much trying to shock, as he is pleased to understand something.)* Pregnant! She was pregnant! *(There is much giggling and tittering.)*

Mother: All right now, that's enough. We all know that Mary was pregnant. *(MOTHER continues reading, under the BETH-ALICE dialogue),*... And it came to pass, while they were there, that the days were accomplished that she should be delivered, and she brought forth her firstborn son....

Alice: *(to BETH)* I don't think it's very nice to say Mary was pregnant.

Beth: Well, she was.

Alice: I don't think *your mother* should say Mary was pregnant. It's better to say 'great with child.' I'm not supposed to talk about people being pregnant, especially in church.

Mother: *(reading)*... and wrapped him in swaddling clothes and laid him in a manger, because there was no room for them in the inn....

Leroy: What's a manger? Some kind of bed?

Mother: Well, they didn't have a bed in the barn, so Mary had to use whatever there was. What would you do if you had a new baby and no bed to put the baby in?...

Claude: What were the wadded up clothes?

Mother: The what?

Claude: *(pointing in the Bible)* It said in there... she wrapped him in wadded up clothes.

Mother: *Swaddling* clothes. People used to wrap babies up very tightly in big pieces of material, to make them feel cozy....

Imogene: You mean they tied him up and put him in a feedbox? Where was the Child Welfare?

To Alice, described by the author of the play as a "prim, proper pain in the neck," familiar words like *pregnant* show a lack of reverence in this particular context. Yet stage directions—the italicized comments that appear within parentheses—show that nothing of the kind was ever intended. Thus, the play introduces an important issue about language and paraphrase. As America becomes more and more culturally diverse, it becomes less and less appropriate to assume that any one phrasing of ideas or information is inherently better, clearer, or more appropriate than all others. Consider how the same chapter from the Gospel of St. Luke has been translated in a more recent version of the Bible:

At that time Emperor Augustus ordered a census to be taken throughout the Roman Empire. When this first census took place, Quirinius was the governor of Syria. Everyone, then, went to register himself, each to his own home town.

Joseph went from the town of Nazareth in Galilee to the town of Bethlehem in Judea, the birthplace of King David. Joseph went there because he was a descendant of David. He went to register with Mary, who was promised in marriage to him. She was pregnant, and while they were in Bethlehem, the time came for her to have her baby. She gave birth to her first son, wrapped him in cloths and laid him in a manger—there was no room for them to stay in the inn.

There were some shepherds in that part of the country who were spending the night in the fields, taking care of their flocks. An angel of the Lord appeared to them, and the glory of the Lord shone over them. They were terribly afraid, but the angel said to them, "Don't be afraid! I am here with good news for you, which will bring great joy to all the people. This very day in David's town your Savior was born—Christ the Lord! And this is what will prove it to you: you will find a baby wrapped in cloths and lying in a manger."

Suddenly a great army of heaven's angels appeared with the angel, singing praises to God:

"Glory to God in the highest heaven, and peace on earth to those with whom he is pleased!"

When the angels went away from them back into heaven, the shepherds said to one another, "Let's go to Bethlehem and see this thing that has happened, which the Lord has told us."

This particular version of the Bible uses more familiar words, like *pregnant,* in relating the Christmas story. Yet few educated adults would be likely to view it as a less reverent account.

Paraphrasing a Different Style   EXERCISES

1. The following newspaper editorial responds to a proposal to reduce state funding for the marine sciences program at the University of North Carolina at Wilmington. The editorialist is sensitive to the fact that this proposal was made by professors at a larger, more established public university "upstate." Notice how the writer opens his argument with one type of language in the first three paragraphs, then restates it (particularly in the third from last paragraph) in a different type of language.

UNCW Marine Science Has Earned Respect

Far as fancypants p'fessahs upstate is concerned, onliest thang we rednecks down hyeah know about marine science is go runnin' and screamin' onto a beach, shootin' and throwin' hangernades.

Hogwash. We ain't mo-rons. We know it has to do with stuff like how come sheepsheads hang around pier pilin's and how to sneak up and gig yourself a big ol' flounder for Christmas dinner.

But these ear ovah-educated boys is mad as *far,* cuz some experts has said that UNC-Womanton ought to git a new lab and maybe, some day, be the university system's top dog when it comes to makin' marine science doctors—you know, the kind what don't make house calls. The folks upstate thanks we's to stoopid fuh that sorta thang.

Au contraire.

In point of fact, gentlemen, the marine biology program at UNC-Wilmington is ranked seventh in the country. More than 400 undergraduates are enrolled in marine-related degree programs.

UNCW offers joint doctorates in marine biology with N.C. State University.

UNCW is doing research not only in American waters, but also in waters off Costa Rica, Ecuador, Malaysia, Mexico, the Philippines, Portugal and Venezuela.

Congress just voted to fund the UNCW undersea research program.

In other words, this is a serious, well-respected operation. And it's located on the coast—where the water is.

Putting a first-class lab here, and inviting scientists and students at other UNC campuses to share it, makes perfect sense. Nobody is talking about shutting down programs elsewhere.

Of course, this is the kind of proposal that can be expected to start a turf battle between existing programs and the upstart new one. It has done that.

But as UNCW Chancellor Jim Leutze said, the tone of the complaints conveys something other than predictable protectiveness. It also conveys snobbery—about this often-forgotten corner of the state and about a regional university whose growing strengths it is inconvenient to acknowledge.

UNCW isn't hoping to take over the university system's marine science program. It is hoping to bolster it.

Sadly, it appears that some scientists on other campuses care more about protecting their prestige and perks than in strengthening marine education and research in North Carolina.

Try to construct an editorial that employs the same strategy (adopting an exaggerated voice, then paraphrasing your point of view in more conventional editorial language). For example, an editorial rebutting the claims made in "UNCW Marine Science Has Earned Respect" might open with a tone of exaggerated snobbishness:

During a recent sojourn to the maritime provinces, we encountered an editorial in the February 2 issue of your quaint publication. Upstate, the subject of crustaceans is more typically addressed in the food section of the newspaper than in the editorial pages. On the whole, we believe that the anatomy of marine organisms is an area of study best left to restaurateurs and domestic servants. Nevertheless, universities in our region of the state offer a few academic programs in fields less erudite than lyric poetry and modern dance.

Then, the writer might adopt a more earnest tone:

Seriously, folks, the issue here is not regional pride or snobbery, but quality education—which institution can provide the best program for the money. State University already has doctoral programs in biology and oceanography. Consequently, it already has in place many of the personnel and facilities needed to establish a first-class program in marine science.

You might consider one of the following as a context for your editorial:

a. Your college administration has just rejected a proposal to include student representatives on policymaking committees.

b. A recent study has suggested that students who have attended private schools are better prepared for college than students who have attended public schools (or vice versa).

c. A letter to the editor of your campus newspaper argues that the admission of older, nontraditional students should be curtailed.

2. Every poem expresses meaning in a unique way, and certainly in a way different from prose writing. For that reason, it is probably impossible to provide a faithful prose paraphrase of a poem. The experience of reading prose just isn't the same.

Nevertheless, if you recognize that limitation, you will find that paraphrasing a poem causes you to think hard about its meaning and may help you gain a better understanding of it. Paraphrase the following poem by A. E. Housman (1859–1936). Make sure your paraphrase captures the meaning, not just of individual words and phrases but of the poem as a whole. In other words, your paraphrase will present *your* interpretation of Housman's poem.

Loveliest of Trees, the Cherry Now

Loveliest of trees, the cherry now
Is hung with bloom along the bough,
And stands about the woodland ride
Wearing white for Eastertide.

Now, of my threescore years and ten,
Twenty will not come again,
And take from seventy springs a score,
It only leaves me fifty more.

And since to look at things in bloom
Fifty springs are little room,
About the woodlands I will go
To see the cherry hung with snow.

Paraphrasing an Argument

One of the more difficult tasks you may face as a writer is paraphrasing, accurately and fairly, an argument with which you disagree. Nevertheless, the ability to do so helps to portray you as a person of good will and integrity whose views deserve to be taken seriously.

The need to paraphrase an argument with which you disagree may arise under various circumstances, but let's consider one of the most familiar. Suppose you want to refute a commonly held opinion. You may wish to begin by demonstrating that you understand, have considered, and respect that opinion. One obstacle can be your *personal commitments*. The following sentences appear in an essay by Paul McBrearty, who argues for the elimination of anonymous evaluation of college professors by their students:

> Anonymity in student evaluations virtually assures lowered academic standards and inflated grades. The pressures on teachers to *give* good grades so as to *get* good grades are severe, pervasive, unremitting, and inescapable.

The original passage

Though we happen to disagree with this argument, we would not consider the following to be an objective paraphrase of McBrearty's first sentence:

> Some college professors fear that students will use anonymous evaluations as a way of getting even for unfair grades.

An unacceptable paraphrase

What this paraphrase does is to *project* certain attitudes or views that are not clearly there. It implies that the writer condones arbitrary grading practices, when in fact he supports grading that is both demanding and fair.

Another obstacle to paraphrasing an argument accurately can be overdependence on familiar patterns or *schemas*. Schemas are recurrent structures that allow us to make predictions about what a writer or speaker is going to say next. Most of the time, schemas help us read and listen more efficiently. For example, the fourth sentence in the previous paragraph—"One obstacle can be your personal commitments"—leads most readers to expect that at least one other obstacle will be discussed in a subsequent sentence or paragraph. The danger, of course, is that a reader can take too much for granted and make a hasty assumption about what the writer is going to say. Consider, for instance, the second sentence taken from Paul McBrearty's essay:

The original passage

The pressures on teachers to *give* good grades so as to *get* good grades are severe, pervasive, unremitting, and inescapable.

At first glance the following sentence might seem to be a fair paraphrase:

A hasty paraphrase

Professors are tempted to bribe students with high grades.

Because we have heard this argument before, we might be tempted to conclude, upon reading the sentence cited above, that McBrearty is making the same claim. Later, however, he says:

The original passage

Whenever student evaluations are used in any way by administrators as a basis for the denial of promotion, retention, or salary increase, or for assigning a less-than-satisfactory rating to a faculty member, the faculty member is denied the constitutional right of due process if not permitted to confront what are in effect his or her accusers.

Although we still may not accept the validity of McBrearty's argument, we should recognize that he is not suggesting that his colleagues are offering bribes, but that they are responding to pressure in order to protect their jobs. Therefore, a much fairer paraphrase of this sentence would be:

A fairer paraphrase

Professors fear that they will be penalized with poor student evaluations if they grade rigorously.

Sometimes, writers are called upon to paraphrase arguments that challenge not only their opinions, but their personal values. On such occasions, the best strategy is to be explicit in attributing arguments to sources. Suppose, for example, a writer opposed to all forms of censorship needed to paraphrase the following argument from an essay by Barbara Lawrence titled "Four-Letter Words Can Hurt You":

The original passage

Obscene words . . . seem to serve a similar purpose: to reduce the human organism (especially the female organism) and human functions (especially sexual and procreative) to their least organic, most mechanical dimension; to substitute a trivializing or deforming resemblance for the complex human reality of what is being described.

Such a writer might show that Lawrence's argument is incompatible with his own views by using what we have called a "descriptive paraphrase." In other words, he might precede his paraphrase with an **acknowledgment phrase** like "According to Barbara Lawrence" or perhaps one of the following alternatives:

In an essay often cited by proponents of censorship, Barbara Lawrence argues . . .

Barbara Lawrence presents an argument raised by feminists who wish to suppress pornography . . .

Paraphrases acknowledging the author

On the other hand, it probably would not be fair or appropriate to use a slanted or "loaded" acknowledgment phrase like "According to radical feminist Barbara Lawrence."

Earlier in this chapter, we spoke of the occasional need to paraphrase a source that uses language offensive to most readers. Another reasonable concern is how to paraphrase arguments that violate the fairly permissive boundaries of academic inquiry and conversation. While it is usually best to accord respect to persons with whom you disagree, occasionally you may encounter ideas so hateful that you feel compelled to express disapproval. A number of years ago, one of our students complained that he had found in the university library a publication that he considered insulting to homosexuals and religious minorities. In a letter voicing his indignation to the director of the library, this writer wanted to paraphrase some of the views expressed in the offending publication. The writer used judgmental phrases like the following:

Here we find the familiar homophobic belief that . . .

Overt anti-Semitism emerges later, when . . .

Judgmental paraphrases

Exactly when a writer is justified or wise in expressing judgments about paraphrased sources—or in deciding that a particular opinion is out of bounds and therefore unworthy of paraphrase—is a sensitive issue in the academic community. However, it is usually best to avoid judgmental citations unless there are clear and compelling reasons for their use.

Paraphrasing an Argument   EXERCISE

Try to paraphrase each of the following arguments, which appear in reading selections elsewhere in this book:

a. Indulging one's fancy in an unthreatening, vaguely iconoclastic café . . . makes people feel individualistic.
   —Faith Popcorn quoted by Mark Schapiro in "Muddy Waters: The Lore, the Lure, the Lowdown on America's Favorite Addiction"

b. Yes indeedy, buying a three-dollar cup of multilayered coffee makes [the patrons of trendy coffee shops] *very different* from those Sanka-swilling wage slaves trudging by the café's picture windows.
   —Helen Cordes, "Imperialism, Sexism, Rapacious Capitalism, and Mindless Conformity! Four Steaming, Frothing Rants against the New Coffee Chic"

c. If the Founding Fathers ever envisioned an ideal social order, it was surely. . . a system under which people succeed mainly on the basis of ability and effort.
   —Robert J. Samuelson, "America the Open: Faddish Attacks on the Meritocracy Are Nuts"

d. In America today. . . we keep an excessive share of our resources tied up in the legal, medical and financial [professions], while business and government wither.
   —Nicholas Lemann, "The Curse of the Merit Class: America's Ruling Caste Is Bad News for the Country"

Paraphrasing in Research Papers

As we have said earlier in this chapter, research writing often paraphrases sources in order to cite important facts or information, to place a topic or issue in context, or to support an interpretation or opinion. In these cases, a writer must be especially careful to cite sources by name (usually in the form of parenthetical notes, which will be explained in Chapter 6).

Uses of paraphrase in research writing—particularly conventions of style and documentation—are explained in greater detail in Chapter 12. The following examples simply illustrate various contexts in research writing that might call for paraphrase.

Using Paraphrase to Cite Facts or Information

Suppose you are writing a research paper arguing that the United States should cut its consumption of beef in order to preserve the environment and alleviate world hunger. Using a direct quotation, you might open your paper as follows:

In his recent book, *Beyond Beef: The Rise and Fall of the Cattle Culture,* Jeremy Rifkin cites the following facts:

Using a
quotation to
cite facts

> Some 100,000 cows are slaughtered every twenty-four hours in the United States. In a given week, 91 percent of all United States households purchase beef. . . . Americans currently consume 23 percent of all the beef produced in the world. Today, the average American consumes 65 pounds of beef per year. (154)

On the other hand, you might paraphrase the quotation to better effect. Consider this alternative:

Better: using a
paraphrase to
cite facts

> We are so addicted to beef that every week 91 percent of American families purchase it. Because of this dietary preference, our country lays claim to nearly a fourth of the world's supply. Individually, each of us devours 65 pounds of beef a year, requiring a daily slaughter of 100,000 cows (Rifkin 154).

Although it might have been easier simply to quote Rifkin, there is no compelling reason to do so. There is nothing particularly unusual about the words he uses; the basic facts he cites can be rendered just as effectively in your own words.

Using Paraphrase to Place a Topic or Issue in Context

Suppose curtailment of air conditioning during the summer months has been introduced as a conservation measure on your campus. Responding to outcries of opposition, you write an objective, carefully researched study of the consequences of this measure—both its savings and its drawbacks. In order to establish the need for such objective inquiry, you open your paper by addressing the commonly held notion that air conditioning has become an indispensable feature of everyday life. You might do this by paraphrasing the following passage from an essay by Frank Trippett:

The original
passage

> [Air conditioning has] seduced families into retreating into houses with closed doors and shut windows, reducing the commonality of neighborhood life and all but obsoleting the front-porch society whose open casual folkways were an appealing feature of a sweatier America. Is it really surprising that the public's

often noted withdrawal into self-pursuit and privatism has coincided with the epic spread of air conditioning? Though science has little studied how habitual air conditioning affects mind or body, some medical experts suggest that, like other technical avoidance of natural swings in climate, air conditioning may take a toll on the human capacity to adapt to stress.

Your opening paragraph might look like this:

> Although most of us regard air conditioning as an unqualified blessing if not an absolute necessity, our dependence on it carries seldom-examined consequences. Author Frank Trippett enumerates some of these consequences. For one thing, air conditioning has impoverished Americans' notions of neighborliness by luring people away from their front porches and into rooms that are shut off from outside air. This seclusion may contribute to certain antisocial tendencies, such as self-absorption and extreme competitiveness. Also, Trippett suggests that while it remains only a theory, some scientists think that air conditioning may impair our ability to cope with stress (75).

A paraphrase

Notice that the source, Frank Trippett, has been identified at the beginning of the paraphrase rather than within the parenthetical note at the end. (The parenthetical note is retained, however, to identify the precise location of the ideas that have been borrowed—page 75 of the publication in which Trippett's article appeared.)

Using Paraphrase to Support an Interpretation or Opinion

Suppose that you are writing a paper arguing that the recording industry has grown too powerful. In the course of your research, you run across the book *Music for Pleasure* by Simon Frith, a scholar of popular culture. Frith argues that one consequence of the recording industry's power is the suppression of certain kinds of musical talent:

> The industrialization of music means a shift from active musical production to passive pop consumption, the decline of folk or community or subcultural traditions, and a general loss of musical skill. The only instruments people like me can play today are their record players and tape decks.

The original passage

A paragraph in your research paper might open as follows:

> One consequence of the recording industry's power is the disappearance of musical talent. Simon Frith, a scholar of popular culture, has argued that the marketing of records has discouraged music-making by amateurs and has undermined regional and ethnic traditions, thus inhibiting the development and exercise of musical talent. Says Frith, "The only instruments people like me can play today are their record players and tape decks" (11).

A paraphrase

There are two things to note in regard to this paragraph. First, when you paraphrase a source to support your opinion or interpretation, the chances are you will choose someone regarded as an authority. Therefore, it is likely that you will identify that source in an acknowledgment phrase rather than in a parenthetical note at the end. Notice, too, that the basis for regarding Frith as an authority—the fact that he is a scholar of popular culture—is mentioned as well. (Obviously, if your source were a universally recognized person like Albert Einstein or Hillary Clinton, you would not need to do this.) The other thing you may have noticed about this passage is that it contains a quotation as well as a paraphrase. Since there really isn't any way to put the last sentence in words fundamentally different from Frith's—at least not without losing something—it is best to quote that sentence directly.

EXERCISE	**Paraphrasing in Research Papers**

Write a paraphrase of each of the following quotations—one that is appropriate to the situation at hand. Remember that you may choose to name the source before you start paraphrasing, or you may prefer to put the last name(s) of the source in a parenthetical note at the end, along with page number.

a. You are writing a research paper that takes a position regarding sex education in the public schools. You wish to use facts set forth in the following quotation to demonstrate that many young people are not well informed about sex.

Source: Sol Gordon and Judith Gordon, researchers at Syracuse University's Institute for Family Research and Education. The quotation appears on page 14 of an article by the Gordons.

Quotation:
The 1,200,000 teenage pregnancies a year and the 2,000,000 new cases of sexually transmitted diseases among those under 25 belie the myth that young people "know it all."

b. You are writing a research paper that analyzes the readership of several popular magazines. You want to introduce a section on the *New Yorker* with a paraphrase of the following quotation.

Source: Louis Menand, contributing editor of the *New York Review of Books*. The quotation appears on page 10 of an article in that publication.

Quotation:
The *New Yorker* was enormously attentive to the insecurity of its readers. It pruned from its pieces anything that might come across as allusive or knowing, and it promoted . . . a sensibility that took urbanity to be completely compatible with a certain kind of naiveté. The *New Yorker* made it possible to feel that being an antisophisticate was the mark of true sophistication.

c. You are writing a research paper that deals with differences in the dining habits in Great Britain and the United States. You wish to use a paraphrase of the following quotation to explain the way Britons view the American preference for serving beverages ice cold.

Source: British food critic Andrew Barr. The quotation appears on page 30 of his book, *Wine Snobbery: An Exposé.*

Quotation:
European commentators have struggled to explain the American obsession with refrigeration. . . . The underlying explanation appears to be the reverence that is accorded to the role of technology in the development of the United States. . . . It is an American habit to make use of technology in order to distance oneself as far as possible from the primitive and brutal life of the frontier.

GUIDELINES for Effective Paraphrasing

The general principles set forth in this chapter can be summed up in the following guidelines for effective paraphrasing:

- Paraphrasing involves a special kind of reading and response, appropriate when the occasion calls for close literal reading and accurate reporting.

- When you paraphrase a passage to make it suitable for a different audience, you should make appropriate adjustments in style, vocabulary, and degree of formality.

- When you paraphrase an argument, particularly one with which you disagree, you must be careful to be fair and objective.

- When you paraphrase a research source, you must completely recast the source's words in your own language and in your own style. Simple word substitution does not constitute a legitimate paraphrase of another's language; neither does the rearrangement of word order.

 ## READING SELECTION

The following article describes the reported benefits of the "miracle drug" melatonin, originally marketed as a sleeping pill but now viewed as a possible means of retarding the effects of aging.

Melatonin

GEOFFREY COWLEY

Turning back the clock has long been the domain of crackpots and charlatans. Take one look at the claims that enthusiasts are making for melatonin, a hormone sold as a supplement in health-food stores, and you'll quickly sense that nothing much has changed. "Senescence, the downward spiral that we have come to associate with aging, does not have to occur," Drs. Walter Pierpaoli and William Regelson declare in their forthcoming book, *The Melatonin Miracle.* "Melatonin can stop the spiral." 1

Strip away the bombast, and it turns out these guys are on to something interesting. Like most animals, we produce melatonin abundantly throughout early life. But the levels in our blood drop slightly before puberty and decline steadily into old age. When Pierpaoli, an Italian immunologist, restores youthful levels of the hormone in mice, they outlive their life expectancies by nearly a third. And his findings are consistent with a burgeoning scientific literature. Recent studies suggest that supplementing the hormone may bolster our immune systems, keep our cells from disintegrating, slow the growth of tumors and cataracts, and ward off heart disease. All that while helping us sleep better. 2

3   Proven or not, melatonin is poised to become one of the hottest pills of the decade. It's cheap and readily available—a month's supply costs less than $10 in health-food stores—and it's gaining popularity among people who've heard nothing about its anti-aging properties. Travelers and office workers are using it as an antidote to jet lag, stress and insomnia. And sales are soaring. One manufacturer, Source Naturals of Scotts Valley, Calif., expects to move a million jars of lozenges this year—three times the number it sold in 1993. Skeptics cringe at the thought of people gulping down a supplement whose long-term effects are largely unknown. But since studies have yet to document any hazards, even scientists are taking the plunge. "I take a milligram or less every night," says Russel Reiter, a University of Texas cellular biologist who has studied melatonin for 30 years. "I want to die young as late in life as possible, and I think this hormone could help."

4   First identified just four decades ago, melatonin is now recognized as one of life's most ubiquitous molecules. It turns up in such diverse organisms as people and protozoa, suggesting it dates back a billion years or so. Humans secrete it cyclically from the pineal gland, a pea-size structure nestled at the center of the brain, in response to the amount of light hitting our eyes. Physiologists know melatonin as the hormone that keeps us in sync with the rhythms of the day and the season. Through its actions on other hormones, it helps determine when people sleep and horses breed, when birds migrate, dogs shed their coats and certain frogs change color. But cellular biologists have recently discovered that melatonin has an even more basic function, which is to protect oxygen-based life from the toxic effects of . . . oxygen.

5   Yes, oxygen. As we metabolize this life-sustaining gas, we generate highly reactive molecules called free radicals, which can corrode our cellular membranes and damage our DNA. The process, known as oxidation, weakens our minds and muscles as we age, and contributes to at least 60 degenerative diseases, including cancer, heart disease and Alzheimer's. The body produces several enzymes to inhibit oxidation, and nutrients such as vitamin C, vitamin E and beta carotene can provide extra protection. But most of these so-called antioxidants work only in certain parts of certain cells. Melatonin readily permeates any cell in any part the body—including the brain. And as Reiter's research team has recently shown in animal experiments, the hormone can protect tissues from an amazing array of assaults.

6   The evidence started stacking up just two years ago, when Reiter and his colleagues showed that a small dose of melatonin could shield rats from a cancer-causing chemical called safrole. Given alone, safrole quickly oxidizes liver cells, causing extensive DNA damage. But when rats got tiny doses of melatonin before their safrole shots, they exhibited 41 percent less damage than their untreated counterparts—and those receiving a slightly larger dose of melatonin suffered just *1 percent* as much liver damage as the controls. In more recent studies, Reiter's team has shown that melatonin's antioxidant action can protect rats from ionizing radiation (halving the death rate from a normally lethal dose), and can shield the animals' lungs from the deadly herbicide paraquat. Melatonin may also help prevent cataracts, the cloudy lesions that appear on our eyes as oxidation damages cells in the lenses. When the Texas researchers gave 18 newborn rats a toxic compound called BSO, all 18 developed cataracts within two weeks. But when 15 animals got the same treatment plus melatonin, 14 maintained perfectly clear eyes.

7   Oxidation isn't the only reason we fall apart as we age. We also lose our immune function. The thymus gland shrinks over time, sapping our ability to generate infection-fighting T cells, and we produce fewer of the antibody molecules that bind with and neutralize foreign invaders, such as viruses and bacteria. Could all of this follow from a

loss of melatonin? Test-tube studies have identified receptors, or specialized portals, for melatonin on the cells and glands of the immune system. And animal experiments are showing that the hormone can preserve, or even restore, a creature's defenses.

One of the best examples comes from Pierpaoli's mouse lab. A few years ago he   8
paired 10 young mice with 10 old ones and had a microsurgeon switch their pineal glands (old to young and vice versa). Before long, the youngsters were hobbling around with cataracts in their eyes and bald patches on their backs. The old ones gained muscle and energy, and their coats grew thick and shiny. Autopsies revealed what was probably part of the reason. The young mice had all but lost their thymus glands after the pineal transplant. The oldsters had had theirs restored.

In other animal studies, Italian researchers have shown that a nightly melatonin sup-   9
plement can boost the performance of immune systems compromised by age, drugs or stress. And scientists in Israel and Switzerland have found that when mice receive melatonin, their odds of surviving infection with an encephalitis virus more than double.

No one knows just how neatly any of these findings will apply to people. But   10
together they suggest that melatonin could help us prevent, and even treat, the most common afflictions of old age. Where cancer is concerned, the evidence isn't limited to mouse studies. Autopsy studies suggest that pineal calcification (a condition that hardens the gland and reduces melatonin output) is most common in countries with high rates of breast cancer and least common in countries where breast cancer is rare. By the same token, women taking chlorpromazine, an antipsychotic medication that raises melatonin levels, enjoy unusually low rates of the disease.

The explanation, says Dr. Michael Cohen of Fairfax, Va., involves estrogen. Pro-   11
longed exposure to that hormone (due to early puberty, infrequent childbearing or late menopause) increases a woman's risk of breast cancer. But melatonin dampens the release of estrogen. In fact, high melatonin levels can temporarily shut down the reproductive system. That's why females in most species are fertile only at certain times of year. Exploiting this principle, Cohen has combined a stiff (75 mg) dose of melatonin with progestin to create a new oral contraceptive. The drug, called B-Oval, has performed as well as conventional birth-control pills in European studies involving 1,000 women, and has shown no toxicity. Cohen plans to launch U.S. trials within two years, but his goal is not simply to market another contraceptive. If his hypothesis about melatonin, estrogen and breast tumors bears out, the new pill could help women prevent cancer as well as unwanted pregnancies.

Melatonin may also prove useful for fighting existing malignancies. Several studies   12
have shown that it can slow the growth of human tumor cells in a test tube, and some cancer specialists are now testing its effects on patients. In a 1992 study, Dr. Paoli Lissoni and his colleagues at San Gerardo Hospital in Monza, Italy, found that a nightly melatonin supplement (10 mg) significantly improved one-year survival rates among patients with metastatic lung cancer. The same lab has since reported that melatonin can enhance the effect of interleuken-2 shots (IL-2 is a hormone that helps T cells proliferate) on cancers of the lung, kidney, liver, colon and pancreas. IL-2 causes horrific fevers and nausea at the doses normally required to tame tumors. But Lissoni's group found that the compound is effective at a fraction of the usual dose when accompanied by melatonin.

Defining this hormone's true powers as an antidote to aging and chronic illness will take   13
years, if not decades. There are countless leads to follow. Animal studies suggest that besides combating cancer, melatonin might help control cholesterol, regulate blood pressure and modulate the release of heart-killing stress hormones. But today's users aren't overly concerned with any of this. Most just want a decent night's sleep—and

many will tell you they've found it. Robbie Felix, a 40-year-old employment consultant in Silicon Valley, says she was a "chronic insomniac" until two years ago, when she read about melatonin on the Internet. Since then, she has taken 15 to 20 milligrams every night (three to four times the typical dose), and slept soundly. "With traditional sleeping pills you're groggy the next day," she says. "Not with this." Dr. Steven Bock of Rhinebeck, N.Y., author of a new book titled "Stay Young the Melatonin Way," says he has given the stuff to 300 patients and never seen a bad reaction. Dr. Ray Sahelian of Los Angeles (author of *Melatonin: Nature's Sleeping Pill*) is just as excited. 'I think eventually this will make prescription sleeping pills all but obsolete," he says.

14   There's more at work here than the power of suggestion. Researchers have been documenting melatonin's sleep-inducing properties since the early 1980s, when Dr. Richard Wurtman of MIT's Clinical Research Center started giving volunteers what are now recognized as megadoses (240 mg). Controlled studies have since established that as little as a tenth of a milligram can hasten the onset of sleep, whatever the time of day. Researchers have also shown that a brief nightly regimen of 5 milligrams can help airline workers adjust to new time zones. And Dr. James Jan of Vancouver, British Columbia's Children's Hospital, has reported that bedtime doses of 2.5 to 10 milligrams help establish normal sleep patterns in kids with neurological problems such as autism, epilepsy, Down syndrome and cerebral palsy. "We had tried everything," Jan recalls of the first child he treated with melatonin, "but nothing worked." After one dose of the hormone, "the parents called me and said, 'It's a miracle! A miracle!' The child slept through the night."

15   There are plenty of drugs that can bring on sleep, but they have well-known drawbacks. They tend to suppress the restorative dream state known as REM. They lose their effect over time. They're addictive if used too often, and at high doses they can kill you. Researchers have yet to report any of these problems with melatonin. When government scientists set out to find melatonin's "LD 50"—the dose that's lethal to 50 percent of the animals receiving it—they couldn't make a rich enough concentrate to kill a mouse. And when researchers fed human volunteers 6 *grams* (6,000 mg) of the stuff every night for a month, stomach discomfort and some residual sleepiness were the only reported side effects.

16   Even so, experts differ sharply on whether melatonin should be sold like seaweed in health stores. "Every time someone writes about this stuff," says Wurtman, "I get the sinking feeling that more people are going to run out and take it." Wurtman is as excited as anyone about the hormone's potential. His own company, Interneuron Pharmaceutical, has a patent pending on a melatonin-based sleeping pill (the chemical itself can't be patented). But he worries that we know less about the hormone than we think we do. "Is it safe to take while you're pregnant?" he asks. "Is it safe to take with Prozac? No one really knows." If the FDA regulated melatonin as a drug, manufacturers would have to address such questions before marketing it. They would also have to show that their ingredients were pure and their production methods sound. Says Wurtman, "You'd have a better idea of what you were buying."

17   For now, consumers are stuck deciding for themselves whether to trust what they read on a label. There's no reason to assume that melatonin is any more hazardous than other unregulated supplements. And as enthusiasts like to point out, regulated prescription drugs still carry plenty of risks. So far, the FDA has shown little interest in controlling melatonin. The agency simply warns users that they take it "without any assurance that it is safe or that it will have any beneficial effect." It's a worthy admonition but it's not likely to turn people away. The promise is too rich: a good night's sleep, complete with dreams of a rip-roaring 105th birthday party.

Freewriting

Freewrite for ten to fifteen minutes about the possible consequences of finding a cheap and widely available drug that would allow most people to lead healthy and productive lives of more than a hundred years. First, write about some of the obvious benefits—relief from the pain and anxiety caused by disease, greater ability to plan for the future, longer relationships with family members and friends, more time to achieve financial security. Then, consider some of the potential drawbacks—overpopulation, concentration of wealth and power among the elderly, the need to redefine retirement. After considering both points of view, try to assess the desirability of finding and distributing such a drug.

Group Work

Share freewritings with your group by having each member read aloud as others take notes. As you listen to each person read, jot down notes in two columns, listing the most persuasive or unusual advantages and the most serious drawbacks for finding a drug that would drastically retard the aging process. After everyone has read, try to formulate the most compelling arguments for and against the development of such a drug. Report your findings to the class as a whole.

Review Questions

1. What makes melatonin a more effective antioxidant than such familiar substances as vitamin C and beta carotene?

2. What roles do the thymus and pineal glands play in the process of aging? How are they affected by melatonin?

3. What are the advantages of melatonin over other sleeping drugs?

Discussion Questions

1. Most scientists would say that it is never wise to take a drug when its long-term effects are unknown. Why might they consider melatonin an exception to the rule?

2. Do you think many people would abandon exercise and good nutritional habits if they could obtain the same benefits from drugs?

3. Why do you suppose the Food and Drug Administration has shown little interest in regulating melatonin?

Writing

1. Since the article on melatonin appeared originally in *Newsweek,* it is less technical and detailed (and perhaps less rigorously objective) than a piece in a more specialized magazine or professional journal might be. Consult one or more of

the following articles and write a brief comparison of the vocabulary, style, and factual detail found in each source:

a. "Overnight Sensation: Melatonin May Cure Your Insomnia, but Will You Regret It in the Morning?", by Benedict Carey, published in the September 1995 issue of *Health,* pages 36–38.

b. "Drug of Darkness: Can a Pineal Hormone Head Off Everything from Breast Cancer to Aging?", published in the May 13, 1995, issue of *Science News,* pages 300–01.

c. "Melatonin—the Hormone of Darkness," by Robert D. Utiger, published in the November 5, 1992, issue of the *New England Journal of Medicine,* pages 1377–79.

2. If you can ask a person with special knowledge or expertise (e.g., a chemist, biologist, nutritionist, or pharmacist, or perhaps a fellow student who is majoring in one of these fields) to read the article that ends this chapter, ask him or her to assess its completeness and objectivity. Present your findings in a brief report addressed to the other members of your class.

3. Write an objective presentation of both of the arguments you considered in carrying out the group work detailed above. Take into account the observations of other groups as they reported to your entire class.

4 Reading for the Main Idea

THE READING strategies discussed in Chapter 2 have many purposes, one of the most important being to help you see, quickly and clearly, what the writer is getting at. Good readers always have one question before them as they read: What is this about? Or, in other words, what is the *main idea* of the passage? Being able to recognize, understand, and restate the main idea of a passage is a valuable skill that you will use in carrying out a variety of academic tasks, including library research.

Defining *main ideas* as a concept is not as easy as it may sound. Chapter 2 demonstrated how active readers *create meaning* when they experience a written text. Because people carry into their reading different backgrounds and personal histories, it seems improbable that any two readers will experience a long or complicated piece of writing (the novel *Moby Dick,* for example) in precisely the same fashion. In an effort to account for this diversity, one modern philosopher has declared that "every reading is a misreading." In the face of such views, you may ask how it is possible to determine anything like the main idea of a reading.

There is no easy answer to that question. However, it seems safe to say that the meaning of a written text does not belong entirely to the writer; nor does it belong entirely to the reader. Instead, the two, acting in collaboration, negotiate meaning. At least that's how reading operates under ideal circumstances. But in order for the processes of negotiation to work smoothly and predictably, both writer and reader must recognize and abide by certain established conventions. When you tried reading a passage in Chapter 2 that defied one of those conventions—it lacked an informative title—the collaboration between you and the writer broke down.

Basically, writers plant clues and signals, and readers respond to them in predictable and relatively uniform ways. This chapter focuses on some of these conventions. Your familiarity with them should help you hold up your end of the transaction between writer and reader.

 ## GENERAL AND SPECIFIC STATEMENTS

If the main idea of any piece of writing were stated in a sentence, that sentence would be a *general* statement, much broader than the other sentences in the text, which are more *specific.* The difference between general and specific statements is an important one for readers to grasp. It can be demonstrated briefly with a few examples. Here are some words and phrases listed in order from the most general to the most specific:

more general

things
life forms
animals
mammals
humans
students
first-year students
members of Professor Filbert's comp class

more specific   Chip Holzclaw

Each term in the list is more specific, and therefore less general, than the one before it. As a category, each includes fewer members. The first term includes everything (every *thing*) in the universe, while the last includes only one single individual. Chip belongs to each category; his dog Jack belongs just to the first four; and Jack's flea collar is a member only of the most general category, things.

Some statements can also be arranged in order from most general to most specific:

- Some people have qualities not shared by everyone.
- Jo Ann has many exceptional traits.
- Most notable is her superhuman will power.
- She can stick to her diet no matter how great the temptation.
- Last week when I offered her a hot fudge sundae topped with real whipped cream for dessert, Jo Ann turned it down and ate half an apple instead.

Again, each statement is a more specific instance of the statement before it. Each bears a *for example* relationship to the one it follows, and the examples cover less and less territory. The last one is a very specific and **concrete** statement, one that presents a picture that you can visualize in your imagination—here describing a specific event at a specific time involving specific people. In contrast, the first one is a very general and **abstract** statement, one that calls up an idea but not any particular event that you can see with your mind's eye. Being aware of the difference between general, abstract statements and specific, concrete ones is essential for readers.

EXERCISES   General and Specific Categories

1. Arrange the following lists in order from the most general to the most specific:

    a. loafer
       foot covering
       casual shoe
       entity

Mr. MacLennan's right shoe
garment
product
shoe

b. The College of Arts and Sciences
higher education
Natural History of Intertidal Organisms 553
The Marine Biology Option
State University
Department of Biology
school
Division of Physical Sciences

c. Mrs. Drumble lacks concern for her fellow creatures.
Mrs. Drumble cuts off the tails of blind mice with a carving knife.
Mrs. Drumble tortures rodents.
Mrs. Drumble is a heartless person.
Mrs. Drumble is cruel to animals.

d. Words can affect their hearers.
Patrick Henry aroused sentiment for independence with his cry, "Give me liberty or give me death."
Political oratory can be particularly stirring.
Some statements provoke people's emotions.

2. For each of these items, supply two others: one that is more general and another that is more specific.

a. chair

b. circus performer

c. Bert loves Felicia.

d. Parents often urge their teenage children to do well in school.

 DEDUCTIVE AND INDUCTIVE ORGANIZATION

Within any passage, some statements are more general than others. Often the way an author arranges general and specific statements is important. Notice, for example, that the sample passage on page 62, which you examined in Chapter 2, contains four levels of generality. Here we have numbered those levels from 1 (the most general) to 4 (the most specific) and arranged the sentences on the page with more specific levels indented farther to the right:

1 Scarfe was always a tyrant in his household.
   2 The servants lived in constant terror of his fierce diatribes, which he would deliver whenever he was displeased.

3 One of the most frequent causes of his displeasure was the food they
served him.

4 His tea, for example, was either too hot or too cold.

4 The soup had either too much or too little seasoning.

3 Another pet peeve was the servants' manner of address.

4 God help the butler who forgot to add "sir" to every sentence he
spoke to Scarfe, or the chauffeur whose tone was deemed not properly deferential.

4 On the other hand, when one of the more timid parlor maids
would hesitate in speaking so as to be certain her words did not
give offense, he would thunder at her, "Out with it, you stupid
girl!"

2 Scarfe's wife and children were equally the victims of his tyranny.

Notice that the most general sentence, at level 1, states the main idea of the
entire passage—that Scarfe was a tyrant in his household. The two sentences at
level 2 give examples of his tyranny. In the same way, sentences at level 3 present
examples of statements made at level 2, and level-4 statements are examples of
what is said at level 3. For the most part, then, sentences in the passage are arranged
in a general-to-specific sequence.

Unlike the Scarfe passage, the explanatory paragraph you just read ("Notice
that . . . ") is arranged in a specific-to-general order. Its first three sentences make
specific statements, and then the last sentence sums them up in a general conclusion.

In general-to-specific, or **deductive,** passages, the writer first states the main
idea in a general way and then demonstrates it with specific examples or explanations. In specific-to-general, or **inductive,** passages, the writer takes you through a
sequence of discovery, with the main idea coming as a conclusion reached after the
specific evidence has been presented.

Deductive arrangements are far more common than the reverse order, but
probably few passages that you meet will be as neatly organized or as multileveled
as the Scarfe example.

EXERCISES | Deductive and Inductive Passages

1. Decide whether each of the following passages is arranged in a deductive (gen-
    eral-to-specific) or inductive (specific-to-general) order:

    a. Delaware, it should be known, does possess an indigenous, if contradictory, cul-
        ture. It's a state of point-to-point horse races and countless chicken farms. It's an
        unreconstructed Cheeverscape where preppies with names like Frolic and Pepper
        toss back G&Ts and shag to Herb Alpert records; yet it's also Flannery O'Connor
        territory, where good ol' boys with crosses tattooed on their biceps chew deer jerky
        and go scramblin' on their Harleys down on Slaughter Beach. The Delaware accent
        (yes, such a thing exists) is an intriguingly nasal Baltimoron squawk mixed with top
        notes of Yankee lockjaw and honeyed bottom notes of southern y'all-ness—a reflec-
        tion of the fact that Delaware fought for the Union while remaining a slave state.
        —Elissa Schappell, "Cipherland, U.S.A."

    b. If you enjoy working out the strategy of games, tit-tat-toe or poker or chess; if you
        are interested in the frog that jumped up three feet and fell back two in getting
        out of a well, or in the fly buzzing between the noses of two approaching cyclists,

or in the farmer who left land to his three sons; if you have been captivated by codes and ciphers or are interested in crosswords puzzles; if you like to fool around with numbers; if music appeals to you by the sense of form which it expresses—then you will enjoy logic. You ought to be warned, perhaps. Those who take up logic get glassy-eyed and absent-minded. They join a fanatical cult. But they have a good time. Theirs is one of the most durable, absorbing and inexpensive of pleasures. Logic is fun.

—Roger W. Holmes, *The Rhyme of Reason*

c. There are various reasons for the appeal of sparkling wine. From the point of view of the wine maker, carbon dioxide accentuates the acid taste in wines and therefore makes them seem fresher. This is very useful for white wines made in hot climates, which tend to suffer from a lack of acidity. It also protects wine from decay, because the pressure of gas trying to escape prevents air from entering the bottle. When the "champagne method" was developed last century, making it possible to produce sparkling wines at will, it was used to preserve white wines while they were waiting for customers. . . . From the point of view of the consumer, the carbon dioxide enhances a drink's appearance, diminishes the taste of alcohol (which many people dislike), and at the same time enables the alcohol to be absorbed much more rapidly by the gut, thereby producing a much more rapid effect. This has rendered sparkling drinks sexually useful.

—Andrew Barr, *Wine Snobbery: An Exposé*

2. This paragraph from a student paper has sentences on several different levels of generality, but the pattern of arrangement is mixed. Discuss its use and arrangement of specific and general statements.

> Outside pressures are often the cause of early marriages. Tom and Emily have been dating since junior high. She wears his class ring, and each of them is rarely seen without the other. They are such a familiar item that friends expect them to get married and talk of it openly. These expectations from their peers constitute an unspoken but real pressure on them to marry. They are also faced with pressure from their parents. Tom's mother is a close friend of Emily's, and they often discuss the wedding as if it were a certainty. Emily's parents have dropped several hints about her moving out of the house and of "making us grandparents." As a result of these pressures from peers and parents, Tom and Emily have announced their engagement to be married next June.

3. As was done with the Scarfe passage on pages 115–16, number the sentences in each of the previous passages to represent their levels of generality.

4. Write another version of the second paragraph of the Scarfe passage. Begin with the final sentence ("Scarfe's wife and children ... "), and invent details for your sentences as needed. Make the sentences in your paragraph follow this organization for levels of generality: 2, 3, 4, 4, 3, 4, 4.

 ## THESIS STATEMENTS AND TOPIC SENTENCES

Sometimes, as several examples have demonstrated, writers condense the main idea of a passage into a single sentence. When one sentence states the main idea for an entire essay (or for any longer passage, such as a research paper or a book chapter), it is called a **thesis statement.** When a statement within an individual paragraph states its main idea, it is called a **topic sentence.**

Identifying Topic Sentences

Not every paragraph you encounter in your daily reading will have a topic sentence (in fact, fewer than half of them will), just as not every longer passage will have an explicit thesis statement. When topic sentences and thesis statements do occur, however, they are among the most valuable reading clues; they help you see the writer's intentions and anticipate what is to follow. It pays to attend to them. Since a deductive arrangement is much more common than an inductive one, topic sentences appear most frequently at the beginnings of paragraphs, introducing and preparing for the supporting sentences that follow. Less often, they come after some preliminary statements, summing up or drawing conclusions from them. As you read the following paragraphs, see if you can identify their topic sentences.

> The effect of an ice age is dramatic. It does not just ice up the poles but drops temperatures everywhere around the world by about ten degrees centigrade. The world's wildlife gets squeezed into a band near the equator and even here life is hardly comfortable. The vast polar ice packs lock up a lot of the earth's water, disrupting rainfall and turning previously lush tropical areas into drought-stricken deserts.
> —John McCrone, *The Ape That Spoke*

> In the Medieval Glass of Canterbury Cathedral, an angel appears to the sleeping wise men and warns them to go straight home, and not return to Herod. Below, the corresponding event from the Old Testament teaches the faithful that each moment of Jesus's life replays a piece of the past and that God has put meaning into time—Lot turns round and his wife becomes a pillar of salt (the white glass forming a striking contrast with the glittering colors that surround her). The common theme of both incidents: don't look back.
> —Stephen Jay Gould, *The Flamingo's Smile*

The first paragraph opens with a topic sentence that is perfectly straightforward: *The effect of an ice age is dramatic.* Such a sentence is an aid to reading, since it signals what will follow: specific examples that illustrate the topic sentence—in this case, three dramatic consequences of an ice age. The second paragraph is arranged inductively and provides no such clues at the beginning. Its author begins with specific evidence: He describes the stained-glass depiction of two Biblical episodes. A topic sentence is presented as the final sentence, which draws a general conclusion from the evidence: the two scenes illustrate the same theme.

EXERCISE | **Topic Sentences**

1. Identify the topic sentences in each of the sample paragraphs in Exercises 1 and 2 on pages 116–17.

2. Identify the topic sentence in each of these passages:

a. There is no such thing as the artistic personality—not in poetry, not in the visual arts. Michelangelo's personality was just one of the colorful range on offer. He was paranoid about his productions, keeping his drawings secret not only from his contemporaries who might include potential plagiarists, but also from posterity itself. As his days drew to a close he made two large bonfires, and not a drawing or cartoon was found in his studio after his death. And this paranoia extended to his relations with other artists. He did not "bring on young talent." He appears to have surrounded himself deliberately with no-hopers, and it is easy to imagine that it was the skill, not the shortcomings, of Giambologna that drove him into such a rage.
—James Fenton, "A Lesson from Michelangelo"

b. On all parts of the giant building, statuary and stone representations of every kind, combined with huge windows of stained glass, told the stories of the Bible and the saints, displayed the intricacies of Christian theology, adverted to the existence of highly unpleasant demonic winged creatures, referred diplomatically to the majesties of political power, and, in addition, by means of bells in bell towers (manned in [Victor] Hugo's time by the hunchback Quasimodo) told time for the benefit of all of Paris and much of France. It was an awesome engine of communication.
—Paul Berman, "Dos Misérables"

c. When it was over and I escaped through the ropes, shaking, bleeding a little from the mouth, with rosin dust on my pants and a vicious throbbing in my head, I knew all there was to know about being hit in the prize-ring. . . . I knew the sensation of being stalked and pursued by a relentless, truculent, professional destroyer whose trade and business it was to injure men. I saw the quick flash of the brown forearm that precedes the stunning shock as a bony, leather-bound fist lands on a cheek or mouth. I learned more (partly from photographs of the lesson, viewed afterwards, one of which shows me ducked under a vicious left hook, an act of which I never had the slightest recollection) about instinctive ducking and blocking than I could have in ten years of looking at prizefights, and I learned, too, that as the soldier never hears the bullet that kills him, so does the fighter rarely, if ever, see the punch that tumbles blackness over him like a mantle, with a tearing rip as though the roof of his skull were exploding, and robs him of his senses.
—Paul Gallico, *Farewell to Sport*

 ## RESTATING THE MAIN IDEA

Identifying topic sentences is more than a mere exercise. It is important that you remember the point of what you have been doing. Good reading means recognizing what the writer is getting at; that includes seeing and understanding the main idea. When a topic sentence states the main idea very neatly for you, it is a valuable help. Sometimes, however, topic sentences are not as straightforward as they are in the preceding examples. Read the following paragraphs, keeping a lookout for each writer's main idea:

Our files show that most men are unhappy with the state of their bodies. They would prefer to have the kind of torso that provokes ooohs and aahs from admiring women. They would like to have bulging biceps that will win the respect and envy of other men. They are seeking the feeling of pride and confidence that comes from

possessing a truly well developed physique. They want the kind of body that any man can build by subscribing to the Jack Harrigan Dyna-Fit Program.
—An imagined magazine advertisement

Almost everyone has hitherto taken it for granted that Australopitheca [our female hominid ancestor who lived more than a million years ago], since she was primitive and chinless and lowbrowed, was necessarily hairy, and the artists always depict her as a shaggy creature. I don't think there is any reason for thinking this. Just as for a long time they "assumed" the big brain came first, before the use of tools, so they still "assume" that hairlessness came last. If I had to visualize the Villafranchian hominids, I'd say their skin was in all probability quite as smooth as our own.
—Elaine Morgan, *The Descent of Woman*

In the paragraph from the body-building ad, you might question whether the first or the last sentence should be called the topic sentence. A case can be made for either. The first sentence is a general statement, contending that most men are dissatisfied with their physiques. The remaining four sentences then restate that contention more specifically. On the other hand, the writer's main idea is not just to state this dissatisfaction but to imply a conclusion from it, namely that men (more specifically, the readers) should want to spend their money on the company's fitness program. Perhaps, then, the last sentence is more appropriately viewed as the topic sentence. Actually, since the main idea of the whole paragraph combines information from the first and last sentences, together with what you infer about the author's intentions, you could state the main idea in a concise general statement of your own: *Men who wish to improve their physiques should invest in the Harrigan Dyna-Fit Program.*

A similar question about the topic sentence arises with the paragraph about Australopitheca. Here the author's main idea is stated twice—first in the short second sentence and then again more concretely in the final sentence. But neither sentence expresses the entire idea of the paragraph, and so once again you could formulate your own statement of its main idea, perhaps like this: *Despite most people's assumption to the contrary, Australopitheca was probably no hairier than modern woman.*

Paragraphs with Implied Main Ideas

Many paragraphs have no explicit topic sentence. Often it is because they deal with several different ideas joined together for convenience, as in this example:

The first Mormon community was at Kirkland, Ohio, but in order to approach the Lost Tribes, it moved to a spot on the east bank of the Mississippi which the Prophet named Nauvoo. At first the Mormons were welcomed in Illinois, courted by both political parties, and given a charter that made Nauvoo practically an autonomous theocracy. The settlement grew rapidly—even faster than Chicago. It was at Nauvoo that Joseph Smith received the "revelation" sanctioning polygamy, which he and the inner circle of "elders" were already practicing. Although supported by Isaiah iv. 1, "And in that day seven women shall take hold of one man," this revelation split the church. The monogamous "schismatics" started a paper at Nauvoo; Smith caused the press to be broken up after the first issue; he and his brother were then arrested by the authorities for destruction of property and lodged in the county jail, whence they were pulled out by a mob and

lynched. Brigham Young, who succeeded to the mantle of the Prophet, and to five of his 27 widows, directed retaliation, and for two years terror reigned in western Illinois. The Mormons were a virile, fighting people, but the time had come for them to make another move, before they were hopelessly outnumbered.
—Samuel Eliot Morison and Henry Steele Commager, *Growth of the American Republic*

This paragraph narrates a series of events in the early history of the Mormon church, but no one sentence summarizes all of them.

Sometimes a single-topic paragraph does not need a topic sentence because the main idea can be easily inferred from the context. Here is an example of such a paragraph without a topic sentence:

Thin soup served in a soup plate is eaten from the side of the spoon, dipped into the liquid away from you. Thick soup may be eaten from the tip and dipped toward you. Soup served in bouillon cups is usually sipped (silently) from the spoon until cool and then drunk—using one handle or both. Eat boneless and skinless fish with a fork, but to remove skin or bones it is necessary to use a knife. According to the best modern practice, you may cut a piece of meat and lift it at once on the fork in the left hand to the mouth while holding the knife in the right.
—*Britannica Junior* (1956), "Etiquette"

If the authors had wanted to introduce this paragraph with a topic sentence, they would have written something like this: *Polite people follow certain rules of table etiquette when they eat.* But since the preceding paragraphs had described other examples of table manners, they felt that no topic sentence was needed here. Many times, however, topic sentences are useful. One of the mistakes often made by inexperienced writers is to omit such sentences when they would aid the reader.

Restating the Main Idea

1. Being able to label a topic sentence when one occurs in a passage is useful, but the really important thing is to recognize the main idea of the passage. Remember that the two will not always coincide.

    For each of the following paragraphs, try first to identify a topic sentence. If no one sentence adequately states the author's main idea, write your own one-sentence statement of that idea. Then consider whether the readability of the passage would have been improved if the author had used your topic sentence. If so, should it go at the beginning, middle, or end of the passage?

    a. The tradition of linking the divine and the material is particularly strong among Catholics, whose devotional lives have long included saying the rosary, blessing the home with holy water and lighting candles in front of statues. American Protestants have also depended on objects and images; during the 19th century, Protestant women embroidered pious mottoes and carved crosses out of wax, setting them in the parlor with the family Bible. Mass-produced prints of Jesus and other biblical characters began finding their way into homes, churches and Sunday schools.
    —Colleen McDannell, "In Defense of Material Christianity"

    b. In terms of its effects on the body, caffeine is a drug that stimulates the central nervous system—increasing heartbeat, respiration, metabolic rate, and the production of stomach acid and urine. Some people are far more sensitive to its effects than others, and regular caffeine consumption increases your tolerance (a fact that can skew research, which sometimes fails to note whether subjects are habitual caffeine consumers, who can down several cups of coffee without effect, or caffeine dabblers, who may get inordinately stimulated by one cup). Caffeine also causes a physical dependency. A 1992 *New England Journal of Medicine* study of 62 healthy adults—71 percent of them female—found that after cutting out caffeine for days, even moderate coffee drinkers (those sipping an average of two and a half cups a day) experienced withdrawal symptoms: depression, anxiety, low vigor, and fatigue. A whopping 52 percent had moderate to severe headaches. (Of course, if you never stop drinking coffee, this isn't a problem.)

—Marjorie Ingall, "Caffeine: The (Mostly) Good News"

2. In the following passages, topic sentences have been replaced by ellipses (. . .). Use the remaining context to discover the main idea of each paragraph and try to guess what the author's topic sentence might have been.

    a. . . . He is a writer pretty much everyone in the English-speaking world has heard of, if they have heard of writers at all. He is regularly read by many people who don't read many other writers. And, along with Danielle Steel and a few others, he is taken to represent everything that is wrong with contemporary publishing, that engine of junk pushing serious literature out of our minds and our bookstores. The English writer Clive Barker has said, "There are apparently two books in every American household—one of them is the Bible and the other one is probably by Stephen King." I don't know what Barker's source is for this claim, but I wonder about the Bible.

       —Michael Wood, "Horror of Horrors"

    b. On a recent trip to St. Petersburg, I visited Smolny, one of the holiest shrines of Soviet history. A handsome yellow neoclassical structure erected by Catherine the Great, Smolny served as headquarters for Lenin and his victorious Bolsheviks during the Russian Revolution. For decades after October 1917, Smolny was mythologized in Soviet film, literature and song as the cradle of the world's first Socialist government. . . .

       —Harlow Robinson, "Leningrad Was Here"

3. Like an inductive paragraph, which ends by stating a conclusion, many scientific experiments can be called inductive, in that they lead to a discovery. So too the following could be called an inductive exercise, which asks you to draw conclusions from your discoveries.

    a. In books, magazines, or other texts, find one example of a paragraph that begins with a topic sentence and another of a paragraph that ends with a topic sentence. Copy (or photocopy) them and bring them to class.

    b. Examine an example of each of the following:
       • college-level textbook
       • novel
       • biography (book or essay about a person)
       • newspaper article
       • magazine article

    From each, select ten paragraphs at random and see how many (1) begin with a topic sentence, (2) end with a topic sentence, (3) have a topic sentence placed elsewhere, (4) have an implied topic sentence, or (5) have no unifying concept at all.

c. Now draw conclusions from your experiment: How easy was it to find topic sentences? When they occur, where are topic sentences more likely to be placed? Are certain types of writing more likely than others to make use of topic sentences? If so, why do you think that is? Are there any general conclusions that you can now draw about how writers use paragraphs?

Discovering Implications

As the preceding section demonstrated, in many paragraphs a topic sentence is implied rather than explicitly stated. Discovering the main idea is a task left for the alert reader. But it is only one of many such tasks. Writers leave many gaps in the meaning they intend to communicate, and they expect their readers to fill them in.

Even in everyday conversation, we do not always put everything that we mean into words. Consider, for example, the ***implication,*** the unspoken but intended meaning, in the following conversation between two students:

Aaron: I signed up for Professor Phrisby's Organic Chemistry class.

Caitlin: I hope you've got a large supply of caffeine tablets.

Without saying it in so many words, Caitlin is implying that Professor Phrisby's course is difficult and requires much studying into the late hours. For Aaron to understand her meaning, he must make connections, relying on his past experience with college life and with how people use language. A less sophisticated listener, such as an eight-year-old, might not be able to bridge the gap between what Caitlin says and what she actually means.

Being a sophisticated listener or reader demands skill at drawing inferences.* Not everyone will derive the same meaning in each circumstance. Sometimes the gaps in our messages are open to more than one interpretation. In the preceding example, Aaron was probably already aware of the reputation of Professor Phrisby's course and understood exactly what Caitlin meant. But someone else overhearing Caitlin's response might draw a different conclusion, inferring perhaps that Professor Phrisby's classes are boring and students have difficulty staying awake. Success in communication depends upon knowing your audience and adapting your message to allow them to draw the inferences you intend.

Writers rely on implication just as speakers do. Consider the following paragraph, taken from an essay about the bizarre treatment its author often receives as a result of his blindness:

For example, when I go to the airport and ask the ticket agent for assistance to the plane, he or she will invariably pick up the phone, call a ground hostess and whisper: "Hi, Jane, we've got a 76 here." I have concluded that the word "blind" is not used for one of two reasons: Either they fear that if the dread word is spoken, the

---

*The words *imply* and *infer* are often confused. A speaker like Caitlin who communicates an idea without stating it explicitly is *implying* an unspoken meaning. A listener like Aaron who understands the implication is *inferring* meaning. In other words, speakers imply and listeners infer.

ticket agent's retina will immediately detach, or they are reluctant to inform me of my condition of which I may not have been previously aware.

—Harold Krents, "Darkness at Noon"

The writer leaves it for us to infer from the passage that a "76" is an airline code for a blind passenger. He also assumes we will infer that the ticket agents whisper into the phone because they do not want people in the vicinity, including Krents himself, to hear their words. Earlier in the essay, Krents had written, "There are those who assume that since I can't see, I obviously also cannot hear." Having read that, a reader might infer that the whispering agents mistakenly believe that Krents will neither hear nor understand their words. The final sentence of the paragraph demands even more sophistication from readers in drawing implications. Krents probably expects his readers to infer a meaning that might be spelled out like this:

> The agents don't really believe they will go blind if they say the word, and Krents isn't sincere when he suggests that they do. The agents also can't really believe that Krents doesn't know he is blind. But as silly as those conclusions are, the real reasons for the agents' behavior are even more foolish: They apparently think of blindness as a condition too embarrassing to be spoken of to a blind person. They aren't giving Krents credit for having come to terms with his blindness or for being able to notice that they are evading the topic. Worse, they aren't even able to realize that a blind person is a human being with the same capacities of hearing and thinking as everyone else.

You can easily see that the passage, with its unspoken implications, is far more effective than if Krents had spelled out everything he meant. By causing us to think for ourselves and to draw conclusions, Krents has enlisted us as partners with him in the creation of meaning. That sense of partnership makes us all the more receptive to his purposes for writing. After reading his paragraph, you may have drawn the following more general conclusion:

> Perhaps I, the reader (now that I see the agents' behavior as foolish), should give some thought to how I treat blind people or others with disabilities.

Drawing inferences is an important part of reading, and good readers are as alert to meaning that is implied as to that which is explicitly stated.

EXERCISES   Implications

1. Imagine you overheard the following conversational exchanges. What would you infer in each case?

    a. **Restaurant patron:** I'll have a vodka tonic.
       Waiter: Sir, this is a family restaurant.

    b. **Husband:** When are we having supper?
       Wife: It isn't even six o'clock yet.

2. The words in the following passages may state a clear and explicit meaning, but the words do not state everything that was on their authors' minds. What inferences do you draw as you read them?

a. Anxiety, stress, dread: faced with getting out of bed in the morning, some people, even the congenitally driven, sometimes just break down a little and get an ailment. Then they go out and talk about it. Not long ago, all you heard about was the stress-related ailments—temporomandibular-joint syndrome, and attention-deficit disorder, with the ultra stylish Epstein-Barr filling the occasional lull. But lately, at small dinner parties and anywhere else food is present, people have been bewailing "lactose intolerance," a physiological condition whereby the digestive system has an unattractive reaction to anything with milk in it. From the decibel level in Manhattan, you might think its incidence is greatest among twenty-somethings.
— "The Talk of the Town," *The New Yorker*

b. "Orientation is designed to disorient you," announced Stanford professor James Adams to an auditorium of 1,600 puzzled freshmen at the beginning of the new school year. Assembled for one of many orientation-week programs on "diversity," the freshmen soon learned what he meant. A lesbian activist spoke first about "challenging your sexuality," and encouraged the 17- and 18-year-old students to "overcome" their "fears of being queer." Next, a black musician performed an electric-guitar solo as police sirens wailed in the background. He concluded his demonstration by dropping suddenly to the floor and convulsing his body in a re-enactment of the Rodney King beating.
—David Sacks and Peter Thiel, "Freshman Disorientation"

c. I always assumed that my modest contribution to the church collection plate purchased assault rifles for Sandinista-type guerillas, because, as any newspaper reader knows, that's where mainline Protestant churches invest their money.

So imagine my surprise upon learning that my alms finance legitimate, peaceable and socially redeeming activities.

Unbeknownst to many, the United Church of Christ . . . is now the country's most vocal defender of the 1990 Children's Television Act.
—Alex Beam, "One Church Takes on Goliaths"

 ## A FURTHER COMMENT ON PARAGRAPHS

We should repeat and reemphasize our earlier statement that most paragraphs that you encounter in reading do not have straightforward topic sentences. In actual practice, the paragraph is a far less structured unit of thought than is often claimed. Most writers, most of the time, do not think in terms of paragraphs as they compose. They develop ideas as they write, and they use the paragraph break as a form of punctuation, sometimes to signal the start of a new idea or a change in direction, at other times to provide emphasis for dramatic effect. At still other times, long topics are divided rather arbitrarily into several paragraphs to give the reader a sense of pausing and to make the writing appear less formidable.

Eye appeal is frequently a factor in paragraphing. Essays written in a sprawling handwriting are likely to have (and need) more paragraph breaks than will more compact-looking typewritten essays. Newspapers, with their narrow columns of type, prefer shorter paragraphs than those found in books. Psychologists have discovered that readers find material easier to read when it is divided into short to medium-length paragraphs than when it is presented in long paragraphs.

For all these reasons, no two writers create their paragraphs in exactly the same way. Given a passage (such as those in the following exercise) from which all paragraph breaks have been omitted, it is unlikely that any two professional writers or writing teachers chosen at random would be in full agreement about where the breaks should go.

Supplying Paragraph Breaks

1. Paragraph breaks have been removed from the following passages. Decide where you would put them and indicate your choices, using the paragraph sign (¶). Remember that there are many different yet appropriate responses to this exercise.

   a. "Happy Birthday to a man with incredible 'savoir-faire'. . . . That's French for 'deadly farts that could gag a maggot.' " I am starting to panic. I'm afraid I'll walk out of here without a card. I'm afraid I'll walk out of here with one. I wonder how it would feel to receive a birthday card like this. I prepare myself. My birthday happens to fall on the same day as my special man friend's. Is he standing in a card shop right now, laughing his guts out over a joke about dog feces, cat litter, hair balls or flatulence? Is this the kind of card I will get? "Birthdays are like garlic toast. . . . The more you have, the less people want to kiss you." Ha, ha, ha! Your body is decaying into worm food. Better you than me. Get it? I do. But I don't particularly want to. I just want a little clever mass-produced sincerity for my special man friend. Is this too much to ask? Apparently it is. The greeting-card planet seems to be massing around two poles: sweet, sappy, sunset-type cards and these gross joke cards. I know; they're only greeting cards. . . . But Americans will buy 7.4 billion of them this year, by the Greeting Card Association's estimate. That's a lot of private discourse going on between friends. Meanwhile, stores are stocking gross joke cards by the gross. What are we saying to each other?
   —Jeanne Marie Laskas, "Greet Expectations"

   b. What is different about group generalizations based on race? Generalizations that discriminate against blacks have been outlawed for obvious historical reasons. But what about group generalizations that discriminate in favor of blacks? How are they different from the group generalizations that are the warp and woof of everyday life? The answer cannot be that they are different simply because race is innate and immutable. So, according to its enthusiasts, is I.Q.—yet opponents of affirmative action generally wish to see the role of such innate characteristics (if not I.Q., then "merit" or "talent") enhanced, not reduced. The answer must be that race is such a toxic subject in American culture that it should not enter into calculations about people's places in society—even in order to benefit racism's historic victims. That is a respectable answer. But it understandably rings hollow to many blacks, who see this sudden and ostentatious anathema on racial consciousness a bit too convenient. Where was color blindness when they needed it?
   —Michael Kinsley, "The Spoils of Victimhood"

2. Compare your responses to the first exercise with those of your classmates. Was there general agreement about the number of paragraph breaks you supplied? Did you agree with the authors of the two passages (who, as it happens, presented them as eight paragraphs and one paragraph, respectively)? What conclusions might you draw from the exercise?

READING SELECTION

If you have ever taken a psychology course, you are probably familiar with types of conflict (e.g., approach–avoidance, approach–approach, double approach–avoidance) and how people are thought to negotiate them in making decisions. Assume that you have been asked to read the following article to prepare for a class discussion of conflict and decision making. Annette Kornblum, the author, is a freelance writer with particular interests in health and business. She recently published a book titled *Wear It in Good Health: A Nurse's Guide to Professional Image.*

Maybe, Maybe Not

With Too Many Choices, Americans Make up Their Minds to Think Things Over

ANNETTE KORNBLUM

1 Remember when the only choice in diapers was white cloth? Remember when you could correspond on a typewriter and not have to choose among software packages that require doctorate-level expertise in computer technology? Remember Henry Ford, who made control over destiny simple with his Model T marketing decree: You can have any color you want, as long as it's black.

2 If only the automobile baron's edict was still the commanding sentiment, then maybe the excess of choice wouldn't be driving us crazy. But Henry has long since died and so has the ethos that said: "Let us make your life easy. We'll decide what kind of car, medical insurance, long-distance company, retirement plan, career path that's best for you."

3 Choice is now our national creed, with the result that decision-making today is overwhelming, never-ending. A woman I know has pondered for weeks whether to buy a striped or solid sleep sofa, while a publishing house has had my book on hold as long as it takes to deliver a baby.

4 All talk, no action. Hurry up and wait. Gridlock. It is the pressure-cooker '90s when people take months to make up their minds about things that once were settled quickly and decisively.

5 To a large degree, the indecision can be blamed on our bewildering array of options—the multitude of products and alternatives that are constantly laid before us, that entice but also confuse us. Yet, perhaps *because* the choices have grown exponentially, we have also become more averse to making decisions: Why make a firm decision when delay and compromise will help us cover all bases?

6 And so people waver about everything. Contracts, investments, corporate strategy, hiring and firing, even commitment to interpersonal relationships are put on hold long enough to make any sane person have self-doubts. Friendships fall apart after agonizing indecision about where to eat, what to wear, when to meet.

7 In an age when predictability is out and uncertainty about the future in, decision deflection reigns. And it is everywhere:

8 • A 1993 National Association of Homebuilders study found that, compared with a decade back, new homebuyers now take twice as long to sign a contract on a new house.

9   • Ben Long, president of Travaille Executive Search in Washington, says the organizations he works for used to take three to six months to find and hire top managers. Now, six months is routine and top spots are left vacant up to a year while the waffling and wavering drags on.

10   • It took nine years for Hollywood to make "Forrest Gump," the 1994 runaway hit about a guileless resolute hero, a movie that, ironically, became victim to the industry's dependence on so-called high-concept test-marketing. The problem was that the movie didn't fit into the traditional genre of Hollywood—thriller, adventure, comedy—and so deciding whether to produce it and when was the subject of unending debate. The flick would have stayed on ice, observers agree, but for the tenacity and pull of its producer, Wendy Finerman.

11   What we are left with is a country being devoured by Decision Avoidance Syndrome. It is now the hallmark of such disorders as phobias, depression, lack of self-esteem, obsession with perfection, fear of making mistakes or aversion to accepting what a bad decision might say about you, the decision-maker.

12   "To some extent indecision reflects uncertainty about the world and one's self," says Baruch Fischoff, a self-described behavioral decision-theorist in the Department of Social and Decision Sciences at Carnegie-Mellon University in Pittsburgh. "On some level, people realize they are not good at making decisions and will be judged unduly harshly if they make the wrong one."

13   For some, it is a paralyzing phenomenon: The 60-year-old wife of a local retailing titan died recently never having completely furnished her home or chosen an avocation.

14   "It was never a question of money but wanting something so perfect she could never find exactly what she wanted," recalls her close friend. "She left tags on things in case she changed her mind and wanted to return them. Everything she wore was the best, but understated out of fear of not being absolutely right."

15   It is no wonder so many of us are traumatized by indecision. Even those responsible for society's exploding panoply of choices can't decide what they're doing. Today's clothing fashions, for example, herald the optimum in merchandising insecurity: a little bit of this, a little bit of that, without any strong point of view on the part of those doing the designing. Seventh Avenue's once-bold dictates of vibrant reds, wild patterns and shimmering fabrics have retreated into tamer, classic, earthy naturals.

16   The message in women's fashion has been mixed for years. But now it's fusion: anything goes. Today, designers are showing four or five lengths in skirts and dresses, from midway up the thigh to barely above the ankle, with several alternatives in between. A new fall catalogue from one prominent clothier offers the same dress in not one but three different lengths. For those who cannot make up their mind, the pants suit has made a comeback.

17   Or remember when there used to be one color that was "In"? Or when men knew how wide a tie was supposed to be, either as broad as an envelope or as thin as a ruler? Now, of course, we can't decide: in between seems good, or maybe not. And what about casual Fridays, asks Patrick McCarthy, executive editor of *Woman's Wear Daily* and *W*? Are jeans okay? Do you follow the lead of senior people or those who you think are hip?

18   At first glance, this may seem empowering. After all, an industry that used to dictate to us what we should wear is now letting us decide. But there is something unsettling about not knowing what's "In" and what's not, what's acceptable and what isn't.

19   "If you know that this year's big color is green and the hemline is right above the knee then you have a clear choice," says Michael Mazis, a professor of marketing at the American University School of Business. "But if there are many different hemlines, col-

ors and fabrics, you have more choice but less satisfaction because decision-making takes so much longer."

Our colloquialisms too have absorbed the collective wavering of society at large. **20** The in-rhetoric is littered with "actually" or "the truth of the matter" or "I would say so" or "maybe later" or "probably" or "take stock" or "doesn't quite work for us" or "not quite right."

An unconditional "yes" or "no" is a rarity. **21**

"The standard here in L.A. is 'We'll do lunch,'" confides one frustrated Hollywood **22** agent. "You think you're a genius until you never hear from the guy again and sit there wondering—when? No news here is always bad news."

I grew up believing the United States was uninhibited by time-honored, plodding **23** European or Third World traditions. People here said what they meant, did what they wanted, worried not about fallout but about the new frontiers ahead. In the everyday cadence of daily journalism, you went with what you got. This is now passe—not just in the worlds of fashion and fad but in the realm of business and politics where, presumably, tough decisions affecting the fates of nations are made every day.

One might expect that the pressures of modern life would have prompted more deci- **24** siveness among those at the top. In fact, the opposite may have occurred: No one wants to be proven wrong or have a view renounced in a world where politicians, executives, and everyone who works for them are in a cut-throat competition to survive.

Zur Shapira, a professor of marketing at New York University's Sterne Business **25** School who specializes in decision theory, recently interviewed 750 managers here and in Israel for a new book on risk-taking behavior. "Managers who are considering an investment in a new plant or venture tend to consider the hazard zone, the worst-case scenario, rather than the benefit and what they can gain," Shapira explains.

You might think that fax machines, computers, e-mail, the information superhigh- **26** way and cell phones would move things along, but they only bring on more choices, more data, more indecision. In a scene dizzy with information overload, bureaucratic oversight, overwhelming special interests and experts dissecting every aspect of a problem, the business of uninterrupted musing is booming.

The only guarantee in this fuzzy cerebral equation is prolonged deliberations with no **27** clear resolution. Hearings, seminars and retreats last hours without a mission statement, common goal, vision or timetable. Simple invoices take weeks to approve. Memos with fresh ideas for retooling never see the light of day. "He's in a meeting," "it hasn't been acted on," "she's thinking about it" are mantras for big-budget, high-level paralysis.

What in business life is infuriating has become the accepted code of conduct in the **28** indecisive world of politics. The garden-variety disinclination to act, take a stand, move forward, has become a socially-acceptable dysfunction in a town where leisurely thought and negotiation have become the very essence of the democratic process.

One of the greatest hesitaters since Hamlet is Bill Clinton, whose every pause in for- **29** eign, domestic and economic policy has given him the unenviable reputation of a vacillator. Like many of his colleagues in Washington, he prefers posturing to definite action, talking tough and then backing down on Bosnia, on welfare reform, on his appointees and his personal life.

"The problem is our leaders are going in so many different directions or consumed **30** by trying to figure out what the public wants that they can't get past the deliberation stage," said Sheila Mann, a political scientist at the American Political Science Association.

The courts are another common venue for indecisiveness, as seen most vividly in the **31** nine-month trial of O.J. Simpson. The prosecution, particularly, seemed irresolute in its approach, one week deluging the jurors with scientific minutia, the next appealing to their moral duty to extinguish domestic violence. In the end, the prosecuting team's lack of focus and complex strategy could well have cost them the case.

32   Why all the deliberation? Why now? Perhaps it's a sign of age.

33   Baby boomers, in facing their own mortality and insecurity, are losing that effervescent itch to say "What the hell; Go for it." And so they resist painful choices. They defer decisions on how to think, act and interact. They fear being sued, or being wrong. Or taking the wrong path.

34   And yet, when all is said and done, people most regret things they failed to do, risks they never took, people they never embraced or gave the benefit of the doubt.

35   As a precocious 7-year-old actor told a network executive, "I'd rather have a fast no than a slow yes." And yet, judging by recent official surveys that find children and "Generation X" increasingly cynical and afraid of the future, the youngster's wish may be on hold for some time.

36   It doesn't have to be this way. We could just decide to end this indecision.

37   Even the much-maligned Richard Nixon saw the wisdom of expedient forcefulness: "If the U.S. is to continue to lead in the world," he wrote in his last book, "it will have to resolve to do so and then take those steps necessary to turn resolution into execution."

38   With that dictum guiding global leaders, there's no reason we shouldn't resolve to be equally bold on matters of everyday life. And so I urge you from this point out: Get on with it. Let it go. Do it. And remember, it's better to make a mistake than do nothing at all.

Freewriting

In your notebook, write for ten minutes about your own experience with and opinions about decision making. You might start by listing some of the difficult choices that you confront—from those as momentous as deciding on a career to others as trivial as picking out an article of clothing or an item off a restaurant menu. You might write about individuals you have observed or read about who seem to be effective or ineffective as decision makers. You might assess various explanations for the trend that Annette Kornblum describes, including some that she may have overlooked. If you have studied decision making in a course in some other field, such as psychology or business, try to apply what you have learned to some of the ideas found in this article.

Group Work

Listen carefully and take notes as each freewriting is read aloud. Decide if members of your group report similar experiences or express similar views. What generalizations about the causes and effects of indecision can you agree upon? Do group members identify with the problem Kornblum examines?

Review Questions

1. How does a person's self-esteem presumably affect decision-making ability?

2. How does the fashion industry contribute to indecisiveness?

3. Where in public life has indecision become especially evident?

Discussion Questions

1. What is the main idea of the article? In which paragraph does Kornblum state it explicitly? How does she use general and specific statements to create meaning?

2. Decide whether each of the longer paragraphs has a topic sentence. If so, identify it. Are ¶s 7, 16, and 27 arranged in a deductive or inductive order? Essays or parts of essays can also be organized inductively or deductively. Is the arrangement of the first three paragraphs deductive or inductive?

3. Why does Kornblum preface her quotation of a former president in ¶37 with "Even the much-maligned Richard Nixon saw the wisdom. . . "? That is, what assumptions does she seem to be making about how many of her readers might respond to the quotation?

4. This article appeared in the op-ed (opinion and editorial) section of the Sunday issue of the *Washington Post*. What clues does the article offer about Kornblum's perception of the audience she is addressing? Do you feel the article is well adapted to that group of readers?

Writing

1. Select a paragraph (or two) from Kornblum's article and analyze it according to the concepts discussed in this chapter. For example, observe whether it contains specific and general statements, how they relate to each other, and how they are arranged. Note whether the paragraph has a topic sentence and whether the paragraph can stand as an independent unit of thought or whether it depends on adjacent paragraphs for context. As a related matter, analyze whether the placement of paragraph breaks before and after the paragraph is logical or arbitrary.

2. Write a personal essay about your own decision-making processes. You might consider how those processes operate, what kinds of experiences have influenced you to adopt them, and how effective they are.

3. Interview several students about their decision-making processes and then try to draw some generalizations about the topics mentioned in writing suggestion 2, above.

5   *Writing a Summary*

A **summary** of a text or a passage is a shortened version of it. The writer of a summary keeps only the main ideas and essential information from the original, while eliminating most supporting details, such as the examples and illustrations. Many summaries are written to save readers time, but they can have other purposes as well, such as to focus readers' attention or to refresh their memories. Many of your textbooks, for example, conclude each chapter with a summary of contents designed to solidify what you have learned. Most scientific and technical articles begin with an **abstract,** a brief summary of their findings so you can see the point quickly and even decide if you want to read the text in its entirety.

As a student, you are no stranger to summary writing. A book report or "report on the literature" requires you to summarize the contents of one or more works. A lab report includes an abbreviated account of your experimental procedures and results. An argumentative paper, like a trial lawyer's case, may conclude with a forceful summation of the evidence you have presented. Although it may be less familiar to you now, one of the most extensive uses of summaries comes when you do research. You read articles and books filled with detailed information. Since you cannot tell your readers everything you have learned, you must decide what is most important and appropriate, and you record only that on your note cards. In fact, the entire research paper is by nature a summary, a carefully condensed and focused presentation of what you have discovered in the course of your investigation.

Whenever you read, your mind does something like summarizing: seeking out the main ideas, making connections between them (and connections with your other experiences), and creating a framework for efficient storage in your memory. You can assist that process when you write notes on your reading. For example, a student reading a textbook to learn how the human eye works might write this summary note in the margin:

The textbook passage

In the human visual system the initial encoding of the image occurs in the *retina,* a layer of neural cells at the rear of the eyeball. The retina contains a two-dimensional layer of sensory cells, called *rods* and *cones,* which are sensitive to light. Each of these cells is capable of generating a neural signal when struck by light.

—Neil A. Stillings, "Vision," from *Cognitive Science: An Introduction*

Rods and cones in the retina encode images

A student's summary note in the margin

Writing the note helps the student see the main point of the passage and remember it.

 ## SUMMARY AND PARAPHRASE

Sometimes the reading notes that you write in the margins of your textbooks *paraphrase* passages, but the preceding brief note *summarizes* the original passage as well, since it omits many details, including the definitions of terms. As you will see, summary and paraphrase share similarities in both form and function. Before introducing those similarities, however, we need to consider two ways in which summary and paraphrase differ. First, unlike a paraphrase, a summary may quote a phrase or two, or even a short sentence, from the original source, provided that it is set off with quotation marks. Second, a summary involves decisions about what is most important and what can be left out. In the following passage, a British author writes about the processing and marketing of food products.

> All these techniques, originating in the United States and vigorously marketed by American businessmen, have spread across the industrialised communities of Europe. There have been several social consequences.
>
> One of these has been a significant change in shopping habits. When food retailers still purchased their supplies in bulk—flour and sugar by the sack, tea in a chest, butter in a keg and cheeses whole—the local store was a place of resort. It was a social centre as well as a distribution point. Standard articles, prepackaged and preserved by canning or freezing in a large-scale modern factory, are distributed with more efficiency, even if with the loss of social intercourse, in an equally efficient large-scale supermarket. Hence it is reasonable to suggest that one of the effects American food technology has had on the character of European society has been to accelerate the extinction of the general store on the street corner, of the specialised butcher, baker, greengrocer, and dairy and to substitute the supermarket. Great Britain, moving forward a decade behind the United States, possessed 175 supermarkets in 1958, 367 in 1960 and 4,800 in 1971.
>
> —Magnus Pyke, "The Influence of American Foods and Food Technology in Europe"

The original passage

Notice the difference between a paraphrase and a summary of this passage. A student wishing to use the information from this passage in a research paper might paraphrase it as follows:

> New methods of processing and distributing food, developed in America and sold overseas, have brought social change to Europe. For one thing, many Europeans no longer shop for groceries as they did when stores bought large containers of flour, sugar, tea, and butter and whole cheeses. In those days, the food store was a place to meet friends as well as to buy groceries. Though impersonal by comparison, today's supermarkets are more efficient, selling products that come individually packaged from the factory, where they have been canned or frozen to keep them fresh. Consequently, American methods have led to the gradual disappearance of butcher shops, bakeries, produce markets, and dairy stores, all of which have been supplanted by supermarkets. The number of supermarkets in Britain, which is about ten years behind trends established in the U.S., grew from 175 in 1958 and 367 in 1960 to 4,800 in 1971 (Pyke 89–90).

A paraphrased version

The paraphrase changes the writer's language, but it retains all of his ideas, including examples and minor details. The following summary, on the other hand, presents only the most important ideas in a much shorter version:

A summary

> American innovations in the production and distribution of food have brought supermarkets to Europe. Once a neighborly "place of resort," the corner store has been supplanted by the more efficient, though less sociable, supermarket (Pyke 89–90).

Notice that the summary eliminates details and examples found in the paraphrase. Nevertheless, the summary provides a faithful account, taking into consideration the author's ideas and attitudes. You may have noticed also that this particular summary retains a phrase from the original source, placed in quotation marks.

A good summary, like a good paraphrase, makes the author's ideas clear, possibly even clearer than they are in the original. However, the writer of a summary has the advantage of being able to quote a phrase or short sentence from the source, provided that it is set off with quotation marks. Finally, you should notice that both the paraphrase and the summary acknowledge their common source with a parenthetical note.

EXERCISE   ## Paraphrase and Summary

A process for writing summaries is offered in the next section of this chapter, but you already are able to summarize a passage whose main idea you recognize. The following passage comes from an essay by Pamela Malcolm Curry and Robert M. Jiobu, who show how American eating habits are as arbitrary and symbolic as those of a Polynesian group, the Tekopia. First paraphrase the passage; then write a brief summary of it. Both your paraphrase and your summary should be composed in your own language, although you may wish to quote a short phrase or two in the summary. Avoid making reference to the authors' names, and end both paraphrase and summary with a parenthetical note: (Curry and Jiobu 248–50).

> Eating is surrounded by norms and folkways, many of which are also rituals and habits. This makes life easier since day-to-day decisions, once converted to habit, require less time and effort and once ritualized provoke less anxiety. . . . We use a specially decorated cake to symbolize many ceremonial occasions: birthdays, christenings, weddings, anniversaries, and retirements to name a few. . . . Once we begin to catalog them, other iconic foods and rituals associated with holidays and ceremonies pop into mind: Christmas cookies for carolers; chocolate rabbits and hunting decorated eggs for Easter; turkey and the gathering at Grandmother's for Thanksgiving; and champagne toasts for New Year's Eve.

 ## WRITING SUMMARIES

To summarize a single paragraph, the procedure is about the same as the one you practiced in the previous chapter when you created topic sentences for paragraphs whose main ideas were implied but not stated: *You can read the passage once or twice until its meaning is clear, put it aside, and then write a brief summary from memory.*

As the length of an essay increases, however, your ability to remember it decreases, and the process of summarizing becomes more difficult. Throughout your college career, you are going to be asked to write a variety of summaries. Some will be routine, such as the summary of a single brief essay; others will be more complex summaries of several essays or books. In any case, you will need a workable method that can help you create polished summaries with the most efficient use of your time and energy.

The following sequence of steps can save much time and frustration. As in all types of writing, time well spent in the preliminary stages pays off later on.

A Process for Summarizing Longer Passages

1. *Read carefully.* When you summarize a passage, you must be sure you understand it fully. Read it, look up any confusing words, and discuss its meaning with others.

2. *Read with a pencil.* Whenever you read, underlining and making marginal notes can increase comprehension. Be selective; underline only main ideas. Use your own symbols and marginal comments to highlight important ideas. Good notes and underlining make later rereading quick and easy, so it pays to concentrate the first time through.

3. *Write a one-sentence paraphrase of the main idea.* If the text has a thesis statement, you can paraphrase it. If not, state what you take to be the main idea in your own words. This sentence can serve as an umbrella for everything else in the summary.

4. *Write the first draft.* Create a miniature version of the passage based only on the portions you have underlined and the marginal notes you have written. Keep this draft simple by following the order of ideas from the original. Paraphrase where possible, although parts of the first draft may still be close to the phrasing of the original.

5. *Paraphrase your first draft.* Treat your first draft like a passage to be paraphrased. Restate its ideas and information in your own style and language, quoting no more than an isolated phrase or two or perhaps a single sentence if there is an idea you cannot express as capably in your own words. Remember that a summary is a miniature essay that should express the ideas of the author not just succinctly but also smoothly and clearly. Help your readers by inserting transitions, eliminating unnecessary words, combining ideas, and clarifying any confusing syntax.

We can illustrate this procedure with an example. Suppose you have been asked to summarize the following essay on stereotyping from a book on semantics, the study of how language can affect the way we think. First, read it with care until you are certain you understand it (step 1).

After you are satisfied that you have understood the essay, go back and reread it with a pencil, underlining or paraphrasing the main ideas (step 2). Here is the passage as it was marked by one reader. Since each reader is unique, it is unlikely that you would have marked it in exactly the same way.

Stereotyping: Homogenizing People

We all carry around images of what members of particular groups are like. For instance, what image is conjured in your mind for a dope smoker, New York cab driver, black athlete, college professor, construction worker? These images are often shared by others. Typically, they stress similarities and ignore differences among members of a group. These images, then, become stereotypes—the attribution of certain characteristics to a group often without the benefit of firsthand knowledge.

Stereotypes are judgments of individuals not on the basis of direct interaction with those individuals specifically but based instead on preconceived images for the category they belong to. Stereotypes, however, are not inherently evil. Some stereotypes, when predicated upon personal experience and empirical data, can be valid generalizations about a group.

There are several potential problems with stereotypes, however. First, these preconceived images of groups may produce a frame of reference, a perceptual set in our minds concerning the group as a whole. Then when faced with an individual from the group, the preconceived image is applied indiscriminately, screening out individual differences. Individuals become mere abstractions devoid of unique qualities, pigeon-holed and submerged in the crowd, a crowd that is thought to be homogeneous.

Indiscriminate application of stereotypes is particularly troublesome because stereotypes are not necessarily grounded on evidence or even direct experience. The classic study of stereotyping by Katz and Braly (1933) clearly revealed that stereotypes are often formulated in ignorance. They reflect attitudes toward labels—racial, ethnic, and others—frequently without benefit of actual contact with members of the group stereotyped. Student subjects held Turks in low esteem, yet most had never interacted with any member of this group.

A second problem with stereotypes is what general semanticists term *allness*. This is the tendency to characterize an individual or an entire group in terms of only one attribute or quality. This one characteristic becomes all that is necessary to know about a person. Once you realize that the person is a woman, or a Jew, or a Southerner, no more information is sought. This unidimensional view of a person is nothing more than a simplistic conception of an individual. You may be a Jew but also a brother, son, brilliant lawyer, charming compassionate individual, devoted father, loving husband, and so forth. Allness sacrifices complexity and substitutes superficiality. Racial and ethnic characteristics do not lend themselves to change, yet racial or ethnic labels may be the prepotent characteristic that supersedes all others. In fact, allness orientation may produce exaggerated perception of group characteristics. Secord et al. (1956) showed "prejudiced" and "unprejudiced" subjects several pictures of blacks and whites. The prejudiced observers exaggerated the physical characteristics of blacks such as thickness of lips and width of nose. Racial labels accentuated the stereotyped differences between "races" for prejudiced (allness oriented) subjects.

A final problem associated with stereotyping is that it can produce frozen evaluations. Juvenile delinquents or adult felons may never shed their stigmatizing label despite "going straight." Zimbardo and Ruch (1977) summarize studies conducted at Princeton University over several decades regarding

[Margin annotations:] Some stereotypes are valid !?

① The group becomes more important !

②

③

stereotypes by Princeton students of various ethnic groups. While the stereotypes did change, they tended to do so relatively slowly. In 1933, blacks were deemed superstitious by 84 percent of Princeton students, 41 percent in 1951, and 13 percent in 1967. Thirty-four years is a very long time for people to acquire an accurate image of blacks on this one item.

When we see stereotypes we can't see changes in people!!

Stereotypes are thus troublesome because they are often indiscriminate, exhibit an allness orientation, and can produce frozen evaluations. Considering the pervasiveness of stereotyping in our society, one should not take it lightly. When we stereotype we define a person and this definition, superficial at best, can be quite powerful.

Summary of above

To stereotype is to define and to define is to control, especially if the definition is widely accepted regardless of its accuracy. In a male dominated society women may be stereotyped as empty-headed and illogical. The fact that the stereotype has persisted for years manifests the control men have over women, control that excludes women from executive positions and relegates them to mindless housekeeping duties. Women's liberation is fundamentally the struggle to define, to reject male stereotypes of females.

Stereotypes are sometimes seductive, however. When women are told repeatedly that they are stupid, they may begin believing it. A self-fulfilling prophecy may develop. Low self-esteem produced from male definitions of women as unintelligent can lead to poor performance and the consequent belief that the stereotype has merit. The stereotype is thus nurtured and perpetuated. Stereotyping can thus control, insidiously imprisoning its victims in constraining roles.

vicious circle

So while stereotyping isn't intrinsically evil, most stereotypes lack empirical foundations and are assertions of power and dominance over less powerful groups. Reduced to an abstraction, victims of stereotyping must struggle to define themselves or be content to accept roles others have carved out for them. It is little wonder our society has been experiencing turmoil.

—J. Dan Rothwell, *Telling It Like It Isn't* (pages 76–78)

SUMMARY ☆

Now write the thesis, the sentence that you have decided covers most of the material (step 3):

> Stereotypes are judgments of people based on preconceived images about a group they are supposed to belong to.

Thesis

Next, a first draft might look like this (step 4):

> We all carry around images of what groups are like, and these images are often shared. They stress similarities and ignore differences. So stereotyping is giving a group certain characteristics without benefit of firsthand knowledge.
>
> Stereotypes are judgments of individuals based on preconceived images, not on direct interaction. However, stereotypes are not inherently evil. Some are valid.
>
> Nevertheless, there are some problems with stereotypes. When you have a preconceived image of a group, it produces a perceptual set that screens out individual differences. Indiscriminate stereotypes are not grounded on evidence and are often formulated in ignorance without actual contact. A second problem of stereotyping is allness: characterizing an individual or a group in terms of only

A first draft

one attribute or quality. When you realize someone is a woman, a Jew, or a Southerner, you may stop looking for other information. This is a very simplistic idea of a person. It is superficial and not complex as real people are.

A final problem with stereotypes is frozen evaluations: judgments that have stayed the same for a long time and change relatively slowly.

So we can see that stereotypes are dangerous because they are indiscriminate, are inclined toward allness, and give a frozen evaluation. They also define and control people if the stereotypes are widely accepted. Women, for example, have to struggle to reject men's stereotypes of females. Sometimes stereotypes are seductive. People believe these images, so they become self-fulfilling. An image can control its victims, imprisoning them in roles. Even though most stereotypes aren't valid, victims of stereotyping must either struggle to define themselves or accept the bad image others have made up for them.

The final step is to revise and proofread (step 5). Here you can concentrate on condensing, on avoiding repetition, and on focusing the sentences around the thesis. Because you are seeking economy, see if your first draft can be shortened. The result is a final draft that is, in effect, a summary of a summary, as in this final version:

The final draft

Stereotypes are judgments of individuals based on preconceived images about a category they belong to. Although some stereotypes can be valid, they cause three problems. First, stereotypes prevent us from judging people as individuals. Second, they cause us to characterize people or groups on the basis of only one superficial attribute, a problem known as *allness*. Third, stereotypes become frozen and take years to change. If these false images are widely accepted, they can define and control people so strongly that unless the victims struggle against the stereotypes, they may come to believe them themselves (Rothwell 76–78).

EXERCISES   **Writing Summaries**

1. Use the process outlined on page 135 to write a brief summary of the following paragraph, taken from page 40 of "Testing the Limits in a Culture of Excess," an article published in the *New York Times*. In this paragraph, the author, Vicki Goldberg, talks about how notions of decency and censorship in art and entertainment have changed rapidly.

    When the increasingly blatant use of sexual imagery in the popular culture began some 30-odd years ago, it was partly a response to long-term repressions. From 1934 until the movie ratings were introduced in 1968, the Hollywood Production Code kept the lid on, forbidding the display of kisses longer than 30 seconds, "intimate items of underwear," women's breasts (Howard Hughes had a huge row with the Hays Office, which administered the code, over Jane Russell's bosom in *The Outlaw*) or illicit affairs (*For Whom the Bell Tolls* was another thorny problem).

    Today, a Rip Van Winkle who had slept for 30 years might suppose that someone had inserted mandatory nakedness quotas into the commercial equation to make up for the old cover-up rules. (The more modest movie stars demand breast stand-ins, who might be called the cinema league's designated bodies.) Renoir, say, could paint only 60 nudes in a lifetime, but popular culture has the means to churn out nudes by the millions. It seems that once repressive and hypocritical barriers were knocked down, the result was less liberation than binge. We have achieved a stunning triumph of excess.

2. Summarize the following excerpt from page 62 of an article in *Newsweek*, "Sexism in the Schoolhouse," by Barbara Kantrowitz.

Sexism may be the most widespread and damaging form of bias in the classroom, according to a report . . . by the American Association of University Women. The report, which summarized 1,331 studies of girls in school, describes a pattern of downward intellectual mobility for girls. The AAUW found that girls enter first grade with the same or better skills and ambitions as boys. But, all too often, by the time they finish high school, "their doubts have crowded out their dreams."

In elementary school, the researchers say, teachers call on boys much more often and give them more encouragement. Boys frequently need help with reading, so remedial reading classes are an integral part of many schools. But girls, who just as often need help with math, rarely get a similar chance to sharpen their skills. Boys get praised for the intellectual content of their work while girls are more likely to be praised for neatness. Boys tend not to be penalized for calling out answers and taking risks; girls who do the same are reprimanded for being rude. Research indicates that girls learn better in cooperative settings, where students work together, while boys learn better in competitive settings. Yet most schools are based on a competitive model. The report also indicates that schools are becoming more tolerant of male students sexually harassing female students.

Despite these problems, girls get better grades and are more likely to go on to college, according to the report. But even these successful girls have less confidence in their abilities than boys, have higher expectations of failure and more modest aspirations. The result, the report concludes, is that girls are less likely to reach their potential than boys.

The differences between the sexes are greatest in science. Between 1978 and 1986, the gap between the national science achievement test scores of 9- and 13-year-old boys and girls widened—because girls did worse and boys did better. Girls and boys take about the same number of science courses, but girls are more likely to take advanced biology and boys are more likely to take physics and advanced chemistry. Even girls who take the same courses as boys and perform equally well on tests are less likely than boys to choose technical careers. A Rhode Island study found that 64 percent of the boys who had taken physics and calculus in high school were planning to major in science or engineering, compared with only 18.6 percent of the girls who had taken those courses.

More than two thirds of the nation's teachers are women. Presumably, their gender bias is unintentional but no less apparent. American University researchers Myra and David Sadker have taped hundreds of hours of class sessions in schools around the country and have studied how teachers react to boys and girls. "When researchers have asked teachers to remember their favorite students, it always ends up being kids who conformed to gender stereotypes," says David Sadker. "The ones they like best are assertive males and the ones they like least are assertive females."

USES OF SUMMARY

Thus far, we have said little about why a writer might summarize a text or a passage, beyond the obvious reasons of saving paper and sparing the reader any wasted time. Basically, however, summary serves most of the same purposes as paraphrase. The marginal note beside the textbook passage on page 132 shows how summary, like paraphrase, can help a reader understand and come to terms with complex and important ideas. A writer also can use summary to make a relatively difficult passage more accessible to readers who may not be familiar with its terminology and references. Our summary on page 134 of Magnus Pyke's account of European grocery shopping provides an example of that.

Summarizing an Argument

Another frequent use of summary is to demonstrate understanding of a controversial point of view or an argumentative text. Suppose you need to summarize the following excerpt from an essay about nonsexist language written by conservative columnist William Safire.

> It makes sense to substitute *worker* for *workingman* . . . , *firefighter* for *fireman* and *police officer* for *policeman.* Plenty of women are in those occupations, and it misleads the listener or reader to retain the old form. . . .
> But do we need *woman actor* for *actress,* or *female tempter* for *temptress?* And what's demeaning about *waitress* that we should have to substitute *woman waiter* or the artificial *waitron?* We dropped *stewardess* largely because the occupation was being maligned—a popular book title suggesting promiscuity was *Coffee, Tea or Me?*—a loss that also took the male *steward* out the emergency exit, and now we have the long and unnecessarily concealing *flight attendant.* We were better off with *steward* and *stewardess.*
> The abolition of the *-ess* suffix tells the reader or listener, "I intend to conceal from you the sex of the person in that job." Thus, when you learn that the *chairperson* or *chair* is going to be Pat Jones or Leslie Smith, or anyone not with a sexually recognizable first name like Jane or Tarzan, you will be denied the information about whether that person is a man or a woman.
> Ah, that's the point, say the language police, sex-eraser squad: it should not matter. But information does matter—and does it really hurt to know? What's wrong with *chairwoman* or *Congresswoman?* Let's go further: now that the antisexist point has been made in this generation, wouldn't it be better for the next generation to have more information rather than less?

Regardless of whether you agree with the opinions expressed here, you probably would want to attribute them to your source with an acknowledgment phrase, rather than to present them as if they were your own. Notice how the underlined phrases in the following summary do that:

> <u>Some purists argue</u> that certain forms of nonsexist language are awkward and unnecessary, contributing little if anything to gender equity. <u>These writers contend</u> that occupational titles like *flight attendant* and *waitron* are awkward or silly and that they conceal relevant information about people's identities. <u>One such</u>

critic, <u>William Safire, believes</u> that the injustices of sexist language have been sufficiently addressed already and that some traditional job designations should be retained (10).

Summarizing an Argument

EXERCISE

The following excerpt is taken from pages 19 and 20 of "The Censorship of Neglect," an article by Mexican American author Rudolfo Anaya. The article, originally published in *English Journal,* is addressed to teachers of English, primarily those at the high-school and middle-school levels. Write a brief summary of Anaya's argument and supporting evidence. Since your summary will refer to the author by name, the closing parenthetical note should cite only page numbers.

> We have not been free to teach. We have accepted the literature presented to us by publishers, those producers of books who have a direct link and a vested interest in the status quo. Big publishers have neglected or refused to publish the literature of minority communities of our country; their lack of social responsibility has created a narrow and paternalistic perspective of our society. The true picture of this country is not narrow; it is multidimensional; it reflects many communities, attitudes, languages, and needs. Our fault, as teachers, is that we have accepted the view of those in charge: teacher-training programs, publishers, politicians, and sectarian interests.
>
> And yet we know better. We know one approach is not best for all; we know we have to incorporate the many voices of literature into the curriculum. . . .
>
> If you are teaching in a Mexican American community, it is your social responsibility to refuse to use the textbook which doesn't contain stories by Mexican American writers. If you teach Asian American children, refuse the textbook that doesn't portray their history and social reality. This kind of activism will free you to teach. . . . But you don't have to be teaching in a Mexican American barrio to insist that the stories and social reality of that group be represented in your textbook. You shortchange your students and you misrepresent the true nature of their country if you don't introduce them to all the communities who have composed the history of this country.

Summarizing in Research Papers

Summary can serve basically the same purposes as paraphrase in research writing: to cite important facts or information, to place a topic or issue in context, or to support an interpretation or opinion. It is, of course, just as important to use parenthetical notes to identify summarized sources as paraphrased sources. The following examples illustrate contexts for using summary in research writing.

Summarizing to Cite Facts or Information

Suppose you are writing a research paper about homelessness in the United States. One of your sources, an article by David Levi Strauss titled "A Threnody for Street Kids," cites the following facts:

> "Home" has increasingly become a site of violent conflict and abuse. Half of all homes are "broken" by divorce; many more are broken by spousal abuse. Child

The original source

abuse in the home is a national epidemic. Poverty kills twenty-seven children every day in America. Ozzie and Harriet are dead and the Cosbys don't live around here.

Every year in the United States a million and a half kids run away from home. Many of them end up on city streets. Right now, today, there are some 30,000 kids living on the streets of New York City. Contrary to popular belief, most of them run away not because they want to but because they have to; because even the streets are safer than where they're running from, where many of them have been physically and sexually abused by their families. Even so, they are not running *to* anything but death. Nationwide, more than 5,000 children a year are buried in unmarked graves.

A summary of these facts might prove useful in a paragraph that dispels certain myths about homelessness. Among those myths is the belief that homeless people are primarily adults who have made conscious, deliberate choices. Your summary might look like this:

A brief summary

> One of the most brutal facts about homelessness is the number of its victims who are minors. Driven from their families by domestic violence, huge numbers of children (30,000 in New York City alone) have taken to the streets, vainly hoping to find safety. Thousands of them die (Strauss 753).

Basically, these sentences summarize facts, while citing one statistic. Though obliged to cite your source in a parenthetical note, you probably would not name David Levi Strauss in an acknowledgment phrase, since there is nothing in the facts themselves that is uniquely his. If, on the other hand, you wanted to quote a bit, you probably would include such a phrase. A slightly longer summary, therefore, might look like this:

A longer summary that quotes the source

> One of the most brutal facts about homelessness is the number of victims who are minors. One reason is the dramatic increase in domestic violence, especially in poor neighborhoods. As journalist David Levi Strauss puts it, "Ozzie and Harriet are dead and the Cosbys don't live around here." Strauss points to some alarming facts: on any given day, 30,000 children are homeless in New York City; thousands of homeless children die every year in the United States (753).

Summarizing to Place a Topic or Issue in Context

Suppose a member of the student government association on your campus has raised objections to Black Culture Week, arguing that such an event is unwarranted without a comparable celebration of white culture. If you wished to examine and refute this familiar argument in a research paper, you might demonstrate that most white Americans know far less about African culture than they think they do—certainly a great deal less than most African Americans know about European culture. In the course of your research, you might locate an article by Neal Ascherson titled "Africa's Lost History," which reviews a recently published book. Ascherson's article contains the following paragraph:

The original passage

> This is a book perfectly designed for an intelligent reader who comes to the subject of Africa reasonably fresh and unprejudiced. Unfortunately, those are still fairly uncommon qualifications in Europe. The first category of baffled consumers

will be those who until yesterday spent much energy denying Africans their history. They did not quite say, like [one] Cambridge professor, that Africa had no history at all. They said that anything ancient, beautiful, or sophisticated found on the continent could have had nothing to do with the talentless loungers incapable of making a decent cup of tea or plowing in a straight line. The ruins of Great Zimbabwe had been built by Phoenicians, the Benin bronzes were probably Portuguese, and all ironwork was Arab. A more sophisticated version of this line was that although Africa had made a promising start, some unknown disaster or lurking collective brain damage had immobilized Africans halfway down the track. This meant, among other things, that the history and archaeology of Africa belonged to the Europeans, who had dug it up and were alone able to understand it. Back to Europe it went and there, to a great extent, it remains.

A summary of this passage would allow you to place Black Culture Week in a different context from the one in which your fellow student views it. Consequently, your paper might include a paragraph like this somewhere in its introduction:

> Black Culture Week is more than just an occasion for celebrating African heritage. It is an opportunity to dispel some of the demeaning misconceptions and stereotypes that diminish respect or even curiosity among white Americans. Among these is the belief, held by many educated Europeans, that Africa has no native history and culture at all—that whatever artifacts can be found there were brought by non-Africans, who are the only people capable of understanding or appreciating them (Ascherson 26). Black Culture Week, therefore, is not so much a matter of promoting African heritage as it is a matter of correcting pervasive misinformation so that educated people can decide whether they wish to study a field that many assume to be nonexistent or unworthy of attention.

Incorporating a summary into your essay

Summarizing to Support an Interpretation or Opinion

In Chapter 3, when we talked about paraphrasing arguments, we considered the effects of various methods of attributing views to a source. Specifically, we considered the following options:

- Stating an argument with no direct reference to its source, but putting both the author's name and the appropriate page number(s) in a parenthetical note.

- Identifying the source within the summary by means of an acknowledgment phrase, leaving only page number(s) in the parenthetical note. (For example, attribution phrases that might introduce a paraphrase of Barbara Lawrence's argument appear on pages 102–103.)

- Expressing judgment about the credibility of the source in an acknowledgment phrase. (Judgmental acknowledgment phrases used in a letter to a library director are found on page 103.)

The effects of attributing an opinion to its source are equally important in the case of summary. Consider the following passage from an essay by Charles R. Lawrence, III, a professor of law at Stanford University. Lawrence makes the controversial argument that racial insults are not protected by the constitutional guarantee of free speech when they occur on college campuses.

A source
expressing an
opinion

If the purpose of the First Amendment is to foster the greatest amount of speech, racial insults disserve that purpose. Assaultive racist speech functions as a preemptive strike. The invective is experienced as a blow, not as a proffered idea, and once the blow is struck, it is unlikely that a dialogue will follow. Racial insults are particularly undeserving of First Amendment protection because the perpetrator's intention is not to discover truth or initiate dialogue but to injure the victim. In most situations, members of minority groups realize that they are likely to lose if they respond to epithets by fighting and are forced to remain silent and submissive.

Courts have held that offensive speech may not be regulated in public forums such as streets where the listener may avoid the speech by moving on, but the regulation of otherwise protected speech has been permitted when the speech invades the privacy of the unwilling listener's home or when the unwilling listener cannot avoid the speech. Racist posters, fliers, and graffiti in dormitories, bathrooms, and other common living spaces would seem to clearly fall within the reasoning of these cases. Minority students should not be required to remain in their rooms in order to avoid racial assault. Minimally, they should find a safe haven in their dorm rooms and in all other common rooms that are a part of their daily routine.

I would also argue that the university's responsibility for insuring that these students receive an equal educational opportunity provides a compelling justification for regulations that insure them safe passage in all common areas. A minority student should not have to risk becoming the target of racially assaulting speech every time he or she chooses to walk across campus.

If you were arguing in favor of a campus speech code that prohibits racial insults, you could cite Lawrence to support your views. Thus, you might summarize the passage as follows:

Use of the
source in an
argumentative
paper

The First Amendment was designed to protect the free exchange of ideas, but racial insults are designed to injure or intimidate others, to discourage rather than to promote discussion. It would be different if minority students were able to walk away from such insults, but when these insults are placed in dorms and other university buildings, offended students are compelled to endure them (Lawrence B1).

If you wanted to add authority to this opinion, you might introduce the same summary with an acknowledgment phrase—for example, "Stanford law professor Charles Lawrence concludes that . . . " or "It is the opinion of some legal experts that . . . "

If, on the other hand, you disagreed with Lawrence and saw danger in efforts to abridge free speech on college campuses, you would certainly want to precede your summary with an acknowledgment phrase that places some distance between you and Lawrence's view—for example, "Professor Charles Lawrence's views are typical of those who argue that protecting minorities must take priority over preserving unrestricted free speech." You might even consider a more judgmental acknowledgment phrase—for example, "Professor Charles Lawrence rationalizes the abridgment of free speech on college campuses by arguing that it serves to promote racial justice."

Summarizing in Research Papers

Write a summary of each of the following passages—one that is appropriate to the given situation. Remember that you may choose to identify the source at the beginning of your summary or put the last name(s) of the author(s), along with page number(s), in a parenthetical note at the end.

a. *Source:* The following passage comes from page 54 of an article by Max Frankel, who examines the enduring appeal of *Fortune* magazine's annual list of the four hundred wealthiest Americans. Frankel speculates on why some people actively seek inclusion and why others who are not wealthy take interest in the list.

Situation: You are writing a paper about class consciousness in the United States and wish to show that financial success is frequently defined in terms of status and recognition as well as by wealth.

Passage:
   The first explanation for this need of notice can be found in Alexis de Tocqueville's account of his travels in 19th-century America. "When the reverence that belonged to what is old has vanished, birth, condition and profession no longer distinguish men," he noted. "Hardly anything but money remains to create strongly marked differences between them and to raise some of them above the common level." And as David Reisman observed of us a century later, the truly acquisitive, fully selfish person "is not interested in himself but only in others' evaluation of himself. . . . He is their satellite, even when he dominates them."
   And we "others"—why do we pine for Barbara Walters to lead us past the gates of estates? Why do we let the *Wall Street Journal* pretend to be the diary of the American dream? Why do we pay $5 to fondle *Forbes*'s list, upon which none of us will ever appear?
   Surely the answers are neither greed nor envy. If our democracy held a majority of the truly avaricious, then people earning an average of $30,000 to $75,000 a year would never tolerate, no less venerate, a roll of 96 billionaires and their train of 300. The happy portraits of so many of them at work and play betray not even a whisk of concern about a covetous multitude. They know us well. They trust the ethic of success that defines community in America, the ethic that envelops both the richest and the poorest so long as they all continue to strive.

b. *Source:* The following passage is taken from pages 106–08 of a book about courtship and marriage in Renaissance Italy. Its author, Gene Brucker, a professor of history, is describing how economic factors determined who could marry whom.

Situation: You are writing a paper demonstrating the traditional inequality of partners in marriage. You wish to summarize information from the following passage to introduce your topic.

Passage:
   Wealth and its derivation were one criterion for measuring a family's reputation and thus its place in the complex and vaguely defined hierarchy of social rank. The evaluation of fluctuating reputations was a major preoccupation of Florentine parents responsible for arranging marriages for their children. In these operations the marriage

market was not unlike a modern stock exchange; indeed, marriageable girls were sometimes characterized as "merchandise" *(mercatanzia).* The operations of the market are revealed in rich detail in the correspondence of Alessandra Strozzi, a Florentine widow who was actively engaged for more than two decades, from 1447 to 1471, in finding spouses for her daughters Caterina and Alessandra and her sons Filippo and Lorenzo, who were then living in Naples. A letter written by her son-in-law Marco Parenti to Filippo Strozzi in July 1465 graphically describes aspects of that enterprise. Marco had investigated the qualifications of two girls from the Adimari and Tanagli families as prospective brides for Filippo; he concluded that they were the best candidates in the current market. Their dowries were of equal size; their physical appearance was similar. Marco conceded that the Adimari were more "noble" than the Tanagli, but that advantage was neutralized by the fact that the Adimari girl was an orphan with no brothers, and her close relatives (uncles and cousins) were undistinguished men. Though the Tanagli lineage did not rank so high in the social order as the Adimari, "they are old and worthy, and this branch is descended from knights.". . . "So that," Marco concluded, "balancing one and the other, there is not much difference, and we leave it to your judgment."

c.   *Source:* The following passage appears on page 49 of a review of the catalogs for two exhibitions of the works of the seventeenth-century painter Nicholas Poussin. The author of the review is Francis Haskell.

    Situation: You are writing a paper that examines artistic license, specifically the way writers and painters sometimes incorporate historical inaccuracies in their work. A summary of facts and information in this passage can refute the common assumption that such inconsistencies reflect the artist's ignorance or carelessness.

    Passage:
      Like Rubens, [Poussin] was keen to draw attention to the accuracy of his antiquarian researches, but success in this respect obviously depended on their being recognized and appreciated. "In this picture," he writes at the end of a meticulous description of the exotic rituals to be seen in his *Holy Family in Egypt* (Hermitage), "I have put in all these things to give pleasure through their novelty and variety and to show that the Virgin is in Egypt." Surprisingly, however, he does not refer to the fact that, having taken so much trouble over the priests of Serapis and the sanctuary of Ibis, he has included at the back of the picture what appears to be some of the most famous buildings in ancient Rome.
      Poussin's "mistakes" (inconsistencies, rather), which would attract little, if any, comment were they to be found in the works of most of his contemporaries, are disturbing because he often insisted that his pictures had been thought out with the utmost care. Was he perhaps alluding, in the Hermitage picture, to the eventual triumph of Christianity in Rome itself? The suggestion is given some weight because of the inclusion in the distance of a medieval tower surmounted by a very small and barely visible cross, but it is odd that he did not bother to mention this in his detailed letter.
      It is odder still that in the Oxford *Exposition of Moses* the architecture is entirely Roman. Could this be because Rome appeared to provide a timeless setting for his biblical narrative? But what about the papal palace of the Belvedere set in the landscape in which we see the ascetic Diogenes renouncing the last of his worldly goods? Or the reconstructed temple of Palestrina in the hills above the (heavy-handed) satirical scene depicting Achilles disguised as a girl among the daughters of Lycomedes, and betraying his true identity by showing greater enthusiasm for manly weapons than for a casket of jewels? It will surely be very difficult indeed to detect the symbolism that could account for such inconsistencies. In the absence of any convincing solution to them, it

seems that we can do little more than accept the hypothesis that Poussin was not *always* the idiosyncratic artist that he himself and his early biographers made out and that the degree of his commitment to syncretism or to archaeological accuracy may have varied according to the expectations of his clients. To acknowledge this will only appear disparaging to those who believe that the moral stature of an artist is in some way to be measured by the intellectual complexity of his sources.

GUIDELINES FOR EFFECTIVE SUMMARIZING

The general principles set forth in this chapter can be summed up in the following guidelines for effective summarizing:

- Like paraphrasing, summarizing calls for close literal reading, but it also involves discerning main ideas—distinguishing them from minor points and illustrative examples.

- Like a paraphrase, a summary is written in your own language, although it may contain a short quotation or two—never more than a single sentence.

- Although there is no single correct way to compose a summary, one workable process is detailed on page 135.

- Summaries serve the same basic functions in research writing as paraphrases do.

 # READING SELECTION

The following article, which appeared on the front page of the *Wall Street Journal*, describes the experiences of bright, gifted students in an environment hostile to academic success. As you read the article, you may find yourself drawing comparisons and contrasts between Ballou Senior High in Washington, DC, and the schools you have attended.

Against All Odds

In Rough City School, Top Students Struggle to Learn—and Escape

RON SUSKIND

Recently, a student was shot dead by a classmate during lunch period outside Frank W.   1
Ballou Senior High. It didn't come as much of a surprise to anyone at the school, in this city's most crime-infested ward. Just during the current school year, one boy was hacked by a student with an ax, a girl was badly wounded in a knife fight with another female student, five fires were set by arsonists, and an unidentified body was dumped next to

the parking lot. But all is quiet in the echoing hallways at 7:15 A.M., long before classes start on a spring morning. The only sound comes from the computer lab, where 16-year-old Cedric Jennings is already at work on an extra-credit project, a program to bill patients at a hospital. Later, he will work on his science fair project, a chemical analysis of acid rain.

2   He arrives every day this early and often doesn't leave until dark. The high-school junior with the perfect grades has big dreams: He wants to go to Massachusetts Institute of Technology.

3   Cedric is one of a handful of honor students at Ballou, where the dropout rate is well into double digits and just 80 students out of more than 1,350 currently boast an average of B or better. They are a lonely lot. Cedric has almost no friends. Tall, gangly and unabashedly ambitious, he is a frequent target in a place where bullies belong to gangs and use guns; his life has been threatened more than once. He eats lunch in a classroom many days, plowing through extra work that he has asked for. "It's the only way I'll be able to compete with kids from other, harder schools," he says.

4   The arduous odyssey of Cedric and other top students shows how the street culture that dominates Ballou drags down anyone who seeks to do well. Just to get an ordinary education—the kind most teens take for granted—these students must take extraordinary measures. Much of their academic education must come outside of regular classes altogether. Little gets accomplished during the day in a place where attendance is sporadic, some fellow students read at only a fifth-grade level, and some stay in lower grades for years, leaving hardened, 18-year-old sophomores mixing with new arrivals.

"Crowd Control"

5   "So much of what goes on here is crowd control," says Mahmood Dorosti, a math teacher. The few top students "have to put themselves on something like an independent-study course to really learn—which is an awful lot to ask of a teenager."

6   It has been this way as long as Cedric can remember. When he was a toddler, his mother, Barbara Jennings, reluctantly quit her clerical job and went on welfare for a few years so she could start her boy on a straight and narrow path. She took him to museums, read him books, took him on nature walks. She brought him to church four times each week, and warned him about the drug dealers on the corner. Cedric learned to loathe those dealers—especially the one who was his father.

7   Barbara Jennings, now 47, already had two daughters; her first born while she was in high school. Cedric, she vowed, would lead a different life. "You're a special boy," she would tell her son. "You have to see things far from here, far from this place. And someday, you'll get the kind of respect that a real man earns."

8   Cedric became a latch-key child at the age of five, when his mother went back to work. She filled her boy's head with visions of the Ivy League, bringing him home a Harvard sweatshirt while he was in junior high. Every day after school, after double-locking the door behind him, he would study, dream of becoming an engineer living in a big house—and gaze at the dealers just outside his window stashing their cocaine in the alley.

Seduced by Failure

9   Ballou High, a tired sprawl of '60s-era brick and steel, rises up from a blighted landscape of housing projects and rundown stores. Failure is pervasive here, even seductive. Some 836 sophomores enrolled last September—and 172 were gone by Thanksgiving. The junior class numbers only 399. The senior class, a paltry 240. "We don't know much about where the dropouts go," says Reginald Ballard, the assistant principal. "Use your imagination. Dead. Jail. Drugs."

On a recent afternoon, a raucous crowd of students fills the gymnasium for an assembly. Administrators here are often forced into bizarre games of cat and mouse with their students, and today is no exception: To lure everyone here, the school has brought in Washington Mayor Marion Barry, several disk jockeys from a black radio station and a rhythm-and-blues singer.   **10**

A major reason for the assembly, though, has been kept a secret: to hand out academic awards to top students. Few of the winners would show up voluntarily to endure the sneers of classmates. When one hapless teen's name is called, a teacher must run to the bleachers and order him down as some in the crowd jeer "Nerd!"   **11**

The announcer moves on to the next honoree: "Cedric Jennings! Cedric Jennings!" Heads turn expectantly, but Cedric is nowhere to be seen. Someone must have tipped him off, worries Mr. Ballard. "It sends a terrible message," he says, "that doing well here means you better not show your face."   **12**

Cedric, at the moment, is holed up in a chemistry classroom. He often retreats here. It is his private sanctuary, the one place at Ballou where he feels completely safe, and where he spends hours talking with his mentor, chemistry teacher Clarence Taylor. Cedric later will insist he simply didn't know about the assembly—but he readily admits he hid out during a similar assembly last year even though he was supposed to get a $100 prize: "I just couldn't take it, the abuse."   **13**

Mr. Taylor, the teacher, has made Cedric's education something of a personal mission. He gives Cedric extra-credit assignments, like working on a sophisticated computer program that taps into weather satellites. He arranges trips, like a visit with scientists at the National Aeronautics and Space Administration. He challenges him with impromptu drills; Cedric can reel off all 109 elements of the periodic table by memory in three minutes, 39 seconds.   **14**

Most importantly, earlier this year, after Cedric's mother heard about an M.I.T. summer scholarship program for minority high schoolers, Mr. Taylor helped him apply.   **15**

Now, Cedric is pinning all of his hopes on getting into the program. Last year, it bootstrapped most of its participants into the M.I.T. freshman class, where the majority performed extremely well. It is Cedric's ticket out of this place, the culmination of everything that he has worked for his whole life.   **16**

"You can tell the difference between the ones who have hope and those who don't," says Mr. Taylor. "Cedric has it—the capacity to hope."   **17**

• • •

That capacity is fast being drummed out of some others in the dwindling circle of honor students at Ballou. Teachers have a name for what goes on here. The "crab bucket syndrome," they call it: When one crab tries to climb from a bucket, the others pull it back down.   **18**

Just take a glance at Phillip Atkins, 17, who was a top student in junior high, but who has let his grades slide into the C range. These days he goes by the nickname "Blunt," street talk for a thick marijuana cigarette, a "personal favorite" he says he enjoys with a "40-ouncer" of beer. He has perfected a dead-eyed stare, a trademark of the gang leaders he admires.   **19**

Phillip, now a junior, used to be something of a bookworm. At the housing project where he lives with both parents and his seven siblings, he read voraciously, especially about history. He still likes to read, though he would never tell that to the menacing crowd he hangs around with now.   **20**

Being openly smart, as Cedric is, "will make you a target, which is crazy at a place like Ballou," Phillip explains to his 15-year-old sister Alicia and her friend Octavia Hooks, both sophomore honor students, as they drive to apply for a summer-jobs program for   **21** disadvantaged youths. "The best way to avoid trouble," he says, "is to never get all the answers right on a test."

22   Alicia and Octavia nod along. "At least one wrong," Octavia says quietly, almost to herself.

23   Cedric tries never to get any wrong. His average this year is better than perfect: 4.02, thanks to an A+ in English. He takes the most advanced courses he can, including physics and computer science. "If you're smart, show it," he says. "Don't hide."

24   At school, though, Cedric's blatant studiousness seems to attract nothing but abuse. When Cedric recently told a girl in his math class that he would tutor her as long as she stopped copying his answers, she responded with physical threats—possibly to be carried out by a boyfriend. Earlier, one of the school's tougher students stopped him in the hallway and threatened to shoot him.

25   The police who are permanently stationed at the school say Ballou's code of behavior is much like that of a prison: Someone like Cedric who is "disrespected" and doesn't retaliate is vulnerable.

26   Worse, Cedric is worried that he is putting himself through all this for nothing. Scores are in, and Cedric has gotten a startling low 750 out of a possible 1600 on his PSAT's, the pretest before the Scholastic Aptitude Test that colleges require. He is sure his chances of getting into the M.I.T. program, where average scores are far higher, are scuttled.

27   He admits that he panicked during the test, racing ahead, often guessing, and finishing early. He vows to do better next time. "I'm going to do better on the real SAT's, I've got to," he says, working in Mr. Taylor's room on a computer program that offers drills and practice tests. "I've got no choice."

28   At his daily SAT Preparation class—where Cedric is the only one of 17 students to have completed last night's homework—Cedric leads one group of students in a practice exercise; Phillip leads another. Cedric races through the questions recklessly, ignoring his groupmates, one of whom protests faintly, "He won't let us do any." Phillip and his group don't bother trying. They cheat, looking up answers in the back of the book.

29   Janet Johns-Gibson, the class teacher, announces that one Ballou student who took the SAT scored a 1050. An unspectacular result almost any place else, but here the class swoons in amazement. "Cedric will do better than that," sneers Phillip. "He's such a brain." Cedric winces.

30   In truth, Cedric may not be the smartest student in his class. In a filthy boys' room reeking of urine, Delante Coleman, a 17-year-old junior known as "Head," is describing life at the top. Head is the leader of Trenton Park Crew, a gang, and says he and "about 15 of my boys who back me up" enjoy "fine buggies," including a Lexus, and "money, which we get from wherever." There is a dark side, of course, like the murder last summer of the gang's previous leader, Head's best friend, by a rival thug from across town. The teen was found in his bed with a dozen bullet holes through his body.

31   But Head still feels invincible. "I'm not one, I'm many," says the 5-foot-3, 140-pound plug of a teenager. "Safety, in this neighborhood, is about being part of a group."

32   Head's grades are barely passing, in the D range. Yet Christopher Grimm, a physics teacher, knows a secret about Head: As a sophomore, he scored above 12th-grade-level nationally on the math section of a standardized basic-skills test. That's the same score Cedric got.

33   "How d'you find that out?" barks Head when confronted with this information. "Well, yeah, that's, umm, why I'm so good with money."

34   For sport, Head and his group like to toy with the "goodies," honor students like Cedric who carry books home and walk alone. "Everyone knows they're trying to be white, get ahead in the white man's world," he says, his voice turning bitter. "In a way, that's a little bit of disrespect to the rest of us."

Phillip tests even better than Head, his two F's in the latest quarter notwithstanding. On the basic-skills test, both he and Cedric hit a combined score—averaging English, math and other disciplines—of 12.9, putting both in the top 10% nationwide. But no one seems to pay attention to that, least of all Phillip's teachers, who mostly see him as a class clown. "Thought no one knew that," Phillip says, when a visitor mentions his scores. **35**

Heading over to McDonald's after school, Phillip is joined by his sister Alicia and her friend Octavia, both top students a grade behind him. Over Big Macs and Cokes, the talk shifts to the future. "Well, I'm going to college," says Alicia coolly, staring down Phillip. "And them I'm going to be something like an executive secretary, running an office." **36**

"Yeah, I'm going to college, too," says Phillip, looking away. **37**

"Very funny, you going to college," snaps Alicia. "Get real." **38**

"Well, I am." **39**

"Get a life, Phillip, you got no chance." **40**

"You've got nothing," he says, starting to yell. "Just your books. My life is after school." **41**

"You got no life," she shouts back. "Nothing!" **42**

The table falls silent, and everyone quietly finishes eating. But later, alone, Phillip admits that, no, there won't be any college. He has long since given up on the dreams he used to have when he and his father would spin a globe and talk about traveling the world. "I'm not really sure what happens from here," he says softly, sitting on the stone steps overlooking the track behind the school. "All I know is what I do now. I act stupid." **43**

Phillip of late has become the cruelest of all of Cedric's tormentors. The two got into a scuffle recently—or at least Phillip decked Cedric, who didn't retaliate. A few days after the McDonald's blowup, Phillip and a friend bump into Cedric. "He thinks he's so smart," Phillip says. "You know, I'm as smart as he is." The friend laughs. He thinks it's a joke. **44**

• • •

Cedric is on edge. He should be hearing from M.I.T. about the summer program any day now, and he isn't optimistic. In physics class, he gamely tries to concentrate on his daily worksheet. The worksheet is a core educational tool at Ballou: Attendance is too irregular, and books too scarce, to actually teach many lessons during class, some teachers say. Often, worksheets are just the previous day's homework, and Cedric finishes them quickly. **45**

Today, though, he runs into trouble. Spotting a girl copying his work, he confronts her. The class erupts in catcalls, jeering at Cedric until the teacher removes him from the room. "I put in a lot of hours, a lot of time, to get everything just right," he says, from his exile in an adjoining lab area. "I shouldn't just give it away." **46**

His mentor, Mr. Taylor, urges him to ignore the others. "I tell him he's in a long, harrowing race, a marathon, and he can't listen to what's being yelled at him from the sidelines," he says. "I tell him those people on the sideline are already out of the race." **47**

But Cedric sometimes wishes he was more like those people. Recently, he asked his mother for a pair of extra-baggy, khaki-colored pants—a style made popular by Snoop Doggy Dogg, the rap star who was charged last year with murder. "But my mother said no way, that it symbolizes things, bad things, and bad people," he reports later, lingering in a stairwell. "I mean, I've gotta live." **48**

Unable to shake his malaise, he wanders the halls after the school day ends, too distracted to concentrate on his usual extra-credit work. "Why am I doing this, working like a maniac?" he asks. **49**

50   He stretches out his big hands, palms open. "Look at me. I'm not gonna make it. What's the point in even trying?"

• • •

51   Outside Phillip's house in the projects, his father, Israel Atkins, is holding forth on the problem of shooting too high. A lyrically articulate man who conducts prayer sessions at his home on weekends, he gives this advice to his eight children: Hoping for too much in this world can be dangerous.

52   "I see so many kids around here who are told they can be anything, who then run into almost inevitable disappointment, and all that hope turns into anger," he says one day, a few hours after finishing the night shift at his job cleaning rental cars. "Next thing, they're saying, 'See, I got it anyway—got it my way, by hustling—the fancy car, the cash.' And then they're lost.

53   "Set goals so they're attainable, so you can get some security, I tell my kids. Then keep focused on what success is all about: being close to God and appreciating life's simpler virtues."

54   Mr. Atkins is skeptical about a tentative—and maybe last—stab at achievement that Phillip is making: tap dancing. Phillip has taken a course offered at school, and is spending hours practicing for an upcoming show in a small theater at the city's John F. Kennedy Center for Performing Arts. His teacher, trying hard to encourage him, pronounces him "enormously gifted."

55   At Ballou, teachers desperate to find ways to motivate poor achievers often make such grand pronouncements. They will pick a characteristic and inflate it into a career path. So the hallways are filled with the next Carl Lewis, the next Bill Cosby, the next Michael Jackson.

56   But to Phillip's father all this is nonsense. "Tap dancing will not get him a job," he says. It is all, he adds, part of the "problem of kids getting involved in these sorts of things, getting their heads full of all kinds of crazy notions."

• • •

57   As Cedric settles into his chair, the teacher's discussion of the Great Depression echoes across 20 desks—only one other of which is filled.

58   But Cedric has other things on his mind. As soon as school is over, he seeks out his chemistry teacher, Mr. Taylor. He isn't going to enter a citywide science fair with his acid-rain project after all, he says. What's more, he is withdrawing from a program in which he would link up with a mentor, such as an Environmental Protection Agency employee, to prepare a project on the environment. Last year, Cedric had won third prize with his project on asbestos hazards. Mr. Taylor is at a loss as his star student slips out the door.

59   "I'm tired, I'm going home," Cedric murmurs. He walks grimly past a stairwell covered with graffiti: "HEAD LIVES."

60   The path may not get any easier. Not long after Cedric leaves, Joanne Camero, last year's salutatorian, stops by Mr. Taylor's chemistry classroom, looking despondent. Now a freshman at George Washington University, she has realized, she admits, "that the road from here keeps getting steeper."

61   The skills it took to make it through Ballou—focusing on nothing but academics, having no social life, and working closely with a few teachers—left Joanne ill-prepared for college, she says. There, professors are distant figures, and students flit easily from academics to socializing, something she never learned to do.

"I'm already worn out," she says. Her grades are poor and she has few friends. Ten-   62
tatively, she admits that she is thinking about dropping out and transferring to a less rigorous college.

As she talks about past triumphs in high school, it becomes clear that for many of   63
Ballou's honor students, perfect grades are an attempt to redeem imperfect lives—lives
torn by poverty, by violence, by broken families. In Cedric's case, Mr. Taylor says later,
the pursuit to flawless grades is a way to try to force his father to respect him, even to
apologize to him. "I tell him it can't be," Mr. Taylor says. "That he must forgive that
man that he tries so hard to hate."

• • •

Behind a forest of razor wire at a prison in Lorton, Va., Cedric Gilliam emerges into a vis-   64
iting area. At 44 years old, he looks startlingly familiar, an older picture of his son. He
has been in prison for nine years, serving a 12- to 36-year sentence for armed robbery.

When Cedric's mother became pregnant, "I told her . . . if you have the baby, you   65
won't be seeing me again," Mr. Gilliam recalls, his voice flat. "So she said she'd have an
abortion. But I messed up by not going down to the clinic with her. That was my mistake, you see, and she couldn't go through with it."

For years, Mr. Gilliam refused to publicly acknowledge that Cedric was his son, until   66
his progeny had grown into a boy bearing the same wide, easy grin as his dad. One day,
they met at a relative's apartment, in an encounter young Cedric recalls vividly. "And I
ran to him and hugged him and said 'Daddy.' I just remember that I was so happy."

Not long afterward, Mr. Gilliam went to jail. The two have had infrequent contact   67
since then. But their relationships, always strained, reached a breaking point last year
when a fight ended with Mr. Gilliam threatening his son, "I'll blow your brains out."

Now, in the spare prison visiting room, Mr. Gilliam says his son has been on his   68
mind constantly since then. "I've dialed the number a hundred times, but I keep hanging up," he says. "I know Cedric doesn't get, you know, that kind of respect from the
other guys, and that used to bother me. But now I see all he's accomplished, and I'm
proud of him, and I love him. I just don't know how to say it."

His son is skeptical. "By the time he's ready to say he loves me and all, it will be too   69
late," Cedric says. "I'll be gone."

It is a Saturday afternoon, and the Kennedy Center auditorium comes alive with a   70
wailing jazz number as Phillip and four other dancers spin and tap their way flawlessly
through a complicated routine. The audience—about 200 parents, brothers and sisters
of the school-aged performers—applauds wildly.

After the show, he is practically airborne, laughing and strutting in his yellow "Bal-   71
lou Soul Tappers" T-shirt, looking out at the milling crowd in the lobby.

"You seen my people?" he asks one of his fellow tappers.   72

"No, haven't," she says.   73

"Your people here?" he asks, tentatively.   74

"Sure, my mom's over there," she says, pointing, then turning back to Phillip.   75

His throat seems to catch, and he shakes his head. "Yeah," he says, "I'll find out   76
where they are, why they couldn't come." He tries to force a smile, but manages only a
grimace. "I'll find out later."

• • •

Scripture Cathedral, a pillar of Washington's thriving apostolic Pentecostal community,   77
is a cavernous church, its altar dominated by a 40-foot-tall illuminated cross. Evening

services are about to begin, and Cedric's mother searches nervously for her son, scanning the crowd of women in hats and men in bow ties. Finally, he slips into a rear pew, looking haggard.

78   From the pulpit, the preacher, C. L. Long, announces that tonight, he has a "heavy heart": He had to bury a slain 15-year-old boy just this afternoon. But he launches into a rousing sermon, and as he speaks, his rolling cadences echo through the sanctuary, bringing the 400 parishioners to their feet.

79   "When you don't have a dime in your pocket, when you don't have food on your table, if you got troubles, you're in the right place tonight," he shouts, as people yell out hallelujahs, raise their arms high, run through the aisles. Cedric, preoccupied, sits passively. But slowly, he, too, is drawn in and begins clapping.

80   Then the preacher seems to speak right to him. "Terrible things are happening, you're low, you're tired, you're fighting, you're waiting for your vision to become reality—you feel you can't wait anymore," the preacher thunders. "Say 'I'll be fine tonight 'cause Jesus is with me.' Say it! Say it!"

81   By now, Cedric is on his feet, the spark back in his eyes. "Yes," he shouts. "Yes."

82   It is a long service, and by the time mother and son pass the drug dealers—still standing vigil—and walk up the crumbling stairs to their apartment, it is approaching midnight.

83   Ms. Jennings gets the mail. On top of the *TV Guide* is an orange envelope from the U.S. Treasury: a stub from her automatic savings-bond contribution—$85 a week, about one-third of her after-tax income—that she has been putting away for nine years to help pay for Cedric's college. "You don't see it, you don't miss it," she says.

84   Under the *TV Guide* is a white envelope.

85   Cedric grabs it. His hands begin to shake. "My heart is in my throat."

86   It is from M.I.T.

87   Fumbling, he rips it open.

88   "Wait. Wait. 'We are pleased to inform you . . .' Oh my God. Oh my God." He begins jumping around the tiny kitchen. Ms. Jennings reaches out to touch him, to share this moment with him—but he spins out of her reach.

89   "I can't believe it. I got in," he cries out, holding the letter against his chest, his eyes shut tight. "This is it. My life is about to begin."

Freewriting

In your notebook, write for ten to fifteen minutes responding to the predicament of academically gifted students at Ballou Senior High. You might want to draw connections to your own experience and observation as a high-school student; you might consider various causes and explanations for conditions described in the article; or you might want to speculate on the possible future that awaits each of the students profiled. If you attended a high school vastly different from the one described in the article, you might think about strategies that you have adopted as a college-bound student.

Group Work

Listen carefully and take notes as each freewriting is read aloud. Try to characterize the attitudes of group members toward the academically gifted students who attend Ballou Senior High School. Do the members of your group agree unanimously on what forces create such an environment? If not, try to understand and articulate competing opinions and explanations. What kind of a future do your peers forecast for the students profiled in the article, particularly Cedric Jennings? How do they feel they would cope with the stress and danger that Cedric endures?

Review Questions

1. What roles have the parents of Cedric Jennings played in motivating him to succeed academically?

2. What special initiatives has Clarence Taylor, Cedric's chemistry teacher, undertaken as a mentor?

3. How have Phillip Atkins and Delante Coleman channeled their academic talents?

Discussion Questions

1. Of all the possible explanations for Cedric's academic success—for example, innate genius, parental encouragement, dedicated teachers, personal effort—which do you feel are the most and least significant?

2. Of all the possible impediments to Cedric's success—for example, being poor, living in a single-parent household, being harassed and intimidated by peers, attending a supposedly inferior school—which do you feel are the most and least significant?

3. Although this article is an ostensibly objective profile, how do you think the author, Ron Suskind, views his subject? Do you suppose he hopes to arouse any particular response? Be sure to consider Suskind's audience, readers of the *Wall Street Journal*.

Writing

1. Write a summary of Suskind's article and compare it with the summary of a classmate whose educational background differs substantially from your own. In particular, see if there are any significant differences in what each of you takes to be the main ideas in the article. Consider, in writing, whether or not a person's understanding of main idea is affected by her or his background and experience.

2. Combining what you have learned from Suskind's article with what you have experienced and observed as a student, write an essay that speculates on the causes of academic achievement (or over- or under-achievement).

3. Arrange an opportunity to observe an educational setting that you are unfamiliar with (e.g., an adult-literacy class; community-service instruction in an art, craft, or sports activity; a pre-kindergarten class). Report on what you learn in a profile essay like Suskind's or like Julie Swain's essay in Chapter 1 of this book.

6 Synthesizing Sources: Writing a Summary Report

I**N PREVIOUS** chapters, you worked with individual sources, paraphrasing or summarizing them in isolation. More typically, your research on a topic will lead you to consult several sources, and you will need to present the information you find in a way that combines, or *synthesizes,* those sources. If, for example, you wanted to learn more about dirigibles or about the early history of your hometown, you probably would consult books and articles. If you reported your findings, you would synthesize the information acquired from these sources.

There are several strategies for synthesizing multiple sources, and we begin with the simplest. It consists of two steps: writing separate summaries or paraphrases of the individual sources and then linking them with transitional passages. What follows is an example.

 WRITING A BRIEF SUMMARY REPORT

Suppose that you have been asked to examine recent trends in coffee consumption and some of their implications. You have chosen the following articles from a list of sources provided by your instructor. As a first step toward writing your report, read each of the articles with care, searching for important ideas and underlining noteworthy information.

Muddy Waters
The Lore, the Lure, the Lowdown on America's Favorite Addiction*
Mark Schapiro

Cuppa joe—jack—crank—java—mud—ink. Cup of misery. Take it midnight (black) or take it slippery (white). You may never again hear those colorful gems of American argot conjuring coffee in all its forms. Today "latté" rolls off the tongues of 14-year-olds as the cafés and espresso bars blossoming like seedlings on our street corners and in our malls transform America's gritty coffee culture.

*This article appears in its entirety on pages 58–65 of the November–December 1994 issue of *Utne Reader.* The excerpt reprinted here appears on pages 58–60.

Nighthawks, Edward Hopper's haunting portrait of a coffee drinker hunched over a diner counter—symbolic of the days when coffee was a dime and you drank it at Formica countertops by the tankful—is now imitated on the side of a Starbucks coffee mug like a fondly remembered relic of a bygone era. Today you'd need some hardwood paneling and chrome to convey the transfiguration of coffee into the liquid fuel of the information age.

Some call it a sweet buzz; others call it tachycardia; the FDA may someday call it a "caffeinated delivery system." The lowly coffee bean—exalted into unprecedented combinations, flavors, and espresso-based concoctions—has landed in the hearts and minds of American consumers, as law-abiding citizens show their affection for what is undoubtedly the most popular unregulated drug in America. Fifty-two percent of Americans drink at least one cup a day (an estimated 130 million daily cups), while the number of coffee bars, as opposed to Hopperesque coffee shops, has leapt from barely 250 nationwide 15 years ago to over 5,500 today, and will reach an estimated 10,000 by the end of the century. The unabated taste for coffee has made this human engine starter into the second most actively traded commodity on the planet, right after oil—that other form of black gold.

The United States has long had a love affair with coffee, consuming one-third of the world's yearly production. But over the past five years, espresso and its innumerable cousins have become a $2 billion-a-year business as this higher-grade coffee begins coursing into the veins of America's mainstream. From coffee mainstays like Seattle, Vancouver, and San Francisco, cappuccino is now hitting the heartland. "Three new cafés opened this spring in Peoria," exults Ted Lingle, executive director of the Specialty Coffee Association, the trade group representing the interests of processors and sellers of higher-quality coffees. Even McDonald's is testing espresso machines in its fast-food outlets in the Northwest. If espresso once had the luster of the elite, that is no longer the case as coffee stands are sandwiched between shoe stores in shopping malls across the country—barely recognizable miniatures of the New York or San Francisco cafés that link them, by a tenuous thread, to America's coffeehouse culture.

New York's Greenwich Village and San Francisco's North Beach have left us a legacy of cafés that became centers of creative fermentation for artists, writers, and musicians, providing a collective space in which one could languidly indulge in the combination of caffeine and conversation. Many of their offspring, however, provide the substance—high-quality coffee—without the soul that once propelled New York's legendary Cafe Figaro (now a tourist attraction) or San Francisco's Caffé Trieste into the heart of America's dissident political and artistic culture.

Until recently, the café business was almost exclusively an enterprise of aficionados; for 80 percent of the new café owners, it is their first time owning a business, according to Lingle. Even the phenomenally successful Starbucks, which now has close to 400 stores across the country and earned $163 million in revenues last year, started as a smattering of coffee kiosks in Seattle. But as the profit margins become clear (the average coffee bar pulls in about $300,000 in revenues a year), the picture is changing. Gloria Jean's is one of the fastest-growing franchises in the country, targeting over 200 malls with its manufactured and transitory version of reproducible bonhomie based on specialty coffee drinks. A group of Dartmouth Business School graduates recently started Minneapolis-based Caribou Coffee after seeing the profit potential of chains like Starbucks. And they know the market—young people with money to spare in search of not only a good coffee but also the intangible taste of being "in" on a new means of defining themselves. . . .

Pop psychologists tell us that yuppie baby boomers went to Europe and came back with a palate newly sensitized to the nuances of high-quality coffee. The fact that people enthusiastically spend up to three dollars for a coffee drink that costs seven cents to make (plus the accessories: another 10 to 15 cents for napkins, sugar, spoons, etc.) is an indication of how willing we are to spend money on the small luxuries when hard economic times constrain purchase of the big things—a car, a house. Naturally, trendmeister Faith Popcorn has even given this trend a name: "small indulgence syndrome." Of course, coffee is also the least toxic indulgence left to health-obsessed baby boomers besieged by bad news about everything from secondhand cigarette smoke to AIDS. And indulging one's fancy in an unthreatening, vaguely iconoclastic café, says the upbeat Popcorn, makes people feel "individualistic, like it's their own local place. Cappuccino has more arty, poetic, intellectual associations than the old 'cuppa java.' "

Or maybe it's the fact that coffee seems to have replaced Stoli as the elixir of seduction, as coffee bars become the new "singles" bars—an observation confirmed by café owners across New York City. Liquor consumption is down, coffee consumption is up. And while recent studies confirm that alcohol increases women's sexual drive, a new breed of sociopundits claims that coffee revs up the mind-body equation on both sides of the table—if one accepts the premise that stimulating conversation stimulates desire. "It's more of an intellectual than a sexual pickup scene," comments David Gomez-Pearlberg, who has witnessed many caffeine-fed romances as co-owner of Eureka Joe's, a living-room-style café on New York's lower Fifth Avenue. "It's a safer, lighter place to meet than a bar."

Grounds for Concern

Caffeine Works—It Really Can Pick You Up and Make You More Alert.
But It Also Can Cause Trouble*

Marilyn Dickey

A 45-year old cabinetmaker walked into the sleep clinic at Boston's Brigham and Women's Hospital complaining of feeling groggy. He took naps every day, would drop off to sleep unexpectedly, and was usually in a foul mood. "This guy was irascible," says Dr. Quentin Regestein, the psychiatrist who took the case. "He was argumentative and unlivable with his family. When he came here, he got into a set-to in the parking lot with someone who had grazed his fender."

In an effort to stay awake, the patient was drinking six or seven cups of coffee a day and took caffeine pills on top of that.

Before embarking on a sleep study, Regestein has patients eliminate anything that could interfere with sleep. The cabinetmaker was told to taper off his use of coffee and pills gradually, to minimize withdrawal symptoms. He did—and his grogginess vanished. It wasn't the first time Regestein had a patient who was suffering uncontrollable fatigue from drinking caffeine.

Six months ago, a woman in her early 30s walked into psychotherapist Jerilyn Ross's office at DC's Ross Center for Anxiety and Related Disorders. The woman suffered from crippling panic attacks, often several a day. Doctors had put her through a battery of tests but found nothing. She was jovial but uneasy—she

*This article appears on pages 25 and 26 of the May 1994 issue of *Washingtonian*.

fidgeted, talked at a fast clip, and gestured nervously. Ross, the center's director, asked her about caffeine.

"She had this thing about iced tea," says Ross. "She would make this huge pot in the morning and another in the afternoon and would just set it on her desk and keep sipping it slowly. She told me she was drinking two gallons a day."

Ross suggested that the woman wean herself from the tea. A month later, she called Ross back. She had been caffeine-free for a week and hadn't had an attack in that time. It was the most dramatic example Ross had seen of caffeine-induced anxiety.

This is the paradox of caffeine. It can make you tired or make you jittery. It can relieve migraines or make them worse. And some of the symptoms of withdrawal—headaches, lethargy, irritability, anxiety—can be much the same as the symptoms of caffeine intoxication. This tangle of contradictions makes it hard to diagnose caffeine-related problems.

"Someone who has anxiety could be overindulging or withdrawing," says Thomas Uhde, until recently a researcher at the National Institute of Mental Health and now chairman of the psychiatry department at Wayne State University, in Detroit. "What makes that even more complicated is that the people who go into withdrawal are often the people who overindulge. So it can get into a vicious cycle. What you should do under those circumstances is stabilize the intake and then gradually taper it down."

Regestein cites a study done among college students in the '60s that found a link between caffeine consumption and morning grogginess. "You can say, sure, sleepy people are drinking coffee," he says. "But it turns out that upon quitting coffee, the morning grogginess clears up. I think with the heavy caffeine users, withdrawal occurs in the night, so they wake up groggy."

Regestein doesn't think that's what was at work in the cabinetmaker's case, though he isn't sure what was. "You can spin a lot of tales, but the fact is that there are vast differences in the nervous systems of different people."

Scientists think they can explain why caffeine can work either way on migraines. One thing caffeine does is constrict blood vessels, a process called vasoconstriction. Both vasoconstriction and vasodilation are involved in migraines. "So depending on when you take the caffeine, you can either relieve the migraine or make it worse," says John Hughes, a psychiatrist at the University of Vermont.

Part of caffeine's appeal is its ability to impart a sense of well-being. But in a study at NIMH, Uhde had patients drink fairly heavy doses—480 milligrams, about what you'd get from five cups of coffee. Several people went on a brief crying jag, he said. " It would last only a few minutes," he says, "but it was very profound."

Does that mean caffeine can cause depression? No one knows for sure, says Hughes. "We know that depressed people drink more coffee, but whether it causes depression we don't know at this point."

It has been shown that caffeine can exacerbate psychotic symptoms in some patients with mental illness.

Caffeine isn't a dangerous drug. It doesn't appear to cause cancer. There are conflicting reports about whether pregnant women can safely drink it, but many experts say using it in moderation is probably okay. In a person unaccustomed to it, caffeine can cause a temporary rise in blood pressure, but people who consume it regularly develop a tolerance. Probably the worst it can do—and this can be serious—is to rob you of calcium, promoting osteoporosis, but one glass of milk a day can offset that effect.

The good side is that repeated studies have confirmed what many people suspect: Caffeine helps them think more clearly and accomplish routine, repetitive tasks with greater efficiency. For certain people, in the right doses, it is pleasantly stimulating.

But not for everyone. Sometimes people have medical problems related to caffeine without realizing it and wind up in a doctor's office complaining of headaches, flu-like symptoms, or stress-related problems. And people with fibrocystic breast disease, palpitations, infertility, or heartburn are often told to curb or cut out caffeine.

Caffeine can interfere with sleep, but some people can drink a cup of strong coffee right before bedtime and nod off with no trouble. Those people, says Uhde, are really hooked. "If someone requires a cup of coffee in order to sleep well, he has a significant dependence until proven otherwise."

The irony about losing sleep is that once you're sleep-deprived, drinking the amount of caffeine you normally do can have a much more powerful impact. In his sleep studies, Uhde has found that healthy people who were deprived of sleep and then took a dose of caffeine that normally wouldn't faze them sometimes experienced panic attacks.

Withdrawing from cigarettes can heighten caffeine's effects, too, according to Hughes. Nicotine makes you metabolize caffeine more quickly. "When people stop smoking, their blood levels of caffeine go up about 50 percent, even though they keep their caffeine intake the same," says Hughes. "Some people think that some of nicotine withdrawal, which includes things like restlessness, difficulty concentrating, anxiety, and trouble sleeping, is actually due to caffeine intoxication. One thing we do for people who quit smoking is tell them to cut back on their caffeine intake. We wouldn't want to tell them to stop it completely, because there would be not only nicotine withdrawal but caffeine withdrawal, too."

People who take birth-control pills eliminate caffeine more slowly, as do women in the latter stages of pregnancy and most people as they age.

Caffeine can hide in the most unexpected places. It's in soft drinks like Sunkist Orange, Mello Yello, and Mountain Dew. It's sometimes in diet pills, extra-strength pain killers, antihistamines, and other over-the-counter and prescription medications. It's also in chocolate, and in significant quantities in some coffee-flavored yogurt.

Teas contain about half as much caffeine as brewed coffee. Though herbal teas often are assumed to be caffeine-free, not all are: Morning Thunder packs a powerful punch.

In studies at Johns Hopkins University, Roland Griffiths has found that as little as 100 milligrams of caffeine spread out over the course of a day can cause dependence in some people. Withdrawal symptoms—like headaches, fatigue, anxiety, depression, nausea, and other flu-like symptoms—usually peak 24 to 48 hours after you quit and completely disappear in the next few days, Griffiths found. But, as is typical with caffeine, there are contradictory reports. Some people complain of sleepiness long after quitting. The cabinetmaker who quit caffeine didn't completely overcome his fatigue for six weeks.

Ten years ago, less than 5 percent of the coffee sold at Starbucks, the coffee-house chain, was decaffeinated. Today the figure is 20 percent.

Psychotherapist Jerilyn Ross thinks people are growing more alert to caffeine's downside. Fifteen years ago, most of her patients hadn't made any connection between caffeine and anxiety; now most have withdrawn on their own before coming to see her.

Ross has found that she, too, has a low caffeine threshold. Five years ago, she was celebrating her birthday at Dominique's. "We were having this wonderful meal. I was with a friend I hadn't seen in a while, and we were talking, talking, talking, catching up. There was a couple at the next table, and somehow we got engaged in each other's conversation, and they weren't finished eating yet, so we ordered dessert and lingered a while. The waiters kept filling my coffee cup, and all of a sudden, here in the middle of this celebration, I had the most whopping panic attack I've ever had. My heart was pounding. I wanted to run out of there. And then it dawned on me: I had gotten caught up in the evening and forgotten to ask for decaf.

"That's the last time I ever had more than one cup of coffee."

The Latest on Coffee?

Don't Worry. Drink Up.*

Jane E. Brody

With coffee bars proliferating from Seattle to Boston, and the specialty coffees they feature promising to turn around a decades-long decline in American coffee consumption, the news about coffee's effects on health is surprisingly good.

A substantial amount of research, including several large studies done in the last few years, has turned up very little solid scientific evidence to indict a moderate intake of coffee or caffeine as a serious or even minor health threat.

"Some of the most serious hazards that were linked to caffeine in the past have not panned out," said Dr. James L. Mills, who studies caffeine's effects on pregnancy at the National Institute of Child Health and Human Development in Bethesda, Md.

After peaking in 1962 at 3.12 cups per person a day, coffee consumption endured a 30-year slide in popularity, finally stabilizing in the mid-1990's around 1.7 cups, according to a survey conducted last winter by the National Coffee Association.

Of course, caffeine is also present in black and green teas and in soft drinks. Eighty percent of Americans consume at least one beverage containing caffeine every day, and among Americans over 18, the per capita consumption of caffeine is about 200 milligrams a day.

Dr. Mills noted that heavy caffeine consumers—those who drink eight or more five-ounce cups of coffee a day—tend to be "very overworked, driven people who are generally not the best health risks."

For the average healthy person, about the most serious charge science can levy against caffeine is that it may be addictive. After 18 to 24 hours, its absence, even in those who consume it moderately, sometimes results in withdrawal symptoms, including severe headaches, fatigue, depression and poor concentration.

---

*This article begins on page C1 and continues on page C6 of the September 13, 1995, late edition of the *New York Times*.

Concerns about the effects of caffeine on pregnancy and fetal development also persist. Despite a score of studies on the relationship between caffeine and a woman's ability to conceive and deliver a full-term, full-size, healthy infant, researchers are still arguing about the reproductive risks of even relatively high doses of caffeine before or during pregnancy. All relevant studies have suffered from one or more methodological limitations that might invalidate their findings, scientists say.

And while moderate consumption—usually defined as two to four five-ounce cups of coffee daily—has thus far received a relatively clean bill of health even in people at high risk for developing heart disease or cancer, new studies have linked heavier daily intakes to heart attacks and bone loss in women. And in men with mild high blood pressure, several recent studies have shown that a significant rise in blood pressure can occur after just two or three cups of coffee, especially if caffeine is consumed before exercising.

Along with these cautionary findings has come encouraging news about caffeine's potential role in weight control. Caffeine raises the rate at which the body burns calories for three or more hours after it is consumed, according to studies of healthy volunteers of normal weight in Denmark. Just 100 milligrams of caffeine—the amount in one cup of coffee or two cans of cola—can raise the metabolic rate by 3 to 4 percent, and larger intakes raise it even higher. If the consumer also exercises, the caloric burn stimulated by caffeine is greater still. But caffeine is no free lunch for dieters because it also effects the release of insulin, causing blood sugar to fall, which induces hunger pangs.

Caffeine's ability to bolster physical performance is well known among professional athletes. A recent study by Dr. Terry Graham and Dr. Lawrence L. Spriet at the University of Guelph in Ontario indicated that even a moderate amount of caffeine—1.5 milligrams per pound of body weight—had a potent exercise-enhancing effect. Caffeine helps to mobilize body fat and make it available as fuel for exercising muscles, allowing them to work longer before they fatigue.

Caffeine, known chemically as 1,3,7-trimethylxanthine, is one of a class of methylxanthine compounds found in 63 plant products, including tea leaves, cocoa beans and coffee beans. Similar to amphetamines but milder in its effects, caffeine stimulates the sympathetic nervous system, which regulates the body's automatic function. As a central nervous system stimulant, it makes people feel more alert, temporarily relieves fatigue and promotes quick thinking. Its contrary effects on blood vessels often render it medically useful: it dilates arteries feeding the heart, increasing blood flow, and constricts arteries in the head, helping to counter migraine headaches.

But caffeine is only one, albeit the best known, of some 500 chemicals in coffee. Indeed, caffeine was recently absolved of at least one of coffee's reputed ill effects—the ability to raise serum cholesterol levels. That drawback, researchers in the Netherlands say, stems not from caffeine but from the oils in coffee beans that are extracted when the grounds are boiled. Those oils are not a problem when coffee is brewed through a paper filter, because the oils are left behind.

Decaffeinated coffee has lately captured a growing body of devotees who spurn caffeine's stimulating effect but still covet coffee's flavor and social attributes. Yet, research sponsored by the National Institutes of Health and directed by Dr. H. Robert Superko while at Stanford University has suggested that decaffeinated coffee is more likely than its caffeine-rich counterpart to raise levels of artery-damaging LDL cholesterol. He says this condition may occur because stronger-flavored coffee beans, known as robusta, are typically used to prepare decaffeinated coffee to compensate for the flavor lost in the decaffeinating process. These same beans are used to prepare instant coffees with and without caffeine. But most brewed coffee containing caffeine is prepared from milder arabica beans. This finding has not yet been confirmed by other studies.

Sorting out the health effects of drinking coffee, with or without caffeine, is complicated by the fact that coffee drinkers are, on the whole, a different breed from drinkers of other beverages, including caffeine-containing tea. At least three large studies conducted here and in Europe have shown that coffee drinking, especially at high levels, is associated with behavior that is linked to serious illnesses, like cigarette smoking.

Furthermore, decaf drinkers are different from those who drink coffee with caffeine. In a study of 2,677 adults by Alan Leviton and Elizabeth N. Allred of Harvard Medical School and Boston Children's Hospital, which was published last year, women who drank only decaffeinated coffee behaved more like women who drank no coffee at all than like women who consumed coffee with caffeine. Decaf drinkers in the study were more likely than other women to take vitamin supplements, eat vegetables in the cabbage family, use seat belts routinely and exercise regularly. The men who drank decaf exclusively typically weighed less and were more likely to consume a low-fat diet and to eat such vegetables.

To determine whether drinking coffee increases the risk of disease, researchers must take into account many "life style" factors, since these factors and not coffee or caffeine could be responsible.

Heart Disease. In studies that have taken other risk factors into account, people who consume fewer than four or five cups of coffee a day seem to incur no added cardiac risk, even if they already have clogged coronary arteries or irregular heart rhythms. Several studies found no drop in blood cholesterol levels when people with or without high cholesterol switched to decaf. But cardiac trouble begins to accrue at five or more five-ounce cups of coffee a day among both smokers and nonsmokers and especially in people with high blood pressure.

Cancer. In 1981, coffee aficionados were momentarily dismayed by a report from Harvard researchers linking coffee (with and without caffeine) to pancreatic cancer, a disease with a very poor prognosis. But at least seven major studies, including one conducted last year in a large retirement community, have failed to find such a link, and five years after the initial scare, the Harvard researchers, after further analysis of their data, retracted their findings.

Likewise for breast cancer and benign fibrocystic breast disease. Despite widespread publicity given to anecdotal findings that linked caffeine and other methylxanthines to symptoms of fibrocystic breast disease, no well-designed studies have confirmed a clear-cut relationship. And in several large studies, including a continuing Harvard-based study of 121,700 nurses, no risk of breast cancer associated with coffee drinking has been found. In fact, among the nurses, coffee drinkers have developed fewer breast cancers than abstainers so far.

A similar inverse relationship was found between heavy coffee consumption and cancers of the colon and rectum in a study of 1,255 cancer cases and 3,883 matched patients with unrelated conditions. Those who consumed five or more cups of coffee a day had a 40 percent lower risk of developing colon cancer, according to a research team headed by Dr. Lynn Rosenberg of the Boston University School of Public Health.

The first link reported between coffee and cancer concerned the bladder. But cigarette smoking, a known cause of bladder cancer, apparently accounted for the relationship (smokers drink more than twice the amount of coffee that nonsmokers do). After analyzing 35 studies of the coffee-bladder cancer relationship, Yale University researchers concluded in 1993 that regular coffee consumption was not a "clinically important" risk factor for bladder cancer in men or women. Soon after, however, another study linked heavy coffee consumption to bladder cancer in nonsmokers. And so the debate continues.

Bone Disease. Caffeine has an undisputed negative effect on calcium metabolism. When exercise levels and smoking are taken into account, women who consume caffeine lose more calcium in their urine and have less dense bones than do nonconsumers, and thus may be more prone to fractures. Indeed, the nurses' study linked caffeine intake to an increased risk of hip fractures but not wrist fractures in postmenopausal women. Among those who consumed the most caffeine (more than 817 milligrams a day), the risk of suffering a hip fracture was nearly three times higher than for those who did not consume caffeine.

But among more moderate coffee consumers, drinking just one glass of milk a day can offset the calcium loss induced by the caffeine in two cups of coffee, a recent study of nearly 1,000 postmenopausal women in southern California showed.

Pregnancy. In 1980, following a study in which pregnant rats that were force-fed the human equivalent of 56 to 87 cups of strong coffee gave birth to pups with missing toes, the Food and Drug Administration warned pregnant women to avoid or at least moderate their consumption of caffeine. Two years later, the agency's concerns were reinforced by a study of 12,000 pregnant women that linked drinking four or more cups of coffee daily to premature birth and low birth weight. But while smoking turned out to be the chief culprit, the agency has yet to ease its warning.

Studies of caffeine and pregnancy continue to produce conflicting results. One study of 2,800 fertile women found no effect of caffeine on their chances of conceiving, while another study of 1,900 women linked drinking more than 300 milligrams of caffeine daily to a delay in conception. A study of more than 7,000 Canadian women linked increasing doses of caffeine to a rising risk of fetal growth retardation, but there was no rise in premature births or low birth weight. And the newest study, published this year by researchers at the University of North Carolina, also failed to document a link between caffeine consumption during pregnancy and pre-term births.

Still, enough research has suggested that caffeine may delay conception, increase the risk of miscarriage and slow fetal growth to prompt many public-health specialists to advise women planning pregnancy, as well as those who are already pregnant, to eliminate caffeine or restrict its consumption to the amount in one or two cups of brewed coffee a day. "Based on the better studies, I don't think caffeine is a problem," said Dr. Mills of the child health institute. "But during pregnancy, you should be cautious about any substance that has metabolic effects."

A simple strategy for your report is to summarize these sources individually and then to present the three summaries, linked with connecting comments if necessary. Writing the summaries should be easy enough, but you also want your report to have unity. Like the readings you have studied in this book, it too should have a unifying idea.

For your report to be unified, you will need to discover a theme that relates to all three sources. Certainly they all concern coffee drinking. But can a single statement be made that would connect all three? To find out, you can start by paraphrasing the main idea of each source as we have done here:

- As coffee drinking has grown trendy, the typical consumer is more likely to be urbane, educated, and health conscious.
- The physiological effects of caffeine, though they vary from one individual to another, are often unpleasant if not dangerous.
- Recent medical research challenges earlier findings that link caffeine consumption to a variety of serious diseases.

Does any theme present itself here? Certainly we can make some observations about these three ideas:

- The sophisticated clientele that has popularized gourmet coffee includes many health-conscious consumers.
- There is apparently some cause for concern about the physiological effects of caffeine.
- Many of the presumed effects of caffeine consumption have been false or exaggerated.

From these observations, you may discern a central idea, one that can provide a unifying theme for your report. For example, you might focus a paper on this theme: *The sophisticated, health-conscious consumers who have popularized gourmet coffee must consider conflicting evidence about the effects of caffeine.*

Writing the report now becomes easier. You can begin with two or three sentences introducing the topic, state your central idea, then follow it with summaries of the three sources, as in the essay that follows. Notice too that these sources of information are acknowledged both by notes (within parentheses) and in a list of works cited at the end of the report. (Parenthetical notes and lists of works cited are explained at the end of this chapter.)

To Satisfy a Craving for French Roast:

Following Fashion at the Expense of Fitness?

The past year has brought three new coffee bars to

Lexington. Like their fashionable counterparts in other

cities, they serve an array of exotic brews to a clientele of

urbane patrons who abhor cigarette smoke, curtail their

intake of fat, and exercise rigorously. Determined to avoid

so many other health risks, these coffee drinkers confront a

perplexing dilemma. The sophisticated, health-conscious

consumers who have popularized gourmet coffee must consider

conflicting evidence about the effects of caffeine.

Once an unpretentious beverage associated with blue-

collar diners and rural cafés, coffee is now popular among a more elite social class. Unlike their less discriminating predecessors, these new coffee drinkers demand a variety of fresh-ground coffees and savor such trendy derivatives as espresso, cappuccino, and latté. One reason for the appeal of these drinks is the belief that, compared to other forms of self-indulgence, coffee consumption is relatively safe, if not harmless (Schapiro 58-60).

Not all scientists, however, accept that appraisal. In recent years, caffeine addiction has been linked with a number of ailments and discomforts. But what complicates the findings of research is that people respond differently to caffeine, and often the effects of addiction are not easy to distinguish from those of withdrawal. Nevertheless, recent studies have raised enough concern to increase the popularity of decaffeinated drinks (Dickey 25-26).

Perhaps the best news for inveterate coffee drinkers is that studies that discourage caffeine comsumption may have been scientifically flawed. Some have overlooked other factors (like correlations between coffee consumption and addiction to other substances or compulsive personality traits). Furthermore, until recently, scientists have been less eager to investigate the possible benefits of caffeine. On the whole, there is good reason to think that health risks once attributed to coffee drinking have been exaggerated (Brody C1, C6).

Trends come and go, and public tastes often change rapidly. However, the long-standing tradition of coffee drinking in the United States, coupled with our persistent concerns about health and fitness, almost guarantees that the dangers and possible benefits of caffeine will be a subject of future study and debate.

Works Cited

Brody, Jane E. "The Latest on Coffee? Don't Worry. Drink

Up." <u>New York Times</u> 13 Sept. 1995, late ed: C1+.

Dickey, Marilyn. "Grounds for Concern: Caffeine Works--It

Really Can Pick You Up and Make You More Alert. But It Also

Can Cause Trouble." <u>Washingtonian</u> May 1994: 25-26.

Schapiro, Mark. "Muddy Waters: The Lore, the Lure, the

Lowdown on America's Favorite Addiction." <u>Utne Reader</u>

Nov./Dec. 1994: 58-65.

The result is a brief but effective synthesis of the three sources. There are several things to note about the writing of this paper. First, the report ends with a paragraph that draws conclusions; it is, in effect, an extension of the main idea, which is stated in the opening paragraph. Second, the report is divided into several paragraphs: one for the introduction, one for the conclusion, and one for each summary. Although this report could have been written as a single paragraph, the indentations help the reader, each one signaling a new topic. On the other hand, if the writer had used more sources or longer sources or had taken more information from each article, additional paragraphs might have been appropriate.

There are, of course, other ways of synthesizing these sources. For example, a writer might have dealt with the emotional and behavioral effects attributed to caffeine in the third paragraph and with the possible links between coffee drinking and physiological diseases in the fourth paragraph. (Each paragraph would have drawn information from both Brody and Dickey.)

Regardless of how such a report is structured, it is called *objective* because it presents information from sources without overtly expressing any opinions of the writer who is synthesizing them. (In Chapter 7, we consider subjective, critical reporting, in which the writer analyzes and evaluates sources.) Nevertheless, objectivity is relative. Notice, for example, that the writer has placed a bit more emphasis on the health consciousness of the "new" coffee drinkers than the sources themselves do. That emphasis may reflect his personal history and experience or recent observations—things that readers bring to bear on almost any text. Suppose, for a moment, that the same three sources had been read by someone very different from this particular writer—a business major or amateur investor, a medical researcher, or a person whose religion forbids the use of all stimulants. An objective report by the business major might focus on how recent research into caffeine addiction might influence investment in certain stocks or in coffee futures. The medical researcher might infer, objectively, that the press is unduly influenced by popular trends when it reports on scientific topics. The reader who avoids coffee for religious reasons would probably find Brody's article less encouraging. The point is that each of these readers and, indeed, all readers unavoidably—and often unconsciously—draw connections among the sources they read and other sources or texts they have encountered previously.

In short, no synthesis is ever entirely objective. Nor is it ever an entirely finished or complete report on a topic. Consider, for example, how the writer of the foregoing synthesis might change his approach after reading the following article as a fourth source.

Imperialism, Sexism, Rapacious Capitalism, and Mindless Conformity!
Four Steaming, Frothing Rants against the New Coffee Chic*
Helen Cordes

Don't get me wrong. I love the stuff. If it wasn't for the sad fact that for me, coffee equals insomnia, I'd swig a flagon of dark, creamy caffeine-crammed brew whenever I dang well felt like it. But I can't. So here's why you shouldn't either.

1. The trendmeisters confirm what I've observed in oh-so-cute coffee bars from Boulder to Berkeley, from Minneapolis to Austin: Simply by their presence at this ultrahip spot, patrons are proclaiming their—as trend queen Faith Popcorn puts it—"individuality." Yes indeedy, buying a three-dollar cup of multilayered coffee makes them *very different* from those Sanka-swilling wage slaves trudging by the café's picture windows. Mm-hmmm. With both independent and chain coffee bars breeding like roaches in every mall and small town, these iconoclastic café-goers are marching to marketers' tunes like lemmings to latté. Here's my advice: Coffee doesn't make you hip, *you* do. Read some good books and magazines, exercise some independent thinking, laugh more, talk to people. They'll think you're cool.

2. Coffee is a capitalist tool. Don't believe me? Believe the *New York Times*—they ought to know.

The very day I was writing this, the business pages carried a story about the Silicon Valley bean wars. It seems that high-tech companies are one-upping each other by replacing the office Bunnomatics with sleek espresso and cappuccino makers—often putting machines in each poobah's office—and trading in Maxwell House for 12-bucks-a-pound designer blends. While the *Times,* of course, chalks this up to the need for companies to be able to compete for employees and "build morale," a revealing quote from a software CEO tells the rest of the story: "We want a work environment that both attracts the best engineers and is conducive to productivity."

There you go. Is it mere coincidence that ever since offices were invented, they've come with coffeemakers attached? Those Mr. Coffees are no thoughtful worker perk; they're sugar-coated productivity-prodding poison machines. So now those ever-so concerned employers are offering high-octane work fuel—and the treadmills in our tiny straw-lined cages whir even faster. I'm warning you, there's a capitalist conspiracy here. Workers of the world: Stop sipping! If you're getting a regular buzz on so you can work harder, why? Besides, having looked at coffee clouds from both sides now, I'm convinced that that burst of caffeine energy is inevitably paired with an energy bogdown later and, furthermore, that low- or no-caffeine productivity is often superior overall to the big buzz.

3. If you don't buy that conspiracy, try this one: Why was the only other recent era of high coffee consumption the 1950s?

---

*This article appears on pages 68 and 69 of the November–December issue of *Utne Reader.*

Let's see, the '50s: According to history—or sitcom reruns—the '50s were when Dad tanked up first thing in the morning with a pot of java, which set him on his jaunty way to a job that siphoned away his lifeblood in exchange for lifelong employment, a two-car garage, and Mom's charge card. In between shopping and cleaning, Mom and other neighborhood gals coffee-klatched, assuring one another that a life spent servicing hubby, kids, and house, plus those charge cards, made them the luckiest women in the world.

And now the '90s. According to increasingly insistent "expert" voices, the United States could be a world leader again if more workers had a work ethic like they used to, and women stayed home with the kids (who, according to them, have all become juvenile delinquents with no work ethic at all because Mom works) like they used to.

The two decades' common factor: increased caffeine intake. So go ahead—sit in your boho joe hole, eyeballing that shaved-head babe, and pretend you are some kind of anti-establishmentarian. Next thing you know, you're some neo version of Updike's Rabbit, putting the moves on a latter-day June Cleaver.

4. We all know the characteristics of a really good caffeine buzz. Coffee makes us feel smarter, more articulate, more ambitious, and more organized. And at least until the buzz wears off and needs reviving—more in control. So what does it mean that more people are drinking more and stronger coffee? Not to make light of real issues and anxieties, but should we be covering up our problems with a whitewash of black gold? Prozac's a stimulant, too, you know—does anybody else see the correlation between the increasingly inappropriate use of Prozac and the demands for more and stronger coffee? A person who is really in control is in control of coffee. A stimulant should not determine the success of your days or your life.

Now I know that you're thinking I'm a judgmental twit. Guilty as charged. And I'm not suggesting that coffee is best banished—remember, I'm an addict too, even if my fix is limited to one prissy little part-decaf cup per morning. But looking deep into the dregs of my addiction has made me think about ways coffee could be an occasional pleasure rather than a crutch, a pretension, or an imperialist tool.

If the writer who synthesized the first three sources considered this article, he might now draw a different conclusion. For example, he might connect his sources with a thesis like this: "The current resurgence in coffee drinking raises some complex and controversial medical and economic issues."

Writing a Brief Summary Report   EXERCISE

Write a report synthesizing information found in the following two sources and in "Against All Odds" by Ron Suskind, the reading that concludes Chapter 5 (pages 147–54). Follow this procedure:

a. Read each source (including Suskind's) with a pencil, underlining important information.

b. Write a one-sentence summary of each source's main idea.

c. Consider whether a theme links these three articles. If so, state this theme in a sentence that can serve as the thesis statement for your report.

d. Write the report. Begin with your thesis statement, follow it with three summaries (in whichever order you feel is most appropriate) linked with transitional phrases if necessary, and end with a general concluding statement. For now you can omit parenthetical notes and a list of works cited, both of which are discussed later in this chapter.

The Ghetto Preppies
Giving Kids "A Better Chance" Is Not So Easy*
Marcus Mabry

Growing up on the South Side of Chicago, Walter Clair had to duck bullets and gangs to get to school. He was one of eight children and his mother was on welfare. But he was intelligent—and lucky. A relative heard about a program called A Better Chance, Inc., that sent smart inner-city kids to private schools, and submitted Walter's application. In short order, the exclusive St. Mark's School, in Southborough, Mass., accepted him for the fall of 1969. After four years, he moved on to Harvard, earning three degrees including his M.D. Today, he is a cardiologist at Duke University Medical Center. He says he could not have done it without A Better Chance: "It's one of those quiet programs that makes a difference. It ranks right up there with Head Start."

Not all ABC stories have such happy endings. In 1976, Tony Ashby left the South Bronx for the Groton School in Massachusetts. He did well there, and he, too, went on to Harvard. But, along the way, things fell apart: Ashby lost his drive to "get out" of the ghetto. Since he finished Harvard in 1986 he has bounced from job to job. He lived in a cramped tenement in Harlem until his landlord recently kicked him out.

Founded in 1963 by a group of Ivy League administrators and prep-school head-masters, ABC epitomized the idealism of the times: by sending poor kids to elite private schools, they would adopt the mannerisms and mind-sets of their white preppie peers and thus be lifted from poverty. It hasn't always worked out that way. Making the transition from one world to the other was difficult for most students, impossible for some. The most famous failure was Edmund Perry, the Exeter alumnus who was killed in 1985 while allegedly mugging an undercover New York City policeman.

The program has prospered—growing and spawning imitators. Wealthy benefactors from Manhattan's Perfumed Stockade to the Hollywood Hills have embraced whole classrooms of inner-city kids, guaranteeing them college educations if only they'll finish high school. But like ABC before them, they've found that helping kids to succeed is more complicated than giving well-intentioned grants. Poor kids—like rich kids—need guidance; they need adults who can muffle their culture shocks and hear their frustrations. The help can take many forms—counselors, summer-long retreats, an autumn walk in the woods—but it's as essential as the tuition check itself. Poor kids—like privileged kids—need a chance to fail, a break from being the best little person their neighborhood ever produced. Poor kids—like rich kids—need space to be themselves; the process of absorbing the refined values of elite prep schools and colleges must not come at the cost of feverish self-hatred. And rich benefactors must understand that some kids are still going to fail.

*This article begins on pages 44 and 45 and continues on page 48 of the November 4, 1991, issue of *Newsweek*.

Reaching Out. To its enduring credit, ABC made mistakes and learned from them. By the mid-'70s, the program was reaching out to find kids from ever more abject circumstances. Those youngsters needed the most support, but as funding dried up ABC had to abandon its summer-long residential pre-prep program. As a result, admittees lacked mentors like Clair's, and more kids had trouble in school. Unable to reinstitute the summer orientation, ABC adjusted its recruiting, shifting toward kids from lower-middle-class and poor but stable families.

Despite the changes, ABC administrators insist that the program's goal remains the same. "Sometimes people come to us who can afford to send their children to school," says Judith Griffin, president of ABC. "But we look in the Bronx and on the South Side of Chicago. We look for these kids and there they are and they are poor." Griffin says that a third of ABC children still come from welfare families. This year about 1,100 students are scattered among 160 schools. More than two thirds are African-American; most of the rest are Latino.

Over the years, more than 7,000 students have graduated from ABC. *Newsweek* has chosen three—Clair ('74), Ashby ('81) and Lisa Partin ('89)—to illustrate ABC's slow and sometimes painful evolution and the inevitable collision of idealism with the realities of race and class:

The Winner. During his first year at St. Mark's, Clair received some rude lessons in the peculiar code of the prep school. He was relieved to hear that at some meals he could ditch his coat and tie for "casual" clothes. He made the mistake of wearing his crisp new blue jeans, freshly pressed white T shirt and gleaming white Converse All-Stars sneakers to his first casual meal; he was turned away by a teacher. No jeans, even fresh ones, in the dining hall. Meanwhile, he recalls, his shabby genteel classmates were free to wear "Topsiders so ragged that they had to be held together by hockey tape, tennis shirts with holes and corduroy pants so worn that the seat was smooth."

Clair may have been unprepared for the cultural niceties of prep life, but he learned more important lessons at ABC's summer-orientation program before he was sent off to St. Mark's. For six weeks at beautiful Williams College, ABC admittees got a dose of discipline; they ate, slept, studied and played sports on a strict schedule. The ABC mentors instilled a sense of pride in Clair. "They reminded us that we were special kids and that any individual failure was a failure of the program," he says. "That was the feeling that kept me going at St. Mark's."

His first year was harrowing academically. He almost failed English. And even in classes where he did well, he encountered prejudice. Once, he yawned in Latin class without covering his mouth: "The teacher slapped me. He said, 'That's why we bring you kids here, to teach you some manners.'" Still, Clair says the experience was positive. Despite low faculty expectations of African-American kids, his grades improved. And, through sports and extracurricular activities he formed strong friendships. He says, "As I adjusted to St. Mark's socially and did well academically, people viewed me as another Anglo-American who just had black skin."

That is, until it came time to apply to college. A classmate dubbed senior year "the year of the nigger," for the preference the black kids would get in college admissions. Most of his St. Mark's classmates assumed that "their social standing meant they would never have to compete with [blacks]," says Clair. "It was only when our blackness became an advantage that it was a problem. Even living as intimately as one could, as the stakes got higher, people's intolerance and their own feelings of being threatened got harder to hide. I saw it in college and again in medical school."

Clair is grateful for his St. Mark's education, and he says he might even send his own sons, ages 4 and 8, there someday. But he's a realist. Whatever advantages their school ties give them, the disadvantage of having two black parents in America "will have a larger influence on their lives."

The Drifter. The first thing Tony Ashby noticed when he stepped onto the Groton campus was the sprawling playing fields. The campus was awash in deep greens late that New England summer; the concrete of the South Bronx was far away. The fields were the focal point of Ashby's years at Groton; he played football, lacrosse and basketball. The plaques in the field house that list team captains for football and lacrosse will "forever bear my name," he says proudly. "[Groton] challenged me to be my best." Unfortunately, for Ashby, prep school turned out to be preparation for nothing so much as prep school. The larger world, as he would find, did not play by the rules he learned at Groton.

Ashby and other ABC students of his time weren't sure if they were storming the barricades of the privileged or were being co-opted by the white establishment. ABC itself did little to help Ashby sort through his conflicts; during his five years at Groton, he says he never met an ABC representative. "ABC just puts you there and forgets you," he said.

But if ABC stumbled—grants were disappearing even as kids admitted into the program came from ever more difficult backgrounds—Groton became a haven. If anything, the school was perhaps too protective, too paternalistic, too good at making Ashby feel at home. "At Groton we were taught fair play," he says. When he got to Harvard "it was kill the next guy at any cost." To make things worse, Harvard was racially divided as well: blacks and whites usually did not mix. Ashby felt a tension between his allegiance to African-American peers and his comfort with his largely white group of friends. That tension finally drove him from many of his white friends after graduation. "Living with white people got to be too much after 10 years," he says. Ashby drifted between New York and Boston and worked as, among other things, a teacher, a paralegal and a youth counselor.

In his last interview, he sat in his cramped Harlem apartment and spoke with some defiance and some self-pity. "The one thing that no one can take away from me is my years at Groton," he said. "Groton gave me a lot of cultural refinement." When his landlord kicked him out, he left no forwarding address.

The New Ideal. Beginning in 1983, Lisa Partin commuted daily from Harlem to The Spence School on Manhattan's Upper East Side. She was from a stable, two-parent, working-class household. "There was always an emphasis on education in my house," she says. "My experience is very different from most kids' in Harlem because of my parents." For ABC, Partin was an ideal candidate.

Not only had ABC changed by the 1980s, but attitudes at prep school had changed as well. "My best friends were white and we're still in touch," she says. By the '80s blacks were a part of most prep schools. Few people questioned their qualifications to be there: most teachers searched for ways to make the curriculum and the faculty more inclusive. In fact, class, not race, was the most important difference for Partin. After vacation "girls came back from Europe and I had only gone to Florida," she says. The irony, she says, is that "a lot of them envied me. They were raised by nannies and they envied me for my parents."

After Spence, Partin went to Harvard. "My close friends were almost all black. We had a lot more in common, the parties we went to, the music we liked. We all went to the same place to get our hair done," she says. Still, she got along better with whites than some other blacks did, thanks to her prep-school experience. "I couldn't imagine going in as a (black) freshman and having to adapt." She earned her bachelor's degree in three years and then joined the Bank of Boston as a management trainee. Along the way, she has run into the other "smart girls" from her Harlem junior-high-school class. "During an internship at an investment bank in New York I ran into a girlfriend who competed with me for grades: she was a secretary there. Another is a cashier and another one has a baby. The only difference is that I was given a chance."

Returning Formal Education to the Family

Experiencing the Alternative*

Omonike Weusi-Puryear and Muata Weusi-Puryear

We started our parental adventure by choosing natural childbirth, followed by breast-feeding, with a deep concern for our children's health care. We avoided the negative aspects of our surroundings and turned toward the positive aspects of our African heritage. The decision to teach our children at home came as a normal development of our parental style. In contrast, we saw our peers, in reaction to the public and private school environment, spend more effort to unteach and reteach their children than it would have taken them to do the entire job themselves. We concluded that we could do a better job of educating our children than any local public or private school system could do.

As parents, we were concerned for our children's physical well-being, their emotional, social, and intellectual development. In traditional African culture the extended family and community taught children the social, intellectual, and work skills that were needed to perpetuate the culture. This model seemed to us to be a sound one. The problem for us, however, was how to raise African-American children who would perpetuate the ideals of our family while living in a country dominated by a different culture.

It seemed unrealistic to expect the dominant culture to teach the values we prized. For example, the dominant culture favors competition over cooperation as the general way in which people should interact. We, however, value the dynamics of cooperation, especially within the family.

Without discussion, we independently concluded that "cultural transmission" was as important a concern in education as "the three R's." We envisioned that the new Weusi-Puryears would be proud Black people capable of receiving the cultural baton, carrying it forward, and then passing it on to the next generation.

In January 1977 we agreed upon the following guidelines for our children's education. Education should produce young people who:

1. understand, accept, and practice the Nguzo Saba
2. accept the African concept of family
3. have knowledge and pride in the history of Black people, their family, and themselves
4. understand their physical, cultural, political, and social environment
5. understand the world's development (physical, cultural, political, biological, and social)
6. exhibit good communication skills (i.e. can read, write, speak, listen, observe, and act effectively)
7. have arithmetical and algebraic skills and knowledge of science and scientific methods
8. have knowledge and appreciation of folk arts, and have skill in African arts
9. have practical skills in farming, animal husbandry, carpentry, plumbing, domestic science, weaving, camping, hunting, fishing, and preventive medicine
10. have reached a healthy level of physical development and have demonstrable skills in the martial arts
11. have acceptable social graces (including respect for elders)
12. have knowledge about nutrition and have the ability to apply nutritional information on a day-to-day basis

*This essay appears on pages 228–32 of the book *Black Male Adolescents: Parenting and Education in Community Context,* edited by Benjamin Bowser and published in Lanham, Maryland, by University Press of America in 1991.

Schooling was sometimes very informal, but became more formal as the children grew older. There were no dress codes; in the beginning, instruction was conducted at the breakfast table in pajamas. School was an integral part of the parent/child interaction. It was continuous: it started with each son's naming day ceremony and continued without breaks until his manhood ceremony. There were no summer vacations from schooling, but the seasonal changes did result in major activity changes. Soccer lessons, music lessons, Tai Chi lessons, tennis lessons, swimming lessons, among others, were conducted by nonparent teachers but were considered a part of growing up (learning to be an adult).

One of the advantages we had was that we started from scratch. We were in control before a peer group could establish negative norms. We did not have to unteach —that is, change attitudes or correct statements learned in another educational system. Our children played most with the children of our (culturally) Black friends.

The success of teaching our children at home can be attributed to planning, organizing, scheduling, and following the plan/schedule as consistently as common sense allowed. We tried always to keep in mind our philosophy (or the reasons why we were teaching our children at home) and an appreciation for each child's individuality. Our success is also due in part to our decision to forgo the luxuries of a two-income household so Omonike could apply her teaching/management skills full-time to the education of our children.

A typical school day started with breakfast at 7:00 a.m. The family sat at the table with a wholesome meal of hot, whole grains and fruit or vegetables and homemade whole-grain bread. Breakfast was a time to "chat" before school started.

The boys cleared the table after breakfast, transforming it into the teacher's assignment desk. Each child in turn met with Omonike to go over the assignments he had done the previous day. Meanwhile, his brothers worked on assignments in the classroom, a room specifically set aside for school work. Later the children developed a degree of independence and could successfully anticipate assignments. This gave them a sense of control that aided in their enthusiasm for education. At mid-morning there was usually a break for a snack. Lunch was at noon followed by recreation. Sometime between 1:00 p.m. and 3:00 p.m. each child had from sixty to ninety minutes to lead a discussion of his written work and/or to do some oral reading.

The local public libraries became important adjuncts to the home education process. When the boys were too young to catch the bus to the library, we chauffeured them two or three times per month. We brought home dozens of books at a time. We censored their reading. We would pick some "must read" books. They would pick many "would like to read" books. Before we went to the checkout desk, a parent would give a "yes" or "no" judgment to each of the "would like to read" pile. Books about Black people, social studies, science, science fiction, literature, crafts, cookbooks, riddles, and magic usually got a "yes" judgment. By the time they could catch the bus by themselves, adult censorship was no longer needed.

Public television programs were a vital part of the curriculum. "Sesame Street," "3-2-1 Contact," "Reading Rainbow," "Square One," "Cover to Cover," "Vegetable Soup," and "Newton's Apple" were among the "educational" programs they watched. Other programs received the same censorship that their choice of library books received. When they were young, the television set was placed on a special shelf that was hung from the ceiling, so only an adult could control it. Sex, violence, and most cartoons shows were censored.

Because of Muata's work (educational computer software), we always had either a computer or a remote computer terminal in the house. The boys early learned to use computer programs and enjoyed learning how to program in the LOGO and BASIC languages.

The recreational facilities of our city and county—tennis, swimming, and parks— were used to provide the physical aspects of their education. Vacations were also a part of the learning process. A geography lesson caused the family to tour the U.S.A. by train to various Black American historical sites. The trip also gave us a chance to show the children the extent of our family in the U.S.A.

We felt the boys needed positive social interaction with their peers. Therefore, Omonike helped organize a family support group that had activities for adults and children. The group, along with the children, met once a month and usually planned several outings for the children and several family activities. Children's activities included a chess workshop, roller skating parties, a computer workshop, and camping trips. There were many family picnics. Museum visits, nature preserves, book readings by noted Black writers and concerts were among the enrichment activities for our sons.

We were fortunate to be living in a state in which the laws allowed for private tutoring as an alternative to public education. We expected (and were prepared for) state inspections of our activities. We keep good records but were never called upon to justify what we did. Often we used surplus texts and educational materials from public schools. We can imagine how much more difficult it would have been if we had been in constant battle with local school authorities.

WRITING AN OBJECTIVE REPORT ON SOURCES

Sometimes you are asked to report not just on a particular topic (that is, on the information *in* your sources), but on the sources themselves. Such a research task can be approached in much the same way as the previously described summary report. The major difference is that a report on sources refers specifically to these sources by name. It says, in effect, "Source A says this; Source B says this; Source C says this. . . . " A report on sources can be subjective (presenting your own analysis and opinions of them), but for now we will consider just the objective report. What follows is an example.

Suppose that you have been asked to report on two editorials that debate the desirability of meritocracy, the distribution of wealth and power on the basis of intelligence and achievement. Since you will be presenting the opinions of two different writers, rather than your own views, it is important that you refer specifically to your sources in the essay.

Before reading the following editorials, examine their titles, which clearly indicate that one writer views meritocracy as a threat to democratic ideals and that the other writer does not. Next, as you begin reading each essay, see how far you have to get into it before you find a statement of the author's position. Finally, read the articles with a pencil, searching for important information and opinions.

The Curse of the Merit Class
America's Ruling Caste Is Bad News for the Country*
Nicholas Lemann

We've gotten used to the idea that when Japanese officials get up to tell us what's wrong with American culture, we're going to be treated to an exercise in factory-worker bashing. So it was refreshing, in a way, when Prime Minister Kiichi

*This article begins on page B1 of the February 9, 1992, issue of the *Washington Post*.

Miyazawa decided the other day to lecture about the shortcomings of the people at the *top* of our society. Miyazawa charged that American college graduates take jobs on Wall Street rather than running factories, "with the result," said Japan's prime minister, "that the number of engineers who produce goods has gone down quickly."

This is perfectly true, and it's only one aspect of a much larger change in this country: the steady rise to dominance, since World War II, of a group that might be called the Meritocratic Upper Class.

Today, the Meritocratic Upper Class is a distinctive group with its own values and way of life—perhaps not as fully articulated, yet, as those of what E. Digby Baltzell once identified as the Protestant Establishment, but the Meritocratic Upper Class is still quite new. . . .

The Meritocratic Upper Class is probably somewhat larger than the Protestant Establishment was. Its members live in metropolitan areas, particularly on the East and West coasts. (Yuppies, if they are literally young urban *professionals* rather than just affluent city dwellers, would be a subset of the Meritocratic Upper Class, most of whose members are former yuppies who have become suburban and middle-aged.) They marry within the class—Baltzell is right when he says that the dean of admissions is the new marriage broker—and usually form two-career couples. They work as what Robert Reich calls "symbolic analysts"—as lawyers, doctors, investment bankers, management consultants, professors, and, increasingly, in the fields of journalism, entertainment and information processing.

Members of the Meritocratic Upper Class have a distinctive taste in clothing, cars, architecture, books, movies and food. These tastes change regularly, but as a general rule, meritocrats prefer things that can be described with words like "authentic" or "understated" or "quality" or "old," so long as they aren't seedy; they also have a weakness for well-designed high-tech stuff.

They make a lot of money but don't accumulate "fortunes" in the manner of members of the Protestant Establishment in its great days. Partly for this reason, and partly because they've had to run a gauntlet to get where they are, meritocrats tend to feel somewhat aggrieved. For example, they often complain about "stress" and feel that they don't live as well as they deserve to and that their taxes are too high.

Meanwhile, as Reich has observed, many members of the Meritocratic Upper Class have engineered an Ayn Randian exodus from any involvement with the public sector through the use of security guards, private schools and Federal Express. They don't serve in the military. Their taxes have been cut while almost everyone else's have gone up. And while they can't be absolutely certain of passing on their status and isolation to their children, their focus in childrearing is trying to maximize the odds of their kids' success by stressing education and the development of the psychological tools necessary for high achievement. . . .

In favor of the Meritocratic Upper Class, it can be said that it is not nearly as prejudiced and cosseted as the Protestant Establishment was. Its social life is carried out in restaurants rather than private clubs (and to the extent that private clubs are still important, they're the more meritocratic ones, like the Century in New York and the Cosmos in Washington); some of its children go to public schools (though only in the suburbs, and even there, the number is decreasing); and it isn't mono-ethnic. Access to it is probably more open than access to the Protestant Establishment was, and its children's ultimate place in life is determined at birth to a lesser extent.

On the other hand, at this fairly early point in its history, the Meritocratic Upper Class is more Darwinian, more convinced of its own superiority, than the Protestant Establishment was—the meritocrats made it by running the educational gauntlet and therefore qualify as self-made, don't they? Also, the Merito-cratic Upper Class, already fairly isolated from the rest of the country, is becoming more so. Because of their taste in way of life, its members have very little spare time or money. All this breeds a lack of familiarity, empathy, concern and respon-sibility with respect to everybody else.

With any established upper class—especially if it becomes a caste—there is a danger that it will use its power to protect those aspects of the society from which it derives its position. To the extent that the Meritocratic Upper Class really does replenish its ranks by seeking out the talented from every nook and cranny of the country and bringing them together in the best universities, it then substantially wastes the talent by channeling it so heavily into the professions. In America today, this means we keep an excessive share of our resources tied up in the legal, medical and financial worlds, while business and government wither.

There is a temptation to regard the reforming of the Meritocratic Upper Class as a silly project—isn't reform supposed to be directed at solving people's prob-lems, rather than modifying the career paths of people whose lives are pretty cushy? But even those who don't believe there should be a coherent, quasi-hered-itary upper class of any kind (let alone one that absorbs reformist energy) should realize that rectifying the shortcomings of the Meritocratic Upper Class is a noble cause, since to do so would be to make the Meritocratic Upper Class less coherent and less quasi-hereditary.

Its isolation is an easy problem to address, at least partially; it could be done by instituting compulsory national service. The problem of restricted access to the class could be solved in part by trying hard to find ways to make big personnel decisions later in life and on the basis of performance rather than credentials.

Lifer and Talent venues like the military, the corporate world, Hollywood and Silicon Valley tend to have more varied leadership groups than the meritocrati-cally controlled professions, because they don't have to decide who makes it and who doesn't before the age of 30, when inherited advantages are at the peak of their potency.

If we can move the professions in this direction, it will help solve the Merito-cratic Upper Class's economic productivity problem, too: If a six-figure income were no longer virtually assured for everyone who enters an elite law school or medical school and became instead merely a possibility, we'd stop seeing more than half the graduates of our best colleges becoming doctors and lawyers.

All this would certainly help stave off the Meritocratic Upper Class's metamor-phosis into a caste—and it might even, dream of dreams, broaden access so much that the country would be led by an ever-changing group of people who were not members of a discernible class, or establishment, at all.

America the Open

Faddish Attacks on the Meritocracy Are Nuts*

Robert J. Samuelson

If the Founding Fathers ever envisioned an ideal social order, it was surely a meritocracy: a system under which people succeed mainly on the basis of ability and effort. We are probably closer to that ideal now than ever before. More Ameri-cans go further in school, and our best colleges and universities are more open to

*This article appears on page 48 of the July 31, 1995, issue of *Newsweek*.

students of all backgrounds. The executive ranks of business have been similarly, if less decisively, democratized. And yet, the meritocracy is now under furious intellectual assault.

The indictment, crudely, is that we are creating a caste society unfairly dominated by upscale snobs. Richer than other Americans, they are increasingly insulated from popular beliefs and tastes (so it's said). Worse, they perpetuate their position by sending their children to elite private universities that are gateways to the best jobs. In a book a few years ago, Labor Secretary Robert Reich called the new upper tier "symbolic analysts." Charles Murray and the late Richard Herrnstein termed it "the cognitive elite" in *The Bell Curve*. And Michael Lind calls it "the overclass" in his book *The Next American Nation*.

As with most stereotypes, this one contains some truth. Managers and professionals—the core of this new class—have exploded. Since 1940 the labor force has slightly more than doubled to 119 million in 1993. Meanwhile, managers quadrupled (from 3.8 million to 15.4 million) and engineers quintupled (from 300,000 to 1.7 million); doctors and lawyers expanded sharply (lawyers went from 182,000 to 777,000 and doctors from 168,000 to 605,000). With more managers and professionals, they can be treated as a cohesive class that can be analyzed, criticized or satirized.

It's a setup. We don't live in a classless society (and never will), but we do live in an enormously fluid one. That is the central point that all these analyses miss or minimize. The meritocracy is no monolith. It has its own cultural, economic and political fissures (doctors vs. lawyers on malpractice, for example). And the success of the people at the top does not cause the poverty of the people at the bottom. If elite universities didn't produce successful graduates, you'd wonder: why not? They do. But if a prestige degree was the only path to advancement, you'd worry: is America a closed society? It isn't.

One report in the mid-1980s on 2,729 top executives at 208 major corporations found that 17 percent of them didn't go to college or dropped out; an additional 28 percent had bachelor's degrees from nonprestige schools. At *Newsweek*, Editor Maynard Parker graduated from Stanford; but his boss, Editor-in-Chief and President Richard Smith, went to Albion College. Jack Welch and John Smith, the heads of General Electric and General Motors, both graduated from the University of Massachusetts.

I am not denying the obvious. In life, it helps to come from a high-income, well-educated family and to go to a well-known college. But the image of a pampered elite that can easily program its own future is vastly overdrawn. I graduated from Harvard; my father had no college degree. The odds that any of my three children will go to Harvard—assuming they want to—are low; the chances of all of them going are zero. Indeed, elite colleges have become less accommodating of alumni. As late as 1961, almost a quarter of Yale freshmen were sons of Yale College graduates. In 1994, only 9 percent were.

In America, the paths to fame and fortune (and even contentment) are many and ever changing. Two of the nation's most powerful men today, Bill Gates and Rush Limbaugh, are college dropouts. People have different talents, ambitions, drives and luck. Brothers and sisters pursue different life goals with varying success. Nor have those with higher incomes been entirely sheltered from economic upheaval. Managers and professionals have suffered from "downsizing." By one government study, job security (though still considerable) eroded as much in the 1980s for college as for high-school graduates.

It is precisely the realization, among better-educated and higher-income Americans, that they cannot fully guarantee their own futures—let alone their children's—that has raised society's audible anxiety. Down the economic ladder, people have always faced possible layoffs and interrupted incomes. Hardly anyone loudly complained. Upscale society imagined itself immune to these possible upsets, and the recognition that this is an illusion has triggered outcries. But change and insecurity define both a competitive economy and a meritocracy.

Our new class theorists downplay this endless turbulence and, in the process, forget history. In a recent book, the late Robert Christopher described the "de-WASPing of America's power elite"—that is, the decline of the stranglehold of white, Anglo-Saxon Protestants on our major business and cultural institutions. Wrote Christopher:

> When I left to enter the Army in late 1942, my hometown of New Haven, Connecticut was a place where marriage between Irish and Italian Americans [still raised] eyebrows on both sides, where social intercourse between WASPs and Italian or Jewish Americans was still minimal and generally awkward, and where no one of Polish or Greek heritage could sensibly hope ever to win the presidency of a local bank or brokerage house.

The social barriers of Christopher's youth have been battered by intermarriage, more education and new social norms. In 1940, less than 5 percent of Americans had a college degree; now nearly 25 percent of young Americans do. At Yale (whose records are very good), about 70 percent of freshmen came from private schools in 1940. In 1994, nearly 60 percent came from public schools. Almost half were women, first admitted in 1969. About 10 percent were black, 7 percent were Hispanic and 16 percent were Asian-American. Two fifths received financial aid.

Our meritocracy has flaws and hypocrisies. Doctors, lawyers and managers often act in self-interested ways, just as unions do. There are advantages of privilege and connections; "affirmative action" is another wrinkle. But whatever its defects, the meritocracy is a huge advance over the preceding barriers of race, sex, religion and ethnicity. Life is unfair, John Kennedy once said. it always will be—but it is not rigged, at least not in America.

As in the case of the previous report, a logical step now is to formulate briefly the main idea of each article:

- In an op-ed essay appearing in the *Washington Post,* Nicholas Lemann argues that a relatively small elite has gained too much wealth and power in America.

- In a *Newsweek* editorial, Robert J. Samuelson rejects the argument that membership in America's meritocracy is unduly exclusive and undemocratic.

Following the steps used in the exercise on pages 169–70, we can now write the report:

```
     Meritocracy and Democratic Idealism: A Conflict?

     Editorialists Nicholas Lemann and Robert J. Samuelson

disagree about the practical consequences of what is often

called meritocracy--the allocation of wealth and power to

those who possess the most impressive academic credentials.
```

Lemann decries the growth of a "Meritocratic Upper Class"
because with it has come a withdrawal from civic responsibility
Members of this class, he contends, avoid military service,
shun public schools, resent equitable taxation, and generally
show little concern for the needs and interests of others.
Lemann proposes compulsory national service and more open
access to the professions as remedies to the "curse" of
meritocracy (B1, B4).

Robert J. Samuelson, on the other hand, derides "faddish
attacks on meritocracy." Granting the existence of a privileged
elite in the United States, he contends that it is not a
monolithic group and that it is far less dominant than critics
like Lemann believe. What critics of meritocracy fail to
consider, says Samuelson, is that Americans from every social
class face an increasingly insecure future, both for themselves
and their children; hereditary privilege is more and more a
thing of the past. Samuelson is convinced that despite its
flaws, the idea of distributing rewards according to merit
has meant greater inclusiveness and has thus brought us closer
to the ideals of American democracy (48).

Works Cited

Lemann, Nicholas. "The Curse of the Merit Class: America's
    Ruling Caste Is Bad News for the Country." Washington
    Post 9 Feb. 1992: B1+.

Samuelson, Robert J. "America the Open: Faddish Attacks on
    the Meritocracy Are Nuts." Newsweek 31 July 1995: 48.

Three things should be noted about the way this report is written. First, you
may have noticed that it lacks a concluding paragraph or statement. Although one
could have been added, a short report like this does not usually require a separate
conclusion, since the reader does not need to be reminded of what it was all about.
Conclusions are unnecessary also when you have nothing new to add to what you

already have written. Second, note that the report is presented in two paragraphs. Since the introduction is only a single sentence, the first editorial does not need to be introduced with a paragraph break. There is a break for the second paragraph, however, because here the reader needs to be alerted to the change in subject. Finally, note that the report aims to be objective, presenting the views of the editorialists without commentary. When the writer says, "Lemann decries . . . " in the first paragraph, she shows the reader that the opinion expressed in that sentence is not necessarily that of the person writing the report. One question you can ask yourself, however, is whether the order in which the two summaries are presented makes a difference. Would the report have a different effect if the editorials had been summarized in reverse order?

 ## ACKNOWLEDGING SOURCES—THE OBLIGATION OF SCHOLARSHIP

Whenever you compose a summary report or any other type of writing that relies on sources, you create something new for others to read. Although what you produce may seem less than earth-shaking in significance, you are nevertheless adding, in however small a way, to the sum of the world's knowledge. You are making a contribution to the domain of scholarship. That may sound lofty, yet it is still true that your writing makes you a member of the fellowship of scholars, past and present, subject to all the benefits and obligations of that august body.

One of the principal benefits of being a scholar is that you are entitled to read— and to use—the scholarship of others. You have a right, for example, to write a summary report based on any sources you can find. Presenting your research and ideas for others to use is in fact one of the obligations of scholarship. We must work together, sharing our findings, if humanity's search for knowledge and understanding is to progress.

Another of your obligations as a scholar is to acknowledge your sources. For example, in the summary report found on pages 165–67, the writer uses parenthetical notes and a list of works cited to identify sources of information. In the report on sources found on pages 179–80, the writer makes it clear that the ideas and opinions being presented have been expressed by others.

Whenever your writing is based on research, you should make sure readers know which ideas and discoveries are your own and which you have taken from your sources. You must give your readers accurate and complete information about what those sources are and where they can be found. Acknowledging your sources is important for two reasons:

- Credit must be given where it is due. Creators of ideas deserve to be recognized for them. Whenever you present material without acknowledging an outside source, readers assume that you are its author. When students err in this regard, they usually do so unintentionally, as a result of inexperience. However, when writers deliberately present another's work as their own, they are guilty of ***plagiarism*** (see pages 315–18 for a further discussion).

- Readers need to know where they can locate your sources so they can consult the original versions. This allows them not only to check the accuracy of your citations, but also to find additional material beyond what you have presented.

Besides naming them within the text itself, writers acknowledge sources in two principal ways. One is to use ***notes*** (such as parenthetical notes or footnotes) to credit sources of specific ideas and statements. The second way is to append a ***list of works cited,*** which acknowledges all the sources from which words have been quoted or from which information or ideas have been derived. A detailed discussion of lists of works cited and notes can be found in Chapters A and B in the reference section of this book. For now, however, a brief introduction should suffice.

The List of Works Cited

A writer appends a list of works cited to a research paper to identify sources. This list provides enough information for readers to identify each source and to locate it if they wish. Although this information might be presented in various ways, writers generally follow a standardized *format,* a prescribed method of listing information. Different fields have their own preferred formats. If you are writing a paper for a psychology course, for example, you may be expected to use a format different from the one you would use in a history paper. The lists of works cited for the two sample papers found in this chapter follow a format known as ***MLA style,*** the format prescribed by the Modern Language Association, an organization of English and foreign-language scholars. Research papers written for composition classes use this format more often than any other, and it is the one we follow throughout this book. Other widely used formats are explained in Chapters E and F in Part II of this book.

Each different type of source—a book, say, or a government document or a television program—is presented in a particular way in an MLA-style list of works cited. For now we will examine only four of the most common kinds of sources: books, articles in magazines, items in newspapers, and essays in edited anthologies or collections. Formats for other sources, as well as more detailed information about MLA-style documentation, can be found in Chapter A of Part II.

Suppose that you used a passage from a book titled *Possible Lives* by Mike Rose. Here is how you would cite that source in an MLA-style list of works cited:

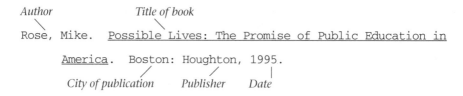

The entry consists of three general categories of information, each of which is followed by a period. They are presented in this order:

1. *The author's name.* Give the author's last name, followed by a comma, and then the author's first name(s).

2. *The complete title of the book, including any subtitle.* Capitalize the first word of the title (and of the subtitle, if there is one) and of all subsequent words except for articles *(a, an, the)*, conjunctions *(and, or, but, nor)* and prepositions *(in, from, to, between,* and so on). Underline (or italicize) the title.

3. *Information about publication:*

    –The city (and state, if the city is not a major one) in which the book was published. Follow this with a colon.

    –A shortened form of the publisher's name. This shortened form always omits articles, business abbreviations (Inc., Corp., Co.), and words such as *Press, Books,* and *Publishers.* If the name of the publisher is that of an individual (e.g., William Morrow), cite last name only; if it consists of more than one last name (e.g., Prentice Hall), cite only the first of them. If the name contains the words *University Press,* they must be included with the abbreviation *UP.* Follow the publisher's name with a comma.

    –The year of publication. End the entry with a period.

Now suppose that another source is an article from *Newsweek*. Here is how you would cite it:

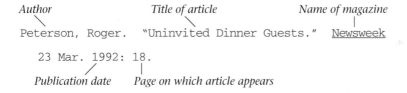

This entry consists of the same three categories of information, with only slight variations in the last two. Instead of being underlined, the title is now placed in quotation marks. Information about publication is cited in the following way:

1. *The name of the magazine.* Underline (or italicize) it. Do not follow it with any punctuation.

2. *The publication date.* List the complete date—day, month, and year for a weekly or biweekly magazine; month and year for a monthly magazine; or season and year for a quarterly magazine. Abbreviate all months except May, June, and July. Follow the date with a colon.

3. *Page numbers.* List the page numbers on which the entire article appears. Do not include the word *page(s)* or an abbreviation such as *pg., p.,* or *pp.* If the pages are not continuous (if, for example, an article begins on pages 8 and 9 and then skips to page 50), cite the number of the first page only, followed by the symbol +.

Entries for newspaper items are much the same as those for magazine articles. Following are two typical examples:

Author   *Title of article*

Powers, William F.   "Airstream of Consciousness."

Washington Post 9 July 1995: E1+.

Name of newspaper   Publication date   Pages on which article appears

Levine, Philip.   "Keats in Detroit."   New York Times 29 Oct.

1995: late ed.: sec. 4: 13.

Edition of newspaper   Section Page

One difference between these entries and the example for magazine articles is that a section of the newspaper is cited. When the section is designated by a letter, as in the first instance, it is incorporated into the page number; when it is designated by a number, it is cited separately, as in the second instance. You will notice also that the second entry cites "late ed.," since the *New York Times* appears in two editions: the late and national editions.

An entry for an essay in an edited anthology cites author and title of the essay, followed by the title of the anthology and the name of its editor. Information about publication is followed by page numbers of the essay:

Author   *Title of essay*

Ellerby, Janet.   "Narrative Imperialism in Rushdie's The

Satanic Verses."   Multicultural Literacies through

Feminist/Poststructuralist Lenses.   Ed. Barbara Frey

Waxman.   Knoxville: U of Tennessee P, 1993.   173-89.

Title of anthology   Editor   Pages on which essay appears

List entries in alphabetical order according to the first word in each entry. If the author of a particular work is not named, introduce the entry for that work with its title and alphabetize accordingly. Do not number the items. Indent each entry the reverse of the way that paragraphs are normally indented; that is, begin the first line of each entry at the left margin, but indent the second and subsequent lines a half inch (five typed spaces). Notice how this format is applied in the following list of works cited from a report on birth order:

Leman, Kevin.   Growing Up First Born: The Pressure and

Privilege of Being Number One. New York: Delacorte,

1989.

```
Leonard, Joan.  "Reflections of a Second Child."  Parents

     Mar. 1990: 57-59.

Woodward, Kenneth L.  "The Order of Innovation: A Study

     Finds Scientific Rebels Are Born, Not Made."  Newsweek

     21 May 1990: 76.

"Your Place in the Family."  Current Health May 1991: 12-13.
```

Consult Chapter A of Part II for more complete information about lists of works cited.

| **A Brief List of Works Cited** | EXERCISES |

1. Suppose you have been asked to write a report on bisexuality based on the following sources. Write an MLA-style list of works cited for the report. Be certain to follow the format guidelines precisely.

   a. A book by Marjorie Garber titled *Vice Versa: Bisexuality and the Eroticism of Everyday Life,* published in New York by Simon and Schuster in 1995.

   b. An article by John Leland titled "Bisexuality," published in the July 17, 1995, issue of *Newsweek,* on pages 44–50.

   c. An article titled "What Do Bisexuals Want?", published in the spring 1992 issue of *Out-Look,* on page 21. No author is cited.

   d. An article by Lynn Darling titled "Bisexuality," published in the June 1995 issue of *Harper's Bazaar.* The article begins on page 136 and is continued in back pages of the magazine.

2. Create a list of works cited for the summary report you were asked to write for the exercise on pages 169–75. (Remember that one of the three sources on which the report is based, "Against All Odds," is found at the end of Chapter 5. That article began on page 1 and was continued on page 8 of section A of the May 26, 1994, issue of the *Wall Street Journal.)*

Parenthetical Notes

A list of works cited identifies your paper's sources *in their entirety.* A **parenthetical note**—a note placed in parentheses within your paper—identifies the *specific* location within a source from which you have taken a bit of paraphrased information or a quotation. Unlike the more complicated and cumbersome footnotes and endnotes, parenthetical notes employ a form of shorthand: They supply the least amount of information needed to identify a source.

The beauty of parenthetical notes is their simplicity. MLA-style notes usually give only two items: the author's last name and the page(s) from which the paraphrased information or quotation was taken. For example, assume that one of your sources was the article on meritocracy by Nicholas Lemann on pages 175–77. You would cite that article in the list of works cited at the end of your paper as follows:

```
Lemann, Nicholas.  "The Curse of the Merit Class: America's

     Ruling Caste Is Bad News for the Country."  Washington

     Post 9 Feb. 1992: B1+.
```

Any notes within your paper need only refer the reader to this citation. To indicate that the following sentence is a paraphrase of a passage found on page B4 of that article, you would provide a brief parenthetical note:

```
Although the children of meritocrats aren't guaranteed

a lifetime of privilege, their parents do provide them with

every benefit conducive to high achievement (Lemann B4).
```

The note is placed at the end of the sentence but preceding the period. Observe also that the note tells you only the *specific page* from which you have taken this particular idea. (In contrast, the entry in the list of works cited shows the pages on which the *entire article* is printed.) However, when notes refer to an article as a whole—as do the notes on page 166—then they too give all the pages on which the article appears.

When the author's name is unknown, cite instead the first word or two of the title. Suppose, for example, that you wanted to paraphrase something from the last item in the list of sources concerning birth order. That anonymous article is cited as follows:

```
"Your Place in the Family."  Current Health May 1991: 12-13.
```

Your parenthetical note might look like this:

```
("Your Place" 12)
```

If your paper states the author's name (or, in the case of an anonymous article, its title) so that your source is already identified, then a parenthetical note provides only the page number(s). See, for example, the two notes for the report "Meritocracy and Democratic Idealism: A Conflict?" on pages 179–80. As you can see, the theory behind parenthetical notes is to present the least information needed to identify sources.

Complete information about parenthetical notes can be found in Chapter B of Part II.

EXERCISE   **Supplying Parenthetical Notes**

Suppose you have based a report on birth order on the list of works cited found on page 184. Show what the following notes would look like:

a. A note referring to information on page 18 of Leman's book.

b. A note referring to the article in *Current Health* as a whole.

c. A note referring to information taken from the first two pages of Leonard's article.

 READING SELECTIONS

The following articles address the issue of whether provocative or hate speech, particularly that which is heard on radio talk shows, contributes to political terrorism and other forms of violence. The last two articles appeared soon after the bombing of the Federal Building in Oklahoma City in April 1995.

Talk Radio or Hate Radio?
Critics Assail Some Hosts*

TIMOTHY EGAN

1   Talk radio thrived by allowing people to say the kind of things that were discouraged by liberal orthodoxy, according to many talk show hosts. But, critics say, some programs have gone too far, bordering on hate talk.

2   The subjects that seem to bring out the most extreme passion are racial minorities, homosexuals and guns.

3   In Phoenix, Bob Mohan, a talk show host on the top-rated KFYI, has come under criticism for a recent show about Jim Brady, the former press secretary for President Ronald Reagan, who was wounded in the assassination attempt on Mr. Reagan. Criticizing Mr. Brady's wife, Sarah, and her campaign for gun control, Mr. Mohan said Mrs. Brady "ought to be put down."

4   According to a partial transcript of Mr. Mohan's show, which was printed in the Dec. 21 edition of *The Arizona Republic,* Mr. Mohan said of Mrs. Brady:

5   "You know, she ought to be put down. A humane shot at a veterinarian's would be an easy way to do it. Because of all her barking and complaining, she really needs to be put down."

6   According to the newspaper's transcript, Mr. Mohan also said, "I wish she would just keep wheeling her husband around to go to speaking engagements—wiping the saliva off his mouth once in a while—and leave the rest of us damn well alone." Mr. Mohan could not be reached late in the week to comment on his remarks.

7   Guns also figured in a decision by the talk show host Don Baker, of KVOR in Colorado Springs, Colo., to step down briefly from his show. Mr. Baker, who had encouraged listeners during the summer to take guns to Washington to protest moves to ban assault weapons, took himself off the air after his callers accused him of inspiring a Colorado Springs man, Francisco M. Duran, to fire shots at the White House. Mr. Duran has

*This article appears on page 22 of the January 1, 1995, late edition of the *New York Times.*

8   been charged with attempting to shoot the President; Federal officials have never commented on whether or not talk radio played a role.

8   In taking himself off the air in mid-November, Mr. Baker, who sometimes broadcasts from a Colorado Springs gun shop, responded to news reports that his crusades on gun control and the President had incited Mr. Duran by saying that talk radio was not to blame.

9   Referring to Mr. Duran as "the jerk, the wacko, the creep," Mr. Baker said on the air in November, "If this man thinks I or Rush Limbaugh are the reason he went out there, he needs psychiatric counseling."

10   Mr. Baker returned to the air in December, after being told by his producer to tone down his remarks. In the past, he had said of Attorney General Janet Reno that, "We ought to slap Janet Reno across the face" and "send her back to Florida where she can live with her relatives—the gators."

11   The Duran shooting prompted Mr. Baker's station to "sit up and take notice—we're more potent than we thought," said Don Seidholz, general manager for KVOR. He said the station now has a formal policy against advocating violence or retribution.

12   A staple of some talk show hosts, following the lead of Rush Limbaugh a few years ago, is to make fun of the way some black people talk.

13   Bob Grant of WABC in New York has called South African blacks "savages." Recently, he apologized for making a profane reference to Dr. Martin Luther King, Jr.

14   Some hosts have noted that black talk radio stations make fun of white people, and that what they are doing is only fair play.

15   "Before, blacks were a sacred cow," said Robert Namer, a far-right talk show host for two stations near New Orleans, WASO and WTIX. "Now, it's open season." He added, "People realize you don't have to placate black people any more."

16   But others say such talk encourages open racism and hatred. The Rev. Francis X. Mazur, a Roman Catholic priest who is interim director of the Buffalo Area Metropolitan Ministries, which represents clergy members of about 30 faiths, said talk radio brings out the worst in some people.

17   "The part that scares everyone is the amount of hate, prejudice and racism that still exists out in the public," Father Mazur said.

Toxic Speech

As Clinton Connects the Bombing to Right-Wing Hate Radio, the Resurgence of America's Incendiary "Paranoid Style" Is Finally under Scrutiny*

JONATHAN ALTER

1   Let's assume that President Clinton's attack on "loud and angry voices" and "promoters of paranoia" was motivated by political expediency. So what? His critics are so accustomed to impugning motives that they've lost sight of the substance of what he said. Clinton argued simply that these extremists "leave the impression, by their very words, that violence is acceptable." If anything, he was late on hate. The president might have taken a cue from his Sister Souljah triumph during the 1992 campaign and made

*This article appears on pages 44 and 46 of the May 8, 1995, issue of *Newsweek*.

denunciation of incendiary rhetoric on both the left and the right a regular feature of his presidency. Instead he once again backed off last week, as aides scampered to insist that the president wasn't really talking about right-wing talk radio.

Actually, he was. All week long on his radio show, Rush Limbaugh played the victim like a pro. But Clinton was really aiming at the likes of G. Gordon Liddy, the second most popular conservative talk-radio host. When Liddy tells listeners to murder agents of the Bureau of Alcohol, Tobacco and Firearms who enter their homes ("Head shots, head shots—kill the sons of bitches!") or laughs about using pictures of the Clintons as target practice; when self-styled "patriots" plot armed rebellion on short-wave radio or pass along bomb recipes on computer bulletin boards; when Bob Mohan of KFYI Phoenix says of handgun-control advocate Sarah Brady, "She ought to be put down. A humane shot at a veterinarian's would be an easy way to do it"; when gun shows sell bumper stickers that say, FIRST LINCOLN, THEN KENNEDY, NOW CLINTON?—then it's time to draw a line. Now, finally, we're beginning to take a hard look at our whole Vulture Culture—the endless shouting and demonizing that doesn't necessarily lead to violence but coarsens and worsens us all.

The left has its share of vultures; their rancid words must be challenged, too. And it's cynical to tar all conservatives with the right-wing brush. But when Limbaugh says on the air that the Oklahoma City terror was perpetrated by anarchists, not right-wingers, he undermines his widely hyped powers of perceptions. Would Limbaugh and the Oklahoma GOP senators who echo him deny that the members of the Weather Underground of the late 1960s and early 1970s were left-wing extremists? These terrorists took mainstream liberal antiwar views and made them extreme left-wing views. From what we already know of the Oklahoma City crime, it's clear that the bombers took mainstream conservative ideas—resistance to gun control, the United Nations and a powerful federal government—and made them extreme-right views. All the defensive bombast in the world won't change that fact.

Perceived threats: The bully-boy right should, of course, be distinguished from what the late historian Richard Hofstadter called "the paranoid style in American politics." In his 1965 book of that name, Hofstadter argued that groups spouting overheated conspiratorial fantasies have always been with us. Some of the perceived threats—from Jews, internationalists, high government officials and gun control—have remained consistent for generations; others—from Masonic orders to fluoridated water—have changed with the times. Because the dark forces are seen as threatening "a nation, a culture, a way of life" and not just individuals who think someone is out to get them, the paranoia can find a wider audience.

Hofstadter argued that paranoid groups often ape the characteristics of those they fear. Thus the KKK, which attacks not just blacks and Jews but Roman Catholics, began dressing in vestments, and the John Birch Society, which saw communists everywhere, formed in cells. Today's militia movement, which sees its enemy as federal authority, takes the form of the most potent symbol of that authority—the army.

Sometimes the American strains of puritanism and paranoia combust; more often they just overlap and confuse. We've never before been quite so mixed up about the meaning of hurtful words, so simultaneously tolerant and intolerant of toxic speech. It's come to this: the same epithets that get you fired from a university get you hired on talk radio. Maybe it's a class thing—different standards for gown and town. A student at the University of Michigan mentions casually that he believes homosexuality is a disease that can be cured by therapy. He is immediately hauled before a disciplinary board. A custodian at the same university, Mark Koernke, repeatedly goes on short-wave radio describing how to kill government officials. He is almost totally ignored—until it turns out that one of the suspects in the Oklahoma City bombing may be a follower, at which point his short-wave program is finally yanked by the "Christian" station that was airing it.

7   It's strange: Mark Twain's masterpiece *Huckleberry Finn* is banned in many areas because it contains the word "nigger." At the same time, when a big-time radio talk-show host in New York, Bob Grant, helps promote neo-Nazis and white supremacists and tells a caller who disagrees with him about O.J. Simpson and Oklahoma: "What I'd like to do is put you against the wall with the rest of them, and mow you down with them," guess what happens to him? Capital Cities/ABC, which airs Grant's show, defends him with a statement acknowledging that he "*may be* [emphasis added] controversial." Yes, ABC, and you may be in it for the money.

8   ABC's larger defense was that Grant shouldn't be "censored." This was the argument of choice for talk-radio hosts last week. They can call the president "Coward in Chief" and imply he killed Vincent Foster, but if he mildly criticizes them, it's censorship. Sorry. It would be censorship if the government tried to revoke their licenses or seize their studios. Clinton was talking about responsibility. That doesn't mean that hate purveyors are responsible for wackos' blowing up buildings, but that they—and everyone else—are responsible for trying to *prevent* such violence. Responsibility is when people in positions of authority (including movie, TV, radio and recording executives) assess the possible social consequences of what they disseminate. This should be elemental and obvious, but it isn't.

9   And so we need to remind ourselves of what we were supposed to have learned years ago—the fourth "R." Responsibility is Neal Boortz, a conservative talk-show host at Atlanta's WSB, who, when a caller said recently that government was now the enemy, replied: "If you want a revolution, go to the ballot box." Responsibility is Bill McNulty, general manager of KCKC-AM in San Bernardino, Calif., who last week yanked Liddy's show from his station. "I felt that there was a sincere influence on some of those unstable individuals," McNulty explained.

10   Liddy said last week that his listeners are smart enough not to take his violent talk seriously. But it was Liddy himself who, when working in the Nixon White House, took seriously Jeb Stuart Magruder's offhand remark that it would "be nice if we could get rid of" columnist Jack Anderson. He began plotting to kill Anderson before being restrained by Magruder. "If Liddy could misinterpret the words of a man who was sitting in the same room—a man he knew very well—and set off on an assassination mission, how could he not understand the potential danger of his remarks to strangers on the air?" asks columnist William Raspberry. Indeed, it was only last year that Francisco Duran, who listened to incendiary Colorado Springs radio host Don Baker, set off for Washington to try to kill Clinton.

11   **Shouting sells:** Maybe there's no connection. After all, Duran's deranged. And maybe there's no connection between the Oklahoma City bombing and voices of hate, either; terrorists shouldn't be able to "blame society" any more than gangbangers can. Repressing free speech in order to stop crime has never worked in the past, and it's not likely to work now. Besides, shouting sells, and selling is even more American than paranoia.

12   But before we let the Vulture Culture off the hook, remember: it may not have the power to demolish buildings, but it does have the power to erode faith in democratic life. As Roger Conner of the American Alliance for Rights and Responsibilities puts it, "A process dominated by extremes is a process that produces anger and withdrawal. People listening to all the shouting *know* that it's not all black and white. So they opt out; they say, 'If you have to know you're this certain of your beliefs in order to participate, count me out'." Now *there's* a causal link: anger breeds withdrawal breeds profound alienation and a new, lonelier civic existence. If we lower our voices, we won't necessarily save any lives. But we may help save our ability to reason and govern together.

In Defense of Prejudice*
Why Incendiary Speech Must Be Protected

JONATHAN RAUCH

The war on prejudice is now, in all likelihood, the most uncontroversial social move-   **1**
ment in America. Opposition to "hate speech," formerly identified with the liberal left,
has become a bipartisan piety. In the past year, groups and factions that agree on nothing else have agreed that the public expression of any and all prejudices must be forbidden. On the left, protesters and editorialists have insisted that Francis L. Lawrence
resign as president of Rutgers University for describing blacks as "a disadvantaged population that doesn't have genetic, hereditary background to have a higher average." On
the other side of the ideological divide, Ralph Reed, the executive director of the Christian Coalition, responded to criticism of the religious right by calling a press conference
to denounce a supposed outbreak of "namecalling, scapegoating, and religious bigotry."
Craig Rogers, an evangelical Christian student at California State University, recently
filed a $2.5 million sexual-harassment suit against a lesbian professor of psychology,
claiming that anti-male bias in one of her lectures violated campus rules and left him
feeling "raped and trapped."

In universities and on Capitol Hill, in workplaces and newsrooms, authorities are   **2**
declaring that there is no place for racism, sexism, homophobia, Christian-bashing, and
other forms of prejudice in public debate or even in private thought. "Only when racism
and other forms of prejudice are expunged," say the crusaders for sweetness and light,
"can minorities be safe and society be fair." So sweet, this dream of a world without prejudice. But the very last thing society should do is seek to utterly eradicate racism and
other forms of prejudice. . . .

What is especially dismaying is that the purists pursue prejudice in the name of pro-   **3**
tecting minorities. In order to protect people like me (homosexual), they must pursue
people like me (dissident). In order to bolster minority self-esteem, they suppress minority opinion. There are, of course, all kinds of practical and legal problems with the
purists' campaign: the incursions against the First Amendment; the inevitable abuses by
prosecutors and activists who define as "hateful" or "violent" whatever speech they dislike or can score points off of; the lack of any evidence that repressing prejudice eliminates rather than inflames it. But minorities, of all people, ought to remember that by
definition we cannot prevail by numbers, and we generally cannot prevail by force.
Against the power of ignorant mass opinion and group prejudice and superstition, we
have only our voices. If you doubt that minorities' voices are powerful weapons, think
of the lengths to which Southern officials went to silence the Reverend Martin Luther
King Jr. (recall that the city commissioner of Montgomery, Alabama, won a $500,000
libel suit, later overturned in *New York Times* v. *Sullivan* [1964], regarding an advertisement in the *Times* placed by civil-rights leaders who denounced the Montgomery
police). Think of how much gay people have improved their lot over twenty-five years
simply by refusing to remain silent. Recall the Michigan student who was prosecuted for
saying that homosexuality is a treatable disease, and notice that he was black. Under
that Michigan speech code, more than twenty blacks were charged with racist speech,

*This article begins on pages 37–39 and continues on pages 42–46 of the May 1995 issue of *Harper's*. The first
two paragraphs of this excerpt are printed on page 37, and the remainder comes from pages 45 and 46.

while no instance of racist speech by whites was punished. In Florida, the hate-speech law was invoked against a black man who called a policeman a "white cracker"; not so surprisingly, in the first hate-crimes case to reach the Supreme Court, the victim was white and the defendant black.

4   In the escalating war against "prejudice," the right is already learning to play by the rules that were pioneered by the purist activists of the left. Last year leading Democrats, including the President, criticized the Republican Party for being increasingly in the thrall of the Christian right. Some of the rhetoric was harsh ("fire-breathing Christian radical right"), but it wasn't vicious or even clearly wrong. Never mind: when Democratic Representative Vic Fazio said Republicans were "being forced to the fringes by the aggressive political tactics of the religious right," the chairman of the Republican National Committee, Haley Barbour, said, "Christian-bashing" was "the left's preferred form of religious bigotry." Bigotry! Prejudice! "Christians active in politics are now on the receiving end of an extraordinary campaign of bias and prejudice," said the conservative leader William J. Bennett. One discerns, here, where the new purism leads. Eventually, any criticism of any group will be "prejudice."

5   Here is the ultimate irony of the new purism: words, which pluralists hope can be substituted for violence, are redefined by purists *as* violence. "The experience of being called 'nigger,' 'spic,' 'Jap,' or 'kike' is like receiving a slap in the face," Charles Lawrence wrote in 1990. "Psychic injury is no less an injury than being struck in the face, and it often is far more severe." This kind of talk is commonplace today. Epithets, insults, often even polite expressions of what's taken to be prejudice are called by purists "assaultive speech," "words that wound," "verbal violence." "To me, racial epithets are not speech," one University of Michigan law professor said. "They are bullets." In her speech accepting the 1993 Nobel Prize for Literature in Stockholm, Sweden, the author Toni Morrison said this: "Oppressive language does more than represent violence; it is violence."

6   It is not violence. I am thinking back to a moment on the subway in Washington, a little thing. I was riding home late one night and a squad of noisy kids, maybe seventeen or eighteen years old, noisily piled into the car. They yelled across the car and a girl said, "Where do we get off?"

7   A boy said, "Farragut North."

8   The girl: *"Faggot* North!"

9   The boy: "Yeah! Faggot North!"

10   General hilarity.

11   First, before the intellect resumes control, there is a moment of fear, an animal moment. Who are they? How many of them? How dangerous? Where is the way out? All of these things are noted preverbally and assessed by the gut. Then the brain begins an assessment: they are sober, this is probably too public a place for them to do it, there are more girls than boys, they were just talking, it is probably nothing.

12   They didn't notice me and there was no incident. The teenage babble flowed on, leaving me to think. I became interested in my own reaction: the jump of fear out of nowhere like an alert animal, the sense for a brief time that one is naked and alone and should hide or run away. For a time, one ceases to be a human being and becomes instead a faggot.

13   The fear engendered by these words is real. The remedy is as clear and as imperfect as ever: protect citizens against violence. This, I grant, is something that American society has never done very well and now does quite poorly. It is no solution to define words as violence or prejudice as oppression, and then by cracking down on words or thoughts pretend that we are doing something about violence and oppression. No doubt it is easier to pass a speech code or hate-crimes law and proclaim the streets safer than actually

to make the streets safer, but the one must never be confused with the other. Every cop or prosecutor chasing words is one fewer chasing criminals. In a world rife with real violence and oppression, full of Rwandas and Bosnias and eleven-year-olds spraying bullets at children in Chicago and in turn being executed by gang lords, it is odious of Toni Morrison to say that words are violence.

Indeed, equating "verbal violence" with physical violence is a treacherous, mischievous business. Not long ago a writer was charged with viciously and gratuitously wounding the feelings and dignity of millions of people. He was charged, in effect, with exhibiting flagrant prejudice against Muslims and outrageously slandering their beliefs. "What is freedom of expression?" mused Salman Rushdie a year after the ayatollahs sentenced him to death and put a price on his head. "Without the freedom to offend, it ceases to exist." I can think of nothing sadder than that minority activists, in their haste to make the world better, should be the ones to forget the lesson of Rushdie's plight: for minorities, pluralism, not purism, is the answer. The campaigns to eradicate prejudice—all of them, the speech codes and workplace restrictions and mandatory therapy for accused bigots and all the rest—should stop, now. The whole objective of eradicating prejudice, as opposed to correcting and criticizing it, should be repudiated as a fool's errand. Salman Rushdie is right, Toni Morrison wrong, and minorities belong at his side, not hers.

14

Freewriting

Each of these texts deals with the cherished ideal of free speech, addressing controversies about if and when limitations are appropriate. After reading all three, take a few moments to compile a list of instances in which you have observed hate speech (spoken or written), experienced its effects, or perhaps even engaged in it yourself. After listing a few such instances, make a conscientious effort to speculate (engaging in as few moral judgments as possible) on the motives of the speaker or writer and on the feelings of the person or group targeted. Choosing one particular instance (or perhaps several, if you prefer), try to explain objectively the motives and feelings of both parties, as you are able to understand them. Do this in a ten-minute freewriting. Finally, in a second freewriting, make the strongest case you can in favor of regulating hate speech; then offer the strongest case you can make against regulating it.

Group Work

Share both freewritings with members of your peer group by having each member read aloud as others take notes. Look for these patterns:

1. Where is hate speech most often encountered (e.g., talk radio, anonymous letters or phone messages, graffiti)?

2. What motivates people to engage in hate speech? Is there any circumstance in which it is justified or excusable?

3. How can a victim of hate speech respond most effectively?

4. Are there any circumstances under which hate speech should be regulated? If so, when and how?

Review Questions

1. How, according to Timothy Egan's article, do some talk-show hosts defend remarks that many consider dangerously provocative?

2. What distinction does Jonathan Alter try to draw between exercising censorship and trying to prevent violence?

3. How does Jonathan Rauch use Toni Morrison and Salman Rushdie as contrasting examples? What point is he making with them?

Discussion Questions

1. Do the more extreme talk radio shows merely reflect hatred, anger, and fear that were widespread before they became so popular? Or do they actually help to increase those feelings?

2. Is the distinction that Alter draws between censorship and responsibility a valid one? Why or why not?

3. Would you predict that limitations on freedom of speech will become more or less of an issue in America during the next century?

Writing

1. Write a brief summary report using these three sources and following the guidelines set forth in this chapter. Include a list of works cited.

2. Write an objective report on sources using the articles by Alter and Rauch. Include a list of works cited.

3. Develop your response to any of the discussion questions above into an essay.

4. Write an essay arguing for specific restrictions on a specific form of hate speech. Or, you may wish to argue that such restrictions are never warranted.

7 Analytical Reading and Writing

Talking with friends in the college cafeteria, you might be asked what you thought about the latest music video by a currently popular group. "I didn't like it," you might say. "It seemed repetitive. It's like I've heard and seen it all before. They've lost their edge." After some half-hearted agreement or disagreement with this appropriately vague comment, the conversation might drift to a recent party, an upcoming exam, the weather, or maybe lunch. That is the way with informal talk; it wanders almost aimlessly from here to there, rarely pausing to pursue a topic in depth.

But if the context were to change, your offhand comment could be disastrous. If, for example, you wrote that same answer on the exam for a seminar in popular culture, you would fail. In that situation, the response would not be specific enough. There is a thesis ("I didn't like it") and some support ("repetitive," "lost their edge"), but both are inappropriately thin for formal writing.

Sometimes it is difficult to make the transition from the looseness of informal spoken language to the tightness of writing. But the difference between them is significant. You rarely need much support for your ideas and opinions in conversation, but you do in writing. It is not a matter of right or wrong; it is just that each way of communicating has different conventions. As a literate member of a college community, you should know and observe these special conventions. If you were asked in the cafeteria what you thought about a recent video, a developed 500-word analysis of the cinematography would not be a smart answer. The "correct" response would be the appropriately brief one. In any situation the needs and interests of the audience should determine the ideas you will explore, the specificity of detail you will provide, and the level of language you will use.

As we noted in Chapter 4, the foundation of writing lies in the interplay between the general and the specific, the way a writer brings abstract ideas down to earth. Writers need to support general statements with appropriate details, reasons, examples, and illustrations. They are part of a special community of people who must demonstrate not only what they think, but also their reasons for thinking it. In a sense their ideas are promises to their readers, promises that they must keep by linking one idea to another. If they don't keep those promises, their readers will be disappointed. That's why good writers deliver.

Good readers also deliver. At this stage of your education, you do not want to be merely a passive consumer of ideas. If you are to be a contributing member of a college community, you must be an active, analytical reader and writer. By writing about your reading, you learn to read more carefully, and you develop more acute skills of perception. The purpose of this chapter is to explore ways for you to analyze your reading so that you can become a more informed receiver and creator of knowledge.

ANALYZING THE PARTS

Whenever you analyze anything, whether it is a chess move, an automobile engine, a political theory, or a poem, you try to break down its complexity by dividing it into component parts. Then you can look at the parts individually, seeing first their detail and then examining the way they work together.

To understand anything that is complex, observers must first analyze the parts. Political scientists, for example, constantly analyze the differences between free-market and managed economies—how they produce and deliver consumer goods, what profits their industries are allowed to make, what restrictions they place on imports. Experts compare the systems by analyzing money, people, goods, laws, attitudes, and other components. They take the whole apart to see how each element works and then study the ways those elements operate together.

When you analyze a reading, you should do the same thing—consider separate aspects individually and then see how they function together as a whole. Writing is an extremely flexible medium of communication, and just as there is no set formula for writing an essay—one can write in many different ways, and the success of a work may even depend on the writer's originality—so too there is no set formula for analysis. How you view a reading depends on what it is and why you are reading it. You look for different qualities in an epic poem, a comic satire, and a scientific report. You approach a work that you read for pleasure differently than you approach a source for a research paper.

Nevertheless, there are some features common to all written works that you should consider. Every piece of writing tries to do something with concepts or information, addressing and developing a main idea in an organized sequence so that readers can understand what is being discussed. The following five aspects of a work should be considered in an analysis:

- The **purpose** for which the work was written
- The way the author has directed the work to its intended **audience**
- The **main idea** of the work
- The **development** or **support** for that idea
- The **organization** and **coherence** of the work

We will first look at each of these five aspects individually and then see how they can be put together into a more comprehensive analysis of a reading.

Purpose

Every work must be judged in terms of what it is attempting to accomplish. You can't be upset with a zany movie for not being sufficiently philosophical or with a journal in comparative linguistics for lacking humor or with a fantasy adventure for being unrealistic.

Some writers want to change our minds; others simply want to tell us something we didn't know before. Some want to provoke us to action; others hope to entertain, cajole, shock, or educate us. As a college reader, you must be alert to these possibilities. If you misinterpret a writer's intention, the whole point may be lost; sometimes the result of such an error can be tragic—or hilarious.

Although we cannot always know exactly what an author is thinking, the general purpose of most writing is evident enough. Nevertheless, things are not always what they seem. You must be alert for satire as well as for attempts to manipulate your beliefs. You must notice the writer's biases and be wary of both slanted evidence and outright deception. Sometimes writers are candid about where they stand; but at other times you may have to read between the lines, basing your judgments about intentions on your past reading experiences and your knowledge of human nature.

In a passage cited earlier in this book, David Sacks and Peter Thiel make no effort to conceal their bias—a disdain for the efforts of many universities to raise consciousness about issues of cultural diversity:

> "Orientation is designed to disorient you," announced Stanford professor James Adams to an auditorium of 1,600 puzzled freshmen at the beginning of the new school year. Assembled for one of many orientation-week programs on "diversity," the freshmen soon learned what he meant. A lesbian activist spoke first about "challenging your sexuality," and encouraged the 17- and 18-year-old students to "overcome" their "fears of being queer." Next, a black musician performed an electric-guitar solo as police sirens wailed in the background. He concluded his demonstration by dropping suddenly to the floor and convulsing his body in a re-enactment of the Rodney King beating.

After quoting Professor Adams's statement about the objectives of orientation at Stanford, the authors ridicule those objectives by listing the more controversial, possibly outrageous, activities involved. The authors provide various clues to signal their disregard. For example, they place the word *diversity* in quotation marks and describe the audience as "puzzled." A more subtle tactic is their reminding readers in the third sentence that some first-year students are, legally, minors. Since they are so forthright in showing their bias (and since their article was published in the conservative *National Review),* the writers cannot be accused of deception. We may choose to disagree with them—we may even dislike their methods of argument—but at least they have given us every reason to expect a presentation of their topic slanted toward their particular bias. An intelligent reader will examine Sacks and Thiel's ideas critically, aware that these are not the only possible perceptions of freshman orientation at Stanford University.

EXERCISES | **Analyzing Purpose**

1. As you read the following passage, try to decide the author's purpose in writing it:

    During the first week of September, advance copies of John F. Kennedy Jr.'s new political magazine, *George,* appeared on the New York publicity circuit, defined by its founding editor as "post-partisan" and addressed to the kind of people (very upscale, very hip) apt to think—at least until they meet *George*—that politics are boring and nasty and old. . . .

    His magazine looked a good deal like *Vanity Fair* or *Vogue* (280 glossy pages, delicately scented with an assortment of French perfumes), and in response to questions from the two or three skeptics in the crowd, Kennedy explained . . . that *George* was a political magazine from which the politics had been tactfully removed, "a lifestyle magazine" refreshingly devoid of ideas and unencumbered by "any partisan perspective—not even mine," a magazine not unlike a merchandizing catalogue, "exuberantly" and "extravagantly" bent on exhibiting political figures as "pop icons" and made to the measure of sophisticated consumers certain to bring to their reading of the Bill of Rights or a speech by Bob Dole the same standards of judgment (discriminating) and taste (exquisite) that they bring to their appreciation of an Armani suit, a pair of Ferragamo shoes, or a Louis Vuitton suitcase.
    —Lewis H. Lapham, "Eyebrow Pencils"

2. The following item appears in a "survival guide" issued to all first-year students at the university where we teach.

    University Police
    The university police department is a full-fledged, honest-to-goodness police department. The department is staffed with 20 sworn police professionals, five emergency dispatchers, and a support staff that includes security guards. The police department's purpose is to allow you to achieve your educational goals in as safe an environment as possible. Hopefully, while you are a member of the community, you will take the opportunity to get to know the police staff. A primary focus is a community policing program called PAC'N. PAC'N is an acronym that stands for Police and Community Networking. PAC'N includes a ride-along program and presents numerous crime prevention programs aimed at keeping your valuables safe.
    Bicycle registration . . . when you move in, bring your bicycle to one of the registration tents or to the police department and get it registered free of charge. Registration is required for all bicycles.
    Just for women . . . there is a tremendous self-defense class offered called RAD, which stands for rape aggression defense. This program has been well received in the community and is certainly one for which you will want to sign up.
    In the event of an emergency . . . call from any campus phone by dialing 4911. There are also emergency call boxes located throughout campus—just push the button. If you are just calling for information, please dial 395-3184.

    a. Several purposes are addressed in this short passage. How many can you identify?

    b. Do any of these purposes take priority over others? Are some in conflict with each other? Which ones are more challenging to present or justify to an audience of first-year college students?

c. What strategies (e.g., phrasing, order of presentation) does the writer employ to communicate or to elicit compliance with less welcome information and policies? For example, what might be the rationale for inserting the phrase "take the opportunity to" in the fourth sentence of the first paragraph? Why is the last sentence of the second paragraph not used to open that paragraph?

Audience

Although authors sometimes write mainly to express themselves, more often their purpose is to create an effect on outside readers. They usually have a particular audience in mind (for example, in writing this paragraph, we have in mind an audience of college students and their instructors), and they adjust their writing to fit the needs and interests of their intended readers. Likewise, in analyzing a work, readers must consider the audience for which it was intended and judge it on those terms.

In the following brief essay from a newsletter for fourth-graders, the writer has been attentive to the needs of young readers:

Computers Help People with Handicaps

Several million people in the U.S. are handicapped. Some can't speak or make speech signs. Some don't have the use of their arms. Today, some of these handicapped people do things they have never done before. Computers help them talk, play games, and do schoolwork.

Many handicapped people must find special ways to work computers. Some use one finger to press the keys of their computers. Other people use a pencil held in their mouth. Some use their toes.

Computers give many handicapped people a chance to do things without help from others. These people read stories on computers and play computer games. These people also use computers to turn lights on and off and to open and close doors. A handicapped person's computer can get lessons to and from a computer at a school.

Someday people with serious handicaps may be able to get jobs for the first time. Their computers will be connected to computers at places of business.

—*Weekly Reader*

Notice the clear, connected way information is presented. The short sentences, basic vocabulary, brevity, and lack of technical details all suggest the writer's awareness of audience.

It would be unfair to criticize this writer for failing to see complexity in the subject. If you were doing research on computers for a college course, you would be wise simply to look elsewhere. On the other hand, the following piece, written for an audience with special technical expertise, might be equally inappropriate as a source for a college research paper:

Myelography and other invasive procedures designed to show disc rupture and root compression should only be employed where surgical intervention is being considered. These procedures should never be used as routine diagnostic measures. They do form an essential part of a preoperative evaluation. Myelography has two primary purposes: (1) to rule out a neurogenic cause such as a nerve root tumor accounting for the clinical picture; (2) to confirm the level of localization for the suspected disc rupture.

—J. Leon Morris, "Radiologic Evaluation"

Here the assumptions about prior knowledge, the vocabulary, and the main point suggest an audience of medical specialists. Again, to criticize this piece for being dense and unreadable would be comparably unfair.

Audience, however, involves more than just level of vocabulary and assumptions about prior knowledge. It also reflects attitudes and values that readers are expected to share. Consider, for example, the following passage by Allison Glock, who edits a column called "Dr. Sooth" in the monthly issues of *GQ*, a men's fashion magazine:

Dear Dr. Sooth:

I get turned on only by unshaven women, but my girlfriend refuses to stop trimming. She thinks my requests are abnormal. Are they?
Harry Pits

Dear Harry:

Ever consider moving to Vermont? Many women there, and in progressive communities in California and Colorado, eschew the razor for more unaffected pits. Chances are, your own attraction is fueled less by an undue fondness for fur than for the accompanying pungent odor. One of the key carnal lures between couples is scent. All social animals indicate sexual readiness by releasing and sniffing pheromones. . . . Body hair traps that ardent aroma and gives it bite, by letting the pheromones fester, so you in turn feel "friendlier" around chicks with pelts. In addition, you may enjoy the promise of low maintenance and free love that woolliness connotes. Either way, you are verifiably normal. Whether it's kosher to demand a change in your mate's grooming habits is something else. She probably feels about stubble the way you feel about *The Bridges of Madison County*. Your choice? Respect her opinion or buy some Birks and get another, more hirsute babe.

This passage contains one technical term *(pheromones)* and some sophisticated diction *(hirsute)* alongside informal language, some of it *(chicks, babes)* likely to offend certain readers. More important than the vocabulary, however, are the assumptions we might draw about the targeted audience. On the one hand, readers are cast as urbane and liberated, unfazed by a topic embarrassing or disgusting to some. The flippant suggestion about moving to Vermont or to a "progressive community" in California or Colorado suggests an audience of urbanites (or people who want to see themselves that way), while a dismissive reference to "Birks" implies a certain disdain for less fashionable clothing. "Liberated" views are further suggested by the subtle reminder that women should not feel compelled to make themselves sexually desirable to men, but they are undercut by the implication that "normal" men aren't likely to enjoy *The Bridges of Madison County*. In fact, the whole passage reflects a good deal of anxiety about what is normal male taste and behavior. Apparently it is a matter about which the audience needs a certain amount of reassurance—hence the pun in the title of Glock's column, "Dr. Sooth"(e).

To analyze certainly means to take apart, but readers can do so objectively only if they view the work within the context of its intended audience. Sometimes this is little more than determining how much information and vocabulary readers are assumed to possess, but at other times it is more a matter of looking for subtle clues regarding attitudes, values, interests, and experiences shared by a particular community.

Analyzing Audience   EXERCISES

1. The following three excerpts all define obsessive-compulsive disorder, a common form of neurotic behavior. Use clues such as style, vocabulary, content, format, and assumed knowledge to decide if they are intended for different audiences. Which of the excerpts might include you among its targeted readers? Analyze how each text is adjusted to meet the needs of readers.

   a. Nearly all her life, Mary, now a 54-year-old suburban Dallas housewife, has been a prisoner of the ludicrous, unrelenting preoccupations that plague at least five million Americans who suffer from obsessive-compulsive disorder (OCD). How ludicrous? Mary's fear of contamination is such that she wakes at six each morning and spends most of her day cleaning her house. She has an anorexic's fear of gaining weight and an agoraphobic's fear of venturing alone outside the safe confines of her home. Like many OCD sufferers, Mary battled the disease in secrecy well into adulthood, but even after her affliction was diagnosed when she was forty, she continued to perform the torturous rituals she concocted to relieve her anxiety. "They tell me I shouldn't think this, but I know I'm crazy," she says in a voice that sounds thoroughly sane if a bit wounded. "That's the hardest part."
   —Jim Atkinson, "A Perfect Mess" (article in *Texas Monthly* magazine)

   b. Another psychoneurotic disorder is the *obsessive-compulsive reaction,* which may include obsessions, compulsions, or both. An obsession is an *idea* that constantly intrudes into a person's thoughts. An obsessive parent may think constantly that something has happened, or will happen, to the children. A person may be obsessed with the idea that he will kill himself, or someone else, in an auto accident. A compulsion, on the other hand, is an *act* that intrudes into a person's behavior. One compulsive person may wash his hands every few minutes; another must count all the steps she climbs; another cannot sleep at night without stacking the day's change on the bureau—quarters on the bottom, then nickels, then pennies, and dimes on top. But some people are compulsive in a more general way; they cannot tolerate disorder or uncertainty, and they strive for orderliness of thought, in dress, and at work. Indeed any undue emphasis on "doing things the right way" is in some degree compulsive.
   —Clifford T. Morgan, *A Brief Introduction to Psychology,* 2nd ed.

   c. **Diagnostic Criteria for**
      300.3. Obsessive-Compulsive Disorder
      A. Either obsessions or compulsions:
         Obsessions as defined by (1), (2), (3), and (4):
         (1) recurrent and persistent thoughts, impulses, or images that are experienced, at some time during the disturbance, as intrusive and inappropriate and that cause marked anxiety or distress

(2) the thoughts, impulses, or images are not simply excessive worries about real-life problems

(3) the person attempts to ignore or suppress such thoughts, impulses, or images, or to neutralize them with some other thought or action

(4) the person recognizes that the obsessional thoughts, impulses, or images are a product of his or her own mind (not imposed from without as in thought insertion)

Compulsions as defined by (1) and (2):

(1) repetitive behaviors (e.g., hand washing, ordering, checking) or mental acts (e.g., praying, counting, repeating words silently) that the person feels driven to perform in response to an obsession, or according to rules that must be applied rigidly

(2) the behaviors or mental acts are aimed at preventing or reducing distress or preventing some dreaded event or situation; however, these behaviors or mental acts either are not connected in a realistic way with what they are designed to neutralize or prevent or are clearly excessive

—Reprinted with permission from the *Diagnostic and Statistical Manual of Mental Disorders,* Fourth Edition. Copyright 1994 American Psychiatric Association.

2. The following passage comes from a syndicated advice column for investors that appears in newspapers across America. The author, Malcolm Berko, is responding to a letter from "S. T." of Woodland Park, Colorado, who, though deeply in debt, contemplates using an inheritance of $105,000 to finance his son's college education. Try to determine any attitudes, values, interests, and experiences shared by Berko's audience. As much as possible, connect the inferences you draw to specific details in Berko's response.

Don't be stupid. You guys are in hock up to your earballs, and soon as you get a gift from God you're hot to trot to spend it. Suckers like you who pledge their incomes 10 years hence are seldom given a second chance . . . in life. And most that do fail because they can't discipline themselves for the future. It must be genetic! . . .

Forget Junior's college education. Frankly, many of today's colleges are nursery schools for teenage high school mutants. Most colleges have lowered their testing standards so that almost anyone with sixth-grade qualifications can get a degree. And the College Board in March 1994 made its SAT questions so simple that applicants with room-temperature IQs earn acceptable scores.

In my opinion college degrees are fraudulent diplomas certifying an education that never happened. Today's students believe that paying four years of tuition entitles them to a degree, and so many colleges have acquiesced that we have created a new national social disease called the "dumbing down of America." Tell Junior to join the armed services. . . .

Main Idea

As you saw in Chapter 4, the central question a reader must ask about a work is what, specifically, it is about. Many writers announce their main point in a single sentence—the thesis statement. But since so many good writers develop their ideas in other ways, you cannot always expect to find a one-sentence statement of the main idea at the beginning of a text. Sometimes writers state the main idea in the middle; sometimes they put it at the end; and some other times they make their point throughout the course of a work without ever summarizing it in a single sentence. And since not every writer is a good one, sometimes writers wander from point to point without ever achieving a focus.

Important questions that you must ask, then, in any analysis of a text are these: (1) What is its main idea? (2) Has the writer kept to the topic, providing a unified essay that is indeed about that idea? The best advice for discovering a main idea is to read attentively and to become actively involved in your reading. Reread where necessary and read with a pencil, underlining and writing comments in the margin whenever feasible. Then try to summarize the main idea in your own words.

Analyzing the Main Idea

EXERCISES

1. As a review of the skills studied in Chapter 4, read the following essay carefully, underlining the important statements and then stating the main idea in your own words.

Frat Boys Make Good Grown-Ups . . .
Mark Adams

Ten years ago, when I received my SAE pledge pin at the University of Illinois, the fraternity boy was still an innocuous icon of goofy campus high jinks, still living the cliché of the beanie-wearing, goldfish-eating scamp. But the young bucks who pulled into places like Ann Arbor, Berkeley and Chapel Hill for the first time this fall are being greeted with a much different portrait, that of a date-raping, hate-mongering scoundrel who epitomizes the decline of the American university. Nowadays, complete strangers expect me to break down sobbing like Jimmy Swaggart—*I have sinned!*— when my fraternity past is "outed." America's puritanical contempt for fraternities, like its contempt for adult bookstores, is exceeded only by its fascination with what goes on inside them.

Unlike federal crimes, the misdeeds of a frat boy have no statute of limitations. I confess to being guilty of most of them: dispensing silly nicknames derived from bodily functions; engaging in intricate handshakes; and making the occasional foray into pyromania (the house had too many futons anyway). But mark you, I learned more about how the world operates in that beery house than I did in any economics class—and I'm referring to more than my discovery that you can catapult a melon great distances using two-by-fours and surgical tubing. The acquaintances of mine who most disapprove of my past—typically Ivy Leaguers who proudly shunned the "elitist" Greek system and instead erected DIVEST NOW shantytowns on the quad—often scold me for having associated with what they unfairly assume was a homogeneous mob of uncouth, right-wing assholes. As every member of the Greek system knows, a fraternity house is an ego crucible in which one quickly develops the peace-making skills that prevent each semester from becoming a repeat performance of *Lord of the Flies*.

Now, I won't pretend for a moment that I joined a frat because I thought it would make me a better human being. Like any repressed postadolescent freshly dumped on a collegiate playground, I was out for a good time. I found it. My fraternity brothers and I spent our weekends up to our armpits in unlimited sausage products, rivers of Schlitz and 500-watt stereos seemingly incapable of emitting anything but Rush and Van Halen. And we drank that beer with dozens of gorgeous women—the house's "little sisters"—who actually enjoyed hanging around the building we lived in. A fraternity is your average 18-year-old male's dream: a low-rent version of the Playboy Mansion, with a lot less sex and a lot more punching other guys in the shoulder.

The question I'm asked most frequently and accusingly about frat life is, "What did you have to do to get in?" Granted, the first, or "pledge," year can be harrowing. (Confidential to the SAE class of 1999: Beware the mysterious appearance of large vats of vanilla pudding.) But the bulk of pledge-year unpleasantness involves performing menial tasks and memorizing inane house history, not having intercourse with goats and electrical appliances. Like Woodstock stories, hazing tales tend to grow exponentially in outrageousness over time. I wish I'd kept a list of all the objects I've been told that someone's friend's second cousin was supposedly forced to copulate with or pick up between his butt cheeks. ("It's *true!*") The media don't help matters, habitually blowing out of proportion stories about purported fraternal atrocities while taking a "kids will be kids" attitude toward the rest of the student body's indiscretions. A few years ago, when I saw a front-page headline in the *New York Times* about the bust of three houses at the University of Virginia, I expected to read how the Delts had kidnapped a troop of Camp Fire Girls and used them to smuggle Stinger missiles to Cuba. What I found instead was a tale of overzealous drug agents gloating over a haul of pot and mushrooms that wouldn't last from Chicago to Milwaukee on the Black Crowes' tour bus. Drugs on campus—*who knew?*

What gets lost in the maelstrom of fraternity horror stories is the sense of tolerance and commitment that living with a hundred guys between the ages of 18 and 21 forces you to learn. If someone gets on your nerves in the dorms, you can petition to switch rooms. In a fraternity, escape isn't the answer—compromise is. Remember the jazz-dance major who struggled with his gender? I showered beside him every morning without puerile, knee-jerk, "don't drop the soap" fear. The farm boy who chewed tobacco while he ate? He sat next to me at dinner. That's why fraternity men make such good brokers and congressmen—they already know that in the real world one has to cut deals with cretins and idiots, and that you can't run away from everyone whose interests and foibles don't jibe with your own.

One of my fondest college memories involves an SAE brother of mine whose views on virtually everything were so opposite my own that a warm friendship grew out of our mutual antipathy. He was a huge country-boy ROTC cadet, and his loyalty saved me one snowy night from a well-deserved pummeling outside a club in downtown Champaign. My beer-loosened tongue had irked three of my fellow undergrads— Rugby players, no less. Just as my antagonists were circling in for the kill on a deserted corner, my fraternity brother came charging through the blizzard in full army uniform. He strode past my would-be attackers and, without breaking his lockstep, tossed me over his shoulder like a sack of De Kalb corn. He carried me the half mile back to the house, muttering the entire time about how a strong U.S. military had once again made it possible for a wiseass liberal to shoot his mouth off.

In the spirit of compromise, I didn't disagree.

2. The following is an excerpt from the opening handout in an upper-level college course. A list of class policies is not usually considered to have a main idea apart from the policies themselves. Nevertheless, do you find a theme, a central idea running through these policies? If so, how can you summarize it?

Attendance policy: Your regular attendance is an essential requirement of the course, and attendance will be taken at each meeting. While there is no penalty for up to three absences, each absence beginning with the fourth, unless excused for a legitimate reason, will result in a one-letter lowering of your final course grade. Students missing more than six classes (for any reason) will have missed too much of the course to receive credit for taking it and should withdraw to avoid a failing grade. Attendance will be taken at the beginning of each class. (Please do *not* submit excuses for the first three absences—no matter how noble—since none is needed.)

Late arrival: You are also required to be here on time. Late arrival causes a disruption of the class and is strongly discouraged. Consequently, three arrivals after attendance is taken will be counted as equivalent to one absence. Should you arrive late, it is *your* responsibility to check with me after class to be marked present; otherwise, you will be recorded as absent.

Reading assignments: You are expected and required to be well prepared for each class meeting. In order for you to contribute constructively to class discussions and to profit from lectures, it is essential that you have read the assignments with care. Unannounced quizzes will be frequent; results will be a significant factor in final grading decisions, since they reflect the seriousness of your participation in the course. Continuous studying and keeping up are essential; this is not a course in which students can wait until exam-time to begin studying.

Exams: Four exams will be given, after each quarter of the semester. Failure to take any of the four exams at the assigned time will result in a failing grade for the course. Make-up exams will not be given, except for a documented medical or other emergency. Any make-up will be given during the final exam period (following the final exam) and will be more difficult than the regularly scheduled exam. It is your responsibility to know the date and time of the final exam and to make advance plans accordingly. Make-up exams will *not* be given to accommodate conflicting engagements, outside jobs, or early vacations.

Course grades: Your final grade will be based principally on the four exams and a writing assignment. Passing grades on the exams and paper range from A+ (4.33) to D– (0.67). Failing grades are F (0), F– (–1.0) and F– – (–2.0). The five grades will be averaged to determine the course grade. Quiz grades will be the deciding factor when a student's average is within 0.1 of another grade. Absences in excess of six, cheating, failure to take an exam, or failure to submit the assigned paper will automatically result in a failing grade for the course. Please take note: The course grade will be determined strictly by calculation based on your performance. The professor does not "give" grades; the grade you receive in this course will be the grade you have earned for yourself.

A final observation: As you can see from the above, you are expected to be a serious, self-disciplined, conscientious student in this class, and responsibility for your actions and performance is entirely yours, not the instructor's. In the past, students who have worked conscientiously and who have consistently come to class prepared have done well in this course. Persons with poor work habits have found themselves having to repeat it.

Development

If stating an idea were enough, there would be no books or essays. Each piece of writing would consist only of a topic sentence. Of course, more is needed. Writers must explain, expand, and support their ideas. Sometimes facts or logic is called for, sometimes narration of events, and sometimes examples, illustrations, and reasons. A mathematics textbook calls for clear, step-by-step reasoning, with many examples and exercises to reinforce each lesson. New interpretations of historical events call for background information, direct evidence, and support from authoritative sources. The way that an author chooses to develop a main idea depends on the work's purpose and its intended audience.

Writers develop their ideas successfully when they support them with specific, concrete evidence. In the following excerpt, the writer answers her opening question with a series of examples.

Who were the influential male models of appearance and behavior in turn-of-the-century America? Sports figures like boxer John L. Sullivan were important, as were businessmen and industrialists. In addition, western cowboys were also admired. They had inherited the mantle of the frontiersmen and Indian fighters after Owen Wister apotheosized their lives as cattle raisers into a saga of gunslinging drama in his 1901 novel *The Virginian*. But there were others whose image was softer and whose aggressive masculinity was countered by sophistication and humor.

Cosmopolitan men of the theater, for example, were popular. This was the age, after all, when the Barrymores first rose to prominence. In the 1890s many stationery and jewelry stores displayed in their windows photos of Maurice Barrymore holding an elegant demitasse cup and saucer in his hand and garbed in full dress as in one of his famed portrayals. . . .

—Lois W. Banner, *American Beauty*

In much of the writing that you do in college, you will need to conduct additional research to develop your ideas. Outside sources can provide you with the information you lack, and expert sources can lend your paper the prestige of their authority. In the following excerpt, the authors rely on research sources to support their own ideas about science classrooms:

The design of this science classroom . . . is also based on the notion that schools are not just buildings, and that all people are life-long learners. The need for relevance in the experiences of school children and for applicability and currency in teacher-training programs is not a new one; however, these needs are not often met.

In *Educating Americans for the 21st Century*, a National Science Board report, technology and an understanding of technological advances and applications were recognized as basic. While initial effects of the infusion of computers into instruction might not have produced desired results (Greenberg 107), the relevance of technology education is still apparent. Kids learn differently today, differently from the learning modes familiar to us. In the 20th century people were "paper" trained. Youngsters of the 21st century are "light" trained, i.e., comfortable with video- and computer-based material. Matching learning styles with delivery systems is crucial for success.

—Richard J. Reif and Gail M. Morse, "Restructuring the Science Classroom"

The authors make their thesis about technology in classrooms more persuasive by citing support from a report of the National Science Board. Even when they cite another authority who disagrees with their contention (Greenberg), they score points by showing they are well informed and have considered all sides of the issue.

EXERCISE | **Analyzing Development**

Read each of the following passages and answer these questions: What is its main idea? What specific facts, ideas, or examples does the author present to support and develop that idea? What in the passage, if anything, helps to convince readers of the author's authority in addressing that idea? Would a different approach (for example, more citing of research sources or of personal experiences) have been more effective?

a. **Living Too Long**
    Michael Norman

Only Aunt Millie survives. She is 88 now, a widow with alabaster hair and skin like parchment. Some days she seems more frail than others, and it is on these melancholy days that she begins to muse. Her eyes fill with doubt and she says things like: "Why? Why are the scientists breaking their brains to get us to live longer? I want to know, what's the point?"

She keeps going, of course, because she has the habit of living. She cooks her own meals and cleans her own house, an apartment on a narrow street in Brooklyn where she has lived since 1941—three rooms and a tiny kitchen with a blue step-stool.

I visit her twice a month. I take her to the podiatrist and the supermarket. I sit on the step-stool and listen.

She is my grandmother's younger sister, the only survivor of that clan and now the family's grand matriarch. My mother and cousins worry about her health—her hypertension, loss of hearing, dizzy spells (one tumble broke her wrist), a minor stroke, chronic fatigue, periodic insomnia, polyuria. I worry about her soul, her state of being.

"It's no good," she once told a friend. "I'm living too long already. What's the point?"

In fact, these days the old are living so long that they have created nothing less than a new stage of life. Since 1900, the life expectancy of the average American has increased from 47 years to 74 years. At the end of World War II, only 8 percent of the population was over 65. Today that number is nearly 13 percent; by 2050 it is likely to be 20 percent: an estimated 100 million elderly men and women.

We can thank—"blame," Aunt Millie would surely say—science for this. In a thoughtful book called *The Journey of Life: A Cultural History of Aging in America,* a historian named Thomas R. Cole says that in the last 200 years the social and biomedical sciences have thought of old age as only "an engineering problem to be solved or at least ameliorated." But by reducing old age to a "problem," science has impoverished it, Cole says.

Science has robbed old age of the rich symbolism and purpose it had for most of our history. In other words, old age no longer stands for anything. It is empty, purposeless, without meaning. And as "spiritual animals, we need meaning," Cole says, no less than we need sustenance and health.

At the moment, more than 31 million Americans are over 65. So many people are living so long that retirement is no longer just a transient afterpiece, the brief interregnum before death. The species has achieved something new, a second summer, if you will.

b. **Where Woman Was, There Gal Shall Be**
    Natalie Angier

We women are so fickle. We just can't decide what we want to be called. Back in the pre-Cambrian era of the early feminist movement —you know, two or three decades ago—we renounced the use of the word "girl" to describe adult females. Even worse was "lady," with its hint of class structure, petticoats and Emily Post. Out went the silly Audubon argot, the "chicks" and the "birds"; out, too, went the Raymond Chandleresque "dames" and "broads." And use the nasty B word, buster, at the risk of a kick in the T's.

We are Woman. Hear us snore.

Restless once again, we are struggling to find a word that conveys snazziness and style, a casual term for the double-X set, a word without condescension or sneer, something more relaxed than "woman," something less fussy than "female," our equivalent of guy. A delicious egalitarian word like . . . gal.

After years of dangling in lexical limbo, not a putdown but not quite kosher for general usage either, the word gal lately has gained legitimacy, even a mild cachet. It has appeared about 70 times in the *New York Times* this year, roughly double the usage of six years ago. In the *Washington Post,* gal was used 85 times in 1995, compared to 58 times in 1989. O.K., newspapers may not exactly be arbiters of hipness, but keep in mind that most of these uses occur in quotations of real men and women.

As for trendiness, who is a better judge of it than the young? Kate Clinton, a columnist for *The Progressive* and a self-described "gal comedian," said she started incorporating the word into her routines after hearing women in their 20's talk about their gal pals.

"I like the word gal; it's a great-feeling word to say," she said. "It has a guttural quality to it, it sort of rolls around in the right side of your mouth. Ms. Clinton appreciates the sense of it as well. "It's a sororal, flapperish, Dorothy Parker word," she said. "A career gal is somebody who has a need for smart martinis after work." During a recent performance, she introduced a variant, "your galship."

Those trying to resuscitate the old word from its storage in Broadway musicals know that gal has a rich and prismatic quality to it. A gal is a grown person with a sense of humor whom you'd better take seriously. A gal is a sexy subject rather than a sexy object. A gal can be any age as long as she's too old to be in a Calvin Klein ad. A gal looks after herself. If she's a musician, she's either in rock or country and western; if she's a good sport, it means she plays sports.

Charles S. Mechem, commissioner of the Ladies Professional Golf Association, would no more refer to his athletes as ladies than the head of the N.A.A.C.P. would call its members colored people. No, Mr. Mechem boasts about his gals, their ferocity, their tenacity, the way they can swing a club cleanly.

Part of the reason why it has taken time for gal to catch on as thoroughly and uneventfully as did the word "guy" is the word's etymology. Gal is an alteration of that dread word, girl. Anne Soukhanov, lexicographer supreme, suggests that the word arose as a spelling of a British dialectical variation, when girl might have come out sounding almost like "gel." According to the *Random House Historical Dictionary of American Slang,* the first citation of the word dates to about 1770, in "Mother Goose":

> *What care I how black I be,*
> *Twenty pounds will marry me;*
> *If Twenty won't, Forty shall,*
> *I am my Mother's bouncing gal.*

Whatever the word's origins, gal no longer implies "little girl," and according to Ms. Soukhanov, it is less a slang term than an informal one. "Unlike other terms for the female of the human species, this one doesn't seem to be overloaded with any kind of historical putdown," she said.

Not everybody is willing to embrace the expression. Lydia Sargent, an editor at *Z* magazine, a left-wing political publication, uses gal constantly in her column "Hotel Satire," but she means the term sarcastically. "It's a user-friendly word for girls," she said. "I think it's a pathetic description of women. I've never liked these cutesy words that imply we're all these cutesy giggling girls sitting around gossiping."

Mother Love, a radio personality in Los Angeles, said that when she aired a program recently on the subject of sexual harassment, listeners called in to give their opinions of various words for women, and some said they found gal offensive. But Ms. Love herself, an outspoken woman known for her down-to earth drama, said she sees the usefulness of gal and other informal words, depending on the context. She's girlfriend to her good friends. She's a broad when she stands toe to toe to a man. But she is *never* to be called the other sort of B. "Those are fighting words to me," she said.

In fact, nobody likes to be called by that other word, which may explain why a recent story in the *New York Times* referred to a certain breed of female dog as, yes, a pit bull gal.

Organization and Coherence

Good writing abides by a standard of courtesy. Like good hosts, writers treat their readers well. Of course, many great poets and novelists challenge their readers by experimenting with new ways to experience time, character, and ideas. But nonfiction writers, whose purpose typically is to inform or persuade their readers, are more straightforward. They usually make their point early and stick to it. Their readers have a right to expect clarity, order, and a fair amount of logic. As one writing theorist, Kenneth Burke, has claimed, writers have a duty to take their readers by the hand, walking them through the essay and helping them see connections between ideas, sentences, and paragraphs.

An analytical reader can ask the following questions about organization and coherence: Does the writer provide indications of where the passage is heading? Can you follow the movement of ideas, or are you sometimes puzzled, lost, or taken by surprise? Is there a logic to the way the text is put together? Is there a clear link between the main idea and the support (reasons, examples, and explanations)? Is the supporting material arranged in an order that makes sense? Does the writer make the passage readable by providing transitions when new ideas are introduced?

Not every writer gives readers the help they need. The following passage leaves its readers to shift for themselves; it is so poorly organized that a reader can never be certain where it is aiming to go next. The writer builds up expectations about one topic but suddenly heads off in another direction.

> You wouldn't believe my son Jason. He was so unbelievably wild and inconsiderate yesterday I got one of my headaches. They come on with a vengeance, with no warning. I was so crazy with pain last week, it will be a miracle if my sister-in-law ever speaks to me again. I've been to specialist after specialist and none of them can find the problem. A lot of money they get paid, for what? Fancy offices and fancy diplomas so they can charge fancy fees. When I think about doctors I get another headache. My head throbs and my eyes don't focus. I don't want anything to do with people, and I'm as miserable to Jason as he usually is to me. Maybe Jason will be lucky enough to become a doctor someday and then the money will stay in the family.

This writer has given no thought to organization, writing whatever comes into his head. He leads us to think the paragraph will be about his son's behavior, but it turns into a discussion of his headaches, with frequent detours to other topics. Later we expect to learn what he said to his sister-in-law, but that topic is abandoned with no awareness of the reader's unsatisfied curiosity. The topic of doctors is introduced, then forgotten, and finally returned to at the end, with no thought for logical ordering.

In contrast, the essays in the following exercise are coherent, readable, and logical because the writers spent days, perhaps weeks, thinking about the best shape for their readers. They took pains to organize the movement of their ideas and to provide examples, signposts, and transitions.

EXERCISE | *Analyzing Organization*

A short essay and the introduction to a fairly lengthy magazine article follow. Read each carefully. Then explain as specifically as you can how the author has put each text together. Why is the text arranged as it is? How does the writer move from one idea to the next? What are the links between sentences and paragraphs? Has the writer provided help to guide you through the text?

Not Hopeless
Ernest van den Haag

In 1971 Richard Herrnstein, co-author with Charles Murray of [a 1994 book, *The Bell Curve*], published an article in *The Atlantic Monthly* arguing that success—status, income, power—now depends on intelligence. We are becoming a "meritocracy" with great hereditary inequalities. *The Bell Curve* lucidly organizes an immense amount of data demonstrating empirically that, despite costly efforts to stave it off, meritocracy is becoming a reality. Before continuing, let me dispose of two distractions which have produced hysterical and silly columns—e.g., in *The New Republic* (unexpected) and the *New York Times* (expected); although, to be fair, elsewhere the *Times* was rational.

1. *The Bell Curve* shows that cognitive ability measured by IQ tests reliably predicts success—professional, academic, pecuniary—and that, on average, African-Americans have an IQ about 15 points below that of Caucasians, whose IQ, in turn, is lower (by about 5 points) than that of East Asians. Success differs accordingly. However, the point would be the same if all low- and high-IQ persons were Caucasians. Ethnic differences in IQ cause political complications but do not otherwise affect the hereditary social stratification described and predicted by *The Bell Curve*. (Incidentally, why should anyone expect all ethnic groups to have the same average IQ? Why not the same skin color?)

2. The authors establish the predictive validity of IQ tests for all groups and estimate that 60 per cent of the variation in measured intelligence is due to genetic differences, which means that nearly half of the variation depends on environmental factors. The proof of this point seems fairly conclusive, based on identical twins separated at birth and on adopted children. Yet if intelligence depended exclusively on environmental influences, if it were entirely an acquired trait, that would hardly make a difference. We have no way of influencing the average cognitive ability of any group, regardless of whether it depends on environmental or genetic factors. Whatever other benefits they may yield, Head Start and similar schemes do not permanently raise the IQ of disadvantaged groups. Perhaps in the future we will find a way to increase cognitive ability genetically or environmentally. So far we have not. Thus it matters little whether the cognitive ability of groups is inherited or acquired. (Needless to say, there may be a genius within a low-IQ group and dolts within a high-IQ group; what applies to averages does not apply to individuals.)

Without distractions, what does *The Bell Curve* tell us? Past societies have offered very unequal opportunities and, linked to them, very unequal outcomes. Education was distributed unequally, depending on parental status. So was everything else. Individual status was ascribed rather than achieved. Little depended on intelligence, much on inherited status and wealth. This has changed. Opportunity has become more and more equal, inherited social privileges less and less important. College education is widely distributed, and the best colleges are available to the talented poor. By now, intelligence on the average predicts outcomes better than parental privilege.

Liberals believed that, once opportunity was equal, outcomes would become equal too: they thought unequal outcomes were due largely to unequal opportunities. However, Herrnstein and Murray show conclusively that inequalities won't disappear. This may account for the liberal media's rancorous reception of *The Bell Curve.* Individuals are born not as *tabulae rasae,* as many liberals believe, but with different intelligences, which produce very unequal outcomes.

Equal opportunity redistributes social inequalities but does not diminish them. It may increase them. God is not an egalitarian, much as Jefferson thought it "self-evident" that He is. People are born unequally gifted. If they have equal opportunity to use their unequal gifts, major social inequalities are unavoidable.

These inequalities may be augmented because people usually marry others with similar IQs. The poor transmit their low IQs and therewith their poverty. Their fertility exceeds that of the more intelligent and produces a permanent and growing underclass. Unwed mothers have low IQs on the average and provide environments not likely to help their children. They help to perpetuate the underclass. Criminals also come from low-IQ groups. With our egalitarian ideology we will have major social problems with the increasing inherited inequalities predicted. Their congruence with ethnic groupings will accentuate political problems.

The data Herrnstein and Murray provide are convincing, but I do have reservations about their more speculative inferences. People with low IQs will not be left hopeless, as they imply. Many kinds of socioeconomic success are independent of intelligence. A low-IQ youth may become a baseball player or a pop singer and do better than any professor. A low-IQ girl may become a supermodel. Such careers require neither stupidity nor intelligence. Sure, the (non-IQ) talents needed for these careers are rare and, therefore, such outcomes are statistically insignificant. But psychologically they generate hope, just as lotteries do. Success is possible, if not probable, for the low-IQ individual. Further, even those confined to the lowest jobs need not dwell in misery. In any future society practically all can be reasonably comfortable regardless of talent (unless they are highly self-destructive). The prediction of *The Bell Curve* that people with low IQs have to become wards of the government is rank speculation. We cannot predict future social policies and conflicts. Remember Karl Marx?

In any case, the structure of a future society does not really tell us how people will feel about it. The authors mention that intelligence is only one factor in prestige or self-esteem; but they hardly note that, in most high schools currently, intelligence is a negative factor, athletic ability (or attractiveness) a positive one in prestige and self-esteem. I do not know whether people in a future society will go far beyond these high-school evaluations. Will mathematicians be esteemed more and will they earn more than former high-school athletes?

The authors rightly commend individualism as an answer to group dissatisfactions based on low IQs and low success. Yet "affirmative action" and similar anti-individualist capers show that neither liberal politicians, nor bureaucrats, nor the favored groups want individualism. It would take another volume to explore why they have prevailed. Will they in the future? Charles Murray is just the man to explore this question.

Scientists, Politicians and the Public
Lucy Horwitz

What a strange place we've reached in the history of the complex relationship between science and society. Never has science made so much progress so rapidly. The Hubble telescope is expanding our knowledge of the universe on an almost daily basis; new disease-causing genes are discovered every week; the top quark has been found; and there's even the recent discovery (creation?) of a new phase state of matter—the

Bose-Einstein condensate. Yet the political climate has not been so unfriendly to science since the Scopes trial. Not only do we read that more people believe in alien abductions than accept Darwinian evolution, but the creationists are actually getting their nonsense into school text books and curricula. Congress is cutting basic research to the bone, and the public is up in arms because there is still no cure for AIDS or cancer. What is going on here?

There are two distinct aspects to the current anti-science climate, the practical and the ideological. On the practical level, the public mistrusts science first of all for its failure to solve all the problems it would like to see dealt with. The phrase "If we can go to the moon, why can't we cure the common cold" may be passé, but the attitude is very much alive. And not only do scientists fail to solve all problems, they even make mistakes and get things wrong. Worse yet, they change their minds. One day hormone replacement therapy is a must, the next it's a danger. First we're told to eat margarine instead of butter, then margarine is out and it's olive or canola oil. Canola who? What's a person to believe?

Not only does science provide little useful guidance, it creates horrible dangers: the atom bomb, agent orange, and now with all this genetic manipulation, who knows what monstrous things will be produced? And finally it costs too damn much. The government is spending tax dollars on all sorts of hare-brained schemes. Imagine financing that thing in Texas that no one could understand the use of, and then not building it anyway, billions of dollars later. Yes, seeing a man on the moon was exciting, but what did we ever get out of the space program but Mylar and Tang?

The other kind of problems that some members of the public have with science are cultural or ideological. The conflict between science and religion on such issues as evolution vs. creationism on the part of fundamentalists, and abortion and birth control on the part of Catholics and the religious right are the most obvious examples. But a distaste for science as a way of seeing the world need not be based on religion; it can be the result of a culture clash of a very different kind. To some, science is an elitist activity that excludes the less affluent and less educated from its benefits, both material and cultural. There's real fear of a coming two-tiered society—or is it here already?

Politicians, as representatives of the people, are caught in the middle. But they are people too, and may share in one or more of the attitudes just described. They have the power to act on their beliefs, which creates a separate set of problems. There are politicians who don't understand science, and feel all the resentments described above. They are free to cut and slash funds and programs, or to pass laws of the henceforth-π-will-equal-3 variety. There are politicians who don't understand science and are at the mercy of whatever experts tell them. There are politicians who don't care one way or another about science but will do whatever it takes to get re-elected. And of course there are those who do care and do try to understand, but have a difficult time making their way through the forest.

It's a mess, isn't it?

An interesting contrast to our current state of affairs is offered by [Bernard] Cohen in *Science and the Founding Fathers.* Of course, our founding fathers had the advantage of living in the Age of Reason. Newton's *Principia* appeared in 1687, Locke's *An Essay Concerning Human Understanding* in 1691. Benjamin Franklin, born in 1706, was a renowned scientist in his day, who, with his original research in electricity, had a part in shaping the new scientific view of the world. Jefferson, born in 1743, was educated at a time when that new world view had been accepted, and even digested, by most educated people.

The role that science played in society as whole was very different from what we see today. In many ways, our founding fathers lived in a much less democratic society than we do. Slavery was practiced not only in the South, but in all the colonies. Even among free men, vast educational disparities were taken for granted. A reputation for scientific knowledge was generally a cause for admiration, not envy and resentment.

Cohen makes a point of how greatly Franklin was respected in London and Paris for his work as a scientist, and how this furthered his diplomatic missions.

Of course, the relationship between science and government was also very different. Washington was not faced with funding a supercollider. Pursuit of science was left entirely to private enterprise. Cohen notes that the only mention of science in the Constitution says: "To promote the progress of Science and useful arts by securing for limited times to authors and inventors, the exclusive right to their respective writing and discoveries." In other words, the only encouragement of science was the awarding of patents.

Another interesting difference is the comparative lack of friction between science and religion. Certainly there were those who were violently opposed to science (William Blake was one), but not necessarily on religious grounds. The scientists of the day seemed little troubled by clashing beliefs. Newton, for example, wrote the following defense of atomic theory in *Opticks:* "It seems probable to me that God in the Beginning formed Matter in solid, massy, hard, impenetrable, moveable Particles, of such Sizes and Figures, and with such other Properties, and in such Proportion to Space, as most conduced to the End for which he formed them."

So what was the importance of science in the deliberations of our founding fathers? More than anything else, it was a turn of mind, a way of thinking, an approach to the world that said, "Let us observe, and we will find the truth." For example, Cohen tells of a highly charged and politicized controversy that arose over the relative merits of pointed versus blunt lightning rods.

He quotes Benjamin Franklin as saying he "never entered into any controversy [about his] philosophical opinions." They should "take their chance in the world. If they are *right,* truth and experience will support them; if *wrong* they ought to be refuted and rejected."

Both Franklin and Jefferson began by holding the prejudices of their day with regard to African slaves—that they were inherently inferior to white men. However, through observation and experience, both men came to change their minds. Jefferson's case is particularly interesting in that he was apparently always an abolitionist. He tried to include an abolitionist statement in the Declaration of Independence, but was voted down. Nevertheless, he held some extreme prejudices. In the same *Notes on the State of Virginia* in which he advocated the emancipation of all slaves, he wrote "in memory they are equal to the whites," in "reason [they are] much inferior." Five years later, Jefferson received a manuscript from one Bannaker, a black self-taught astronomer and mathematician. Jefferson publicized the manuscript with statements to the effect that the Africans' limitations mentioned in his *Notes* were no doubt due to the limited opportunities available in the slave state. He further hoped to see them become reestablished "on an equal footing with the other colors of the human family."

The founding fathers were true sons of the Age of Reason in that science formed the basic framework of their thinking. Cohen points out that they saw the creation of a new form of government as a scientific experiment whose success would validate it just as the return of a comet validates its orbit. There are countless examples of the use of just this kind of scientific metaphor in political discussions of the day. It was used to explain, to persuade and to inspire, as well as to inform the thinking of the founders. The notion of the balance of powers may well have been built on Newtonian physics (both accurate interpretations and misunderstandings), as well as being defended by metaphorical references to gravitational forces.

Cohen concludes with the following remarks:

> The metaphors drawn from the sciences give us an index of the high esteem then accorded to the study and understanding of nature. Even more important, the analysis of these metaphors indicates an implied set of values and cherished beliefs that enlarges both our view of history and our understanding of the inner forces that motivated some of the primary founders of our country.

WRITING A BRIEF READING ANALYSIS

Purpose, audience, main idea, development, organization and coherence—these are the most important, but by no means the only, aspects you can consider when you analyze a reading source. In addition to these general topics, each work must be considered on its own terms. Each work has its unique identity, and an analytical reader will find much in it to consider and talk about. And because readers take an active part in their reading, so too each reader's analysis will be different. It is important when you analyze a work to see it clearly, but it is also wise not to worry about being "right." In analyzing what you read, you must be willing to trust your own judgment.

Now that you have analyzed different elements of readings in isolation, you should have a better sense of how those elements work together. An analysis of the whole text should consider all five aspects. Read the following text carefully and analytically, asking yourself questions about each of the elements we have considered so far.

Black Pride for White People

Are You *Sure* You Don't Have an African Ancestor?

Adrian Piper

The fact is that the longer a person's family has lived in this country, the higher the probable percentage of African ancestry that person's family is likely to have—bad news for the Daughters of the American Revolution, I'm afraid. And the proximity to the continent of Africa of the country of origin from which one's forebears emigrated, as well as the colonization of a part of Africa by that country, are two further variables that increase the probability of African ancestry within that family. It would appear that only the Lapps of Norway are safe.

A number of years ago I was doing research on a video installation on the subject of racial identity and miscegenation, and came across the Phipps case of Louisiana in the early 1980s. Susie Guillory Phipps had identified herself as white and, according to her own testimony (but not that of some of her black relatives), had believed that she was white, until she applied for a passport, when she discovered that she was identified on her birth records as black by virtue of having one thirty-second African ancestry. She brought suit against the state of Louisiana to have her racial classification changed. She lost the suit but effected the overthrow of the law identifying individuals as black if they had one thirty-second African ancestry, leaving on the books a prior law identifying as black an individual who had any African ancestry—the "one-drop" rule that uniquely characterizes the classification of blacks in the United States in fact though no longer in law. So according to this long-standing convention of racial classification, a white who acknowledges any African ancestry implicitly acknowledges being black—a social condition, more than an identity, that no white person would voluntarily assume, even in imagination. This is one reason that whites, educated and uneducated alike, are so resistant to considering the probable extent of racial miscegenation.

No reflective and well-intentioned white person who is consciously concerned to end racism wants to admit to instinctively recoiling at the thought of being identified as black herself. But if you want to see such a white person do this, just peer at the person's facial features and tell her, in a complimentary tone of voice, that she looks as though she might have some black ancestry, and watch her reaction. It's not a test I find or any black person finds particularly pleasant to apply (that is, unless one dislikes the person and wants to inflict pain deliberately), and having once done so inadvertently, I will never do it again. The ultimate test of a person's repudiation of racism is not what she can contemplate *doing* for or on behalf of black people, but whether she herself can contemplate calmly the likelihood of *being* black. If racial hatred has not manifested itself in any other context, it will do so here if it exists, in hatred of the self as identified with the other—that is, as self-hatred projected onto the other.

When I was an undergraduate minoring in medieval and Renaissance musicology, I worked with a fellow music student—white—in the music library. I remember his reaction when I relayed to him an article I'd recently read arguing that Beethoven had African ancestry. Beethoven was one of his heroes, and his vehement derision was completely out of proportion to the scholarly worth of the hypothesis. But when I suggested that he wouldn't be so skeptical if the claim were that Beethoven had some Danish ancestry, he fell silent. In those days we were very conscious of covert racism, as our campus was exploding all around us because of it. More recently I premiered at a gallery a video installation exploring the issue of African ancestry among white Americans. A white male viewer commenced to kick the furniture, mutter audibly that he was white and was going to stay that way, and start a fistfight with my dealer. Either we are less conscious of covert racism twenty years later, or we care less to contain it.

Among politically committed and enlightened whites, the inability to acknowledge their probable African ancestry is the last outpost of racism. It is the litmus test that separates those who have the courage of their convictions from those who merely subscribe to them and that measures the depth of our dependence on a presumed superiority (of any kind, anything will do) to other human beings—anyone, anywhere—to bolster our fragile self-worth.

When I turned 40 a few years ago, I gave myself the present of rereading the personal journals I have been keeping since age 11. I was astounded at the chasm between my present conception of my own past, which is being continually revised and updated to suit present circumstances, and the actual past events, behavior, and emotions I recorded as faithfully as I could as they happened. My derelictions, mistakes, and failures of responsibility are much more evident in those journals than they are in my present, sanitized, and virtually blameless image of my past behavior. It was quite a shock to encounter in those pages the person I actually have been rather than the person I now conceive myself to have been. My memory is always under the control of the person I now want and strive to be, and so rarely under the control of the facts. If the personal facts of one's past are this difficult for other people to face too, then perhaps it is no wonder that we must cast about outside ourselves for someone to feel superior to, even though there are so many blunders and misdeeds in our own personal histories that might serve that function.

For whites to acknowledge their blackness is, then, much the same as for men to acknowledge their femininity and for Christians to acknowledge their Judaic heritage. It is to reinternalize the external scapegoat through which they have sought to escape their own sense of inferiority.

If you were in a class of college students assigned to write an analysis of Adrian Piper's text, you could begin by freewriting about each of the five elements. You might produce preliminary notes such as these:

Purpose: Adrian Piper tries to rouse us from the comfortable, self-righteous certainty that our country and we as individuals have overcome racism. By the time we reach the last paragraph, we're uncomfortable with the smug assumption that we're more enlightened than members of the DAR, whom she ridicules in the first paragraph. We get the sense that Piper is going to share a good laugh with us at the expense of overtly racist snobs—that she's going to cut them down to (our) size. It's like Piper starts out "with" us, sharing a jibe at the expense of an easy target, but then she turns the tables, putting us on the defensive.

Audience: Piper is addressing an audience of well-educated readers who deplore racism. However, they're not the kind of people who might call up Donahue or Oprah and naively (or angrily) insist that there is no vestige of racism in their particular neighborhood or community. These readers understand that because racism is part of our cultural history, it's built into so many societal institutions that it's almost invisible at times. It's tempting to say that Piper is addressing a white audience, but that may not be the case. However, black readers are likely to respond to Piper's ideas differently than white readers.

Main Idea: Piper is saying that a white person's inability to acknowledge the possibility that she might have an African ancestor is "the litmus test" for covert racism. The last two paragraphs, however, seem to extend that idea a bit, to offer some observations about self-honesty and the need to feel superior to others.

Development: Piper uses a variety of evidence to support her observations. Though her claims in ¶1 aren't documented or developed, they sound authoritative. That impression is reinforced by the research into legal cases evident in the following paragraph. After ¶3, Piper begins to rely more on personal observation and experience. Most of these observations and experiences must be painful to recollect and write about, and they're likely to discomfort most readers.

Organization and Coherence: The first paragraph opens with an authoritative assertion ("The fact is that . . . ") but ends with a touch of irony ("only the Lapps of Norway are safe"). The next paragraph is rather dry and factual by comparison, though it ends with some disquieting assertions about *all* whites, "educated and uneducated alike." The next paragraph is pivotal because it's here that the reader gets drawn in—implicated, if you will—when Piper says. . . . "But if you want to see . . . a white person do this. . . . " This paragraph ends with an important assertion, signaled by the word *ultimate,* followed by a sentence that explores the practical consequences of that assertion—an "if . . . then" statement. This is the first suggestion that Piper is talking about racism as a symptom of something much larger—self-hatred. In ¶4, she tests these ideas against personal observation. In the following short paragraph, she extends her ideas a bit further, then returns to personal experience in ¶6, before stating her conclusions in the last paragraph. In fact, throughout her text, Piper alternates between inferences in odd-numbered paragraphs and personal observations (signaled by the pronoun *I*) that support them in even-numbered paragraphs.

These notes are only a rough beginning. You could then write a draft of the paper, which you would edit and revise. Your polished analysis might look like this:

Analysis: "Black Pride for White People"

Adrian Piper has written an essay likely to discomfit

most white readers and to confirm the perceptions of many

African Americans. Whites in America, especially those who are privileged, tend to consider themselves immune to racial prejudice. While they may recognize and deplore racism as a societal problem, they assume that they can transcend it as private individuals. Striving to undermine this smug assumption, Piper confronts readers with the observation that while most Americans have at least some African ancestry, very few whites will acknowledge it freely. Their refusal, often vehement and hostile, is, in Piper's view, proof of covert racism.

Piper pursues a careful strategy that may catch some white reader unawares. She does this by distancing racism at first, associating it with the Daughters of the American Revolution, an organization toward which few of her readers will feel loyalty or empathy. But by the third paragraph, it becomes clear that Piper is also implicating "reflective and well-intentioned" whites in her critique. This becomes even more evident when she supports her claims in the following paragraph with personal experiences involving a university student and a museum patron. Many of Piper's white readers will find it harder to distance themselves from these educated elites.

A careful look at the structure of this text reveals that Piper alternates between shorter paragraphs that make assertions (paragraphs 1, 3, 5, and 7) and longer ones that support those assertions with details drawn from personal observation and experience (paragraphs 2, 4, and 6). In fact, the further she proceeds, the more personal those details become: paragraph 2 summarizes a research project undertaken by the author (the pronoun *I* appears only in the first sentence); paragraph 4 presents the author's observation of unexpected racist behavior by two educated whites; paragraph 6 describes the author's own attempts to confront self-hatred.

Paragraph 6 completes a subtle shift in focus that Piper has introduced earlier when she first refers to "self-hatred projected onto the other." What makes racism so pernicious and difficult to eradicate, Piper asserts, is the way it reinforces a basic human drive to distance those aspects of the self that a person is ashamed of. Having someone else, who is completely different in some very visible way (like race or gender), enables a person to cope more easily with this self-hatred. Piper seems to suggest, then, that eliminating racism would contribute to the self-esteem of all Americans.

ASSIGNMENT   Writing a Brief Reading Analysis

Analyze the reading selection that follows, using this procedure:

1. Read the essay twice; underline main ideas and write comments in the margin.
2. Freewrite comments about each of the five elements for analysis.
3. Prepare a carefully edited and revised analysis of about three hundred to four hundred words. Begin with a description of the essay (its purpose, audience, and main idea), and then analyze its support, organization, and coherence. Polish your draft so that it is a unified, readable paper.

 READING SELECTION

The following essay was written by a twenty-three-year-old copywriter for a software-development company and appeared in the December 4, 1995, issue of *Newsweek*.

Family Resemblances

Not long ago, I was embarrassed to be likened to my mother.
Now I'm pleased that I am.

JENNIFER NATHANSON

1   I was concerned recently when I felt something unstoppable taking over my life. It was a kind of transformation. Then it became clear: I'm becoming my mother. Not so long ago, I was mortified to be caught shopping with my mother. When we went to the store, I'd be embarrassed by her handful of coupons and her uncanny timing. "Why do you need to have the designer brand? This $5.99 shirt is just as good," she'd say, at the precise moment one of my school's "popular kids" was turning the corner.

2   Occasionally, it was my mom's turn to drive the carpool. My friends' parents had expensive cars with leather seats. Our car was a gold Ford Maverick leaking some oily substance that, we once were warned, was highly flammable. I used to scrunch down in my seat, my head barely discernible from outside—just in case I might be photographed for the front page of the local newspaper. The headline, I thought, would read LOOK! THAT'S JENNIFER IN HER TOTALLY UNCOOL CAR WITH HER TOTALLY UNCOOL MOTHER!

3   Salesmen would ask if Mom and I were sisters. My mother would giggle, knowing that the "you're so young-looking that your daughter must be your sister" compliment is an old sales ploy. Still, she seemed to believe it, even if I was only 10 years old. This was a precursor to a phrase everyone would pronounce as soon as they saw us together: "Why, you look like twins!" Upon hearing this, my mom would stand tall and smile. I, on the other hand, in a classic adolescent maneuver, would frown, gasp or make gagging noises.

4   At the time, my mother was working night shifts as a nurse. Her days were sprinkled with intermittent naps, that never really helped the fatigue. Even so, she was unfailingly available for me. Yet through the eyes of a pre-teenager, this was a curse. I wanted to be independent. I wanted to be the boss. And I would make these intentions clear by rolling my eyes, crossing my arms and glaring, or by stomping to my room with door slamming and sulking for hours.

5   When college beckoned, I went far away from my Miami, Fla., home to Ohio's Oberlin College. There I was finally free of maternal scrutiny. I was able to dye my hair red, then black, then red with black streaks—all without being subjected to the "tsk tsk" eyes of my mother. During one visit home to Miami, I had my nose pierced and my hair colored fuchsia—on the same morning. I looked like Ronald McDonald on a bad hair day. My mother took one look at me, wisely recognized that I would do whatever I wanted—and righted herself just before she could faint. I was so proud of her!

6   When I got back to college, my chain-smoking, eyebrow-pierced friends thought I looked wonderful. Later, I began to grow tired of hair falling out from the chemicals that were regularly poured onto my scalp. So I colored my hair to my natural color, brown, and removed the nose ring. Fortunately, the fuchsia metamorphosis lasted only three weeks.

7   Now I work full-time in Iowa, take graduate courses at night and live with my boyfriend, who is investing serious time in a doctoral program. The change in my attitude, hair color and behavior has been dramatic. One day, I'm trying to get into a bar with a fake ID. The next, I'm taking careful note of the Frugal Gourmet's recipes. Rather than looking like Cyndi Lauper, I'm getting more akin to my mother.

8   A few months ago I was summoned home for my father's 50th-birthday party. I was thankful that my hair no longer caused anyone—especially my relatives—to have spasms. If any of them knew I'd once harbored a nose ring, they would have choked on their conch-fritter hors d'oeuvres.

9   Upon seeing me, distant cousins warmly embraced me. "I don't know if we've met, but you must be Gail's daughter," they said, a smile directed at the inescapable resemblance between me and the mother from whom I always tried to escape. I felt flattered. Pride welled up inside of me.

10   As the night wore on, a few of the relatives got together near the beach for an after-midnight drink. I was sure that my mom would pass on the invitation. Her nights usually ended right after the late news. Still, she went and she laughed and chatted into the night while I struggled to keep my eyes open. Wasn't it only a few years earlier that I was out dancing in the clubs until dawn?

11   When it was time to leave, I found that—unlike the college student who used to run to the airport at the end of every vacation, multicolored hair flying in the wind—I wanted to stay. From the moment I returned to Iowa, I realized that the transformation was complete. I picked up stray papers and ran for the Lysol before I could set the luggage down. I asked my boyfriend whether our dog had been fed and walked. I checked the basement for signs of small creatures and I winced at the pile of dishes in the sink.

12   Then I called my mother. "Well, I'm home—tired, but safe and sound," I told her. "Me too. Planning this party was an energy drain," she said, the tone and lilt of her voice almost indistinguishable from mine. Then we exchanged recipes and launched into a discussion of the party. We chatted about an annoying family acquaintance ("Well, I didn't think he'd actually show up," she reasoned) and that weird cousin, our views nearly identical.

13   "You know, Mom, I feel like I'm turning into you," I told her. "I know. I'm so sorry," she said, the predictability of her familiar sarcasm washing over me like the comforting rhythm of a warm summer rain shower. We laughed simultaneously and on cue, both of us knowing that her knack for self-deprecating humor was indiscernible from mine.

14   When peering into the mirror, I often catch myself checking for signs of gray hair. A patch has started to peek through near my right temple, similar to the graying that appeared on my mom in her 20s. These hairs represent more than age and heredity. They represent learning, accepting, nurturing and loving—the change from child to adult. And they remind me of family, a notion that once upset me but now makes me smile. It's a smile that my mother, looking into her mirror, just might recognize.

Freewriting

Write in your notebook for ten minutes in response to the essay. Among the questions you might consider are these: Can you draw any connections between Jennifer Nathanson's relationship with her mother and relationships among members of your own family? Is this the way that relationships between mothers and daughters typically develop? Do relationships between fathers and sons often follow the same pattern? What about relationships between parents and children of the opposite sex?

Group Work

After each freewriting has been read aloud to the group by its author, discuss the five elements described in this chapter (purpose, audience, main idea, development/support, and organization/coherence). See where the group is (and is not) able to reach agreement in its analysis of the essay.

Review Questions

1. What specific things about her mother used to embarrass Nathanson?

2. Why did Nathanson choose to attend Oberlin College? Do you sense that it proved to be a good choice?

3. What event has led to Nathanson's discovery that she has become like her mother?

Discussion Questions

1. Why do you suppose Nathanson makes reference to her mother's working hours (¶4)? How do they relate to what used to embarrass her about her mother?

2. Nathanson does not mention having any siblings. After you first read the essay, did you assume that she had one or more brothers or sisters or that she was an only child? How might your response to the essay change if you adopted totally opposite assumptions about this?

3. In her final paragraph, Nathanson says that her gray hairs remind her of "family, a notion that once upset me but now makes me smile." Her essay, however, makes only one reference to her father (¶8). Would you say that this essay is more about family in general than it is about mother–daughter relationships in particular?

Writing

1. Using the methods discussed in this chapter, write an analysis of Nathanson's essay.

2. Write a personal essay about your perception of and experience with some important type of familial relationship. Focus on how that kind of relationship tends to change over time.

8   *Beginning a Research Project*

SUPPOSE you are a smoker who has finally decided to kick the habit. Knowing that your addiction will be hard to overcome, you wonder if you should try to cut down in successive stages, or if you should take the more drastic step of quitting cold turkey. Determined to succeed, you visit the library and find that people who quit all at once have the best results. You also learn that you can expect withdrawal symptoms, but that after seventy-two hours, the worst of these are over. You grit your teeth, toss your remaining cigarettes in the garbage, and resolve that you, not tobacco, will prevail.

In Chapter 1, you learned that research is another name for finding out what you need to know. In the case at hand, reading about nicotine addiction carries a clear personal benefit. However, research often helps others as well. A college **research project** is an undertaking that should not only satisfy your own curiosity but also inform anyone else who reads the paper in which you present your findings.

THE RESEARCH PAPER

A **research paper** is one way to report your findings. However, the paper itself is only the final step in a project that seeks out and discovers information about a particular topic. After making your discoveries, evaluating and selecting among them, and then organizing the material you wish to report, you finally present what you have learned in a documented paper. Of course, not all research papers are alike; in years to come you probably will make frequent use of research in your writing, though not always in what you may think of as "research papers."

Although papers that draw on research can take many different forms, most fall into one of two categories. The more common of these two is the **research-based paper.** Papers of this type consist largely of information found through research; the writers of such papers present relatively few of their own opinions or discoveries. For example, a student seeking to learn whether the fearsome reputation of great white sharks is justified could write a paper based almost entirely on what she found from reading and from interviewing experts. Her own observations on the subject might play only a small part in her paper. In contrast, the **research-supported paper** presents the writer's own ideas, with research findings used to support or supplement them. Argumentative essays are frequently research-supported. For example, a student arguing for increased funding for intramural athletics could use research in part of his paper; he could demonstrate feasibility by citing published budgetary figures, and he could support his own arguments with expert testimony on the need for greater fitness. Still, his original ideas would constitute the heart of his paper.

In practice, the distinction between research-based and research-supported writing is far from absolute. It is not possible to present information in a completely impersonal or neutral way. Assume, for example, that the student writing about great white sharks tried to make her paper objective and impersonal, presenting only the facts and ideas she had learned from her reading and offering no personal opinions or speculations. Even so, the paper she wrote would be very much hers, since it was she who interpreted her sources, selected which facts and ideas to include, and shaped the material so that it represented her understanding of what great white sharks are like. Whatever type of research writing you engage in, you are expected to *think;* even research-based papers are written by human beings, not by computers.

 ## PRIMARY AND SECONDARY RESEARCH

We can also distinguish between types or methods of research. Most library research undertaken for college papers is *secondary research,* so called because it involves the second-hand discovery of information. Through secondary research we learn what others have previously discovered or thought about a topic. In contrast, when we make our own original discoveries, we engage in *primary research.* To give an example of primary research, an agricultural scientist might plant a standard variety of corn in one field and a new hybrid variety in another to test which provides higher yields and is more resistant to drought and disease. On the other hand, a farmer who reads a report written by that scientist to find out the best seed to plant is engaging in secondary research.

As a college student, you will have opportunities to undertake both primary and secondary research. When you conduct an experiment to test the behavior of laboratory rats or survey voter reactions to a presidential speech, you engage in primary research. When you read a history or a chemistry textbook, consult an encyclopedia, or get a printout from a computer database, you engage in secondary research.

However, not every use of a print source is secondary. Written sources can be either primary or secondary. A historian researching the slave trade in colonial America would seek sources from that era. Newspaper stories about slavery, diaries written by freed slaves and slave owners, slave auction notices and bills of sale, tracts written by abolitionists, and census figures and other records from that time are all examples of *primary sources.* In addition, the historian would consult such *secondary sources* as books and articles by other historians who have also researched and written about the slave trade.

In your upcoming research project, you may have occasion to make both secondary discoveries (in library works) and primary discoveries (by interviewing or corresponding with sources). The research you do is determined by the nature of your project and the resources at your disposal.

BENEFITS OF DOING RESEARCH

If research papers were not a requirement in composition classes, it is doubtful that many students would have the opportunity or motivation to undertake such projects on their own. By the same token, few instructors are surprised when students, after their projects are completed, say that they were glad to have had the opportunity. Often students say they have gained more from the experience than they expected. They find that research writing can have unanticipated benefits.

Learning an Essential Skill

One aim of this book is to help you become a competent college researcher with all the tools you need to produce quality research papers. A more general—and important—aim is to give you the confidence and skills to discover and use available information about any topic that arouses your curiosity.

It is likely that you will need to write many research papers during your college career and afterward. In other classes, you may be asked to gather information on a topic and report what you discover. After college, in your professional career, you may be faced with questions that you will have to answer through research. In these cases, you will need to consult what others have written, to evaluate and select what is pertinent from this information, and to write reports on your findings.

One reason you are being asked to do one or more research projects in your current course is to give you the experience you will need to conduct future projects with confidence. Practice now will make things easier later. When you are assigned to write a research paper in an art history, marketing, or anthropology class, for example, your instructor will not have time to tutor you in the basics of research. And after you graduate, you will have no instructor at all. College students and college graduates are simply expected to have mastered these skills. Now is the time for you to become an experienced researcher.

While students in a college composition course have the opportunity to learn research skills, they are also at a disadvantage compared with other researchers. Others do research not to practice a skill but to learn about specific topics. What they are discovering is important to them, and the research process is merely a means to that end. In the composition class, however, learning about the research paper can be an end in itself, and the topic you are writing about may seem of only peripheral importance. In that regard, your research project may seem artificial to you, an exercise that is useful in teaching skills for later use but one that has no real importance of its own. This *can* happen, but it is up to you to make sure it does not. For that reason, it is essential for you to choose with care the topic that you will research and write about. Because you will be spending much time and effort on this project, you should become as involved as you can with your topic. If you pursue a topic you genuinely care about, you will gain many rewards: not only will you spend your time profitably, but you will also write a far better paper and, in the process, learn what you need to know about research methods. If you take an interest in your topic and pursue it avidly, the skills you are seeking to acquire will take care of themselves.

Contributing to Scholarship

Although competence in research and research writing are practical skills, there is yet another reason to engage in research besides its personal usefulness to you. By doing research and then making your discoveries public in a paper, you are benefiting your readers as well.

Research is at the very heart of education—it represents the cooperation that is essential to learning. Most knowledge that you have gained is a result of such cooperation. None of us would have been able to figure out the principles of algebra, to mention just one example, if we had been left entirely on our own. Fortunately, throughout the centuries, mathematicians have shared the results of their discoveries with each other and (through our school algebra classes and textbooks) with us as well. A major function of higher education is to share with students the most important thoughts and discoveries of other scholars.

School classes are not the only means by which scholars share their work with us. They also publish their findings so that we and other scholars can have access to them. To make this sharing even easier, the books and articles they produce have been gathered in a central, accessible place: the college library. Engaging in research is simply taking advantage of what other scholars have learned. Like all scholars, you have the right to read about and learn from the discoveries of others. But scholarship is more than just passively receiving the gift of knowledge. As a scholar, you play an active role. Even when you write a research-based paper reporting on the findings of others, you are still creating something new, a fresh synthesis of information, shaped with your own wisdom and insights, a *new source* that was not available to scholars before. Every research paper makes at least a modest contribution to the domain of knowledge. As a student researcher, you are fully entitled to think of yourself as a scholar engaged in a scholarly enterprise. It is for this reason that you are expected to share your findings in a written, public form.

Gaining Personal Knowledge

In traditional college research writing, the author's aim is to report findings, to share information with readers. Authors of these papers keep their writing focused on their topic, while directing attention away from themselves as authors. (The word *I* rarely appears in conventional research writing.) But while you write such a paper to inform others, no one benefits more from your project than you yourself. Before you can inform your readers, you must first inform yourself about your topic through research. Research writing is a sharing of the knowledge you have gained.

Even the act of writing contributes to your learning. Creating a focused, unified paper forces you to see your topic in new ways. It causes you to bring together information from various sources, to make connections, to take vague ideas and make them concrete. Writing has been properly called a *learning tool;* research writers continue to gain personal knowledge while they are writing about what they have read.

On some occasions, however, personal benefit is not just a byproduct but your principal motive for conducting research. At times, you need to seek answers to questions important to you personally. Writing about such privately motivated research can be just as beneficial and worthy as carrying out conventional research projects. For that reason, one type of paper that has become increasingly popular in composition courses is the ***personal research paper.**** Unlike the standard research paper, this paper does not call for impersonal writing; as its name implies, it aims to be intensely personal. If you write a personal research paper, you should pick a topic that has real importance to you—or as one author puts it, you should let a topic pick you (Macrorie 66).† Perhaps your research will help you make a decision, such as what major or career to choose, or even which motorcycle to buy or what vacation to take. Perhaps it will just satisfy some strong curiosity. In any case, a personal research paper is a record of your quest for answers. You write your paper not only about *what* you found but also about *how* you went about finding it. The word *I* appears often in personal research writing. Even when such projects are approached with purely personal goals in mind, they provide far wider benefits. Besides being informative, they can be especially instructive because a strong motivation to find answers is the best teacher of research skills. Although personal papers center on the writer's interest and focus on the writer's experiences, readers often find them interesting. The writer's deep involvement in the subject usually translates into lively writing.

 ## THE RESEARCH PROCESS

Like all other forms of writing, a research paper does not happen all at once. Many steps are involved. Although a research paper may seem complicated and difficult, you can learn to produce one quite capably if you take one step at a time. This and the next five chapters examine each stage in the research process. To illustrate the tasks involved, we will trace the experiences of two first-year college students as they undertake research and write papers for their composition classes. By examining the steps they follow, the problems they encounter, and the solutions they discover to overcome them, you can observe the skills that go into writing a research paper. The same procedure can be adapted for research writing in your other courses and in your future career.

 ## A RESEARCH ASSIGNMENT

In any given semester, students in different composition classes receive a wide variety of assignments for research projects. Some are given open-ended assignments with many options, whereas others are assigned more focused tasks, such as projects related to a particular theme the class has explored in reading and discussion.

Helen Veit and Molly MacLaren, first-year college students enrolled in composition courses, were given different assignments by their instructors. In Helen's class, each student was asked to write a standard college research paper. Students

---

*It was also given the name "I-search paper" by Ken Macrorie in his book *The I-Search Paper,* rev. ed. (Portsmouth, NH: Boynton, 1988).

†As Chapter 6 explained, "Macrorie 66" is a form of shorthand that tells the reader that the authors are citing an idea raised by Ken Macrorie on page 66 of his book (identified in the preceding footnote).

in Molly's class were offered the option of writing either a standard or a personal research paper. In both classes, students were asked to choose their own topics.

Following is an assignment similar to the one that students in Molly's class received. Your own research assignment may differ from it, and your instructor may provide additional criteria for the length, scope, and format of your paper. Make careful note of any ways in which your own instructor's assignment differs from the one given here.

Research Paper   **A S S I G N M E N T**

Investigate a question or problem that intrigues you and write an informative essay, based on your findings from research. Observe the following guidelines, depending on the option you choose or are assigned.

Option A: The Standard College Research Paper

- *Subject:* Frame your research task in the form of a question that you want your investigation to answer. You may explore any subject that arouses your curiosity and interest. You might choose a topic related to your career goals or the field you plan to major in. Perhaps a certain topic in one of your other courses has aroused your curiosity. Perhaps an event or person from recent or earlier history would be worth learning more about. Perhaps in your reading, in conversation, or in viewing a film or television program you have encountered a subject you would like to explore.

- *Audience:* Assume that the other members of your class are your audience. Write a paper that is appropriate for this audience—one that they will find informative and interesting.

- *Voice:* You are the author of this paper, and it should be an honest presentation of what you have learned. But remember that your readers' interests, not yours, should come first. Although sometimes research writers use the word *I* in their papers (e.g., when they present their personal experience as a source), the focus of the paper should be on the subject matter, not on you as a person.

- *Information and opinion:* Be certain that your paper is principally based on the findings of your research rather than on personal speculation. This does not mean, however, that your paper must avoid any ideas and opinions of your own. Your paper may adopt a point of view, but if it does, you should make it clear to your readers from the beginning.

- *Length:* A typical paper is six to twelve pages long, but the length of your paper should be determined by the nature of your subject.

- *Sources:* Your paper should be based on a variety of research, including (where appropriate) such secondary sources as books, periodicals, and newspapers. If you find that additional sources are appropriate for your topic, you should also interview or correspond with experts or participants. Most papers will cite between eight and sixteen sources. In upcoming classes, you will learn how to locate appropriate sources, how to make use of what you learn from them, and how to acknowledge them in notes and in a works-cited page—that is, how to give your sources credit for their contributions to your paper.

Option B: The Personal Research Paper

Most of the guidelines for the standard research paper apply here as well, but there are some differences.

- *Subject:* You should pick a topic that is already a personal concern in your life. That is, you should seek a question you have a good reason to answer, one that can benefit you directly. Any topic that can help you make a decision or that can provide you with information that will enhance your life in some way is likely to be a good choice.

- *Voice and audience:* You should write honestly and unpretentiously about your research experience. Since your topic is of personal interest to you, the word *I* may occur often in your paper. However, you should also write so as to inform readers who may share your interest.

- *Form:* Unlike the standard paper, which is limited to the subject of the writer's research, the personal paper tells about the writer's process of discovery as well. Although no pattern for what to include and how to arrange it is right for all papers, here is a typical pattern suggested by Ken Macrorie. If you choose, your paper can follow this general outline, found in Macrorie's book *The I-Search Paper:*

  1. What I Knew (and didn't know about my topic when I started out).
  2. Why I'm Writing This Paper. (Here's where a real need should show up: The writer demonstrates that the search may make a difference in his life.)
  3. The Search [an account of the hunt, usually in chronological order; what I did first, what I did next, and so on].
  4. What I Learned (or didn't learn. A search that failed can be as exciting and valuable as one that succeeded). (Macrorie 64)

  Parts 3 and 4 can be merged if it makes sense to combine your accounts of what you found and how you found it.

- *Sources:* Interview experts, people who are likely to have the answers you want or who know where you can find answers. Consult these primary sources as well as library materials and other secondary sources.

You are also asked to keep a research notebook (explained on page 256) throughout your research project. Save all your notes, outlines, and rough drafts (more about these later), and submit them in a folder with your completed paper. Your current priority is to choose one of these options and to begin focusing on a specific topic. Use the time between now and our next class to think more about potential topics for your paper.

When their instructors announced the assignment, Helen and Molly had a reaction typical of most first-year college students in this situation: a sinking feeling in the stomach, followed by varying degrees of anxiety. It seemed more intimidating than the papers they had written before. Although both are competent writers, they weren't sure they could do it. At least momentarily, they were afraid their deficiencies would be exposed, that they would be revealed as imposters impersonating college students.

As grim as this sounds, there is nothing unusual about what Helen and Molly felt. All writers are apprehensive at the beginning of an assignment, especially one as unfamiliar and as complex as this research paper seemed. But despite their early fears, Helen and Molly not only wrote their papers but also received high grades for them. Afterward they admitted that the project was not the ordeal they had expected. In fact, it was not only rewarding but also interesting, informative, and, despite much hard work, even enjoyable.

What Helen and Molly did you can do. The trick is to divide the long project into a sequence of smaller, manageable tasks. As we examine these tasks, we will consider these two students' experiences as examples—following the progress of research from chaos to clarity, from panic to finished product. Since you will be making a similar trek, the journeys of Helen and Molly are worth your attention.

 ## THE FINISHED PRODUCT

Before you examine all the steps Helen and Molly took to produce their papers, first look at where they ended up. Their polished, final drafts—the completed papers that were the result of all their work—appear on the following pages.

A Sample Standard Research Paper

First is Helen's response to option A, her research paper on whether fairy tales are harmful. Note that despite her impersonal voice, Helen's paper includes ideas of her own about the topic.

Helen Veit

English 102

Prof. Robert Byington

3 April 1996

Fairy Tales on Trial

Once upon a time, almost all children grew up hearing stories of wonder and fantasy. Successive generations shared a knowledge of fairy tales passed down through books and oral story telling. Recently, however, this tradition has been called into question by concerned parents, educators, and psychologists who fear that such tales are actually detrimental to the happiness and security of children.

Consider the tale of Little Red-Cap, better known as Little Red Riding Hood. A sweet young girl and her sickly grandmother are easily duped by a clever wolf. He swallows them whole, but a resourceful hunter rips open the wolf's belly with scissors, rescuing the still-living females. The hunter sews heavy stones into the body of the animal, who then dies and is skinned by the hunter. The girl learns her lesson: "I will never by myself leave the path, to run into the wood, when my mother has forbidden me to do so" (Grimm and Grimm).

Is this a violent tale? Undoubtedly. Does it stereotype females as naive, helpless victims; males as predators and protectors; even wolves as evil creatures

Veit 2

deserving extermination? Undeniably so. Surely, think
some, hearing such tales can only brainwash and brutalize
children. But against all expectations, many other experts
deny that fairy tales will leave children emotionally
handicapped; on the contrary, they assert that these
stories are actually vital to the healthy development of
children.

Violence in Fairy Tales

Foremost among concerns is the violence in almost
every tale. Evil mothers plot to murder their own
children. Vanity is routinely punished with grotesque
disfigurement. Villains meet excruciating deaths. These
macabre elements have been targeted and censored by parents
and publishers. There is evidence, however, that
eliminating violence in fairy tales may only feed the fears
of children. A nine-year-old in one study remarked on the
punishment of the witch in Hansel and Gretel: "Somebody
said to me that the witch could have been put in prison.
But that can't be. The witch would have found her way out
by magic. And then she'd be free again" (qtd. in Messner
11).

Such anxiety is not uncommon. For example, one
revision of the Three Little Pigs omitted the wolf's death
over a fire and inserted instead a mild burn and a panicked
dash to the nearby woods. Instead of reassuring children

of life's security, the new version actually created anxiety that the wolf would return. One little girl, convinced that the wolf was only biding his time until he could reattack, had persistent nightmares. Only when the original version including the wolf's death was substituted for her regular story could the child believe that the wolf was truly gone for good (Tunnell 609).

Although children are often obsessed with violence, that does not seem to be a problem, according to psychologist Ann Trousdale. She states that children tend to "omit gratuitous violence" when retelling the story and only keep the violence that is necessary for justice (76). Fairness is very important to young people. "Children are innocent and love justice," observes author and critic G. K. Chesterton, "while most of us are wicked and prefer mercy" (qtd. in Tunnell 608). So a parent and offspring reading a fairy tale aloud may have very different reactions; what seems to be violent to the parent may seem only fitting to the child.

Another important factor affecting the perception of brutality is the extreme nature of the fairy tale itself. Indeed, the heights of savagery and wonder balance each other out, for, as Max Lüthi writes, "a princely reward or a sentence of death is but one of the many contrasts used in the fairy tale." Children don't regard these outcomes

Veit 4

as they would in a realistic narrative. They merely accept them as "rule[s] of the game" (152).

Lüthi goes further to say that not only are the violent elements harmless, but they are actually crucial to children's development and perception of the world around them. By demonstrating that dragons can be slain, these fantastic stories teach children to master their dilemmas rather than blame themselves or others (154). Ann Trousdale points out that children can deal with anger by identifying with villains who have great power and are therefore able to strike out and take control. For children, who often have minimal control in their lives, this identification can be fulfilling. It is necessary, however, that the villain be eventually conquered (72).

In his landmark study, The Uses of Enchantment, Bruno Bettelheim speaks of the danger of censoring violent elements:

> Those who outlawed traditional folk fairy tales
> decided that if there were monsters in a story
> told to children, these must all be friendly--but
> they missed the monster a child knows best and is
> most concerned with: the monster he feels or
> fears himself to be, and which also sometimes
> persecutes him. By keeping this monster within
> the child unspoken of, hidden in his unconscious,
> adults prevent the child from spinning fantasies

Veit 5

around it in the image of the fairy tales he

knows. Without such fantasies, the child fails

to get to know this monster better, nor is given

suggestions as to how he may gain mastery over

it. (120)

Trousdale cites one little girl in her study as an

example of the positive use of a typical fairy-tale

villain. The evil fairy in Sleeping Beauty was in fact the

girl's favorite character until the fairy's rage got out of

control as she turned into a giant. The girl herself had

not been invited to a friend's party and had been upset for

some weeks. The story allowed her to vent her anger and

simultaneously feel relief when the evil fairy is killed at

the end. Her "dangerous impulses" had been controlled

(74).

Gender Stereotypes

Most experts agree that the violence in fairy tales

provides both an outlet for children's frustrations and

representations of their ability to conquer their problems.

On the other hand, the blatantly stereotypical gender roles

in fairy tales are usually met with much less enthusiastic

responses. From the straw-spinning heroine of

Rumpelstiltskin, who is incompetent in her given occupation

without male help (Zipes 49), to the Snow White/Sleeping

Beauty type who is so passive that she falls into a

Veit 6

comatose state, the role of females in traditional fairy

tales does not meet up to the standards of modern

womanhood.

For little girls, the problem seems to originate in

their subconscious association with the heroine (Davies and

Banks 22). The docility, dependence, and sacrifice

glorified in most fairy-tale women make "female

subordination seem a romantically desirable, indeed an

inescapable fate" (Rowe 209). Balanced with a variety of

different types of stories, however, fairy-tale gender

roles can be enjoyed for the glimpse they give children

into the past. Alone, the outdated perceptions can cripple

children who will grow up in a world with very different

expectations.

As with violence, case studies have examined the

effects of gender stereotyping in fairy tales. One group

of elementary students was asked to draw pictures of their

favorite characters from a story read to them and to write

their own tale. Ella Westland, who conducted the study,

observed that girls seemed torn between a yearning for

traditional femininity--most drew beautiful princesses--and

a desire for independence that was apparent in their

tomboyish writings. Overall, the boys seemed content with

the straightforward fairy-tale scenario, embellished with

gore picked up from television. Westland concludes that

while the inner conflict of the girls indicates turmoil,

they are winning the struggle. She suggests the group to be worried about is the boys, who accept their stereotyped roles without reflection (237-45). And although "politically correct" fairy tales have been revised to place women and minorities in control, no effort has been made to place males, particularly fathers, in a more flattering light (Brott).

A Place for Fairy Tales

The harm attributed to fairy tales has been denied by many experts. Taken a step further, these stories are actually used by teachers and therapists to solve problems. As part of a "values-based" curriculum, high school students use the Sleeping Beauty story to examine their views about love and sex ("Using"). Some counselors read folk tales to battered wives to confront abuse and open up discussion of male and female attitudes and alternative solutions (Ucko 414-17). A similar process that encourages identification with Cinderella and other heroines is used in the treatment of women with eating disorders (Hill 585). In these functions, fairy tales are useful to teenagers and adults as well as to children.

Fairy tales have been a source of controversy for almost a century. The gender roles acceptable when these tales were rewritten by the Victorians are under scrutiny today for the sexual stereotypes they extol. On the other hand, the violent elements do not seem to promote actual

Veit 8

violence, but rather provide outlets for the otherwise
repressed frustration of children. In this manner, and in
the use of folklore in therapy, fairy tales are fulfilling
a crucial role in our society. And while knowledge about
this subject continues to unfold, it seems safe to conclude
that children who are read fairy tales have as good a
chance as any of living happily ever after.

Veit 9

Works Cited

Bettelheim, Bruno. <u>The Uses of Enchantment: The Meaning
    and Importance of Fairy Tales</u>. New York: Knopf, 1976.

Brott, Armin A. "Not All Men Are Sly Foxes." <u>Newsweek</u>
    1 June 1992: 14-15. <u>InfoTrac: Expanded Academic
    Index/ASAP</u>. Online. Information Access. 16 Mar.
    1996.

Davies, Bronwyn, and Chas Banks. "The Gender Trap: A
    Feminist Poststructuralist Analysis of Primary School
    Children's Talk about Gender." <u>Journal of Curriculum
    Studies</u> 24 (1992): 1-25.

Grimm, Jakob, and Wilhelm Grimm. <u>Grimms' Fairy Tales</u>.
    Online. Carnegie Mellon U. Library. Internet.
    Available: http://www.cs.cmu.edu/Web/books.html.
    20 Mar. 1996.

Hill, Laura. "Fairy Tales: Visions for Problem Resolution
    in Eating Disorders." <u>Journal of Counseling and
    Development</u> 70 (1992): 584-87.

Lüthi, Max. <u>The Fairytale as Art Form and Portrait of Man</u>.
    Trans. Jon Erickson. Bloomington: Indiana UP, 1984.

Messner, Rudolf. "Children and Fairy Tales--What Unites
    Them and What Divides Them." <u>Western European
    Education</u> 21.2 (1989): 6-28.

Rowe, Karen E. "Feminism and Fairy Tales." <u>Don't Bet on
    the Prince: Contemporary Feminist Fairy Tales in North</u>

Veit 10

<u>America and England</u>. Ed. Jack Zipes. New York:

Methuen, 1986. 209-26.

Trousdale, Ann. "Who's Afraid of the Big, Bad Wolf?"

<u>Children's Literature</u> 20.2 (1989): 69-79.

Tunnell, Michael O. "The Double-Edged Sword: Fantasy and

Censorship." <u>Language Arts</u> 71 (1994): 606-12.

Ucko, Lenora Greenbaum. "Who's Afraid of the Big Bad Wolf?

Confronting Wife Abuse through Folk Stories." <u>Social</u>

<u>Work</u> 36 (1991): 414-19.

"Using Books to Teach Values." Associated Press News

Service. 2 May 1995. <u>CD NewsBank Comprehensive</u>.

CD-ROM. NewsBank. Apr. 1996.

Westland, Ella. "Cinderella in the Classroom: Children's

Responses to Gender Roles in Fairy-tales." <u>Gender and</u>

<u>Education</u> 5 (1993): 237-49.

Zipes, Jack. "Spinning with Fate: Rumpelstiltskin and the

Decline of Female Productivity." <u>Western Folklore</u> 52

(1993): 43-59.

A Sample Personal Research Paper

True to the nature of personal research papers, Molly's paper on choosing a career as a writer, which follows, is indeed more personal and informal than Helen's paper on fairy tales. Molly's style, however, is fully appropriate for the kind of paper she is writing.

Molly MacLaren

ENG 102

Prof. Janet Adams

19 April 1996

The Power of the Pen:

Should I Become a Professional Writer?

I.　Why I Am Writing This Paper

　　Ernest Hemingway once said, "The hardest trade in the world is the writing of straight, honest prose about human beings" (qtd. in Stafford 25). For most of my life, I have wondered whether I could meet such a challenge. Do I have what it takes to follow giants like Hemingway, Cather, and Faulkner? Could I sit at my desk day after day, summoning forth eloquence and creativity? Could I withstand the rejection that comes with the trade? And could I make enough money to create a stable existence for myself? In short, could I be a writer?

　　As a college freshman, I have some time before I have to decide on a career or even a major. However, I want to make an educated decision based on hard facts rather than childish dreams. My research has helped me compare my fantasy with reality. If nothing else, I have come to understand the time, dedication, and investigative labors that are demanded of a professional writer.

MacLaren 2

II. What I Knew

When I began my research, I had an idealized portrait
of writers. I thought of them as romantic figures who
shunned the public light but loved cigarettes, black
coffee, and jazz. In my mind, writers spent hours living
in a fantasy world of their own making. It was almost as
if I believed that writers were a like-minded fellowship
who left their typewriters only at night. Although the
rational part of my mind realized that this picture was
wrong, I have still been surprised to learn how normal most
writers are.

Because I have wanted to be a fiction writer since the
age of five, I already knew something about the hardships
of the business. Writing, like acting, is a career where
success is determined by the public's response. I saw
creative writing as a less stable career than one as a
salaried journalist. However, I didn't know exactly how
easy (or difficult) it would be to sell stories and novels.
I also had no idea how much money one could make as a
writer. Could average writers support themselves by their
pens alone?

Extensive reading has introduced me to many
informative sources. I had heard of the obstacles to
getting one's words into print, and I knew that some great
authors were stymied by a formidable, sometimes hostile
publishing industry. I remembered that now-celebrated

MacLaren 3

writers such as Jack London, Tillie Olson, and even Dr.
Seuss met only rejection until late in their careers.
Information such as this made me hesitant about my own
abilities and chances for success.

III. The Search

The vast number of volumes in our public and college
libraries was itself comforting evidence that many writers
do get published. Among these thousands of reassuring
reminders, I began my search.

I wanted to obtain an overview of the writing profession
before I undertook more specific research. I had to find a basic
job description that included average income, educational
requirements, employment rates, and expected income growth.
Using the OPAC, I found vocational handbooks and
encyclopedias that gave me more than enough information.

When I began my in-depth research, I consulted various
how-to books and articles. Some showed how an aspiring
writer should create plot, characters, setting, and other
aspects of fictional narratives. Although helpful, they
did not provide the information I needed for my project.
Others included tips from experienced professionals on how
a new author can get published. These were far more
helpful because they discussed the difficulties of a
writing career. They also helped me envision the long and
strenuous journey into print.

MacLaren 4

I also found many books that provided inspiration and insight. Biographies and autobiographies revealed the habits and secrets of famous writers. Their advice to the beginning writer varied greatly, but I always found the accounts interesting. The most helpful were <u>On Being a Writer</u>, edited by Bill Strickland, and <u>Parting the Curtains: Interviews with Southern Writers</u> by Dannye Powell. These books shattered one of the myths I held: I discovered that individual writers are as different as the novels they publish.

Although I had a rudimentary understanding of writers and their jobs, I still needed to find out how difficult it would be for me to succeed at a career in writing. I searched InfoTrac and NewsBank under "writ* career*" to find newspaper and magazine articles that related to the writing profession. Although several magazines, such as <u>Writer's Digest</u>, are geared toward writers, I found few articles that answered my questions. I photocopied the most promising of these for further reference. I also made an appointment with Rebecca Lee, a professor of creative writing. As a successful writer of fiction and creative nonfiction, she gave me a revealing insider's look at the business. She was also an encouraging model for me, writing regularly for the <u>Atlantic Monthly</u> and other prestigious publications while still in her twenties.

MacLaren 5

My research so far had given me insight into the work
of successful creative writers, but what about the
thousands who never achieve success, much less celebrity?
In particular, what about those who turn for their
livelihoods to the workaday world of journalism? I spoke
to my aunt, Elizabeth Flagler, and my grandfather, Fred
Flagler, both of whom have long experience in the newspaper
business. Both were helpful and frank about the stressful
realities of newspaper work. Since they know me, they were
also able to judge how well I would do in a journalistic
career.

Finally, to test my own aptitude to be a writer, I
visited the Career Planning Office on campus, where I took
a computer-generated test called SIGI-Plus. It provided a
printout with an assessment of my interests and a list of
compatible occupations. At the conclusion of my research,
I felt that I had much valuable information and was well
prepared to begin my paper.

IV. What I Found

Writers are not all-wise and all-seeing gods. They
are merely people who see the world through discerning
eyes, observing life and transforming it into the written
word. As mere mortals, writers contend with the harsh
realities of survival. They must work painstakingly to meet
stressful deadlines. They must deal with writer's block and

rejection. They must also pay bills and put food on the
table.

It sometimes seemed that no one could fit the mold of
the ideal writer. Of course one needs to write well, which
means that a writer "should be creative and able to express
ideas clearly" (Hopke 621). The model writer is also
"gutsy, brazen, brave, . . . hardworking, determined,
confident and disciplined" (Carr 23). Other qualities are
also advantageous: "curiosity, persistence, initiative,
resourcefulness, an accurate memory, and physical stamina"
(Hopke 621). I realize that some of these virtues are not
my strong points, but I am willing to work hard to develop
these traits.

In my research, I found the writer's soul described in
turbulent terms. Writers are both "blessed" and "damned,"
according to fiction writer and essayist Harlan Ellison
(8). Allan Gurganus observed that writers must exist in a
state of painful "obsession" to achieve a worthwhile
product (qtd. in Powell 165). Often, a writer will spend
enormous time, money, and effort on a manuscript only to be
turned down by an editor. One of the factors contributing
to success is the ability to withstand such rejection. In
order to do this, a writer must be an exceptionally strong
person.

I got a taste of such rejection from the computer
program SIGI-Plus, which seemed to have reservations about

MacLaren 7

my becoming a writer. Having analyzed my responses to its
questions, it listed seventeen occupations that matched my
interests and abilities, but writer was not one of them.
Occupations on this surprising list included foreign
service officer, historian, English professor, teacher,
public relations specialist, fund-raiser, and even member
of the clergy. Since a writer must be optimistic, I choose to
note that the proposed professions involve communication
with others, a writer's stock-in-trade.

Financial success is also a concern. Novelist Robyn
Carr states frankly, "[I]t's hard to make money in this
business" (22), and Carr's emphasis on "hard" is scary.
Every writer has financial horror stories, and these all-
too-real tales frighten me. At one point in his life, even
Alex Haley, the author of Roots, possessed only eighteen
cents and two cans of sardines (Powell 179).

Fortunately, one vocational handbook was more
encouraging: "In the 1990's, beginning writers and
researchers receive starting salaries of about $20,000 a
year" (Hopke 623). Although this is not a princely income,
it is encouraging news; I could certainly support my
present lifestyle on that amount. Another handbook,
America's 50 Fastest Growing Jobs, ranks the weekly
earnings for writers as "very high," its highest rating
(Farr 10B). Freelance writers, or those who sell their

MacLaren 8

work to a variety of publications, "may earn from $5,000 to $15,000 a year." The key word, however, is "may," for the next sentence is short, cold, and to the point: "Freelance earnings vary widely" (Hopke 623). Until they "make it," many writers have to work two or three "day" jobs to support themselves. Rebecca Lee reports that most of her writer friends, like her, have undertaken a second profession. Teaching English seems to be most common.

While fiction is my first love, my research made it abundantly clear that it would be only practical to consider other options as well. Previously, I had assumed that writing careers fell into only a few categories, such as fiction, nonfiction, and journalism. However, I soon discovered many other options:

> Writers develop fiction and nonfiction ideas for plays, novels, poems and other related works; report, analyze, and interpret facts, events, and personalities; review art, music, drama, and other artistic presentations; and persuade the general public to . . . favor certain goods, services, and personalities. (Hopke 619)

Writers have a place in nearly every large business. Even huge chemical corporations need people to write reports and summarize data. Writers can find work in advertising firms, publishing companies, television and radio

MacLaren 9

broadcasting stations, government agencies, and educational institutions (Trainor 1-5). The thought that writing jobs such as these exist in abundance was reassuring. Although these jobs may not be a fiction writer's dream, they are available if one needs them and searches hard enough.

A variety of different jobs are available within the field of journalism. Here, one finds columnists, editors, cartoonists, critics, and news writers (Hopke 620). Reporters write articles about breaking news and other subjects that may be interesting to their readers. Critics evaluate books, plays, movies, TV shows, concerts, and restaurants. Columnists provide editorial comment on current events, humor, advice, or slants on local news.

Many of my relatives work for newspapers and magazines around the country. My aunt, Elizabeth Flagler, worked at the Sun-Sentinel, a Fort Lauderdale paper with a circulation of 375,000. She started as a copy editor and specialized in design when she became the graphics editor. She stressed that advancement in the newspaper business is possible, especially if you supervise the work of other people; however, a management job is not very appealing to me. A more attractive aspect of journalism is a steady paycheck, and at least one job manual was optimistic, reporting that employment in newspapers and magazines "is expected to increase about as fast as average" (Farr 16A). However, a less optimistic note about the future of the

MacLaren 10

newspaper business was expressed by my grandfather, Fred Flagler, who recently retired as the managing editor of the <u>Winston-Salem Journal</u>: "One day you're not going to have newspapers. They cost more and more to produce. All the afternoon papers are out of business. I just don't think it would be a worthwhile career anymore." Even the most viable newspapers are downsizing, which means fewer and fewer jobs.

Having encountered considerable discouraging news in my research, I approached my interview with Rebecca Lee with real doubts about my future as a writer. As we talked, I told her I was worried that I had not completed many stories. She dispelled my fears by saying that she had not decided to become a writer until she was in college. "Writing is one of the only arts where you don't find many prodigies," she said. She told me that such doubts are inevitable but that a beginning writer needs to believe in herself. If I wanted to become a writer, the best thing I could do would be to read constantly and to adopt a disciplined writing schedule. The writing craft requires a long apprenticeship. Since a writer learns the trade and develops a style only through practice and experimentation, I should be "willing to write poorly" in my early efforts. The odds against success are great, but no writer can succeed who is unwilling to face those odds.

MacLaren 11

Ms. Lee's words mirrored what I learned about success from my reading. Everyone knows the big names in writing--the novelists whose names blaze across the <u>New York Times</u> Best Seller list. Robyn Carr offered encouraging words: "It <u>is</u> possible to be great. It <u>is</u> possible to be a star" (22). However, a writer cannot depend on what F. Scott Fitzgerald called "that first wild wind of success" (qtd. in Burnett and Burnett 175). I appreciate the wisdom of Carr's further advice: "Fame should be a by-product and <u>not</u> a goal" (22). One of Ray Bradbury's comments also made a lot of sense to me. He said, "Money is not important. The material things are not important. Getting the work done beautifully and proudly is important" (qtd. in Filosa 56). One should write because one loves to write; so much the better if fame and glory follow.

V. Conclusion

After all my research, my dream of becoming a writer is still alive. True, my shining, idealized image of the writer is a bit tarnished, but the power of the written word still exercises a strong attraction. Despite uncertain financial prospects, writing offers a mystique that is not attached to any other career. I still regard the writer as a special creature; it would be a worthy challenge to become one. Yes, writers undergo rejection, criticism, starvation, and poverty, but if all goes well, they experience the freedom and exhilaration of creating a manuscript and seeing it set in print for the world to read. Like Ray Bradbury, I will write "because it is an adventure to watch it come out of [my] hands" (qtd. in Filosa 57).

In order to achieve my dream, I will take two creative writing courses next semester. Ms. Lee has offered to help me with any questions I might have, which is wonderful. I also intend to submit stories to local literary magazines and other publications. An internship at my local newspaper, the <u>Morning Star</u>, will give me the chance to see whether journalism is my forte. I also intend to enter writing contests for young adults. It is my hope and intent that these decisions will put me well on the road to becoming a writer.

MacLaren 13

Works Cited

Burnett, Hallie, and Whit Burnett. Fiction Writer's
        Handbook. New York: Harper, 1975.

Carr, Robyn. "Do You Have What It Takes?" Writer's Digest
        Apr. 1994: 20-23.

Ellison, Harlan. "Harlan Ellison." Strickland 2-8.

Farr, J. Michael. America's 50 Fastest Growing Jobs.
        2nd ed. Indianapolis: JIST, 1995.

Filosa, Frank. "Ray Bradbury." Strickland 52-57.

Flagler, Elizabeth. Personal interview. 24 Mar. 1996.

Flagler, Frederick James, II. Personal interview. 24 Mar.
        1996.

Hopke, William E., ed. "Writers." The Encyclopedia of
        Careers and Vocational Guidance. 4 vols. Chicago:
        Ferguson, 1993. Vol. 4.

Lee, Rebecca. Personal interview. 20 Mar. 1996.

Powell, Dannye Romine. Parting the Curtains: Interviews
        with Southern Writers. New York: Blair, 1994.

SIGI-Plus. Diskette. Princeton, NJ: Educational Testing
        Service, 1995.

Stafford, Edward P. "Ernest Hemingway." Strickland 21-26.

Strickland, Bill, ed. On Being a Writer. Cincinnati:
        Writer's Digest, 1989.

Trainor, Linda. "Advertising." Jobs For Writers. Ed.
        Kirk Polking. Cincinnati: Writer's Digest, 1980.
        1-8.

Molly's paper is about a career choice, an important decision in her life. Personal research projects also work well with less momentous topics; any question that arouses your curiosity is a worthy candidate for such a paper. Helen's project on fairy tales, for example, would also have worked as a personal paper, just as Molly could have written a standard research paper about career opportunities for writers. You might try to imagine what each of these papers would have been like if its author had chosen a different format for it.

EXERCISE | ## Analysis and Discussion

Before reading on to learn how Helen and Molly went about researching and writing their papers, answer these questions about their final drafts:

a. What is your impression of the strengths and weaknesses of each paper? Does each have a clear focus; that is, can you give a brief summary of its topic or central idea? Do you find it interesting? informative? clearly written? well organized? Did the author seem to do an adequate job of researching her topic?

b. If you were the author's instructor, how would you respond to each paper? If you were the author, would you change it in any way to improve it?

Both Helen's paper about fairy tales and Molly's about her career decision impressed their instructors and classmates, but they did not get that way all at once. Many stages involving much labor, some frustrations, and many changes preceded the final versions. The history of their creation is as informative as the papers themselves.

■ YOUR RESEARCH SCHEDULE: PLANNING IN ADVANCE

Writing a research paper is a labor-intensive project. Between now and the time you submit your final draft, you will be busy. You will be choosing a topic, exploring it, refining it, chasing down leads, riffling through sources, taking notes, thinking, jotting down ideas, narrowing your project's focus, doing more research and more thinking, writing a tentative draft, revising and revising again.

Obviously, a research project cannot be completed in a day or two. You need to plan now so that you have enough time to undertake each step in the process and so that you can make efficient use of your time. Like Helen Veit, you may be assigned separate deadlines for the various steps in your project. Or you may be given only the final deadline for submitting the completed paper, in which case you should establish your own intermediate deadlines for completing each stage. Helen's instructor gave the class a form much like the one shown in Figure 8.1, with a date for each deadline. You can use the form for recording your own schedule.

RESEARCH PROJECT

Principal Deadlines: **Due Dates:**

1. Research prospectus due, including a
    statement of your research topic and a
    working bibliography (see page 301):   _____

2. Note cards and preliminary outline due
    (see page 306):   _____

3. In-class editing of completed draft
    (see pages 369–70):   _____

4. Typed good draft due (see page 394):   _____

5. Final draft due (see page 394):   _____

Figure 8.1 A schedule for a research project.

Some instructors may supply an even more detailed schedule, which may include dates for such additional activities as library orientation, additional editing sessions, and student–instructor conferences. Whatever your schedule, your instructor will certainly concur in this advice: Budget your time wisely, and get started on your project without delay.

THE BENEFITS OF WORD PROCESSING

An extended discussion of the format for your completed paper appears in Chapter C of Part II. It includes settings for your word-processing program such as margins, line spacing, and justification. But the word processor itself is such a valuable tool at *every* stage of the research process that we need to give it some attention from the beginning.

Chapter 1 discussed the benefits of word processing (writing with a computer). Perhaps you have already found that word processing is the quickest and easiest way to write and that it makes you a better writer and researcher. When you compose, you can make as many changes as you wish in your writing, instantly and without mess. When you edit, you can produce a printed copy of part or all of what you have written—at the press of a button. You can easily rearrange sentences or whole sections of your paper to improve its organization. You can use the spelling-check feature to find and correct errors. Moreover, since printing a copy of your work is so easy, you can make alterations and corrections up to the last moment. And, of course, the copy you produce has a professional, error-free appearance.

Word processing also helps long before you begin the actual writing of the research paper. It can simplify and improve your work in many preliminary stages of research such as generating ideas, maintaining your working bibliography, outlining, and taking notes.

Use of the word processor has become indispensable in all areas of academic, business, and professional life. Your current research project can present an ideal opportunity for you to develop this essential skill. If you do not own a computer, your college may have computer rooms for student use. The basic operating instructions are usually not difficult, and instruction may be provided to help you get started.

 # A RESEARCH NOTEBOOK

At the beginning of your project you may already have a clear vision—or only the vaguest notion—of what your final draft will eventually look like. Nevertheless, it is probably safe to say that your final paper will be very different from anything you currently imagine. A research project involves many discoveries, and the act of writing usually inspires us to rethink our ideas. Rather than being *assembled*, research papers typically *evolve* through a process of development and change. Prepare for an adventure in which you discover what eventually emerges on paper.

Your finished paper is the end product of that adventure, the last of several stages in the research process. What you learn during that process is probably more important in the long run than the paper itself. It was for this reason that Helen's and Molly's instructors asked each student in their classes to keep a **research notebook.** At every stage of the project, researchers were expected to keep a personal record of their progress. The research notebook is like a diary. In it Helen and Molly recorded what they were doing and what they were expected to do. They wrote about what they had found, the problems they were facing, and their plans for their next steps. Molly used her notebook as the raw material for the "search" section of her personal research paper.

The writing you do in a research notebook should be informal, not polished. Unlike the research paper itself, the notebook is written to yourself, not to outside readers. When you are finished, you have a record of your research process. But there is also another benefit to keeping a notebook. Both Helen and Molly found that it helped them to make decisions and to focus their thoughts. In addition, many of the passages both writers used in their papers came from ideas they had scribbled in their notebooks.

You should use a spiral notepad that you can carry with you when you do research, though you may also want to use your word processor (if you have one) to record some entries. You will start using your notebook from the very beginning—now—as you select and focus your research topic.

 # YOUR RESEARCH TOPIC

Only on rare occasions do researchers have to *choose* a topic. Such an occasion might come about for a freelance writer of magazine articles who wants to select not only a fresh subject that will interest readers and an editor but also one about which she can find enough information through interviews, legwork, and library research.

In most cases, however, researchers already have their topics before them. A situation arises that demands exploration. For example, in order for a detective novelist to write convincingly about a counterfeiting ring, he must do research to learn how counterfeiters actually operate. A historian with a theory about the causes of the Russian Revolution would have to discover the available facts about the period as well as learn what theories other historians have proposed. A lawyer writing a brief for a criminal case must research legal precedents to know how similar cases have been decided in the past and to provide herself with convincing arguments. Most researchers begin with a strong curiosity about a topic and a need to know.

As you begin your own research project, you may already have decided on a topic. Perhaps your class has been reading and talking about an interesting issue such as nuclear policy, teenage suicide, the future of the family farm, or dating practices in foreign countries. Your discussion may have raised questions in your mind, questions that you can answer only through research. Besides satisfying your own curiosity, you can perform a service for your instructor and classmates by informing them about what you have learned. For you, a research paper is a natural.

On the other hand, you may not yet have chosen a specific topic. Perhaps your instructor, like Helen's and Molly's, has left the selection of a topic up to you. Perhaps you have been given a choice within a limited area, such as a current event, the life and views of a public figure, or your career goals. In any case, it is important for you to select a topic you can work with. Because many hundreds of topics may appeal to you, deciding on any one can be hard.

You begin with your curiosity. Your research is aimed at answering a question in your mind, at satisfying your urge to know. For that reason, it is usually helpful at the outset of a project to state your topic in the form of a *research question.* Rather than just naming a general area for your paper, such as "racial policy in the armed forces," it is often more useful to frame your project as a question to be answered, such as "How has the military dealt with discrimination?" or "How has the struggle against discrimination in the American armed forces compared with the struggle in the civilian world?" Perhaps you have formed a *hypothesis,* a theory that you would like to test. In this case your question would begin, "Is it true that. . . ?" For example, in reading about the plagues that devastated Europe during the thirteenth century, you might have speculated that in spite of modern scientific advances, the reactions of people to epidemics have not changed much in seven hundred years. If you decided to test this hypothesis through research, your question might be, "Are effects of the AIDS epidemic on our society similar to the effects of the Black Death on medieval Europe?"

Three factors are critical in framing a good research question. Your topic should have the following qualities. It should be

1. *Appealing.* This is the most crucial factor. Your research should be aimed at answering a question that genuinely arouses your curiosity or that helps you solve a problem. If you are not involved with your topic, it is unlikely that you will write an essay that will interest readers. The interest you have in your topic will also determine whether the many hours you spend on it will be rewarding or agonizing.

2. *Researchable.* You may be curious about the attitudes of college students in Japan toward religion, for example, but if you can locate only one or two sources

on the subject in your local libraries, you will not be able to write a research paper about it.

3. *Narrowed.* If your question is "What is astronomy?" you will find no shortage of materials. On the contrary, you will certainly discover that your topic is too broad. You can find hundreds of books and entire journals devoted to astronomy. However, you cannot do justice to so vast a topic in a paper of a few thousand words. You will need to narrow your topic to one you can research and cover adequately. You may decide to concentrate on black holes, for example, as a more focused topic. Later on, as you continue your research and begin writing, you may narrow the topic still more, perhaps to a recent theory or discovery about black holes.

GENERATING IDEAS

Unless you already have a question in mind that you are eager to answer, or unless you are facing a pressing decision for which you need information, you will have to do some exploring and thinking about a general subject before you arrive at a properly appealing, researchable, and narrowed research question. Several techniques for stimulating ideas can help you in your selection, including brainstorming and clustering.

Brainstorming

If you were asked right now to declare some possible research topics, you might find it difficult to do so. After a few minutes of wrestling with the problem, you might finally come up with a few topics, but you might find them to be neither original nor exciting. Yet there are literally hundreds of topics that you not only would enjoy researching but also could write about well. The trick is to stimulate your mind to think of them. ***Brainstorming*** is one helpful technique. It is simply a way of forcing your mind to bring forth many possible topics, under the theory that one idea can lead to another and that, if enough ideas are brought forth, at least one will click.

On the day they announced the assignment, Helen's and Molly's instructors led their classes through several activities to stimulate their thinking. Following are some examples of brainstorming exercises.

EXERCISES | **Brainstorming: Random Listing**

1. We start with a light and unintimidating exercise. The following is a random list of concepts in no particular order and of no particular significance. Read the list rapidly and then, in your research notebook, begin your own list, adding as many items to it as you can. Give free play to your imagination. List whatever comes to mind without regard to whether it is serious or would make a reasonable research topic. Save those concerns for later. For now, write rapidly, and have some fun with your list.

surnames
clowns
cans
lip sync
lipstick
war paint
juggling
teddy bears
cave dwellers
haircuts
ways to fasten shoes
high heels
hit men
cheerleaders
revenge
bicycles
televangelists
silicon chips
college colors
company logos
roller skates
tractors
warts and birth-
    marks
freckles
tattoos

water fountains
sea horses
con artists
cremation
hiccups
blueprints
Russian roulette
triplets
women's weight-
    lifting
chocolate
frisbees
coffins
chain letters
tanning
baldness
wigs
facial hair
earrings
longevity
boomerangs
fuel injection
fertility
nomads
film editing
spelunking

swimsuits
salesmanship
pro wrestling
campaign buttons
prep schools
sponges
snuff
fads
cavities
advertising jingles
plastic surgery
bartending
mirrors
juke boxes
icebergs
mermaids
tribal societies
fast food
cyclones
Beetle Bailey
toilets
laughing
cable cars
Mardi Gras
free gift with
    purchase

2. Because one idea leads to another in brainstorming, the ideas of other people can stimulate your own thinking. You can cross-fertilize your imagination by looking at other students' lists. After you have listed items for a few minutes, you can (a) exchange lists with one or more classmates or (b) join members of your class in calling out items (perhaps in orderly turns, perhaps randomly) as one or more people write them on the blackboard.

3. Stimulated by these new ideas, resume listing for another few minutes.

4. When you have finished, reread your list and circle the items that seem most interesting to you. What about these items stimulates your curiosity? See if you can now pose five or six questions about them for which you would like answers.

You may be concerned that some of the topics you listed or some of the questions you posed are not particularly serious or do not seem scholarly or deep. You need not worry, since any subject that provokes your genuine interest and curiosity is worth exploring and can be given serious treatment in a research paper. The item "lipstick" in the preceding list, for example, may seem frivolous at first, but it can lead to many serious questions: What is lipstick made of (now and in the past)?

How long have people been using lipstick? How has society regarded its use in earlier times? Does it symbolize anything? Is its use widespread throughout the world? Is it ever prohibited by governments or by religions? Why do American women use it but not (for the most part) American men? Such questions point to an interesting and rewarding research project. A student who pursued them would find much information. In the course of research, the student could certainly narrow the topic—perhaps to "What has society thought about lipstick?"—and write an informative, worthwhile paper.

EXERCISE   ## Brainstorming: Focused Listing

This brainstorming exercise is more focused than the preceding one. In your notebook, list as many ideas as you can in response to the following questions. Write rapidly, listing whatever comes to mind. List phrases, rather than complete sentences. If one topic strikes you as having possibilities as a research topic, keep listing ideas about it until you have explored it to your satisfaction. You do not need to answer every question, but do not stop listing ideas until your instructor tells you that time is up.

- What have been your favorite courses in high school and college? What topics in those courses did you find interesting? For each topic, write as many phrases associated with it as you can.

- What major are you considering? List some particular subjects you hope to explore in your major.

- What career are you considering? What specific branches of that field interest you? What jobs can you imagine yourself holding in the future? List several possibilities.

- What recent or historical events or discoveries are associated with your career interests or major field? What notable persons are associated with these areas? List some things you know about them.

- List magazine articles, books, movies, and memorable television programs that you have encountered lately. List some specific ideas or topics that they bring to mind.

- List some events or controversies that concern you. What news stories have aroused your interest or concern? What historical events have you wanted to learn more about? What do you consider the major changes that have taken place during your lifetime in world affairs? in science and technology? in the way we lead our lives? What problems face us in the future?

- What topics have you read about because you needed or wanted to learn more about them? What problems do you now need to resolve?

- What decisions will you have to make soon? Decisions about school? career? lifestyles? morality? romance? friends? family? purchases? leisure time?

- What areas are you an expert in? What are your chief interests and hobbies?

- What are some of the major gaps in your background? What should you know more about than you do?

- What notable people do you most admire? What people have had achievements that mean something to you? Think of men, women, historical figures, living people, scientists, artists, athletes, politicians. What famous people do you pity or consider villains?

Helen's class spent about fifteen minutes listing ideas for the preceding exercise. Afterward, students shared lists with classmates and discussed their ideas. They also jotted down any new ideas that came to them. Helen's list filled several pages in her notebook. Here is an excerpt from it:

. . . Favorite courses
 English (literature, writing, esp. creative)
   —literature
    Shakespeare
     Romeo and Juliet—is she strong or weak?
    short stories: Poe, O. Henry, Kate Chopin
    Romantic and Victorian lit.: Bronte, Austen, Dickens
     movies about their books
    folktales
     —origins, effects (fairy tales)
     —Cinderella myth
     —Snow White
 History
   —Middle Ages
   —Renaissance
    Michelangelo
    families: Medicis, Borgias (dysfunctional)
 Theater
   children's
   Romeo and Juliet (read vs. on stage) . . .

Helen's list was not an orderly, logical outline, nor was it meant to be. However, this short excerpt shows her mind actively at work, shaping ideas that would eventually lead to a research topic. The complete list included other ideas as well, most of which turned out to be dead ends. The excerpts shown here include "hot spots" or "centers of gravity"—ideas and phrases that engage the writer's interest, or that of her peer respondents, when reviewing all that has been jotted down. From these parts of her brainstorming list, Helen's topic began to emerge.

Here are some excerpts from Molly's list:

. . . III. Careers
  1. English-related field → author, playwright, professor, teacher, or freelance
  2. Journalism → columnist, editor, reporter
  3. History → research historian, genealogist, museum curator, preservationist, teacher
  4. Biology → environmental scientist, geneticist

... V I. Events and controversies
       1. Will books become obsolete because of computer technology?
       2. Loss of quality when a book is turned into a movie
       3. The abilities of children who are read to versus those who are not read to
       4. Quality of public school system
       5. Effects of DNA engineering
   VII. Decisions to make
       1. Major
       2. Career
       3. Do I want to aim for graduate school?
       4. Part-time job...

Developing an Idea: Clustering

A more concentrated form of brainstorming can be called *clustering* or *mapping.* It is a technique designed to stimulate the development of many ideas related to one given idea. Helen's instructor gave her class the following exercise.

EXERCISE | **Clustering Ideas**

Review the lists you have made thus far and circle all the items that look promising as research topics. If you have time, ask one or two classmates to do the same thing, each using a different color ink. Finally, select one possible topic (this is not a final commitment) and write it in the center of a blank page in your notebook. Using it as a starting point, radiate from it whatever ideas come to mind. Helen's clustering is shown in Figure 8.2.

Finally, Helen's instructor asked class members to call out questions that arose from the ideas they had listed (or new ones that occurred to them), while he wrote them on the board. Here are some of the questions offered by the class:

- What effect will the deforestation of the Amazon have on the planet?
- Is fraternity hazing a worthwhile ritual or barbaric torture?
- What motivates serial murderers?
- How are children affected by parents' divorce?
- How can you cope with the death of a family member?
- How were air bags developed?
- What treatments are available to vets to cope with tick-borne diseases?
- Is police corruption an epidemic?
- Is coral bleaching in the Caribbean an omen of environmental disaster?

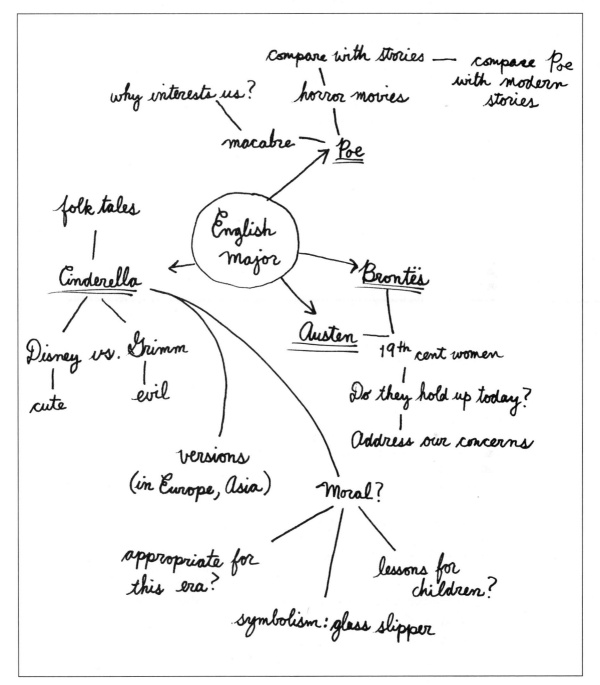

Figure 8.2 Helen's clustering.

- Does the Beat Generation speak to us today?
- Is Bill Gates an American hero?
- How can school teachers cope with depression in students?
- What can identical twins tell us about the effects of heredity and environment on personality?

Also on the list was a question from Helen, "What is the meaning of the Cinderella story?"

Prewriting exercises are not magic formulas that instantly produce the perfect research topic. Instead, if all goes well, they begin a chain reaction that leads you, however circuitously, to your eventual topic. The idea-generating exercises that Helen and Molly engaged in pointed them in helpful directions. Molly was the exception who found her topic rather easily. She first considered several ideas about problems facing the elderly, largely because of her after-school job in a nursing home. But she was also facing a difficult career choice, and she quickly decided to take advantage of what seemed a perfect opportunity to investigate a career as a professional writer. Helen's path to her topic was less direct, and she would not settle on her final topic until well after beginning her research. Her favorite subject, literature, prompted several ideas that proved to be dead ends. An offshoot was folklore and folktales in particular. She considered narrowing her topic to the Cinderella story, which had long fascinated her and about which she had recently been reading. She did not yet know that her research would lead her to an even more interesting topic: the debate about whether traditional fairy tales are harmful to children.

A research project is like a puzzle. When you begin it, you can never know how it will turn out. After all, the purpose of research is to answer questions for which you do not currently have answers. When you start, you cannot know what answers you will find. You cannot even be sure your questions are good ones. These discoveries are made only as you undertake the actual research and as you begin to write about your findings. You are almost certain to find that the research paper you end up writing will be quite different from your current expectations. What you learn along the way will cause you to change plans and go in new and often unexpected directions. You are sure to meet surprises. A good researcher must be flexible, able to adapt to whatever new ideas and information present themselves. For this reason you need not be concerned if you now have only a tentative idea of the topic for your paper. Your topic will take firmer shape (and perhaps a very different shape) as you undertake your research. The following chapters show you how to conduct research.

9 *Tools for Finding Sources*

 BEGINNING YOUR RESEARCH

Having generated ideas about likely topics for papers, Helen and Molly needed to do preliminary research to learn more about these topics and to bring their research questions into sharper focus. A visit to the library and some exploration of the resources available to them via computer were the logical next steps. From their instructors they received assignments similar to the one that follows.

Preliminary Research	ASSIGNMENT

Do some preliminary research to explore the topic you are considering.

- Learn more about your topic by reading about it in encyclopedias and other general reference sources. If the topic seems appropriate, take notes and see if you can narrow your focus to a specific question.

- See if your topic is researchable by assembling a working bibliography of about a dozen sources that you intend to consult. (Working bibliographies are further explained in Chapter 11.) Use a variety of search tools (explained in this chapter), and include books, periodicals, newspapers, and electronic media, as appropriate for your topic. If, for example, you are writing about a recent event, newspaper articles will be a significant source of information. On the other hand, if you are writing about an event from ancient history, you may not discover any newspaper sources.

- If adequate sources are not available, see if you can broaden your topic or switch to another one. If you find too many sources, read more about the subject and narrow your paper's focus within more manageable limits.

- Make sure your sources are available. Find out if the library has the periodicals and newspapers you are seeking. Check books out. If necessary, order books from other libraries through InterLibrary Loan. Ask the circulation desk to recall desired books that have been checked out by others. If most of the books are gone, however, someone else is probably writing on your topic, and the sources you need may not become available in time. If so, avoid needless frustration by switching now to another topic.

- Do some quick reading in your sources to learn more about your topic. It might be wise to ask a professor or some other authority on your subject for suggestions about the topic and for further research sources.

- Decide what additional sources can provide valuable information for your project. Write letters to request information, if necessary. Arrange interviews in advance by setting up appointments. (Letters and interviews are discussed in Chapter 10.)

- Be sure to record your discoveries, questions, and other experiences with locating sources in your research notebook.

As they begin their first research project in college, few students are experts in using the library. Many are confused and intimidated by electronic resources such as online databases and the World Wide Web. By the time students have finished the project, however, they have learned how to find information in their library as well as to access other sources throughout the world via electronic communication.

 ## YOUR CAMPUS LIBRARY

Your purpose in conducting a research project is not only to inform yourself about your topic by discovering information but to inform others as well by making your discoveries available in a paper. Learning is, after all, a cooperative venture, and scholars have an obligation to pass on to others what they have learned. For that reason, a wealth of important information and ideas produced by scholars has been collected and located in a convenient place for your use—your college library.

As any quick browse through the library will make abundantly clear, there are a great many potential sources out there—written about an almost unlimited number of topics. Finding information about any particular topic might seem an impossible task. Fortunately, however, the means are available for locating almost anything you are looking for. Your library offers not only *research sources* themselves, such as books and periodicals, but also *search tools,* which allow you to discover what research sources are available for your topic and to locate them. These tools include the library's book catalog, printed and computerized guides to periodical and newspaper sources, and even reference librarians. Search tools can give you a great deal of power, allowing you to discover information on almost any topic. Of immediate interest to you, of course, is that they allow you to find sources for your research paper. This chapter, with its accompanying exercises, is intended to make you proficient in the use of various search tools.

 ## ELECTRONIC RESOURCES

No area of the university has undergone more rapid and sweeping change in recent years than the library. Electronic media have revolutionized the search for information. A computerized catalog called an *OPAC* (pronounced *OH-pack* and short for *online public-access catalog)* has replaced the card catalog as the gateway to the library's holdings. Electronic indexes have superseded printed indexes as tools for finding periodical and newspaper articles. Even sources themselves may be "published" in electronic format. For example, reference works such as encyclopedias and dictionaries are now available in CD-ROM format. In fact, computers have made us expand our concept of "the library" to include more than just the building where books and other print media are stored. Many college libraries are tied into electronic networks that allow you to "visit" them without leaving your dorm workstation or your home computer. If your computer has a **modem** (a device that lets it communicate with other computers through regular telephone lines), you can have the same access to your library's OPAC that you would have at a library computer terminal.

Linking up with your library from home is certainly a convenience and a time-saver, but it represents only a small part of the research power now available to you through computers. For example, if you wanted, you could also search the holdings of a university library in Australia, copy a file stored on a computer in Scotland, or ask a question of a scholar in Nigeria. Before we explore the various tools for locating sources, both within and outside the library, we need some general background about electronic resources. To understand electronic resources and acquire skill in using them, there is no substitute for hands-on practice, but the following can provide a useful introduction.

A collection of material that is available electronically (by computer) is generally referred to as a **database.** Databases can be classified as either portable or online. A **portable database** is one that can reside within a particular computer, such as a program on a floppy disk or a CD-ROM file. In contrast, an **online database** is located at a distant site, such as a host computer or another computer on a network. For you to access it, your computer must communicate with that site. A vast and ever-growing number of databases is available online. These include valuable search tools such as indexes that enable you to locate sources, electronic encyclopedias, and whole libraries of data. Because millions of people can "post" as well as read databases, they also include less useful, even frivolous items such as "chat-line" conversations about soap operas, ads for questionable products, and "pages" devoted to someone's pet cat.

Networks

To gain access to an online database, your computer terminal needs to be connected to another computer containing the database. Such an arrangement by which a number of computers can contact each other is called a **network.** We will consider three kinds of networks that allow you to access online databases: your college library network, the Internet, and commercial networks. Although you may not have access to each of these networks, it is still worthwhile to be aware of them.

Your **college library network** is accessible through terminals in the library. In fact, it may be connected to a larger network for your college and be accessible at other sites on campus, such as classrooms and dormitories, and you may be able to access it through your home computer as well. The library network will certainly include its OPAC: the catalog of its collection of books and other materials. In many libraries the network will also give you access to bibliographic indexes, abstracts, online reference works, and more. Other indexes may be available in CD-ROM form at individual computer workstations (that is, in portable rather than online form). These library resources are discussed more fully in the following pages.

By far the most extensive network, connecting millions of computers across the world, is the ***Internet.*** Originally begun by the U.S. government, this network has grown to allow computer users almost everywhere on the planet to communicate and share information with each other. The Internet is actually the interconnection of thousands of local networks, so it is likely that a connection to your campus network can provide Internet access as well. Since colleges put restrictions on who may use their network, you may need to apply for an ***account*** and receive an ***address*** and a ***password.***

Any Internet user can send a message directly (and almost instantly) to any other user, through a process known as ***e-mail.*** For example, you could direct an inquiry about your research question to a scholar in Finland, provided you knew that person's Internet address. You could also join one of countless ***discussion lists*** devoted to particular topics. A message sent to a list is automatically forwarded to all of its subscribers. For instance, if you were researching voting patterns of women, you might post an inquiry on the PoSciM list, which is devoted to discussion of political science issues (and maybe also to WmSt-L, a women's studies list). Other subscribers interested in your topic would be likely to reply. Another way of following an ongoing e-mail discussion about a particular topic is by consulting a ***newsgroup*** or a ***bulletin board.*** These are very much like actual bulletin boards, where anyone can read and post messages. Unlike discussion lists, where all items are e-mailed directly to subscribers, newsgroups and bulletin boards are "places" on the network that you can "visit" whenever you choose, but no messages are sent to your e-mail in-box.

Another component of the Internet is the ***World Wide Web,*** which allows users to read (and create) attractive presentations of text, graphics, and sound known as ***Web pages.*** Because virtually anyone can post material on the Web, there is no limit to the variety of available presentations. For example, you can explore your college's ***home page,*** which is linked to many other Web pages containing information about its programs, faculty, and resources. You can also read electronic "magazines" (often called *zines)* on the Web or consult the Web for instant news, weather, and sports updates. The variety is so great that "surfing the Net" has become a recreational obsession for many.

A third source of online material is the ***commercial networks,*** such as America OnLine, CompuServe, and the Microsoft Network. Subscribers, who pay a fee for their connect time, can access many databases, download programs, communicate with other subscribers, and even connect to the Internet. Note that the network on your college campus may also provide you with wide access to databases, including Internet access, and may charge you only a small fee or none at all. Consult your instructor, librarian, or campus computing center for more information about network access.

 ## USING YOUR LIBRARY'S RESEARCH TOOLS

It is important to remember that while search tools can give you access to a vast quantity of information, the *quality* of that information varies widely. More than ever, student researchers need to use careful judgment about the reliability of their sources and the usefulness of information they encounter. Since the number of channels by which you can access research sources is so great, the following sections of this chapter will focus on those most likely to be helpful. Still, many such tools—old and new—are described, and they can seem intimidating at first. Don't allow yourself to be overwhelmed. It is not necessary for you to absorb all the information in a single sitting. Nor do you need to memorize the names of all the available reference sources and the procedures for using them. Instead, regard this chapter as a guide that you can consult whenever you need it, now and in years to come. By examining the resources that are described here one at a time and by gaining experience with their use through the practice exercises, you will soon develop a solid and confident command of the tools needed for doing college research.

Using Your Library's OPAC

Your library's holdings, including its books, videocassettes, periodicals, and many other materials, are indexed in an online electronic catalog called an OPAC. Because it is such a powerful and convenient search tool, your college library's OPAC is usually the best place to begin your search for research sources.

Several different companies sell OPAC systems to libraries, each with its own format, so the sample screens you see on the following pages may differ somewhat from the screens you will find at your library. Fortunately, most OPAC systems work in a similar way, and they are designed to be user-friendly. With the information in this section and a little practice, you should be able to make good use of the OPAC on your campus. Check also to see if a hands-on introductory workshop on using the OPAC (and other search tools) is available in your library.

You begin your use of the OPAC from its main menu screen, which provides a list of options from which to choose. The sample main menu shown in Figure 9.1 (page 270) offers nine choices (remember: your college OPAC may look somewhat different from this one). Not only could you use this OPAC to search the library catalog to find books and other materials (option S), but you could also access many other search tools (I, U, and O). This OPAC would allow you to learn more about library services (L), see what materials your instructors have put on reserve (R), obtain materials from another library (G), or even check when books you have borrowed are due or what fines you may owe (C). Choosing any of these options would lead you to another screen. For example, if you selected option S, you would then see the catalog search menu in Figure 9.2 (page 271).

Searching Library Holdings

In the now-outdated card catalogs that preceded today's electronic OPACs, each book was catalogued by several cards filed alphabetically in drawers: an author card, a title card, and one or more subject cards. As you can see from the sample catalog search screen in Figure 9.2, OPACs offer many different ways of locating books. Searching for a book when you know its author (an **author search**) or title (*a **title search***) is fairly straightforward, so we will focus on ways of finding what books might be available about a particular research topic.

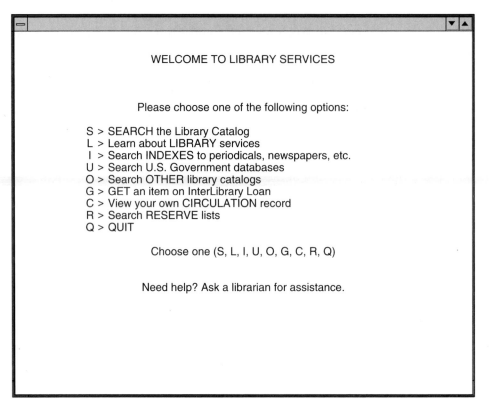

Figure 9.1 A typical OPAC main menu screen.

One option is to do a *keyword search.* When you choose this option (in Figure 9.2, by selecting W), you are then asked to type one or more words that might appear in the work's title, in its subject, or in catalog notes about its contents. Imagine, for example, that you are interested in researching the threat posed by so-called "killer bees." If you entered "bee," you would find that dozens of works in your library are referenced by this keyword, including books about beekeeping, quilting bees, and spelling bees—and even literary works (we found one entry for the poem "What the Bee Is to the Flow'ret") and sound recordings (we found the song "Woolie Boogie Bee"). Since these are not relevant to your research, you could narrow your search by including two or more words, such as "killer bee." This would limit the search just to entries containing both of those words—not necessarily together or in that order. A keyword search for "bee killer" would produce precisely the same results as a search for "killer bee." One limitation to keyword searches is that a computer is very literal minded. If you include the word "bee," it will ignore instances of "bees" or "beehives." Most OPACs allow you to use a *wildcard symbol,* usually an asterisk, to represent optional characters. For example, if you typed "bee*," you would find instances of both "bee" and "bees," but unfortunately also of "beer," "beefeaters," and "Beethoven." Nevertheless, by a judicious choice of keywords, you can conduct a successful search. By entering the words "killer bee*" in a keyword

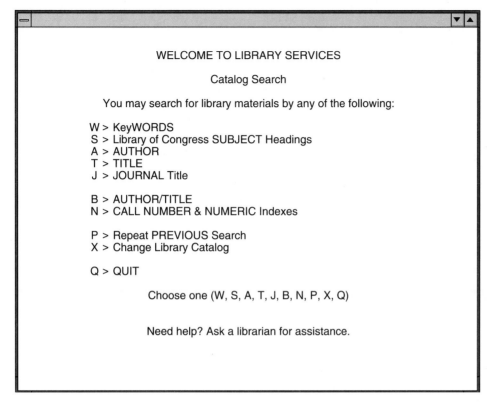

Figure 9.2 A typical OPAC catalog search screen.

search on our OPAC, we learned that "killer" occurred in 72 listings, "bee*" in 650 entries, but that only three entries contained both words. The results of our search are shown in Figure 9.3 (page 272), in which the three titles are listed on the screen.

You could examine either of these entries by selecting it. For example, if you typed the number 3 using this OPAC, you would be shown the record for the third entry, *Living with Killer Bees,* as in Figure 9.4. This screen gives much information about the book, including its author, complete title, publisher, and length (144 pages). The fact that the book was published in 1993 is one indication of how current it is. The information in the box tells you that the library has one copy of the book, located in its general collection. Unfortunately, this copy has been checked out by another patron. If you needed to consult it before its due date, you could ask the circulation desk to send a ***recall notice*** to the borrower, but you would have no guarantee that it would be returned on time.

In addition to giving information about the book itself, the record shown in Figure 9.4 (page 273) offers three useful pieces of information that could help you locate *other* works on this topic. The book includes a ***bibliography*** (on pages 137 and 138), which you could consult to find a list of other works on the subject. Second, the record gives the book's ***call number,*** its location in the stacks. Since works with similar subjects have similar call numbers, you could visit the stacks where

```
┌─────────────────────────────────────────────────────────────────────┐
│ ─                                                              ▼ ▲    │
│                                                                       │
│                        KEYWORD SEARCH                                 │
│    You searched for the WORD: killer bee*                             │
│    ▓3 entries found, entries 1-3 are:▓▓▓▓▓▓▓▓▓▓▓▓▓▓▓▓▓▓▓▓▓▓▓▓▓▓▓▓▓▓▓ │
│    1   Killer bees/Africanized bees: January 1981-September . . .     │
│    2   Killer bees: the Africanized honey bee in the Americas . . .   │
│    3   Living with killer bees: the story of the Africanized . . .    │
│    ─────────────────────────────────────────────────────────────    │
│                                                                       │
│                                                                       │
│                                                                       │
│                                                                       │
│    ─────────────────────────────────────────────────────────────    │
│    Please type the NUMBER of the item you want to see, OR             │
│    N > NEW Search                    D > DISPLAY Title and Author      │
│    A > ANOTHER Search by WORD        L > LIMIT this Search             │
│    P > PRINT                         + > ADDITIONAL options            │
│    Choose one(1-3, N, A, P, D, L, +)                                  │
│                                                                       │
└─────────────────────────────────────────────────────────────────────┘
```

Figure 9.3 Results of a keyword search.

this book is shelved in hopes of finding other books on killer bees. A much handier alternative would be to conduct a ***call number search*** on the OPAC (selecting option N in Figure 9.2). By typing in the first part of this book's call number (QL568), you would be shown all holdings with similar numbers.

Third, the record lists ***subject labels*** associated with the book. Figure 9.4 shows that the book is classified under two subject labels, "Africanized honeybee" and "Bees." Books in almost all U.S. college libraries are classified according to a standard list of subjects, known as ***Library of Congress Subject Headings.*** If you conduct a ***subject search*** on the OPAC (choosing option S in Figure 9.2), you could type in the subject "Africanized honeybee" to find all works listed under that subject heading. Note that only a subject listed by the Library of Congress can be used. For example, if you were to try "killer bees," you would find it was not an accepted subject. A useful strategy is to first find relevant works through a keyword search, then examine their listings for useful subject headings, and then conduct a subject search as well.

It should also be noted that your search need not be limited to the holdings in your own library. A work found in another library can be borrowed by your library through an ***InterLibrary Loan.*** You may find it useful to check the collections of libraries likely to specialize in your subject. For example, we used our OPAC (Fig-

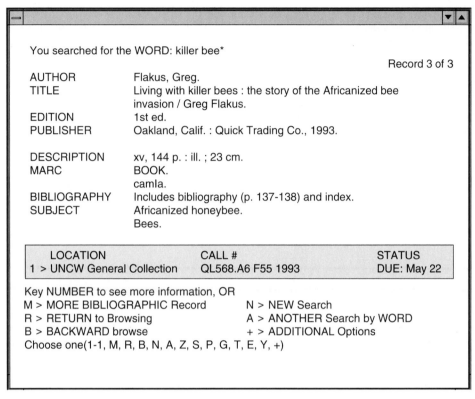

Figure 9.4 A typical OPAC entry for a book.

ure 9.1, option O) to connect with the OPAC at Texas A&M University, which has a large agricultural school. There we found seventeen listings under "Africanized honeybee," compared to three at the library on our campus. Similarly, if you were researching manatees, you would expect to find more works on the subject at the University of Miami than, say, at the University of North Dakota. Ask your librarian for help in searching the collections of other libraries.

Using Your Library's OPAC   EXERCISES

Use your college library's OPAC to answer the following questions. Although these exercises may remind you of a scavenger hunt, they are intended to familiarize you with the resources in your library and to practice important research skills that you will use many times in the future.

1. These questions can be answered by doing an author search on your college library's OPAC:

   a. How many authors with the surname Churchill have works in your library?

   b. How many listings are there for Sir Winston Churchill (1874–1965)?

c. View the record for one book by Sir Winston Churchill (and print it, if your library's OPAC terminals are connected to printers). What is the book's full title? its call number? Is the book currently available in your library, or has it been checked out? In what city was the book published? by what publisher? in what year? How many pages long is the book? What subject headings could you use in a subject search to find similar works on the same topic?

2. Do a subject search, using one of the subject headings found in 1c, above. How many works does your library have on that subject? What are the title, author, and call number of one of those works (other than the Churchill book)?

3. Find an author whose last name is the same as or close to your own. Record the title and call number of one book by this author.

4. How would you use your OPAC to locate works *about*, rather than by, Sir Winston Churchill? How many works does your library have about him? Record the author, title, and call number of one such book.

5. How many books does your library have with the title (or partial title) *Descent of Man*? Who are the authors of these books?

6. Do a call number search on the OPAC to answer these questions: How many works are there in your library whose call numbers begin with TL789? What subject(s) are books with this number about? Record the author, title, and call number of one such book.

7. To answer this question, you may need guidance from your instructor or librarian: How can you limit your call number search to only those works (with call number TL789) that were published after 1990? How many such works are there in your library's collection? Can you limit your search to TL789 works with the word "flying" in the title? How many such works are in your library?

8. Do a keyword search to find works on your research project topic (or another topic that interests you). What subject headings do you find for these works? Use the most appropriate of these headings to do a subject search. Record information about works likely to help you in your research project.

Encyclopedias and Other General Reference Works

General reference works, books, periodicals, newspapers, and microforms are some of the resources in college libraries. Because so many sources are available, it is helpful to approach a search for information with a strategy in mind and to turn first to resources that are most likely to be of help. Before you search in particular directions, you need a broad overview of your topic. General reference works are often a good place to begin.

General reference works, such as encyclopedias and almanacs, offer information about many subjects. They are located in the reference section of your library, where they can be consulted but not checked out. Many encyclopedias, dictionaries, and almanacs are also available in CD-ROM format, and most commercial online services give their customers access to these works. In addition to text and pictures, some online works allow you to view film clips and hear audio as well. Another advantage of online encyclopedias is that they are frequently updated, and the latest edition is always available to you.

General encyclopedias have alphabetically arranged articles on a wide variety of subjects. *Encyclopedia Americana* and *Collier's Encyclopedia* both contain accessible articles that can provide you with helpful introductions to unfamiliar subjects. The *New Encyclopaedia Britannica* is somewhat more complicated to use in that it is divided into various sections, including the "Micropaedia," which consists of short articles and cross-references to other articles in the set, and the "Macropaedia," which consists of longer, more detailed articles. Encyclopedias published on CD-ROM disks or available online include *Encarta* and *Grolier's Encyclopedia*. One-volume **desk encyclopedias,** such as the *New Columbia Encyclopedia,* can be quick and handy guides to basic information about a subject. **Almanacs,** such as *Information Please Almanac, Atlas and Yearbook* and *The World Almanac & Book of Facts,* contain tables of information and are handy sources of much statistical information.

Specialized encyclopedias, restricted to specific areas of knowledge, can provide you with more in-depth information about specific topics. Many such works are available—the OPAC at the university where we teach lists over a thousand works under the subject heading "Encyclopedia." By way of example, here are just a few from the beginning of the alphabet: *Encyclopedia of Adolescence, Encyclopedia of African-American Civil Rights, The Encyclopedia of Aging and the Elderly, The Encyclopedia of Alcoholism, Encyclopedia of Allergy and Environmental Illness, The Encyclopedia of Amazons, Encyclopedia of American Social History, The Encyclopedia of Animated Cartoons, Encyclopedia of Arms Control and Disarmament,* and *Encyclopedia of Assassinations.* You can use your college OPAC to locate a specialized encyclopedia dealing with your research topic. You can also browse the reference section in the appropriate stacks for your topic; sections are marked by Library of Congress call numbers (for example, BF for psychology, HV for crime, N for art, and so on).

Using General Reference Works

EXERCISES

1. Locate a specialized encyclopedia dealing with your research topic or another topic that appeals to you.

2. Look up that same topic in the *New Encyclopaedia Britannica* (look first in the index, which will direct you to either the "Micropaedia" or the "Macropaedia") and then in *Encyclopedia Americana* or *Collier's Encyclopedia*. Finally, if possible, consult an online or CD-ROM encyclopedia. Compare the treatment and coverage of the topic in these different works.

3. Determine if information about the same topic can also be found in a desk encyclopedia or in an almanac.

4. Finally, write a one-page account of what you discovered. In particular, what kinds of information are found in the different reference works? How do the treatments of the topic differ?

FINDING ARTICLES:
MAGAZINES, JOURNALS, AND NEWSPAPERS

Articles in magazines, journals, and newspapers are among the sources used most frequently by student researchers in composition classes, for several reasons: Articles are written on a variety of subjects; they make timely information available right up to the most recent issues; and, being relatively brief, they tend to focus on a single topic. Your college library is likely to have recent issues of hundreds of magazines and journals and of many local, national, and international newspapers. In addition, back issues of these publications are available either in bound volumes or on *microforms* (miniaturized photographic copies of the material). The use of an *electronic database* or a *printed index* will help you find articles on the topic you are looking for.

Locating Periodicals

If you are in doubt about whether your library has a magazine or journal you are looking for, you can consult a list of all the periodicals your library owns. Such a list is usually found on the library's OPAC (for example, in Figure 9.2, by selecting option J) and possibly also in a printout, rotary file, or microfiche file located in the periodicals section. In most libraries, current issues of magazines and journals are shelved on open stacks; back issues are collected and bound by volume or copied onto microforms. Recent back issues, not yet bound, are sometimes available at a periodicals or service desk. If you have difficulty finding an article, ask at the periodicals or reference desk for assistance.

Microforms

As a space-saving device, many libraries store some printed materials on microforms, miniaturized photographic copies of the materials. The two principal types of microforms are *microfilm,* which comes in spools that resemble small movie reels, and *microfiche* (pronounced *MY-crow-feesh*), which comes in individual sheets of photographic film. The images they contain are so small that they can store large quantities of material. At the same time, a projector is required to enlarge these images so they can be read. Most college libraries have projectors for both microfilm and microfiche. Some projectors also allow for photocopying of what appears on the projector's screen. Follow the directions on these machines or ask a librarian for assistance. Although sturdy, microforms are not indestructible, so it is important to handle them with care and to return them in the same condition as you received them.

Library Vandalism—A Crime against Scholarship

Since scholarship is a cooperative enterprise, it is essential that all scholars have access to sources. Students who steal, deface, or mutilate library materials commit a crime against the ethics of scholarship. An unforgivable sin is to tear articles from magazines, permanently depriving others of their right to read them. Many a frustrated scholar, looking for a needed source only to find it stolen, has uttered a terrible curse upon the heads of all library vandals—one that it might be wise not to incur. On the more tangible side, most states have also made library vandalism a criminal offense, punishable by stiff fines and in some cases jail sentences.

Actually, there is no excuse for such vandalism. Short passages can be hand-copied. Longer excerpts, to be used for legitimate academic purposes, can be photocopied inexpensively. Most libraries have coin-operated or debit-card photocopy machines in convenient locations. (Some photoduplication violates copyright laws; consult your instructor or librarian if you are in doubt.)

 ## USING ELECTRONIC DATABASES

Most college libraries provide links to electronic databases, which have replaced printed indexes as the most popular means for students to locate articles, electronic files, and other materials related to their research topics. These databases are either online (through an electronic connection to the database host site) or portable (stored on a CD-ROM disk). **Online databases** are usually accessed through the library's OPAC (for example, by selecting option I in Figure 9.1). **Portable databases** are usually accessed at computer terminals, with the databases on CD-ROM disk. From the user's point of view, both online and portable databases work alike, but the former often have the advantage of being more frequently updated by the database company. However, even portable databases are quite current, since disks are replaced with updated versions at regular intervals.

College libraries usually have dozens of databases, either online or portable, and the number is increasing at a rapid rate. Look for a list in the reference section or ask your librarian for information about available databases. The library may have a large collection of databases on CDs, and you may have to ask a librarian to install the one you wish to use.

In this chapter we will introduce a few of the more popular and useful databases, but you should explore your library to learn what databases are available.

InfoTrac Databases

One of the most widely used databases (actually a collection of several different databases) is **InfoTrac**. Through InfoTrac, you can obtain bibliographic references to magazine, newspaper, and journal articles.

Instructions for using InfoTrac are often available in the library, but users can learn to navigate the databases with a little hands-on practice. You can also press the Help key (identified as the "{" key in Figure 9.5, page 278) whenever you have a problem. Following are some general guidelines for using InfoTrac.

Libraries usually subscribe to more than one of the InfoTrac databases, and your first step is to select the one you want from an on-screen menu (Figure 9.5). Each of the many databases is an index to articles on specific subjects. Use the up and down arrow keys to move the highlight bar to the database you wish to search and press the Enter key.

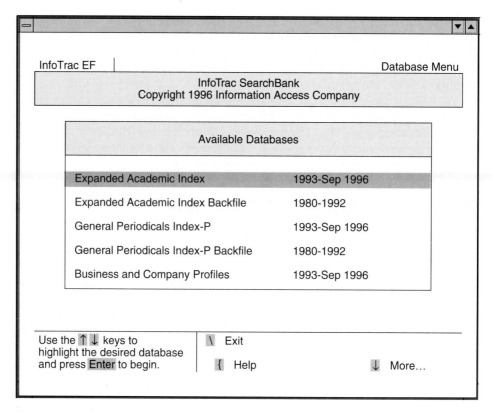

Figure 9.5 InfoTrac Database Menu screen.

Several InfoTrac indexes allow a broad search covering a wide variety of publications. The *Academic Index* is a tool for finding articles in over 400 scholarly and general-interest publications. Covered subject areas include the social sciences, humanities, general sciences, and current events. The *Expanded Academic Index* is similar but indexes over 900 publications. The *General Periodicals Index* indexes over 1,000 general-interest and scholarly publications, including the *New York Times,* the *Wall Street Journal,* and the *Christian Science Monitor.* Covered subject areas include the social sciences, general sciences, humanities, business and management, economics, and current affairs. The *National Newspaper Index* provides a single, in-depth reference to five major newspapers: the *New York Times*, the *Wall Street Journal,* the *Christian Science Monitor*, the *Washington Post,* and the *Los Angeles Times.* Many of these indexes come in versions with the suffix "ASAP" (for example, Expanded Academic Index ASAP), which provide the articles themselves online.

Indexes on more specialized topics include the *Health Index* for medical and health-related articles; *Business Index, General BusinessFile,* and *Business and Company ProFile* for business-related articles; *Government Publications Index* for national and state government documents; and *LegalTrac* for articles related to the law.

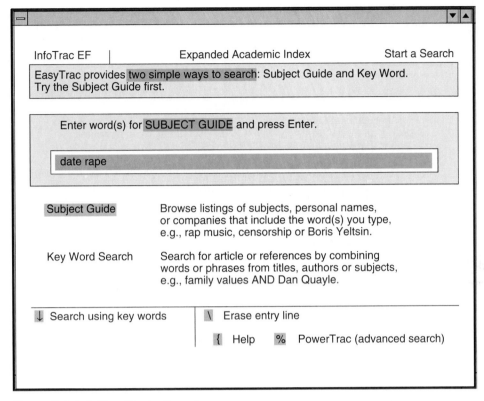

Figure 9.6 InfoTrac Start a Search screen.

We will introduce you to the Expanded Academic Index, but since all Info-Trac databases work alike, you can apply these procedures to any of them. For example, let us imagine you are searching for sources for a research paper about date rape.

1.   Once you have selected the desired InfoTrac database, the Start a Search menu appears (Figure 9.6). As with a search of your library catalog, you can do either a subject search or a keyword search. Generally it is advantageous to start with a subject search; if the words you enter do not match an accepted subject, InfoTrac will conduct a keyword search instead. You can type in "date rape" (or any other topic, such as "AIDS education," "animal behavior," or "insider trading").

2.   Since "date rape" does not turn out to be a recognized subject heading in this database, InfoTrac performs a keyword search using the words "date" and "rape." You learn that these words are found in eleven citations, which are shown on a Brief Citations screen (Figure 9.7, page 280). You can use the arrow keys to scroll through the citations. For example, you could stop at the fifth of the eleven citations, as in Figure 9.7. The citation contains much useful information:

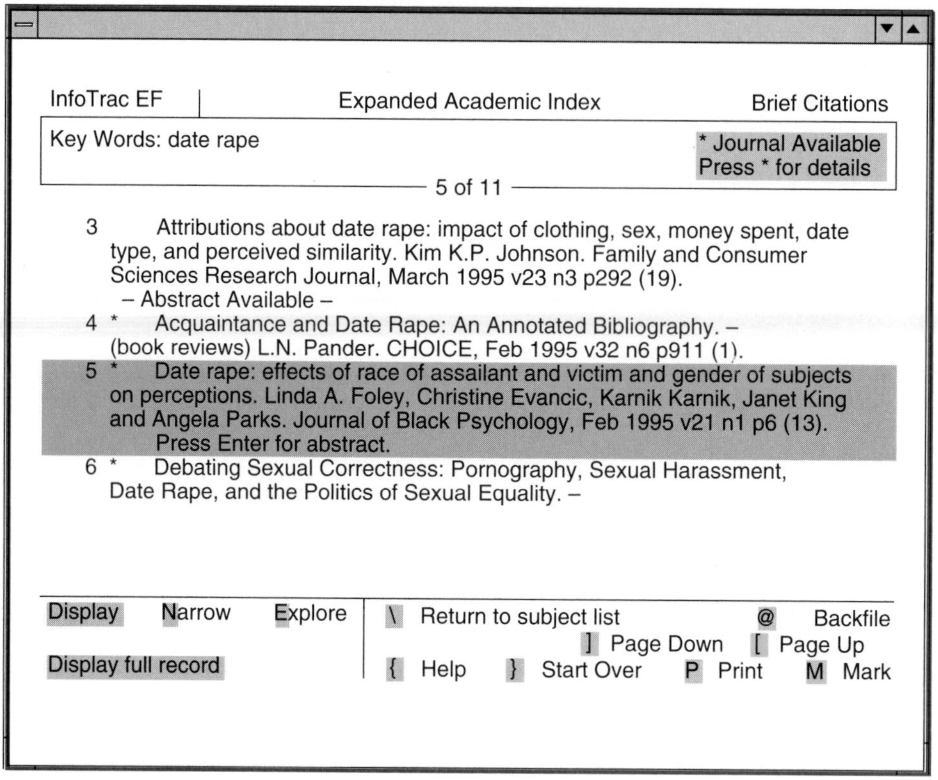

```
┌─────────────────────────────────────────────────────────────────────────┐
│ ═                                                                  ▼ ▲     │
├───────────────────────────────────────────────────────────────────────────┤
│                                                                           │
│  InfoTrac EF    │      Expanded Academic Index          Brief Citations   │
│  ┌──────────────────────────────────────────────┐  ┌───────────────────┐ │
│  │ Key Words: date rape                          │  │ * Journal Available│ │
│  │                                                   │ Press * for details│ │
│  └───────────────────────────── 5 of 11 ─────────────────────────────┘  │
│                                                                           │
│      3      Attributions about date rape: impact of clothing, sex, money spent, date │
│             type, and perceived similarity. Kim K.P. Johnson. Family and Consumer │
│             Sciences Research Journal, March 1995 v23 n3 p292 (19).        │
│             – Abstract Available –                                         │
│      4  *   Acquaintance and Date Rape: An Annotated Bibliography. –       │
│             (book reviews) L.N. Pander. CHOICE, Feb 1995 v32 n6 p911 (1).  │
│      5  *   Date rape: effects of race of assailant and victim and gender of subjects │
│             on perceptions. Linda A. Foley, Christine Evancic, Karnik Karnik, Janet King │
│             and Angela Parks. Journal of Black Psychology, Feb 1995 v21 n1 p6 (13). │
│             Press Enter for abstract.                                      │
│      6  *   Debating Sexual Correctness: Pornography, Sexual Harassment,   │
│             Date Rape, and the Politics of Sexual Equality. –              │
│                                                                           │
│                                                                           │
│  ─────────────────────────────────────────────────────────────────────  │
│  Display    Narrow    Explore  │  \  Return to subject list      @   Backfile │
│                                │              ]  Page Down    [  Page Up  │
│  Display full record           │  {  Help    }  Start Over    P  Print  M  Mark │
│                                                                           │
│                                                                           │
└───────────────────────────────────────────────────────────────────────────┘
```

Figure 9.7 InfoTrac Brief Citations screen.

> 5   *   Date rape: effects of race of assailant and victim and gender of subjects
> on perceptions. Linda A. Foley, Christine Evancic, Karnik Karnik, Janet King
> and Angela Parks. *Journal of Black Psychology*, Feb 1995 v21 n1 p6(13).
> Press Enter for abstract.

The citation can be interpreted as follows:

> The article "Date Rape: Effects of Race of Assailant and Victim and Gender of
> Subjects on Perceptions" was written by the five authors whose names are given.
> It appeared in the *Journal of Black Psychology* in the February 1995 issue (volume
> 21, number 1). The article begins on page 6 and is 13 pages long.

The asterisk in front of the article's title (and the highlighted note in the upper right
of the screen) tells you that this issue of the journal is available in your library. Typing an asterisk would tell you where in your library to find it. Some libraries subscribe
to a version of InfoTrac databases that can display the full text of many of the articles.

3.   Rather than having to copy the citation by hand, you can print a copy (if your
terminal is connected to a printer) by pressing the P key. You could also press the M
key to mark this and other citations that interest you. When you are ready, you can
then print all the marked citations at one time.

```
┌─────────────────────────────────────────────────────────────── ▼ ▲ ─┐
│ ─                                                                     │
│                                                                       │
│   InfoTrac EF    |        Expanded Academic Index      Full Records   │
│  ┌────────────────────────────────────────────────────────────────┐  │
│  │ Key Words: date rape                          * Journal Available│  │
│  │                                               Press * for details│  │
│  │                       ─── 1 of 11 ───                            │  │
│  └────────────────────────────────────────────────────────────────┘  │
│      Source:  Journal of Black Psychology, Feb. 1995 v21 n1 p6 (13).  │
│                                                                       │
│       Title:  Date rape: effects of race of assailant and victim and gender of subjects │
│               on perceptions.                                         │
│      Author:  Linda A. Foley, Christine Evancic, Karnik Karnik, Janet King │
│               and Angela Parks.                                       │
│                                                                       │
│    Subjects:  Acquaintance rape - Surveys                             │
│                                                                       │
│          RN:  A16790175                                               │
│                                                                       │
│    Abstract:  Survey of 75 students of a medium size public university in the │
│    Southeast in the US, including 43 white females and 10 black males from │
│    an introductory psychology class and a literature class, on the effect of race │
│    of the assailant and gender of the victim of a date rape reveals that black │
│  ─────────────────────────────────────────────────────────────────  │
│   Display    Narrow    Explore  │ \  Brief citation display    @  Backfile │
│                                 │ +  Next          ]  Page Down  [  Page Up │
│   Display brief citations       │ {  Help    }  Start Over   P  Print   M  Mark │
│                                                                       │
└───────────────────────────────────────────────────────────────────┘
```

Figure 9.8 An InfoTrac Full Records screen, including an abstract.

4. At the end of the highlighted citation are the words "Press Enter for abstract." If you do so, a Full Records screen for that citation will appear (Figure 9.8). The abstract that begins at the bottom of the screen is a summary of the article's contents and your best guide to whether you will wish to consult the article itself.

5. In the bottom left of Figure 9.8 are two additional options that can help you find sources related to your topic. The first is to narrow your search by pressing the N key. You are then asked to enter an additional word or words. For example, if you wanted to limit the search on date rape just to occurrences on college campuses, you could add the word "campus" to your search. (Alternatively, you could type "NOT campus" to limit the search to citations with the keywords "date" and "rape" but *not* the word "campus.")

6. A second option is to explore related subject areas by pressing the E key. The screen in Figure 9.9 (page 282) would then appear, telling you that 47 articles are cited under the subject "Acquaintance Rape." You could press Enter to see these citations, or you could highlight the next line to examine the 18 subdivisions of the topic; you would learn that these include "Acquaintance rape—causes of," "Acquaintance rape—psychological aspects," and others that may be of particular interest for your research project.

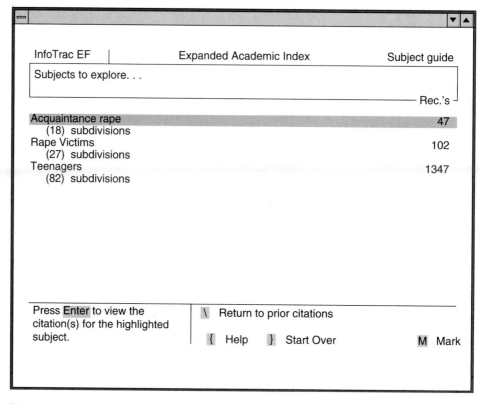

Figure 9.9 InfoTrac Subjects to Explore screen.

Using InfoTrac

1. In Figure 9.5, what is the difference between the Expanded Academic Index and the Expanded Academic Index Backfile?

2. At the Start a Search screen of the Expanded Academic Index (Figure 9.6), how might you find articles about the effect of television violence on children?

3. Who wrote article number 3 on the Brief Citations screen (Figure 9.7)? In what journal did it appear? How can you tell if that article is available in the library? (Hint: Look in the upper right of the screen.)

4. From the screen in Figure 9.7, how could you:

   a. view the abstract for article number 3?

   b. print items 4, 5, and 6 (in one step, rather than one at a time)?

   c. narrow your search to items about date rape involving alcohol?

   d. start a new subject or keyword search?

Use InfoTrac to answer these questions:

5. Which InfoTrac databases does your library subscribe to?

6. Which of these InfoTrac databases would you use to find articles on:

   a. modern art?

   b. a speech last week by the vice president of the United States?

   c. muscular dystrophy?

   d. Burger King's profits?

   e. reviews of a recent movie?

7. Describe what happens when you do a subject search for "modern art."

8. What is the date of the most recent article about the vice president? Print the abstract of this newspaper article about the vice president. Print the abstract of another recent article about the vice president. (If printers are not provided, copy the first sentence of each by hand.)

9. How many articles are there related to muscular dystrophy? Print (or hand-copy pertinent information from) the record of one article that can be found in your library. How many articles are there when you narrow the search by including "telethon"? Print (or copy pertinent information from) one of these records.

10. Find the phone number of the Burger King company. What is the "ultimate parent company" of Burger King? How many articles are there about Burger King profits? Print (or copy pertinent information from) the record for one of them.

11. Finally, find articles on your research project topic (or another topic that interests you), using the appropriate InfoTrac databases. Print (or copy pertinent information from) the records of works likely to help you in your research project.

NewsBank Databases

Like InfoTrac, *NewsBank* is a collection of many different databases. As with Info-Trac, you can access different databases from a single menu screen (see Figure 9.10, page 284). Two of them, *CD NewsBank Comprehensive* and *NewsBank Reference Service Plus,* are particularly valuable for finding newspaper articles. Others include *NewsBank Index to Periodicals, Business NewsBank,* and *Foreign Broadcast Information Service (FBIS),* which references translated broadcasts and articles from around the globe. NewsBank Comprehensive references over 450 different newspapers. NewsBank Reference Service Plus references articles from fewer newspapers (over 100), but it provides the full text of the articles in electronic form, in the database itself.

Imagine that you wish to research patterns of smoking by teenagers and you are looking for newspaper sources. After you select the NewsBank Comprehensive database (Figure 9.10), you might enter "teen* and smoking" as keywords; NewsBank will search for articles that contain any of the words *teen, teens, teenager,* and

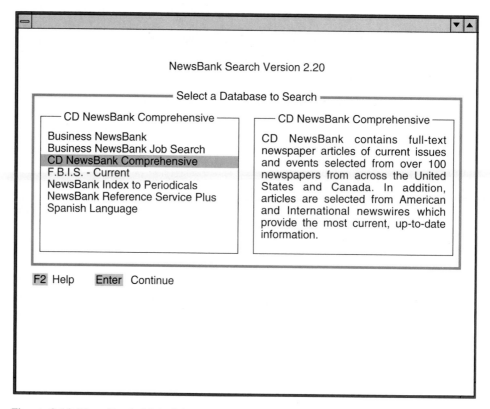

Figure 9.10 NewsBank Main Menu screen.

teenagers—as well as the word *smoking.* You learn that 80 such articles are available (Figure 9.11), and you can scroll through a list of their dates and headlines (Figure 9.12, page 286). If you select the headline "Teen Smoking Surge Blamed on Marketing Push," you are shown a screen with information about the article (Figure 9.13, page 287), and if you scroll down, the text of the article appears. You can either print the article or download it onto a diskette to view later on your computer at home.

ERIC

The **ERIC** (Educational Resources Information Center) database consists of two integrated files: ERIC Journal (EJ), which indexes articles from over 750 professional journals in education and related disciplines, and ERIC Document (ED), which indexes a variety of documents that are available on microfiche, including research reports, curriculum guides, handbooks, and conference papers. Because the word *education* is used in the broad sense, ERIC is a good place to look for nonpublished sources on a broad range of topics. For example, an inquiry about teenage smoking yielded 71 records. Figure 9.14 (page 288) shows the printout for one of them, a paper about teen smoking delivered at a conference. The article itself is available in the ERIC microfiche collection.

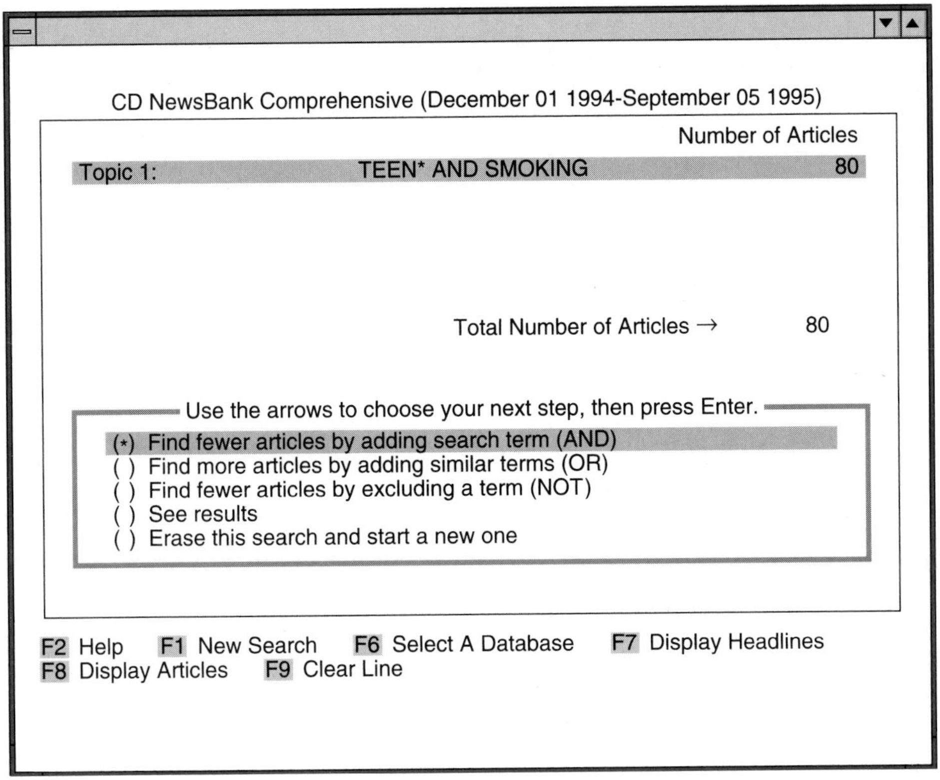

```
┌────────────────────────────────────────────────────────────────── ▼ ▲ ┐
│ ─                                                                        │
│                                                                          │
│   CD NewsBank Comprehensive (December 01 1994-September 05 1995)          │
│  ┌────────────────────────────────────────────────────────────────┐    │
│  │                                                  Number of Articles│   │
│  │  Topic 1:              TEEN* AND SMOKING                    80    │    │
│  │                                                                   │    │
│  │                                                                   │    │
│  │              Total Number of Articles →         80                │    │
│  │                                                                   │    │
│  │  ┌──── Use the arrows to choose your next step, then press Enter. ──┐ │
│  │  │ (*) Find fewer articles by adding search term (AND)              │ │
│  │  │ ( ) Find more articles by adding similar terms (OR)             │ │
│  │  │ ( ) Find fewer articles by excluding a term (NOT)              │ │
│  │  │ ( ) See results                                                │ │
│  │  │ ( ) Erase this search and start a new one                      │ │
│  │  └────────────────────────────────────────────────────────────┘ │
│  │                                                                   │    │
│  └────────────────────────────────────────────────────────────────┘    │
│                                                                          │
│  F2 Help    F1 New Search    F6 Select A Database    F7 Display Headlines │
│  F8 Display Articles    F9 Clear Line                                     │
│                                                                          │
└──────────────────────────────────────────────────────────────────────┘
```

Figure 9.11 NewsBank Keyword screen.

GPO and Other CD-ROM Databases

Many of the databases we have described are available in online and CD-ROM versions. Many of the latter are distributed by a company called SilverPlatter. Although not all of them look alike, you should have little difficulty using them, especially if you are familiar with other indexes. In addition to ERIC and General Academic Index, SilverPlatter distributes CD-ROM versions of *Reader's Guide to Periodical Literature* (an index to articles in popular magazines), *Biography Index* (an index to works about notable people), and *Essay and General Literature Index* (an index to essays and shorter works within books). In addition, it offers many field-specific indexes, such as *Applied Science & Technology Index* (an index to many fields such as aeronautics and space science, artificial intelligence, engineering, textiles, mathematics, and robotics), *Art Index* (coverage includes archeology, architecture, art, film, and photography), *General Science Index* (includes sciences from astronomy to zoology), *Humanities Index* (includes literature, history, and other fields in the humanities), *PsycLIT* (an index to material related to psychology), and *Social Sciences Index* (an index to such fields as anthropology, crime, economics, law, medicine, political science, psychology, and sociology). The following section describes one SilverPlatter index, *GPO on SilverPlatter,* an index to government documents.

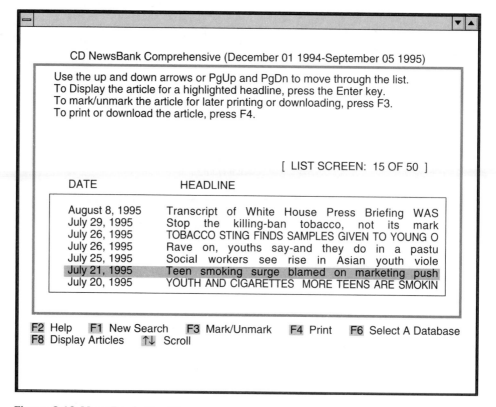

Figure 9.12 NewsBank Headlines screen.

GPO—Finding Government Publications and Pamphlets

The vast array of documents published by the United States government constitutes another useful resource for research in almost any field of study. Each state has at least one designated depository library that receives all documents distributed by the Government Printing Office, as well as several other partial depository libraries that receive selected government publications. Items not in your college library can usually be borrowed through the InterLibrary Loan service.

Government documents are usually shelved in a special library section and identified by a special call number called a *SuDoc* number (short for the Superintendent of Documents Classification number). Library OPACs do not usually index government documents with their book holdings. To find documents and their SuDoc numbers, you need to consult one of several indexes. The *Monthly Catalog of U.S. Government Publications* is issued in bound volumes. It is also available as an electronic database through several companies, one of which is **GPO on SilverPlatter.** Figure 9.15 (page 289) shows the printout for one GPO citation under the topic "rain forest." (The database comes in Windows and DOS versions; Figure 9.15 shows the DOS version.) The document, written by Ariel E. Lugo for the U.S. National Committee for Man and the Biosphere and published by the U.S. State Department, can

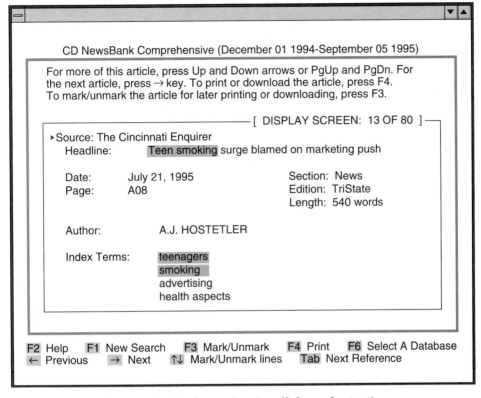

Figure 9.13 NewsBank article information (scroll down for text).

be found in the library's government documents section under its SuDoc number, S1.2:P39/3.

Using NewsBank, ERIC, and GPO

EXERCISES

1. In Figure 9.10, which NewsBank databases would you use to find newspaper articles on your research topic? Which would you use to find magazine articles? Which database references English translations of articles from foreign countries?

2. In Figure 9.11, how could you restrict your search to articles about teen smoking in every state except California? How could you expand the search to cover smoking by both teens and children? How could you restrict it to advertisements related to teen smoking?

3. In Figure 9.13, how would you display the text of the article? How would you print the article?

4. At what conference was the paper shown in the ERIC record in Figure 9.14 delivered? Which of the subject headings shown might be used to find other articles on teen smoking?

```
You searched for the WORDS: teen* smoking                            ERIC
                                                          Record 4 of 71
ERIC #        ED361805.
AUTHOR        Pashupati, Kartik.
TITLE         The Camel Controversy: Same Beast, Different Viewpoints.
                 A Position Paper.
ABSTRACT      A coalition of health groups wants the R. J. Reynolds Tobacco
                 Company(RJR) to discontinue the use of the Joe Camel cartoon
                 character in its cigarette advertisements. RJR has denied the
                 findings of the three studies published in the "Journal of the
                 American Medical Association" and cited by the health groups—
                 these studies contend that these ads lead children and adoles-
                 cents to smoke. The controversy can be viewed from three per-
                 spectives: (1) the regulatory perspective of the Federal Trade
                 Commission; (2) the perspective of the advertiser, with empha-
                 sis on First Amendment rights; and (3) the advertising strategy
                 perspective. RJR's decision to use Joe Camel as a mascot for
                 its cigarettes is defensible from the viewpoint of both the
                 First Amendment rights of the advertiser and the marketing com-
                 munication viewpoint. However, the adoption of an extremely
                 defensive stance by the marketer is not likely to earn the com-
                 pany much goodwill from consumers or lawmakers. It is concluded
                 that since RJR claims that it is not interested in targeting
                 children and teenagers with its marketing efforts, it should
                 have little hesitancy about using the charismatic charms of Joe
                 Camel in an intensive media campaign advising teenagers and
                 young adults of the negative consequences of cigarette smoking.
                 (Contains 37 references.) (Author/RS)
PUB DATE      Aug 93.
PUB TYPE      SPEECHES, CONFERENCE PAPERS.
              VIEWPOINTS (Opinion Papers, Position Papers, Essays, etc.)
COUNTRY       U.S.; Michigan.
NOTE(S)       19p.; Paper presented at the Annual Meeting of the Association for
                 Education in Journalism and Mass Communication (76th, Kansas
                 City, MO, August 11-14, 1993)
              Paper & fiche.
LANGUAGE      English.
MAJOR SUBJ    Advertising.
              Audience Awareness.
              Mass Media Effects.
MINOR SUBJ    Children.
              Elementary Secondary Education.
              Freedom of Speech.
              Health Education.
              Media Research.
              Merchandising.
              Smoking.
              First Amendment.
MAJOR IDEN    Advertising Effectiveness.
              Joe Camel.
CLEARINGH #   CS508317.
```

Figure 9.14 Printout of an ERIC record.

5. This exercise can be undertaken by one or two students who can report their findings to the class. Find out if your college library is your state's regional depository for U.S. government documents or a partial depository. If the latter, what percentage of available government items does it receive? Where in the library are government documents shelved? How can students gain access to government documents not in your library?

6. Use NewsBank, ERIC, and GPO (if available) to discover sources related to your research topic or to some other topic that interests you. Report on what you find.

7. Consult a field-specific index that is appropriate for your project, such as Business NewsBank, PsycLIT, or General Science Index. Report on what you find.

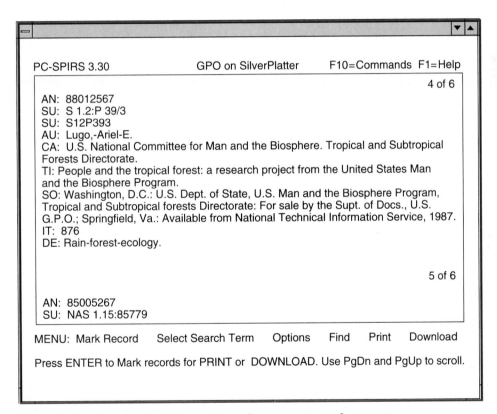

Figure 9.15 Printout of a GPO citation of a government document.

INTERNET RESOURCES

Library sources can be accessed in systematic ways; by contrast, finding sources on the Internet is much more a hit-or-miss affair. Whereas the library's staff controls its collection and creates an index of all of the library's holdings (its OPAC), no one runs the Internet, much less controls access to it or creates a comprehensive index.

The Internet is really a vast interconnected network of smaller networks, which virtually anyone can access and where virtually anyone can publish anything at all. Navigating the Internet and finding resources that can aid your research project require much practice, some skill, and considerable luck.

The best Internet tutorial comes from hands-on exploration, aided by your curiosity and an adventurous spirit. Here we can give only some brief information and hints to get you started.

World Wide Web Files

World Wide Web files contain text, often graphics, and sometimes even sound or animation. Figure 9.16 shows a typical Web page, which happens to be an index to sources of data supplied by the U.S. Department of Education. This sample page is in graphical format, but users whose computers lack graphics capability can read the Web in text-only format. A valuable feature of Web pages (as documents on the World Wide Web are called) is that they usually contain links to other pages, known as *hypertext.* For example, if you had Figure 9.16 on your computer screen, you could use your mouse to click on any of the boxes or highlighted items—for example, on "USA Counties: 1969–1994"—and a guide to information about any county in the country would then appear on your screen. Following Web links from page to page is one of the most useful (and addicting) aspects of the Internet.

Web pages are usually accessed using a Web *browser,* a software program such as Netscape Navigator, the Microsoft Internet Explorer, or Lynx. Netscape and Internet Explorer show graphics as well as text (a Netscape screen is pictured in Figure 9.16); Lynx is a text-only browser. To access a World Wide Web document, enter its *address,* also known as its *URL,* or uniform resource locator, usually a rather lengthy string of letters and characters. For example, the URL for the document in Figure 9.16 is:

http://govinfo.kerr.orst.edu

Internet addresses are often long and must be entered exactly. Fortunately, most of the time you move from page to page by pointing and clicking, rather than by typing in URLs.

Web Search Engines

When you seek Web sources for a research project, you will probably not know the addresses for specific files. Although no comprehensive index to the millions of Web files exists, several commercial indexes (known as *search engines*) provide access to a large number of files, either by keyword or subject searches. Among the more prominent search engines and their URL addresses are:

AltaVista	http://altavista.digital.com
Excite	http://www.excite.com
InfoSeek	http://www.infoseek.com
Lycos	http://www.lycos.com
Magellan	http://www.mckinley.com

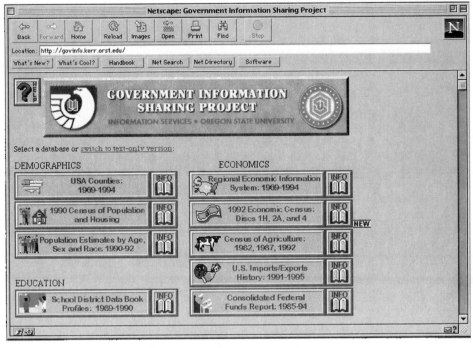

Figure 9.16 A typical World Wide Web page.

WebCrawler   http://webcrawler.com

Yahoo   http://yahoo.com

Browsers such as Internet Explorer and Netscape offer their own search pages that provide easy access to many search engines. These can be accessed by clicking on a button (for example, the "Net Search" button in Figure 9.16) or by entering one of the following URLs:

Microsoft Internet Search   http://www.msn.com/access/allinone.asp

Netscape Internet Search   http://home.netscape.com/home
                                internet-search.html

Figure 9.17 shows a Yahoo search screen. If you type in a topic in the Search box, Yahoo will show you a list of sites related to that topic. You can then visit one of those sites by clicking on its name. Search engines can also be used for subject searches. Yahoo allows you to choose from many broad topics (for example, *arts*), then to narrow the search (perhaps to *humanities,* then to *history,* then to *19th century,* then to *Irish potato famine).*

A word of caution about Web documents and other Internet resources is in order. Students should evaluate them with a careful, critical eye. Find out who has created the document and how reliable or comprehensive it is. For example, if you are researching a scandal in the widget industry, you might find one or more widget Web pages. Knowing if the page is created by a widget trade organization

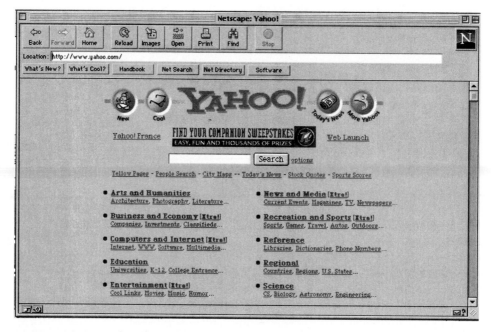

Figure 9.17 A Web Search page.

(which would be expected to have a pro-widget bias) or by an anti-widget consumer group (with the opposite bias) is essential if you are to assess the source and determine whether and how to use it.

EXERCISES   **Using the World Wide Web**

Do the following exercises if you have access to the World Wide Web.

1. See what you can find on the Web on the following three topics: identical twins, Peru, and archery. Use one or more of the above search engines to explore these topics. Follow links from page to page as your curiosity leads you. Write a narrative describing your search and discoveries.

2. The Yahoo search engine is organized around a number of topics (Arts, Business, etc.). Select one that interests you, and continue to choose from among options until you arrive at an interesting page. Print the page (if equipment allows) or summarize its contents.

3. Use other search engines to find Web sources on your research topic.

Finding Other Internet Resources

No comprehensive index helps you locate Internet resources. Many online indexes exist, but each covers only a small part of what is available. The on-screen menu of your college or library network is a good starting place to look for Internet indexes. Look too for a **gopher server,** a system of easy-to-use menus. Through a gopher you can use two programs for finding information named *Archie* and *Veronica.* Archie searches for names of files, and Veronica searches for topics. Both can be accessed on the Web at these addresses:

Archie   http://hoohoo.ncsa.uiuc.edu/archie.html

Veronica   gopher://veronica.scs.unr.edu:70/11/veronica

Instructions for using these search tools are usually provided on the screen.

THE REFERENCE LIBRARIAN— THE MOST RESOURCEFUL RESOURCE

By far the most valuable resource in any library is the librarian, a professional who knows the library well and is an expert in locating information. Use the other resources in this chapter first, but if you become stuck or do not know where to look or cannot find the sources you need, do not hesitate to ask a librarian for help. College libraries have *reference librarians* on duty, usually at a station marked as the *reference desk.* Their job is to assist when you need help in finding sources. Reference librarians are almost always helpful, and they have aided many students with the same kinds of research problems and questions that you are likely to have.

There are some limits, however, to the services reference librarians can provide. One librarian requested that we mention some problems they are sometimes asked to solve but cannot. They cannot pick a topic for you, interpret your assignment, or answer questions about the format of your bibliographic citations. Those questions should be addressed to your instructor. The librarian's job is to assist when you need help in locating library sources.

Although printed and electronic materials are of great value to researchers, they are not the only sources available. Chapter 10 discusses ways to use other sources in your research project.

10 Finding Sources outside the Library: Conducting Interviews and Writing Letters

 INTERVIEWING SOURCES

In addition to print sources, interviews with experts can provide valuable material for your paper. Because the people you interview are primary rather than secondary sources, the first-hand information they provide is exclusively yours to present—information that readers will find nowhere else. Therefore, interviewed sources can make a favorable impression, giving readers the sense that they are getting expert testimony directly and reliably. Your own reliability and credibility may also be enhanced, since you demonstrate the initiative to have extended your search beyond the usual kinds of sources.

On a college campus, professors are an accessible source of expert information. Being familiar with research in their individual fields, they also can suggest published and unpublished resources you might not have found in your library research. In her research on a writing career, Molly MacLaren interviewed Rebecca Lee, a professor of creative writing on her campus. Molly found it invaluable to talk with someone who had succeeded in the career she was researching and who could give her first-hand advice.

You may also find experts living in your local community. Molly spoke at length with two of her relatives in the newspaper business, but she also could have talked with writers for her community newspaper or with technical writers and public relations officers employed by local corporations.

Other valuable sources include participants and eyewitnesses. If you were researching, say, the Vietnam War or the Bosnian mission, you could interview relatives and neighbors with experience in the military. Be resourceful in considering interviewees who can contribute to your knowledge and understanding.

Conducting interviews may not be the first order of business in your research project, but because interviews require advance planning, it is important to set up appointments as early as possible—even before you are ready to conduct them. Soon after Molly had decided on her topic, she knew she would want to talk to a professional writer. She wanted to do some reading first in order to be sufficiently informed to ask intelligent questions, but she also knew that authors guard their writing time jealously and that it would be wise to arrange an interview well in advance. She also visited the Career Services office on her campus to schedule a session to test her aptitude for a writing career.

Arranging the Interview

Like every other stage in a research project, arranging interviews can lead to inevitable frustrations. For example, if you were researching a career in psychiatry, you might find it difficult to arrange an interview with a psychiatrist. After all, psychiatrists spend their days talking with patients; they may have little interest in giving up their precious free time to talk with someone else (and without compensation).

When you telephone someone you don't know, be courteous and explain your purpose simply and clearly. For example, if you were calling an executive at a computer company to ask for an interview, you might say something like this:

> Hello, Ms. Smith, I'm [your name], a student at [your school]. I'm conducting a research project concerning the future of computers in the workplace. I'm particularly interested in talking to a person in the industry with your expertise, and I would like to learn your views on the topic. I wonder if I could meet with you briefly to ask you a few questions.

You can expect the person to ask you further questions about the nature of your project and about the amount of time the interview will take. If you are courteous and open and if your purposes seem serious, people are likely to cooperate with you to the extent that they are able. Be prepared to meet at a time and place convenient to the interviewee. Many interviews can be conducted in fifteen to thirty minutes. If you wish to tape-record the interview, ask for permission at the time you arrange the meeting.

Professors are usually available to students during office hours, but business people and other professionals are usually not so easy to reach. Before talking to the executive, you might have to explain your need to a receptionist or secretary, who might be reluctant to connect you. Often a letter written in advance of your telephone call can be effective in securing an interview. For example, a student who wishes to arrange an interview with a computer executive might send a letter like this one:

```
                        202 Willow Street
                        Wilmington, NC 28401
                        2 March 1997

Ms. Denise Smith
Vice-President for Research and Development
CompuCosmos Corporation
Wilmington, NC 28401

Dear Ms. Smith:
     I am a student at the University of North Carolina
at Wilmington engaged in a research project concerning
the future of computer use in business offices.  I have
learned much about the topic from written sources,
but I still have some unanswered questions.  Your
observations and expert opinions would be invaluable
```

```
for my report.  I know your time is valuable, and I
would be grateful if I could meet with you for a brief
interview.  I will telephone Wednesday morning to see
if I can arrange a meeting.  If you wish, you can reach
me by phone at 555-1893.
```

Sincerely,

Blair Halliday

Blair Halliday

Conducting the Interview

Some interviews may consist of a simple question or two, designed to fill specific gaps in your knowledge about your topic. Others may be extended question-and-answer sessions about a variety of topics. The success of your interviewing depends on your preparation, professionalism, and interpersonal skills. The following guidelines should be followed when you conduct an interview.

1. *Before the interview:*

    • **Be well prepared.** The most important part of the interview takes place before the questions are posed. Become as informed about your subject as you can so that you can ask the right questions. Use your reading notes to prepare questions in advance.

    • **Dress appropriately for the interview.** How you dress can influence how the interviewee behaves toward you; people are most comfortable talking with someone who dresses as they do. Business and professional people, for example, are more likely to take you seriously if you are wearing standard business attire. On the other hand, formal attire would be inappropriate when interviewing striking factory workers, who might be reluctant to speak freely with someone who looks like management.

    • **Arrive on time for your appointment.** Not only is arriving on time a matter of courtesy, but it is essential in assuring the interviewee's cooperation.

2. *During the interview:*

    • **Take careful and accurate notes.** If you intend to quote your source, you must be certain that you have copied the person's words exactly. A tape recorder can give you an accurate transcript of your interviews.

    • **Behave politely and ethically.** Be certain you have the interviewee's permission if you tape-record the conversation. If you take notes, offer to let the interviewee check the transcript later to ensure accuracy (doing so may elicit further elaborations and additional statements that you can use).

    • **Be relaxed and friendly.** People who are not accustomed to being interviewed are often nervous at first about having their comments recorded. By being friendly and relaxed, you can win their confidence and put them at ease. The most fruitful parts of interviews occur when interviewees become absorbed in what they are saying and forget they are being recorded. Begin with general questions that can be answered with ease and confidence. Later introduce more specific and pointed questions. (For experienced interviewees, these precautions may not be necessary.)

• **Make your recording as unobtrusive as possible.** Many people will not speak freely and naturally when constantly reminded that their comments are being recorded. Place the tape recorder out of the interviewer's direct line of sight. Do not write constantly during the interview; write down key phrases and facts that will allow you to reconstruct the conversation immediately after the interview.

• **Be interested in what the interviewee says.** People will speak much more freely with you if they sense that you are responsive to their comments. It is a mistake for an interviewer to read one prepared question after another, while barely listening to the interviewee's responses. Such wooden interviewing produces an uncomfortable atmosphere and strained responses.

• **Stay flexible.** Do not be a slave to your prepared questions. Listen with real curiosity to what the person says and ask further questions based on what you learn. Request explanations of what is not clear to you. Ask probing questions when a topic is raised that you would like to learn more about.

• **Let the interviewee do the talking.** Remember that it is the interviewee's ideas that you are interested in, not your own. Avoid the temptation to state your own opinions and experiences or to argue points with the interviewee.

3. *After the interview:*

• **End the interview professionally.** Check your notes and questions to determine if any gaps still need to be filled. Thank the interviewee. Ask if the person would like to check your use of statements and information for accuracy, and whether you can call again if you have further questions. Offer to send the interviewee a copy of your paper when it is completed.

• **Be fair to the source.** When you write the paper, be certain that any ideas or statements you attribute to the source are true reflections of the sound and spirit of the person's answers and comments. Be accurate in quoting the person, but eliminate slips of the tongue and distracting phrases like *uh* and *you know*.

• **Send a thank-you note.** Whether or not you send a copy of your paper to the interviewee, you should send a note expressing your appreciation for the help that the person provided.

Molly prepared the following list of questions before she interviewed Rebecca Lee, a professional writer who taught at her college:

Possible Interview Questions for Rebecca Lee

• When did you decide to become a writer? Why?
• How did you get started?

- Did you have second thoughts? Are you glad you became a writer?
- Was it difficult?
- Did you have any mentor(s)?
- How possible is it to make enough money to live as a writer?
- Is it more difficult for a woman?
- What are your current projects?
- What courses do you teach?
- Would you recommend writing as a career?
- Do you have any advice for an aspiring writer?

Although she used her prepared questions as a point of reference, Molly found herself departing from them as she responded to Professor Lee's comments. During her interview, Molly took notes in her research notebook. Here are some excerpts (in a few cases we have recast them to make them clearer to other readers):

Notes from the Interview with Rebecca Lee

—never officially decided to become writer; liked to write; found herself doing it more and more

—wrote bad poetry in high school; took creative writing courses in college

—"I have second thoughts" almost every time she writes, especially first draft. Moments when she writes better than she expected make her want to keep writing

—Writing always has been difficult for her; "I feel sort of inefficient and slow"; in some ways, easier than other professions: flexible hours, no boss

—making money "a realistic goal"; most work at other professions as well; too much pressure if writing sole means of support

—difficulty for woman? tempting to think so when a rejection comes, but that has not been her experience

—would recommend it to someone who feels compelled to write and enjoys solitude; few external rewards at first so writing must be a reward in itself

—aspiring writer: read a lot; most lessons for writers "absorbed through reading"; aspiring writer "should be willing to write poorly at times"; you have to write your way into fine ideas, beautiful images

After the interview with Professor Lee, Molly reviewed her notes, expanded them while her memory of the conversation was fresh, and wrote down observations in her notebook. She then transcribed the material she thought she would use in her paper onto note cards (discussed in Chapter 11).

 ## WRITING FOR INFORMATION

It frequently happens that information helpful to your project is unavailable in the library. For example, if you were doing a project on nutrition in children's breakfast foods, you might visit a supermarket to record nutritional information and ingredients of various brands from the sides of cereal boxes. You could also write letters of inquiry to cereal manufacturers, such as the one that follows.

November 3, 1996

Public Relations Officer
Breakfast Foods Division
General Foods Corporation
250 North Street
White Plains, NY 10625

Dear Public Relations Officer:

As a student at [your university], I am undertaking a research study of nutrition in breakfast cereals. I am particularly interested in learning if there is a market for low-sugar cereals targeted specifically for the children's market. Could you please tell me the sales figures for your low-sugar Post Crispy Critters cereal? I would also appreciate any additional information you could send me related to this subject.

I would be grateful if you could respond before [date], the deadline for my research paper.

Sincerely,
[your signature]
[your name]

Business directories in the reference section of your library, such as *Directory of Corporate Affiliations,* can help you find company addresses. If you need further assistance, consult with the reference librarian.

It is wise to tell correspondents how you plan to use the information you are requesting. They are more likely to respond if convinced that your project will not be harmful to their interests. (Some businesses, such as tobacco or liquor companies, are understandably leery about supplying information for studies that may attack them.) You can increase your chances of getting a response by including a self-addressed stamped envelope with your letter. If time is short, a telephone call or a fax may get a speedier response than a letter.

 ## STILL OTHER SOURCES

Researchers can avail themselves of many other sources besides library materials, interviews, and letters. *Lectures, films, television programs,* and ***audio recordings*** are among the sources often cited in student research projects. In your paper, for example, you might quote a person who appeared in a television documentary, or you might describe an event portrayed in a news program. A song lyric or a line from movie dialogue might effectively illustrate a particular theme.

On many campuses there is a ***media center*** in which videotapes (including television documentaries), films, and various audio recordings are available. It may be housed in the library or in a separate building. Some campuses belong to a regional network of media centers that share their materials, usually with little or no charge to the borrower. If your campus has a media center, ask how you can find what sources are available on your topic and whether it is possible for you to gain access to materials from other campuses.

11 *Putting Your Sources to Work*

 A RESEARCH PROSPECTUS

A *prospectus* is a statement of your plans for a project. During the early stages of their projects, Helen Veit and Molly MacLaren were asked by their instructors to submit a research prospectus. Helen's class received the following assignment.

Research Prospectus   **ASSIGNMENT**

Bring to our next class a prospectus of your research project. It should consist of the following elements:

1. *A statement of your research question.* Your topic may be tentative at this point, so you needn't feel locked into it. In upcoming days, you may decide to alter your question or shift its focus as you conduct further research and learn more about the subject.

2. *A paragraph or two about your progress so far.* You can summarize why you chose your topic, what you already know about it, and what you hope to discover. You can also discuss any problems or successes you have had with focusing your topic and finding sources.

3. *A working bibliography* (a list of the sources you have located so far). Use the MLA format (explained in Chapter A of Part II) for your bibliography. After each entry, write in brackets the name of the bibliographic source that you used to discover it (for example, OPAC or InfoTrac General Periodicals Index). This is a list of raw sources—sources you have not yet had much chance to examine and evaluate—so it is likely to contain some items that you will not use in your paper and therefore will not appear in the works-cited page of the final draft.

Helen and Molly had by now a general idea of their topics. They had done some browsing in encyclopedias and other reference works, and each was beginning to assemble a list of potential sources. Following are some excerpts from

Helen's research notebook, written during and after early visits to the library. Helen's notes were informal, in the style of journal entries. We have edited them somewhat to make them clearer for other readers.

> I'm thinking of tracing the Cinderella story through different countries and from its earliest known beginnings to the present. In the library, I found several of the classic versions, an Old South version called "Moss Gown," an Appalachian version, and a Korean version. I thought I was doing well until I got on the Internet and found a goldmine. On the World Wide Web, I used InfoSeek to search "Cinderella" [see Chapter 9 for information about Web search engines—authors]. First on the list was a page called "Cinderella Stories," which turns out to be an incredible bibliography. It lists dozen of books and articles about Cinderella. One book by Judy Sierra has "24 Cinderella stories from a wide range of cultures." Another book published in 1893 has 345 variants. Another source is *The Uses of Enchantment* by Bruno Bettelheim, which is one of my mother's favorite books. . . . The page also has links to other Internet sources. One is to the Cinderella Project at the University of Southern Mississippi. I opened it and it has twelve different versions starting from 1729, and they're all online. . . .

Here is another entry from Helen's notebook written a few days later:

> . . . *The Uses of Enchantment* is fascinating. He talks about Cinderella but writes mainly about fairy tales being good for children. I looked up both "Cinderella" and "fairy tales" on InfoTrac, and there were many articles about whether fairy tales are too violent for children or are sexist. I looked up a few out of curiosity, but now I think that topic is even more interesting because it involves controversy. I have many Cinderella sources, and I will make it the center of my paper, or I may just do the controversy. . . .

After more searching with the OPAC, periodical databases, and the Internet, Helen and Molly had settled on their topics and were ready to write their prospectuses. Helen's prospectus and working bibliography are shown in Figure 11.1 (pages 304–05). By now she had abandoned her original idea of writing about the Cinderella story and placed her focus entirely on the debate about the suitability of fairy tales.

 ## THE WORKING BIBLIOGRAPHY

A *bibliography* is a list of research sources. One of the last tasks in your search project is to type a *list of works cited* at the end of your paper—a formal bibliography or listing of all the sources you have used in writing it. But this occurs much later in the research process. For now, your task is to continue gathering sources; that is, you need to use the library indexes and other research tools described in Chapter 9 to locate books and articles for your paper. The list of possible sources you draw up now as you begin your search is your *working bibliography.* You add to the working bibliography during the course of your project as you discover additional sources, and you subtract from it as some sources on the list turn out not to be helpful.

A working bibliography is tentative, informal, and practical. The only requirement for a good working bibliography is that you are able to use it conveniently.

Since it is for your own use—not part of the paper itself—you can record the information you need in any way you like. For example, when you find a likely book from a subject citation in the OPAC, you can jot down in your notebook the key information that will enable you to locate it—perhaps only its title and call number. On the other hand, there are advantages to including more complete information in your working bibliography, as Helen did, in that you will use this information later, at the end of the project, when you type your works-cited page. Therefore, you can save considerable time by including in your working bibliography all the information you may need later. For that reason, it is important for you to be acquainted with the standard conventions for citing sources. Those conventions are detailed in Chapter A of Part II.

Once you have completed your prospectus and have had it approved by your instructor, you are ready to put your sources to work.

USING YOUR WRITTEN SOURCES

The early stages of your project may have been easier than you expected. You selected a topic, did some preliminary browsing in the library, and assembled a list of sources to work with. So far so good. But now what? Is there some simple technique that experienced researchers use to get ideas and information *out* of their sources and *into* their writing?

In fact, there is a reasonably uncomplicated and orderly procedure for putting your sources to use, but it isn't exactly simple. You can't just sit down before a stack of sources, read the first one and write part of your paper, then read the second one and write some more, and so on until you are finished. Obviously, such a procedure would make for a very haphazard and disjointed paper.

You can't write your paper all at once. Because you have a substantial body of information to sort through, digest, select, and organize, you have to use good management skills in your project. Your course of action needs to consist of manageable subtasks: You need to (1) *read* your sources efficiently and selectively and (2) *evaluate* the information you find there. As you learn more about your topic, you should (3) *narrow your focus* and (4) *shape a plan* for the paper. And to make use of new ideas and information, you need to (5) *take notes* on what seems important and usable in the sources. Only then are you ready to begin the actual drafting of the paper.

This chapter examines each of these tasks in turn, but do not think of them as separate operations that you can perform one after the other. They must interact. After all, how can you know what to read and take notes on unless you have some plans for what your paper will include? On the other hand, how can you know what your paper will include until your reading reveals to you what information is available? In working on your paper, you can never put your brain on automatic pilot. As you read and learn from your sources, you must continually think about how you can use the information and how using it will fit in with (or alter) your plan for the paper.

Veit 1

Helen Veit

Research prospectus

1.   Research question: Are fairy tales harmful to children?

2.   I've always been interested in different types of literature--particularly folklore and fairy tales. My mother always read fairy tales to me when I was a child, but the principal of the school I went to between the ages of two and seven believed that fairy tales were a negative influence on children. Therefore, she discouraged parents from reading fairy tales to their children.

My mother, a sociologist herself, initiated a friendly debate with the principal. One source my mother used to argue her point was The Uses of Enchantment by Bruno Bettelheim. The principal was at least partially convinced and began to encourage or at least tolerate fairy tales (in some circumstances). I had forgotten that story until I came across Bettelheim's name when I began research on Cinderella. I started reading the book, and I found many other articles on the topic as well. Jack Zipes is another advocate of fairy tales, but there are many who firmly contradict them. I realized that the debate "begun" by my mother and my principal has been raging in psychological circles for decades. I also realized I had found a very interesting and fertile research topic.

Figure 11.1 Helen's research prospectus.

Veit 2

3. Working bibliography

Bettelheim, Bruno. <u>The Uses of Enchantment: The Meaning</u>
    <u>and Importance of Fairy Tales</u>. New York: Knopf, 1976.
    [InfoSeek: bibliography in "Cinderella Stories" page]

Brott, Armin A. "Not All Men Are Sly Foxes." <u>Newsweek</u>
    1 June 1992: 14-15. [InfoTrac: Expanded Academic
    Index/ASAP]

Hill, Laura. "Fairy Tales: Visions for Problem Resolution
    in Eating Disorders." <u>Journal of Counseling and</u>
    <u>Development</u> 70 (1992): 584-87. [ERIC]

Lüthi, Max. <u>The Fairytale as Art Form and Portrait of Man</u>.
    Trans. Jon Erickson. Bloomington: Indiana UP, 1984.
    [OPAC]

"Only in America." <u>Fortune</u> 13 Nov. 1995: 266. [InfoTrac:
    Expanded Academic Index/ASAP]

Rowe, Karen E. "Feminism and Fairy Tales." <u>Don't Bet on</u>
    <u>the Prince: Contemporary Feminist Fairy Tales in North</u>
    <u>America and England</u>. Ed. Jack Zipes. New York:
    Methuen, 1986. 209-26. [OPAC]

Tunnell, Michael O. "The Double-Edged Sword: Fantasy and
    Censorship." <u>Language Arts</u> 71 (1994): 606-12. [ERIC]

"Using Books to Teach Values." Associated Press News
    Service. 2 May 1995. [CD NewsBank Comprehensive]

Zipes, Jack. "Spinning with Fate: Rumpelstiltskin and the
    Decline of Female Productivity." <u>Western Folklore</u> 52
    (1993): 43-59. [bibliography in Rowe article]

Figure 11.1 (continued)

Helen and Molly received an assignment like the following from their instructors.

ASSIGNMENT   **Note Cards and a Preliminary Outline**

Continue your research by reading your sources, evaluating them, taking notes on note cards, narrowing your focus, and shaping a plan (a preliminary outline) for your paper. This is the most time-consuming stage of your research project, so be sure to begin working on it right away. Continue to record your experiences and observations in your research notebook.

Reading Your Sources

At this stage, you need to undertake several tasks, the first of which is to **read your sources.** A research paper should be something new, a fresh synthesis of information and ideas from many sources. A paper that is largely a summary of only one or two sources fails to do this. Become well informed about your topic by reading widely, and use a breadth of information in your paper. Most likely you have found many sources related to your topic, and the sheer volume of available material may itself be a cause for concern. Because your time is limited, you need to use it efficiently. Following are some practical suggestions for efficient reading.

• **Read only those sources that relate to your topic.** Beginning researchers often try to read too much. Do not waste valuable time reading sources that do not relate specifically to your topic. Before reading any source in detail, examine it briefly to be sure of its relevance. Chapter titles in books and section headings or even illustrations in articles may give you a sense of the work's usefulness. If you find dozens of books devoted solely to your topic, that topic probably is too broad to treat in a brief paper, and your focus should be narrowed. (Narrowing your paper's focus is discussed later in this chapter.)

• **Read each source selectively.** Do not expect to read every source from cover to cover; rather, read only those passages that relate to your topic. With a book, for example, use the table of contents in the front and the index in the back to locate relevant passages. Skim through promising sections, looking for passages relating directly to your topic—only these should you read carefully and deliberately.

• **Think as you read.** Ask yourself if what you are reading relates to your topic. Is it important and usable in your paper? Does it raise questions you want to explore further? What additional research do you need to do to answer these questions? Find new sources as needed, discard unusable ones, and update your working bibliography.

• **Read with curiosity.** Do not let your reading become a plodding and mechanical task; don't think of it as plowing through a stack of sources. Make your reading an act of exploration. You want to learn about your topic, and each source

M Y   T U R N

Not All Men Are Sly Foxes

BY ARMIN A. BROTT

If you thought your child's bookshelves were finally free of openly (and not so openly) discriminatory materials, you'd better check again. In recent years groups of concerned parents have persuaded textbook publishers to portray more accurately the roles that women and minorities play in shaping our country's history and culture. "Little Black Sambo" has all but disappeared from library and bookstore shelves; feminist fairy tales by such authors as Jack Zipes have, in many homes, replaced the more traditional (and obviously sexist) fairy tales. Richard Scarry, one of the most popular children's writers, has reissued new versions of some of his classics; now female animals are pictured doing the same jobs as male animals. Even the terminology has changed: males and females are referred to as mail "carriers" or "firefighters."

There is, however, one very large group whose portrayal continues to follow the same stereotypical lines as always: fathers. The evolution of children's literature didn't end with "Goodnight Moon" and "Charlotte's Web." My local public library, for example, previews 203 new children's picture books (for the under-5 set) each *month*. Many of these books make a very conscious effort to take women characters out of the kitchen and the nursery and give them professional jobs and responsibilities.

Despite this shift, mothers are by and large still shown as the primary caregivers and, more important, as the primary nurturers of their children. Men in these books—if they're shown at all—still come home late after work and participate in the child rearing by bouncing baby around for five minutes before putting the child to bed.

In one of my 2-year-old daughter's favorite books, "Mother Goose and the Sly Fox," "retold" by Chris Conover, a single mother (Mother Goose) of seven tiny goslings is pitted against (and naturally outwits) the sly Fox. Fox, a neglectful and presumably unemployed single father, lives with his filthy, hungry pups in a grimy hovel littered with the bones of their previous meals. Mother Goose, a successful entrepreneur with a thriving lace business, still finds time to serve her goslings homemade soup in pretty porcelain cups. The story is funny and the illustrations marvelous, but the unwritten message is that women take better care of their kids and men have nothing else to do but hunt down and kill innocent, law-abiding geese.

The majority of other children's classics perpetuate the same negative stereotypes of fathers. Once in a great while, people complain about "Babar's" colonialist slant (little jungle-dweller finds happiness in the big city and brings civilization—and fine clothes—to his backward village). But I've never heard anyone ask why, after his mother is killed by the evil hunter, Babar is automatically an "orphan." Why can he find comfort only in the arms of another female? Why do Arthur's and Celeste's mothers

Mothers work and give care. Fathers just work.

Fathers still negatively stereotyped

Figure 11.2 Annotation of a photocopied source.

holds the potential to answer your questions. Search out answers, and if you don't find them in one source, seek them in another. There are many profitable ways for researchers to think of themselves: as explorers discovering unknown territory, as detectives following a trail of clues, as players fitting together the pieces of an intriguing puzzle.

• *Use your hand as well as your eyes when you read.* If you have photocopied an article or book chapter, underline important passages while reading, and write yourself notes in the margins. (Of course, don't do either of these things unless you own the copy; marking up material belonging to the library or to other people is a grave discourtesy.) Getting your hand into action as you read is a good way of keeping your mind active as well; writing, underlining, and note-taking force you to think about what you are reading. An article from *Newsweek* that Helen photocopied and then annotated is shown in Figure 11.2.

• *Write notes about your reading.* Use your research notebook to "think on paper" as you read. That is, write general comments about what you have learned from your sources and the ideas you have gained for your paper. Use note cards to write down specific information that you might use in writing your paper. (Note cards are discussed in detail later in this chapter.)

Evaluating Your Sources

All sources are not equally reliable. Not all writers are equally competent; not all periodicals and publishers are equally respected; and not all statements from interviewees are equally well informed. Certainly not every claim that appears in print is true. Because you want to base your paper on the most accurate, up-to-date, and authoritative information available, you need to exercise discretion in *evaluating your sources.* Following are some questions you can ask about a source:

- *Is the publication respectable?* If you are researching flying-saucer sightings, for example, an article in an astronomy or psychology journal commands far more respect than an article like "My Baby's Daddy Came from a UFO" in a lurid supermarket tabloid. Between these two extremes are popular magazines, which cover a wide range of territory. Information that appears in a news magazine such as *Newsweek* or *U.S. News & World Report* is more likely to be accepted as balanced and well researched than information taken from a less serious publication such as *People* or *Teen.* You must use your judgment about the reliability of your sources. Because sources differ in respectability and prestige, scholars always identify their research sources so as to allow readers to make their own judgments about reliability. (Acknowledging sources is discussed in Chapter B of Part II.) As a general rule, works that identify their sources are more likely to be reliable than those that do not.

- *What are the author's credentials?* Is the author a recognized authority? An astrophysicist writing about the possibility of life in other galaxies will command more respect than, say, an amateur flying-saucer enthusiast who is a retired dentist. Expert sources lend authority to assertions you make in your paper—another reason for the standard practice of identifying your sources to your readers.

- *Is the source presenting information at first-hand?* Are the writer's assertions based on primary or secondary research? For example, articles about cancer research in *Reader's Digest* or *Time* may be written with a concern for accuracy and clarity, but their authors may be reporters writing second-hand on the subject— they may not be experts in the field. You can certainly use these sources, but be certain to consider all factors in weighing their reliability.

- *Does the source demonstrate evidence of careful research?* Does the author show by way of notes and other documentation that the statements presented are based on the best available information? Or does it appear that the author's statements derive from unsupported speculation or incomplete research? A source that seems unreliable should either not be used at all or else be cited as an example of one point of view (perhaps one that you refute using more reliable sources).

- *Is the source up-to-date?* Clearly you do not want to base your paper on information that is no longer considered accurate and complete. For example, a paper on a dynamic field such as nuclear disarmament or advances in telecommunications would be hopelessly out-of-date if it is based on five-year-old sources. If you are writing a paper on a topic about which new findings or theories exist, your research should include recent sources. Check the publication dates of your sources.

- *Does the source seem biased?* Writers have opinions that they support in their writing, but some writers are more open-minded than others. Is the author's purpose in writing to explain or to persuade? Does the author provide a balanced presentation of evidence, or are there other perspectives and evidence that the author ignores? Be aware of the point of view of the author and of the publication you are examining. An article in a magazine of political opinion such as *National Review* can be expected to take a conservative stance on an issue, just as an article in *The Nation* will express a more liberal opinion. Your own paper, even when you are making an argument for a particular viewpoint, should present evidence for all sides. If you use opinionated sources, you can balance them with sources expressing opposing points of view.

- *Do your sources consider all viewpoints and theories?* Because many books and articles are written from a single viewpoint, it is important to read widely to discover if other points of view exist as well. For example, several works have been written claiming that ancient monuments such as the pyramids are evidence of past visits to our planet by extraterrestrials. Only by checking a variety of sources might a student discover that scientists have discredited most of the evidence on which these claims are based. Students writing about such topics as astrology, subliminal advertising, Noah's flood, holistic healing, Bigfoot, or the assassination of President Kennedy should be aware that these areas are controversial and that they should seek out diverse points of view in their research so they can be fully informed and can present a complete picture of the topic to their readers.

Narrowing Your Paper's Focus

If you are like most students, the research paper assigned in your composition course may be the longest paper you have had to write, so you may feel worried about filling enough pages. Most students share that concern at this stage, but they soon find so much material that having *too much* to say (not too little) becomes their concern.

The ideal topic for your paper is one to which you can do justice—one you can write about with some thoroughness and completeness—in a paper of the length you are assigned. Most student researchers start out with a fairly broad conception of their topic and then make it more and more limited as their research and writing progress. As you learn how much information is available about your topic and as you discover through your reading what aspect most intrigues you, you should **narrow your paper's focus**—that is, bring your topic into a sharper and more limited scope.

From your first speculations about a topic for your research project until the completion of your final draft, your topic will probably undergo several transformations, usually with each new version more narrowly defined than the one before. For example, Helen Veit's prewriting shows that as she was deciding on a topic, she began with the general area of *literature,* her favorite school subject. She then considered several more specific areas of literature, including *folktales,* which she then narrowed to one specific tale, *Cinderella.* Finally, her topic became even more specific as she considered *tracing different versions of the Cinderella story.* Until this point, her discovery of a topic moved, as the following diagram illustrates, from a more general (broader) to a more specific (narrower) focus.

Progress toward a topic is not always consistently linear, as Helen's case demonstrates. Continued research in this area suddenly caused her to detour in a slightly different direction, as she changed her project's focus to the effects of fairy tales on children—which she later actually *broadened* to include some effects on teenagers and adults as well. Most of the time, however, student researchers find their projects moving in a generally more narrow and specific direction as they determine their topic. As another example of a topic becoming more sharply focused, a student might begin with the general concept of his major, oceanography, and narrow it through successive stages as follows:

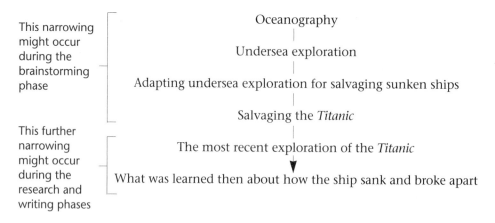

Narrowing a Topic

1. Speculate how each of the following general topics might be successively narrowed in the course of a research project. Write each topic in your notebook, and beneath it give three or four additional topics, each more specific and more narrowly focused than the one above it. (For example, if you were given the topic *oceanography,* you might create a list something like the one above.)

    Warfare   Music   Famous people   Luxury goods

2. Now take your own research topic and make a general-to-specific list of its successive stages. First list the most general idea you started with and show how it narrowed to your present topic. Then speculate on how your topic might be narrowed even further as you complete work on your project.

Formulating and Refining a Plan

Writing is never an exact science or a tidy procedure, and the business of planning and organizing is the untidiest part of all. It would be nice if you could start by creating a full-blown outline of your paper, then take notes on the areas you have outlined, and finally write your paper from your notes, exactly as first planned. However, any writer can tell you it rarely if ever works that way.

Research papers evolve as you do research, and they continue to evolve as you write them, so it is important to remain flexible. As you learn more about your subject—as you read and take notes, and even as you begin writing—new directions will suggest themselves to you. Be prepared to adjust the focus and organization of your paper at every stage, right up to your final revision. Many a student has expected to write one paper, only to discover something quite different actually taking shape on the page. There is nothing wrong with making these changes—they are a natural part of the writing process. Writing is as much a process of discovery for the writer as it is a medium for communicating with readers.

As you start examining your sources, you may have only a hazy notion of the eventual contents of your paper, but the beginnings of a plan should emerge as you learn more and more. Shortly into your research you should be ready to pause and sketch a very general *informal preliminary outline* of where your paper seems to be going. Helen's first rough outline, shown in Figure 11.3, makes no pretense of being complete or final or even particularly pretty—nor should it at this stage. Helen was "thinking on paper," making sense of her own thoughts and trying to bring some vague ideas into focus. She was doing it for her own benefit, not trying

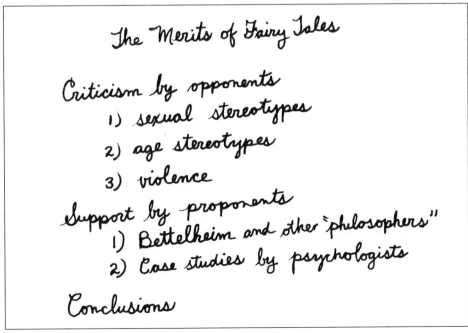

Figure 11.3 Helen's rough outline.

to impress any outside readers. Having established some sense of her paper's parts, Helen was then able to resume reading and taking notes with greater efficiency. She had a clearer idea now of what she was looking for. She was also aware that the organization of her paper would probably change as she continued writing.

Begin with a very general outline, perhaps listing just a few of the main topics you expect your paper to include. As you continue reading, taking notes, and thinking, your outline may become more fleshed out, as you continue to refine your preliminary plans. Remember that an informal outline is an aid to you in organizing and writing your paper. It is not a part of the paper and does not need to be in any kind of polished, orderly form. A formal outline, if you do one, can be written as one of the last steps of your project. (Formal outlines are discussed in Chapter C of Part II.)

Taking Notes on Note Cards

Clearly, you cannot put into your paper everything you read in the course of your research. Some sources will be more useful than others, but still you will use only a small portion of any one source. Note-taking is a way of selecting what you can use. It is also a way of aiding your memory and storing the information and ideas you find in a convenient form for later use when you write the paper.

Good notes, then, have the virtue of being both selective and accessible. You could take notes in your notebook, but a notebook is far less easy to work with than *note cards,* which have the advantage of flexibility. Unlike entries in notebooks or on long sheets of paper, notes on index cards can be easily sorted, rearranged, and weeded out. When you are ready to write, you can group note cards according to topics and arrange them in the order in which you expect to use them in the paper. This greatly simplifies the task of writing.

Besides being selective and convenient, good notes have another quality— accuracy. You are obliged as a scholar to be scrupulously accurate in reporting and acknowledging your sources. In research writing, you must quote your sources accurately and paraphrase them fairly. (Quoting and paraphrasing sources are discussed more fully in Chapter 12.) Moreover, you should give credit to sources for their contributions and make it clear to your readers which words in the paper are your own and which are taken directly from sources. You can use your sources fairly and accurately only if you write from notes that you have taken with great care.

For an example of how a writer takes notes, look first at this passage that Helen read in one of her sources, "Who's Afraid of the Big, Bad Wolf?" an article by Ann Trousdale. Trousdale is describing a seven-year-old's reaction to the death of the witch in the story of Sleeping Beauty. Henbane, the witch, had cast a spell on Sleeping Beauty because Henbane had not been invited to the girl's christening party.

A passage from a source

> Rebecca seemed to be drawn to the powerful, manipulative, and vindictive Henbane until the fairy's desire for revenge got out of hand and turned her into an evil monster. When the evil became uncontrollable, Rebecca was frightened— and relieved when the monstrous Henbane was destroyed.
> Rebecca's responses to the dangerous figure in "The Sleeping Beauty" indicate that the figures in fairy tales do provide children the opportunity to objectify inner conflicts, as Bettelheim and Yolen have suggested. As I was attempting to

Topic label

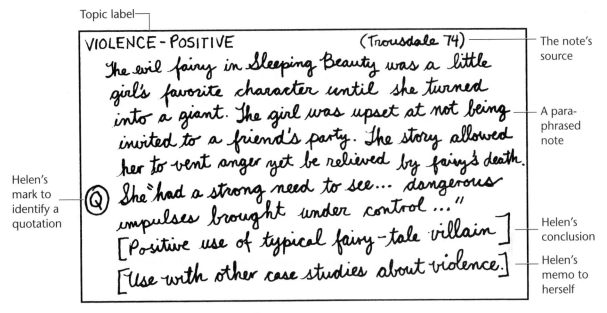

VIOLENCE - POSITIVE   (Trousdale 74)

The evil fairy in Sleeping Beauty was a little girl's favorite character until she turned into a giant. The girl was upset at not being invited to a friend's party. The story allowed her to vent anger yet be relieved by fairy's death. She "had a strong need to see... dangerous impulses brought under control..."

Ⓠ

[Positive use of typical fairy-tale villain]

[Use with other case studies about violence.]

The note's source

A para-phrased note

Helen's mark to identify a quotation

Helen's conclusion

Helen's memo to herself

Figure 11.4 A sample note card.

understand Rebecca's responses to Henbane, I asked her father whether Rebecca had recently had the experience herself of not being invited to a party. He told me that several months previously a little girl in the neighborhood had had a birthday party and had not invited Rebecca, who had been very much upset. Rebecca seemed to use the figure of the evil fairy to explore angry impulses within herself, within the safety of a story form. Her reaction to the battle between the fairy and the prince suggest that she had a strong need to see these dangerous impulses brought under control at the end of the story.

Figure 11.4 shows the note card that Helen made for this passage. Later, when Helen wrote her paper, she used this card to write the following paragraph:

    Trousdale cites one little girl in her study as an
example of the positive use of a typical fairy-tale villain.
The evil fairy in Sleeping Beauty was in fact the girl's
favorite character until the fairy's rage got out of control
as she turned into a giant. The girl herself had not been
invited to a friend's party and had been upset for some
weeks. The story allowed her to vent her anger and
simultaneously feel relief when the evil fairy is killed at
the end. Her "dangerous impulses" had been controlled (74).

Helen's use of the note card in her paper

There are various systems for taking notes on cards, and you should use consistently a system that meets your needs. All good note-card systems have several features in common. In making note cards you should follow these guidelines:

• *Put no more than one unit of information on a note card.* That is, use one card for each important fact or idea. (If you try to economize by crowding many unrelated notes from a source onto a single card, you will sacrifice flexibility later when you try to sort the cards by subjects.) Some cards may contain long notes, whereas others may contain only a word or two. One source may provide you with notes on a dozen different cards, whereas another may give you only a single note (or no notes at all).

• *Label each card by topic.* A topic label helps you remember what a note card is about so that after you have finished taking notes from all your sources, you can easily arrange your cards according to topic. Helen selected the label *VIOLENCE-POSITIVE,* writing it in the upper left corner of the card. The same label appeared on two other cards that Helen prepared while reading different sources. When she was ready to organize her notes, Helen gathered these three cards together, discarded one of them that she knew she would not use, and arranged the remaining two in the order she was likely to use them in a first draft of her paper.

You should consider following a procedure similar to Helen's. Whenever you take a note, consider where within your subject the information might fit and give the note a label. The label may correspond to one of the divisions in your preliminary outline. If it does not, that may suggest that the organization of your paper is developing and changing and that you need to expand or revise your outline to reflect those changes.

• *Identify the source of each note precisely.* In the upper right corner of her note card, Helen identified her note's source: *(Trousdale 74).* This is an example of a parenthetical note (explained in Chapter B of Part II), and its purpose is to tell Helen that the information on the card comes from page 74 of the article written by Trousdale. Helen had recorded the full information about that source in her working bibliography, so she needed only the author's last name to identify it.

It is important for each note card to contain all the information you will need in order to cite its source when you write your paper—so you can give the source credit in a parenthetical note. You will find nothing more frustrating as a researcher than having to search through sources at the last minute to find page references for a passage that you forgot to identify on a note card. It is smart to identify each source, as Helen did, just as you will identify it in the paper itself—with a parenthetical note. For that reason, you should consult Chapter B before you begin taking notes.

• *Clearly identify the kind of information your note contains.* Three principal kinds of information can appear on note cards; you must make it clear which is which, so you do not get confused later if you use the card in writing the paper:

   –**Direct quotations.** The passage "had a strong need to see . . . " on Helen's card is quoted directly from the author, Ann Trousdale. *Any time you put a source's own words on a note card, place them within quotation marks.* Do so even if everything on the card is a quotation. It is essential that when you read a note card later, you can tell whether the words are a direct quotation or your own paraphrase of the source. For this reason, you might even use a backup procedure for identifying quotes, as Helen did. She put a circled Q next to each quotation on her cards to be doubly sure she knew these were her source's exact words.

–**Your own comments.** When you write a note from a source, it may inspire some additional thoughts of your own that you will want to jot down. You may also want to remind yourself later of how you intend to use the note in your paper. *Put your own comments in brackets.* For example, at the bottom of Helen's note card, she expressed her own conclusion in brackets: "[Positive use of . . .]." She also wrote a note to herself about where she might use the material in her paper: "[Use with other case studies . . .]." She placed these comments in brackets to alert herself that these were her own ideas, not those of her source.

–**Paraphrase.** Like Helen's, your cards should consist largely of paraphrases of what you have found in your sources. *Anything on a card that is not in quotation marks or in brackets is assumed to be your paraphrasing of the source.* To paraphrase, recast the source's words into your own language, using your own phrasing and style.

- *Be selective in your note-taking.* Because many beginning researchers fear they will not have enough material to use in writing their papers, they often take too many notes. When it comes time to write the paper, they soon discover that if they were to make use of every note, their paper would be dozens of pages long. In fact, for each student who cannot find enough source material for a paper, many others discover to their surprise that they have more than enough.

With experience, researchers learn to be selective, restricting their note-taking to material they stand a good chance of using. Of course, no one makes use of every note card. Especially in the early stages of reading, a researcher does not have a clear notion of what the paper will include or of what information is available. As reading continues, however, those hazy notions become more substantial, and the researcher can take notes more selectively.

Figure 11.5 shows two additional cards that Helen wrote when she read the *Newsweek* article on page 307.

 ## AVOIDING PLAGIARISM

To ensure that you use your sources fairly and accurately, you should observe one additional guideline when you take notes: *Do your paraphrasing on the note card, not later.* If you do not intend to use a source's exact words, do not write those words on your card. (When you should and should not quote a source directly is discussed on pages 340–44.) It is wise to translate important information into your own words right after you read. This will save time and help you avoid unintentional *plagiarism*—using the source's words without quotation marks—when you begin

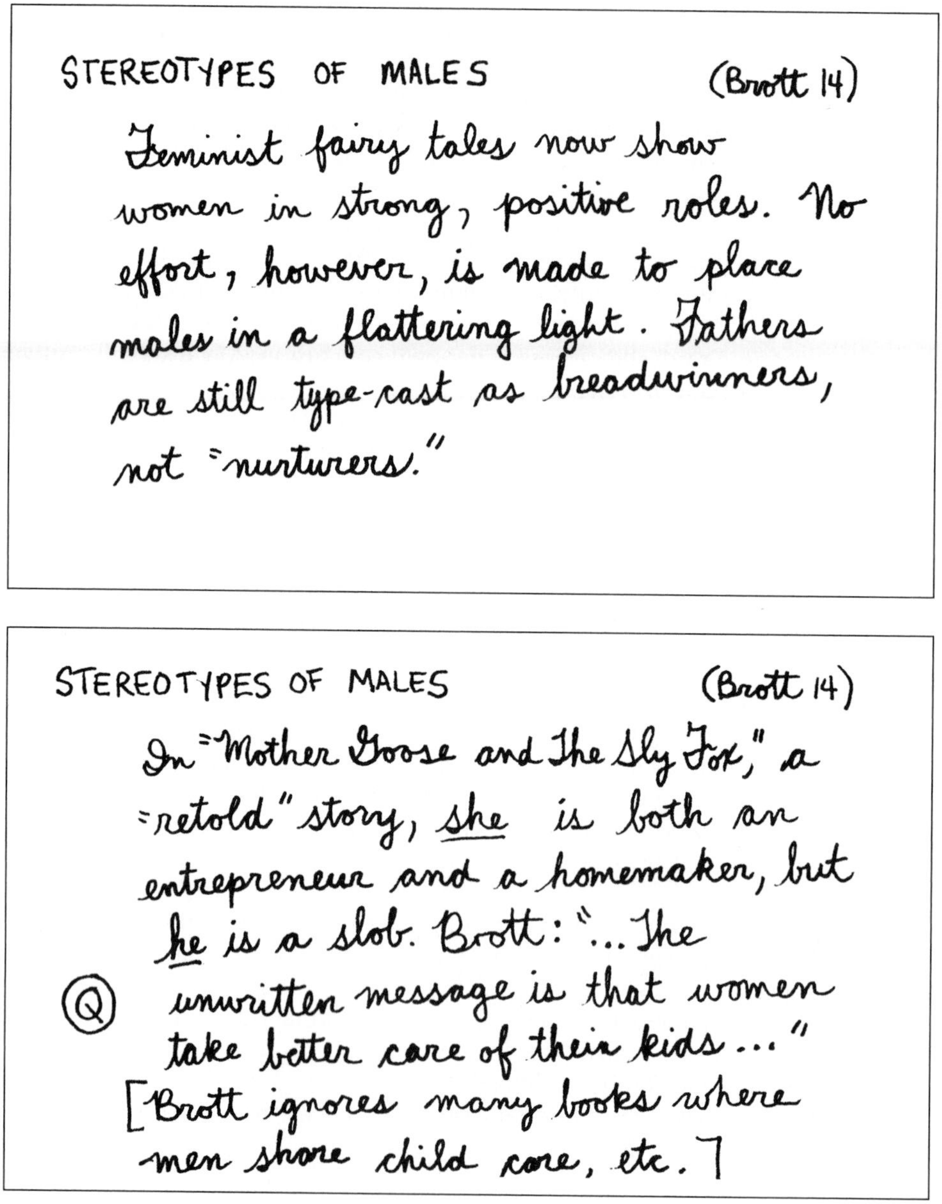

STEREOTYPES OF MALES   (Brott 14)

> Feminist fairy tales now show women in strong, positive roles. No effort, however, is made to place males in a flattering light. Fathers are still type-cast as breadwinners, not "nurturers."

STEREOTYPES OF MALES   (Brott 14)

Ⓠ In "Mother Goose and The Sly Fox," a "retold" story, she is both an entrepreneur and a homemaker, but he is a slob. Brott: "...The unwritten message is that women take better care of their kids..." [Brott ignores many books where men share child care, etc.]

Figure 11.5 Two additional note cards.

to write from your notes. Paraphrasing and summarizing your sources now will also give you more focused notes, as well as force you to read and analyze your sources more carefully.

Since you cannot use everything in your sources, no matter how interesting, it is often necessary to boil down what you find into brief summaries of what is important. In general, the procedure for paraphrasing and summarizing a source is as follows:

1. When you have discovered a passage that you may want to use in your paper, reread it with care.

2. After you have reread it, put it aside and think about the essential idea you have learned. Then write that idea on your card in a brief version, using your own words and style. It is often best not to look at the passage while you write the note, so as to be less likely to plagiarize the original language.

Do not forget to indicate on your note card the specific source of the paraphrase.

Consider how Helen wrote the first note card that appears in Figure 11.5. First, read the exact words of her source, Armin A. Brott:

> There is, however, one very large group whose portrayal continues to follow the same stereotypical lines as always: fathers. . . . [M]others are by and large still shown as the primary caregivers and, more important, as the primary nurturers of their children.

The original source

If Helen had written a note like the following, instead of her actual note card, she might have plagiarized the passage when she used the note card to write her paper:

> Mothers are now shown as the primary caregivers and nurturers of their children. Fathers, however, are one group who continue to be portrayed along the same stereotypical lines as always.

A plagiarized note

Notice how this passage—while it selects from the original, changes some words, and rearranges the order of sentences—relies too closely on Brott's original wording. In contrast, Helen's note states her understanding of Brott's ideas in her own language:

> Feminist fairy tales now show women in strong, positive roles. No effort, however, is made to place males in a flattering light. Fathers are still type-cast as breadwinners, not "nurturers."

A legitimate note

Putting source information into your own words does *not* mean substituting a few synonyms now and again as you copy your source's sentence onto your note card. For example, consider how it would be possible to misuse the following sentence from the passage by Ann Trousdale, quoted earlier:

> Rebecca seemed to be drawn to the powerful, manipulative, and vindictive Henbane until the fairy's desire for revenge got out of hand and turned her into an evil monster.

The source's words

If Helen had written the following on her note card, she would still have been guilty of plagiarism:

> Rebecca appeared to be attracted to the exploitative, forceful, and vengeful Henbane until the desire for vengeance by the witch went out of control and changed her into a wicked giant.

A plagiarized note

Observe how this is really the Trousdale sentence with a few word substitutions (*appeared* for *seemed, attracted* for *drawn,* and so on). Putting sources aside when you write note cards is one way to avoid this plagiarism-by-substitution. It also assures that your paraphrase will be a genuine expression of your own understanding of a source's ideas. Of course, if the exact words are particularly memorable or effective, you may wish to copy them down exactly, within quotation marks, for possible use in your paper. Notice how Helen has done this with one particular sentence—*She "had a strong need to see . . . dangerous impulses brought under control. . . . "* When it came time to use this note, it was clear to her that this was a direct quotation from her source. Although she decided to paraphrase it in writing her paper, she kept one phrase from the original, which she placed within quotation marks:

Use of a
quotation

Her "dangerous impulses" had been controlled (74).

The foregoing can be summed up as follows:

GUIDELINES for Avoiding Plagiarism

1. Whenever you use ideas or information from a source but do not intend to quote the source directly, paraphrase the source. You must restate the material in your own words, using your own phrasing and style. Merely substituting synonyms for the source's words or phrases is not acceptable. Do your paraphrasing at the time you take notes.

2. Whenever you intend to use the source's words, copy those words exactly onto a note card and place them within quotation marks. To be doubly sure that you will not later mistake the author's words for your own, place a circled letter Q (or some other prominent device) on the card next to the quotation.

3. For any borrowed material—whether a direct quotation or your paraphrase of it—carefully note the source and page number(s) on your note card so that you can cite them in your paper.

4. In your paper, you will give full credit to the sources of all borrowed material, both those you quote directly and those you paraphrase. The only exception is for commonly available factual information. (For further guidelines, see the section "When Are Notes Needed?" in Chapter B of Part II.)

5. Observe the rules for acknowledging sources in your paper by providing acknowledgment phrases, parenthetical notes, and a list of works cited. (Further information about giving credit to sources can be found in Chapter 6 and Chapter B.)

EXERCISES   **Note-Taking**

Following are passages that Helen Veit encountered in her research into fairy tales. Suppose that you were researching the same topic. Using the guidelines provided in this chapter, write notes for these sources. On your note cards, you may want to paraphrase some passages, quote others, and offer your own comments or responses. You may take more than one note from a passage.

1. In this passage from page 607 of an article titled "The Double-Edged Sword: Fantasy and Censorship," scholar Michael O. Tunnell argues that fairy tales improve children's mental health:

   . . . [C]oping devices may act like the safety valve on the boiler of a steam engine and have helped many a child (and adult) deal with stress. A small child, for instance, is completely controlled by an adult world—told what to eat, when to sleep, what to wear. But in fairy tales, it is often the youngest son or daughter or the weak, seemingly less able character, rather than parents or other power figures, who wins the day: Hansel and Gretel, Cinderella, or the youngest son in Grimm's "The Water of Life." Children vicariously vent frustrations in healthy ways by subconsciously identifying with such heroes.

2. In her article "Who's Afraid of the Big Bad Wolf? Confronting Wife Abuse through Folk Stories," Lenora Greenbaum Ucko claims that folk stories are useful therapeutic tools in counseling battered women. The following passage is quoted from page 415:

   Wives often interpret the violence against them as having been caused by their own limitations. They tend to apologize for their actions, promise to do better and adapt their behavior to what they think their husbands want, all in the often vain hope that the violence will cease. Women rarely examine the attitudes of their husbands. They take for granted the man's dissatisfaction with them and then try somehow to please him.

   Battered women need encouragement to recognize and evaluate the man's point of view as well as their own attitudes in battering situations. From an examination of various folk stories, men's views of wife battering are as follows:

   - Men regard wife beating as normal behavior.
   - Men believe that the world at large, and especially other men, expect them to resort to wife beating to get their own way.
   - Men see themselves as the final arbiters of women's behavior.
   - Men do not feel accountable and are not held accountable for battering their wives.

   Folk-story wives, on the other hand, tend to be controlled by abusive treatment from their husbands, apologize for their behavior despite the ill treatment they receive, and change their behavior to suit their husbands after being beaten.

Before reading your sources and taking notes, you should consult the following chapter, where conventions of quoting and paraphrasing are more fully explained. Chapter B of Part II demonstrates appropriate ways of acknowledging sources with parenthetical notes.

12 *Reporting on Sources: Paraphrase and Quotation*

MOSTLY when you *do* research on sources, you find out what other people have thought, discovered, said, or written. When you *report* on your research, you tell your readers what you have learned. The following very different passages could all be called examples of reporting on research sources.

1. My old man says he can lick your old man.

2. "If man does find the solution for world peace," wrote General George C. Marshall in 1945, "it will be the most revolutionary reversal of his record we have ever known."

3. Senator Woodling made it clear today that she would shortly declare herself a candidate for the presidency.

4. The first words ever transmitted by telephone were spoken by Bell to his assistant: "Mr. Watson, come here, I want you."

5. The Stoics argued that it was the highest wisdom to accept triumph without elation, tribulation without regret.

6. V. O. Key, Jr., a leading political scientist, offered this positive assessment of the role played by interest groups in American politics:

   > At bottom, group interests are the animating forces in the political process. . . . The chief vehicles for the expression of group interest are political parties and pressure groups. Through these formal mechanisms groups of people with like interests make themselves felt in the balancing of political forces. (Qtd. in Lowery 63–64)

These six passages all report on sources, since each of them communicates what has been learned from someone else. They certainly do so in different ways and with different effects. The first statement, you might guess, is spoken by one child to another, reporting on what he learned from his father. As for its authority, a listener might be wise to doubt that his father said any such thing. The last statement, in contrast, is surely an example of writing, not speech, since it has all the earmarks of a passage from a scholarly paper or article. Its very form, its direct quotation, its acknowledgment of its source and claim for his expertise (*V. O. Key, Jr., a leading political scientist*), and its careful source citation (*Qtd. in Lowery 63–64;* that is, the quotation was found on those pages in a work by Lowery) all lend it an impressive authority. The four middle passages could be either spoken or written.

There are other differences among them as well. Passages 2, 4, and 6 all present their sources' words through *direct quotation,* with the original language repeated in a word-for-word copy. Passages 1, 3, and 5, on the other hand, *paraphrase* their sources, with the source's ideas and information recast in different words. The identity of the sources in each statement is generally clear, although we are not told where the author of passage 5 learned about the Stoic philosophy; still, it is evident that the ideas presented are those of the Stoics and not the author. Of all these passages, however, only number 6 with its *parenthetical note* gives a careful *citation* of its source, the exact location from which the quotation was taken.

 ## THE CONVENTIONS OF REPORTING

Like the reporting of journalists, the reporting of scholars aims to get at and present the truth. To ensure accuracy and clarity, both types of writing follow careful rules and procedures.

Often these practices are identical in both fields. Both journalism and scholarship, for example, require that sources be acknowledged and identified. Both pay scant attention to unsupported opinions. On the other hand, both pay great respect to expert testimony. In reporting on sources, both fields observe the same time-honored conventions, including rules for paraphrasing, quoting, and even punctuating quotations. If there is one outstanding difference between scholarship and journalism, however, it is that scholarly writing, with its careful conventions of documentation, follows even more stringent procedures for identifying the precise sources from which ideas and information are taken.

This chapter is in large part devoted to these conventions. While some of it is given up to technicalities (e.g., does a comma go to the left or right of a quotation mark?), even they are important extensions of the care that researchers take to be accurate and truthful. While you are expected to become familiar with most of the conventions here, you should also regard this chapter as a resource that you can turn to often throughout your college career for guidance in presenting the results of your research.

 ## OPTIONS FOR PRESENTING SOURCES

Whenever you report on your research, you need to find a way of presenting to your readers what you have learned from your sources. Sometimes the appropriate method will be paraphrase; at other times, quotation. In fact, you have several options.

Imagine, for example, that in an introductory anthropology course, your instructor has assigned a research paper in which you are to analyze some aspect of American culture. You have chosen to write about the way Americans express their emotions, and in your research you come upon the following passage from page 248 of Ashley Montagu's book, *The American Way of Life:*

> To be human is to weep. The human species is the only one in the whole of ani-
> mated nature that sheds tears. The trained inability of any human being to weep
> is a lessening of his capacity to be human—a defect which usually goes deeper
> than the mere inability to cry. And this, among other things, is what American
> parents—with the best intentions in the world—have achieved for the American
> male. It is very sad. If we feel like it, let us all have a good cry—and clear our
> minds of those cobwebs of confusion which have for so long prevented us from
> understanding the ineluctable necessity of crying.

The passage expresses an interesting opinion—that American men have been
trained, unnaturally, not to cry—and you want to use it in your paper. You can do
so in many ways; the following are examples of your options.

Paraphrase

You can restate an author's ideas in your own words:

```
Montagu claims that American men have a diminished

capacity to be human because they have been trained by

their culture not to cry (248).
```

Direct Quotation of a Sentence

You can quote an author's exact words, as in these three examples:

```
In his book, The American Way of Life, Ashley Montagu

writes, "The trained inability of any human being to weep

is a lessening of his capacity to be human--a defect

which usually goes deeper than the mere inability to cry"

(248).
```

```
According to Montagu, "To be human is to weep" (248).
```

```
"If we feel like it," writes Ashley Montagu, "let us all

have a good cry--and clear our minds of those cobwebs of

confusion which have for so long prevented us from

understanding the ineluctable necessity of crying" (248).
```

Quoting Part of a Sentence

You can incorporate part of an author's sentence into a sentence of your own:

```
One distinguished anthropologist calls the American

male's reluctance to cry "a lessening of his capacity to

be human" (Montagu 248).
```

```
Montagu finds it "very sad" that American men have a

"trained inability" to shed tears (248).
```

Quoting Longer Passages

You can quote more than one sentence:

```
Anthropologist Ashley Montagu argues that it is both
unnatural and harmful for American males not to cry:
                To be human is to weep. . . .  The trained
                inability of any human being to weep is a
                lessening of his capacity to be human--a defect
                which usually goes deeper than the mere
                inability to cry. . . .  It is very sad. (248)
```

In this chapter, we will study these options in some detail. We will first examine the precise methods of presenting sources through paraphrase and quotation. Afterward, we will look at strategies for using sources: when and where to use the options at our disposal. Chapter B of Part II considers the techniques for citing these sources in parenthetical notes.

ACKNOWLEDGING SOURCES

Whether you paraphrase or quote an author, it is important that you make it clear that it is the author's ideas, not your own, you are presenting. This is necessary for the sake of clarity and fairness—so that the reader knows which words, ideas, and discoveries are yours and which are your source's. Parenthetical notes, which cite a page reference and, if needed, the author's name, do that. Notice, too, that each of the preceding examples makes its indebtedness to its source clear through an *acknowledgment phrase,* such as "Montagu claims that. . . . " Other acknowledgment phrases that we might have used include the following:

```
Ashley Montagu maintains that . . .

Ashley Montagu, author of The American Way of Life,
    says that . . .

Montagu also believes that . . .

Professor Montagu argues that . . .

According to Ashley Montagu, the eminent
    anthropologist, American men . . .
```

Acknowledgment
phrases

A quotation should never be placed in a paper without acknowledgment. Even a parenthetical note is not enough to identify a quotation. You must always introduce a quotation, telling your readers something about it. Avoid writing passages like this with a "naked" quotation in the middle:

Bad:
unacknowledged
quotation

When my grandfather died, all the members of my family--men
and women alike--wept openly. We have never been ashamed
to cry. "To be human is to weep" (Montagu 248). I am
sure we are more human, and in better mental and physical
health, because we are able to express our feelings
without artificial restraints.

Even though the parenthetical note identifies the source, readers find it awkward to read a quotation without knowing its origin in advance. Forcing them to skip ahead to find the note creates an undesirable interruption of the flow of the paper. These problems would not arise if the writer had used a simple phrase (e.g., *As anthropologist Ashley Montagu observed,*) to introduce the quotation:

Better:
acknowledged
quotation

When my grandfather died, all the members of my family--men
women alike--wept openly. We have never been ashamed to cry.
As anthropologist Ashley Montagu observed, "To be human is
weep" (248). I am sure we are more human, and in better mental
and physical health, because we are able to express our
feelings without artificial restraints.

Not only does the reader better understand the quotation's function with the introductory phrase, but the quotation has more impact as well because it has been attributed to a recognized authority.

Always give your readers enough information to identify your sources. The first time you refer to a source, give both the person's first and last names. Unless the source is a well-known figure, identify him or her so that the reader can understand why this particular person is being quoted.

First references

Winston Churchill said, . . .

Cynthia Bathurst, author of <u>The Computer Crisis</u>,
     believes that . . .

According to Valerie Granville, British ambassador to
     Bhutan during the Sherpa Riots, . . .

Rock star Mick Jagger gave a flip answer: . . .

After the first reference, the source's last name is sufficient:

Subsequent
references

Churchill said that . . .

Later Jagger remarked, . . .

Although acknowledgment phrases almost always introduce quotations, they are sometimes unnecessary with paraphrased material. As a general rule, use an acknowledgment phrase when the paraphrased material represents an original idea or opinion of the source, when the source's credentials lend the material authority, or when you wish to distance yourself from opinions with which you disagree.

<table>
<tr><td>

Anthropologist Ashley Montagu argues that crying is a distinctively human activity--as appropriate and necessary for males as for females (248).

</td><td>

Acknowledgment phrase for paraphrased material

</td></tr>
</table>

However, an acknowledgment phrase is not needed for largely factual information, as in these passages:

<table>
<tr><td>

At one point in his life, even Alex Haley, the author of <u>Roots</u>, possessed only eighteen cents and two cans of sardines (Powell 179).

One study has found that firstborns score better in achievement tests that measure language and mathematics skills (Weiss 51).

</td><td>

No acknowledgment phrase is needed for factual information

</td></tr>
</table>

In such cases, the parenthetical notes provide adequate recognition of sources. (Parenthetical notes are discussed in Chapter B of Part II.) Use your best judgment about whether an acknowledgment phrase is called for with paraphrased material. When in doubt, however, provide the acknowledgment phrase. It is better to err on the side of *over-* rather than *under-*recognition of your sources.

 ## RELYING ON EXPERTS

Besides being fair, acknowledging the contribution of a source can also add force to your own writing. In most cases, the sources you present will have greater expertise than you on the subject; a statement from one of them can command greater respect than an unsupported statement from you, a nonexpert. To illustrate this, assume that, in writing a research paper, you quote Montagu on the subject of crying and identify him to your readers as an eminent anthropologist. Could you have made the point equally effectively if instead you had written the following?

> I think it is wrong that men in America have been brought up to think it is not manly to cry. Crying is natural. Our macho-man mentality takes a terrible toll on our emotions.

While you are entitled to your opinions, a reader who doubts your expertise on the subject is likely to question whether you have considered all aspects and implications of your position. After all, what reason does the reader have to trust you? However, when an expert such as Montagu is quoted, many of the doubts are removed and the statement carries greater weight.

This is not to say that experts are automatically right. Experts do not always agree with each other, and progress in humanity's quest for truth often comes as new ideas are introduced to challenge old ones. What it does mean is that experts are people who have studied their subjects thoroughly and have earned the right to be listened to with respect. Since you will not often begin with a thorough knowledge of the subjects you write about in research papers, your writing will rely heavily on what you have learned from expert sources.

 ## PARAPHRASING SOURCES

Most of the time when you present ideas or information from sources, you will paraphrase them. To *paraphrase* a statement or a piece of writing is to recast it into different words. Paraphrase is the least cumbersome way of communicating what a source has said, as well as the easiest to read. Often the source is too technical for your readers or too wordy; you can present the source's point more clearly and succinctly using your own words. When you paraphrase a source, be accurate and faithful to what your source wrote, but use your own style and phrasing. Imagine, for example, that you wished to make use of this passage as a research source:

> Nearly forty years ago Damon Runyon nearly collapsed in laughter when he covered the trial of George McManus, a gambler, who was accused of shooting Arnold Rothstein, another gambler, who thereupon died. The cause of Damon Runyon's mirth was the sight of the witnesses and jurors in the case running out into the halls during court recesses to place bets with their bookies—even as they considered the evils of gambling in the city.
> —Edwin P. Hoyt, *The Golden Rot*

You can paraphrase this information in a briefer version, using your words:

Good

    According to Edwin P. Hoyt, Damon Runyon was highly
    amused that both witnesses and jurors in a gambling trial
    would place bets with their bookies during court
    recesses.

What you must *not* do is simply change a word or two while keeping the structure of the original intact:

Bad

    Edwin P. Hoyt writes that about forty years ago Damon
    Runyon almost fell down from laughing when he was a
    reporter for the trial of gambler George McManus, accused
    of murdering another gambler, Arnold Rothstein.

You can avoid word-substitution paraphrase, as well as unintentional plagiarism, if you paraphrase from memory rather than directly from the original copy.

Chapters 3 and 11 describe the best method as follows: *Read the passage so that you understand it; then put it aside, and write your recollection of its meaning on a note card, in your own words.* Be certain to observe the guidelines for avoiding plagiarism (see page 318).

Paraphrasing a Source

EXERCISE

Imagine that each of the following is a source for a research project. Write a paraphrase of important information from each quotation as you would on a note card. Then write it as you would in the paper itself, giving credit to your source with a suitable acknowledgment phrase. *(Note:* You do not need to present all of the information from each passage in either your paraphrases or your acknowledgments.)

a. *Source:* Linus Pauling. He won Nobel Prizes for both Chemistry (1954) and Peace (1962).

Quotation:
Science is the search for truth—it is not a game in which one tries to beat his opponent, to do harm to others. We need to have the spirit of science in international affairs, to make the conduct of international affairs the effort to find the right solution, the just solution of international problems, not the effort by each nation to get the better of other nations, to do harm to them when it is possible.

b. *Source:* Edwin P. Hoyt. This quotation is from his book, *The Golden Rot: A Somewhat Opinionated View of America,* published in 1964.

Quotation:
Let there be no mistake, the pressures on government for destruction of wilderness areas will grow every time the nation adds another million in population. The forest service has been fighting such pressures in the West for fifty years. Any national forest visitor can gauge the degree of success of the "multiple use program" of the forest service very nicely by taking a fishing rod and setting out to catch some trout. He will find mile after mile of the public waters posted by private landowners who do not allow fishing or hunting on their property—or on the government property they lease. Inevitably this includes the best beaver dams and open stretches of water along the streams.

c. *Source:* Marvin Harris. He is an anthropology professor and author of several books on human behavior throughout the world.

Quotation:
The trouble with the "confessions" is that they were usually obtained while the accused witch was being tortured. Torture was routinely applied until the witch confessed to having made a pact with the Devil and having flown to a sabbat [a witches' meeting]. It was continued until the witch named the other people who were present at the sabbat. If a witch attempted to retract a confession, torture was applied even more intensely until the original confession was reconfirmed. This left a person accused of witchcraft with the choice of dying once and for all at the stake or being returned repeatedly to the torture chambers. Most people opted for the stake. As a reward for their cooperative attitude, penitent witches could look forward to being strangled before the fire was lit.

d. *Source:* Jessica Mitford. She was a well-known muckraker, an investigative journalist who specialized in exposing scandals and abuses.

Quotation:
True, a small minority of undertakers are beginning to face the facts and to exhibit more flexibility in their approach to customers, even to develop some understanding and respect for people who as a matter of principle do not want the full funerary treatment ordinarily prescribed by the industry. But the industry as a whole, and particularly the association leaders, are unable to come to grips with the situation that confronts them today because their whole operation rests on a myth: the assumption that they have the full and unqualified backing of the vast majority of the American people, that the costly and lavish funeral of today, with all its fabulous trimmings, is but a reflection of American insistence on "the best" in all things. It is particularly hard for them to grasp the idea that a person who has lived well or even luxuriously might *prefer* the plainest disposition after death.

QUOTING SOURCES

In research writing, sources are quoted less often than they are paraphrased, but quotation is more complicated and requires more explanation.

Punctuating Quotations

The conventions of punctuation have driven many a student nearly to distraction. They seem arbitrary and often illogical. If you were to set about tinkering with the rules of punctuating, you could very likely make some worthwhile improvements in the current system. Nonetheless, the system as it stands is well established and unlikely to change. Your consolation is that, even if it is complicated, it can be mastered, and it does serve its purpose of giving readers helpful signals that make reading easier. In the case of quotations, punctuation makes it clear just which passages are your own and which belong to your sources.

The following are the most important punctuation conventions for presenting sources. You should learn these guidelines and follow them carefully.

1. *Use double quotation marks (" ") before and after a source's words when you copy them directly.*

    At the Battle of Trafalgar, Admiral Nelson exhorted his

    fleet: "England expects every man to do his duty."

Double
quotation marks

    The phrase "bats in the belfry" was coined by the writer

    Eden Phillpotts.

2. *Use single quotation marks (' ') before and after quoted material when it occurs within other quoted material—that is, when it occurs inside double quotation marks.*

    Charles and Mary Beard contend that the American

    government was not established as a <u>democracy</u>: "The

Constitution did not contain the word or any word lending countenance to it, except possibly the mention of 'We, the people,' in the preamble."

We used this example earlier in the chapter: "According to Ashley Montagu, 'To be human is to weep.'"

Single quotation marks

3. ***Indent a quotation that takes up more than four lines in your paper.*** In typing, indent one inch (ten spaces) from the left margin. Do not indent any additional spaces from the right margin. If you are quoting a single paragraph or less, do not indent the first line of the quotation any additional spaces:

The millionaire Andrew Carnegie believed that free enterprise and private charity, not government social programs, offered the best solution to the problem of poverty:

> Thus is the problem of Rich and Poor to be solved. The law of accumulation will be left free; the laws of distribution free. Individualism will continue, but the millionaire will be but a trustee of the poor; entrusted for a season with a great part of the increased wealth of the community, but administering it for the community far better than it could or would have done for itself.

Indent the left margin one inch (10 spaces). Do not indent the right margin.

However, if the indented quotation consists of two or more paragraphs, indent the first line of each paragraph an additional quarter inch or three spaces:

Florence Nightingale questioned the unequal treatment of men and women in Victorian England:

> Now, why is it more ridiculous for a man than for a woman to do worsted work and drive out every day in the carriage? Why should we laugh if we see a parcel of men sitting around a drawing room table in the morning, and think it all right if they were women?
>
> Is man's time more valuable than woman's? or is the difference between man and woman this, that women have confessedly nothing to do?

Indent paragraphs an additional quarter inch (three spaces)

These passages demonstrate other guidelines as well:

- **An indented quotation is never placed within quotation marks.** Quotation marks are unnecessary since the indenting already makes it clear that the passage is a quotation.

- **When typing, do not skip extra lines before or after an indented quotation.** The entire paper, including such quotations, is double-spaced.

4. *Accuracy is essential in quoting a source.*

- **Copy a quoted passage exactly as it is printed.** The only exception is for obvious typographical errors, which you should correct. Otherwise, make no changes in a quoted passage, even if you disagree with its wording or punctuation. For example, if you, rather than Andrew Carnegie, had been the author of the quotation on page 329, you might have used a colon or dash after the word *poor* instead of a semicolon. But since Carnegie used a semicolon, that is the way it must appear when you copy it.

- **Insert *[sic],* the Latin word meaning "thus," in brackets, immediately after an apparent error.** Do so only if you feel it necessary to identify it as your source's error, not your error in copying the passage.

  The régime posted a proclamation on every streetcorner: "Amnesty will be granted all mutineers who lay down their arms. Die-heart [sic] traitors who persist in rebellion will be shot."

  This device should be used only rarely. Avoid using *sic* to belittle a source with whom you disagree.

5. *Use punctuation to separate a quotation from an acknowledgment phrase or sentence.*

- **Use a comma (,) or colon (:) when the phrase comes before the quotation.** A comma is preferred when the introduction is not a complete sentence:

The introduction is not a complete sentence

  Jacques Delille wrote, "Fate chooses our relatives, we choose our friends."

  As Al Jolson remarked, "You ain't heard nothin' yet, folks."

- **A colon is preferred when the introduction is a complete sentence:**

  Edmund Burke believed that sadism is a component of human nature: "I am convinced that we have a degree of delight

and that no small one, in the real misfortunes pains
of others."

The last words in Act II are spoken by Hamlet: "The
play's the thing / Wherein I'll catch the conscience of
the King."

The introduction
is a complete
sentence

- **Use a colon to introduce an indented quotation:**

From his jail cell Martin Luther King wrote about the law:

> An unjust law is a code that a numerical or power
> majority group compels a minority group to obey
> but does not make binding on itself. This is
> <u>difference</u> made legal. By the same token, a just
> law is a code that a majority compels a minority
> to follow and that it is willing to follow itself.
> This is <u>sameness</u> made legal.

Colon

- **However, no punctuation is needed when a quotation is a continuation of the introductory sentence:**

According to the Library Bill of Rights, libraries are
forums for information and ideas, and they have

> . . . the responsibility to provide . . . all
> points of view on all questions and issues of
> our times, and to make these ideas and opinions
> available to anyone who needs or wants them,
> regardless of age, race, religion, national
> origin, or social and political views.

No colon

- **Use a comma when the acknowledgment phrase comes after the quotation, unless the quotation ends in a question mark or exclamation point:**

"When you have nothing to say, say nothing," wrote
Charles Caleb Colton.

Comma

But:

"Who can refute a sneer?" asked William Paley.

No comma

- **When the acknowledgment phrase is inserted within a quoted sentence, begin and end it with commas:**

"Politics," said Bismarck, "is not an exact science."

Commas

- Use no punctuation at all (other than quotation marks) when you make quoted words part of your own sentence:

No comma

Robert E. Rogers's advice to the Class of 1929 at MIT was to "marry the boss's daughter."

The word *that* incorporates a quotation that follows it into your sentence. Note carefully the difference in punctuation among the following three sentences:

–Quotation treated as an independent sentence:

Comma

Henry Ford said, "History is more or less bunk."

–Quotation incorporated into the sentence:

No comma

Henry Ford said that "history is more or less bunk."

–Quotation paraphrased:

No comma

Henry Ford said that history is nonsense.

6. *Capitalize the first word of a quotation when it is treated as an independent sentence. Do not capitalize it when it is incorporated into your own sentence.*

Uppercase letter

Margaret Hungerford gave us the famous saying, "Beauty is in the eye of the beholder."

Lowercase letter

Like Margaret Hungerford, many psychologists believe that "beauty is in the eye of the beholder."

7. *The trickiest rules apply to punctuation at the close of a quotation. Refer to the following examples whenever necessary.*

- **Commas and periods are always placed inside a closing quotation mark:**

Comma inside the quotation mark

"From the sublime to the ridiculous is but a step," wrote Napoleon.

Period inside the quotation mark

Martin Joseph Routh offered timeless advice over a century ago: "You will find it a very good practice always to verify your references, sir."

Period inside single and double quotation marks

Judge Learned Hand wrote, "I should like to have every court begin, 'I beseech ye in the bowels of Christ, think that we may be mistaken.'"

- **Colons (:), semicolons (;), and dashes (—) are placed outside closing quotation mark:**

Colon outside the quotation mark

"Blood, toil, tears and sweat": these were the sacrifices Churchill promised to his country.

On his deathbed, O. Henry said, "Turn up the lights--I
don't want to go home in the dark"; then he expired.

Semicolon
outside the
quotation mark

- Questions marks (?) and exclamation points (!) go inside the closing quotation mark when they belong to the quotation, but outside when they do not:

Macbeth asked, "What is the night?"

Question mark belongs to quotation

Who said, "Cowards die many times before their deaths"?

Question mark does not belong to quotation

Colonel Sidney Sherman first shouted, "Remember the Alamo!"

Exclamation point belongs to quotation

How dare you respond, "No comment"!

Exclamation point does not belong to quotation

- For punctuation following a parenthetical note, see pages 459–60 or the quick reference guide on the inside back cover.

8. *Follow these conventions for quoting poetry:*

- Use a slash (/) with a space before and after it to divide quoted lines of poetry:

Ogden Nash wrote, "Candy / Is dandy / But liquor / Is
quicker."

Space, slash, space

- Longer passages of poetry are indented:

Emily Dickinson wrote:

> "Faith" is a fine invention
>
> When Gentlemen can see--
>
> But Microscopes are prudent
>
> In an Emergency.

Indent the left margin 10 spaces

Like other indented passages, poetry is not placed within quotation marks. The word *"Faith"* is in quotation marks because Dickinson punctuated it that way in her poem.

Punctuating Quotations

EXERCISES

1. The following passages that appear in brackets are quotations, printed with their original capitalization and punctuation. Remove the brackets and add whatever punctuation is necessary. Make whatever additions and changes are necessary to put each sentence into proper form.

   a. Anne Morrow Lindbergh wrote [The wave of the future is coming and there is no fighting it.].

b. Rachel Carson was among the first to warn against the pollution of the environment [As crude a weapon as the cave man's club, the chemist's barrage has been hurled against the fabric of life.].

c. [Gentlemen of the old régime in the South would say, "A woman's name should appear in print but twice—when she marries and when she dies."] wrote Arthur Wallace Calhoun in 1918.

d. [Gentlemen] wrote Anita Loos [always seem to remember blondes.].

e. How many students today believe with James B. Conant that [He who enters a university walks on hallowed ground.]?

f. William Morris called this a [golden rule] [Have nothing in your houses that you do not know to be useful, or believe to be beautiful.]; a rather different conception of what a house should be is presented by a statement of architect Le Corbusier [A house is a machine for living in.].

g. Freud never underestimated the role of religion in human culture [If one wishes to form a true estimate of the full grandeur of religion, one must keep in mind what it undertakes to do for men. It gives them information about the source and origin of the universe, it assures them of protection and final happiness amid the changing vicissitudes of life, and it guides their thoughts and motions by means of precepts which are backed by the whole force of its authority.].

h. Poverty is not portrayed as romantic in Keats's poem "Larmia"
[Love in a hut, with water and a crust,
Is—Love, forgive us!—cinders, ashes, dust.]

i. Gloating on his pact with the devil, Doctor Faustus asked [Have not I made blind Homer sing to me?].

j. [We was robbed!] shouted manager Joe Jacobs into the microphone in 1932, when the decision went against his fighter, Max Schmeling.

2. Create sentences that incorporate quotations according to the following guidelines.

a. Use this quotation by Mark Twain in a sentence that begins with an acknowledgment phrase:

Man is the only animal that blushes. Or needs to.

b. Use the following quotation by Havelock Ellis in a sentence that ends with an acknowledgment phrase:

The place where optimism most flourishes is the lunatic asylum.

c. Use the following quotation by George Santayana in a sentence with an acknowledgment phrase inserted within it:

Fanaticism consists in redoubling your efforts when you have forgotten your aim.

d. Incorporate a paraphrase of this quotation into a sentence that acknowledges its author, Congressman Grimsley Buttersloop:

My opponents have accused me of embezzlement, drinking, fooling around, and falling asleep during committee meetings. The only thing they haven't accused me of is not loving my country, and that they can never do.

e. When you quote the following, let the reader know that its author, Frank Winslow, deliberately misspelled the word *souperior* in a letter to his aunt, Martha Fleming:

All I can say of your clam chowder is that it was positively souperior.

Altering Quotations

Sometimes when you write about your research you will want to use a quotation that does not precisely fit. Either it lacks a word or a phrase that would make its meaning clear to your readers, or else it contains too much material—unnecessary words that are not relevant to your point. For example, imagine that you found this quotation from a person named Vanessa O'Keefe:

> I absolutely long to prove to the world, as I said in an interview yesterday, that a perpetual motion machine is not an impossibility.

Assume you wanted to introduce it with the phrase *Vanessa O'Keefe announced that she. . . .* Fortunately, there are methods that allow you to alter such a quotation to fit your needs. By using them, you can write:

```
Vanessa O'Keefe announced that she "absolutely long[ed] to
prove to the world . . . that a perpetual motion machine
is not an impossibility."
```

As you can see, you can make certain alterations in quotations to suit your needs. When you do so, however, you must obey these two guidelines:

1. You must make it completely clear to your readers precisely what changes you have made.
2. Your alterations must not distort the meaning or essential phrasing of a quotation or make it appear to say something other than what the author intended.

The following methods may be followed to alter quotations:

Adding to Quotations: Brackets [ ]

Whenever a word, phrase, or suffix needs to be added to a quotation to make its meaning clear, you may insert it within **brackets.** Brackets are most commonly used to explain a reference. For example, it would not be evident to a reader of this quotation that it was the United States that José Martí was referring to as "the monster":

```
I have lived in the monster and I know its insides; and
my sling is the sling of David.
```

By using brackets when you quote this sentence, you can make the reference clear:

```
In a letter to Manuel Mercado, Martí wrote, "I have lived
in the monster [the United States] and I know its
insides; and my sling is the sling of David."
```

Insertion in
brackets

Similarly, you can insert modifiers in brackets. The following insertion makes it clear which frontier is being referred to:

> Churchill said, "That long [Canadian-American] frontier
> from the Atlantic to the Pacific Oceans, guarded only by
> neighborly respect and honorable obligations, is an
> example to every country and a pattern for the future of
> the world."

Another use for brackets is to provide brief translations of foreign or archaic words:

> Chaucer wrote, "A fol [fool] can not be stille."

Unusual terms may also require explanation. For example, if you used the following quotation in writing about doctors performing unnecessary operations, you might need to explain the term *arthroscopic surgery* to your readers.

> According to Dr. Robert Metcalf, who teaches orthopedic
> surgery at the University of Utah, the problem exists in
> his field as well: "There's considerable concern that
> arthroscopic surgery [a technique for repairing damaged
> knees] is being overutilized and is sometimes being done
> in a manner damaging to healthy cartilage."

When the unclear term is a simple pronoun, you can replace it altogether with the noun it refers to. For example, in the following quotation, instead of "They [the Americans] are the hope of the world," you can write:

> Baron de l'Aulne expressed a more favorable opinion in
> 1778: "[The Americans] are the hope of the world."

Instead of brackets, however, sometimes the simplest solution is to incorporate the unclear portion into your own sentence:

> Writing about Americans in 1778, Baron de l'Aulne
> expressed the more favorable opinion that "they are the
> hope of the world."

Or better still:

> In 1778, Baron de l'Aulne expressed the more favorable
> opinion that Americans are "the hope of the world."

The best rule is to use brackets when they provide the simplest way of making the source's meaning clear to your readers. As you can see, bracketing is a useful tool that can solve several writing problems. At the same time, it should not be overused. As with other devices, when brackets appear again and again in a paper, readers will find them distracting.

Subtracting from Quotations: Ellipsis Dots (. . .)

You can omit irrelevant parts of a quotation and replace them with ***ellipsis dots,*** three typed periods separated by spaces. The part you omit can be a word, a phrase, one or more sentences, or even a much longer passage. As with brackets, however, there is one important condition: You must not distort the author's meaning or intentions.

Good writers edit their writing, paring away what is unnecessary, off the point, or distracting. Quotations are used most effectively when you select them carefully and when you take only the pertinent parts and omit what is not needed. As an example, consider again the passage by Ashley Montagu quoted earlier:

> To be human is to weep. The human species is the only one in the whole of animated nature that sheds tears. The trained inability of any human being to weep is a lessening of his capacity to be human—a defect which usually goes deeper than the mere inability to cry. And this, among other things, is what American parents—with the best intentions in the world—have achieved for American males. It is very sad. If we feel like it, let us all have a good cry—and clear our minds of those cobwebs of confusion which have for so long prevented us from understanding the ineluctable necessity of crying.

As interesting as this passage is, you might be best able to make your point if you quote only parts of it. For example:

```
Anthropologist Ashley Montagu argues that it is both
unnatural and harmful for American males not to weep:
          To be human is to weep. . . .  The trained
          inability of any human being to weep is a
          lessening of his capacity to be human--a defect
          which usually goes deeper than the mere
          inability to cry. . . .  It is very sad.
```

Ellipsis dots
indicate a
deletion

Whole sentences have been removed from the passage and replaced with three dots (the fourth dot represents the period between sentences). Parts of a sentence can also be omitted and replaced with three dots, as follows:

```
Montagu feels that "the trained inability . . . to weep is
. . . a defect which usually goes deeper than the mere
inability to cry."
```

As with brackets, there is a danger in overusing ellipses. Not only can they become distracting to the reader, but they can also defeat your purpose in quoting, as with this monstrosity:

```
Montagu feels that "the . . . inability . . . to weep is
. . . a defect which . . . goes deeper than the . . .
inability to cry."
```

Bad

The preceding sentence makes so many changes in the original quotation that it can no longer be said to communicate Montagu's phrasing, and the point of using direct quotation is lost. Paraphrase would make much more sense; for example:

Better

```
Montagu feels that the inability to cry is a more
significant defect than might be realized.
```

Ellipsis dots are not needed when it is already obvious that the passage you have quoted is only a part of the original:

Ellipsis dots are not needed

```
A man's inability to cry, according to Montagu, is a
"lessening of his capacity to be human."
```

You should use ellipses, however, when it is not obvious that you are quoting only a portion of the source's complete sentence:

```
Montagu wrote, "The trained inability of any human being
to weep is a lessening of his capacity to be human . . . ."
```

When the omission comes at the front of a quoted sentence, you may capitalize the first word if you put the first letter in brackets:

```
Montagu offered this advice: ". . . [L]et us all have a
good cry. . . ."
```

EXERCISES   Using Brackets and Ellipsis Dots

1. The following is part of the transcript of a reporter's interview with a political candidate, Paul Shawn. Read it and comment on the quotations that follow.

    Q: Your opponent, Darla Stowe, says you hunger for money. Is that true?

    A: If you mean, do I want to earn enough for my family to live decently, then yes, I hunger for money. I think that's true of almost everyone. But I hunger for other things as well: peace, justice, brotherhood, and national prosperity.

    Q. Your opponent also says you are using this race as a stepping-stone to higher office. Is this true?

    A: Actually, I'm quite certain I have no more desire for higher office than she has.

    Which of the following quotations can be justified on the basis of this interview? Explain why each of them is fair or unfair, and discuss its use of brackets, ellipses, and paraphrase.

    a. Paul Shawn says he "hunger[s] for . . . peace, justice, brotherhood, and national prosperity."

    b. Shawn admitted, ". . . [Y]es, I hunger for money."

    c. Shawn's opponent accuses him of using this race to seek further political advancement, but he responds, "I have no more desire for higher office. . . . "

d. Shawn believes that a "hunger for money" is "true of almost everyone."

e. Quick in responding to an opponent's accusation, Shawn retorted that he has "no more desire for higher office than [Darla Stowe] has."

f. While admitting he has the same interest as most people in earning a comfortable living for his family, Shawn says he has other goals as well: "peace, justice, brotherhood, and national prosperity."

2. Use quotations from the following passages according to the instructions given for each. Introduce each quotation with an acknowledgment phrase.

a. *Quotation:*
I always dreamed of it as being a kind of earthly paradise where no troubles ever intruded.
Speaker: Linnea Aycock
Instructions: (1) Introduce the quotation with the acknowledgment phrase *Linnea Aycock said,* and use brackets to show that Aycock is talking about Tahiti. (2) Write another version, this time quoting only part of her sentence. Without using brackets, show that she is talking about Tahiti.

b. *Quotation:*
Our inspiration was a cartoon that appeared in a children's magazine.
Speaker: A NASA scientist
Instruction: Use brackets to indicate that the cartoon inspired the design of a new space helmet.

c. *Quotation:*
My generation never thought of college in terms of making ourselves employable. It was OK to be interested in Plato or T. S. Eliot or Freud, but never in IBM or General Mills. It was easy then to regard jobs with contempt since there were so many of them. It is very different with today's job-conscious generation. The response to Shakespeare now is likely to be, "How will he help me in my job?"
Writer: Ronni Jacobsen
Instruction: Quote two or three sentences that communicate the main idea of this passage. Use ellipsis dots to represent what you omit.

d. *Quotation:*
My message to all you students is that hard work and self-discipline are the keys— and you should never forget this—to success in your college and business careers.
Speaker: Cyrus T. Pierpont
Instruction: Begin with *Cyrus T. Pierpont told students that.* Omit unnecessary parts of the quotation, including the first eight words and the part that is surrounded by dashes. Although it is not necessary, you can change *your* to *their.*

e. *Quotation:*
If idiots drive motor vehicles when they are drunk, this should happen: they should lose their licenses and be sent to jail—for 90 days or longer.
Speaker: Sergeant Robert Symmes
Instruction: Introduce the quotation with the words *Sergeant Robert Symmes said that.* Alter the quotation by deleting the word *if,* inserting *who* after *idiots,* omitting *this should happen:,* and making whatever other changes are necessary.

WHEN TO QUOTE AND WHEN TO PARAPHRASE

One of the questions beginning research writers often ask their instructors is: "How many quotations should I put in my paper?" Their uncertainty is not usually allayed by the appropriate answer: "It depends." What it depends on are the circumstances of the individual case—and your own good judgment. While there is no easy answer to the question, some useful guidelines can help you decide how to use your sources.

1. ***Do not overquote.*** In fact, do not quote very much at all. Most beginning researchers quote far too much in their papers. Quotations should be saved for special occasions, and with good reason: Readers find papers that are filled with quotation after quotation unpleasant and hard to read. (By now you are probably tired of reading quotations in this chapter!) When they encounter a great many quotations, readers will often skim them or skip them entirely. No one likes to read a passage like this:

Bad (too many quotations)

> "Early [Roman] amphitheaters," according to Fredericks, "were temporary wooden structures that often collapsed under the weight of spectators, with the result of great loss of life" (40). Bennett reports:
>
> > The most famous of all buildings of this kind was the Flavian Amphitheater in Rome. Also called the Colosseum because of its size, it was begun by the emperor Vespasian and dedicated by his son Titus in A.D. 80. . . . After the 6th century it was used as a fortress and a quarry. (101)
>
> Fredericks says, "Although accounts of the time report it held more than 80,000 spectators, modern estimates place its capacity at 50,000" (42). The architectural historian Anne Ramsey wrote:
>
> > Structurally and functionally, the Roman Colosseum has been rivaled by no comparably sized arenas until the most recent age. Even today it remains a model of planning for rapid crowd access and exit and for unobstructed spectator sight lines. (17-18)

Of these four quotations, piled one upon the other, all but the last, which expresses the opinion of an authority, should be rephrased in the writer's own words. The passage then becomes much more readable:

The first Roman amphitheaters were temporary structures   Better
built of wood. Because they could not long support the
great crowds who attended the spectacles, they often collapsed
in terrible disasters (Fredericks 40). Later they were
replaced by permanent facilities, the most famous of which
was the Flavian Amphitheater, better known as the Colosseum.
Begun by the emperor Vespasian, it was dedicated in A.D. 80
by his son, Titus. It served as a sports and gladiatorial
arena with a capacity of 50,000 spectators until the sixth
century. It was then allowed to deteriorate, being used
occasionally as a fortress and frequently stripped of its
stone for use in other buildings (Bennett 101). Nevertheless,
it survived and remains today one of the most widely admired
Roman buildings. Architectural historian Anne Ramsey writes:

> Structurally and functionally, the Roman
> Colosseum has been rivaled by no comparably
> sized arenas until the most recent age. Even
> today it remains a model of planning for rapid
> crowd access and exit and for unobstructed
> spectator sight lines. (17-18)

The rule can be restated as follows: *If you have a choice between quoting and paraphrasing a source, paraphrase it.*

2. ***Always paraphrase a source, except when a direct quotation is needed.*** You should paraphrase most of your sources most of the time, especially under the following conditions.

- **Paraphrase if the source provides factual information.** Avoid quotations like the following:

The collapsing of bridges was a considerable problem in   Unnecessary
the past: "In the latter half of the 19th century,   quotation
American bridges were failing at the rate of 25 or more
per year!" (Worth 29).

Instead, state this factual information in your own words:

A century ago American bridges were far more dangerous than   Better
today, collapsing at an annual rate of 25 or more (Worth 29).

- **Paraphrase if you can say it more briefly or clearly in your own words.**

Wordy

Sun worshiper Andrea Bergeron claims that "Solists face grave and persistent discrimination, not the least of which is that which prohibits a fair hearing for our beliefs. Because our beliefs are not traditional we are dismissed as cultists" (202).

Very likely, you would need nothing more elaborate than this brief paraphrase to make your point:

Better

Andrea Bergeron feels that she and her fellow Solists (sun worshipers) are discriminated against and their religious views are not taken seriously (202).

3. *Quote a source directly when the source's words work better than your own.* If you use them sparingly, quotations can be effective in your research writing. Use them in the following cases:

- **Quote when the source's words are phrased in a particularly eloquent or memorable way.** Paraphrase could not do justice to the following quotations:

General Patton wrote, "A pint of sweat will save a gallon of blood" (987).

In 1947, physicist J. Robert Oppenheimer expressed the unease felt by many scientists about their role in developing the atom bomb: "In some sort of crude sense which no vulgarity, no humor, no overstatement can quite extinguish, the physicists have known sin; and this is a knowledge which they cannot lose" (1055).

You may not always find it easy to decide whether a statement from a source is so well phrased that it should be presented to readers directly. Use your best judgment. In cases where you are in doubt, the wisest course is to paraphrase.

- **Quote when you are writing about the source or the source's words:**

Ginter was never modest in his self-descriptions: "When I was born 42 years ago to a family of humble asparagus farmers, none suspected I would one day be the world's leading transcriber of baroque music for the banjo" (37).

The advertisement promised "luxury villas with a spectacular ocean view," but only by leaning far out the windows of our ancient bungalow could we gain even a distant glimpse of the sea.

Victor Hugo called Jean Henri Fabre "the Homer of the Insects" with good reason. Few naturalists wrote such vivid metaphors as Fabre does in this description of the praying mantis:

> To judge by the term Prègo-Diéu, we should look to see a placid insect, deep in pious contemplation; and we find ourselves in the presence of a cannibal, of a ferocious spectre munching the brain of a panic-stricken victim. (Qtd. in Lynch and Swanzey 51)

- **Quote when the source is an expert whose exact words will lend authority to a claim that you make:**

Paratrupus schusterensis, the common swamp frogwort, is a delicacy among scavenger gourmets. Florence Demingo, author of A Field Guide to Edible Weeds, exclaims: "Ah, the frogwort! No other plant offers such a thrill to the palate while fortifying the liver with such potent dosages of Vitamin B-8" (188).

The public is often outraged when technicalities decide the outcome of important court cases, but as Justice Felix Frankfurter observed in 1943, "The history of liberty has largely been the history of the observance of procedural safeguards" (37).

As anthropologist Ashley Montagu observed, "To be human is to weep" (248).

Usually, however, you can paraphrase an authority with the same good results:

Florence Demingo, author of A Field Guide to Edible Weeds, finds the frogwort both tasty and rich in Vitamin B-8 (188).

And one final consideration for quotation in research papers:

- **Do not restrict your quoting to already quoted material.** Many students only quote passages that appear within quotation marks in their sources; that is, they quote writers they have found quoted by other writers. It never occurs to them to quote their sources directly. Of course, you should not overquote, but on the other hand, do not be afraid to quote your sources themselves. If, for example, you were using this very paragraph as a research source, you could quote from it:

```
Veit, Gould, and Clifford advise, "Do not restrict your
quoting to already quoted material" (344).
```

EXERCISE   **Judging When to Paraphrase and Quote**

Decide if any of the quotations in the following passages should instead have been paraphrased by the writers. For those quotations, write a paraphrase that could be substituted for the inappropriate quotation. Omit any notes that you decide are unnecessary.

a. Pott's disease is "tuberculosis caries of the vertebrae, resulting in curvature of the spine. It was named after the physician who described it, Percival Pott (1714–88)" (Gleitman 110).

b. Geologists and seismologists are uncertain how to interpret the cryptic note found in McPhilibar's hand after the cave-in: "Major discover [sic]—8th strata, fault line demarcation—earthquake predictor. Eureka!" (Donnelly 192).

c. Harris argues that the animal-powered agriculture of India is not necessarily a problem to be corrected:

    To convert from animals and manure to tractors and petrochemicals would require the investment of incredible amounts of capital. Moreover, the inevitable effect of substituting costly machines for cheap animals is to reduce the number of people who can earn their living from agriculture. . . . Less than 5 percent of U.S. families now live on farms, as compared with 60 percent about a hundred years ago. If agribusiness were to develop along similar lines in India, jobs and housing would soon have to be found for a quarter of a billion displaced peasants. (12)

d. Humans are not entirely logical creatures. Often we take our guidance from emotional and spiritual voices within us. As the philosopher Pascal observed, "The heart has its reasons which reason knows nothing of" (40).

e. "The word *ain't*," says Phillips, "has generated its share of controversy" (64). Frelling writes, "*Ain't* is widely accepted in casual conversation. It is rarely used in formal discourse and in writing" (6). A controversy arises especially over its use as a contraction for *am not*. Dwight Macdonald speaks in its behalf, noting that "there is no other workable contraction, for *amn't* is unpronounceable and *aren't* is ungrammatical" (144). Theodore Bernstein, on the other hand, says, "There can be no doubt that *ain't I* is easier to say than *aren't I* and *amn't I*, and sounds less stilted than *am I not*. Nevertheless, what should be not always is" (13–14).

A FURTHER NOTE ON PLAGIARISM

Undoubtedly, the most often repeated exhortation in this book is your obligation as a scholar to acknowledge your sources. The message is so important that we don't want to risk its being missed. Feel free to make use of sources (after, all, that is what research is all about), but by all means give them full credit when you do so. Failure to acknowledge a source, thereby making someone else's work appear to be your own, is plagiarism.

The most glaring cases of plagiarism are deliberate acts of cheating: students handing in papers that they did not write or copying out articles from magazines and passing them off as their own work. These are dishonest acts that rank with library vandalism as among the most serious breaches of the code of scholarship. They are dangerous as well, since penalties for them are understandably severe, and instructors are much better than most plagiarists realize at spotting work that is not a student's own.

A less serious offense, but also one to be avoided, is an unintentional act of plagiarism. Most of the time when students plagiarize they do so innocently, unaware that they are violating the rules of scholarship. They copy a sentence or two from an article, not knowing that they should either quote or paraphrase it. They change a few words in copying a sentence, sincerely believing that they are paraphrasing it. They do not provide a parenthetical note because they do not know that one is needed. They are not trying to cheat; they are not even aware that they are cheating. It is just that no one ever told them to do otherwise. Perhaps when they were in the fifth grade, they wrote papers that consisted of copying out passages from encyclopedia articles. That may have gone unreprimanded in grade school. It is never tolerated in college.

There is certainly no need to plagiarize, because you are allowed to use sources provided that you acknowledge them. In fact, there is no advantage in it either: Papers based on expert sources, fairly acknowledged, are what is wanted of scholars. They are exactly what instructors are looking for.

 ## PRACTICE WITH USING SOURCES

The first part of this chapter—in which you learned to paraphrase and quote individual sources—can be compared to the on-the-ground instruction given to would-be parachutists. It is essential background, but the real learning doesn't take place until the first jump. In the rest of this chapter, we intend to push you out of the plane. Your jump will involve taking a selection of sources and using them to write a brief research-based essay.

Writing a Brief Objective Research Essay

When you do research, you have a purpose in mind: You are seeking to learn more about a certain topic and, often, to inform others about what you have discovered. As an example to illustrate the process involved in a brief research project, imagine that you have been assigned to report briefly to your political science class on a controversy surrounding the Constitution's Bill of Rights. Let's suppose that, having narrowed your topic, you decide to review the "Schillinger case." Here are excerpts from five (fictitious) sources that you have discovered in your research:

The following is a news article from the *Essex Herald-Journal,* 5 August 1996, on page 6:

State Seeks to Force Cancer Treatment

State authorities have asked the courts to grant them custody over the 13-year-old daughter of a clergyman so that she can receive the anti-cancer treatment doctors say she needs to stay alive.

The Rev. and Mrs. Paul Schillinger and their daughter, Cathy, are members of the Children of Prophecy church, which rejects all medical treatment and relies on faith to cure ailments. The Schillingers are contesting the state's attempt to force Cathy to undergo chemotherapy. Doctors say that she suffers from leukemia and will die within six months without treatment.

Claiming in his brief to the court that "the first duty of the state is to protect its citizens," State's Attorney J. Walker Dodson says he is "reluctantly" undertaking the action to save the girl's life.

At a press conference outside the courthouse, Cathy Schillinger affirmed her own opposition to the state's action. "I know there is a better place waiting for me in heaven. If God calls me, I am ready to die," she said.

If the court rules in favor of the state, the girl will be placed in Memorial Hospital until the course of treatments can be completed.

A ruling is expected later this month.

This excerpt is from an article by Cathy's father, the Rev. Paul Schillinger, "Leave Our Daughter Alone," printed on page 20 of the *Lexington Post,* 9 August 1996:

. . . I know in my heart I am doing God's will. He holds the power of life and death, and if in His infinite goodness and wisdom He wants us to live we will live, and if He wants us to die we will die. No state and no court can say otherwise. The judge and the doctors are trying to play God, and they are committing a damnable blasphemy. My daughter is willing to die if she must, because she knows there is a better place for her waiting in heaven.

The following is an excerpt from page 67 of the September/October 1996 issue of *American Religion.* It appeared in an article by Mark Signorelli, "A Church-State Battle over Child Custody," printed on pages 65–67:

Interviewed outside court, State's Attorney Dodson said, "Cathy Schillinger's life is in imminent danger, and only this action can save her. If it were her father or any other adult, we would not intervene. But Cathy is a minor, not yet able to make an informed decision about a complicated matter, nor is there evidence that she fully understands the issues involved. It is our policy not to interfere with the parents' raising of their children as they see fit unless the child is abused or in danger. Here the child's right to life takes priority."

This is a letter to the editor of *National News Weekly,* appearing in the 16 August 1996 edition, on page 17:

Dear Editor:

Once again our fundamental American rights and freedoms are being trampled by the very government that was established to protect them. Freedom of religion and the right of parents to raise their children in their own beliefs and values mean nothing to the prosecutors. As a neighbor, I have known the Schillingers for years. They are a loving family, and the parents want Cathy to live. But they and Cathy believe that medical treatment is sinful, and the government must respect that. People must respect the beliefs of others, even if they do not agree with them.

Helen Bridgeman

This is the first sentence from a front-page article in the 17 August 1996 *Essex Herald-Journal*. The headline is "Girl's Death Ends State Attempt at Custody":

The state's effort to gain custody over 13-year-old Cathy Schillinger was made moot this morning when the girl died of leukemia in her sleep.

No one can read about this case without having an opinion, very likely a strong emotional one. You probably also recognize with the rational part of your brain that the issues here are complicated ones with profound implications and that there is much to be considered on both sides before you can reach a wise decision about their merits.

You can use these sources to write either *subjectively* or *objectively* about the case; that is, you can express your opinion, or you can simply present information to the reader without offering views of your own. As an example of the difference between objective and subjective writing, note that the reporter who was author of the first source wrote objectively. By reading that article you cannot tell the reporter's personal feelings about the case. On the other hand, there is nothing objective about Helen Bridgeman's letter to the editor. You know exactly where she stands. She and the reporter were clearly writing for two different purposes.

Often it is wise to write objectively about a controversial matter before expressing an opinion. This ensures that you at least examine the merits of both sides before rushing in with a judgment.

In this imaginary paper, let's assume that you have decided first to present the facts from the case objectively and afterward to draw subjective conclusions from what you have found. For this earlier part of the paper, then, you will write a brief objective report on the Schillinger case, informing your readers of the nature of the case and the issues involved.

How do you begin writing an objective report from the five sources that you have discovered? They consist of two tersely written news stories, quotations from some of the principal participants on opposing sides, and an opinion from an outside reader. All of them might offer material you can use. But what do you do with them?

Unlike the summary reports you produced in Chapter 6, you cannot simply summarize each source individually and then present the summaries one after the other. Instead you must interweave your materials. Since you have important statements from participants, you will also want to quote some of their words. You will need, then, to select material from your sources and produce a synthesis. Here is how one student, Keith Pearsall, Jr., wrote a report from these five excerpts:

Keith's paraphrase of a source

The Schillinger case, another prominent instance of conflicting rights and freedoms, involved a 13-year-old girl with leukemia. On one side of the case stood the girl and her parents, who rejected all medical treatment on religious grounds. On the other stood the state, which sought to force the medical care doctors say she needed to remain alive ("State" 6).

Keith's thesis statement

Parental and religious rights were in conflict with the right to life itself and with the obligation to protect minors.

Quoting a source directly

One question that is raised by the case is the extent to which parents have the right to raise their children in their own religious beliefs and practices. The father of the girl, a minister in the Children of Prophecy church, believed that God alone "holds the power of life and death, . . . and if He wants us to die we will die." The minister also believed that in seeking to counteract the divine will, the state was committing a "damnable blasphemy" (Schillinger 20). The daughter, Cathy, subscribed to her parents' beliefs and expressed her willingness to die if necessary rather than undergo

A note for paraphrased material

treatment they believed to be sinful ("State" 6).

According to State's Attorney J. Walker Dodson, on the other hand, the issue was not one of religious freedom but of the state's "first duty . . . to protect its

A note for a quotation

citizens" (qtd. in "State" 6). Dodson argued that the girl was too young to make an informed decision about a matter of vital interest to her and that the state was obliged to protect her right to life (Signorelli 67).

No note for widely available information

Legal questions in this controversial case have still not been answered, since the girl died before the courts could reach a decision.

Keith has taken five sources and from them has written something that is new and his own. The report is objective, since nowhere are Keith's opinions evident, but he still remains in control throughout. He is aware of the point of the entire report, and he shapes it with several of his own sentences. For example, the last sentence of the first paragraph and the sentence following it are topic sentences, expressing his summary of the main ideas of the passage.

In his handling of sources, Keith avoids three mistakes often made by inexperienced research writers; that is, he observes three important rules:

1. *Don't just quote.*
2. *Don't just quote quotations.*
3. *Don't just note quotations.*

Examples from Keith's report can demonstrate what the rules mean:

Don't Just Quote

Many beginning researchers quote too much, tediously stringing together one quotation after another. Keith avoids that mistake. His three direct quotations all make perfect sense in his report. In addition, he selects only the words from his sources that are most relevant, and he introduces them so that the reader always knows who is being quoted and why. More often than quoting, however, Keith paraphrases his sources. For example, in the first three sentences of his report and the last sentence of his second paragraph, he has rephrased material from his sources into his own words. The result is a clear, readable, effective report.

Don't Just Quote Quotations

Some students quote only material that appeared within quotation marks in their sources. It never occurs to them to quote the sources themselves. Note that Keith does both: The first source contains quotations, and Keith uses them in his report. Although the second source has no quotation within it, Keith quotes from it as well. This may seem obvious, but many students are unaware of this valuable way researchers can use their sources.

Don't Just Note Quotations

Another mistake made by inexperienced research writers is to give parenthetical notes only for direct quotations. Notice that Keith provides notes not only for sources he has quoted, but also for sources he has paraphrased, such as his citation of the first source in his opening paragraph.

Not every source you use will receive mention in notes. Each of the sources played a role in Keith's writing of the report, but only three of them are noted in parentheses. The fourth source, the neighbor's letter, gave Keith some general ideas, but since it did not provide him with any specific information, he decided not to paraphrase it or quote from it. Therefore, it did not receive a note. Although the fifth source, the mention of Cathy's death in a news story, did contain the information used in Keith's last paragraph, that information is so readily available (found in news accounts throughout the country) that acknowledgment is not necessary.

Because Keith quoted or paraphrased only three of his five sources (and cited them in parenthetical notes), he omitted the two other sources from his list of works cited, which follows:

```
                    Works Cited
Schillinger, Paul.  "Leave Our Daughter Alone."
    Lexington Post 9 Aug. 1996: 20.
```

Signorelli, Mark.   "A Church-State Battle over Child
        Custody."   American Religion Sept./Oct. 1996: 65-67.
"State Seeks to Force Cancer Treatment."   Essex Herald-
        Journal 5 Aug. 1996: 6.

EXERCISE | **Writing an Objective Research Essay**

Imagine that in writing a paper about how Americans have kept track of time through the years, you discovered the following (purely fictitious) sources. Part of your paper will concern a recent proposal to change our current time zones. Use these sources to write a brief objective report on what you have learned. Acknowledge your sources with parenthetical notes and provide the list of works cited that you would include in your final paper.

1. This news story appeared last year in the May 22 issue of *Birmingham Star-News* in section B, page 4. Dina Waxman wrote the article under the headline, "Parent Tells Dangers of Time Zone Change."

   Congressional hearings on a proposal to have all the country's clocks tell the same time continued today with testimony from a parents' group opposed to the plan.
   The proposal, put forth by Edna Odom of Muscatine, Iowa, would eliminate the four time zones that now divide the country. She would replace them with a single nationwide zone.
   Testifying against Odom's plan was Floyd Rugoff, president of the Eureka, California, PTA. He argued that it would endanger school children, who would travel to or from school in darkness.
   Under the proposal, clocks in the Eastern zone would be set back one and a half hours, while Pacific zone clocks would be set ahead by the same period. Central and Mountain zone clocks would receive half-hour adjustments. Alaska and Hawaii would be exempt from the proposal.
   In his testimony Rugoff said, "In December it's already dark in the morning when children leave for school. If we change, California children won't see the sunrise until 8:30, and in New England it will have set by the time children come home from school. We're going to see a big increase in accidents involving children."

2. These excerpts are from Edna Odom's article, "It's About Time," in *Future and Change* magazine. It appeared in last year's January issue on pages 76 to 78.

   If all of the country operated by the same clock, businesses would reap an enormous advantage. Communication from coast to coast would be simplified. Now, with four time zones, companies operating from nine to five on the two coasts have only five working hours in common, and only three if you remove the two lunch hours. Under my proposal, if an executive in Tucson needs to reach her main office in New York at 4 P.M., she can call and get through. The way it is now, the time in the East would be 7 P.M., and she'd have to wait until Monday morning for the New York office to reopen. Television networks, airlines, and neighboring communities that now straddle time zones would all reap enormous benefits. [page 77]
   . . . It isn't as if we were being asked to switch day with night. An hour and a half change isn't that big. The claims of opponents are vastly exaggerated. We already move the clocks an hour twice each year, and everyone adjusts easily. There is nothing that says that the sun has to be overhead at noon. If it's dark at 6 A.M., why can't a

farmer milk the cows at 8 instead? Schools could open later or earlier to accord with the sunlight. Why are people so hidebound? If the human race isn't flexible enough to make small adjustments, heaven help us when a major catastrophe strikes. [page 78]

3. "Farmer Ticked by Time Scheme" is the headline for an article that appeared without byline last May 23 on page 24 of the *Riverside Ledger:*

> In his testimony against the OUT (Odom Unified Time) proposal, farmer Duane Wentworth of Millinocket, Maine, argued that the proposal would wreak havoc with livestock producers.
>
> "Animals operate by the sun, not the clock," he said, "and we can't convince them otherwise. If we have to get up at 4 in the morning to tend them, we'll be eating lunch at 9 and going to bed by 8. We'll be out of sync with the rest of the country."

Writing a Brief Subjective Research Essay

Not all writing is objective writing; sometimes your purpose is to express your own opinion in order to convince others. Chapter 14 considers argumentative writing in detail, but here we will take a brief look at how writers can use research sources to support and strengthen an argument. Of course, you are always free to offer an opinion without any outside support at all, but the support of experts can greatly help your case. By taking your facts from sources, you also show your readers that you have gone to the trouble of researching the issue, and you make yourself seem more worthy of their trust. When you quote or paraphrase authorities in support of your opinions, those opinions seem much more impressive than they otherwise would.

For a brief example of how subjective writing can be supported by sources, imagine that you are arguing your own views on the unified time zone plan that was introduced in the exercise above. You can use those sources effectively to support your argument:

> Edna Odom's proposal to synchronize all the nation's clocks within a single time zone may seem attractive at first glance, but closer inspection of the scheme reveals serious flaws. Although Odom rightly points out the benefits to TV networks and airlines of eliminating time zone differences, she is too quick to dismiss her plan's opponents as "hidebound" and its problems as "exaggerated" (77–78).
>
> The proposed change would have the most impact on the two coasts, where clocks would be altered by an hour and a half from current settings. While Odom sees this as small, the effects would be considerable for farmers and school children, to take only two examples. Since livestock regulate their lives by the sun, farmers on the east coast would need to rise as early as 4 A.M. to tend animals at sunrise ("Farmer" 24). And as the president of a California PTA chapter observed in testifying before Congress, it would be dark in winter as western children traveled to school and as eastern children returned home from school. He predicted that the number of auto accidents involving children pedestrians would increase sharply (Waxman 4).
>
> A principal advantage that Odom claims for her scheme is that it would aid communication by standardizing business schedules. But she also recommends that schools and other institutions adjust their opening and closing times to conform with the sun (77–78). She can't have it both ways. If California schools open

according to the sun, three hours after New York schools, parents will demand that businesses where they work do likewise, and the uniformity that Odom promises will be lost.

While it would be wonderful if time were the same in all parts of the country—and of the world, for that matter—the fact is that the sun refuses to cooperate. Any proposal that is based on human wishes, without regard for the realities of nature, is doomed to certain failure. Imperfect as our current time system is, it is at least preferable to the alternative.

The list of works cited for this essay would be the same one that you listed for the objective essay in the exercise.

The writer of this essay argues the case against the plan. The sources he uses buttress his arguments and lend it authority. For example, because he has supported it with sources, readers are more likely to accept his claim that the plan would hurt farmers and school children; the reader can see that this is not just the writer's unfounded speculation.

Notice that the writer has used sources to help make his point. At the same time, he has not been a slave to the sources. While he takes several arguments from sources, much of the language and thought behind the paper is entirely his own. His introduction and conclusion are original, and in the third paragraph he has applied his own logical twist to turn Edna Odom's argument against her.

Sources, in other words, are tools that require the ingenuity of writers to make use of them. There is nothing in the three sources that led inevitably to this paper. In fact, another writer with different views about time zones could use them to write an equally effective paper supporting Edna Odom's proposal.

EXERCISE | **Writing Subjective Research Essays**

1. Write a subjective essay arguing your views on the Schillinger case. Use the five sources found on pages 346–47 to support your essay. Acknowledge your sources in notes and include a list of works cited.

2. Write a subjective essay that argues in favor of Edna Odom's time zone proposal. Support your position, using the sources in the exercise on pages 350–51.

13 Writing and Revising the Research Paper

 GETTING ORGANIZED

Once Helen Veit and Molly MacLaren had gathered material from their sources and taken notes on index cards, they were ready for the next step: the actual writing of their papers. While writing proved less time-consuming than source-gathering, it was no less important, and, like earlier stages of the research process, it consisted of several substeps. Helen and Molly each received an assignment similar to the following for the first of these substeps:

Do the following before our next class meeting in preparation for writing your first draft:

- Complete your note-taking on index cards.

- Formulate a thesis statement; that is, state in a sentence or two your concept of the main idea of your paper.

- Sort your note cards by topic.

- Prepare an updated informal working outline for your first draft.

- Put new topic titles on your note cards as necessary, arrange them in the order suggested by your outline, and put aside (but do not discard) the ones you do not expect to use.

Formulating a Thesis Statement

When Helen began her project, she was afraid she would not have enough to say about her topic. However, halfway through her first source, she had fifteen cards' worth of notes. Aware that she was taking too many notes, Helen concluded that she would need to be more selective. Like almost every other student researcher, she found that a shortage of material would not be a problem for her after all. She sharpened her focus and began to take fewer but more carefully chosen notes. Even so, she ended up taking notes on over a hundred cards, several dozen more than she would end up using.

After discovering that her original topic, the Cinderella story, was too broad, Helen narrowed it to a comparison of the many versions of that story that have appeared around the world. Still, she was not entirely satisfied with her topic, and, in the course of her research, she stumbled on a related topic that she liked much better. Her Cinderella research introduced her to a controversy over whether fairy tales are harmful to children. After examining several articles relating to this controversy, she decided to change her focus, even though she had already taken a few dozen notes on the Cinderella topic.

As she continued her research, Helen encountered criticism of the violence and gender stereotypes found in many fairy tales, though most experts seemed to defend the violence. Although fewer defended the stereotypes, the preponderance of informed opinion supported the tales as more beneficial than harmful to children. As is usually the case in research, Helen found contradictory evidence and an absence of black-and-white, clear-cut patterns. Because of these mixed opinions, Helen did not become entirely sure of her paper's thesis until she was well into an early draft of the paper itself. She was then able to formulate a *thesis statement*, a brief summary of what she expected to be her main focus:

Thesis: Some parents, educators, and psychologists fear that fairy tales are harmful to children, but many experts claim that such stories are vital to the healthy development of children.

Helen's thesis statement might be criticized for failing to take a definitive stand, but her purpose in the paper was not to argue for one side or the other but to present a balanced view of her research findings. Being balanced and fair, however, does not mean being unable to analyze or draw conclusions, and the final draft of Helen's paper made it clear that most of her sources (and, apparently, Helen herself) were in the pro-fairy-tale camp.

Student writers are sometimes misled by the advice to *start* a research project with a thesis that is clear, unified, and restricted. Like an outline, a thesis ought to assist the processes of searching, thinking, and composing; it should never become a straitjacket. As we have seen, Helen's preliminary research caused her to narrow and then even shift her focus. Molly faced less difficulty in formulating a thesis statement. She simply expressed in plain language the goals of her project:

Thesis: I have always wanted to be a fiction writer, but I want to find out if my image of the profession is accurate and whether I can make a living with my pen.

As we have seen, premature commitment to a thesis can become a hindrance to thorough, objective inquiry. Nevertheless, many writers prefer to locate a cohesive theme during the early stages of research. They have found that keeping such a theme in view—often in the form of a preliminary thesis statement—can help focus their work. If you have difficulty finding such a focus, try the following procedure:

Tips for Formulating a Thesis Statement

1. *Think about your project in general terms.* In your notebook, write a quick informal paragraph describing what you expect your paper to say and do. It may help to respond to these questions: What main topic have your efforts become focused on? What question(s) have you been trying to answer? What have you learned from your research? Do you now have a point of view about your topic—a conclusion or insight that you want to express in your paper?

2. *Make your general idea specific.* Review the paragraph you have written, and see if you can summarize its main idea in a single sentence.

As you continue your work, you should think often about how each part of your paper supports your focus. Be prepared to eliminate any sections that stray from the main topic. You may, of course, adjust your focus as you proceed with your project. In the final draft of her paper, Helen introduced her readers to her subject in a three-paragraph introduction which concluded with this summary of her thesis:

```
Surely, think some, hearing such tales can only
brainwash and brutalize children.  But against all
expectations, many other experts deny that fairy tales
will leave children emotionally handicapped; on the
contrary, they assert that these stories are actually
vital to the healthy development of children.
```

Sorting Your Note Cards

With an evolving conception of her topic, Helen recorded in her notes material that she thought was usable. While her note cards were a distillation of all she had learned from her reading, they still represented a formidable mass of data. She now had to select and arrange her cards into an order she could use. She read through them and sorted them by topic.

Since Helen had written a topic label at the top of each note card, she was able to group many of her cards together by subject. She found that most of her cards fell into a half dozen general categories: "defense of violence," "violence case studies," "gender stereotypes," "adult therapy," and so on. As she sorted she also set aside many discards—notes it was now clear she could not use. There were also many strays—single cards that did not fit conveniently into categories with any others. Helen had to decide if these belonged in her paper and, if so, how she might use them. In some cases, she would not know for sure until the actual writing.

Even with a good plan and a working outline, the final form of a paper can rarely be predicted in advance. Like Helen, you might follow this procedure:

1. ***Read through and sort your note cards.*** Sorting your cards into piles on a large table or on the floor can be helpful. Be sure you sort the cards by *topic* (not by any other principle, such as by source). Some piles will contain note cards from several different sources.

2. ***When your cards are sorted, think about how they can be used and arranged.*** Write about your ideas in your research notebook; think as you write, using the opportunity to work out ideas for organizing your paper. But do not be dismayed if you encounter loose ends at this stage. You will make many further decisions about your paper's organization as you write it.

3. ***Put aside any cards you do not expect to use.***

The best way to create an organizational plan for a paper is to think first in terms of the most general categories. Helen wrote this about her project in her research notebook:

> I expected writers to say the violence wasn't all that bad and that positive messages made up for it, but they actually say that the violence is <u>good</u> for children. Who would expect that? People don't say the same about the stereotypes about roles. There is criticism, but some, like Ella Westland, say that girls are able to handle it. . . . Possibilities are to do all the criticism first, then all the support—or I can do first violence pro and con, then stereotypes pro and con. . . . Using fairy tales for adult therapy ~~relates~~ for battered wives relates to the gender issue—or maybe a separate section.

Helen wasn't sure of the best organization for her paper, but we can see her mind working here—even making decisions as she wrote. She was confident that she had good materials to work with, and she had enough ideas for at least a tentative organization that she could try out.

Updating Your Outline

Having thought about the parts of her paper and how she might put those parts together, Helen needed a clearer idea—a diagram of what her paper might look like. That is, she needed an ***informal working outline,*** an updated plan for organizing her paper.

When you create an outline, the headings you use will correspond, in theory, to the topic labels on your note cards. In reality, though, you will need to make adjustments to both the cards and the outline as a clear conception of the shape of your paper gradually forms in your mind. Try to put your ideas on paper in a handy visual form: A working outline is nothing more than a way of making these ideas visible and concrete.

Checking and rechecking her note cards, Helen developed the parts of an outline and, after several revisions, created an informal scheme, shown in Figure 13.1, to use in writing her first draft. Although some of the details would change in the final version of her paper, Helen found this outline helpful as she wrote, especially in getting started.

During her next class, Helen showed her outline and note cards to the other students in her editing group. She discussed her plans, received suggestions, and—even

Helen Veit

Thesis and Working Outline

Fairy Tales: Do They Harm or Help Children?

<u>Thesis</u>: Some parents, educators, and psychologists fear that fairy tales are harmful to children, but many experts claim that such stories are vital to the healthy development of children.

Introduction

　　　Explanation of objections

　　　Statement of thesis: others find stories helpful

Violence in fairy tales

　　　Against: harmful to children

　　　For: Helpful

　　　　　Dealing with adversity

　　　　　Problem-solving

　　　Case studies

Stereotypes

　　　Against: males dominant, females subordinate

　　　For: less harmful than expected

Other uses: therapy for battered wives and eating disorders

Conclusion: on balance, more good than bad

Figure 13.1 Helen's thesis and working outline.

more valuable—answered questions. Explaining and defending her outline helped Helen notice strengths and weaknesses in her plan. An added benefit of the session was that it familiarized everyone in each editing group with classmates' projects.

 # WRITING THE FIRST GOOD DRAFT

Having a tentative plan for organizing their papers, Helen and Molly received an assignment like the following from their instructors:

ASSIGNMENT   **Writing the Paper**

You are now ready to write a careful draft of your paper. Do so, and revise it until you are satisfied that it is as clearly written, well organized, interesting, and informative as you can make it. Be sure to document your sources carefully with parenthetical notes and include an updated list of works cited. You should also consult the guidelines for editing and revising on pages 366–69.

Research Writing: General Guidelines

Helen soon discovered that her outline was only a starting point. In fact, she made changes in her organization from almost the moment she began her actual writing. She encountered difficulties with her opening, and, as her rough drafts would show, she went through at least six versions of the introductory section before she felt ready to move on. Her preliminary outline rapidly became obsolete, but it had served its purpose. It had forced Helen to think about her paper as a whole—about how the individual parts might work together. Once she had made the outline, her concept of what she would accomplish in her writing became considerably less vague.

Although later parts of her draft went more smoothly, Helen discovered there is more to writing a paper than following a plan. Certainly, it is not just a matter of first writing about note 1, then about note 2, and so on throughout the paper. It will help to consider the following guidelines in writing your paper:

1. *Keep your goals in mind.* Novices can easily be overwhelmed by the procedures and details of research writing. Because of the many steps—all the procedures for assembling a list of sources and making note cards, outlines, and parenthetical notes—it is easy to lose sight of what a research paper is really about. The goal of your research is to learn something, to discover truth. In writing your paper, your goal is to present what you have learned so that your readers can also become informed. It follows that your writing should be readable and honest, informative and interesting. Never lose sight of these important goals as you write. Do not be blinded by procedures for their own sake.

2. *Remember that principles of good writing apply to research writing, too.* Like any other type of paper, a research paper should be clear and lively, not stodgy and pompous. It should be written so it can be read with enjoyment and without difficulty. Quotations and other source material should be neatly integrated into your writing so they are not obtrusive or awkward.

Like any other author, you have a responsibility to make the reader's job easier. Use topic sentences to help the reader know what to expect. Provide paragraph breaks to signal changes in topic or emphasis. Where appropriate, use transitional words and phrases (such as *on the other hand, also, for example,* and *consequently)* to make clear the relationship between successive sentences and paragraphs.

3. *Most of your paper should be you, not your sources.* While your sources may provide you with most of the information that you present in your paper, *you* are the one writing it. Write in your own voice. Your research paper should communicate what you have to say—just like any other paper you write. Remember, too, that your use of sources is simply a means to the goal of informing your readers; it is not an end in itself. Don't let your paper become simply a vehicle for presenting sources. Don't let your sources get in the way of clear writing.

4. *Don't be a slave to your note cards and outline.* Whenever you use a note from one of your cards, think about how it contributes to the point you are making. If a note isn't useful, don't include it. If it isn't clear, explain it. If you realize that your paper would be improved by adding new topics or rearranging your outline, by all means do so.

5. *Don't rely too heavily on one or two sources.* Inevitably, a few of your sources will have proved more helpful than the rest, and you will rely on these more than the others in writing your paper. Remember, however, that it is not your paper's purpose to restate what has already been said by another source or two. A research paper should present something new, a fresh synthesis of information and ideas from many sources. A paper that is largely a summary of only one or two sources fails to do this. A variety of sources should make substantial contributions to your paper. On the other hand, the opposite extreme—where it becomes an end in itself to squeeze in material from every source you find—should also be avoided. Let common sense guide you between these two extremes.

Some Practical Writing Tips

Following are some practical tips on the act of writing itself:

Don't Put Your Writing Off

Although the pressure of an impending deadline may stimulate great energy, it is unwise to begin writing your paper the night before it is due. You will produce a far better paper if you allow time for careful writing and revision. Start writing as soon as possible. Finishing ahead of your deadline will allow you the valuable opportunity to put the paper aside for a day or so, at which time you can take it up again, read it with fresh eyes, and gain new perspectives for improving it further.

Adopt Methods That Work for You

All writers are different. Use your past experience to decide what writing practices give you the best results.

Write in a place you find comfortable. A quiet library setting may free you from distractions and give you ready access to additional sources. On the other hand, you may prefer sitting at your computer keyboard at home, benefiting from the advantages of word processing. Or perhaps settling into a comfortable easy chair, writing with a pad on your lap and with your note cards on a table by your side, may allow you to do your best work.

Find ways to overcome obstacles. When you get stuck in your writing, perhaps it may help you to pause for a snack or a brief break to recharge your mental batteries—or you may find it best to shift gears, perhaps rereading what you have written or redirecting your attention to another part of the paper.

Adopt Positive Attitudes

Recognize that writing is hard work. Good writers work hard enough to make it *look* easy. Don't be discouraged by the snags that inevitably arise, and be prepared to give your project the time and energy it deserves.

Be persistent in writing. During the hard work of writing, writers are often visited with thoughts of more pleasant things they could be doing. At such times it is tempting to put down the pen or turn off the computer, promising yourself to resume writing later. Such temptations pose stern challenges to one's character and moral fiber. To be a successful writer is to develop self-discipline and to continue when one would rather not. As with any discipline you develop (from losing weight to mastering the cello to training for a triathlon), it is important to set realistic goals and to stick with them. At each writing session, set a goal of writing a certain number of pages or working for a certain number of hours—and meet it faithfully. Writing isn't usually fun, although at times it can be. But writing *is* very satisfying, especially when you know you have worked hard and produced a work you are proud of.

Have confidence in yourself. Even if this is your first research project, there is no reason to think you can't achieve admirable results. Remember, there are no secret formulas that others know and you don't. A paper is nothing more complicated than this: You have learned some information and are simply explaining it to readers who are much like yourself. Keep that in mind, tell your story clearly, let your own interest in the topic come through—and you will write a successful paper.

Getting Started

By the time you are ready to write, the hardest work should be behind you. You have plenty to say, as well as a plan for how you want to say it. You have a stack of note cards, arranged in the order in which you expect to use them. Once you are a page or two into your writing, the work should start to flow more smoothly. After students get past the initial unfamiliarity of working with source material, they usually find research writing little different from any other kind. In fact, because they are so well prepared, it is often easier.

Frequently, the most difficult part is simply getting started. In writing her first draft, Helen began by composing her opening section. She wanted to begin with a brief explanation of the controversy that her paper would describe, followed by a statement of her thesis. After many drafts, she produced this version:

> Once upon a time, almost all children grew up hearing stories of wonder and fantasy. These fairy tales spanned generations through books and oral storytelling. Recently, however, this tradition has been called into question by concerned parents, educators, and psychologists, who fear that fairy tales are actually detrimental to the happiness and security of children. The myriad of stereotypes and the violence inherent in these tales is undeniable. Surely, think some, these aspects will result in children who are brutal or unethical. But against all expectations, the majority of experts agree that fairy tales will not only fail to leave children morally handicapped, they are actually vital to the healthy development of children.

An early draft of Helen's opening

After she had written more of her paper, Helen realized that her introduction was *telling about* the violence and stereotypes in fairy tales rather than *showing* them. She felt her opening needed a specific illustration of what the critics were complaining about, and, after considering several tales, she decided to use the story of Little Red Riding Hood as a clear-cut example. As a result, she changed her opening from one paragraph to three; the final version can be seen on pages 230–31.

Struggling with an opening is not uncommon. Often it is best to wait until after you have drafted the body of a paper before even attempting to write the beginning. Writers sometimes waste time by overlooking the fact that the parts of a paper do not have to be written in the order in which they are to be read. If you are having difficulty getting started or are unsure about where to begin, start with a section that especially interests you or that seems easiest to write. Once you are successfully under way, composing the rest of the paper may be easier.

Writing the Opening

After you have written a draft of the body of your paper, you are in a better position to see what type of opening is most effective. An introductory section can serve many purposes: to inform readers of what your paper is about and where it is going, to generate interest, and to create a smooth transition into the body of the paper. There are many ways to begin a research paper; the following strategies are among those most frequently used:

Option 1: Begin with Background

Because your readers may not be well informed about your topic, you can provide them with a brief overview. The first paragraph of Helen's early draft, quoted above, is an example of such an opening. Notice that her paragraph has an **inductive organization**; it begins with background information (two sentences about the past popularity of fairy tales and three more describing the objections of critics) and ends with the main idea, Helen's thesis statement.

A similar kind of opening is to provide a brief history of events that led up to the subject you are writing about. One kind of background you should *not* use as your beginning is a dictionary definition ("Webster defines a fairy tale as 'a story about fairies, giants, magic deeds, etc.' "). Most readers would find such an opening trite and uninteresting, particularly when the term being defined is already familiar to them.

Option 2: Begin with a Summary of the Paper's Main Idea

The purpose of beginning with a summary of the main idea is to tell your readers immediately what the paper is about. A version of your thesis statement will figure prominently in the opening, which serves as a summary of the entire paper to come. Generally such openings have a **deductive organization**, in which the main idea is stated right away. Helen could have used such an organization to begin her paper:

> Supporters of traditional fairy tales have come to their defense in the face of criticism from those who claim such tales are harmful to children. While some critics have argued that the violence and stereotypes in these tales may harm children emotionally, the majority of experts claim that fairy tales are actually vital to the healthy development of children.

Option 3: Begin with an Interesting Anecdote

Starting with a specific story not only can capture your readers' interest immediately but can also be used to lead into your thesis statement. Helen could have opened her paper with an anecdote:

> In a recently revised version of the famous story of the Three Little Pigs, the wolf, instead of dying over an open fire, suffers only a mild burn and flees in panic into the nearby woods. Ironically, the effect of this less violent version is quite the opposite of what was intended. One little girl, who was told the

story on successive evenings, had persistent

nightmares. She suffered great anxiety, convinced that

the wolf was only biding his time until he could

reattack. Only when the original "violent" version was

substituted for the revised story could the child

believe that the wolf was really gone for good. The

moral of this tale is that traditional fairy tales,

with all their violence and stereotypes, may not be as

harmful to children as many of their critics contend.

Option 4: Begin by Explaining Your Purpose for Writing

A personal research paper often begins with a section headed "Why I Wrote This
Paper" or "What I Wanted to Find Out." Thus, Molly opened her paper as follows:

Ernest Hemingway once said, "The hardest trade in the

world is the writing of straight, honest prose about human

beings" (qtd. in Stafford 25). For most of my life, I have

wondered whether I could meet such a challenge. Do I have

what it takes to follow giants like Hemingway, Cather, and

Faulkner? Could I sit at my desk day after day, summoning

forth eloquence and creativity? Could I withstand the

rejection that comes with the trade? And could I make

enough money to create a stable existence for myself? In

short, could I be a writer?

Many scientific papers also begin by stating specifically what is to come in the
rest of the paper. Conventional research papers, however, generally avoid direct statements by the author about purpose. A rule of thumb in writing for the liberal arts is
that papers should avoid talking about themselves. That is, they should not contain
statements such as "In this paper I will . . . " or "The rest of this paper will examine. . . . " (Note how the other sample beginnings make the theme evident without
any such statements.) The personal research paper is an exception to this rule.

Writing the Conclusion

The one section of the research paper that can be even more troublesome than the
opening is the conclusion. After all, once you have said what you have to say, what

else remains to be done? Fortunately, it is not so hopeless as that. The principal purpose of a conclusion is not to say something new but to draw the ends of the paper together and to leave the reader with a satisfying sense of closure. Simply put, an ending should feel to the reader like an ending.

One strategy, appropriate for a long paper, is to tie together what you have written by summarizing the paper's content. This may be effective if you can summarize the paper in a fresh and insightful way. A summary serves no purpose, however, if it merely states the obvious: if it only rehashes what has already been made evident to the alert reader.

Often a more effective way of ending a research paper and allowing your readers to put what they have read into perspective is to assess (draw conclusions from) what you have learned. In an informative paper, the ending is the most appropriate place to offer your own observations and insights about your topic.

Note how, in her final paragraph, Helen both gave a brief summary of her paper and also drew a conclusion about her topic in the last sentence:

> Fairy tales have been a source of controversy for almost a century. The gender roles acceptable when these tales were rewritten by the Victorians are under scrutiny today for the sexual stereotypes they extol. On the other hand, the violent elements do not seem to promote actual violence but rather provide outlets for the otherwise repressed frustration of children. In this manner, and in the use of folklore in therapy, fairy tales are fulfilling a crucial role in our society. And while knowledge about this subject continues to unfold, it seems safe to conclude that children who are read fairy tales have as good a chance as any of living happily ever after.

Helen also had some fun with her ending. Her final four words ("living happily ever after") allude to the typical ending of fairy tales and complete a theme established with the paper's opening words ("Once upon a time").

In a personal research paper, the final section usually is straightforward. Like Molly's closing paragraphs on pages 251–52, your conclusion can state directly and personally what you have gained from your project. You can tell whether you achieved what you expected, whether your outlook on the subject has changed as a result of your search, and whether the knowledge you have gained has affected your plans or helped you reach a decision.

A word of caution: Strategies such as these are offered as helpful possibilities, not as rules or boundaries. Good writing resists formulas, and good writers continually find original ways of achieving their goals. Adopt whatever strategies work for you, and consider new approaches. That is the best way to extend your range as a writer.

Giving Your Paper a Title

Giving your paper a title may be the final stage of your project. Ideally, your title should both indicate to your readers what your paper is about and arouse their interest. Helen's first tentative title—"Fairy Tales: Do They Harm or Help Children?"—met the first of these requirements, but she decided it was a bit dry and uninviting. She chose as an alternative "Fairy Tales on Trial." A classmate who saw Molly's preliminary draft remarked that her title, "The Power of the Pen," did not give him much information about her topic. Molly briefly considered changing it to "The Pull of the Pen," but she did not want to lose her allusion to the expression "The pen is mightier than the sword." She decided to keep her title but to add a more explanatory subtitle: "The Power of the Pen: Should I Become a Professional Writer?"

Arresting, clever, or witty titles are not easy to create—and not always desirable, as there is a fine line between originality and cuteness. Start with a simple, direct title that captures your theme. If later on you are inspired with a better choice, fine, but if not, no one should object to a plain but clear title.

EDITING AND REVISING

Writers differ in their work habits. Helen is a constant reviser. Composing, rearranging, and editing at the keyboard of her word processor, Helen tends to write a little, pause to read what she has produced, make changes, and then move on. Molly, on the other hand, is more of an all-at-once reviser: She generally writes long passages straight through, forging ahead while ideas are still fresh in her mind. Only after she has written several pages will Molly pause to reread and make changes.

Because of their different work habits, Molly and Helen produced very different kinds of preliminary drafts. Molly wrote several complete drafts, each more polished than the previous one. Helen, on the other hand, emerged with something very close to a final draft after having gradually reached the concluding section of her paper. To call Helen's final paper a single "perfect" draft, however, would be very misleading. Since Helen was constantly rereading, revising, and editing earlier parts of her paper, these parts had actually gone through several drafts by the time she reached her conclusion. Her success was due partly to productive work habits and partly to the fact that Helen kept the structure of her paper clearly in view from the outset.

Both writers achieved success by using methods that worked for them. You, too, should feel free to adopt practices that work for you. Basically, though, you can be an effective editor of your own work if you approach it like a reader. Put aside what you have written for a day or more until you can read it with a fresh perspective. Put yourself in your readers' place, trying to anticipate whether they will find it clear, readable, and effective. You may find it helpful to consult the checklist that begins below, considering each question as if you were responding to a paper someone else has written.

Reworking Your Paper

After completing preliminary drafts, both writers put aside what they had written for a while, then came back and reread them with a pencil in hand. A page from Molly's early draft in which she made particularly extensive changes appears in Figure 13.2. Although Molly makes handwritten corrections on pages composed at a word processor, other writers prefer working entirely on paper, while still others make all their revisions directly at the computer keyboard.

Checklist for Editing and Revising

Topic, Focus, and Support

- Is it clear what the topic of the paper is? Does the writer provide a thesis statement or otherwise make it evident, early in the paper, what the paper is about? Is any further help needed for the reader to see the paper's point?
- Is the topic adequately narrowed—that is, neither too broad nor too limited for the writer to do it justice in a paper of this length?
- Has the writer kept the promises made by the thesis statement? That is, does the paper remain focused on its thesis? Does it stick to the point?
- Is the thesis supported with a variety of details or evidence?
- Is this support clear and convincing?
- In reading the paper, have you learned what you were expecting to learn from it? What questions remain in your mind? What needs to be developed more? What seems to be missing?

Audience, Style, and Readability

- Is the writing style appropriate for its intended audience? What passages do you have trouble understanding?
- Does the paper read smoothly and easily? Does the paper's use of sources and quotations ever become distracting or interrupt the smooth flow of your reading?
- Is the paper free from awkward phrasing, misspellings, typographical errors, and other mechanical flaws?
- Does the paper conform to MLA format (see Chapter C in Part II)?

Organization

- Is the paper organized in a way that makes sense? Can you understand why topics come where they do in the paper? Could any parts be rearranged for greater logic and clarity? Are there passages in different parts of the paper that should be brought together?

1

Molly MacLaren

Editing Draft

The ~~Power~~ *Power / Full* of the Pen: ~~*Should I Become a Professional Writer?*~~ *Say to*

I. Why I Am Writing This Paper

Ernest Hemingway once said, "~~t~~*T*he hardest trade in the world is the writing of straight, honest prose about human beings." *(qtd. in Stafford 25)* For most of my life, I have wondered whether ~~or not~~ *face meet* I could ~~withstand~~ such a challenge. Do I have what it takes to follow ~~in the footsteps of~~ giants like ~~Steinbeck,~~ *Hemingway, Woolf,* Faulkner ~~and~~ Cather? Could I sit ~~in a~~ *at my* desk day after day, ~~bringing~~ *Summoning forth eloquence* ~~continuously pouring forth imagination~~ and creativity? ~~Am~~ *Could* I able to withstand the rejection that comes with the trade? *In short, can I be a writer?* And ~~if I can be a writer,~~ will I make enough money to create a stable existence for myself? ¶ As a freshman ~~in college,~~ ~~I realize that~~ I have some time before I have to ~~actually~~ decide on a career or even a major. However, I want~~ed~~ to ~~be able to~~ make an educated decision based on ~~reality~~ *the truth cold facts hard* rather than childish dreams. My research ~~into the field of writing~~ has ~~definitely~~ helped me ~~discover the reality in~~ *compare* my fantasy *with reality.* If nothing else, I ~~have learned~~ *now know have come to understand* the time, dedication, and ~~legwork~~ ~~research~~ *are demanded of writers* that ~~is involved in writing.~~ *professional*

investigative labors

II. What I Knew

When I began my research, I had an ~~extremely~~ idealized portrait of ~~a~~ writer*s*. I thought that ~~writers~~ *they* were romantic

Figure 13.2 Molly's editing of a draft.

- Does the paper begin with a helpful general introduction to the topic? Can you tell from the introduction where the paper is going? Does the paper capture your interest right from the beginning? Could it be made more lively and interesting?

- Does the writer provide smooth and helpful transitions between subjects? Can you always tell how the part you are reading fits into the paper as a whole?

- Does the paper end with a satisfying conclusion?

Use of Sources

- Is the paper based on a variety of sources? Is the use of sources balanced, or is most of the information taken from only one or two sources?

- Is most of the information from sources paraphrased, rather than quoted directly? Are quotations used excessively? When sources are quoted, is there a reason for doing so? (See pages 340–44 for the proper use of quotations.)

- Does the writer avoid "naked quotations"? That is, is each quotation introduced by a phrase or sentence? (See pages 323–24.) When sources are referred to in the paper, are they adequately identified in acknowledgment phrases? That is, are you given enough information about them so that you can tell who they are and whether they are experts on the subject? (See pages 323–25).

- Are sources documented? Does the paper credit its sources within parenthetical notes? Does it credit paraphrased material as well as direct quotations? (Consult the Quick Reference Guides on the inside covers of this book.)

- Does the writer avoid overnoting (unnecessary notes for commonly available information) as well as undernoting (paraphrasing a source's ideas without providing a note)?

- Is it clear what each note refers to? That is, can you tell what information goes with what note?

- Are the sources listed in a works-cited page following the paper? Are the number and types of sources adequate for the paper?

- Does each note provide the least amount of information needed to refer you to the works-cited page and to identify the specific pages being referenced by the note?

- Except for longer, indented passages, are the notes placed inside the sentences with the period after, not before, the note?

- Does the punctuation in each note and in each entry in the works-cited page follow the prescribed format exactly? (Check the Quick Reference Guides on the inside covers.) Are items in the works-cited page listed in alphabetical order? Has the writer remembered that these items should not be numbered in MLA format?

Getting Advice from Other Readers

No matter how good a job writers do at editing their own writing, they can always benefit from outside help as well. Writers become so closely involved with their work that they can lose the ability to observe it from the reader's perspective. For that reason, good editing often requires advice from a reader who can point out flaws and possibilities that have escaped the writer's notice.

When she was satisfied with her revisions, Molly brought her printed paper to class for editing. (Students in Helen's class met with partners outside of class time to edit each other's papers.) Molly and her classmates were given the following assignment:

Group Editing	ASSIGNMENT

Read the papers written by members of your editing group and offer them the most helpful advice you can give.

Your Role as Editor

- Read each paper with care and interest, as if it were written with you as its intended audience.

- In responding to the paper, think of yourself as a friend trying to help, not as a judge providing a grade or evaluation.

The Editing Procedure

Read each paper at least twice, first for a general impression, then for specific details.

- The first time, read it straight through to gain a general impression. Do not stop to ask questions or write comments. When you have completed your first reading, pause to write a paragraph or two about the paper in general, including the following:

    –State what the paper's main idea seems to be.
    –Describe your general reaction to the paper. What did you learn from it?
    –Tell the author how the paper worked for you. Where was the best writing in the draft? Did the paper develop as you expected it to? As you were reading, did questions arise in your mind that the author answered or failed to answer? Did you ever have trouble following it?
    –Ask any other questions and make any other general comments about the paper as a whole.

- Now read the paper a second time, paying greater attention to specifics. Pause at any time to write comments, according to the following guidelines:

    –Write comments, questions, or ideas in pencil in the margins of the paper. Put checkmarks by passages that you want to talk with the writer about.
    –Point out the paper's strengths (note passages you especially like) as well as weaknesses, but be honest. You will not be much help to the author if you say

that everything is wonderful when you think the paper might be improved. You are not insulting the writer by offering ideas to improve it. Specific suggestions are much more helpful than vague comments like "?" or "Needs work."

–If you are in doubt about an editing or proofreading matter, consult with your instructor.

- Finally, talk with the paper's author. Explain your comments. Describe your response to the paper, what problems or questions you had while reading it, and what suggestions you have for making it better.

Molly received editing suggestions from the two other students in her editing group. The following pages show the comments of Carl, one of her peers.

Molly MacLaren

Editing draft

I wasn't sure what your topic was from this title.

The Power of the Pen

I. Why I Am Writing This Paper   *" The ?*

Ernest Hemingway once said, " the hardest trade in the

world is the writing of straight, honest prose about human

beings." For most of my life, I have wondered whether or

not I could withstand such a challenge. Do I have what it

takes to follow in the footsteps of giants like Steinbeck,

Faulkner and Cather? Could I sit in a desk day after day,

continuously pouring forth imagination and creativity? Am

I able to withstand the rejection that comes with the trade?

In short, can I be a writer? And if I can be a writer,

Maybe you'd want your thesis to come last? Or first?

will I make enough money to create a stable existence for

myself? As a freshman in college, I realize that I have

some time before I have to actually decide on a career or

even a major. However, I wanted to be able to make an

educated decision based on reality rather than childish   *nice*

dreams. My research into the field of writing has

definitely helped me discover the reality in my fantasy.

If nothing else, I have learned the time, dedication and

research that is involved in writing.

II. What I Knew

When I began my research, I had an extremely idealized

portrait of a writer. I thought that writers were romantic

Beginning with your fantasies and illusions works well.

MacLaren 2

Sort of unattractive, like weeds.

creatures who shunned public lights but loved cigarettes, black coffee and jazz. In my mind, writers spent hours living in a fantasy world of their own making. It was almost as if I believed that writers stuck together in a (clump) and never went outside except at night. Although I realized that this picture was wrong, I was still surprised to see that writers are actually normal.

Since I have wanted to be a writer since the age of five, I already knew something about the hardships that are found within the business. Writing, similar to acting, is a career where success is determined through the public *What do you mean?* eye. I believed that free-lance writing was a less stable job when compared to journalistic writing. However, I didn't know exactly how easy (or difficult) it would be to find jobs. I also had no idea how much money one could make through a career in writing. Could the average writerS support themselves from the power of the pen alone?

I read extensively, which has brought me into contact with a number of informative writers. I had heard of the difficulties involved with getting published and I knew that some of the best authors in the world had extreme *oppressive?* problems with the ever distant and impressive publishing world. Even Dr. Seuss was unable to turn his words and sketches into full-fledged books in the first years of his career. Knowledge such as this made me quite hesitant about my own abilities. — *I like how you provide drama. I want to read on.*

III. The Search

I'm not what sure what you mean: Because are there so many books?. MacLaren 3

The amount of volumes in my local library seemed to prove that success was entirely possible. Among thousands of reassuring books, I began my search.

I decided that I wanted to obtain a general idea of what a writer actually did before I did any in depth research. This meant that I had to find a basic job description that included average income, educational requirements, unemployment rate and expected growth. In order to find this information, I visited the career section of the library. Here I found a variety of vocational handbooks and encyclopedias that gave me more than enough information.

When I first began my in-depth research, I consulted various how-to books. Basically, these volumes showed how an aspiring writer should create plot, characters, setting, etc. I found these books helpful, but they did not provide me with the information I needed for my paper. Many more books explained how the average writer could be published, which included tips from those inside the business. I found this second genre extremely helpful because they discussed the difficulties of being a published writer. These books helped me envision the long and strenuous journey to print.

Your style is very honest. It sounds like a real person (you).

In the library, I also found many books that served as a source of inspiration and insight. Many of these were

MacLaren 4

of ?

simply collections of biographies on great authors. I read
many volumes to discover the habits and secrets of famous
writers. Their advice to the beginning writer varied
greatly, but I always found the accounts interesting. The
two volumes that were most helpful were On Being a Writer,
by Bill Strickland, and Parting the Curtains: Interviews
with Southern Writers, by Dannye Powell. In these books,
the first myth was shattered; I discovered that writers are
as individual as the novels they publish.

Although I had a rudimentary understanding of writers
and their jobs, I still needed to find out whether it would
be easy for me to succeed with a career in writing. I
searched the InfoTrac under "writ* career*" to check for
any newspaper or magazine articles that related to the
writing industry. Although there are several magazines
geared toward writers, (like Writer's Digest) I was unable
to find an abundance of articles on writing as a career. I
looked up the three that looked most promising and copied
them for further reference.

After spending many long hours in the library, I had
my own questions about the lives of average writers. The
books had given me insight into the lives of famous
writers, but what about the millions who never become
household names? Most people who write never become famous
and I did not want to neglect the majority. I spoke to my
relatives in the newspaper business, Ms Elizabeth Flagler

MacLaren 5

and Mr. Fred Flagler. They were very helpful and extremely honest about the realities of working at a stressful newspaper. Since they know me, they were also able to judge how well I would do in a journalistic career. I also spoke with Ms Rebecca Lee, a creative writing professor. She gave me an accurate look at the business of writing short stories and novels.

Finally, I visited the Career Planning Office on campus, where I took a test called SIGI-Plus. It provided a printout with an assessment of my interests and a list of compatible occupations. Finally, I felt that I had enough information to begin my paper.

IV. What I Found

Writers are not immortal gods. They are merely people who see the world through different eyes. They take in life and transform it into the written word. As a human, the writer is susceptible to the harsh reality of the world. They must pay bills and bring in money. They must work painstakingly to meet stressful deadlines. They must deal with rejection and writer's block. Every writer has his own private horror stories, and it is these all too real tales that frighten me. At one point in his life, even Alex Haley possessed only eighteen cents and two cans of sardines (Powell 179).

Maybe make it "writers."

Still, this isn't very high

The average writer does not make very much money. As Robyn Carr says, "it's hard to make money in this business" (22). It's the emphasis on hard that is scary. The vocational handbook was somewhat more encouraging. "In the 1990's, beginning writers and researchers receive starting salaries of about $20,000 a year." (Hopke 623). This is not a bad starting salary; I could definitely support myself on $20,000 a year. Just when my future career was looking a little brighter, I realized that this figure is just an average. Some writers make more money, while some make less. Another handbook, America's 50 Fastest Growing Jobs, said that the weekly earnings for writers were "very high." (Farr 10B Appendix A). Once again, however, this is merely an average. Many writers have to work two or three jobs to make money. Freelance writers, or those who sell to a variety of publications, "may earn from $5,000 to $15,000 a year (Hopke 623). The key word appears to be "may earn," for the next sentence is short, cold and to the point: "freelance earnings may vary widely" (Hopke 623). Success depends on my own determination to become an author.

Do you need both of these?

I also learned quite a bit about fame and the writing business, Everyone knows the big names in writing--the current novelists whose names blaze across the New York Times Best Seller List. Such success is more difficult than most people could ever imagine. "Fame should be a by-

MacLaren 7

product and not a goal," Carr says, "It is possible to be
great. It is possible to be a star." (22). However, this
won't happen without a lot of hard work. A writer cannot
depend on "that first wild wind of success," as F. Scott
Fitzgerald called it (Burnett 175). In other words, depend
on the writing and not the fame and glory. *Are you saying that quality is more important than success?*

Success in the writing business depends on many
different factors. In my research, I have heard the soul
of a writer described by many different adjectives.
Writers are both "blessed" and "damned," according to
Harlan Ellison (Strickland 6). Many sources agreed with
this interpretation of the writer/ tortured soul. *I'm not sure what you mean.* Allan
Gurganus once said that "sacrifices have to be made" in
order to achieve success as a writer (Powell 163).
Oftentimes, a writer will spend a lot of time, money and
effort on a manuscript only to be turned down by an editor.
One of the most important factors in achieving success
seems to be the ability to withstand such rejection. In
order to do this a writer must be a truly exceptional
person. It sometimes seemed that no one could fit into the
role of a perfect writer. The ideal writer is "gutsy,
brazen, brave... hardworking, determined, confident and
disciplined" (Carr 23). They also need to write well,
which means that a writer "should be creative and able to
express ideas clearly," (Hopke 621). Other qualities are
also helpful: "curiosity, persistence, initiative,

MacLaren 8

honest and effective

resourcefulness, an accurate memory and physical stamina"
(Hopke 621). I realize that many of these virtues are not
exactly my strong points, but I am willing to develop these
skills.

Obviously, success in the writing business is also in
the eye of the beholder. This doesn't come easy in the
publishing world, which means that minor gains are treated
as major accomplishments. One of Ray Bradbury's comments
made a lot of sense to me. He said, "Money is not
important. The material things are not important. Getting
the work done beautifully and proudly is important"
(Strickland 56). Success is an incredibly personal
experience.

A writer's success can come through a variety of
writing jobs. Not all writers write fiction. Before doing
my research, I assumed that there were only a couple
different kinds of writer: fiction, nonfiction, and
journalistic. These are the basic categories, but there
are also numerous subdivisions. I soon discovered that

indent?

"writers develop fiction and nonfiction ideas for plays,
novels, poems and other related works; report, analyze and
interpret facts , events and personalities; review art,
music, drama, and other artistic presentations; and
persuade the general public to favor certain goods,
services and personalities" (Hopke 619). Writers have a
place in nearly every large business. Even huge chemical

MacLaren 9

corporations need people to write reports and summarize
data. Writers can find work in advertising firms,
publishing companies, television and radio broadcasting
stations, government agencies and educational facilities
(Polking 1-5). The thought that writing jobs such as these
exist in abundance was incredibly reassuring. Although
these jobs may not be a fiction writer's dream, they are
available if one searches hard enough.

A variety of different jobs can be found within the
field of journalism. Here, one is able to find columnists,
editors, cartoonists, critics and news writers (Hopke 620).
News writers write articles about breaking news and other
subjects that may be interesting to their readers. Critics
evaluate books, plays, movies, TV shows, concerts, and
restaurants. Columnists can provide editorial comment on
current events, humor, advice, or comments on local news.
In this field, the pay is steady. Employment in newspapers
and magazines "is expected to increase about as fast as
average" (Farr 16A Appendix A). Many of my mother's
relatives work for newspapers and magazines around the
country. I spoke with my aunt, Ms. Elizabeth Flagler, who
worked at the Sun-Sentinel, a Fort Lauderdale paper with a
circulation of 375,000. She started as a copy editor and
specialized in design when she became the graphics editor.
Ms. Flagler stressed that advancement in the newspaper
business is entirely possible, especially if you want to

MacLaren 10

just manage other people. However, this is not very appealing to me. I also spoke to my grandfather, Fred Flagler, who recently retired as the managing editor of the Winston-Salem Journal. He was not very optimistic about the future of the newspaper business. "One day you're not going to have newspapers. They cost more and more to produce. For example, all the afternoon papers are out of business. I just don't think it would be a worthwhile career anymore." Newspapers are downsizing immensely, which means fewer and fewer jobs.

My interview with Ms Rebecca Lee gave me information concerning freelance and fiction-writing careers. I was slightly worried by the fact that most authors seemed to know that they wanted to enter the writing profession at an early age. While I knew that I wanted to be a writer, I had not written very many completed stories. She dispelled my fear by saying that she had not decided to become a writer until she was in college. "Writing is one of the only arts where you don't find many prodigies," she said. Ms Lee said that if I wanted to become a writer, the best thing I could do would be to read constantly and to be "willing to write poorly." As a professor of creative writing, she knows many other writers. Most of them have other jobs of some kind; teaching English seems to be the most common. This comment made me think about becoming a professor of some sort and then writing on the side.

I'm not sure what she means. Why would you want to write poorly?

Maybe you could put this earlier, with the money questions.

According to Ms. Lee, most writers are forced to do this in order to make money.

Finally, having sought help from books and humans, I turned to the computer. The SIGI-Plus program analyzed my responses to its questions and listed seventeen occupations that matched my interests and abilities, but writer was not one of them. At the top of its list I was surprised to find foreign service officer, historian, English professor, and interior designer. While this is discouraging, several of the proposed professions involve oral and written communication, including teacher, public relations specialist, fund-raiser, and even clergy. — *Do you mean you do or do not want one of these jobs?*

V. Conclusion

Maybe a more positive ending would be good for this section.

After all the research that I did, my dream of being a writer still holds. True, the idolized position of the writer has tarnished some, but the power of the written word is still incredibly strong. Despite the low and unstable salary, writing still has a certain magnetism that no other career possesses. The writer does seem to be a special creature; it would be a challenge to become one. Writers undergo rejection, criticism, starvation and poverty, but they also get to witness the freedom and exhilaration of creating a unique manuscript. I will write "because it is an adventure to watch it come out of [my] hands" (Strickland 57).

In order to achieve my dream of becoming a writer, I will definitely include some creative writing courses in next semester's course load. Ms. Lee has offered to help me with any questions I might have, which is wonderful. I also intend to get involved with local literary magazines and other publications. An internship at my local newspaper, the Morning-Star, will give me the chance to see whether journalism is my forte. I also intend to enter a variety of writing contests for young adults. These decisions should put me well on the road to becoming a writer.

You make a good point, Molly. There are many obstacles to being a writer, but a writer is a person who is willing to face obstacles. You seem like that kind of a person. This is fascinating — plus a little scary.

My one suggestion for revision is to reorganize section IV. Instead of organizing it by source (books, interviews, computer), maybe do it more by topic, like putting all the money questions together.

You found valuable, interesting material and present it well. I hope you pursue your dream.

—Carl

Molly found Carl's comments valuable, because they revealed another reader's response to her paper, as well as useful ideas for improving it. Several of Carl's remarks highlight what worked well for him ("I like how you provide drama"). Others inform Molly about a passage he found unclear ("I'm not sure what she means. Why would you want to write poorly?"). Remarks that specify his difficulty are particularly useful ("Are you saying that quality is more important than success?"). In some of his comments Carl just responds on a personal level to what Molly is saying (for example, about the starting salary she cites, he remarks, "Still, this isn't very high"). Carl's longer commentary at the end of Molly's paper summarizes his overall response. It also includes a particularly thoughtful suggestion for reorganization that Molly adopted in her final draft.

Note that Carl's comments are framed in a positive and unintrusive way. When he offers suggestions, he does so tentatively, making it clear that the paper belongs to Molly and that final editing decisions rest with her ("Maybe you'd want your thesis to come last? or first?"). Even when he offers a minor word substitution, he asks rather than tells ("of?"). Sometimes he notes what does not work well for him (where Molly wrote about a "clump" of writers, he circled the expression and wrote, "Sort of unattractive, like weeds"), but it is clear that Carl's goal is to be as helpful to Molly as possible as she undertakes her revision. His comments are constructive, useful, and confidence-building.

Over the next week, in addition to responding to the valuable suggestions of her classmates and instructor, Molly discovered other ways to improve her paper. Each time she reread her draft, Molly noticed new possibilities for revising it. She spent many hours rephrasing, clarifying, and even rearranging sections of the paper, until she was ready to submit the polished final draft. A comparison of her editing and final drafts (pages 241–53) will show the results of Molly's efforts. Refer particularly to her handwritten changes to her opening page (Fig. 13.2 on page 367) to see how she took Carl's comments into account and made many other improvements in her paper as well.

Consult, too, the final draft of Helen's paper, which we have reprinted on the following pages along with annotations that highlight important elements of research papers.

Veit 1

Helen Veit

English 102

Prof. Robert Byington

3 April 1996

The title is not underlined or placed within quotation marks.

Fairy Tales on Trial

Once upon a time, almost all children grew up hearing stories of wonder and fantasy. Successive generations shared a knowledge of fairy tales passed down through books and oral story telling. Recently, however, this tradition has been called into question by concerned parents, educators, and psychologists who fear that such tales are actually detrimental to the happiness and security of children.

The writer begins with background to introduce the topic. For other opening strategies, see pages 361–65.

Consider the tale of Little Red-Cap, better known as Little Red Riding Hood. A sweet young girl and her sickly grandmother are easily duped by a clever wolf. He swallows them whole, but a resourceful hunter rips open the wolf's belly with scissors, rescuing the still-living females. The hunter sews heavy stones into the body of the animal, who then dies and is skinned by the hunter. The girl learns her lesson: "I will never by myself leave the path, to run into the wood, when my mother has forbidden me to do so" (Grimm and Grimm).

The source of this quotation is identified in a parenthetical note. There is no page reference for an electronic, rather than a printed, source.

Is this a violent tale? Undoubtedly. Does it stereotype females as naive, helpless victims; males as predators and protectors; even wolves as evil creatures

Veit 2

deserving extermination? Undeniably so. Surely, think
some, hearing such tales can only brainwash and brutalize
children. But against all expectations, many other experts
deny that fairy tales will leave children emotionally
handicapped; on the contrary, they assert that these
stories are actually vital to the healthy development of
children.

The writer concludes her opening with a thesis statement.

Violence in Fairy Tales

Section headings are optional.

Foremost among concerns is the violence in almost
every tale. Evil mothers plot to murder their own
children. Vanity is routinely punished with grotesque
disfigurement. Villains meet excruciating deaths. These
macabre elements have been targeted and censored by parents
and publishers. There is evidence, however, that
eliminating violence in fairy tales may only feed the fears
of children. A nine-year-old in one study remarked on the
punishment of the witch in Hansel and Gretel: "Somebody
said to me that the witch could have been put in prison.
But that can't be. The witch would have found her way out
by magic. And then she'd be free again" (qtd. in Messner
11).

Such anxiety is not uncommon. For example, one
revision of the Three Little Pigs omitted the wolf's death
over a fire and inserted instead a mild burn and a panicked
dash to the nearby woods. Instead of reassuring children

Veit 3

of life's security, the new version actually created anxiety that the wolf would return. One little girl, convinced that the wolf was only biding his time until he could reattack, had persistent nightmares. Only when the original version including the wolf's death was substituted for her regular story could the child believe that the wolf was truly gone for good (Tunnell 609).

Although children are often obsessed with violence, that does not seem to be a problem, according to psychologist Ann Trousdale. She states that children tend to "omit gratuitous violence" when retelling the story and only keep the violence that is necessary for justice (76). Fairness is very important to young people. "Children are innocent and love justice," observes author and critic G. K. Chesterton, "while most of us are wicked and prefer mercy" (qtd. in Tunnell 608). So a parent and offspring reading a fairy tale aloud may have very different reactions; what seems to be violent to the parent may seem only fitting to the child.

Another important factor affecting the perception of brutality is the extreme nature of the fairy tale itself. Indeed, the heights of savagery and wonder balance each other out, for, as Max Lüthi writes, "a princely reward or a sentence of death is but one of the many contrasts used in the fairy tale." Children don't regard these outcomes

Parenthetical notes are used for paraphrased material as well as quotations.

When one source is quoted by another source, give the source where the quotation was found.

Transition words and phrases are helpful signals to the reader.

Veit 4

Brackets indicate a word or suffix added by the writer to a quotation for clarity.

as they would in a realistic narrative. They merely accept them as "rule[s] of the game" (152).

Lüthi goes further to say that not only are the violent elements harmless, but they are actually crucial to children's development and perception of the world around them. By demonstrating that dragons can be slain, these fantastic stories teach children to master their dilemmas rather than blame themselves or others (154). Ann Trousdale points out that children can deal with anger by identifying with villains who have great power and are therefore able to strike out and take control. For children, who often have minimal control in their lives, this identification can be fulfilling. It is necessary, however, that the villain be eventually conquered (72).

An acknowledgment phrase marks the beginning of the paraphrased passage.

A note marks the end of the passage.

In his landmark study, The Uses of Enchantment, Bruno Bettelheim speaks of the danger of censoring violent elements:

Longer quotations are indented one inch or ten spaces. No quotation marks are used.

Those who outlawed traditional folk fairy tales decided that if there were monsters in a story told to children, these must all be friendly--but they missed the monster a child knows best and is most concerned with: the monster he feels or fears himself to be, and which also sometimes persecutes him. By keeping this monster within the child unspoken of, hidden in his unconscious, adults prevent the child from spinning fantasies

Veit 5

around it in the image of the fairy tales he

knows. Without such fantasies, the child fails

to get to know this monster better, nor is given

suggestions as to how he may gain mastery over

it. (120)

A note following
an indented
quotation comes
after the period.

Trousdale cites one little girl in her study as an

example of the positive use of a typical fairy-tale

villain. The evil fairy in Sleeping Beauty was in fact the

girl's favorite character until the fairy's rage got out of

control as she turned into a giant. The girl herself had

not been invited to a friend's party and had been upset for

some weeks. The story allowed her to vent her anger and

simultaneously feel relief when the evil fairy is killed at

the end. Her "dangerous impulses" had been controlled

(74).

Other notes
come before
the period.

Gender Stereotypes

        Most experts agree that the violence in fairy tales

provides both an outlet for children's frustrations and

representations of their ability to conquer their problems.

On the other hand, the blatantly stereotypical gender roles

in fairy tales are usually met with much less enthusiastic

responses. From the straw-spinning heroine of

Rumpelstiltskin, who is incompetent in her given occupation

without male help (Zipes 49), to the Snow White/Sleeping

Beauty type who is so passive that she falls into a

The writer gives a
brief summary of
the previous topic
as a transition
into a new topic.

Veit 6

comatose state, the role of females in traditional fairy tales does not meet up to the standards of modern womanhood.

For little girls, the problem seems to originate in their subconscious association with the heroine (Davies and Banks 22). The docility, dependence, and sacrifice glorified in most fairy-tale women make "female subordination seem a romantically desirable, indeed an inescapable fate" (Rowe 209). Balanced with a variety of different types of stories, however, fairy-tale gender roles can be enjoyed for the glimpse they give children into the past. Alone, the outdated perceptions can cripple children who will grow up in a world with very different expectations.

The writer integrates part of a quotation into her own sentence.

As with violence, case studies have examined the effects of gender stereotyping in fairy tales. One group of elementary students was asked to draw pictures of their favorite characters from a story read to them and to write their own tale. Ella Westland, who conducted the study, observed that girls seemed torn between a yearning for traditional femininity--most drew beautiful princesses-- and a desire for independence that was apparent in their tomboyish writings. Overall, the boys seemed content with the straightforward fairy-tale scenario, embellished with gore picked up from television. Westland concludes that while the inner conflict of the girls indicates turmoil,

Veit 7

they are winning the struggle. She suggests the group to be worried about is the boys, who accept their stereotyped roles without reflection (237-45). And although "politically correct" fairy tales, have been revised to place women and minorities in control, no effort has been made to place males, particularly fathers, in a more flattering light (Brott).

A Place for Fairy Tales

The harm attributed to fairy tales has been denied by many experts. Taken a step further, these stories are actually used by teachers and therapists to solve problems. As part of a "values-based" curriculum, high school students use the Sleeping Beauty story to examine their views about love and sex ("Using"). Some counselors read folk tales to battered wives to confront abuse and open up discussion of male and female attitudes and alternative solutions (Ucko 414-17). A similar process that encourages identification with Cinderella and other heroines is used in the treatment of women with eating disorders (Hill 585). In these functions, fairy tales are useful to teenagers and adults as well as to children.

Fairy tales have been a source of controversy for almost a century. The gender roles acceptable when these tales were rewritten by the Victorians are under scrutiny today for the sexual stereotypes they extol. On the other hand, the violent elements do not seem to promote actual

A note for an anonymous work gives the first word or two of the title.

A note gives the author's name when it is not identified in the text.

The writer begins her closing section with a brief summary of her findings.

Veit 8

violence, but rather provide outlets for the otherwise
repressed frustration of children. In this manner, and in
the use of folklore in therapy, fairy tales are fulfilling
a crucial role in our society. And while knowledge about
this subject continues to unfold, it seems safe to conclude
that children who are read fairy tales have as good a
chance as any of living happily ever after.

The writer ends by drawing conclusions from her research.

Veit 9

Works Cited

Bettelheim, Bruno. <u>The Uses of Enchantment: The Meaning</u>
    <u>and Importance of Fairy Tales</u>. New York: Knopf, 1976.

Brott, Armin A. "Not All Men Are Sly Foxes." <u>Newsweek</u>
    1 June 1992: 14-15. <u>InfoTrac: Expanded Academic</u>
    <u>Index/ASAP</u>. Online. Information Access. 16 Mar.
    1996.

Davies, Bronwyn, and Chas Banks. "The Gender Trap: A
    Feminist Poststructuralist Analysis of Primary School
    Children's Talk about Gender." <u>Journal of Curriculum</u>
    <u>Studies</u> 24 (1992): 1-25.

Grimm, Jakob, and Wilhelm Grimm. <u>Grimms' Fairy Tales</u>.
    Online. Carnegie Mellon U. Library. Internet.
    Available: http://www.cs.cmu.edu/Web/books.html.
    20 Mar. 1996.

Hill, Laura. "Fairy Tales: Visions for Problem Resolution
    in Eating Disorders." <u>Journal of Counseling and</u>
    <u>Development</u> 70 (1992): 584-87.

Lüthi, Max. <u>The Fairytale as Art Form and Portrait of Man</u>.
    Trans. Jon Erickson. Bloomington: Indiana UP, 1984.

Messner, Rudolf. "Children and Fairy Tales--What Unites
    Them and What Divides Them." <u>Western European</u>
    <u>Education</u> 21.2 (1989): 6-28.

Rowe, Karen E. "Feminism and Fairy Tales." <u>Don't Bet on</u>
    <u>the Prince: Contemporary Feminist Fairy Tales in North</u>

Sources are not
numbered.

Sources are listed
in alphabetical
order.

Give the date
when you
consulted an
online electronic
source (see
Chapter 10).

Veit 10

<u>America and England</u>. Ed. Jack Zipes. New York:

    Methuen, 1986. 209-26.

Trousdale, Ann. "Who's Afraid of the Big, Bad Wolf?"

    <u>Children's Literature</u> 20.2 (1989): 69-79.

Tunnell, Michael O. "The Double-Edged Sword: Fantasy and

    Censorship." <u>Language Arts</u> 71 (1994): 606-12.

Ucko, Lenora Greenbaum. "Who's Afraid of the Big Bad Wolf?

    Confronting Wife Abuse through Folk Stories." <u>Social

    Work</u> 36 (1991): 414-19.

"Using Books to Teach Values." Associated Press News

    Service. 2 May 1995. <u>CD NewsBank Comprehensive</u>.

    CD-ROM. NewsBank. Apr. 1996.

Westland, Ella. "Cinderella in the Classroom: Children's

    Responses to Gender Roles in Fairy-tales." <u>Gender and

    Education</u> 5 (1993): 237-49.

Zipes, Jack. "Spinning with Fate: Rumpelstiltskin and the

    Decline of Female Productivity." <u>Western Folklore</u> 52

    (1993): 43-59.

Give the date when a CD-ROM database or other portable electronic source was last updated.

TYPING AND PROOFREADING YOUR POLISHED DRAFT

Molly and Helen benefited from the comments and suggestions they received from classmates in their editing groups and from their instructors. They made further revisions in their papers and submitted them in polished form, in accordance with the assignment they had been given, which follows.

ASSIGNMENT   **Submitting Your Portfolio**

Submit the following items in your folder:

- Your typed polished draft.

- All earlier drafts and outlines.

- Your note cards in two packets:

  –those you used in your paper, in the order you used them.
  –those you wrote but did not use.

- Your research notebook.

When you prepare your final draft, be sure that you observe formatting conventions described in Chapter C of Part II, along with any others your instructor may specify. Before you submit your paper, read it through several times, slowly and carefully, looking for errors. Look for typing mistakes, misspellings, missing words, punctuation problems, and any other surface errors that may have escaped your notice in earlier readings. It is especially useful to have a friend proofread the paper as well, because by now you have become so familiar with what you have written that you may have difficulty noticing surface details.

Neatly cross out a minor error with a single line and write the correction above it. Never erase, and do not use correction fluid for making handwritten changes. Any page with a major error or numerous minor errors should be retyped.

After proofreading their final drafts, Helen and Molly brought them to class, where their instructors gave them one final assignment:

ASSIGNMENT   **Final Proofreading**

Read the final drafts of the other students in your editing group. Do not mark on their papers, but if you find an error, point it out to the author so that it can be corrected.

At last, Helen and Molly submitted their final drafts. For both, the project had been difficult but rewarding work. Like their classmates, they had struggled with the previously unfamiliar process of research and research writing. They had uncovered and managed a large body of research materials. From these sources, they had created essays that had substance, form, and interest—essays they were proud of. They had also learned a great deal, not only about their particular topics, but also about research, about college scholarship, and even about the meaning of an education itself. It is likely that after the hard work of your own research project is completed, you too, like Helen, Molly, and many thousands of students before you, will feel a well-deserved sense of satisfaction with what you have accomplished.

14 Argument: Reading, Writing, and Research

Y ou don't have to be hostile or arrogant to be effective at argument. You don't even have to be an expert or have first-hand experience with your topic. In fact, in writing a college-level argument, you should avoid sounding overly confident, too sure you have found the truth. You are expected to be reasonable, fair-minded, and logical. In a strange way, that may be a relief, since you don't have the pressure of needing to win at all costs. Unlike a debater, to whom winning is everything, a writer in a serious argument is above mere victory. The goal is something more important and valuable —the honest search for truth in a world where there are often competing truths. Of course, you always want to make your case convincing enough to have an impact on your audience but you "win" in argumentative writing when you are fair, thorough, and clear. The challenge of writing an argument is to place ideas in a public forum to see if they stand up under scrutiny. College students argue a position not to trick or outmaneuver others, but to test the validity of ideas. That is the intellectual and ethical excitement of argument.

Of course, not all efforts to persuade others have that perspective. Advertisements, for example, are usually concerned not with discovering truth but with selling products. In some cases, ethics and fairness play little part in their attempt to influence consumers to buy.

If you think of argument as a straight line or continuum, at one end would be the rigorous logic and impersonal language of the physical sciences—for example, a geologist trying to convince colleagues that her experiments reverse accepted theories of beach erosion. At the other end might be a richly colored photograph of a dream-like, misty lake that tries to persuade us that mystery and romance await the user of a new shampoo. The two extremes of this continuum would look like this:

Logical reasoning   ◄——►   *Emotional appeal*

EMOTIONAL APPEAL

Although emotional persuasion is not a primary concern in this chapter, we begin by considering the techniques of advertisements. At times their strategies seem obvious. Yet even when we recognize that these ads are out to manipulate us, they can still be surprisingly effective. That is because their creators expect them to be viewed casually on billboards or magazines, not analyzed in college classes. In the right context, these ads apparently work on consumers, since people spend billions of dollars on products that are hardly necessities.

By studying advertising methods, we can become more aware of how ads and other emotional appeals get people to do and believe what their creators want them to. Awareness is the only defense against being manipulated.

The advertisement in Figure 14.1 (page 398) provides an example of this type of persuasion. Like other magazine ads, it is concerned more with stimulating and satisfying emotional needs than with describing specific features of a product. In fact, the advertisement illustrates a formula developed by Hugh Rank, an analyst of advertising and propaganda. First comes *attention-getting*. When they see the ad, most readers are likely to notice, first, dramatic sky above exotic Scottish scenery and, second, the whisky label lit from behind as if by the sun. Next comes *confidence-building*. The reader is told that Scottish weather is easy to predict (with the implied joke that it is almost always raining in Scotland). Then comes *desire-stimulating*. The ad associates this brand of whisky with the appealing Scottish scenery. Finally comes *response-seeking*. The reader is urged to "[t]aste the true flavor of Scotland."

Not every advertisement illustrates Rank's formula quite so clearly as the Dewar's ad. However, a great many ads do emphasize the emotional appeal of a product while providing little if any concrete information about ingredients, specifications, or the like. Ads have been subject to testing and research so that the emotions and desires they evoke coincide with what motivates consumers. As you study the following ads, try to see if you are part of the audience the ad makers had in mind.

Emotional Appeal

EXERCISE

Look carefully at the advertisements on the following pages (Figures 14.2 and 14.3). Be as observant and perceptive as you can, and freewrite for five to ten minutes on each. What audience do the advertisers have in mind, and what response are they seeking to stimulate? How does the advertiser expect people to be persuaded by it? Both ads depict images connected with nature. Do these help the advertisers sell their products? The ad for nuclear energy (Figure 14.2) presents both image and text, while the perfume ad (Figure 14.3) consists almost exclusively of photographic images. Is one ad more logical than the other? Is emotional appeal a component of both ads? Now try to describe ads that would seek to achieve the same results without any recourse to emotional appeals. How would they differ from the ads pictured here? Would they be less or more effective in selling perfume or in persuading readers about nuclear power?

Figure 14.1 Sample advertisement.

To confirm the benefits of nuclear energy, we got an outside opinion.

In the words of the President's National Energy Strategy, "Nuclear power is a proven electricity-generating technology that emits no sulfur dioxide, nitrogen oxides, or greenhouse gases."

In fact, nuclear energy helps *reduce* airborne pollutants in the U.S. by over 19,000 tons every day. That's because the 111 nuclear plants now operating in this country don't burn anything to generate electricity.

The air we breathe is cleaner because of nuclear energy. But we need more nuclear plants. Because the more plants we have, the more energy we'll have for the future of our planet.

For more information, write to the U.S. Council for Energy Awareness, P.O. Box 66080, Dept. BE02, Washington, D.C. 20035.

Nuclear energy means cleaner air.

Figure 14.2 Sample advertisement.

Figure 14.3 Sample advertisement.

Figure 14.3 (continued).

LOGICAL ARGUMENT

In contrast to emotional appeal, most serious argument relies on factual data and logic. Sometimes the logic is presented in a tightly organized pattern, as in the following passage written by a noted biologist who argues for the conservation of wilderness areas.

For species on the brink, from birds to fungi, the end can come in two ways. Many, like the Moorean tree snails, are taken out by the metaphorical equivalent of a rifle shot—they are erased but the ecosystem from which they are removed is left intact. Others are destroyed by a holocaust, in which the entire ecosystem perishes.

The distinction between rifle shots and holocausts has special merit in considering the case of the spotted owl *(Strix occidentalis)* of the United States, an endangered form that has been the object of intense national controversy since 1988. Each pair of owls requires about 3 to 8 square kilometers of coniferous forest more than 250 years old. Only this habitat can provide the birds with both enough large hollow trees for nesting and an expanse of open understory for the effective hunting of mice and other small mammals. Within the range of the spotted owl in western Oregon and Washington, the suitable habitat is largely confined to twelve national forests. The controversy was engaged first within the U.S. Forest Service and then the public at large. It was ultimately between loggers, who wanted to continue cutting the primeval forest, and environmentalists determined to protect an endangered species. The major local industry around the owl's range was affected, the financial stakes were high, and the confrontation was emotional. Said the loggers: "Are we really expected to sacrifice thousands of jobs for a handful of birds?" Said the environmentalists: "Must we deprive future generations of a race of birds for a few more years of timber yield?"

Overlooked in the clamor was the fate of an entire habitat, the old-growth coniferous forest, with thousands of other species of plants, animals, and microorganisms, the great majority unstudied and unclassified. Among them are three rare amphibian species, the tailed frog and the Del Norte and Olympic salamanders. Also present is the western yew, *Taxus brevifolia,* source of taxol, one of the most potent anticancer substances ever found. The debate should be framed another way: what else awaits discovery in the old-growth forests of the Pacific Northwest?

The cutting of primeval forest and other disasters, fueled by the demands of growing human populations, are the overriding threat to biological diversity everywhere. But even the data that led to this conclusion, coming as they do mainly from vertebrates and plants, understate the case. The large, conspicuous organisms are the ones most susceptible to rifle shots, to overkill and the introduction of competing organisms. They are of the greatest immediate importance to man and receive the greater part of his malign attention. People hunt deer and pigeons rather than sowbugs and spiders. They cut roads into a forest to harvest Douglas fir, not mosses and fungi.

Not many habitats in the world covering a kilometer contain fewer than a thousand species of plants and animals. Patches of rain forest and coral reef harbor tens of thousands of species, even after they have declined to a remnant of the original wilderness. But when the *entire* habitat is destroyed, almost all of the species are destroyed. Not just eagles and pandas disappear but also the smallest, still uncensused invertebrates, algae, and fungi, the invisible players that make up the foundation of the ecosystem. Conservationists now generally recognize the difference between rifle shots and holocausts. They place emphasis on the preservation of entire habitats and not only the charismatic species within them. They are uncomfortably aware that the last surviving herd of Javan rhinoceros cannot be saved if the remnant woodland in which they live is cleared, that harpy eagles require every scrap of rain forest around them that can be spared from the chainsaw. The relationship is reciprocal: when star species like rhinoceros and eagles are protected, they serve as umbrellas for all the life around them.

—Edward O. Wilson, *The Diversity of Life*

Even though conservation can be an emotional topic, Professor Wilson appeals to reason. His voice is calm, logical, and confident. A reader may well be convinced that he has authority and reason on his side.

To say that an argument is based on logical reasoning, however, is not to say that the argument is necessarily "right." Two opponents can argue opposite sides of a complex issue, each using logical reasoning in support of his or her position. For example, a proponent of logging in the forests that Edward O. Wilson is seeking to protect could develop an argument based on the economic consequences to the logging industry and to the people and communities that rely on it for their livelihoods. A reader would have to weigh the arguments of both side in deciding which, on balance, has made the more persuasive case.

BALANCED, CREDIBLE ARGUMENT

Both the creators of the ads and the scientist who wrote the piece on species extinction have undoubtedly succeeded in making at least some people see things their way—in the first case, primarily through an appeal to emotion, and in the other case, primarily through reasoned argument. Most serious argumentative writing uses some of both; it relies on sound reasoning (sometimes called *logos)*, but it also recognizes that our minds are more than calculating machines, that they respond to emotional appeals *(pathos)* as well. Consequently, classical rhetoricians understood that effective arguments rely on appeals of both kinds.

The focus of this chapter is somewhere between the extremes of logic and emotion, on the kind of persuasive essays you will read and write in your college courses. In college reading you will analyze the strategies and tactics of arguments, and in your writing you will take positions on topics that are open to debate. You will be required to support your ideas by assembling evidence based on your own logic and experience and on the logic and experience of others. In doing so, you will need to deal with those who disagree with you by noting the strengths and weaknesses of their positions. And throughout, you will want to sound like a person whom readers can believe and trust.

This introduces the third element of argumentation—*ethos* or *persona.* Writers use ethical appeals to persuade the reader by projecting an image of credibility and trustworthiness. This credibility must be earned. It is very difficult to convince someone whom you have alienated through shoddy research, arrogance, or bad writing. As Aristotle pointed out long ago, the persona or personality that the writer projects matters at least as much as the substance and validity of the argument. Readers have to trust you before they will accept your claims. You can inspire trust only by being a careful thinker and writer. For intelligent readers, the credibility of the writer is crucial.

But even if you are reasonable and well prepared, your argument still may not change the minds of those who have strong psychological, social, political, or religious reasons for believing the way they do. After all, the scientific evidence for the dangers of cigarette smoking is impressive, yet millions continue to puff their health away. Even though the surgeon general seems to have won the debate over the hazards of smoking, logic is still not enough to persuade legions of smokers. Atheists and believers rarely change their minds in debates with each other, and sports fans seldom agree with the referee when a close call goes against their team. The old warning not to argue about religion, politics, and sports is sound advice. Apparently there is little hope of changing the minds of those with an emotional commitment to a different outlook. But among open-minded, reasonable people searching for the truth, there are innumerable ideas open to debate. In fact, without intellectual dispute, the life of the mind would be greatly impoverished.

 INFORMAL ANALYSIS OF ARGUMENTS

Intelligent readers try to be on the lookout for false promises and manipulative language in advertisements. It is usually easy enough to see what advertisers are up to. But it is not always easy to see through questionable arguments that appear to be logical. That takes more concentration and more time. In college classrooms professors and students continually put forth their ideas and positions on a wide variety of topics. Textbooks too are full of arguments, usually sound—but not always. Unless you want to be the victim of half-baked ideas and sloppy thinking, you must develop your skills as a reader of arguments. One reasonable tactic in analyzing the soundness of an argument is to take it apart, dividing it into its component elements. Doing this makes the analysis manageable.

Most arguments can be considered in terms of five elements. By asking questions about these, you can get to the heart of an argument:

• *Purpose:* What *audience* does the writer have in mind; that is, whom is the writer trying to persuade? What is the author's reason for wanting to persuade those people? What might their position be on this issue?

• *Thesis* (sometimes called an *assertion* or *proposition*): What is the main idea that the writer is trying to persuade the reader to accept or act upon? Is the writer's position direct and clear? Is the thesis presented as the only reasonable position?

• *Evidence:* What kinds of information does the writer cite to support the thesis? What specific arguments does the author present? Is the evidence sound; that is, is it authoritative, believable, and sufficient? Does it rely on logic or emotion? How is the evidence arranged? Does it convince you?

• *Refutation:* Are the positions of opposing sides presented fairly? Would the opposing sides agree with the writer's understanding of their position? Does the writer show the opposing arguments to be invalid? Are there opposing arguments that the writer has overlooked?

- *Persona:* What is the writer's attitude? Is it hostile, cheerful, irate, reasonable, sarcastic? Does the writer sound believable? Is the writer obviously biased or arguing from a narrow perspective? Does the language used add to the credibility of the author, or is it too offensive or aggressive? Do you trust this person to be fair and open-minded?

Questions in these five areas can be applied to any written argument, and they offer a valuable way of analyzing the writer's methods and the effectiveness of her presentation. If you are interested in exploring your own ideas about a passage you are reading, your analysis does not need to be a formal paper. You can answer these questions in informal notes or freewriting.

As an example of analysis of an argument, let us look at an editorial by Jonathan Alter, an author whose writing has appeared in several national news and opinion magazines.

Cop-Out on Class

Why Private Schools Are Today's Draft Deferments

Jonathan Alter

I'm a part of the so-called overclass—and so are my bosses and many of my colleagues at *Newsweek* and elsewhere in the national media. There's no point in denying it. Whether by birth, effort, ability, luck or some combination, we are more successful and have more options than most Americans, and that inevitably pulls us away from the lives they lead. Neither eating pork rinds (George Bush) nor boasting of humble origins (Bill Clinton) can erase that fact for politicians any more than it can for the rest of the overprivileged. The object should be to achieve consciousness of class, then work hard to make the divisions it creates smaller instead of larger.   **1**

Until the 1970s, race was the rage in public debate. Class remained almost a secret—discussed in private and delineated by taste but subsumed in the assumption growing out of World War II that everyone except the very rich and the very poor was part of the great American Middle.   **2**

Exposing the existence of an overclass began in places like *The Washington Monthly,* a little political magazine. One day in 1970 the wife of the editor, Charlie Peters, was in a bookstore and overheard a hip-looking young man discussing the Vietnam draft. *"Let those hillbillies go get shot,"* he said. When Beth Peters told her husband about the comment, Charlie turned the line into a cause: to convey to American elites the emergence of an unthinking and dangerous class bias in their ranks. Working-class Americans knew that Vietnam, unlike earlier wars in this century, had become a rich man's war and a poor boy's fight. But the people who ran the country hadn't yet faced up to the price of that division.   **3**

Five years later, a young *Washington Monthly* editor named James Fallows drove home the point by graphically describing his feelings of guilt after he starved himself at Harvard in order to flunk the physical for the draft. The widely reprinted article, entitled "What Did You Do in the Class War, Daddy?" angered many veterans, but it kicked off some serious soul-searching among baby boomers about their anti-military, anti-blue-collar bias.   **4**

Unfortunately, the chasm remained. I was too young for Vietnam (and never enlisted). But by the time I joined *The Washington Monthly* in 1981, my generation   **5** was beginning to face its own less bloody yet no less serious class issue: public education. To deny the existence of a class problem in the United States is to ignore the flight from public schools by perpetually anxious, upwardly mobile parents trying to cover their bets on their children's future.

6   I know the feeling, as my parents did before me. Starting in kindergarten, I attended the finest, most diverse private schools and have good memories of them. Yet the fact remains that private schools stand apart from society. They can compensate for that apartness with scholarships and good works but never fully bridge the gap from what America, in its Jeffersonian ideal, is supposed to be. I heard recently that at the tony St. Albans School in Washington, D.C.—alma mater of Vice President Gore—some teachers will tell a badly behaving student that if he doesn't shape up he may have to ship out to public school. They make it sound almost like going to Vietnam.

7   My wife and I have chosen public schools for our children in part because of the eagerness with which other parents we know are abandoning them. Instead of organizing to fix the public schools, they nearly bankrupt themselves escaping, often without even personal visits to see whether their assumptions might be wrong. Here's where race comes in. When they say "bad" they usually mean "black," even if they won't admit it. The result is often overclass children who aren't educated in a larger sense—who don't know their own community and country. They are what my wife calls "underdeprived" kids. They think the world owes them a nice vacation. I know. When I was 12, I was like that, too.

8   **Stay and fight:** Does this mean our three children will never go to private school? No. Children should not have to sacrifice their education to their parents' principles. If the public schools in our area fail—either generally or for our particular children—we'll be gone. But in the meantime we should stay awhile and fight—for high standards, for choice and for accountability. (Beyond safety, a great advantage of private schools is that they can more easily fire bad teachers and administrators.) The single biggest reason for the decline of American public education is that so many capable and committed parents have opted out. That in itself is a bad lesson for their children.

9   Even if they don't send their kids to public schools, successful people should invest time there. Call it the case for Overclass Hypocrisy. "If you feel the public schools can't be changed in the time your kids are that age," says Charlie Peters, "you should take on an extra burden to make sure that the next parents coming along don't have that excuse." My own parents anticipated that point. After putting their children through private school, they now volunteer in Chicago's inner-city public schools.

10   To really break down class divisions, we need a draft that would require every young person to serve either in the military or in the community. John F. Kennedy went to private schools, but he shared a PT boat during World War II with a mechanic and a fisherman. That doesn't happen much today. While some overclass parents make a commendable effort to see that their children meet people from different backgrounds, this risks being just another résumé entry. And many others actually believe that it is supremely important to introduce their children to more People Like Us—to create social shelters instead of real communities.

11   Ambition for yourself and for your kids is good; it's what makes the country go. But what really matters is how you view the rungs below, and how you use all of the extra choices you have for a purpose broader than getting into Princeton. The best answer to American elites is not to bash them or indulge in reverse snobbery. It's to pull them (us) into the great work of the country.

The following is an example of how the questions on pages 404–05 could be used to analyze Jonathan Alter's argument. The responses are written as brief, informal notes, developed extemporaneously:

Purpose: Alter asks well-to-do or upwardly mobile parents to reexamine their beliefs about civic responsibility. He undermines one easy rationalization for shunning public schools: the argument that children should be provided the best education their parents can afford. Alter wants his readers to recognize a civic duty at least equally as important as the interests of individual children.

Thesis: The closest thing to an explicitly stated thesis comes in ¶8, where Alter says that privileged Americans with school-aged children "should stay awhile and fight—for high standards, for choice and for accountability." He goes on to assert that not doing so "is a bad lesson for . . . children."

Evidence: Of course, Alter bases much of his argument on personal experience, both as a student and as a parent. However, he also makes a number of references to current events and recent history, including anecdotal details about Presidents Bush and Clinton, a summary of recent public debates regarding race and class, and references to the role played by one influential journal of opinion (*The Washington Monthly*) and its editor (Charles Peters). Finally, he demonstrates knowledge of American history through references to the Jeffersonian ideal, the social aftermath of World War II, President Kennedy, and Vietnam.

Refutation: Alter acknowledges the appeal of private education (¶6), noting that he himself has enjoyed its benefits. In ¶8 he anticipates the argument that he and his wife are sacrificing the welfare of their children in order to make a political statement. He makes it clear, however, that he is arguing only that public education deserves the benefit of the doubt—that parents should not simply assume that it is necessarily substandard. In his last paragraph, Alter also anticipates and refutes the argument that he is disparaging ambition and competitiveness.

Persona: Alter seems at pains to avoid the perception that he is a liberal elitist. While he does not claim working-class heritage, nor does he offer to speak for people less privileged than he, Alter makes an effort to see things from the point of view of others (especially in ¶s 3 and 4). He also tries to present himself as a patriotic American through references to such widely admired heroes as Thomas Jefferson and John Kennedy.

Informal Analysis of Argument   EXERCISES

1. Two different approaches to argumentation are *Aristotelian* and *Rogerian,* named for the classical philosopher and rhetorician Aristotle and the modern humanist psychologist Carl Rogers.

    In using the Aristotelian style you try to impress the reader, citing authorities and giving overwhelming evidence. You diminish and silence the opposition by creating an irrefutable case. You project the sense that you are right and all reasonable people will agree with you. You win; the opposition loses.

    A Rogerian approach tries to listen to the opposition to see where they are coming from, what their values and assumptions are. In this view of argument, one side does not have to be all wrong; there can be several plausible positions. Typically, you try to paraphrase your opponents' views in a way that they can agree with. You try to engage in dialogue, usually settling for a partial solution.

You try to develop mutual respect, not achieve victory. In Rogerian argument, the writer assumes there are many truths. The Aristotelian approach assumes there is only one.

a. What elements of each appeal can you find in Jonathan Alter's essay?

b. What would you change in Alter's essay to make it more Rogerian or more Aristotelian?

2. You are now ready to analyze an argument yourself. Keeping in mind the previous example, read the following editorial by Donald Kaul, a writer for the *Des Moines Register* whose syndicated column appears in other newspapers across the United States. After reading the editorial, respond to the questions on pages 404–05, which concern the five elements of argument.

We Can't Drive Like Germans

Donald Kaul

I've been studying the letters-to-the-editor columns in newspapers recently, searching for folk wisdom, and I've arrived at this conclusion:

When it comes to speed limits, about half of all Americans are funny in the head.

Not totally deranged, you understand—not like they are about guns—just a little nutsy.

I say that with no sense of superiority; I happen to be a little batty on the subject of fast cars myself. I like to drive at high speeds. It's one of the few vices left to me.

I certainly would not defend the practice, however, nor argue that it is without cost.

Not so the people who write letters to editors. Take this gem, from a recent Midwestern paper: "I'd like to see at least 75 mph. I'd like to see us get into the future here and give some rights back to the citizens, please. Seventy-five or higher."

Or this one: "The speed limit should be eliminated on all roads on days when the weather is good and the roads are in good condition. On days when the weather is bad on a certain road, the speed limit on that road should be 80 mph."

Is that not breathtaking stupidity? Either that or the writer is an undertaker, trying to generate business.

Some of the approaches were more reasonable, of course. Like this one: "I don't think there should be any speed limit. The people will find their own speed limit and it will generally fall within reasonable amounts, just like what the German experience has proven."

Ah, yes, the German experience. It is true that Germany does not have a speed limit on its fastest highways—autobahns, they call them—but it is also true they have horrendous accidents on them.

And this despite the fact that German cars are, for the most part, much better able than American cars to handle high speeds. And Germans are, by nature, a law-abiding people who stay in their own lanes (if you don't count World Wars I and II).

Germany also has a stringent car inspection system that ensures that the cars going 120 mph are at least in good working order.

Still they have terrible accidents.

It's true that people, left to their own devices, will find their own speed limit. Basically, it will be one of these: fast, faster or dead.

And I haven't even mentioned the environmental impact of the faster speeds, not only in increased fuel consumption but in increased motor emissions. The immense Black Forest in Germany is being killed off by highballing German drivers.

I don't get it. Half the population, and all the conservatives, are up in arms because the president has committed American troops to a noble but dangerous mission overseas.

Not one American life should be lost so others might live, the critics in Congress say.

But mention that a 10-mile rise in speed limits will cost thousands of lives a year and they shrug.

The more shameless of them will even produce studies to show that higher speeds don't result in highway deaths, which is like saying you're as likely to survive a fall from a 10-story building as from a garage roof.

These critics, for the most part, also take a completely cavalier attitude toward the carnage produced by our gun laws (or lack of them) and don't even admit that tobacco kills or that environmental laws save lives.

As far as conservatives are concerned, if you're not a solider you're on your own.

If we raise the speed limits, we are going to have a lot of 40-mph drivers in 60-mph cars traveling at 80 mph. That equation wins you a ride in a hearse—one way.

I can live with a higher speed limit. No, wait—let me rephrase that.

I have a car that is built (by Germans) for high speeds and there is a part of me that would like to test its limits. That is the high school part of me.

The part that went to college, however, knows that is a dumb, dumb idea.

We are a nation of rotten drivers. The least we can do is drive badly at low speeds.

 ## WRITING A CRITIQUE OF AN ARGUMENT

As you probably noticed in the previous section, analyzing another writer's arguments is an effective way to understand how ideas are put together. But it can also help you analyze and clarify your own positions on an issue and can provide you with the motivation and ideas to write arguments of your own. All good *writers* of arguments must first be good *readers* of arguments.

Before writing an argument, it is useful to engage in a serious kind of reading analysis—composing a *critique.* A critique is a more formal and objective look at an argument than the informal, subjective analysis described in the previous section, but it does include your own opinions. You begin a critique by answering the same questions, but you try to move beyond these personal responses, becoming more analytical, more detached. After your initial reaction, you try to stand back and look carefully at what the writer has said. Above all, you want to be fair in your judgment.

Critiquing does not mean finding fault. It means weighing the good parts against the bad, arriving at a balanced view. Of course, it might turn out that a particular argument is, in your judgment, not very sound. That's fine. All you can do is make a sincere effort to analyze its strengths and weaknesses. Your purpose is first to search for the truth and then to write a clearly organized evaluation of the writer's whole argument. Not only does critiquing arguments help you see more clearly what writers are saying; it also directly prepares you to write competent and cogent arguments yourself.

The following procedure can be used whenever you write a critique of an argument. Notice how the dialogue that develops between you and the writer can lead naturally into a written critique.

Procedure for Writing a Critique

Preparation

1. Read the passage twice. The second time read with a pencil, underlining important ideas and writing comments in the margin.

2. Respond to the passage subjectively. Freewrite for five minutes, recording any personal response you have: agreement, anger, bewilderment, thoughtfulness, or any other reaction.

3. Respond objectively. Write a brief summary of the passage. Do not insert any of your own ideas.

Analysis

Think through your analysis before writing by responding informally to the questions on pages 404–05. Ask questions about these five elements:

1. Purpose
2. Thesis
3. Evidence
4. Refutation
5. Persona

Writing the Critique

1. Begin the first paragraph with a brief objective summary of the argument and with a thesis statement that presents your judgment of the reading.

2. Support your thesis by analyzing the important evidence presented in the passage.

3. Comment on any of the five elements in your analysis that you consider noteworthy.

Revision

Reread and edit your paper. Ask others to read it. Consider their suggestions as you revise it. Prepare your polished draft and proofread the computer-printed (or typed) copy with care.

To see how you can develop a critique by following this procedure, read the following article from the *New York Times* by Bernard Goldberg, an alumnus of Rutgers University who opposes the development of a major varsity football program at his alma mater. Then observe how one writer has used the suggested sequence to critique Goldberg's argument.

Dear Rutgers: Don't Become a Factory
A Case against the Quest to Hit It Big in Football
Bernard Goldberg

1   Selling your soul is very serious business, so Francis L. Lawrence, the president of Rutgers University, might want to think long and hard before he tries to turn

Rutgers into a football powerhouse. Be assured, it can be done. And also be assured it may not be worth what it will cost.

I was a student at Rutgers in the 1960's and graduated with a degree in journalism. I have been a correspondent with CBS News for more than 20 years. And while I am not a sports reporter, I have seen what big-time college sports programs can do to a university. Yes, they bring in money—lots of it! But the need to win may very well turn Rutgers into a third-rate school with a first-rate football team. **2**

Lawrence fired the head football coach, Doug Graber, on Nov. 27 because Rutgers had just two winning seasons out of six. The university president is impatient, we are told, for a winning program. Who's not for winning? Who's not for packed stadiums and national rankings? It's great when students and alumni can sit side by side and cheer for their team. So much for Norman Rockwell's America. But is Lawrence prepared for the dark side of big-time college sports? **3**

First, there is a danger Rutgers will accept football players into the university who do not belong at the school. Forgive the political incorrectness of those words, but not everyone "belongs" at Rutgers. News accounts say Lawrence is considering adding a "general studies" curriculum to help the eligibility of players of lesser academic standing. Many of these "student-athletes" will enroll for just one reason: to play football. **4**

They will not be a part of the university; they will be apart from it. They will be gladiators: Play for us, bring us money and we will make believe you're getting an education. We will exploit you and you can exploit us. We will take care of you—until your eligibility runs out. If you're not in the pros by then, it was nice knowing you. **5**

When I did a story about the North Carolina State University basketball team (at the time coached by Jim Valvano, a classmate of mine at Rutgers), I interviewed players who took courses called "Introduction to Recreation" and "Leisure Alternatives." Does President Lawrence plan to offer classes like that for "student athletes" who will have to get minimal grades to stay eligible? **6**

And when the new coach understands that his job—his very livelihood—depends on winning, will he do just about anything he has to do to win? There's a good chance he will convince President Lawrence or one of his deans that the kid with rock-bottom Scholastic Assessment Test scores should be admitted "to give him a chance at a better life." **7**

At first, university officials may question that. But not for long. Not when some other school takes him in and he winds up rushing for 150 yards against Rutgers. The coach's argument that "this kid is better off in our structured program than he is on the street" will not only sound good to President Lawrence, it will make him feel like a real humanitarian when he says, "Sure, let's take him into the Rutgers family." **8**

What Lawrence really will be saying is: "If this kid can help us win, if he can get us to a bowl, if he can bring us money, I want him. End of discussion." **9**

And in the process he will be turning a proud university into a field house, into a gymnasium, into a football factory. It doesn't have to be that way, of course, but that depends on just how important winning is to him. **10**

There is no logical reason why one can't have a first-rate sports program and a first-rate university. Problem is, it doesn't usually work out that way. **11**

Have you ever wondered why Harvard or Yale or Princeton doesn't play for the national championship each year? Have you ever wondered why it's so often one of those schools known more for its football team than absolutely anything else? **12**

The answer is simple: The football factories are willing to do what it takes to win. They're willing to look the other way when boosters give cars to star players; **13** they're willing to enroll students with "lesser academic standing"; they're willing to cajole professors into passing kids who by any rational standard should flunk; in short, they're willing to put their morals on hold any time morality interferes with winning.

14   Harvard and Yale and Princeton are not willing to do whatever it takes to win. I'm sure President Lawrence would like to have both—a great team and a great university. So would we all. It could happen, but the odds are it won't, the occasional exception of a Northwestern or Stanford notwithstanding.

15   Lawrence wants his football team to be ranked in the top 10. He thinks that will bring prestige to the school. I want Rutgers to be ranked in the top 10 of academic institutions. That would really bring prestige to the university. Spend more time trying to recruit great teachers and great students and less time recruiting great running backs and we'll all be better off.

16   And while we're on the subject: Why does the Rutgers women's basketball coach earn between $150,000 and $300,000 a year? Do any of the science teachers make that kind of money? How about the English and history professors? I guess it's the law of supply and demand: Good coaches are hard to come by; good teachers are a dime a dozen.

17   Selling your soul, Mr. President, indeed is serious business, but I confess it is not your soul I worry about. It is the soul of Rutgers that has me so concerned.

Here is a freewritten response to Bernard Goldberg's article:

First response: freewriting

Goldberg seems convinced that a big-time football program will hurt the academic reputation of Rutgers. Since I'm a football fan and have taken classes with some varsity athletes (admittedly none of them football players), I tend to resist this idea—or at least Goldberg's complete certainty about it. Is he suggesting that football players aren't as bright as other athletes? Doesn't Rutgers already compete aggressively in other sports like basketball? Maybe it's the violence of contact sports that makes a difference to Goldberg. His reference to gladiators seems to suggest that, and, of course, some college football players do sustain serious injuries that affect them for the rest of their lives. On the other hand, soccer and hockey are also violent, and I get the impression that Goldberg might not have a problem with those sports, since they're all played at Harvard, Yale, and Princeton. Goldberg's references to those other universities makes me think he's a little status-conscious.

This freewriting explores an initial, subjective response. The following objective summary provides perspective:

An objective summary

Bernard Goldberg argues that while students and alumni may enjoy the excitement that comes with a major national football program, the academic reputation of Rutgers will suffer if one is introduced there. He predicts that coaches will be under so much pressure to win that they will persuade administrators to admit inferior or underprepared student athletes who will enroll in a watered-down curriculum. Although they may justify these decisions on altruistic grounds (giving disadvantaged high-school graduates a chance), the real motive will be a cynical commitment to winning football games. Consequently, student athletes will be exploited while the university's reputation suffers. Goldberg believes that supporting a strong football program is incompatible with maintaining a prestigious academic tradition.

An informal analysis of the article helps prepare the writer to draft a formal critique:

Informal
analysis

Purpose: Goldberg hopes to influence administrators at Rutgers, partly through a direct appeal to reason and ethical values but also by applying public pressure. Since the *New York Times* is a national newspaper, this article might arouse some opposition among students and alumni of Rutgers, but also place the university in an unflattering light.

Thesis: The academic reputation of Rutgers University will suffer if the administration follows through on its desire to build a major varsity football program.

Evidence: Goldberg is responding to recent news stories about the firing of a coach whose teams didn't win consistently and about a proposal to establish a "general studies" curriculum for some athletes. Though he is careful to note that he is not a sports journalist, he apparently did some investigative reporting into a scandal involving the basketball program at North Carolina State University during the 1980s. Taking what he observed from that scandal, he forecasts a series of events that would compromise academic standards and threaten the integrity of Rutgers. He ends his article by noting that the universities most respected for their academic programs do not generally promote football.

Refutation: Goldberg concedes at the outset that a big-time football program will bring in money and stimulate excitement, but he says that both will come at great cost. In ¶4, he seems to anticipate accusations of elitism, when he asks readers to forgive "the political incorrectness" of stating that some students aren't academically gifted enough to deserve admission into Rutgers. He tries to disarm those accusations in the following paragraph by arguing that underprepared athletes would be isolated and exploited. Finally, in ¶s 11–14, Goldberg refutes the inevitable argument that a university can be strong in both football and academics; he even cites two notable examples.

Persona: Goldberg tries to present himself as a writer unafraid to take an unpopular stance or at least to discuss in very frank terms some of the unpleasant results of starting a major football program. By making enthusiasm for football seem a naively romantic vision ("Norman Rockwell's America"), he is able to present himself as a hard-headed realist.

Having developed some ideas, the writer is ready to draft her critique. Notice that she begins objectively with a summary and explanation of Goldberg's argument, then examines its persuasiveness, and finally expresses some reservations and disagreement.

A formal
critique

Bernard Goldberg, a broadcast journalist who graduated from Rutgers University in the 1960s, has written an appeal to the administrative officers of his alma mater. Disturbed by reports that the president of Rutgers wants to upgrade the university's football program, Goldberg warns that doing so will lower academic standards and may lead to ethical abuses that would tarnish the university's reputation. While Goldberg may have reason to worry about the impact of such an important change on a school with a distinguished history, he exaggerates the conflict between athletics and academic ideals.

Goldberg is convinced that once a nationally competitive football program is in place, the desire to win at any cost becomes irresistible. He predicts that Rutgers will admit athletes who are academically unqualified and finds evidence for such fears in reports that a special "general studies" curriculum is under consideration. If Rutgers pursues this plan, it will compromise standards and also exploit student athletes. Though conceding that a strong academic tradition might be maintained alongside a major sports program, Goldberg can name only two institutions that have succeeded at this.

Goldberg is undoubtedly right in asserting that the main priority of any university ought to be academic and in noting that a number of schools with big football programs seem to have lost sight of this at times. Recent reports have brought to light flagrant misconduct by coaches, athletes, alumni, and other boosters. And, as Goldberg notes, the disparity between the salaries of some coaches and those of the average faculty member raises troubling questions. He is also correct in observing that, on the whole, the five or six most prestigious American universities invest little in their football programs.

On the other hand, I question Goldberg's assumption that those who support winning football teams either wallow in a sentimentalized "Norman Rockwell" image of sports or try to exploit that image cynically. On the contrary, athletic violations disturb most alumni, and the resulting penalties show how the NCAA investigates abuse and tries to enforce rules. Furthermore, not all reports of abuse involve football: the author's reference to the basketball scandal at North Carolina State shows that.

Perhaps the weakest link in Goldberg's argument is his attempt to equate Rutgers, a multicampus public university, with the most elite members of the Ivy League. Private universities like Harvard, Yale, and Princeton are relatively free to set high admissions standards and to apply them uniformly. But when every citizen of New Jersey pays taxes to support higher education, it is less easy to say that "not everyone 'belongs' at Rutgers." When Goldberg concedes that there is "the occasional exception" to his contention that big-time sports compromises academics, the only examples he cites are Northwestern and Stanford, also highly selective private universities. What about Michigan, North Carolina, and Virginia, all distinguished state universities with top-ranked teams in football, basketball, or both?

Wanting to protect the academic integrity of one's alma mater is commendable, and the alumni and administrators of Rutgers would be unwise to brush aside Bernard Goldberg's concerns. Nevertheless, I believe Goldberg has weakened his case by exaggerating the conflict between athletics and academics and by trying to equate Rutgers with the most elite private universities in the United States.

You may not agree with this critique. The writer attempted to weigh the strengths and weaknesses of Goldberg's argument, but she was alienated by the flaws she saw in its reasoning. Any analysis of an argument should be rigorous and balanced, but in writing a critique, you should be clear about your own ideas. Any issue worth debating has more than one side, and not everyone will take the same position. Another reader might find Goldberg's argument valid and consider this critique too harsh. Critiquing an argument combines both objective and subjective judgments. You might want to try your own critique of Goldberg's essay.

EXERCISES | ## Writing a Critique of an Argument

1. How successful is this critique of Bernard Goldberg's argument? Has the writer been fair in her judgments? Are her arguments reasonable? Did she miss something you would have commented on?

   Which writer do you find more convincing, Goldberg or the author of the critique? Is there a part of each writer's position that makes sense to you? How could each be made more persuasive?

2. Now it is your turn. Use the procedures developed in this section to arrive at a polished written critique of the following essay by Fraser Sherman, a freelance writer who lives in Florida. Use your own ideas to evaluate the author's arguments. Remember that a critique is not necessarily an attack on another person's argument; you may well find yourself in agreement with those you critique. Your critique should discuss whatever successes and flaws you find in the text you are analyzing.

After the Rains Came

If We Live in a Disaster-Prone Area,
We Should Be Prepared for the Cost of Damaged Property

Fraser Sherman

The hurricane season is officially over. I didn't enjoy it. In October Hurricane Opal hit Okaloosa County, Fla., where I live. Sitting in what I thought would be a safe shelter and listening to Weather Channel staffers toss out phrases like "category 5 hurricane" and "Not since Hurricane Camille . . ." left me terrified for a longer period than I'd ever been before.

As it turned out, we got lucky. Although the South took $3 billion in damages, that's nothing compared with what could have been if the hurricane had stayed a category 5. Instead, the eye expanded before Opal made landfall, slowing her down to a category 3. My house and those of my close friends remained unscathed, but if Opal had stayed a 5, I doubt I would be here to write this.

"Lucky," in this context, still hurts. Okaloosa County alone took more than $50 million in damages. The Federal Emergency Management Agency (FEMA) and other government agencies promptly set up local headquarters and began paying out relief: money to rebuild and repair homes, unemployment insurance for those whose jobs were gone (and couldn't receive state payments), payouts for those who participate in the state's wind-damage-insurance and the federal flood-insurance program, low-interest loans for businesses without operating funds.

Is this really such a good idea? We residents of Florida—and the rest of the Gulf Coast—made a conscious decision to live in a hazardous location. Hurricanes happen here (Opal was my second this year) as surely as earthquakes in Los Angeles, or crime in New York and Miami. Ft. Walton Beach, Destin and the other local cities offer beautiful weather, gorgeous beaches and opportunities to fish. But as 1995 reminded us, hurricanes come with the package, sooner or later. Guaranteed.

If we choose to take the risk of living here, why should the government bail us out when the inevitable happens? Should a government that talks about ending welfare as we know it compensate people for putting themselves in the path of a hurricane?

It's not that I like the idea of my neighbors' being unable to rebuild, or of businesses unable to reopen. Lord knows, if I lost my personal property or my home, I'd be right there asking for help. But that's true of many government programs. If you cut off the money, someone has to go without something, whether it's medicine, prenatal care, a lovely home on a barrier island—or a cinder-block home further inland.

For that reason, I'm almost surprised (but not quite) that so many local homeowners have taken advantage of disaster relief. This is a very conservative community. People talk loudly and a lot about government taking from hardworking Americans to support welfare mothers. Apparently, it's OK for the government to take from hardworking voters living inland to support people who want to live near the beach.

I also hear a lot of angry talk about property rights, and how government has no business placing restrictions on someone, just because he or she owns wetlands, or an endangered species lives on the property. Many of the same grumbling landowners see no contradiction between denying government any say over their land and expecting government to pay so that they can afford to live on it.

The urge to have it both ways isn't unique to northwest Florida. People in Los Angeles know they're going to face the Big One someday, people along the Mississippi know they can expect floods. We're all taking risks and expecting someone else to cover it. Some of us don't even try to minimize the cost.

If you decide to save money by not buying storm shutters, which shield windows from windborne debris, and your house is demolished as a result, you can still collect federal aid. If you choose not to buy flood insurance, FEMA will bail you out one time. After that, you buy or lose future relief. Homeowners save money; taxpayers pick up the tab.

And it's only going to get worse. Florida's a growth state, drawing thousands of new residents every year, as does Los Angeles. The more people move in, the more will want aid next time a disaster strikes.

Am I suggesting cutting off FEMA money, federal flood insurance and Small Business Administration disaster-relief loans completely to all disaster-prone areas? Let those who want to live with the danger take the consequences? I don't have the heart to go that far. Thousands of struggling homeowners would wake up and find their property devalued overnight. Even if they wanted to move, they might not be able to afford it. Military families attached to the nearby base don't move here by choice; should they pay for being stationed in harm's way?

The government is hardly likely to demand that much hardship from millions of voters. I wouldn't, if I called the shots. I've seen hurricane damage up close. I couldn't see people lose homes, property and everything else without using my power to help those in need.

What I am suggesting is that we bite the bullet harder than we have been. Living in Florida (or Los Angeles, or along the Mississippi) shouldn't be financially painless. I've read that Hawaii's homeowner-insurance rates have tripled since 1992's Hurricane Iniki, while the steepest home-insurance hike in Florida since Hurricane Andrew has been 68 percent. If rates rise, private insurers can handle more of the damage—though it's unlikely insurers could cover it all, and they do not cover flood damage.

Some homeowners and developers will have to live with risk. I don't think any workable system will be able to cover everyone in a state like mine. There are flood plains along the gulf where the risk is too high even for federal flood insurance, but some developers who've built there want flood insurance anyway. Sorry, guys—you knew the job was dangerous when you took it.

Opal hurt. So did Erin and Andrew; so will the next one. But there's a limit to what government should do to ease the pain.

 ## WRITING AN ARGUMENTATIVE RESEARCH ESSAY

In writing a critique, you were responding to another writer's argument. You expressed either your agreement or disagreement with the writer—or a little of both. In any case your response could not help but take an argumentative form. Still, you were reacting, not presenting your own original argument. This section will discuss how you can write an argument of your own, perhaps even one that others will want to critique and respond to. In particular it will focus on writing an argumentative essay that is also a research paper—that is, one that uses sources to inform its argument, giving it authority and credibility.

Dozens of books are devoted exclusively to the complexities of argumentative writing. The subject has a long scholarly tradition that goes all the way back to Aristotle's *Rhetoric,* a study of argument that is still used as a text to teach theories and tactics for persuading audiences. The scholarly field of rhetorical argument is valuable, but in this chapter we can delve into only a few basic principles.

Arguments take so many forms—writers can find so many different ways to persuade their readers—that it would be impossible to give you an easy formula for argumentative writing. We can give suggestions, however, and some general advice that you can follow to write effective arguments. Like other types of academic writing, an argumentative research paper can seem intimidating if you have had little experience in writing one before. You will find, nonetheless, that you can argue effectively and persuasively. As you did when you critiqued the arguments of others, you need to pay attention to the principal elements that make up an argument. The following sections discuss important ideas that should be considered whenever you write an argument.

Purpose

The best advice of all is to have a real reason for wanting to persuade others and to keep that goal in mind as you write. Argue about a topic you care about and believe in. Argue because you feel it is important for others to learn the truth. Argue to make the world a better place. Without that commitment, argument becomes an empty exercise, offering little prospect for success or satisfaction from it. If you care about your argument, however, it can be an exciting, important activity—and one at which you are likely to succeed.

Although commitment is important, it is also important to retain an open mind and to be willing to be persuaded yourself when better ideas and new information are presented to you. The purpose of college writing, as we have suggested, is not to win a contest or to wield power; rather, it is to test ideas in a sincere search for truth. To that end, you must be honest and fair, but it is also your duty to present the views you believe in as effectively as you can.

Thesis

Although at times writers of arguments feel they can be most effective if they disguise their actual objectives, as a college writer you should make your thesis clear to your readers. State your point in a sentence or two, early in your paper.

Not every thesis is worth arguing. The thesis you write about should meet the following criteria:

- It should be **controversial.** You should address an idea about which reasonable people can disagree. You would waste your time arguing that pollution is wrong, because reasonable people would be unlikely to dispute that thesis. You could, however, argue for or against outlawing internal-combustion automobiles, because you will find reasonable and informed people on both sides of that controversy.

- It should be **arguable.** Argue a position that is open to objective analysis. It is futile to argue about a matter of purely individual taste, like whether racquetball is a more exciting sport than tennis. You cannot profitably dispute likes and dislikes. But you might argue that "racquetball promotes cardiovascular fitness more effectively than tennis does." Research can examine this question, evidence can be gathered, and readers can draw conclusions based on objective criteria.

- It should be **clearly defined.** Words and phrases like *freedom, law and order, murder,* and *obscenity* may be perfectly clear to you, but friendships and even lives have been lost over different interpretations of "obvious" terms. You may want to argue that "pornography should not be shown on television," but if you do, you will have to make very clear what you mean by pornography and to suggest some reasonable method of testing whether a show is pornographic or not.

Audience

Write your argument with your audience in mind. Who is it that you want to persuade? What people do you expect to be reading your argument? What do your readers expect from you and you from them? Why might they ignore you, and what can you do to avoid that? The tone of your writing, the language you use, and the sophistication of your evidence must all be adjusted to the interests, values, and education of your readers. What might appeal to first-year college students might fail miserably with students in either junior high or graduate school. Because of those differences, arguments must be tailor-made for specific audiences; one size does not fit all.

It is not dishonest to write in different ways for different readers. Sometimes it is important to withhold an idea or reason that you believe but that you know will offend or alienate your readers. Mature people know enough not to speak everything that is on their minds. If diplomats at the United Nations said exactly what they thought of each other, there would be few civilized discussions. You cannot get people even to listen to your argument if you threaten them or make them feel defensive. If you are writing to readers who disagree with you, try to understand their point of view, to view reality from their perspective. Not only will this allow you to examine the issue more fully and clearly, but it will help you present your argument in a way that will be most effective with this audience.

Persona

As a writer of arguments, you must be acutely aware of how you sound to your audience. When you write, you want to project a certain image, one that is appropriate to the situation at hand. You might take on the role of a concerned environmentalist, a crusading member of the student senate, or a frustrated commuter campaigning for additional student parking places. Each of these different personas can be adopted sincerely at various times by the same writer. Being your true self means being flexible and honest.

Regardless of how well thought out and researched your arguments are, you must still appear trustworthy enough to be believed. In order to establish a believable persona, it is important to maintain a reasonable tone. Extreme statements and emotional rhetoric work fine at pep rallies or in sermons to the already converted, but they can repel both those who disagree with you and the undecided. You should resist the temptation to belittle the opposition or to engage in name-calling. Shocking audiences may help the writer feel better, but it rarely presents the writer as balanced and fair. Readers need to feel rapport with the writer before they will alter their opinions.

Evidence

In presenting support for your thesis, you can appeal to your readers' emotions, as most advertising does, or to their reason, as participants in scientific debate strive to do. Argumentative writing often contains both kinds of appeals. What you should avoid, on the one hand, is the kind of emotional appeal that ignores reasoning, aiming only at your readers' fears and insecurities. On the other hand, you should avoid a persona so coldly impersonal that your essay may as well have been written by a computer.

You are the author of your own argument, and the ideas you present are a reflection of your own mind. If you are to win your readers' regard in an argumentative essay, your own voice and thoughts should come through. On the other hand, it is also important to win your readers' trust through the authority of your evidence. Research can help. Not only can sources supply you with support for your thesis, but they can also lend their expert authority to your writing and convince your readers that you have studied the subject carefully enough to be trusted. Library research may be most appropriate when you are arguing about a controversy that has received public attention, such as gun control or drunk-driving laws. Observation, interviews, or questionnaires may be appropriate in researching a local issue or an original proposal, such as your plan to improve food services in the campus cafeteria.

Opposition

Remember that any point worth arguing about will have an opposing point of view. You must admit that in your essay. And you must do so in a way that will be fair to your opponents. People do not cooperate or alter their positions when they feel threatened; they become defensive and rigid. It increases your credibility when you admit that those who differ with you are reasonable people. You should also realize that your readers will think of the counterarguments to your position, and it is good strategy to anticipate their objections and to refute them. Experienced writers do so briefly, since they realize that they don't have to devastate the other side. Let the reader see that you know the issue is complex, and then give a reasonable, brief response to opposing arguments. You will seem more trustworthy if you not only defend your position but also acknowledge the opposing view.

Organization

You can organize your essay in many ways, but you may find the following very general arrangement to be helpful, particularly in your first attempts at argumentative writing:

1. *Introduction:* Provide background information so that your readers are informed about the controversy; then state your thesis.
2. *Evidence:* Offer support for your thesis. (This is the longest part of your essay.)
3. *Opposition:* Acknowledge and refute opposing points of view.
4. *Conclusion:* Draw conclusions from the evidence so as to restate the point of your thesis.

You are now ready to research and write an argumentative essay.

ASSIGNMENT   **Writing an Argumentative Essay**

Write an argumentative essay in support of a thesis that you believe in. It can be about a national controversy, such as mercy killing or nuclear weapons policy; about a local issue, such as your school's new requirements for graduation; or about your own proposals for making the world a better place. Support your thesis with evidence from your own reasoning and research. You can invent a purpose and an audience for your essay if you choose. For example, you can write it in the form of a letter to the college Board of Trustees, petitioning the members to provide greater support of the women's intramural program. Acknowledge your sources with parenthetical notes and provide a list of works cited.

 ## A SAMPLE ARGUMENTATIVE RESEARCH PAPER

Following is an argumentative research essay written by a first-year college student named Patrick Krause. Patrick wrote on the controversial topic of whether legislation should be passed to make English the official national language of the United States. You may not agree with Patrick's conclusions, but notice how he used research to explore ideas and bolster his opinions. The result is a paper with great credibility. As readers, we cannot dismiss Patrick's opinion as uninformed; instead, we note the care he has used to research the topic, and we are obliged to treat his presentation with respect.

Krause 1

Patrick Krause

English 102

Prof. William Atwill

4 March 1996

An Official Language Will <u>Not</u> Unite Us

Last year the courts nullified the outcome of a
referendum in Barrow, Alaska, because the ballot measure
had not been accurately translated into the Inupiat Eskimo
language spoken by a majority of Barrow's voters. With a
better translation in the second election, voters in the
nation's northernmost community, 300 miles above the Arctic
Circle, reversed the results of the previous balloting
("Barrow").

This small triumph for democracy was possible only
because of policies that respect the rights of Eskimos and
other language minorities. However, if proposed "Official
English" legislation is passed into law, the Eskimos of
Barrow would no longer be able to use their language to
vote, even though it has been spoken in America for
thousands of years, long before the first English speakers
arrived.

Although English is indisputably the common language
of the United States, that evident fact has never been
legally codified (Daniels, <u>Not Only</u> vii). Since 1981,
however, efforts have been made to amend the U.S.
Constitution to make English our official national language

The writer begins with an anecdote (see pp. 362–63).

The point of the anecdote serves as the introduction to his thesis.

Krause 2

The writer provides background.

Furthermore, numerous politicians and lobbying organizations have supported the introduction of "Official English" and "English Only" laws at the national, state, and local levels. Some laws and legislative proposals have little more than symbolic value (Dorning and Garza). Others go much farther and would limit or prevent the use of languages other than English in governmental activities (such as the Barrow election), in education, and sometimes even in private business.

The writer states his thesis.

While these efforts might at first seem reasonable and beneficial, they are unnecessary at best; at worst, they would have many negative consequences.

At first glance, arguments in favor of such laws appeal to common sense. The most frequently cited argument is that the laws would promote national unity, which proponents consider threatened by the use of other languages. One prominent organization that lobbies for official-English

The writer presents the opposing viewpoint by directly quoting the opposition.

legislation argues that "a shared language provides a cultural guidepost that we must maintain for the sake of our country's unity, prosperity, and democracy" (U.S. English). This widely held view was echoed in a letter to the New York Times by a naturalized Estonian immigrant, who argued that "a national language law . . . will serve as the glue to hold together our culturally and racially diverse society" (Cannon A28).

Krause 3

The need for a "glue" implies that our nation is in danger of coming apart. Behind the arguments for language laws is the fear that our country is being overwhelmed by immigrants who refuse to speak or learn English. This supposed state of affairs is usually contrasted with a rosier past in which immigrants and their descendants became English speakers far more readily than they do today. For example, former U.S. Senator Walter Huddleston, who offered a resolution in 1984 to make English our official language, expressed that view to a Senate committee considering his proposal:

> For over 200 years, the United States has enjoyed
> the blessing of one primary language that is
> spoken and understood by most of its citizens.
> The previous unquestioned acceptance of the
> language by immigrants from every linguistic and
> cultural background has enabled us to come
> together and prosper as one people. (Qtd. in
> Villanueva 79)

The problem with this version of history is that it is based entirely on myth. The idea that the use of English was once nearly universal in the United States is certainly false. In the 1790 census, for example, German-speaking citizens made up 8.7% of the population, a larger percentage than the Spanish-speakers of today (Crawford 54). In the intervening years, large numbers of non-English-speaking

The writer refutes the opposing argument that he has just presented.

Krause 4

immigrants continued to enter our borders. Yet, according

to linguist Dennis Barron, today fully 97% of the country's

residents speak English, a greater percentage than at any

other time in our nation's history (English-Only 177;

"English" 79).

Still the myth persists that today's immigrants and

their descendants are different from their predecessors.

Because of their numbers, Hispanics are frequently singled

out as a threat to our language and our national unity. For

example, former U.S. Senator S. I. Hayakawa, the sponsor of

an official-English amendment to the U.S. Constitution in

1981, said, "The only people who have any quarrel with the

English language are the Hispanics. . . ." (20). Hayakawa,

who was also a founder of U.S. English, the largest

lobbying organization for official-English laws, claimed

that "large populations of Mexican-Americans, Cubans, and

Puerto Ricans do not speak English and have no intention of

learning" (19) and that there is an "aggressive movement on

the part of Hispanics to reject assimilation and to seek to

maintain--and give official status to--a foreign language

within our borders" (21).

The evidence clearly indicates otherwise. Hispanics

today are just as eager to become English speakers as were

earlier generations of German, Scandinavian, Italian, and

Chinese immigrants. In a nationwide survey in 1985, fully

98% of Hispanic Americans believed it was essential for

Again, the writer quotes the opposition and then refutes their argument.

Krause 5

their children to learn to speak "perfect" English in order to succeed--compared with only 94% of non-Hispanics (Villanueva 83; Daniels, "Roots" 4).

Language researchers have noted a consistent pattern of assimilation among immigrants of all nationalities. In most cases, the use of the native language is widespread among first-generation immigrants, but a rapid shift to bilingualism occurs in the second generation, followed by a third or fourth generation that speaks only English (Citrin 31). My own family is typical of this pattern. My great-grandparents, August and Wilhelmina Krause, migrated from Germany in the 1880s and learned to speak halting English. My grandfather was born here and grew up in a bilingual household fluent in both English and German. My father, a third-generation American, spoke only English until he studied French in high school.

That identical pattern can be seen today among America's Hispanic citizens. A study by the RAND Corporation showed that nearly half the permanent Mexican immigrants in California speak English well, and just one-quarter speak only Spanish. Among the second generation--the children of Mexican immigrants--90% are fluent in English, and in the third generation, more than half speak no Spanish (Halton 91). According to census data, nearly 90% of Latinos over the age of four speak English in their households ('Lectric Law Library).

The writer personalizes his argument by citing examples from his family.

Krause 6

Contrary to the claims of official-English supporters, the dominance of English in America is at no foreseeable risk. Only continued immigration, not a failure to adopt English, causes Spanish to be widely spoken in America. If anything, the rate at which Hispanics are assimilating indicates that the long-term survival of the Spanish language in our country is much more uncertain than that of English. This rapid assimilation has caused writer Victor Villanueva, Jr., a third-generation American, to regret that he has lost his Spanish fluency and that his younger sister "cannot even say 'no' in Spanish, or so [his] mother jokes, a sadness in her voice" (83).

The writer shows the effects on individuals to make the statistical information he has cited more immediate to his readers.

Economic and social factors will continue to play a far greater part than laws in keeping the United States an English-speaking nation. Writing in <u>The Christian Century</u>, Mark R. Halton argues that "English does not need to be legislated the official language; gentler forces than those proposed by English-only proponents will produce that end" (92). Simply put, Americans of all backgrounds will continue to speak and learn English not because of laws but because they see that doing so is clearly in their interest.

Far from being the unifying factor that proponents claim, "Official English" and "English Only" laws create divisions by fostering bigotry, mistrust, and discrimination. Certainly, the remarks of some supporters have a nasty anti-Hispanic flavor. During the 1988

Krause 7

campaign to make English the official language of Arizona, reporters uncovered a memo written by John Tanton, the Michigan eye doctor who cofounded U.S. English with Senator Hayakawa. In the memo, Tanton criticized Hispanics for "low educability," a tradition of bribes, and a high birthrate, which he proposed to counteract with forced sterilization. In protest, two prominent members of the Board of Directors of U.S. English, Reagan official Linda Chavez and television journalist Walter Cronkite, resigned from the organization (Draper and Jimenez 14).

Law professor James Harrington cites two recent cases of bigotry against Spanish speakers among the judiciary. In one, a Texas Court of Criminal Appeals ruled that a judge was justified in jailing a man rather than granting him probation, because he spoke only Spanish. In the other, Amarillo District Judge Samuel Kiser accused a woman of child abuse because she spoke to her five-year-old daughter only in Spanish, "relegating her to the position of housemaid" and causing her to be "ignorant." The girl, whose father speaks to her in English, lives in a loving household, and her two older sisters do well in school. Harrington asks, "Since when is a person who speaks two languages 'ignorant'?"

When language legislation is enacted, the result can be discrimination and division, rather than the unity that its supporters claim. The Chicago Tribune reported that,

The writer cites authorities in support of his position.

Krause 8

after English was made Colorado's official language in
1988, some Anglo children told Hispanic children that they
were "unconstitutional," a school bus driver forbade
children to speak Spanish on his bus, and a restaurant
worker was fired for translating a menu item into Spanish
for a South American customer (Barron, English-Only 20).

The fervor for language legislation has led to the
adoption of English-only laws that affect not just government
but private activities as well. For example, a law passed
in Monterey Park, California, made it illegal for businesses
to display storefront signs written only in Chinese. Such
laws infringe against free speech, and, to its credit, U.S.
English opposed this law and other restrictive language
laws that affect activities outside of government (U.S.
English).

The false assumptions, bigotry, and discriminatory
legislation that characterize the current debate about
official English are nothing new in American history. In
1790, when German speakers made up fully a third of the
residents of Pennsylvania, Benjamin Franklin displayed a
surprising ignorance when he complained of dark-skinned
Germans who "will never adopt our Language or Customs, any
more than they can acquire our Complexion." He even warned
that Pennsylvania would soon seem like a foreign country to
English-speakers (Lang 28-29).

The writer
finds support
for his argu-
ments in the
lessons of
history.

Krause 9

Antiforeign hysteria was at its height in the years during and following World War I. A 1919 Nebraska law to eradicate German in the state made it illegal to teach any foreign language before the tenth grade. Robert Meyer, a teacher in a Lutheran school, was convicted and fined because "between the hour of 1 and 1:30 on May 25, 1920," he read a German Bible story to a ten-year-old boy. The lesson was part of the school's program to enable English-speaking children to worship with their German-speaking parents (Barron, English-Only 145). Louisiana's 1921 constitution made it illegal for anyone to speak French on public school grounds, and older Cajuns still remember having to kneel on hard grains of rice or corn as punishment for speaking their language (Dorning and Garza).

The effect of such laws, both today and in the past, is not to unify but to divide and to exclude. University of Texas professor Rodolfo de la Garza finds them an affront to Hispanic Americans: "There is no opposition to learning English. The problem is that many Hispanics have been punished for speaking Spanish, and these laws would further punish people for a cultural difference." Paul Pare, a French-Canadian resident of New Hampshire, was offended by that state's recent English-only amendment: "Subconsciously, we're saying, '. . . If you don't look like us and you don't sound like us, you're not welcome.'" In vetoing his state's official-English bill in 1995,

The writer reinforces his point about divisiveness with a variety of examples.

Krause 10

Maryland Governor Parris Glendening said that immigrants
would see the law "as a message that they are not welcome
in our state" (qtd. in Dorning and Garza).

While summa-
rizing his
arguments in a
conclusion, the
writer turns the
opposition's
arguments
against them by
making a case
for increased,
not less, lan-
guage diversity.

Our nation has survived quite well for over 200 years
without an official language, and the status of English is
more secure than ever before. If any threat is posed to
our country by language use, it comes not from our speaking
languages other than English but from our inability to do
so. In a nation that must compete in a global economy, we
should worry that only ten percent of our citizens can
speak a second language (Barron, English-Only 177). Our
best chance for a united, prosperous country in the next
century will come if we respect the rights and traditions
of all inhabitants of our country, not alienate and divide
them with unwise and unnecessary language laws.

Krause 11

Works Cited

Barron, Dennis. The English-Only Question: An Official
    Language for Americans? New Haven: Yale UP, 1990.

---. "English in a Multicultural America." Social Policy
    21.1 (1991): 5-14. Rpt. in Gallegos 78-87.

"Barrow Voters Approve Another Alcohol Ban." Reuters News
    Service. Online. Internet: WWW. Address: http://
    mouth.pathfinder.com. Pathfinder Politics News. 22
    Feb. 1996.

Cannon, Ilvi J. Letter. New York Times 30 Nov. 1995, late
    ed.: A28.

Citrin, Jack. "Language Policy and American Identity." The
    Public Interest Spring, 1990: 96-109. Rpt. in Gallegos
    30-43.

Crawford, James. "Official English Isn't as Good as It
    Sounds." The American School Board Journal 176 (1989):
    41-44. Rpt. in Gallegos 52-58.

Daniels, Harvey A., ed. Not Only English: Affirming America's
    Multilingual Heritage. Urbana, IL: NCTE, 1990.

---. "The Roots of Language Protectionism." Daniels, Not
    Only English 3-12.

Dorning, Mike, and Melita Maria Garza. "English Language
    Gains New Meaning in National Politics." Chicago
    Tribune 19 Sept. 1995: 1. CD NewsBank Comprehensive.
    CD-ROM. NewsBank. Jan. 1996.

Krause 12

Draper, Jamie B., and Martha Jimenez. "Language Debates in
        the United States." <u>Epic Events</u> 2.5 (1990): 1+. Rpt.
        in Gallegos 10-15.

Gallegos, Bee, ed. <u>English: Our Official Language?</u> The
        Reference Shelf 66:2. New York: Wilson, 1994.

Halton, Mark R. "Legislating Assimilation: The English-
        Only Movement." <u>The Christian Century</u> 29 Nov. 1989:
        119-21. Rpt. in Gallegos 87-92.

Harrington, James. "Racism Taints Texas Justice." Online.
        Internet: WWW. Address: http://www.clark.net/pub/
        jgbustam/english/racism.html. 16 Jan. 1996.

Hayakawa, S. I. "English Language Amendment: One Nation
        . . . Indivisible?" Speech. 1985. Rpt. in Gallegos
        15-21.

Lang, Paul. <u>The English Language Debate: One Nation, One
        Language?</u> Springfield, NJ: Enslow, 1995.

'Lectric Law Library. "English Only." ACLU Briefing Paper
        6. Online. Internet: WWW. Address: http://
        www.inter-law.com/files/con09. 15 Jan. 1996.

U.S. English. Position papers. Online. Internet: WWW.
        Address: http://psych.pomona.edu/kevin/PPA. 16 Jan.
        1996.

Villaneuva, Victor, Jr. "<u>Solamente Inglés</u> and Hispanics."
        Daniels, <u>Not Only English</u> 77-85.

Critiquing an Argumentative Essay

Using the procedure described on page 410, critique Patrick Krause's essay "An Official Language Will *Not* Unite Us." In particular, consider the following: Patrick argued for a controversial viewpoint, one not held by a majority of Americans. Were his arguments sufficient to make others consider his position? If you did not begin the essay in agreement with Patrick, were your views altered as you read his arguments? What kind of arguments and evidence did he use to make his case? Did he give a fair presentation of the opposing arguments? Does he seem interested in fair play? Does he use his research effectively? What kind of persona does he project? Does his style contribute to the effectiveness of his argument?

PART II

Research Paper Reference Handbook

A List of Works Cited (MLA Format)

A *list of works cited*, placed at the end of a research paper, identifies all of the sources you have quoted, paraphrased, or referred to. A *working bibliography* is a list of possible sources that you draw up as you begin your research and that you revise and update throughout your research project. You should provide your readers with citations of your sources to give the authors rightful credit for their contributions to your work and to allow your readers the opportunity to consult your sources directly. Consequently, it is important that you cite sources with care.

BIBLIOGRAPHIC FORMATS

A list of works cited is expected to conform to a certain *bibliographic format*—a prescribed method of listing source information. Every academic field, such as English, sociology, or mathematics, has a preferred format that dictates not only what information about sources should be in the list of works cited but also how it should be arranged and even punctuated.

Unfortunately, each format has its own quirks and peculiarities. Which one you use will depend on the academic discipline in which you are working. If you are writing a paper for a psychology course, for example, you may be required to use a different format than you would use in a chemistry paper. The research papers in Part I follow the *Modern Language Association (MLA) format*, which is widely used in humanities courses (courses in such fields as literature, history, philosophy, theology, languages, and the arts), and it is frequently accepted for use in other courses as well. Two other formats widely used in the social and applied sciences— that of the *American Psychological Association (APA)* and the *numbered references* system—are presented in Chapters E and F. Fortunately, you do not need to memorize the details of these various formats. However, it is important that you know they exist, that you know how to find and use them, and that you follow whatever format you use with care. These chapters can serve as a reference guide to the various bibliographic formats you may encounter throughout your college career.

GENERAL GUIDELINES—MLA FORMAT

The following general guidelines apply to MLA-style bibliographies. Notice how Helen Veit followed the format in her working bibliography on page 305 and in her list of works cited on pages 392–93.

1.   *What to include?* Helen's working bibliography listed the sources she had discovered during the preliminary stages of her project. She had not yet examined all of them, and some she would not use in her paper. Later, in her list of works cited, she would include only the sources she used in writing the paper. You should include a source in your list of works cited if you have quoted or paraphrased from it or if you have made reference to it. Do not list a work if you consulted it but did not make use of it in writing the paper.

2.   *In what order?* Sources are presented in alphabetical order, *not* in the order in which they were used in the paper. Do not number the items in your list.

3.   *What word first?* Each entry begins with the author's last name. When a work is anonymous—that is, when no author's name is given—the title is listed first. If the first word is *a, an,* or *the,* put that word first, but use the next word of the entry to determine its place within alphabetical order.

4.   *What format for titles?* In typed or handwritten papers, titles of longer works, such as books and magazines, are <u>underlined</u> to represent the *italics* used in printing. Do not underline the period that follows a title. Titles of shorter works, such as articles and book chapters (which are published as subparts of longer works), are printed within quotation marks (" "). Thus in Figure A.1 we observe that the article "Not All Men Are Sly Foxes" was published in the periodical *Newsweek*.

5.   *What format for publishers?* Publishers' names are shortened in MLA style. If a publishing firm is named after several persons, only the first is used (e.g., *Houghton* instead of *Houghton Mifflin Co.*). Omit first names (write *Knopf* instead of *Alfred A. Knopf, Inc.*), and omit words such as *Books, Press,* and *Publishers*. Use the abbreviation *UP* to represent *University Press* (e.g., *Indiana UP, U of Michigan P,* and *UP of Virginia*). When questions arise, use your judgment about identifying a publisher accurately. For example, you may write *Banner Books* to distinguish it from *Banner Press*.

6.   *What margins?* The first line of each entry begins at the left margin (one inch from the left edge of the page). The second and all following lines are indented one-half inch (five spaces if typewritten). In other words, each entry is *"out*dented" (also called a *hanging indent),* the reverse of the way paragraphs are *in*dented. The purpose is to make it easy for readers to find the first word of the entry so they can quickly locate individual items from a long list.

7.   *What spacing?* Double-space throughout, both within and between entries. Do not skip extra lines between entries.

8.   *What punctuation?* Punctuation conventions, however inexplicable they may seem, should be observed with care. Follow the models in this book whenever you create a list of works cited, paying close attention to periods, commas, parentheses,

```
                                                              Veit 9
                              Works Cited
Bettelheim, Bruno.   The Uses of Enchantment: The Meaning
       and Importance of Fairy Tales.  New York: Knopf, 1976.
Brott, Armin A.   "Not All Men Are Sly Foxes."  Newsweek
       1 June 1992: 14-15.  InfoTrac: Expanded Academic
       Index/ASAP.  Online.  Information Access.  16 Mar.
       1996.
Davies, Bronwyn, and Chas Banks.   "The Gender Trap: A
       Feminist Poststructuralist Analysis of Primary School
       Children's Talk about Gender."  Journal of Curriculum
       Studies 24 (1992): 1-25.
Grimm, Jakob, and Wilhelm Grimm.   Grimms' Fairy Tales.
       Online.  Carnegie Mellon U. Library.  Internet.
       Available: http://www.cs.cmu.edu/Web/books.html.
       20 Mar. 1996.
```

Figure A.1 Sample MLA Works Cited page.

underlining, quotation marks, and spaces. In the MLA style, most entries have three principal components, each one followed by a period: the author, the title, and the publication information. The most common oversight is to omit the period at the end of each entry.

9. *What heading?* Informal bibliographies do not require any special heading. A formal list of works cited, except in short papers with few sources, should begin on a separate page at the end of your paper. Center the heading

Works Cited

(or *Bibliography,* if you prefer) and double-space (skip one line within and between entries). Do not skip an extra line between the heading and the first entry.

Citing Electronic Sources

Not many years ago, students who wrote research papers encountered almost all of their written sources in print form. Today, many research sources are likely to be gathered electronically. These might include a newspaper article retrieved from an online database, an entry from an encyclopedia on CD-ROM, a file transferred to your computer over the Internet, a World Wide Web page, even a Shakespeare play stored on some distant computer. As with other sources, you are expected to cite electronic sources so as to give credit to their authors and to allow your readers to retrieve and consult them directly.

A problem peculiar to electronic sources, particularly online sources, is that many of them are subject to being updated without notice or moved to another electronic address or even withdrawn altogether, so that someone seeking to consult a source next week may not find it in exactly the same form as another person who consulted it last week—or perhaps may not find it at all. In contrast, a printed work, such as a book, can be cited in the certainty that others who consult it will be able to find exactly the same text that you encountered. Although thousands of copies may be printed, all of them have the same words on the same pages. A book may be updated (for example, the book you are now reading has been updated three times since its initial publication), but each update is identified with a new edition number. (This is the fourth edition of *Writing, Reading, and Research.*)

Being able to identify electronic sources accurately is not a great problem with **portable electronic sources** such as software programs on CD-ROM or diskette, which, like books, are identified with edition or version numbers. **Online sources** such as World Wide Web pages and some databases, however, are subject to being updated or revised. For such sources, it may not be possible to provide a citation that will allow others to consult the source in exactly the same form it took when you consulted it. In your citation of such sources, you should give information that is as adequate as possible, as well as the date when you consulted the source. Consult the models that follow for citing both portable and online electronic sources.

MODEL ENTRIES—MLA FORMAT

You are likely to encounter many different kinds of sources in your research. When you compile a list of works cited using MLA style, you should find the appropriate model for each source from the samples that follow and copy its format with care. If you still have questions about a source you wish to list, consult the *MLA Handbook for Writers of Research Papers*, fourth edition, which can be found in the reference section of most college libraries, or ask your instructor for assistance.

Examine the following model entries and read the explanatory notes. For quick reference later on, you can consult the model MLA citations printed on the inside front covers.

Sources in Books

Citations for books have three main divisions:

```
Author's name.  The title of the book.  Publication
    information.
```

For the ***author's name,*** list the last name first, followed by a comma, followed by the author's other names. Abbreviations such as *Ph.D.* and titles such as *The Rev.* are omitted from citations. The ***book title*** is underlined. List the full title, including any subtitle. When there is a subtitle, place a colon immediately following the main title and then list the subtitle. ***Publication information*** is cited in this format:

```
City of publication: publisher, year of publication.
```

You can find this information on the book's title page and its copyright page (usually the page following the title page). Use the shortened version of the ***publisher's name.*** If the ***year of publication*** is not recorded on the title page, use the most recent year on the copyright page. If more than one ***city of publication*** is listed, give the first. If the city is not widely known, you can also list the state (using standard post office abbreviations—two capital letters, no periods) or foreign country.

A Book with One Author

Brookhiser, Richard. <u>Founding Father: Rediscovering</u>

    <u>George Washington</u>. New York: Free, 1996.

Wheelock, Arthur K., Jr. <u>Vermeer and the Art of</u>

    <u>Painting</u>. New Haven: Yale UP, 1995.

In the Brookhiser example, a colon is placed between the book's title and its ***subtitle***. Publishers' names are abbreviated: *Free* stands for *The Free Press; UP* is the standard abbreviation for University Press, as in *Yale UP.*

A Book with Two or Three Authors

Minnow, Newton, and Craig Lamay. <u>Abandoned in the</u>

    <u>Wasteland: Children, Television, and the First</u>

    <u>Amendment</u>. New York: Hill & Wang, 1995.

Reid, Jo Anne, Peter Forrestal, and Jonathan Cook.

    <u>Small Group Learning in the Classroom</u>. Portsmouth,

    NH: Heinemann, 1990.

The first book is written by Newton Minnow and Craig Lamay. Note that only Minnow's name is inverted (last name listed first), since only the first author's last name is used to determine the work's alphabetized placement in the list of sources. In the second example, Reid's name is listed before Forrestal's and Cook's, because that is the order in which their names appear on the title page. Do not rearrange the authors' names alphabetically. This same principle applies for listing authors of magazine articles and other works. Publishers' names are usually shortened (*Heinemann* instead of *Heinemann Educational Publishers*), but you may give the name in a more complete form, particularly if you are in doubt (*Hill & Wang* rather than *Hill,* to avoid confusion with Ernest Hill Publishing or Lawrence Hill Books). You may use the state abbreviation when you consider it helpful in identifying the city of publication *(Portsmouth, NH)*.

A Book with More Than Three Authors

Boumil, Marcia M., et al. <u>Law and Gender Bias</u>.

Littleton, CO: Rothman, 1995.

The term *et al.* is a Latin abbreviation meaning "and others." It is not underlined (or italicized) in lists of works cited. You may also list all of the authors, if you consider it desirable to acknowledge them by name.

Two or More Works by the Same Author

Asimov, Isaac. <u>Adding a Dimension</u>. New York:

Discus, 1975.

---. "Fifty Years of Astronomy." <u>Natural History</u>

Oct. 1985: 4+.

---. <u>The New Intelligent Man's Guide to Science</u>.

New York: Basic, 1965.

Asimov, Isaac, and John Ciardi. <u>A Grossery of</u>

<u>Limericks</u>. New York: Norton, 1981.

The first three works (two books and a magazine article) are written by the same author, Isaac Asimov. The fourth work is written by Asimov and another author. When you have used more than one work by the same author, your works-cited list should arrange the works alphabetically by title. (In our example, *Adding* comes before *Fifty,* which comes before *New.)* Replace the author's name for all but the first work with three hyphens followed by a period. The reader can then see at a glance that the author is represented more than once and is alerted not to confuse one work with another. Use hyphens only when works have identical authors; notice that Asimov's name is not replaced for the fourth work, since its authors (Asimov and Ciardi) are not identical with the author of the first three works (Asimov).

A Book in a Later Edition

Schaeffer, Richard L. <u>Introduction to Probability</u>

<u>and Its Applications</u>. 2nd ed. Boston: PWS,

1995.

Schaeffer's book is in a second edition.

A Book in a Series

Porterfield, Sally F. Jung's Advice to the

Players: A Jungian Reading of Shakespeare's

Problem Plays. Contributions in Drama &

Theatre Studies 57. Westport, CT: Greenwood,

1994.

Porterfield's is the fifty-seventh book (by different authors) published by Greenwood Press in a series entitled Contributions in Drama and Theatre Studies.

A Book Published in More Than One Volume

When an author gives different titles to individual volumes of a work, list a specific volume this way:

Brinton, Crane, John B. Christopher, and Robert

Lee Wolff. Prehistory to 1715. Vol. 1 of

A History of Civilization. 6th ed. 2 vols.

Englewood Cliffs, NJ: Prentice, 1984.

When individual volumes are not titled, cite the book this way:

Messenger, Charles. For Love of Regiment: A

History of British Infantry, 1660-1993.

2 vols. Philadelphia: Trans-Atlantic, 1995.

If you use only one of these volumes, cite it this way:

Messenger, Charles. For Love of Regiment: A

History of British Infantry, 1660-1993

Vol. 1. Philadelphia: Trans-Atlantic, 1995.

A Book with a Translator or Editor

Mahfouz, Naguib. Children of the Alley. Trans.

Peter Theroux. New York: Doubleday, 1996.

Shakespeare, William. Henry V. Ed. T. W. Craik.

New York: Routledge, 1995.

Mahfouz's book was translated into English by Theroux. Craik edited this edition of the Shakespeare play. Compare how editors are cited in a book written by a single author (the Shakespeare example) with how they are cited in a book consisting of a collection of essays by various authors (the following example).

An Anthology of Essays by Different Authors

> Stimpson, Catherine R., and Ethel Spector Person,
>
>   eds. <u>Women: Sex and Sexuality</u>. Chicago: U
>
>   of Chicago P, 1980.

Stimpson and Person edited this book, an anthology of essays by various writers. It should be noted that occasions when you refer to such a collection *as a whole* in your research will be relatively rare. More frequently, you will use material from an *individual essay* in the collection, and you will cite that specific essay (rather than the collection as a whole) in your list of works cited as in the following examples.

A Work from an Anthology

> Leifer, Myra. "Pregnancy." <u>Women: Sex and</u>
>
>   <u>Sexuality</u>. Ed. Catherine R. Stimpson and
>
>   Ethel Spector Person. Chicago: U of
>
>   Chicago P, 1980. 212-23.
>
> Lichtheim, George. "The Birth of a Philosopher."
>
>   <u>Collected Essays</u>. New York: Viking, 1973.
>
>   103-10.
>
> Rushdie, Salman. "A Pen Against the Sword: In
>
>   Good Faith." <u>Newsweek</u> 12 Feb. 1990: 52+.
>
>   Rpt. in <u>One World, Many Cultures</u>. Ed. Stuart
>
>   Hirschberg. New York: Macmillan, 1992. 480-96.

Leifer's article "Pregnancy" is one of the essays in the collection *Women: Sex and Sexuality* edited by Stimpson and Person. The Lichtheim book in the example does not have an editor; he is the author of all the essays in the book. Rushdie's article originally appeared in *Newsweek*; the person who wrote this listing found it in Hirschberg's book, where it had been ***reprinted*** (*rpt.*). Note also that the ***page numbers*** on which the essays appear within the books are listed. In listing page numbers, omit all but the last two digits of the final page number, unless they are different from those of the first page. For example, you would write: 5–7, 377–79 (not –9 or –379), 195–208, 1006–07 (not –7 or –1007), and 986–1011.

Citing Several Essays from the Same Collection

If several essays are cited from the same collection, you can save space by using ***cross-references.*** First, include the entire collection as one of the items in your list of works cited, as follows:

Stimpson, Catherine R., and Ethel Spector Person,

eds. <u>Women: Sex and Sexuality</u>. Chicago: U

of Chicago P, 1980.

Then you are free to list each article you refer to in your paper, followed by an abbreviated reference to the collection—just the last names of the editors and the pages on which the articles appear, as follows:

Baker, Susan W. "Biological Influences on Human

Sex and Gender." Stimson and Person 175-91.

Diamond, Irene. "Pornography and Repression: A

Reconsideration." Stimson and Person 129-23.

Leifer, Myra. "Pregnancy." Stimson and Person

212-23.

A Book Published before 1900

Nightingale, Florence. <u>Notes on Nursing: What It

Is, and What It Is Not</u>. New York, 1860.

The publisher's name may be omitted for works published before 1900.

A Paperback or Other Reprinted Book

Kerouac, Jack. <u>Big Sur</u>. 1962. New York: Viking

Penguin, 1992.

The book was originally published (in hardcover, by a different publisher) in 1962.

A Book Written by a Group or Government Agency

Institute of Medicine: Commission on Federal

Regulation of Methadone Treatment. <u>Federal

Regulation of Methadone Treatment</u>.

Washington: National Academic, 1995.

Sotheby's. <u>Nineteenth Century European Paintings,

Drawings and Watercolours</u>. London:

Sotheby's, 1995.

The book on nineteenth-century painting is attributed to Sotheby's, the British auction house, rather than to individual authors. Cite the group as author, even when it is also the publisher, as in the Sotheby's example.

A Book Published or Reproduced Electronically

> Bierce, Ambrose. "My Favorite Murder." The
>   Collected Works of Ambrose Bierce. New York:
>   Neale, 1911. Vol. 8. Online. U. of
>   Virginia Lib. Internet. Available FTP:
>   etext.virginia.edu. 11 Nov. 1995.
>
> Darwin, Charles. The Voyage of the Beagle.
>   Harvard Classics 29. New York: Collier,
>   1909. Online. Internet Wiretap. Internet.
>   Address: gopher://ftp.std.com:70/00/obi/book/
>   Charles.Darwin/Voyage.of.the.Beagle.Z.
>   11 Nov. 1995.
>
> Evans, Elizabeth. Anne Tyler. United States
>   Authors Series. Boston: Twayne, 1993. CD-
>   ROM. Twayne's Women Authors on CD-ROM. New
>   York: Hall, 1995.

For books consulted in electronic format, provide standard information for the print source of the reproduced text. (This may not be possible in cases where only the author and title are identified.) For an online source, identify the medium (e.g., online), the source (Bierce's story was downloaded from the depository at the University of Virginia Library), the computer network, the electronic address, and the date of access (the Bierce story was consulted on November 11, 1995). For a portable source, identify the medium (CD-ROM), the title of the CD, and its publisher and year. Because electronic sources vary widely, you may need to use your judgment about how best to identify your source. For a periodical or newspaper article that has been reproduced electronically, see the section on pages 450–51, "A Printed Article Reproduced Electronically."

An Article in an Encyclopedia or Other Reference Work

> Harmon, Mamie. "Folk Arts." Encyclopaedia
>   Britannica: Macropaedia. 15th ed. 1991.
>
> "Wellstone, Paul." Who's Who in America. 50th
>   ed. 1996.
>
> "Yodel." The Shorter Oxford English Dictionary.
>   1973.

The *Britannica* is a printed encyclopedia. Pages need not be listed for reference works whose entries are arranged alphabetically (and therefore can be found easily).

In many reference works, such as *Who's Who in America*, no authors are named for individual entries. Publishers need not be cited for well-known reference books. Provide publisher information for *lesser-known reference works:*

> Hames, Raymond. "Yanomamö." <u>South America</u>.
>
>> Vol. 7 of <u>Encyclopedia of World Cultures</u>.
>>
>> Boston: Hall, 1994.

Electronic reference works are cited as follows:

> "Morocco." <u>Compton's Online Encyclopedia</u>.
>
>> Online. Prodigy. 4 Feb. 1996.
>
> "Yokel." <u>Oxford English Dictionary</u>. 2nd ed.
>
>> CD-ROM. Oxford: Oxford UP, 1992. 14 Dec.
>>
>> 1995.

The "Morocco" entry was consulted through the Prodigy computer network. Because many online reference works upgrade entries regularly, give the date when you consulted the source.

Sources in Periodicals and Newspapers

Entries for different types of periodical and newspaper sources are explained in the following section. Periodical entries are also summarized in Figure A.2.

An Article in a Magazine

> Block, Toddi Gutner. "Riding the Waves." <u>Forbes</u>
>
>> 11 Sept. 1995: 182+.
>
> Maran, Stephen P. "A Deviant Star." <u>Natural</u>
>
>> <u>History</u> June 1983: 24-29.
>
> Robinson, Ann. "Gifted: The Two-Faced Label."
>
>> <u>The Gifted Child Today</u> Jan./Feb. 1989: 34-36.

This format is used for all weekly, biweekly, monthly, or bimonthly periodicals, except for scholarly journals. The Maran article appears on pages 24 through 29. The Block article is not printed on continuous pages; it begins on page 182 and is continued further back in the magazine. For such articles, only the first page is listed, immediately followed by a plus sign (+). Although some magazines may show a volume or issue number on the cover, these are not needed in the entry. Names of months, except for May, June, and July, are abbreviated. Note that there is no punctuation between the periodical's name and the publication date. For a magazine article that has been reproduced on an electronic database (and which you do not consult in its original print version), see the section on pages 450–51, "A Printed Article Reproduced Electronically."

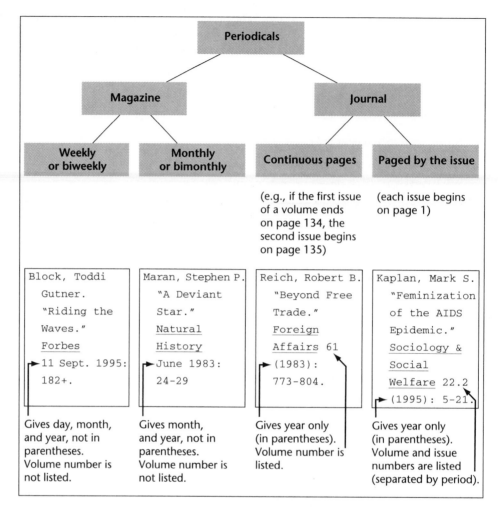

Figure A.2 **Periodical listings for an MLA Works Cited list.**

An Article in a Journal

```
Reich, Robert B.  "Beyond Free Trade."  Foreign Affairs
     61 (1983): 773-804.
```

Journals are usually scholarly publications and are typically published three or four times yearly. Each year begins a new volume. The volume number (61 in this case) is included in the entry for a journal article. Pages in most journals are numbered according to the volume, not the issue. For example, if the Winter issue of volume 61 of *Foreign Affairs* ended on page 742, the Spring issue would begin on page 743. The paging of the next volume (62) would begin again with page 1. Some journals, however, begin each issue on page 1; for these, add a period and the issue number following the volume number, as follows:

```
Kaplan, Mark S.  "Feminization of the AIDS Epidemic."

    Sociology & Social Welfare 22.2 (1995): 5-21.
```

The number 22.2 tells you that the article appeared in volume 22, issue 2, of *Sociology & Social Welfare*. It is not necessary to include the seasonal designation (Winter, Spring, and so on) when there is an issue number. Periodical listings are also shown in Figure A.2. For a journal article that has been reproduced on an electronic database (and which you do not consult in its original print version), see the section on pages 450–51, "A Printed Article Reproduced Electronically."

An Article in a Newspaper

```
Edsall, Thomas B.  "Tensions Divide Elements of

        Potential Coalition."  Washington Post 18

        Feb. 1996: A21.

Ranii, David.  "New AIDS Drug Is Step Closer to

        Approval."  News and Observer [Raleigh] 7

        Nov. 1995: 1D+.

"U.S. Recommends Hepatitis A Vaccine."  New York

        Times 27 Aug. 1995, natl. ed.: sec. 5: 3.
```

The article *The* is omitted from citations of newspapers such as the *Washington Post*. When the newspaper's name does not include the city (e.g., *News and Observer*), provide the city name in brackets; however, do not give a city for national newspapers like the *Wall Street Journal* and *USA Today*. Number pages as they appear in your source. The number of the page of the newspaper where the Edsall article appears is A21 (that is, page 21 of section A), while the newspaper where the Ranii article appears has the section and page numbers reversed (it begins on page 1D). When both the section and page are numbered, present them as in the third example (*sec. 5: 3*). Because the *New York Times* publishes two different editions (called the late and the national editions), it is necessary to specify which edition you used. The third article is listed by its headline because no author is named in a byline. For a newspaper article that has been reproduced on an electronic database (and which you do not consult in its original print version), see the section on pages 450–51, "A Printed Article Reproduced Electronically."

An Editorial

```
"Replace Unfair Tax Law."  Editorial.  USA Today

        28 Aug. 1995: 12A.
```

A Letter to the Editor

```
Cazorlo, Eugenio.  Letter.  History Today Mar.

    1992: 54.
```

A Review

Chesler, Phyllis. "The Shellshocked Woman." Rev.
of <u>Trauma and Recovery</u>, by Judith Lewis
Herman. <u>New York Times Book Review</u> 23 Aug.
1992: 11.

Rev. of <u>Going to the Territory</u>, by Ralph Ellison.
<u>Atlantic</u> Aug. 1986: 91.

Salzman, Eric. Rev. of <u>Bluebeard's Castle</u>, by
Bela Bartok. Katalin Szendrenyi, soprano.
Falk Struckman, baritone. Frankfurt Radio
Symphony. Eliahu Inabel, cond. Compact
disc. <u>Stereo Review</u> Sept. 1995: 102.

The first two reviews are of books; the third is of a recording. Information in review listings appears in this order: the reviewer's name; the title of the review; the work reviewed; its author; performers and performance information, if applicable; and the publication information. Notice that both the second and third review are untitled. In the second review, Ralph Ellison is the author of the book reviewed; the review itself is published anonymously.

A Printed Article Reproduced Electronically

When you consult a magazine, journal, or newspaper article that has been reproduced on an electronic database, provide information as you would for its original print version, followed by the database name, the medium (online, CD-ROM, etc.), and the company that produced or distributed it. For a portable database (such as one on CD-ROM), add the date when the database was most recently updated. For an online database, add the date when the database was consulted.

Bikai, Patricia M., and Deborah Kooring.
"Archaeology in Jordan." <u>American Journal of
Archaeology</u> 99 (1995): 507+. <u>InfoTrac:
Expanded Academic Index/ASAP</u>. Online.
Information Access. 9 Nov. 1995.

Carey, Elaine. "Is Graying of Faculty Turning
University into 'Boring' Place?" <u>Toronto
Star</u> 25 Sept. 1995: A17. <u>CD NewsBank
Comprehensive</u>. CD-ROM. NewsBank. Oct.
1995.

```
Diamond, Nina L.   "Dolphin Sonar: A Biologist and
     Physicist Team Up to Find the Source of Sound
     Beams."  Omni July 1994: 24.   Popular
     Periodicals Standard.  CD-ROM.  NewsBank.
     Oct. 1995.
```

The journal article by Bikai and Kooring was consulted through an online database. The newspaper article by Carey and the magazine article by Diamond were consulted through portable databases on CD-ROM. Bikai and Kooring's article was originally published in the *American Journal of Archaeology* and was reproduced by the Expanded Academic Index/ASAP database, which is distributed by the Information Access Company. Because it is an online database, the date when it was consulted is provided: November 9, 1995. Carey's article originally appeared in the *Toronto Star* and was reproduced in the CD NewsBank Comprehensive database and accessed in CD-ROM format. Because it is a portable database, the month when it was most recently updated is provided: October 1995 (this came from the onscreen information that the database covered articles between December 1, 1994, and October 3, 1995). If you learn about an article through a database but consult the original print form, you do not need to provide information about the database. If you consult a back issue of a publication stored on microfilm, you do not need to state that; note, however, the following entry.

A Printed Article Reproduced by a Microform Reproduction Service

```
"U.S. Forests 'Very Healthy,' Ecologist Reports."
     Wyoming State Tribune 25 June 1991.   NewsBank
     ENV, 1991, fiche 58, grid A1.
```

This newspaper article was indexed in the NewsBank Reference Service database and reproduced in the NewsBank microfiche files.

An Article in an Electronic Publication

```
Plane, Jo.   "Training--How Hard Is Your Workout?"
     Balance Nov. 1995.  Online.  Internet: WWW.
     Address: http://tito.hyperlink.com/balance/.
     18 Feb. 1996.
"World Leaders Condemn Nigerian Executions."
     Reuters 10 Nov. 1995.  Online.  Internet:
     WWW.  Pathfinder News Now.  13 Nov. 1995.
```

The article by Plane was published in *Balance*, an online "zine." Unlike the preceding examples, it did not first appear in print form. It was consulted online on the World Wide Web (WWW). The citation includes the address for the zine's home page and the date when the source was consulted. The second article ("World Leaders") is a news story from the Reuters news agency, consulted on the Internet through a service called Pathfinder News Now. Notice that the date of electronic publication (November 10) and the date of consultation (November 13) are different. The address can be omitted for a temporary posting, which will not be available for others to consult.

Other Sources

An Audio Recording

> Dickinson, Dee. <u>Creating the Future: Perspectives</u>
>
>   <u>on Educational Change</u>. Audiocassette.
>
>   Minneapolis: Accelerated Learning Systems,
>
>   1991.
>
> Mozart, Wolfgang A. Symphony No. 30 in D Major.
>
>   Cond. James Levine. Vienna Philharmonic.
>
>   Compact disc. Deutsche Grammophon, 1986.
>
> Shuster, George N. Jacket notes. <u>The Poetry of</u>
>
>   <u>Gerard Manley Hopkins</u>. LP. Caedmon, n.d.

Audio recordings vary greatly in type and purpose, so do not hesitate to exercise judgment about what information is important. In general, label each recording by medium (compact disc, audiocassette, LP, and so on), although the label is optional for compact discs, which are assumed to be the standard audio medium. For a musical recording, list first the name of the composer, or performer, or conductor, depending on what aspect of the recording you are emphasizing. Recordings are produced by print-media publishers as well as traditional record companies, with the line separating them increasingly blurred; list either the manufacturer and year (as in the second and third examples) or city, publisher, and year (as in the first example). Cite jacket or liner notes as in the third example.

Computer Software

> <u>Morph</u>. Version 2.5. Diskette. San Diego:
>
>   Gryphon, 1995.
>
> <u>Twain's World</u>. CD-ROM. Parsippany, NJ: Bureau
>
>   Development, 1993.

A Film or Video Recording

Ed Wood: Look Back in Angora. Dir. Tim Burton.

  Screenplay by Scott Alexander and Larry

  Karaszewski. Touchstone, 1994.

For a film, give the title, the director, the distributor, and the year of release. You may include other information you consider pertinent, such as the screenwriter and principal performers. For a film viewed on videocassette or videodisc, provide that same information, but also identify the medium, the distributor, and the video release date:

The Little Foxes. Dir. William Wyler. Perf.

  Bette Davis, Herbert Marshall, and Dan

  Duryea. MGM, 1941. Videocassette. Embassy,

  1985.

Cite a nontheatrical video as follows:

The Classical Hollywood Style. Program 1 of The

  American Cinema. Prod. New York Center for

  Visual History. Videocassette. Annenberg/CPB,

  1995.

A Government Document

United States. Dept. of State. Natl. Committee

  for Man and the Biosphere. Tropical and

  Subtropical Forests Directorate. People and

  the Tropical Forest: A Research Project from

  the United States Man and the Biosphere

  Program. By Ariel E. Lugo. Washington: GPO,

  1987.

The country or state producing the document is listed first, followed by the issuing agency or agencies, if any. Individual authors, if known, can be listed after the title. Compare this listing with Figure 9.15 on page 289.

A Lecture

Halme, Kathleen. Class lecture. English 315.

  Swansea College. 7 Apr. 1996.

McKenna, Paula. "Live by Design or Live by
       Default." Public lecture. League of Women
       Voters. Natchez, 20 Oct. 1995.

A Pamphlet

Golden Retriever Club of America. <u>Prevention of</u>
       <u>Heartworm</u>. N.p.: GRCA, 1996.

<u>Who Are the Amish?</u> Aylmer, Ont.: Pathway, n.d.

Pamphlets are treated like books. Use these abbreviations for unknown information: *n.p.* for both "no place" or "no publisher," *n.d.* for "no date," and *n. pag.* for "no pagination" (when the source lacks page numbers). Because pamphlets vary widely, you should exercise judgment to make your listing clear.

A Personal Interview

Lee, Rebecca. Personal interview. 20 Mar. 1996.

A Radio or Television Program

McChesney, John. Report on Comdex and Bill Gates.
       <u>Morning Edition</u>. National Public Radio. 14 Nov.
       1995.

<u>The Missiles of October: What the World Didn't Know</u>.
       Written by Sherry Jones and Peter Jennings.
       ABC-TV. 17 Oct. 1992,

An Unpublished Essay

MacLaren, Molly. "The Power of the Pen: Should I
       Become a Professional Writer?" Essay written
       for Prof. Janet Adams's English 102 class.
       Spring semester 1996.

An Unpublished Letter or E-Mail

Canty, Kevin. Letter to author. 5 Mar. 1996.

Wilkes, Paul. E-mail to author. 29 Dec. 1995.

An Unpublished Questionnaire

Questionnaire conducted by Prof. Barbara Waxman's
       English 102 class. Nov. 1995.

Citation for a project or paper written for a college class need be no more formal than this. An essay meant for wider circulation, however, would need to include the title of the course and the name of the college. Common sense is your best guide in these matters.

A List of Works Cited

This exercise practices many types of bibliographic entries. Imagine that (in a temporary lapse from sanity) you have written a paper called "The Shoelace in History," and you have made use of the following sources. Compile your list of works cited, paying close attention to proper MLA format.

As a first step, circle the word in each of the following items that would begin the listing. Second, order the entries alphabetically. Third, put each listing in proper MLA form. (*Warning:* Some listings contain irrelevant information that you will not use in your works-cited list.) Finally, prepare the finished list.

1. The book *Sandals in Greece and Rome* was written by Sally Parish and published in 1987 by Wapiti Press in Omaha.

2. You found Walter Kelly's article "Shoelaces" on page 36 of volume 12 of the 1984 edition of *Encyclopedia of Haberdashery,* published in New York by the Buster Green Company.

3. During World War II, Fiona Quinn wrote *Knit Your Own Shoelaces* as part of the Self-Reliance Series printed in Modesto, California, in 1942 by Victory Press.

4. On page 36 of its July 23, 1977 edition, *Time* magazine published "Earth Shoes Unearthed in Inca Ruins." No author is given.

5. Two days ago, using the Internet, you downloaded a book by Imelda Markoz, *Never Too Many Shoes,* from the University of Manila library. Two years ago, it had appeared in print, published by Converse Press in Wichita. You downloaded the book by a process called FTP at the address "shoebooks.umanila.edu."

6. Constance Jowett translated a book by Max Philador and Elisaveta Krutsch, *Shoelaces in Africa and the Far East 1800–1914.* It was published in 1994 by Vanitas Publishers, Inc. Cities listed on the title page for Vanitas are Fort Worth, Texas; Chicago; Amsterdam; and Sydney, Australia.

7. On January 5 of this year Louise K. Frobisher wrote you a letter about her father's shoelace research.

8. You found volume 3 of Fiona Quinn's six-volume work of 1950: *The Shoe in the English-Speaking World,* published by S. T. Bruin & Sons of Boston.

9. On pages 711 and 712 of volume 17 of the *Indiana Journal of Podiatry* (November 1974) appears an essay, "Solving the Loose Shoe Problem" by Earl Q. Butz.

10. Leon Frobisher, Werner Festschrift, Ella Fitsky, and Ian McCrimmer published the twelfth edition of *Shoemaking with a Purpose* in 1996. The publisher, Hooton-Muffin of Boston, has published editions of the book since 1939.

11. The Society of Legwear Manufacturers wrote a book, *Laces, Gaiters, and Spats,* in 1901. Provolone-Liederkranz Publishers, Ltd. of Toronto reprinted it in 1955.

12. Mr. O. Fecteau and Ms. Mary Facenda edited a 1993 anthology, *An Ethnography of Footwear,* published in New Orleans by Big Muddy Publications. You found an article on pages 70–81, "Footloose and Sandal-Free," by J. R. R. Frodobaggins.

13. Norman Zimmer thoroughly explores "The Shoelace Motif in Finno-Latvian Sonnet Sequences" in the Fall 1993 edition (volume 43), pages 202 through 295, of a scholarly journal called *PMLA.*

14. Theodore and Louisa Mae Quinn edited a book written by their mother, Fiona Quinn, shortly before her death. The book, *Old Laces and Arsenic,* is published by Capra Press of Los Angeles. Copyright dates given are 1947, 1952, and 1953.

15. In the February 4, 1968 *Hibbing Herald* newspaper, an article, "Lace, Lady, Lace," appears under Robert Dylan's byline. You found the article through a NewsBank index listing: "Minnesota: Hibbing—1968, SOC 54:G13–15." *SOC* stands for the Social Relations category.

16. You draw on information from a television exposé, "The Shoelace Coverup," which appeared last Sunday on the CBS show *60 Minutes.* Leslie Stahl is the narrator.

17. *Dog's Life* is a monthly magazine published in Atlanta. In volume 16, number 3, of that publication (whose date is August 1996), Walter Kelly's article "Little Laces for Little People" appeared. It began on pages 32 to 37 and continued on pages 188 and 189. You found it using the InfoTrac General Periodical ASAP database on CD-ROM, and you downloaded the full text of the article onto a floppy disk to read later on your home computer. The Information Access Company, which distributes the database, updated it last month.

18. You used the World Wide Web to read an article, "Tasteless Laces," by M. R. Blackwell. It appeared this year in the January issue of *Cyberlace,* which calls itself "the e-zine for the well shod." Its address is http://www.knotco.edu/cyberlace/home.html.

Congratulations. Having completed this exercise, you are now prepared for almost any situation that may face you as you prepare lists of sources in the future.

Remember, for quick reference, consult the summary of MLA bibliographic models on the inside front covers.

Parenthetical Notes (MLA Format)

RESEARCH writing has two principal devices for giving detailed information about sources: lists of works cited and notes. The former is a *general,* alphabetized list of all the sources you used in your writing. A **note,** in contrast, acknowledges the *specific* location within a source of a *specific* quotation or bit of information in your paper. For example, if you quoted this very sentence in a paper you were writing, you would include the fourth edition of *Writing, Reading, and Research* in your list of works cited. A note, however, would also be needed with the quotation to tell your readers that it came from page 457 of this book.

TYPES OF NOTES

Notes are of three principal kinds: parenthetical notes, footnotes, and endnotes. Parenthetical notes are by far the simplest kind of notes to use, and they are the standard method for documenting sources within MLA style. Footnotes and endnotes, however, are sometimes used by scholars in such fields as history, theology, and the fine arts. The following case illustrates the differences among these three types of notes.

Imagine that you included the following source in your list of works cited:

> Sternberg, Robert J., and Todd I. Lubart. <u>Defying the</u>
> <u>Crowd: Cultivating Creativity in a Culture of</u>
> <u>Conformity</u>. New York: Free, 1995.

A works-cited listing

Suppose you made use of the following passage about the invention of Post-it notes, which appeared on page 4 of that book:

> Consider, for example, the Post-its on which many people jot reminders of things they need to get done. These "stick-ums" were created when an engineer at the 3M Company ended up doing the opposite of what he was supposed to. He created a weak adhesive, rather than the strong one that was the goal of his working division. But instead of throwing out the weak adhesive, he redefined the problem he was trying to solve: namely, to find the best use for a very weak adhesive. . . . Some of the greatest discoveries and inventions happen when people do just the opposite of what they have been told to do!

A passage from that source

Assume you paraphrased material from this passage in your paper as follows:

Your paraphrase
of the source

```
Creativity consists in seeing possibilities where
others see only dead ends.  For example, the discovery
of a weak adhesive by an engineer who was actually
looking for a strong adhesive led to the invention of
Post-it notes.
```

It is your obligation to identify the specific source you used in writing this paraphrase. Here it is done with a *parenthetical note:*

A parenthetical
note

```
Creativity consists in seeing possibilities where
others see only dead ends.  For example, the discovery
of a weak adhesive by an engineer who was actually
looking for a strong adhesive led to the invention of
Post-it notes (Sternberg and Lubart 4).
```

The note tells your readers that you discovered this information on page 4 of the Sternberg and Lubart book, the complete citation for which can be found in your list of works cited.

By contrast, if you use the footnote or endnote system, you mark your paraphrase with a raised number:

Reference to
a footnote or
endnote

```
Creativity consists in seeing possibilities where
others see only dead ends.  For example, the discovery
of a weak adhesive by an engineer who was actually
looking for a strong adhesive led to the invention of
Post-it notes.[1]
```

The raised number refers the reader to the following note:

A footnote
or endnote

```
     [1] Robert J. Sternberg and Todd I. Lubart,
Defying the Crowd: Cultivating Creativity in a
Culture of Conformity (New York: Free, 1995), 4.
```

As a *footnote,* it would be typed at the bottom of the page on which the reference appeared. As an *endnote,* it would be typed in a list of notes at the end of the paper.

Unless you are using a word processor that automatically formats and arranges your footnotes for you, you will find endnotes easier to type than footnotes. Both, however, involve redundancy; notice that the sample footnote repeats all the information already found in the works-cited listing. In contrast, parenthetical notes are far simpler and more economical than either footnotes or endnotes. In this chapter, we will focus on the MLA parenthetical style, but a full discussion of footnotes and endnotes can be found in Chapter D, and still other styles of notation are explained in Chapters E and F.

 ## PARENTHETICAL NOTES

The rationale for parenthetical notes is that a note should give the least amount of information needed to identify a source—and give it within the paper itself; readers who want to know more can consult the list of works cited for further information. Different academic fields use slightly different formats for parenthetical notes. We consider here one general-purpose format, but you should be aware that papers written for other classes may require some adjustment in their note form. Always ask your instructor for format information if you are in doubt.

In the style used here as a model—the MLA style—a note is placed in the paper at the point where it is needed to identify a source. A typical note consists of two bits of information, in this format: (author pages). That is, the author's last name and the pages from which the information is taken are placed in parentheses. Here is an example of how a parenthetical note is used with a quotation:

> One textbook defines <u>false arrest</u> as "an intentional, unlawful, and unprivileged restraint of a person's liberty, either in prison or elsewhere, whereby harm is caused to the person so confined" (Wells 237).

Observe that the note follows the quotation and that the period is placed *after* the parentheses, not at the end of the quotation. In other words, the note is treated as a part of the sentence. If a quotation ends with a question mark or exclamation point, add a period after the note, as follows:

> Schwitzer taped a quotation from Thoreau to the wall above his desk: "I have never yet met a man who was quite awake. How could I have looked him in the face?" (Johnson 65).

Period follows the note

If the author's name already appears in your sentence, it can be omitted from the note. For example:

> Wells writes that "a false arrest or false imprisonment is an intentional, unlawful, and unprivileged restraint of a person's liberty, either in prison or elsewhere, whereby harm is caused to the person so confined" (237).

For a longer, indented quotation, the note can be placed immediately following the acknowledgment phrase, as follows:

> Historians of the last century maintained a firm belief
> in human progress, according to British historian Edward
> Hallett Carr (324):
>
> > The liberal nineteenth-century view of history
> > had a close affinity with the economic doctrine
> > of laissez-faire--also the product of a serene
> > and self-confident outlook on the world. Let
> > everyone get on with his particular job, and
> > the hidden hand would take care of the
> > universal harmony.

Alternatively, the note can be placed at the quotation's end, as in this example:

> Although the earth is a small planet in a remote corner of
> a minor galaxy, there are reasons for arguing its importance:
>
> > One should not be impressed too much by mere
> > quantity; great dimensions and heavy mass have
> > no merit by themselves; they cannot compare in
> > value with immaterial things, such as thoughts,
> > emotions, and other expressions of the soul. To
> > us the earth is the most important of all
> > celestial bodies, because it has become the
> > cradle and seat of our spiritual values. (Öpik 9)

Period precedes the note in an indented quotation

Notice one oddity of the parenthetical style: When a note is placed after an indented quotation, it follows the final period. (In the other cases we have seen, the period follows the parenthetical note.)

Many students mistakenly assume that notes are used only for quotations, but they are used for paraphrased ideas and information as well. For example:

> John Huston's first movie, The Maltese Falcon, is a
> faithful adaptation of Dashiell Hammett's novel (Fell
> 242).

Note for paraphrased material

Fell's book is the source of the information, but the sentence is not a direct quotation. This point is important and needs to be stressed: *Use notes whenever you make use of a source's ideas and information, whether you quote the source's words directly or paraphrase them.* Since your research paper will contain more paraphrasing than direct quotation, most of your parenthetical notes will follow information written in your own phrasing.

The beauty of parenthetical notes is their simplicity: They provide the *least* amount of information needed to identify a source from the list of works cited, and the same form is used whether the source is a book, a periodical, or a newspaper. Only a few special cases require any variation from this standard form.

Some Special Cases

Notes should be as unobtrusive as possible; therefore, they should contain the least information needed to identify the source. In the following special cases, you will have to include additional information in your notes.

Works with No Author

For works where no author is given, substitute the title (the item that comes first in the entry for that work in the list of works cited; remember that the point of notes is to refer your readers to the list of works cited if further information is needed). For example, consider a note for an anonymous article listed like this:

```
"An Infant's Cries May Signal Physiological Defects."

    Psychology Today June 1974: 21-24.
```

A parenthetical note referring to this article might look like this:

```
("An Infant's" 22)
```

Notice that when a title is long, only the first word or two should be given in the note, with no ellipsis dots. Also notice another difference: The list of works cited locates the complete text of the article, pages 21 through 24, whereas the note lists only page 22. The reason is that a list of works cited gives *all* the pages on which an article appears, whereas a note refers to the *specific* page or pages from which a quotation or piece of information is taken.

Works with Two or More Authors

Notes for works with multiple authors list their names just as they appear in your list of works cited. (You can find the works-cited entries for these two sources on pages 441 and 442.)

```
(Reid, Forrestal, and Cook 52-54)
(Boumil et al. 112)
```

Two or More Works by the Same Author

When two or more works by the same author appear in your list of works cited, add the first word or two from the title to your note to distinguish one work from another. For example, if your paper uses both a book by Isaac Asimov, *Adding a Dimension,* and a magazine article by him, "Happy Accidents," notes for those two sources might look like this:

```
(Asimov, Adding 240-43)

(Asimov, "Happy" 68)
```

Two Authors with the Same Last Name

When two authors with the same last name are cited in a paper, include their first names in notes so as to distinguish between them. For example:

```
(George Eliot 459)

(T. S. Eliot 44)
```

A Multivolume Work

If you are citing a book published in more than one volume, you do not need to list the volume number in the note if it is shown in the list of works cited.

Take, for example, the following entry:

```
Agus, Jacob Bernard.  The Meaning of Jewish History.

        2 vols.  London: Abelard, 1963.  Vol. 2.
```

Since your list of works cited shows that only this one volume is used in your paper, your notes should not list the volume number. For example:

```
(Agus 59)
```

If, on the other hand, your paper uses more than one volume of a work, each note needs to specify the volume as well, as in these examples:

```
(Agus 1: 120)

(Agus 2: 59)
```

Reference to an Entire Work

When you refer to a work as a whole, rather than to a specific passage, no page numbers are needed, as in this example, which refers readers to three different sources found in the list of works cited:

```
At least three full-length biographies of Philbin have

been written since his death (Brickle; Baskin;

Tillinghast).
```

More often, when a work as a whole is referred to, the author's name is mentioned in the paper itself, so no note is needed. For example:

```
Fermin's book on wine-making is sold only by mail-order.
```

Reference to More Than One Work

Sometimes a note needs to refer to more than one work. You can list multiple sources in a note, separated by semicolons:

```
Broadwell's controversial theory about the intelligence of

lizards has been disputed by eminent herpetologists

(Matsumoto 33; Vanderhooten 7; Crambury 450).
```

Reference to Discontinuous Pages

When you have taken source material from discontinuous pages of a work, list the pages, separated by commas:

```
(Witanowski 47, 103)
```

A Source without Pages

Many sources, such as recordings, television programs, and interviews, have no pages. For example, suppose you have conducted an interview for your paper and have this entry in your list of works cited:

```
Philcox, Arthur C.  Personal interview.  17 Oct. 1996.
```

Information from the interview can be cited simply with the interviewee's name:

```
During World War II, children in Hadleyville played at being

civil defense spotters on the levee, searching the skies for

German aircraft (Philcox).
```

If the interviewee's name appears in the passage, no note at all is needed, as shown here:

```
Retired teacher Arthur Philcox says that ballpoint pens did

not replace fountain pens in Hadleyville's grade schools

until the mid-1950s.
```

An Electronic Source

Most electronic sources do not have numbered "pages" in the usual sense, so page numbers cannot be included in notes that refer to such sources. Imagine, for example, that you have consulted the online text of Charles Darwin's book *Voyage of the Beagle*, which you have listed on your works-cited page as follows:

```
Darwin, Charles.  The Voyage of the Beagle.  Harvard

     Classics 29.  New York: Collier, 1909.  Online.

     Internet Wiretap.  Internet.  Address: gopher://

     ftp.std.com:70/00/obi/book/Charles.Darwin/

     Voyage.of.the.Beagle.Z.  11 Nov. 1995.
```

Although the original printed version had page numbers, no page numbers appear with the online text. Consequently, a parenthetical note referring to the text as a whole or to any part of the text would simply be:

```
(Darwin)
```

The same is true for periodical articles that you have not consulted in their original print forms but only as reproduced in an electronic database. For example, the newspaper article in the following works-cited listing appeared on page A17 of the *Toronto Star*.

```
Carey, Elaine.  "Is Graying of Faculty Turning University

     into 'Boring' Place?"  Toronto Star 25 Sept. 1995: A17.

     CD NewsBank Comprehensive.  CD-ROM.  NewsBank.  Oct.

     1995.
```

However, if you read it as reproduced in the database, your parenthetical notes would not include a page reference:

```
(Carey)
```

A Source Reproduced by a Microform Reproduction Service or Database

Reference services such as NewsBank reproduce articles from newspapers on microfiche. No page or microfiche numbers are needed in notes referring to such articles. Assume, for example, that you have included the following item in your list of works cited:

```
"U.S. Forests 'Very Healthy,' Ecologist Reports." Wyoming

     State Tribune 25 June 1991.  NewsBank ENV, 1991, fiche

     58, grid A1.
```

Since the work is anonymous, any note citing the article would refer to the title. No page reference is needed:

```
("U.S. Forests")
```

One Source Cited in Another

Sometimes you wish to quote a source whom you have found quoted in *another* source. In such a case, your note should cite the actual source from which you take the material you are using. Imagine, for example, that in reading a book by an author named Robinson, you encounter a quotation from an article by another author named Amoros. Robinson provided a note *(Amoros 16),* to cite the quotation's location in Amoros's article. However, unless you actually then go to Amoros's article to look up the quotation, you would list Robinson as your source, preceded by *qtd. in* (an abbreviation for "quoted in"):

Quoting a print source found in another source

```
Amoros writes that "successful politicians, like successful

actors and teachers, always stay in character"

(qtd. in Robinson 199).
```

Also use *qtd. in* for notes when the person being quoted was an interview source. For example, if Robinson had interviewed and then quoted someone named Reese, you would give Robinson as your source for the Reese quotation:

> Reese said, "The secret to life is learning how to
>
> write off your losses" (qtd. in Robinson 208).

Quoting an interview source found in another source

However, if you paraphrased Reese, you would omit *qtd. in:*

> Reese believes that people should not dwell on past
>
> setbacks (Robinson 208).

Paraphrasing one source found in another source

Once you have practiced citing sources in your own research writing, you will quickly become familiar with the techniques involved. Observe the way notes are used in the works that you read, as in Helen's and Molly's papers on pages 230–53. In writing your own research papers, refer to the Quick Reference Guide on the inside back covers of this book as needed, and use this chapter for fuller explanations. When unusual situations arise and you are uncertain how to cite a source, the wisest course may be to improvise, guided by your common sense. Always keep in mind that the purpose of notes is to acknowledge your sources in a clear, brief, consistent, and unobtrusive way.

Using Parenthetical Notes

EXERCISE

Assume that the following passages are all taken from the same research paper. Parenthetical notes have been omitted, but information about their sources is given in brackets following each passage. First, write the list of works cited that would appear at the end of the paper (assuming that these are the paper's only sources). Second, insert parenthetical notes in the passages.

1. The world's most advanced bicycle was invented in 1967

   by Swiss inventor Ugo Zwingli.

   [You discovered this information on page 33 of Vilma Mayer's book, *101 Offbeat Ideas,* published by the Phantom Company of Chicago in 1984.]

2. When he first encountered Zwingli's invention, cyclist

   Freddie Mercxx exclaimed: "This will either

   revolutionize road racing or set it back a hundred

   years!"

   [Mercxx wrote this on page 44 of his column, "New Products," which appeared on pages 44 and 45 of the November 1968 *Cyclist's World.*]

3. According to Rupert Brindel, president of the

   International Bicycle Federation, "The cycling world

was in a tizzy about the Zwingli frame. Supporters

called it 'the bike of the future,' while detractors

said it removed the <u>sport</u> from the sport of cycling."

[You found this in Melba Zweiback's book, *Two Wheels,* on page 202. She is quoting from Brindel's article, "The Zwingli Fiasco," which appeared on page 22 of the *Sporting Times* newspaper, April 13, 1983. *Two Wheels* was published in Montreal by Singleday in 1996.]

4. Zwingli had discovered a revolutionary way to reinforce

tissue paper. The result was a frame so lightweight

that it would actually gain speed while coasting

uphill.

[This too was taken from Mayer's book, page 36.]

5. In his <u>Memoirs</u>, Zwingli wrote, "I was overjoyed by how

strong the tissue-paper frame was. The first prototype

held up well under every test--until the first

rainstorm."

[He wrote *Memoirs* in 1978; the quotation is from the bottom of page 63 and the top of page 64. Zigurat Press of Zurich published it.]

6. Zwingli's bicycle was a mere curiosity until the

following year, when he made his second brilliant

discovery: waterproof tissue paper.

[You paraphrased this from "And Now: Non-Absorbent T.P.," an anonymous brief article on page 416 of the July 1968 *Applied Chemistry Bulletin* (volume 28), a journal with continuous paging.]

7. The twin brother of Freddie Mercxx, also a world-class

cyclist, wrote:

> With all other bicycles, the strongest and
>
> fittest cyclist wins the race. With the
>
> Zwingli bike, the lightest racer wins. I'm
>
> tired of being wiped off the track by
>
> skinny guys on tissue paper.

[Otto Mercxx wrote this in a letter to his brother dated 28 January 1970.]

8. The fate of the Zwingli bicycle was sealed in 1985 when

it was outlawed for competition by a vote of 70 to 3 of

the International Bicycle Federation.

[You found this information on page 54 of Melba Zweiback's magazine article, "IBF Disposes of Tissue Paper 10-Speed," published on pages 54, 55, and 56 of the August 1970 *Newsmonth*.]

9. Although the following week's Tour de Finland race was

marred by protests from newly unemployed lightweight riders,

the cycling world soon returned to normal.

[This information appeared on page C17 of the *New York Times-News-Post* newspaper dated August 22, 1970, in an article by Greg LeMoon under the headline "Feather-weight Furor in Finland." You read the article last Tuesday in the AllSportsNews online database, produced by the InfoBank Company.]

When Are Notes Needed?

It is your privilege as a scholar to make use of the scholarship of other people in your writing. It is your obligation as a scholar to make it clear to your readers which words and ideas in your writing are your own and which ones came from your sources. The general rule for when notes are needed is this: *Provide notes for all quotations; provide notes for all paraphrased information that is not commonly available knowledge.* The examples that follow illustrate this rule.

A frequent mistake made by beginning scholars is to give notes only for quotations. Remember that you need to acknowledge your debts to your sources, whether you quote their exact words or only borrow their ideas. You should give a note for information you have used, even if you have phrased it in words entirely your own. For example, assume you are writing an article on the Black Death, the plague that devastated medieval Europe, and one of your sources is Barbara Tuchman's book *A Distant Mirror*. Imagine that you found this passage on page 94:

> . . . Although the mortality rate was erratic, ranging from one fifth in some places to nine tenths or almost total elimination in others, the overall estimate of modern demographers has settled—for the area extending from India to Iceland—around the same figure expressed in Froissart's casual words: "a third of the world died." His estimate, the common one at the time, was not an inspired guess but a borrowing of St. John's figure for mortality from plague in Revelation, the favorite guide to human affairs in the Middle Ages.
>
> A third of Europe would have meant about 20 million deaths. No one knows how many died. Contemporary reports were an awed impression, not an accurate count.

If you wrote any of the following sentences based on this passage, you would need to give credit to Tuchman in a note.

It is widely accepted that about one third of Europe's

population died from the Black Death (Tuchman 94).

> Although a mortality of 20 million Europeans is usually
> accepted for the Black Death, no accurate figures exist
> to confirm this estimate (Tuchman 94).
>
> Even if the usual mortality estimate of one third of
> Europe (Tuchman 94) is not accepted, the Black Death
> still exacted a horrendous toll of the population.

None of these passages is a direct quotation, but since they are based on your source, they require notes. In the first two examples, by placing the note at the end of the sentence, you signal that all the information is from Tuchman's book. In the third example, by placing the note in the middle of the sentence, you indicate that only the material preceding the note is from that source.

You do not need to note information from a source if it is widely available and generally accepted. For example, you might have learned this information in an encyclopedia or almanac: *Oklahoma became a state in 1907.* Although you did not know this fact before you looked it up, it is such common information that it is in effect public property, and you need not acknowledge a source in a note. The facts on the Black Death in Tuchman's article, on the other hand, represent her own research findings, and she deserves full acknowledgment when her ideas are used.

The distinction being drawn here may not always be an obvious one. As is often the case with research writing, your best practice is to let common sense be your guide. You can usually tell when information is public property and when a source deserves credit for it in a note. But when you are in doubt, the safest course is to provide the note.

How Many Notes Are Enough?

In writing a research paper, you are creating something new, even if almost all the ideas and information in it are from your sources. At the very least, your contribution is to synthesize this information and to present it in a fresh way. For this reason your research paper will be based on a variety of sources. A long paper based on only one or two sources serves little purpose since it does nothing new. Consequently, your research papers are likely to have a number of notes, indicating the contributions of your various sources.

Sometimes you will have to use many notes to acknowledge a complex passage that is developed, quite legitimately, from several different sources. For example:

> Herbal folk remedies have been imported to the West with
> mixed results. An East African tea seems to be effective
> against cholera ("Nature's" 6), while moxibustion, a
> Chinese remedy for diarrhea, is still largely untested
> ("Burning" 25). A Chinese arthritis medicine called
> "Chuifong Toukuwan," on the other hand, is a positive
> danger to health (Hunter 8).

The second sentence requires two notes because it is based on two separate sources.

On the other hand, there can be a danger in overloading your paper with notes. One reason the format of notes is so brief is to keep them from getting in the way of what you are saying in the paper. When a paper is filled with note after note, even brief notes call attention to themselves, and they distract and annoy readers. With notes—as with quotations, brackets, and ellipsis dots—there can be too much of a good thing. Avoid passages like this in your writing:

```
In 1948, Isaac Stork ran for president (McCall 80) on the

Anti-Vice ticket (Sullivan 42).  His platform included a

prohibition on all sweetened or alcoholic beverages

(McCall 80), fines for wearing brightly colored outfits

(Stokes 124), and the clothing of naked cats, dogs, and

horses (McCall 81).
```

Bad (too many notes)

The notes here are annoying, not only because they interrupt the passage so often but also because they are unnecessary. It is evident that the writer has done some research and is eager to show off. The writer is deliberately juggling three sources, all of which contain the same information. The first sentence would seem to state commonly available information that does not require acknowledgment. Information in the second sentence might also be considered public property, but to be safe, the writer might provide a single joint note after the final sentence like this:

```
. . . cats, dogs, and horses (McCall 80-81; Stokes 124).
```

Judging When Notes Are Needed

EXERCISE

Imagine that it is some time in the near future and that you are writing a brief research report. Imagine too that, having found the following six passages in your research, you have then written the report that follows them. What remains for you to do is to supply notes for the report.

1. Horseradish *(Armoracia lapathifolia),* a plant of the mustard family, is grown for its pungent, white fleshy root. [*Source:* Elizabeth Silverman's book, *Common Plants of North America,* page 208.]

2. I first met Mr. Finnahey when I stopped by his farm to get forms filled out for his medical benefits. When I asked him his age, he said, "I forget the exact year I was born. It was the same year the Brooklyn Bridge was built." Naturally I didn't believe him since he didn't look a day over 40, and his wife, Becky, was 26. Imagine my surprise when he brought out his birth certificate. [*Source:* social worker Marlys Davenport, quoted on page 35 of a newspaper article written by Lester Grady.]

3. The Brooklyn Bridge was built in 1883. [*Source:* an anonymous article in *Encyclopedia Galactica,* volume 4, page 73.]

4. When I arrived to examine Julius Finnahey, he was eating a lunch of peanut butter and horseradish sandwiches. "Best thing for you," he said. "I eat 'em every day-—

always have." This was my first clue to the cause of his longevity. My research into his diet led to a discovery that may provide humans of the future with lifetimes lasting perhaps two centuries. [*Source:* Chester Vinneman writing on page 19 of his article, "Radish-Legume Combination Slows the Aging Process," in the *New England Medical Report.*]

5. Chester Vinneman discovered that the combination of the trace element *vinnemanium,* which occurs in the common horseradish root, with amino acids in the common peanut retards the decay of the cell wall lining in human tissue. To Vinneman, the increased longevity which his discovery will provide is a mixed blessing: "I find the prospect both thrilling and frightening. The questions and problems that it raises stagger the mind." [*Source:* an unsigned article, "Life Everlasting Now a Reality?" in *Timely* magazine, page 78, continued on page 80.]

6. Chester Vinneman won the Nobel Prize for medicine for his discovery of the miracle age retardant. He is a professor of biochemistry at the University of Manitoba. [*Source: Who's Who,* page 993.]

Here is a section of your report, which is based on the preceding list of sources. Supply the appropriate parenthetical notes.

Important discoveries are often the result of chance occurrences. If it had not been for a routine inquiry by social worker Marlys Davenport, Chester Vinneman might never have won the Nobel Prize for medicine. It was Davenport who confirmed Julius Finnahey's amazing statement that he was born in 1883, "the year the Brooklyn Bridge was built."

Professor Vinneman made the connection between Finnahey's extraordinary youthfulness and his diet of peanut butter and horseradish sandwiches. Horseradish (Armoracia lapathifolia) was not previously thought to have benefits beyond the flavor of its pungent root. Through extensive tests, however, Vinneman discovered a previously unreported trace element in horseradish, which he named vinnemanium. This element, when combined with amino acids such as those found in peanuts, prevents human cell walls from decaying.

Vinneman predicts that as the result of his discovery, human lifetimes may extend in the future to as

```
many as two centuries.  He finds the prospect of such

longevity "both thrilling and frightening.  The questions

and problems that it raises stagger the mind." It

remains to be seen how wisely humankind will cope with

greatly extended lives.
```

Finally, explain why you placed notes where you did and why you provided notes for some statements and not others.

How Much Material Can One Note Cover?

A parenthetical note comes after borrowed material, but how can a writer make clear *how much* of the preceding material is referred to by the note? The following passage illustrates the problem:

```
Haagendazs was considered one of Denmark's premier

eccentrics.  He continually wore the same heavy woolen

sweater, regardless of the occasion or season.  Former

colleagues attest that he worked in near darkness, and he

reportedly kept exotic spiders and beetles as pets

(Noland 18).
```

The extent of the reference is not clear. Is Noland the source for all three examples of Haagendazs's eccentricities or just the latter two (or the last one)? The ambiguity could be avoided, perhaps, by placing a note after each paraphrased sentence. But the paper would then be overloaded with notes, and readers would find it annoying to meet with identical notes sentence after sentence.

A somewhat clearer way to define a long borrowed passage is to mark its beginning with an acknowledgment phrase. For example:

```
Noland reports that Haagendazs was considered one of

Denmark's premier eccentrics.  He continually wore the

same heavy woolen sweater, regardless of the occasion or

season.  Former colleagues attest that he worked in near

darkness, and he reportedly kept exotic spiders and

beetles as pets (18).
```

The acknowledgment phrase marks the beginning of the borrowed passage.

The note marks the end of the passage.

Here it is clear that the entire passage is taken from page 18 of a work by Noland. However, acknowledgment phrases are not commonly used with factual information, and an excess of acknowledgment phrases can be as distracting to readers as an excess of parenthetical notes. Alas, some ambiguity in the scope of your references is probably unavoidable. Rely on your judgment about whether a borrowed passage is adequately marked, but if you are in doubt, supply the acknowledgment phrase. You may also ask your instructor for advice.

EXERCISE | **Judging When Borrowed Material Is Adequately Marked**

Examine the parenthetical notes in the research papers by Helen and Molly on pages 230–53. For each parenthetical note, is it clear how much material is borrowed from the source? If not, can you suggest a way to make it clearer?

 INFORMATION FOOTNOTES

Even when you use parenthetical notes to acknowledge sources, you can still use footnotes to supply information that you feel does not belong in the text of your paper. To mark an *information footnote,* place a raised asterisk (*) in the place where you invite the reader to consult the note, like this:

    . . . domesticated animals such as dogs, cats,* and . . .

At the bottom of the same page, type a line of ten underline bars and present your footnote on the next line, beginning with a raised asterisk, like this:

    _____

        * Witherspoon does not classify the common house cat as
    a "domesticated" animal but as a "wild" animal that merely
    "coexists" with humans (16).

Typing footnotes can be cumbersome. Fortunately, most word-processing programs can place footnotes automatically at the bottom of the proper page.

If you use a second information footnote on the same page, mark it with a double asterisk (**) or dagger (†). You should, however, use information footnotes rarely. Almost always when you have something to tell your readers, it is better to say it within the paper itself. This is in line with the general rule that anything that interrupts the reader or makes reading more difficult should be avoided.

Research Paper Format (MLA Style)

 FORMAT FOR YOUR POLISHED DRAFT

The polished draft of your paper should be either printed (via a computer word processor) or typed. A neatly handwritten paper may be allowed in rare cases, but only a printed or typed paper presents a professional appearance. When you are communicating with others, appearance counts. Although the paper's appearance does not alter the content of your writing, it most certainly does affect the way your writing is received. Instructors try to be as objective as possible in judging student work, but they are still swayed, like all other humans, by appearances. Computer-printed or typed papers give the impression of more serious, careful work, and they are certainly more inviting and easier to read. In the professional world, reports and correspondence are always computer-printed or typed; anything less would be unthinkable. There is no reason to treat your college writing with any less respect.

Computer word processing offers the greatest benefits for composing, revising, copyediting, and printing your paper. With a word processor, you can make additions, deletions, corrections, and rearrangements of passages easily and at any time. The spell-check feature can identify errors in spelling and typing that you might otherwise miss. And, of course, the finished product has a polished, professional appearance.

Use a typewriter only if a computer is unavailable. Most writers find it difficult to compose on a typewriter; it is easier to make changes and corrections in long-hand drafts. But once they have completed a draft, writers find it advantageous to type it. Typing your paper forces you to read it slowly and carefully. For many writers, some of their best ideas for polishing and revising their work come during typing. If you have not learned keyboard skills, you would be well advised to do so at the earliest opportunity; you will be greatly handicapped if you lack direct access to either a computer or a typewriter.

When you print or type your paper, follow the format exemplified by one of the sample papers shown in Chapter 8. In particular, pay attention to the following conventions.

Format for Computer-Printed or Typed Papers

The following are standard format guidelines for research papers. Individual instructors may wish to modify some of them according to their preferences. Check with your instructor if you have questions about the required format.

Paper

For computer printing, use individual sheets of typing paper or plain white, heavy-weight, $8\frac{1}{2} \times 11$-inch fanfold paper that does not leave noticeably ragged edges when separated. If you type, use good-quality, non-see-through, nonoily, non-erasable, 20-pound, $8\frac{1}{2} \times 11$-inch paper. Type on one side of the paper only.

Ribbon

Replace the ribbon in your printer or typewriter if it no longer produces a dark copy. Use only black ink.

Type Font

For computer-printed papers, a laser, ink jet, or dot matrix printer with correspondence-quality type is best. If your word processor allows you a choice of fonts, choose Courier, a monospaced font resembling typewriter type; do not use a proportional-space font that resembles the printing in a book. For typewritten papers, never use a fancy typeface such as script or italic.

Spacing

Double-space (leave every other line blank) throughout the paper. This includes indented quotations and the list of works cited, which are also double-spaced. Do not skip additional lines between paragraphs.

Margins

Leave one-inch margins at the top, bottom, and sides of each page of the paper. The right margin does not need to be straight; do not divide words with hyphens just to achieve a straighter margin. For computer-printed papers, a justified right margin is not desirable; that is, do not have the computer insert extra spaces between words so as to make the right margin straight.

If you wish, you can adjust the bottom margin of any page to avoid a ***widow line*** or an ***orphan***—the typesetting terms for stranded lines. An orphan is the first line of a new paragraph at the bottom of a page; a widow is the last line of a paragraph at the top of a page. To avoid widows and orphans, do not type the first line of a new paragraph at the bottom of a page but begin it instead at the top of the following page. Also, do not begin a new page with the last line of a paragraph; if necessary, type that line at the bottom of the preceding page. Notice how Helen Veit avoided a widow at the top of page 233.

Indenting

Indent one-half inch (five spaces) before beginning each new paragraph. Indent long quotations one inch (ten spaces) from the left margin; do not indent from the

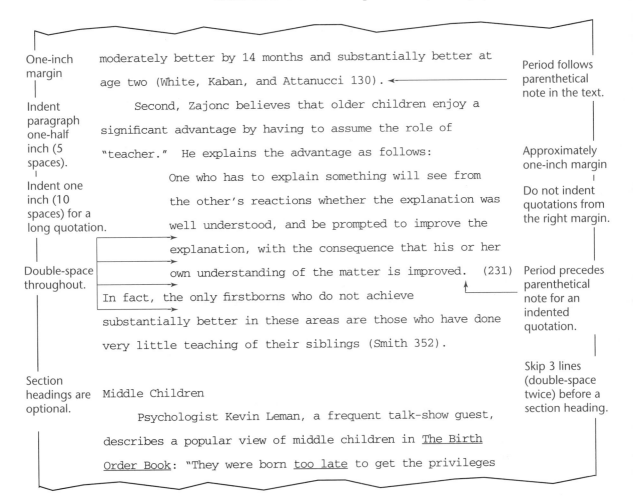

One-inch margin

moderately better by 14 months and substantially better at age two (White, Kaban, and Attanucci 130). ⟵

Period follows parenthetical note in the text.

Indent paragraph one-half inch (5 spaces).

Second, Zajonc believes that older children enjoy a significant advantage by having to assume the role of "teacher." He explains the advantage as follows:

Indent one inch (10 spaces) for a long quotation.

One who has to explain something will see from the other's reactions whether the explanation was well understood, and be prompted to improve the explanation, with the consequence that his or her own understanding of the matter is improved.   (231)

Approximately one-inch margin

Do not indent quotations from the right margin.

Double-space throughout.

In fact, the only firstborns who do not achieve substantially better in these areas are those who have done very little teaching of their siblings (Smith 352).

Period precedes parenthetical note for an indented quotation.

Section headings are optional.

Middle Children

Psychologist Kevin Leman, a frequent talk-show guest, describes a popular view of middle children in The Birth Order Book: "They were born too late to get the privileges

Skip 3 lines (double-space twice) before a section heading.

Figure C.1 Format for the spacing and margins in a research paper.

right margin. (For additional directions, see pages 329–30.) Figure C.1 shows an excerpt from a research paper demonstrating how margins and indentions should be handled.

The First Page

The format of your first page should resemble that of Helen's paper in Figure C.2.

- **Page number.** Type your last name and the number *1* in the upper-right corner of the first page, about one-half inch from the top of the paper.

- **Heading.** Type your full name, course information, and the date in the upper-left corner of the first page, about one inch from the top of the paper. A separate cover page is needed only for lengthy reports (see pages 480–81).

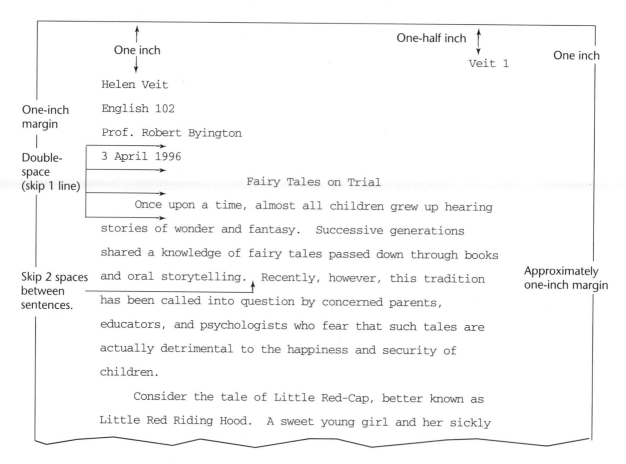

Figure C.2 Format for the first page.

- *Title.* Double-space again (skip a line), and center the title. Only the first letter of each important word in the title should be capitalized; do not capitalize a word such as *the* (article), *and* (conjunction), or *of* (preposition) unless it is the first word of the title or the first word following a colon. Do not underline the title or enclose it in quotation marks. Of course, you should use standard punctuating conventions for titles of works that you include within your own titles. For example:

The Depiction of Old Age in <u>King Lear</u>

and in "The Love Song of J. Alfred Prufrock"

- *Body.* Double-space following the title, and begin your paper. Skip two spaces between sentences. (Notice how Helen skipped two spaces following each period that ends a sentence, each question mark, and each exclamation point in her paper.)

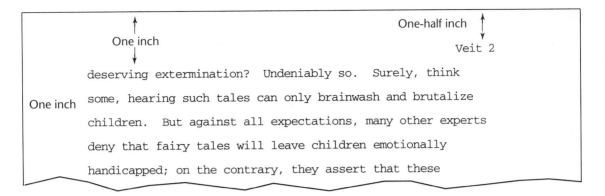

Figure C.3 **Format for subsequent pages.**

Subsequent Pages

The format of subsequent pages is shown in Figure C.3. Type your last name and page number in the upper right-hand corner, about one-half inch from the top of the page. This is a precaution in case pages get misplaced or misarranged. Do not precede the page number with *p.* or *page.* Then double-space twice (skip three lines); the first line of text should begin one inch from the top of the page.

Tables and Figures

You can include *tables*—the presentation of data in columns—and *figures*—drawings, graphs, photographs, or other inserts—in your paper. Tables and figures can be either of your own creation or copied from a source (and duly acknowledged). A sample page from a research paper that includes a table is shown in Figure C.4. Figure C.5 shows a figure that the writer photocopied from a source he acknowledged.

Observe the following guidelines when you include tables and figures:

1. All tables and figures should be referred to within the paper (e.g., "Table 1 shows the variation among . . . ," ". . . as can be seen in Figure 6," and so on). Place the table or figure as close as possible following its mention in the paper.

2. Tables and figures should be numbered consecutively (Table 1, Table 2, Table 3, . . . ; Figure 1, Figure 2, . . .). Each table should be given a clear explanatory label on the following line, and each figure should have an explanatory caption typed on the same line and placed below the figure. Each line begins at the left margin; it is not centered.

3. Double-space throughout, but skip three lines (double-space twice) both before and after a table or figure.

4. Lines may be drawn across the page (as in Figure C.4, for example) to set a table or figure apart from the rest of the paper.

Reagan 8

Other statistics show that although the number of
medical students in their thirties and forties is
increasing, one's chances of being admitted to medical
school decrease with age, as Table 1 demonstrates:

The table is
referred to
within the paper.

Each table or
figure is given
a number and
a label.

Quadruple-space
before and after
each table or
figure.

Raised lower-
case letters are
used for foot-
notes within
tables and
figures.

Table 1

Percentages of Men and Women Accepted by Medical Schools
(1989)[a]

Age	Men	Women
21–23	73	67
24–27	58	55
28–31	49	53
32–34	46	51
35–37	41	46
38 and over	27	34

Each line of a
table begins
at the left
margin (it is
not centered).

Double-space
throughout
the table.

The table
ends with the
source and
footnotes (if
any).

Source: Plantz, Lorenzo, and Cole 115

[a] The chart is based on data gathered by the American
Medical Association.

The paper
resumes
following the
table.

I have learned that there are many criteria other
than age that medical schools consider when reviewing
applications.

Figure C.4   Sample page with table.

material off the diskette and avoids several potential

hazards. The gap between the read/write head and the

diskette is incredibly small, as can be seen in Figure

6. The figure also shows some of the "gremlins" that

cause disk problems.

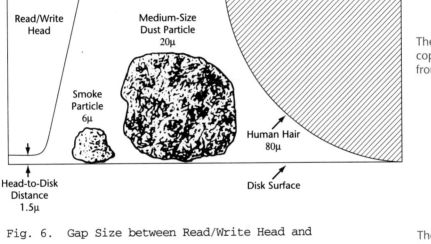

The figure is photo-copied and pasted from the source.

Fig. 6. Gap Size between Read/Write Head and
Diskette(Smith-Richardson 62).

The figure's source is acknowledged.

Figure C.5 Sample page with a figure.

5. A table or figure may be photocopied from a source and pasted onto your page (see Figure C.5). You may then wish to photocopy the entire page again.

6. If the table or figure is taken from a source, acknowledge the source on a line following the table or figure.

7. If you use footnotes (as in Figure C.4), assign them raised lowercase letters (a, b, c, and so on) and place the notes below the table or figure (and source citation, if given).

List of Works Cited

Begin the list of works cited on a new page. (The exception is a very brief list, which you can begin after skipping three lines from the end of the text.)

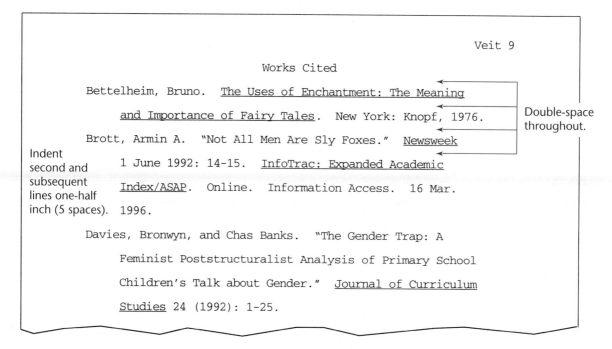

Figure C.6 **Sample Works Cited page.**

- *Title.* Center the title *Works Cited* (or *Bibliography)* about one inch from the top of the page; that is, skip three lines following the page number.

- *Spacing.* Double-space between the title and the first entry and throughout the list. Do not skip additional lines between entries.

- *Entries.* Follow the guidelines in Chapter A. Remember to "outdent" each entry; that is, begin each entry at the left margin and indent the second and subsequent lines one-half inch (five spaces). List items in alphabetical order. Do not number your entries. The list of works cited should include only works that you quoted or paraphrased in writing the paper, not works you consulted but did not use.

Refer to Figure C.6 for a sample works-cited page.

Fastening the Paper

Fasten your paper with a paper clip in the upper left-hand corner. Do not staple or rivet pages together or place your paper within a cover unless you are requested to do so by your instructor.

Title Page

A title page is standard only for a book-length report, a paper with multiple chapters, or a paper with preliminary material such as a formal outline or preface. If you use a title page, it should follow the format shown in Figure C.7.

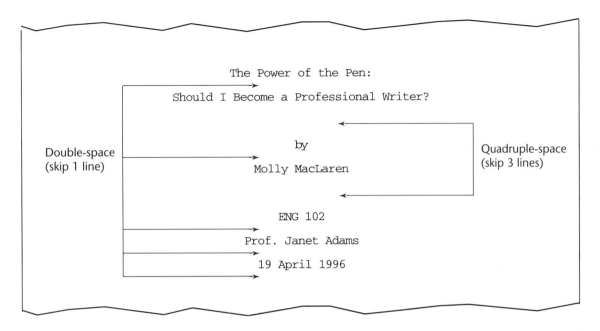

Figure C.7 Sample title page.

Title-page information is typed in the center of the page. Center each line, and leave equal space above and below the typed material. Most word-processing programs can automatically center material on a page from top to bottom. If you type, you can use this formula to determine the number of lines to skip from the top of the page before typing the first line:

1. Count the number of lines of text that will appear on your title page, including skipped lines. (Molly MacLaren's title information takes up 17 lines in the example.)

2. Subtract that number from 66, the total number of lines on a typical page, to get the number of unused lines. (In Molly's case, $66 - 17 = 49$.)

3. Divide that number in half. (Half of 49 is $24\frac{1}{2}$.)

4. Skip that number of lines (in Molly's case, 24 or 25) from the top of the page, and begin typing.

To center each line from left to right, count the number of characters (letters, spaces, and punctuation) in the line (Molly's first line, *The Power of the Pen:*, consists of 21 characters). Backspace half that many spaces from the center of your paper (10 or 11 spaces) and begin typing. If you use a title page, do not repeat title information on the following page. Number the following page as page 1.

Typing Errors

Correction tape is preferable to white correction fluid for removing errors as you type. Never use an eraser. If you use a computer, use the spell-check feature and proofread to make your paper as error-free as possible before you print your final draft.

Errors Discovered during Proofreading

Neatly cross out a minor error with a single line, and write the correction above it. Never erase, and do not use correction fluid for making handwritten changes. Any page with a major error or numerous minor errors should be retyped.

Format for Handwritten Papers

Most of the guidelines for typed and computer-generated papers also apply to handwritten papers, with the following adjustments. Consult your instructor to determine if handwritten papers are acceptable.

Paper

Use lined, non-see-through $8\frac{1}{2} \times 11$-inch loose-leaf paper. Never use sheets torn or cut from a spiral notebook. Paper should be college ruled ($3\frac{1}{2}$ lines per inch) and have a left margin line. Write on only one side of each sheet of paper.

Pen

Use a fine-point pen with dark blue or black ink. Never use a pen that smudges or that leaves small ink blotches when touched to the page.

Handwriting

Write in a neat, clear hand. Hard-to-read, distractingly fancy, or slovenly hand-writing detracts from the effectiveness of your presentation. If you have difficulty with your handwriting, you would be wise to have your paper typed. Do not make your writing excessively large or leave excessive space between words. Handwritten papers with only a few words on each line are unpleasant to read because they demand constant eye movement.

Margins

Leave about a one-inch margin from the top and from the left of each page. That is, begin each page on the second line, and begin each line at the red margin line. Do not leave space for right and bottom margins, unless requested to do so by your instructor. The title and page numbers are placed as in typed papers.

Spacing

Single-space your paper unless you are requested by your instructor to double-space.

Errors

Handwritten papers should be error-free. Neatly cross out a minor error with a sin-gle line, and write the correction above it. Never erase or use correction fluid to

Statley 1

Lisa Statley
English 102
Ms. Virginia Jones
2 April 1995
       First in Family, First in School?
   Scientists long ago discredited the belief that race
or gender can determine intelligence. But what about
birth order? Is it possible that firstborn children possess
an inherent advantage over their younger brothers and
sisters? There are educated people who claim just that. In
fact, some psychologists subscribe to the idea that birth
order and intelligence are related, with firstborn

Figure C.8 Sample first page of a handwritten paper.

Statley 2

relatively short" (234). He claimed that SAT scores gradually
dropped after 1965. because by then fewer high-school
seniors were firstborns, the first wave of post-war
children having already entered college.
   In the years following the publication of Zajonc's
controversial theory, dozens of books and articles have

Figure C.9 Subsequent page from a handwritten paper.

make corrections. Any page with a major error or numerous minor errors should be recopied.

Excerpts from a handwritten paper are shown in Figures C.8 and C.9.

A FORMAL OUTLINE

The general, *informal outlines* that Helen Veit used in writing her early drafts (see pages 311 and 357) helped her to organize her research materials. The length and complexity of a research paper require writers to have a plan for arranging it—one that is general and flexible enough so that they can develop and alter it as they discover new ideas.

Informal outlines are valuable, but most writers—both beginners and professionals alike—find it difficult and limiting to create a detailed, formal outline *before* they write. As you have now read many times in this book, writing is a learning process. Writers rarely know exactly how a paper will turn out before they write it. Even the best-prepared writers are usually surprised by the final form their writing takes. This occurs because our minds are actively at work when we write, and writing stimulates new thoughts that can take our writing in unforeseen directions.

Although a *formal outline* is limited in usefulness when it is prepared before you begin writing, it *can* be useful as part of the revision process—when it is written *after* you have completed a preliminary draft. As a scaled-down map of your paper, the formal outline allows you to see its organization with clarity. It can point out the flaws of your arrangement and suggest new possibilities. Some instructors require that a printed, formal outline be included as a part of the research paper to make sure that their students have considered organization carefully. The detailed formal outline that Helen submitted with her paper is printed on the following page.

Fairy Tales on Trial

I. Introduction

   A. Controversy: effect on children

      1. Traditional role

      2. Modern concerns

   B. Example: Little Red-Cap

   C. Responses: both criticism and support

II. Violence in fairy tales

   A. Examples

   B. Arguments for violence

      1. Violence not harmful

         a. Security in death of villain

            (1) Hansel and Gretel

            (2) Three Little Pigs

         b. Children's differing view of violence

         c. Unrealistic nature of fairy-tale violence

      2. Violence actually helpful

         a. Models of problem-solving

         b. Control over "monster within" children

III. Gender stereotypes in fairy tales

   A. Examples

   B. Arguments concerning stereotypes

      1. Con: romanticizing of female subordination

      2. Pro: glimpse into past

   C. Effects shown by case studies

      1. Girls: successful struggle with conflicts

      2. Boys: acceptance of stereotyped roles

IV. Therapeutic benefits of fairy tales

   A. Teenagers: use in "values-based" curriculum

   B. Adults

      1. Battered wives

      2. Women with eating disorders

V. Conclusion

   A. Summary of arguments

   B. On balance, vindication of fairy tales

An outline can be as detailed—or as general—as you wish. Helen's outline is reasonably complete, but she could have made it either shorter or longer if she wished. Compare it to this excerpt from a less detailed version of Helen's outline:

```
  I. Introduction

     A. Controversy: effect on children

     B. Example: Little Red-Cap

     C. Responses: both criticism and support

 II. Violence in fairy tales

     A. Examples

     B. Arguments for violence

        1. Not harmful to children

        2. Actually helpful to children

III. Gender stereotypes in fairy tales

     A. Examples

     B. Pros and cons of stereotyping

     C. Effects on girls and boys . . .
```

On the other hand, a more detailed outline might expand section III, "Gender stereotypes in fairy tales," as follows:

```
III. Gender stereotypes in fairy tales

     A. Examples

        1. Rumpelstiltskin: incompetent female in need of male

           help

        2. Snow White and Sleeping Beauty: female passivity

     B. Arguments concerning gender stereotyping

        1. Arguments against

           a. Subconscious association with heroines

           b. Glorification of traditional female roles

              (1) docility

              (2) dependence

              (3) sacrifice . . .
```

When you are revising your paper, a detailed outline can help you see how each part fits into the whole. When you have difficulty in creating an outline, the cause is often a problem with the organization of your paper. Your attempts to create a logical outline can often suggest a workable rearrangement of material within your paper. For example, before Helen created her formal outline, she had a separate section of her paper devoted to case studies regarding both violence and stereotyping. Only when she created her outline did she decide that they would be more effective treated separately. That is, she placed the case studies about violence with other materials in a separate section about violence, and she did the same for the case studies about stereotypes.

On the other hand, a writer should not be a slave to a rigidly symmetrical outline. In the final analysis, the nature of your material and not form-for-form's-sake should determine your outline. For that reason, Helen's section II on violence and her section III on stereotypes are similar but not precisely parallel in their structure.

Standard Numbering System

Formal outlines usually follow the format that Helen used. Notice that each major part of Helen's outline is divided into subparts. These subparts are indented and marked with numbers and letters, following this *standard system:*

Paper Title

I. First major part of the paper
II. Second major part
  A. First subpart of II
  B. Second subpart of II
    1. First subpart of B
    2. Second subpart of B
      a. First subpart of 2
      b. Second subpart of 2
        (1) First subpart of b
        (2) Second subpart of b
          (a) First subpart of (2)
          (b) Second subpart of (2)
III. Third major part
  A. . . .
  B. . . .
  C. . . .

Decimal System

The *decimal system* is also widely used for outlines, particularly for scientific papers.

1. First major part
2. Second major part

            2.1 First subpart of 2

            2.2 Second subpart of 2

                  2.2.1 First subpart of 2.2

                  2.2.2 Second subpart of 2.2

                        2.2.2.1 . . .

                        2.2.2.2 . . .

    3. . . .

        3.1 . . .

        3.2 . . .

        3.3 . . .

Some instructors who assign formal outlines require, in the interest of symmetry, that whenever a part is to have subparts, there must be at least two of them; that is, they prefer that there not be a part 1 without at least a part 2, and so on. For example, they would find level A1 in the following to be faulty because it is the only entry on its level (there is no A2):

    IV. Therapeutic benefits of fairy tales

        A. Teenagers

            1. Use in "values-based" curriculum

        B. Adults

            1. Battered wives

            2. Women with eating disorders . . .

It should be stressed that not everyone objects to lone subparts. For those who do, the preceding can easily be adjusted by incorporating the subpart into the part above it:

    IV. Therapeutic benefits of fairy tales

        A. Teenagers: use in "values-based" curriculum

        B. Adults . . .

EXERCISES | Formal Outlines

1. Following are the parts of an outline for an argumentative paper. They appear in the proper order, but they have not been numbered or indented. Number them according to the *standard system* for outlining.

    The Case against Saturday Morning Cartoons
    Introduction
    Background: description of current situation
    Thesis: harm to children by Saturday morning cartoon shows
    Counterarguments (those favoring these shows)
    Positive-benefit arguments
    Benefit to parents: babysitting

Benefits to children
Cartoon violence a harmless outlet for children's aggression
Children taught about life from cartoons
Free-market arguments
Programming determined by ratings, sponsors
Children's viewing up to parents, not networks
Censorship dangerous to our way of life
Refutation of counterarguments
Refutation of positive-benefit arguments
Damage to parents: deprived of interaction with their children
Damage to children
Shown only violent solutions to problems
Shown only the worst aspects of life
Refutation of free-market arguments
Morality, not only profits, a responsibility of networks
Parents unable to judge and screen all programming
Voluntary controls, not censorship, requested
Additional argument: danger to society of children's viewing
A nation of antisocial zombies
A nation of viewers, not doers
Conclusion: a call for reform

2. Renumber the preceding outline entries using the *decimal system.*

Topic and Sentence Outlines

The preceding formal outlines are examples of ***topic outlines,*** in which all the parts consist of phrases rather than complete sentences. In a ***sentence outline,*** the parts consist of complete sentences. For example:

    I. Fairy tales have become a source of controversy.

        A. Their effect upon children is being questioned.

            1. In the past, such tales were an accepted part of
               childhood.

            2. Recently, they have been criticized by parents,
               educators, and psychologists.

        B. Little Red-Cap exemplifies the violence and gender
           stereotypes in fairy tales.

        C. While many have condemned such tales, a surprising
           number of experts have come to their defense.

    II. ...

You can use either the topic or sentence outline method, but whichever you choose, be certain that you follow it consistently.

Like some of the other steps in research writing, the details of outline-writing may strike you as complicated—as undoubtedly they are—but they do serve a purpose. Use your informal and formal outlines to help you organize, write, and revise your paper. But remember that an outline is a tool to help you produce a better paper and not an end in itself. It is important at all times to remember the central goal of your research writing: to communicate what you have discovered in an effective way. Like all parts of the research process, the outline will work best and be of most help to you if you approach it with common sense.

EXERCISE   ## Sentence Outlines

1. Continue revising Helen Veit's outline on page 485 to make it a sentence outline.

2. Rewrite the outline in the preceding exercise (on pages 488–89) to make it a sentence outline. Each line of the outline should be a complete sentence.

D *Footnotes and Endnotes (Alternative MLA Style)*

UNTIL 1984, when the Modern Language Association (MLA) authorized the use of simple parenthetical notes to acknowledge sources (see Chapter B for an explanation of parenthetical format), footnotes and endnotes were the usual method of citation for papers written in the humanities. Since you will certainly encounter footnotes and endnotes in your reading and research and may even be asked to use them in your own research writing, you should be familiar with this style of citation. Although it should not be necessary for you to memorize the details of the format, you should know how to use this chapter as a reference guide whenever you need to write footnotes or endnotes. When you do, consult it carefully and be certain to follow the format exactly, paying special attention to the mechanics of arrangement and punctuation.

Figure D.1 shows how a portion of Helen Veit's research paper would have looked if she had used footnotes instead of parenthetical notes. (Compare it with her use of parenthetical notes on pages 231–33.) The excerpt in Figure D.2 shows what her "Notes" page would have looked like if she had used endnotes.

Footnotes and endnotes serve the same purpose as parenthetical notes—to identify and give credit to your sources for their specific contributions to your paper. In the same place in your paper where you would put a parenthetical note, put a raised number to refer your readers to the note. Number your notes consecutively throughout the paper, starting with number 1. For footnotes, type each note at the bottom of the same page where the reference occurs. For endnotes, type all notes, in numerical order, on a separate page following the paper but preceding the list of works cited.

SAMPLE FOOTNOTES AND ENDNOTES

The models in this chapter show the footnote/endnote format for works cited in Chapter A on pages 440–54. Note that complete information about a source is required only the first time it is cited in a note. Subsequent notes use an abbreviated format. (See sample footnote 5 in Figure D.1.)

Veit 2

said to me that the witch could have been put in prison.

But that can't be. The witch would have found her way out

by magic. And then she'd be free again."[2]

Such anxiety is not uncommon. For example, one

revision of the Three Little Pigs omitted the wolf's death

over a fire and inserted instead a mild burn and a panicked

dash to the nearby woods. Instead of reassuring children

of life's security, the new version actually created

anxiety that the wolf would return. One little girl,

convinced that the wolf was only biding his time until he

could reattack, had persistent nightmares. Only when the

original version including the wolf's death was substituted

for her regular story could the child believe that the wolf

was truly gone for good.[3]

Although children are obsessed with violence, that

does not seem to be a problem, according to psychologist

Ann Trousdale. She states that children tend to "omit

gratuitous violence" when retelling the story and only keep

the violence that is necessary for justice.[4] Fairness is

[2] Qtd. in Rudolf Messner, "Children and Fairy Tales--

What Unites Them and What Divides Them," Western European

Education 21.2 (1989): 11.

[3] Michael O. Tunnell, "The Double-Edged Sword: Fantasy

and Censorship," Language Arts 71 (1994): 609.

[4] Ann Trousdale, "Who's Afraid of the Big, Bad Wolf?"

Marginal notes:

Notes are numbered consecutively throughout the paper. The numbers are raised slightly above the line.

Double-space twice (skip 3 lines).

Double-space within and between footnotes.

Figure D.1 Sample pages from a paper that uses footnotes.

Veit 3

very important to young people. "Children are innocent and
love justice," observes author and critic G. K. Chesterton,
"while most of us are wicked and prefer mercy."[5] So a
parent and offspring reading a fairy tale aloud may have
very different reactions; what seems to be violent to the
former may seem only fitting to the latter.

Another important factor affecting the perception of
brutality is the extreme nature of the fairy tale itself.
Indeed, the heights of savagery and wonder balance each
other out, for, as Max Lüthi writes, "a princely reward or
a sentence of death is but one of the many contrasts used
in the fairy tale." Children don't regard these outcomes
as they would in a realistic narrative. They merely accept
them as "rule[s] of the game."[6]

Lüthi goes further to say that not only are the
violent elements harmless, but they are actually crucial
to children's development and perception of the world around
them. By demonstrating that dragons can be slain, these
fantastic stories teach children to master their dilemmas
rather than blame themselves or others. Ann Trousdale

Footnote
numbers follow
all punctuation.

A line drawn
on the page
signals that the
first footnote
beneath it con-
tinued from the
previous page.

Children's Literature 20.2 (1989): 76.

[5] Qtd. in Tunnell 608.

[6] Max Lüthi, The Fairytale as Art Form and Portrait of
Man, trans. Jon Erickson (Bloomington: Indiana UP, 1984)
152.

After the first
reference to a
source (see
footnote 4),
the abbreviated
form is used.

Figure D.1 (Continued).

Veit 9

Notes

[1] Jakob Grimm and Wilhelm Grimm, <u>Grimms' Fairy Tales</u>, Online, Carnegie Mellon U. Lib., Internet, available: http://www.cs.cmu.edu/Web/books.html, 20 Mar. 1996.

[2] Qtd. in Rudolf Messner, "Children and Fairy Tales-- What Unites Them and What Divides Them," <u>Western European Education</u> 21.2 (1989): 11.

[3] Michael O. Tunnell, "The Double-Edged Sword: Fantasy and Censorship," <u>Language Arts</u> 71 (1994): 609.

[4] Ann Trousdale, "Who's Afraid of the Big, Bad Wolf?" <u>Children's Literature</u> 20.2 (1989): 76.

[5] Qtd. in Tunnell 608.

[6] Max Lüthi, <u>The Fairytale as Art Form and Portrait of Man</u>, trans. Jon Erickson (Bloomington: Indiana UP, 1984) 152.

[7] 154.

[8] Trousdale 72.

[9] Bruno Bettelheim, <u>The Uses of Enchantment: The Meaning and Importance of Fairy Tales</u> (New York: Knopf, 1976) 120.

[10] 74.

[11] Jack Zipes, "Spinning with Fate: Rumpelstiltskin and the Decline of Female Productivity," <u>Western Folklore</u> 52 (1993): 49.

[12] Bronwyn Davies and Chas Banks, "The Gender Trap: A Feminist Poststructuralist Analysis of Primary School

Figure D.2 Sample Notes page from a paper that uses endnotes.

Sources in Books

A Book with One Author

> [1] Arthur K. Wheelock, Jr., <u>Vermeer and the Art of Painting</u> (New Haven: Yale UP, 1995) 52-54.

Note that footnotes/endnotes differ from works-cited entries in several particulars: The first line of each footnote/endnote is indented; the author's first (not last) name comes first; the publisher and date are enclosed in parentheses; and commas (not periods) separate major items. Also, unlike works-cited entries (but like parenthetical notes), footnotes/endnotes give the specific page or pages in the source from which the cited information is taken.

Second and Subsequent References—All Sources

After a work has been cited in one note, you do not need to repeat all the same information in subsequent notes that refer to that same source. For second and subsequent references to a source, footnotes/endnotes should contain the least amount of information needed to identify the source (usually author and page number).

> [2] Wheelock 109.

Note that the content of second footnotes is identical to that of parenthetical notes. Latin terms such as *ibid.* and *op. cit.* are no longer used in notes of any kind.

A Book with Two or Three Authors

> [3] Newton Minnow and Craig Lamay, <u>Abandoned in the Wasteland: Children, Television, and the First Amendment</u> (New York: Hill & Wang, 1995) 88.
>
> [4] Jo Anne Reid, Peter Forrestal, and Jonathan Cook, <u>Small Group Learning in the Classroom</u> (Portsmouth, NH: Heinemann, 1990) 110.

A Book with More Than Three Authors

> [5] Marcia M. Boumil et al., <u>Law and Gender Bias</u> (Littleton, CO: Rothman, 1995) 248-49.

A Book in a Later Edition

> [6] Richard L. Schaeffer, <u>Introduction to Probability and Its Applications</u>, 2nd ed. (Boston: PWS, 1995) 55-58.

A Book in a Series

  [7] Sally F. Porterfield, <u>Jung's Advice to the</u>
<u>Players: A Jungian Reading of Shakespeare's Problem</u>
<u>Plays</u>, Contributions in Drama & Theatre Studies 57
(Westport, CT: Greenwood, 1994) 265.

A Book Published in More Than One Volume

Volumes individually titled:

  [8] Crane Brinton, John B. Christopher, and Robert
Lee Wolff, <u>Prehistory to 1715</u>, vol. 1 of <u>A History of</u>
<u>Civilization</u>, 6th ed, 2 vols. (Englewood Cliffs, NJ:
Prentice, 1984) 303.

Volumes not individually titled:

  [9] Charles Messenger, <u>For Love of Regiment: A</u>
<u>History of British Infantry, 1660-1993</u>, vol. 1
(Philadelphia: Trans-Atlantic, 1995) 388.

A Book with a Translator or Editor

  [10] Naguib Mahfouz, <u>Children of the Alley</u>, trans.
Peter Theroux (New York: Doubleday, 1996) 97-99.

  [11] William Shakespeare, <u>Henry V</u>, ed. T. W. Craik
(New York: Routledge, 1995) 88.

A Work in an Anthology

  [12] Myra Leifer, "Pregnancy," <u>Women: Sex and</u>
<u>Sexuality</u>, ed. Catherine R. Stimpson and Ethel Spector
Person (Chicago: U of Chicago P, 1980) 215.

  [13] George Lichtheim, "The Birth of a Philosopher,"
<u>Collected Essays</u> (New York: Viking, 1973) 103-04.

  [14] Salman Rushdie, "A Pen Against the Sword: In
Good Faith," <u>Newsweek</u> 12 Feb. 1990: 52+, rpt. in <u>One</u>
<u>World, Many Cultures</u>, ed. Stuart Hirschberg (New York:
Macmillan, 1992) 480.

A Book Published before 1900

[15] Florence Nightingale, <u>Notes on Nursing: What It Is, and What It Is Not</u> (New York, 1860) 27.

A Paperback or Other Reprinted Book

[16] Jack Kerouac, <u>Big Sur</u> (1962; New York: Viking Penguin, 1992) 177.

A Book Written by a Group or Government Agency

[17] Institute of Medicine: Commission on Federal Regulation of Methadone Treatment, <u>Federal Regulation of Methadone Treatment</u> (Washington: National Academic, 1995) 44.

[18] Sotheby's, <u>Nineteenth Century European Paintings, Drawings and Watercolours</u> (London: Sotheby's, 1995) 164.

A Book Published or Reproduced Electronically

[19] Ambrose Bierce, "My Favorite Murder," <u>The Collected Works of Ambrose Bierce</u> (New York: Neale, 1911) vol. 8, online, U. of Virginia Lib., Internet, available FTP: etext.virginia.edu, 11 Nov. 1995.

[20] Charles Darwin, <u>The Voyage of the Beagle</u>, Harvard Classics 29 (New York: Collier, 1909), online, Internet Wiretap, Internet, address: gopher:// ftp.std.com:70/00/obi/book/Charles.Darwin/ Voyage.of.the.Beagle.Z, 11 Nov. 1995.

[21] Elizabeth Evans, <u>Anne Tyler</u>, United States Authors Series (Boston: Twayne, 1993), CD-ROM, <u>Twayne's Women Authors on CD-ROM</u> (New York: Hall, 1995).

An Article in an Encyclopedia or Other Reference Work

A well-known reference work:

[22] Mamie Harmon, "Folk Arts," <u>Encyclopaedia Britannica: Macropaedia</u>, 15th ed., 1991.

[23] "Wellstone, Paul," <u>Who's Who in America</u>, 50th ed., 1996.

[24] "Yodel," <u>The Shorter Oxford English Dictionary</u>, 1973.

A lesser-known reference work:

[25] Raymond Hames, "Yanomamö," <u>South America</u>, vol. 7 of <u>Encyclopedia of World Cultures</u> (Boston: Hall, 1994).

An electronic reference work:

[26] "Morocco," <u>Compton's Online Encyclopedia</u>, online, Prodigy, 4 Feb. 1996.

[27] "Yokel," <u>Oxford English Dictionary</u>, 2nd. ed., CD-ROM (Oxford: Oxford UP, 1992) 14 Dec. 1995.

Sources in Periodicals and Newspapers

An Article in a Magazine

[28] Toddi Gutner Block, "Riding the Waves," <u>Forbes</u> 11 Sept. 1995: 182.

[29] Stephen P. Maran, "A Deviant Star," <u>Natural History</u> June 1983: 28.

[30] Ann Robinson, "Gifted: The Two-Faced Label," <u>The Gifted Child Today</u> Jan./Feb. 1989: 34-36.

An Article in a Journal

Pages numbered continuously throughout a volume:

[31] Robert B. Reich, "Beyond Free Trade," <u>Foreign Affairs</u> 61 (1983): 802-04.

Each issue begins on page 1:

[32] Mark S. Kaplan, "Feminization of the AIDS Epidemic," <u>Sociology & Social Welfare</u> 22.2 (1995): 5-6.

An Article in a Newspaper

[33] Thomas B. Edsall, "Tensions Divide Elements of Potential Coalition," <u>Washington Post</u> 18 Feb. 1996: A21.

[34] David Ranii, "New AIDS Drug Is Step Closer to Approval," <u>News and Observer</u> [Raleigh] 7 Nov. 1995: 1D+.

[35] "U.S. Recommends Hepatitis A Vaccine," <u>New York Times</u> 27 Aug. 1995, natl. ed.: sec. 5: 3.

An Editorial

[36] "Replace Unfair Tax Law," editorial, <u>USA Today</u> 28 Aug. 1995: 12A.

A Letter to the Editor

[37] Eugenio Cazorlo, letter, <u>History Today</u> Mar. 1992: 54.

A Review

[38] Phyllis Chesler, "The Shellshocked Woman," rev. of <u>Trauma and Recovery</u>, by Judith Lewis Herman, <u>New York Times Book Review</u> 23 Aug. 1992: 11.

[39] Rev. of <u>Going to the Territory</u>, by Ralph Ellison, <u>Atlantic</u> Aug. 1986: 91.

[40] Eric Salzman, rev. of <u>Bluebeard's Castle</u>, by Bela Bartok; Katalin Szendrenyi, soprano; Falk Struckman, baritone; Frankfurt Radio Symphony; Eliahu Inabel, cond.; compact disc, <u>Stereo Review</u> Sept. 1995: 102.

A Printed Article Reproduced Electronically

[41] Patricia M. Bikai and Deborah Kooring, "Archaeology in Jordan," <u>American Journal of Archaeology</u> 99 (1995): 507+, <u>InfoTrac: Expanded Academic Index/ASAP</u>, online, Information Access, 9 Nov. 1995.

[42] Elaine Carey, "Is Graying of Faculty Turning University into 'Boring' Place?," <u>Toronto Star</u> 25 Sept. 1995: A17, <u>CD NewsBank Comprehensive</u>, CD-ROM, NewsBank, Oct. 1995.

[43] Nina L. Diamond, "Dolphin Sonar: A Biologist and Physicist Team Up to Find the Source of Sound Beams," Omni July 1994: 24, Popular Periodicals Standard, CD-ROM, NewsBank, Oct. 1995.

A Printed Article Reproduced by a Microform Reproduction Service

[44] "U.S. Forests 'Very Healthy,' Ecologist Reports," Wyoming State Tribune 25 June 1991, NewsBank ENV, 1991, fiche 58, grid A1.

An Article in an Electronic Publication

[45] Jo Plane, "Training--How Hard Is Your Workout?" Balance Nov. 1995, online, Internet: WWW, address: http://tito.hyperlink.com/balance/, 18 Feb. 1996.

[46] "World Leaders Condemn Nigerian Executions," Reuters 10 Nov. 1995, online, Internet: WWW, Pathfinder News Now, 13 Nov. 1995.

Other Sources

An Audio Recording

[47] Dee Dickinson, Creating the Future: Perspectives on Educational Change, audiocassette (Minneapolis: Accelerated Learning Systems, 1991).

[48] Mozart, Wolfgang A., Symphony No. 30 in D Major, cond. James Levine, Vienna Philharmonic, compact disc, Deutsche Grammophon, 1986.

[49] Shuster, George N., jacket notes, The Poetry of Gerard Manley Hopkins, LP, Caedmon, n.d.

Computer Software

[50] Morph, version 2.5, diskette (San Diego: Gryphon, 1995).

[51] Twain's World, CD-ROM (Parsippany, NJ: Bureau Development, 1993).

A Film or Video Recording

[52] Ed Wood: Look Back in Angora, dir. Tim Burton, screenplay by Scott Alexander and Larry Karaszewski, Touchstone, 1994.

[53] The Little Foxes, dir. William Wyler; perf. Bette Davis, Herbert Marshall, and Dan Duryea; MGM, 1941, videocassette, Embassy, 1985.

[54] The Classical Hollywood Style, program 1 of The American Cinema, prod. New York Center for Visual History, videocassette, Annenberg/CPB, 1995.

A Government Document

[55] United States, Dept. of State, National Committee for Man and the Biosphere, Tropical and Subtropical Forests Directorate, People and the Tropical Forest: A Research Project from the United States Man and the Biosphere Program, by Ariel E. Lugo (Washington: GPO, 1987) 6-7.

A Lecture

[56] Kathleen Halme, class lecture, English 315, Swansea College, 7 Apr. 1996.

[57] Paula McKenna, "Live by Design or Live by Default," public lecture, League of Women Voters, Natchez, 20 Oct. 1995.

A Pamphlet

[58] Golden Retriever Club of America, Prevention of Heartworm (n.p.: GRCA, 1996) 2.

[59] Who Are the Amish? (Aylmer, Ont.: Pathway, n.d.)

A Personal Interview

[60] Rebecca Lee, personal interview, 20 Mar. 1996.

A Radio or Television Program

[61] John McChesney, report on Comdex and Bill Gates, <u>Morning Edition</u>, National Public Radio, 14 Nov. 1995.

[62] <u>The Missiles of October: What the World Didn't Know</u>, written by Sherry Jones and Peter Jennings, ABC-TV, 17 Oct. 1992.

An Unpublished Essay

[63] Molly MacLaren, "The Power of the Pen: Should I Become a Professional Writer?" essay written for Prof. Janet Adams's English 102 class, spring semester 1996.

An Unpublished Letter or E-Mail

[64] Kevin Canty, letter to author, 5 Mar. 1996.

[65] Paul Wilkes, e-mail to author, 29 Dec. 1995.

An Unpublished Questionnaire

[66] Questionnaire conducted by Prof. Barbara Waxman's English 102 class, Nov. 1995.

E   *APA Format*

 FORMATS OTHER THAN MLA

Although you will use the MLA format to acknowledge sources in papers that you write for humanities courses (such as research papers in a composition class), other disciplines may require you to use different formats. Since many journals establish their own conventions for documenting sources, you are also likely to encounter various other formats when you conduct library research. A glance through scholarly journals in your college library will show you that dozens of different formats are in use—usually varying only in minor ways from MLA format or the formats described in this chapter.

Although it is not practical to describe all the different formats here, you should be familiar with the most commonly used formats for citing sources. It is probably unnecessary for you to memorize the details of any of them, but when you use a particular format you should be prepared to model your own references carefully on sample entries, such as those in this chapter. Note the ways in which these formats differ from MLA format and pay close attention to the information that is presented in each entry, the order in which it is presented, and the punctuation used to denote and separate items.

Two principal formats, besides the MLA, are in wide use among scholars. The APA format gives special prominence to the source's publication date in all citations. In the numbered references format (described in this and the following chapter), each source is assigned a number in the list of works cited; each note in the paper refers to a source by its assigned number.

 APA STYLE

Next to the MLA style, the most common format for documenting sources is that of the American Psychological Association—*APA style.* This format (or a variation of it) is widely used for course papers and journal articles in psychology but also in many other disciplines in both the social and natural sciences. Although APA format differs in many particulars from MLA format, the main difference is the prominence its citations give to the source's publication date.

In fields where new theories and discoveries are constantly challenging past assumptions, readers must know if a writer's sources are up-to-date. Note how the date is featured in the following sample APA citations. Parenthetical notes in APA style always include the date, as in the following:

```
...tendency of creative people to be organized
(Sternberg & Lubart, 1995, p. 246).
```

Following is the listing for that same source, as it appears in the reference page (list of works cited). Notice that the date is given in parentheses immediately following the author's name.

```
Sternberg, R. J., & Lubart, T. I. (1995). Defying the
    crowd: Cultivating creativity in a culture of
    conformity. New York: Free.
```

The particulars of APA reference style are explained in the following sections.

APA Bibliographic Citations (Reference List)

At the end of the paper, all sources are listed on a separate page, under the title *References* (not *Works Cited*). Like the MLA format, the APA also arranges works alphabetically, according to the first word in each item. See, for example, Figure E.4 on page 511.

In addition to the prominence given to publication dates, bibliographic citations in APA style differ from MLA listings in three principal ways:

1. In APA style, only the author's last name is given in full. Initials are used for first and middle names. Thus, an author who would be listed in MLA style as *Sternberg, Robert J.* is listed as *Sternberg, R. J.* in APA style.

2. Except for proper names, only the first word of the work's title (and, if there is a subtitle, the first word following the colon) is capitalized. Thus, a book title that would be listed in MLA style as *Defying the Crowd: Cultivating Creativity in a Culture of Conformity* is listed in APA style as *Defying the crowd: Cultivating creativity in a culture of conformity.*

3. Titles of periodical articles (and other works shorter than book-length) are not enclosed in quotation marks as they are in MLA style.

Other differences can be seen in the following sample entries.

Model Entries

A Book

```
Gabor, A. (1995). Einstein's wife: Work and
    marriage in the lives of five great
    twentieth-century women. New York: Viking.
```

Punctuation following underlined text is also underlined in APA style.

A Book in a Later Edition

    Schaeffer, R. L. (1995). <u>Introduction to
        probability and its applications</u> (2nd ed.).
        Boston: PWS-Kent.

Unlike MLA style, APA does not abbreviate the **names of publishers** (it uses *PWS-Kent* instead of *PWS* and *Alfred A. Knopf* instead of *Knopf*). As in MLA style, words such as *Press*, *Publishers*, and *Company* are omitted.

A Book with a Translator

    Ronchi, V. (1991). <u>Optics: The science of vision</u>
        (E. Rosen, Trans.). New York: Dover.
        (Original work published 1957)

Both dates are given in parenthetical notes: (Ronchi, 1957/1991, p. 22).

A Book with an Editor

    Chapman, G. (1990). <u>Teaching young playwrights</u>
        (L. Barrett, Ed.). Portsmouth, NH: Heinemann.

An Anthology of Essays by Different Authors

    Stimpson, C. R., & Person, E. S. (Eds.). (1980).
        <u>Women: Sex and sexuality.</u> Chicago:
        University of Chicago Press.

APA style does not abbreviate university presses (compare *U of Chicago P* in MLA style).

A Work from an Anthology

    Baker, S. W. (1980). Biological influences on
        human sex and gender. In C. R. Stimson &
        E. S. Person (Eds.), <u>Women: Sex and sexuality</u>
        (pp. 175-191). Chicago: University of Chicago
        Press.

An article's title is not enclosed within quotation marks, as in MLA style. **Page numbers** are preceded by *p.* (for *page)* or *pp.* (for *pages)*. Do not abbreviate page numbers; for example, write *pp. 175–191,* not *175–91.*

A Book Published or Reproduced Electronically

```
Bierce, A. (1911). My favorite murder. In The
     collected works of Ambrose Bierce (Vol. 8).
     New York: Neale. [On-line.] University of
     Virginia Library. Available FTP:
     etext.virginia.edu.
```

A Magazine Article

```
Block, T. G. (1995, September 11). Riding the
     waves. Forbes, pp. 182, 184.
Maran, S. P. (1983, June). A deviant star. Natural
     History, pp. 24-29.
```

Titles of magazines and other periodicals are treated exactly as in MLA style. They are underlined, and every important word is capitalized. Dates are listed in full, with the year first. Months are not abbreviated. If an article does not appear on continuous pages, all page numbers are listed.

A Journal Article

A journal whose pages are numbered continuously throughout a volume:

```
Reich, R. B. (1983). Beyond free trade. Foreign
     Affairs, 61, 773-804.
```

A journal, every issue of which begins on page 1:

```
Kaplan, M. S. (1995). Feminization of the AIDS
     epidemic. Sociology & Social Welfare, 22(2): 5-21.
```

For journal articles (unlike magazine and newspaper articles), neither *p.* nor *pp.* is used before page numbers.

A Newspaper Article

```
Matthews, J. (1995, August 28). More public
     schools using private dollars. The Washington
     Post, p. A1.
U.S. recommends hepatitis A vaccine. (1995, August
     27). The New York Times, national edition,
     section 5, p. 3.
```

An Article in an Electronic Publication

```
Plane, Jo. (1995, November). Training--How hard is
     your workout? Balance. [On-line]. Available:
     http://tito.hyperlink.com/balance/.
```

A Personal Interview

```
Lee, Rebecca. (1996, March 20). [Personal
     interview.]
```

An Anonymous Work

```
L.A. crix nix short pix dis. (1992, November 30).
     Variety, p. 44.
```

A Work with Two or More Authors

```
Reid, J. A., Forrestal, P., & Cook, J. (1990).
     Small group learning in the classroom.
     Portsmouth, NH: Heinemann.
```

APA citations of works with multiple authors differ from MLA citations in three ways:

1. Initials and last names of all authors (not just the first author) are inverted.
2. All authors are listed by name (*et al.* is not used in bibliographic listings for works with multiple authors, although it is used in parenthetical notes for works with more than six authors).
3. An ampersand (&) is used in place of the word *and* before the last author's name.

Two or More Works by the Same Author, Different Years

```
Irvin, E. (1994). New . . .
Irvin, E. (1996, October). Lessons . . .
```

When two or more works have the same author(s), arrange the works chronologically (not alphabetically, as in MLA style). The earliest work is listed first.

Two or More Works by the Same Author, Same Year

```
Bushman, D. (1996a). Developmental . . .
Bushman, D. (1996b). Reduced . . .
```

When author(s) have two or more works in the same year, arrange the works alphabetically by title. Place lowercase letters (*a*, *b*, *c*, and so on) immediately after the year.

A Work Written by a Group or Government Agency

```
Institute of Medicine: Commission on Federal
     Regulation of Methadone Treatment. (1995).
     Federal regulation of methadone treatment.
     Washington: National Academic.
Sotheby's. (1995). Nineteenth century European
     paintings, drawings and watercolours. London:
     Author.
```

Use *Author* for the publisher when the author and the publisher are the same.

Other Sources

Treatment of other sources, as well as detailed information about APA format, can be found by consulting the latest edition of the *Publication Manual of the American Psychological Association*. You can find the book in the reference section of most college libraries.

Notes in APA Style

Parenthetical notes in APA format are handled similarly to the MLA method, but with three notable differences:

1. The year of publication is included in the note.
2. All items are separated by commas.
3. Page numbers are preceded by the abbreviation *p.* or *pp.*

When a work is referred to as a whole, no page numbers are needed:

```
In a study of reaction times (Sanders, 1996), ...
```

Only the year is needed when the author's name appears in the sentence:

```
Sanders (1996) studied reaction times ...
```

Include pages when the source can be located more specifically:

```
"...not necessary" (Galizio, 1994, p. 9).
```

   Give the first word or two from the title when the author's name is unknown. Book titles are underlined; periodical titles in notes (unlike in the reference list) are enclosed in quotation marks; all important words are capitalized (also like reference-list citations):

```
...the book (Culture, 1992).
...the article ("US Policy," 1986).
```

Only the year, not the complete date, is given in notes referring to periodical articles.

For a work with six or fewer authors, the note lists all authors' last names:

```
(Andrulis, Beers, Bentley, & Gage, 1987)
```

However, only the first author's name is given for a work with more than six authors:

```
(Sabella et al., 1996)
```

When the reference list cites two or more works written by the same author in the same year, use lowercase letters to differentiate them, as in reference-list citations:

```
(Bushman, 1996a)
(Bushman, 1996b)
```

These two notes cite different works by Bushman, both written in 1996.

When a note refers to more than one work, separate the references by a semicolon:

```
(Earle & Reeves, 1989; Kowal, 1996)
```

Sample Pages in APA Style

Any paper written using MLA format can also be written in APA format. For example, Helen Veit could have used APA style for her paper on fairy tales.

A cover page is typically used for APA papers. The cover page is numbered as page 1, and a shortened version of the title is placed above the page number on each page, as in Figure E.1.

The title is repeated on the opening page of the paper, numbered as page 2. Compare Figures E.2 and E.3 with pages from Helen's MLA-style paper on pages 476–77. Compare Figure E.4 with Helen's list of works cited on p. 480.

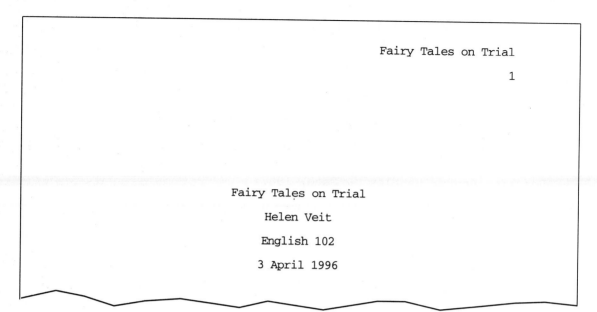

Figure E.1 Sample APA cover page.

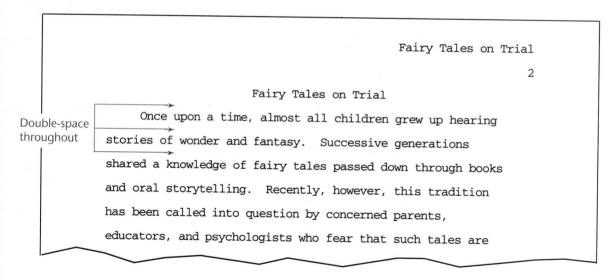

Figure E.2 Sample APA opening page.

Fairy Tales on Trial

4

could reattack, had persistent nightmares. Only when the

original version including the wolf's death was substituted

for her regular story could the child believe that the wolf

was truly gone for good (Tunnell, 1994, p.609).

APA parenthetical notes include the work's date. Page numbers are preceded by p. or pp.

    Although children are often obsessed with violence,

that does not seem to be a problem, according to

psychologist Ann Trousdale. She states that children tend

to "omit gratuitous violence" when retelling the story and

only keep the violence that is necessary for justice (1989,

p. 76). Fairness is very important to young people.

Figure E.3 Sample APA notes.

Fairy Tales on Trial

10

References

Author's last names and first intials are given.

Bettelheim, B.   (1976).   The uses of enchantment: The meaning

    and importance of fairy tales. New York: Alfred A.

    Knopf.

Note the (lack of) capitalization for titles of works.

Brott, A. A.   (1992, June 1).   "Not all men are sly foxes."

    Newsweek, 14-15. [On-line]. InfoTrac: Expanded

    Academic Index/ASAP.

Article titles are placed within quotation marks.

Davies, B., and Banks, C.   (1992).   The gender trap: A feminist

    poststructuralist analysis of primary school

Volume numbers for journals are underlined.

    children's talk about gender. Journal of Curriculum

    Studies, 24, 1-25.

Figure E.4 Sample APA References page.

F *Format Featuring Numbered References*

Another common bibliographic format uses **numbered references** to identify sources. Variations on this format are used most widely in fields such as mathematics, computer science, finance, and other areas in the applied sciences.

Sources are assigned a number in the references page (list of works cited) and are referred to in the paper by that number rather than by the author's name. Items in the references list can be arranged either in alphabetical order or in the order in which references occur within the paper. Figure F.1 shows how the reference list at the end of Helen Veit's paper might have looked if she had used this style. In this case, the references are numbered in the order in which they first appear in the paper.

Here is how the first four sentences with notes in Helen's paper would have appeared if she had used the numbered references style:

```
The girl learns her lesson: "I will never by myself
leave the path, to run into the wood, when my mother
has forbidden me to do so" [1].

"And then she'd be free again" [qtd. in 2, p. 11].

Only when the original version including the wolf's
death was substituted for her regular story could the
child believe that the wolf was truly gone for good [3,
p. 609].

Trousdale states that children tend to "omit gratuitous
violence" when retelling the story and only keep the
violence that is necessary for justice [4, p. 76].
```

This last note—[4, p. 76]—refers to the fourth work in Helen's reference list, the article by Ann Trousdale. Later on in her paper, when she refers again to Trousdale's article, she uses the same reference number:

Veit 9

References

1. Grimm, Jakob, and Wilhelm Grimm. <u>Grimms' Fairy Tales</u>.

    Online. Carnegie Mellon U. Library. Internet.

    Available: http://www.cs.cmu.edu/Web/books.html.

    20 Mar. 1996.

2. Messner, Rudolf. "Children and Fairy Tales--What

    Unites Them and What Divides Them." <u>Western European</u>

    <u>Education</u> 21.2 (1989): 6-28.

3. Tunnell, Michael O. "The Double-Edged Sword: Fantasy

    and Censorship." <u>Language Arts</u> 71 (1994): 606-12.

4. Trousdale, Ann. "Who's Afraid of the Big, Bad Wolf?"

    <u>Children's Literature</u> 20.2 (1989): 69-79.

Figure F.1 Sample list with numbered references.

Trousdale cites one little girl in her study as an
example of the positive use of a typical fairy-tale
villain [4, p. 74].

Apart from the use of reference numbers, there is no uniform style for citing bibliographic sources in this format. Individual items in the bibliography could follow the principles of MLA format, APA format, or yet some other format. If you are required to use numbered references for a course paper, be sure to check with your instructor for specific format details.

Another characteristic of papers using this format is that citation of page references is far less common than in either MLA or APA style. Usually, sources are referred to in the paper solely by their reference numbers, which are usually written within brackets:

Smith and Gurganus [6] showed that...

Often even the authors' names are omitted:

Other examples of this approach are [1,4,5]. In 1976,
[3] analyzed...

Instead of brackets, alternative formats that use numbered references place them either within parentheses:

```
Fort (7) disputes the findings of Byington (3)...
```

or as raised numbers:

```
It has been demonstrated¹ that artifacts that occur...
```

The raised number *1* in the preceding example refers not to a footnote or endnote but directly to the first source in the references list.

Index

Credits

Pages 5–6   From "Against the Grain" by David Bartholomae in *Writers on Writing* (T. Waldrep, ed.). New York: Random House, 1985. Reproduced with permission of The McGraw Hill Companies.

Page 35   "Dressed to Kill" by Eric P. Nash in *The New York Times Magazine,* July 30, 1995. Copyright © 1995 by The New York Times Company. Reprinted by permission.

Pages 35–36   "Shallow Waters Run Deep" by Andrew Chaikivsky in *Esquire,* July 1995. Reprinted by permission of the author.

Pages 36–38   "Eva Perón's Corpse Continues to Haunt Argentina" by Calvin Sims in *The New York Times,* July 30, 1995. Copyright © 1995 by The New York Times Company. Reprinted by permission.

Pages 39–41   Reprinted with the permission of The Free Press, an imprint of Simon & Schuster, from *Passionate Attachments: Thinking About Love* by Willard Gaylin, M.D., and Ethel Person, M.D. Copyright © 1988 by Friends of Columbia Analytic Center, Inc.

Page 46   Excerpt from "I'm Not Sick, I'm Just in Love" by Katherine Davis from *Newsweek,* July 17, 1995. © 1995, Newsweek, Inc. All rights reserved. Reprinted by permission.

Pages 47–50   "Precious Dangers: The Lesson of the Motorcycle" by Melissa Holbrook Pierson. Copyright © 1995 by *Harper's Magazine.* All rights reserved. Reproduced from the May issue by special permission.

Page 59   "Knowing Isn't Everything" by M. T. Spaulding from *Newsweek,* April 3, 1995. © 1995, Newsweek, Inc. All rights reserved. Reprinted by permission.

Pages 66–67   From *Abnormal Psychology: Current Perspectives,* Fifth Edition, by R. R. Bootzin and J. R. Acocella. New York: Random House, 1993. Reproduced with permission of The McGraw-Hill Companies.

Pages 69–72   "Portraiture Is Back, but, My, It's Changed" by Celia McGee in *The New York Times,* January 1, 1995. Copyright © 1995 by The New York Times Company. Reprinted by permission.

Pages 73–74   Excerpt from *The Sound of Mountain Water* by Wallace Stegner. Copyright © 1969 by Wallace Stegner. Reprinted by permission of Doubleday, a division of Bantam Doubleday Dell Publishing Group, Inc.

Pages 76–79   "The West at War" by Michael Elliot with Stryker McGuire from *Newsweek,* July 17, 1995. © 1995, Newsweek, Inc. All rights reserved. Reprinted by permission.

Pages 79–80   Excerpt from *Zen and the Art of Motorcycle Maintenance* by Robert Pirsig. Copyright © 1974 by Robert M. Pirsig. Reprinted by permission of William Morrow and Company, Inc.

Pages 84–86   "Meat Viewed as Staple of Chimp Diet and Mores" by Verne G. Kopytoff in *The New York Times,* June 27, 1995. Copyright © 1995 by The New York Times Company. Reprinted by permission.

Pages 99–100   "UNCW Marine Science Has Earned Respect," *Sunday Star News,* 2 February 1992, p. 6E. Reprinted by permission of Wilmington Star News, Wilmington, NC.

Page 101   "Loveliest of Trees, the Cherry Now" by A. E. Housman from *The Collected Poems of A. E. Housman.* Copyright © 1939, 1940, 1965 by Henry Holt and Company, Inc. Copyright © 1967, 1968 by Robert Symons. Reprinted by permission of Henry Holt and Company, Inc.

Pages 107–10   "Melatonin" by Geoffrey Cowley with Jamie Reno, Mart Hager, and Amy Salzhauer from *Newsweek,* July 17, 1995. © 1995, Newsweek, Inc. All rights reserved. Reprinted by permission.

Page 126   "Greet Expectations" by Jeanne Marie Laskas in *The Washington Post Magazine,* October 15, 1995. © 1995, The Washington Post. Reprinted with permission.

Pages 127–30   "Maybe, Maybe Not" by Annette Kornblum. Reprinted by permission of the author.

Pages 136–37   "Stereotyping: Homogenizing People" in *Telling It Like It Isn't* by Dan Rothwell. Reprinted by permission of the author.

Page 139   Excerpt from "Sexism in the Schoolhouse" by Barbara Kantrowitz from *Newsweek,* February 24, 1992. © 1992, Newsweek, Inc. All rights reserved. Reprinted by permission.

Pages 146–147   Excerpt from an essay by Francis Haskell in *The New York Review of Books,* March 23, 1995. Reprinted with permission from *The New York Review of Books.* Copyright © 1995 Nyrev, Inc.

Pages 147–54   "Against All Odds" by Ron Suskind. Reprinted by permission of *The Wall Street Journal,* © 1994 Dow Jones & Company, Inc. All Rights Reserved Worldwide.

Pages 156–58   Excerpt from "Muddy Waters" by Mark Schapiro in *Utne Reader,* November-December 1994. Reprinted by permission of the author.

Pages 158–61   "Grounds for Concern" by Marilyn Dickey in *Washingtonian,* May 1994. Reprinted by permission of *Washingtonian.*

Pages 161–64   "The Latest on Coffee?" by Jane E. Brody in *The New York Times,* September 13, 1995. Copyright © 1995 by The New York Times Company. Reprinted by permission.

Pages 168–69   "Imperialism, Sexism, Rapacious Capitalism and Mindless Conformity!" by Helen Cordes in

Parenthetical Notes (MLA Style): Quick Reference Guide

Detailed information on parenthetical notes can be found on pages 457–72.

PURPOSE

Use a note to identify the specific source location for a specific idea, piece of information, or quotation in your paper.

FORMAT

Give the specific page reference, preceded by the *least* amount of information needed to identify the source in your list of works cited.

PLACEMENT

Place the note following the passage.

MODEL ENTRIES

Standard Reference

Give the author and page(s):

    A fear of thunder is common among dogs (Digby 237).

Author Identified in the Passage

Omit the author's name in the note:

    Digby noted that dogs are often terrified of thunder (237).

An Anonymous Work (Unidentified Author)

Use the first word or two from the title:

    ("An infant's" 22)

A Work with Two or Three Authors

    (Reid, Forrestal, and Cook 48-49)

A Work with More Than Three Authors

    (Strayer et al. 112)

Two or More Works by the Same Author

Add the first word(s) from the title:

    (Asimov, Adding 240-43)
    (Asimov, "Happy" 68)

Two Authors with the Same Last Name

Include the authors' first names:

    (George Eliot 459)
    (T. S. Eliot 44)

A Multivolume Work

The volume number precedes the page number(s):

    (Agus 2: 59)

Exception: Omit the volume number if only one volume is identified in your list of works cited:

    (Agus 59)

Leifer, Myra. "Pregnancy." Stimpson and
    Person 212-23.

Stimpson, Catherine R., and Ethel Spector
    Person, eds. Women: Sex and Sexuality.
    Chicago: U of Chicago P, 1980.

A Book Published before 1900

Nightingale, Florence. Notes on Nursing:
    What It Is, and What It Is Not. New
    York, 1860.

A Paperback or Other Reprinted Book

Kerouac, Jack. Big Sur. 1962. New York:
    Viking Penguin, 1992.

A Book Published or Reproduced Electronically

Bierce, Ambrose. "My Favorite Murder."
    The Collected Works of Ambrose Bierce.
    New York: Neale, 1911. Vol. 8.
    Online. U. of Virginia Lib. Internet.
    Available FTP: etext.virginia.edu.
    11 Nov. 1995.

Darwin, Charles. The Voyage of the Beagle.
    Harvard Classics 29. New York:
    Collier, 1909. Online. Internet
    Wiretap. Internet. Address: gopher://
    ftp.std.com:70/00/obi/book/Charles.
    Darwin/Voyage.of.the.Beagle.Z. 11 Nov.
    1995.

Evans, Elizabeth. Anne Tyler. United
    States Authors Series. Boston: Twayne,
    1993. CD-ROM. Twayne's Women Authors
    on CD-ROM. New York: Hall, 1995.

An Article in an Encyclopedia or Other Reference Work

A well-known reference work:

Harmon, Mamie. "Folk Arts." Encyclopaedia
    Britannica: Macropaedia. 15th ed.
    1991.

"Wellstone, Paul." Who's Who in America.
    50th ed. 1996.

"Yodel." The Shorter Oxford English
    Dictionary. 1973.

A lesser-known reference work:

Hames, Raymond. "Yanomamö." South America.
    Vol. 7 of Encyclopedia of World
    Cultures. Boston: Hall, 1994.

An electronic reference work:

"Morocco." Compton's Online Encyclopedia.
    Online. Prodigy. 4 Feb. 1996.

"Yokel." Oxford English Dictionary. 2nd
    ed. CD-ROM. Oxford: Oxford UP, 1992.
    14 Dec. 1995.

SOURCES IN PERIODICALS AND NEWSPAPERS

An Article in a Magazine

Block, Toddi Gutner. "Riding the Waves."
    Forbes 11 Sept. 1995: 182+.

Maran, Stephen P. "A Deviant Star."
    Natural History June 1983: 24-29.

Robinson, Ann. "Gifted: The Two-Faced
    Label." The Gifted Child Today
    Jan./Feb. 1989: 34-36.

An Article in a Journal

Pages numbered continuously throughout a volume:

Reich, Robert B. "Beyond Free Trade."
    Foreign Affairs 61 (1983): 773-804.

Each issue begins on page 1:

Kaplan, Mark S. "Feminization of the AIDS
    Epidemic." Sociology & Social Welfare
    22.2 (1995): 5-21.

An Article in a Newspaper

Edsall, Thomas B. "Tensions Divide Elements
    of Potential Coalition." Washington
    Post 18 Feb. 1996: A21.

Ranii, David. "New AIDS Drug Is Step Closer
    to Approval." News and Observer
    [Raleigh] 7 Nov. 1995: 1D+.

"U.S. Recommends Hepatitis A Vaccine." New
    York Times 27 Aug. 1995, natl. ed.:
    sec. 5: 3.

An Editorial

"Replace Unfair Tax Law." Editorial. USA
    Today 28 Aug. 1995: 12A.

A Letter to the Editor

Cazorlo, Eugenio. Letter. History Today
    Mar. 1992: 54.

A Review

Chesler, Phyllis. "The Shellshocked Woman."
    Rev. of Trauma and Recovery, by Judith
    Lewis Herman. New York Times Book
    Review 23 Aug. 1992: 11.

Rev. of Going to the Territory, by Ralph
    Ellison. Atlantic Aug. 1986: 91.

Salzman, Eric. Rev. of Bluebeard's Castle,
    by Bela Bartok. Katalin Szendrenyi,
    soprano. Falk Struckman, baritone.
    Frankfurt Radio Symphony. Eliahu
    Inabel, cond. Compact disc. Stereo
    Review Sept. 1995: 102.

A Printed Article Reproduced Electronically

Bikai, Patricia M., and Deborah Kooring.
    "Archaeology in Jordan." American
    Journal of Archaeology 99 (1995): 507+.
    InfoTrac: Expanded Academic Index/ASAP.
    Online. Information Access. 9 Nov.
    1995.

Carey, Elaine. "Is Graying of Faculty
    Turning University into 'Boring'
    Place?" Toronto Star 25 Sept. 1995:
    A17. CD News Bank Comprehensive.
    CD-ROM. NewsBank. Oct. 1995.

(continued on next page)

List of Works Cited *(continued)*

Dolphin Sonar: A
...ysicist Team Up to
...ce of Sound Beams." <u>Omni</u>
...24. <u>Popular Periodicals</u>
...d. CD-ROM. NewsBank. Oct.

...ted Article Reproduced by a Microform Reproduction Service

"U.S. Forests 'Very Healthy,' Ecologist
   Reports." <u>Wyoming State Tribune</u> 25
   June 1991. NewsBank ENV, 1991, fiche
   58, grid A1.

An Article in an Electronic Publication

Plane, Jo. "Training--How Hard Is Your
   Workout?" <u>Balance</u> Nov. 1995.
   Online. Internet: WWW. Address:
   http://tito.hyperlink.com/balance/.
   18 Feb. 1996.

"World Leaders Condemn Nigerian Executions."
   Reuters 10 Nov. 1995. Online.
   Internet: WWW. Pathfinder News Now.
   13 Nov. 1995.

OTHER SOURCES

An Audio Recording

Dickinson, Dee. <u>Creating the Future:
   Perspectives on Educational Change</u>.
   Audiocassette. Minneapolis:
   Accelerated Learning Systems, 1991.

Mozart, Wolfgang A. Symphony No. 30 in D
   Major. Cond. James Levine. Vienna
   Philharmonic. Compact disc. Deutsche
   Grammophon, 1986.

Shuster, George N. Jacket notes. <u>The
   Poetry of Gerard Manley Hopkins</u>. LP.
   Caedmon, n.d.

Computer Software

<u>Morph</u>. Version 2.5. Diskette. San Diego:
   Gryphon, 1995.

<u>Twain's World</u>. CD-ROM. Parsippany, NJ:
   Bureau Development, 1993.

A Film or Video Recording

<u>Ed Wood: Look Back in Angora</u>. Dir. Tim
   Burton. Screenplay by Scott Alexander
   and Larry Karaszewski. Touchstone,
   1994.

<u>The Classical Hollywood Style</u>. Program 1
   of <u>The American Cinema</u>. Prod. New
   York Center for Visual History.
   Videocassette. Annenberg/CPB, 1995.

<u>The Little Foxes</u>. Dir. William Wyler.
   Perf. Bette Davis, Herbert Marshall,
   and Dan Duryea. MGM, 1941.
   Videocassette. Embassy, 1985.

A Government Document

United States. Dept. of State. National
   Committee for Man and the Biosphere.
   Tropical and Subtropical Forests
   Directorate. <u>People and the Tropical
   Forest: A Research Project from the
   United States Man and the Biosphere
   Program</u>. By Ariel E. Lugo.
   Washington: GPO, 1987.

A Lecture

Halme, Kathleen. Class lecture. English
   315. Swansea College. 7 Apr. 1996.

McKenna, Paula. "Live by Design or Live by
   Default." Public lecture. League of
   Women Voters. Natchez, 20 Oct. 1995.

A Pamphlet

Golden Retriever Club of America.
   <u>Prevention of Heartworm</u>. N.p.: GRCA,
   1996.

<u>Who Are the Amish?</u> Aylmer, Ont.: Pathway,
   n.d.

A Personal Interview

Lee, Rebecca. Personal interview. 20 Mar.
   1996.

A Radio or Television Program

McChesney, John. Report on Comdex and Bill
   Gates. <u>Morning Edition</u>. National
   Public Radio. 14 Nov. 1995.

<u>The Missiles of October: What the World
   Didn't Know</u>. Written by Sherry Jones
   and Peter Jennings. ABC-TV. 17 Oct.
   1992.

An Unpublished Essay

MacLaren, Molly. "The Power of the Pen:
   Should I Become a Professional Writer?"
   Essay written for Prof. Janet Adams's
   English 102 class. Spring semester
   1996.

An Unpublished Letter or E-Mail

Canty, Kevin. Letter to author. 5 Mar.
   1996.

Wilkes, Paul. E-mail to author. 29 Dec.
   1995.

An Unpublished Questionnaire

Questionnaire conducted by Prof. Barbara
   Waxman's English 102 class. Nov. 1995.